BOSTON'S GUN BIBLE

by

Boston T. Party

Published by

JAVELIN PRESS

c/o P.O. Box 31J, Ignacio, Colorado. (81137-0031)
(Without any 4 USC §§ 105-110 *"Federal area"* or *"State."*)
www.javelinpress.com

***Boston on Guns & Courage*:** *March, 1998*
***Boston's Gun Bible*:** *August, 2000*
Boston's Gun Bible (revised): *April, 2002*

**Printed in the united states of America,
without any 4 USC §§ 105-110 *"Federal area"* or *"State."***

10 9 8 7 6 5 4 3 2 / 07 06 05 04

**Library of Congress Catalog Number 00-091704
ISBN 1-888766-06-9**

ACKNOWLEDGMENTS

Huge appreciation goes to my proofreaders and editors (voluntary and not). You know who you are. Douglas P. Bell in particular was a huge help, and often went above and beyond the call of duty!

I am grateful to Tim Mullin, Esq. for his gracious Foreword, and for his generous help in answering questions.

Much of the revised *Boston's Gun Bible* is indirectly due to Fred of Fred's M14 Military Stocks, who kept after me to give the M14/M1A a fairer shake against the FAL. (I did so, and Chapter 10 explains my results.) I also thank Fred for proofing the battle rifle chapters—he found several things that I'd overlooked.

DEDICATION

To the Massachusetts Militia Captain John Parker, and to his present and future successors.

To the "Serial Lecher" Bill Clinton and Hillary, without whom this book would not have been possible, or necessary.

Finally, to Bill and Hillary's pal, Vince Foster, who might be alive today if he'd only had a gun on 20 July 1993.

Works by Boston T. Party:

Good-Bye April 15th!

The untaxation classic—crystal clear and sweeping. Copied, plagiarized, and borrowed from, but never equaled. The most effective and least hazardous untaxation guide. Order the *original* today!

392 pp. (1992) Available for $40 + $6 s&h (in cash).

You & The Police!

The definitive guide to your rights and tactics during police confrontations. When can you *refuse* to answer questions or consent to searches? Don't lose your liberty through ignorance!

128 pp. (1996) Available for $15 + $5 s&h (cash, please).

Bulletproof Privacy

How to Live Hidden, Happy, and Free!

Explains precisely how to lay low and be left alone by the snoops, government agents and bureaucrats. Boston shares many of his own unique methods. The bestselling privacy book in America!

160 pp. (1997) Available for $16 + $5 s&h (cash, please).

Hologram of Liberty

The Constitution's Shocking Alliance with Big Government **by Kenneth W. Royce**

The Convention of 1787 was the most brilliant and subtle *coup d'état* in history. The nationalist framers *designed* a strong government, guaranteed through purposely ambiguous verbiage. Many readers say this is Boston's best book. A jaw-dropper.

262 pp. (1997) Available for $20 + $5 s&h (cash, please).

Boston on Surviving Y2K

And Other Lovely Disasters

Even though Y2K was Y2¿Qué? this title remains highly useful for all preparedness planning. **Now on sale for 50% off!** (It's the same book as The Military Book Club's *Surviving Doomsday*.)

352 pp. (1998) Available for only $11 + $5 s&h (in cash).

Boston's Gun Bible (revised for 2002)

A rousing how-to/*why*-to on modern gun ownership. Firearms are *"liberty's teeth"* and it's time we remembered it. Fully revised for 2002 with 10 new chapters. **Over *200 new pages* have been added!** Much more complete than the 2000 edition. No other general gun book is more thorough or useful! Indispensable!

848 pp. (2002) Available for $28 + $6 s&h (cash, please).

Molôn Labé! (Boston's first novel)

If you liked *Unintended Consequences* by John Ross and Ayn Rand's *Atlas Shrugged*, then Boston's novel will be a favorite. It dramatically outlines an innovative recipe for Liberty which could actually work! A thinking book for people of action; an action book for people of thought. A freedom classic!

454 pp. (2004) Available for $24 + $6 s&h (cash, please).

Visit us at: www.javelinpress.com

TABLE OF CONTENTS

5   After The Smoke Clears...

6   Women & Guns

PART II: BATTLE RIFLES

7   Combat Rifle History

8   Modern Combat Semi-Auto Rifles

12 FAL / L1A1

18   Combat Rifle Optics

PART III: ALL OTHER GUNS

20 Shotguns

21 Bolt-Action Rifle Cartridges

22 Bolt-Action Rifles

23   .50BMG Target Rifles

24   Other Rifles

25   Handguns

PART IV: ACQUISITION

26   My Shopping List

27   You & The BATF

PART V: DISARMAMENT

36   Coercive Buy-up Programs

37   Why I Will Not Obey California's Gun Registration Edict (by Brian Puckett)

38   Confiscation

39   When The Raids Come

PART VI: COURAGE

40   Wealth vs. Liberty

FOREWORD

by Timothy J. Mullin

In 1942, when the threat of invasion from Nazi and Japanese forces seemed very real, Charles Haven and Melvin Johnson, Jr. wrote the delightful little book, *A Comprehensive Small Arms Manual*. In that volume, the authors detailed a wide variety of weapons suitable for the defense-minded citizen of the period. They tested and evaluated these weapons and commented on their usefulness in opposing the designs of foreign socialists and imperialists.

Boston T. Party, in his *Boston's Gun Bible*, has done the same thing for patriots in the first decade of the 21st Century. Of course, that threat persists today because the same foreign ideology is alive and well in Washington, D.C. and other power centers. How best to oppose these insidious forces which destroy our freedoms and traditional way of life?

Money and Time are both precious things to all of us. Boston T. Party has given us a gift of them both by evaluating a long list of weapons so that we do not have to ourselves. Even more critically, he has given us an approach to our dilemma (and an attitude to emulate) to assist us in developing the proper mindset and life-style so essential in a free society.

I have great hope that six decades from now, someone will be reading *Boston's Gun Bible*, much like we today read Haven and Johnson, with a little smirk on our faces about how unnecessary it all was since the invaders never had the nerve—that repugnant philosophies had been eradicated and are now studied in laboratories like the conquered virus of smallpox.

Similarly (and with a lot of luck), we will look back and shake our heads at the notion that any American government agent ever attempted to restrain the free exercise of our constitutional liberties, and that there was ever a time when free-born Americans had anything to fear from their government, federal or State. Hopefully in those years ahead, the freedom-destroyers within certain bureaus and agencies will be viewed as we today view the *Gestapo* thug, the SS executioner, and the maniacal Jap soldier—with a mixture of contempt and amazement that free people ever cowered before such vermin.

Conversely, if the worst ever does occur, we will be ready to at last put what we have learned from *Boston's Gun Bible* to its intended purpose—just like our fathers and grandfathers did who read *A Comprehensive Small Arms Manual* some 60 years ago. Boston's book is precisely the type of work that gives the liberty-haters their nightmares. Make no mistake: Any of you readers who take this book to heart are dangerous to tyranny. *You* will have the proper tools and resolve to assert your liberty. As it said, *"Armed men are citizens; disarmed men are subjects."* Free men need rifles and courage. In this book, you will learn how and where to find them both.

Timothy J. Mullin
April 2000

A former U.S. Marshal, Mullin is the author of *Training The Gunfighter, Testing the War Weapons,* and several other gun books, most of which are available from Paladin Press. Mullin also collaborated in and wrote the Foreword to *Unintended Consequences* by John Ross. They are currently working on the sequel.

PREFACE

Arms are the only true badges of liberty. The possession of arms is the distinction of a free man from a slave.
— Andrew Fletcher, *A Discourse of Government with relation to Militias* (1698), p. 47

My puny philosophical opponents will pigeonhole me as a *"gun nut."* True, I enjoy owning and shooting guns, and am an unabashed enthusiast—however, guns are more a means than an end. I am a *"freedom nut"* and guns—with the responsibility, training, and will to properly use them—are *"liberty's teeth"* (George Washington).

This book is not about hunting. There are already plenty of good hunting books, and yet another one is not direly needed right now. The 2nd Amendment is not *really* about hunting—it is about keeping politicians nervous, honest *servants.* An armed citizenry is the *ultimate* "check and balance" on government. When the ballot box and the jury box no longer work, then it's probably nearing time for the cartridge box.

I can't speak for other nations, but *Americans* merely collectively *delegate* their individual sovereignties to servant government on their *behalf.* When the servant grows haughty it should get corrected or fired. Since, however, the Constitution set up an *insular* arrangement of political correction (only congressmen can impeach and try congressmen), and since voting out the congressional servants has proven to be nearly worthless, concerned citizens are contemplating sterner measures. We should no longer *"spare the rod and spoil the child."*

It's only because congressmen are *not* in fear of their jobs, their fortunes, or their lives that they have the *nerve* to propose repealing the 2nd Amendment, classifying vitamins as prescription drugs, or banning wood-burning stoves. Such D.C. ilk should have been dragged down the streets back in 1933 when they outlawed the private ownership of gold—which they blamed for the Depression!

The thugs who enforced such obscenity should have been strung up from the first day. Since they weren't, they *now* feel free to stomp family pets to death, shoot nursing mothers in the face, and pour helicopter gunfire through the roofs of homestead churches *with women, children, and babies inside.*

Men that are above all fear, soon grow above all shame.
— Trenchard and Gordon, *Cato's Letters* (1755), vol. I, p. 255

Our government, now fearless, has grown above all shame. We *could* have easily pulled these weeds when they first sprouted. *Now* they've got Kevlar vests, night vision devices, and silenced submachineguns. The *National Firearms Act of 1934* was our Reichstag fire, and we acquiesced. The *Gun Control Act of 1968* was our 1936 Rhineland. The "Brady" bill was the March 1938 Austrian *Anschluss*, the *"Crime Bill"* the October 1938 Sudetenland annexation, and the "Terror" bill March 1939 Czechoslovakia. (Gun registration will be 1939 Poland.)

Now we're probably going to have to fight "WWII." And we're not *ready.* (Thankfully, neither are *they.*) Oh, we've got the *guns*—we just don't have the courage. We are nearly perfectly gelded. Never before has such a well-armed people become so utterly apathetic to the preservation of their liberties, so lazy in their thinking, and so cowardly in their actions.

Our domestic Hitlerite gunphobes have called our bluff too many times, and have grown too confident with their progress. A slap in their faces back in 1968 would have saved us incalculable bloodshed a generation later. If there is not a John Ross *Unintended Consequences* scenario *very soon*, then we're in for some extremely nasty business—Civil War 2.

I don't desire this, but if it's inevitable, then let it come. *"Is life so dear, or peace so sweet as to be purchased at the price of chains or slavery?"* No, it's not. It never *was.* **We have the *badges* of liberty, but not the *soul.* We're serfs with guns.** This unprecedented paradox *will* be resolved in one of only two ways: We'll either lose our serfdom, or we'll lose our guns.

If you *won't* fight for your Liberty, then sell your guns to us *now* before they're coercively purchased or confiscated.

Or, read on.

Boston's Gun Bible is about regaining the soul and polishing the badges.

MY GOAL WITH THIS BOOK

Boston's Gun Bible is not the definitive guide to *all* firearms matters. Many subjects worthy of complete books (*e.g,* ballistics, CQB tactics, shooting techniques, countersniping, etc.) are only briefly covered, else this would have been a 1,000 page book not seen before the next round of victim disarmament. We don't have that kind of time, and besides, excellent information on those subjects already exists.

My primary goal was to dispel many potentially dangerous gun misconceptions, and illustrate what you perhaps *don't* know. My secondary goal was to compose the single most useful gun encyclopedia for the modern gunowner, and by nearly all accounts I've succeeded. There's little missing from here that you really need to know.

I've eclectically collected (and rejected) bits from all the Masters. Thus, some of this book is just plain personal opinion and bias. Since guns are *personal* items, bias is to be expected. While I do admit to several gun biases, my reasons for such are clearly explained. Although I'm quite the "Glockaholic" (Glocks work, *period*), if the 1911 or SIG or USP "resonates" better with *you*, then by all means use one of those excellent pistols.

Boston's Gun Bible is a catalog of one civilian's experience and opinions. I don't know everything, but I think you'll get your money's worth. I hope you will find this book a timely, useful, and informative work which stands out above the swill proffered by the misinformed to the ignorant.

What's new in revised *Boston's Gun Bible*?

Totally new chapters for 2002 are:

10	Rating the Battle Rifles
11	M1/M14 (M1A)
12	FAL
13	HK91
15	Rating the Battle Carbines
17	AK74
18	Combat Rifle Optics
19	How To Become A Rifleman
29	Reloading, Zeroing, Shooting, Cleaning, & Caching
46	**excerpts from Boston's upcoming novel,** *Molon Labe!*

These chapters from 2000 have much new/revised material:

1	Terminology
4	Tactics & Training
23	.50BMG Target Rifles
25	Handguns
26	My Shopping List
45	Sources

To make room for the 200+ new pages, I omitted the .264 Boston chapter, and truncated discussion of pre-1899 guns and "curios and relics." I also improved the organization of chapters.

In short, this revised *Boston's Gun Bible* is the gun book I *wish* I had written in 2000, but I didn't then have the time (as I rushed to get it in print before Gore got elected). I've learned much since 2000, and enjoyed sharing that with you here. With 850 pages, you will definitely get your 28 bucks worth!

This is, by the way, the final edition of *Boston's Gun Bible*. I have too many new books to write, and besides, I am *very* pleased with how this revision turned out. We're done here.

ON READING THIS BOOK

Quotes

Quotations are in this form. <u>Any original emphasis is underlined.</u> **Any added emphasis of mine is in boldface.** When I supplement a quote, my nonitalicized comments are within ( ) or [ ]—(like this).

Have a copy of the *Shotgun News*

Not only is *SGN* a great shoppers' guide, it's a reference resource. Page 7 has the issue's list of advertisers.

Gun List is the national classified gun ad paper. A good reference resource to prices and availability.

What I was wrong about in the 2000 edition

That the M1A was not the best .308 MBR. It is (barely).
That the M1 Garand was not really viable as a modern MBR. It is.
That the ArmaLite AR10 was not as unreliable as it is.

My 2000 forecasts which have come true

(I wasn't wrong. I was just too early.)

❖ 1

TERMINOLOGY

Every industry and hobby has its own nomenclature. I assume on your part at least a *basic* knowledge level of shooting verbiage. Here are some bits you might not know. (PolSpeak terms are italicized within quotation marks.)

Ø   **"Federal Reserve Notes"** which are no longer redeemable, in and masquerade as, real $ dollars (gold/silver money). Ancient Chinese proverb (they're *all* ancient, aren't they?): *"The beginning of wisdom is to call things by their right name."* The inverse of that is to stop calling things by their <u>wrong</u> name, which is why I refuse to call FRNs "dollars."

George Orwell made the point that shoddy language results in shoddy politics. Calling dry "wet" and darkness "light" requires the simultaneous, purposeful mental suspension of truth—a 1/100th second bit of insanity—and, in my opinion, <u>evil</u>. To lie to others you must also lie to yourself. Do this enough times (as did the Nazis and Communists) and one's entire thinking (and thus actions) will become deranged and evil.

Make a firm habit of calling things by what they <u>are</u>, not by what sounds cute, kind, acceptable, "politically correct," or expedient.

§   **section.** You'll see this in law quotations.

5.56x45, 7.62x51, 12.7x99, etc.   Metric designation of bullet diameter by case length. The above examples are our .223, .308, and .50BMG.

10mm Boston   My ideal M1 Carbine cartridge, a Czech 7.62x45 case straightwalled to .40, throwing a 200gr at 2000fps for 1777fpe.

15 + 1, etc.   Gun's total capacity: mag capacity plus round in chamber.

.50BMG   .50 Browning Machine Gun. A cartridge used in single-shot or semi-auto target rifles. Very popular with civilians in long-distance (1000-1500yd) shooting matches. The .50BMG throws a 700gr at 2800 for 12,189fpe. *"Gee, willikers, Batman!"*

In 1998 and 2000 I predicted that the .50BMG round would come under increased scrutiny, and I was right. If you can't afford a rifle, then at least buy some ammo. (API at Ø2/round is the best deal for the money) **140/2600 for 2101, etc.** Means a 140gr bullet with a muzzle velocity of 2600fps for a muzzle energy of 2101fpe. Common shooting shorthand.

.264 Boston   My proposed medium-power battle cartridge, offering at least 85% the energy of the .308 in an intermediate 6.5x50 case. My view is that the .223 is too meager (armies should not be equipped with carbines) and the .308 is a bit too much (and rather inefficient at that). (Even if the 7.62x51 were necked down to 7mm or 6.5mm, I'd happily shut up.)

"accident"   A self-serving euphemism for the negligent discharge of a firearm. Guns do not "go off" by themselves any more than cars start themselves up and drive down the road. They must be loaded, chambered, cocked, and fired by a human.

AP   **armor piercing.** We designate it with a painted black tip.

API   **armor piercing incendiary.** Great round!

API-T   **armor piercing incendiary tracer.** The spotting round for API. Tracers go both ways, so beware.

armory   Where guns are *stored.*

arsenal   Where guns are *manufactured.* There is much erroneous transposition of these two words (*Mea culpa!*), which is furthered by gun makers calling themselves an "armory" (*e.g.,* Springfield Armory).

"assault rifles"   Historically, *select-fire* carbines (*e.g.,* StG44, AK47, M16, etc.) of an intermediate rifle caliber (*e.g.,* 8x33, 7.62x39, .223, etc.) with 15-30rd detachable magazine.

"assault weapons"   In modern PolSpeak, *semi-auto* guns that scare Congress. (*"If it looks bad, then it must be bad!"*)

BoG&C   *Boston on Guns & Courage,* my first gun book (1998)

ballistics   The study of objects (*e.g.,* bullets) in flight.

   internal ballistics means bullet behavior between case and muzzle.
   external ballistics means behavior between muzzle and target.
   terminal ballistics means behavior from impact to rest.

BATF   Bureau of Alcohol, Tobacco, and Firearms. (Who's bringing the chips?) A regulatory division of the Dept. of Treasury with *de facto* police power. When a federal law enforcement wanna-be can't get into the FBI, Secret Service, U.S. Marshals, or DEA, only the BATF is left. Considered the "bottom feeders" of feds. Instead of fighting crime (*e.g.,* taking away guns from *gangstas*), the BATF uses stings and entrapments against peaceable gunowners. The BATF is guilty of many civil rights violations, and is not above falsifying warrants (*e.g.,* Waco), planting evidence, shoving against walls pregnant women (who later miscarry), stomping family pets to death, and lying under oath. Beware.

battle carbine A semi-auto military-pattern carbine of lesser cartridge, such as the .223 or 7.62x39. Civilian versions are mistakenly called *"assault rifles"* when such are not select-fire weapons.

battle rifle A semi-auto military-pattern rifle of substantial cartridge, such as the .308. Examples are the M14, FAL, H&K91, and AR10. A battle rifle should be able to deliver 1000fpe at 500yds within 20" (4MOA). 500yds with iron sights is about max for most shooters (even very good ones). Superior power and accuracy belongs to scoped bolt guns in magnum cartridges. An MBR should be effective out to ranges where the sniper rifle begins. 200-300yd carbines in .223 have their place (support, CQB, perimeter, etc.), but riflemen need *rifles*.

bbl **barrel.** Round goes into the chamber; bullet comes out muzzle.

B/C **Boxer/corrosive.** A reloadable case, but extra work to clean.

B/NC **Boxer/non-corrosive.** Reloadable/shootable. Top choice.

BE/C **Berdan/corrosive.** Non-reloadable. Avoid.

BE/NC **Berdan/non-corrosive.** Non-reloadable, but shootable.

BC **ballistic coefficient.** A rating system in decimal points (higher is better) of a bullet's "sleekness"—ability to retain velocity. The less a bullet sheds its velocity, the quicker it gets down range, and the less it drops. Interestingly, BC increases with velocity.

BDC **bullet drop compensator.** Countersniper scopes (and some hunting ones) have BDC cams for certain loads (*e.g.*, M118, etc.), so all the shooter need only dial in the distance and the reticle will be spot on.

boattail Bullets with tapered bases, designed for long-range.

brace A pair (of handguns).

caliber The diameter of a bullet in fractional inch. Not "cartridge."

cannelure A groove around a bullet to hold a case crimp.

cartridge A round of ammunition. Not "caliber."

CCW **concealed carry weapon** permit. (Also called a **CHL**, a concealed handgun license, or a **CCL**, a concealed carry license.) Today, some 31 States have approved a *"shall issue"* form of permit. Don't get too excited, however. If the States really supported your right to bear arms, they'd have simply removed any carry restrictions for non-felon, sane adults (as in Vermont). Millions have obtained permits. A permit means permission. Once Government knows the names, SSNs, and fingerprints of all Americans with the nerve to conceal carry, these permits will be revoked through some future unilateral disarmament measure. CCWs are merely a sneaky form of personal registration.

One good result: CCWs have drawn in million of new gunowners, all with a newly-vested interest in RKBA.

certiorari A Supreme Court hearing of a case. To "deny *cert*" means to refuse to hear the case and let the lower ruling stand.

cheek weld The consistent placement of cheek to buttstock. Precise

and consistent weld is crucial to long-range accuracy.
chamber   The breech end of the barrel. To load a round in the barrel.
clip   Not a magazine, but a stripper clip or revolver moon clip.
COL   **cartridge overall length.** A max COL describes the longest cartridge a magazine and/or chamber will accept and feed.
cold-carry   A kind of method or gun designed for quick disposal.
"compound"   The wooden home of a dissident under federal siege.
concealment   Something which hides you from view (*e.g.*, brush, curtain), but offers little or no protection from incoming fire (as does cover). Concealment is not cover!
Conditions 1-4   Descriptions of a gun's loaded status.
"cop killer bullet"   The KTW Teflon-coated handgun bullet, never sold to civilians, was the origin of that wholly artificial scare. (Never mind that there has not been one case of a cop's vest perforated by criminal handgun fire.)   Because of this crap, and Olympic Arms making a 7.62x39 AR15 pistol, the Chinese steel-core ammo was outlawed.
corrosive   A primer containing corrosive compounds, which are harmful to the bore and gas system (unless quickly removed with hot, soapy water).   Such primers are extremely stable in storage and in cold weather, which is why many 3rd World countries still use them today.
cover   Anything that protects from gunfire, such as a brick wall, car, etc. Cover is usually also concealment, except for bulletproof glass.
cook-off   A chambered round that fired in a hot barrel, without the trigger having been pulled. Only a problem in closed-bolt full-autos.
CQB   **close quarters battle.** Within 25 yards.
"Crime Bill"   The *"assault weapons"* ban of 1994, which had nothing to do with reducing crime. Read the Krauthammer quote on page 32/15.
Cuidado   Spanish for "be careful." (Many readers asked me about it.)
"cult"   Any non-orthodox religious group with fewer than one million national members whose leader does not shave with daily regularity. *"Cultists"* always live in a *"compound"* where they *"hoard"* food. They also *"stockpile"* dangerous *"sniper rifles"* and *"assault weapons"* through *"unlicensed dealer"* purchases (when they aren't reading *"right-wing radical"* and *"anti-government"* material to commit *"hate crimes."*).
cup   **copper units pressure.** A measure of chamber pressure. Guns in identical cartridges (*e.g.*, .45-70) differ in their chamber strength, especially antique vs. modern guns—so beware. Also, know an action's strength before rebarreling it.   (M96 Spanish Mausers are only 45,000cup actions, and were rebarreled to the 7.62 CETME, a .308 Lite.)
DA   **double action**, which describes the first-shot hammer cocking and dropping by the trigger, instead of having to manually cock the hammer (which is a "single action" or SA).
DAO   **double action only.** Some DA pistols cannot be fired from SA,

so as to make successive trigger pulls the same as the first.

DEWAT   DEactivated WAr Trophy. A full-auto G.I. bring-back which has been temporarily deactivated. Since the USG no longer trusts its troops, these were transformed by the *GCA68* into *NFA34 "firearms."*

EER   extended eye relief. Eye relief of over 6", needed for certain scope applications, such as handguns and Scout rifles.

e.g.   exempli gratia. for example, used to preface specific examples. Different from *i.e.* (*id est*–that is to say) which is explanatory.

eye relief The inch distance between your eye and the scope housing. Eye reliefs under 2" risk shooter injury during heavy recoil when the rifle scope slams into the eyebrow, usually causing a deep cut.

FFL   Federal Firearms Licensee. Gun makers must sell their product through the 80,276 FFLs in America. FFLs must charge sales tax, perform background checks, keep those yellow BATF Form 4473s on file, etc. Increased licensing fees and BATF hassles have purposely reduced the number by ⅔rds (from 250,000 in 1994). When have you ever heard of a federal agency actually *reducing* the numbers of its regulated?

firepower Hits per minute, not rounds (*i.e.,* misses) per minute.

FMJ   full metal jacket. A bullet with no exposed core (which can cause feeding problems). Also called "ball" ammo. Used by the military.

fpe   foot-pounds of energy. A unit of work; energy to lift 1 pound 1 foot. (Correctly termed "pounds-feet" but it's never called that.) To calculate fpe, square the velocity, divide by 450,240, and multiply by gr.

fps   feet per second. Bullet velocity. 1087fps is Mach 1 at sea level. Ammo for silenced weapons is subsonic, to avoid the *craaack.*

"fringe" PolSpeak for those on the edge of the sheep herd.

full-auto Multiple shots per single pull of the trigger. *NFA34* regulated.

ga   gauge. In shotguns, the bore size of a 12ga is a lead ball weighing 1/12th of a pound. The smaller the gauge, the larger the bore.

GAO   Government Accounting Office. (Not the GOA.)

GCA68   Gun Control Act of 1968. This mandated the current FFL system and *NFA* control of *"destructive devices"* like 20mm cannons.

GOA   Gunowners of America. Fine 2nd Amendment lobbying group headed by Larry Pratt. (www.gunowners.org)

gr   grains. Measure of bullet and powder weight. There are 7000gr per pound. 1lb of powder will fill 200 cases of 35gr powder loads.

"gun control" Coercive victim disarmament. There is no such thing, by the way, as *"reasonable"* or *"common sense"* gun control. The 2nd Amendment codified an <u>absolute</u> right of individual peaceable Americans to own and carry any gun that they see fit, without any infringement. Period. All *"gun control"* is unconstitutional.

"gun violence" PolSpeak which includes justified self-defense.

"hate crime" Any crime committed by a white against a non-white.

Curiously, the reverse is not considered by law to be a *"hate crime."*
HCl   Handgun Control, Inc.   Headed by that gross opportunist Sarah Brady who has worn out several wheelchairs from trotting out her husband James Brady (who took in the head one of Hinckley's bullets).
headspace   The distance between the base of the cartridge (which, depending on the case, can be the mouth, shoulder, belt, or rim) and the face of the bolt or breechblock. Insufficient headspace will prevent chambering, while excessive headspace can cause a ruptured case (or gun).
"high-capacity magazine"   PolSpeak for normal or full capacity.
HPBT   hollow point boattail. A great long-distance bullet. The best are commercially available from Sierra.
i.e.   id est. that is (to say), which is amplifying explanation. Not the same as *e.g.* After learning the important difference between the two, I'm now tired of seeing continual misuse of the pair.
"illegal arms bazaars"   PolSpeak for gun shows.
IR   infrared. Electromagnetic waves longer than visible light, but less than microwaves. Perceived as heat, seen with NVDs.
IWB   inside waistband. A style of concealed-carry holster.
JPFO   Jews for the Preservation of Firearms Ownership.   Aaron Zelman's very effective 2nd Amendment group. www.jpfo.org
Kalifornia   The People's Democratic Republic of California.
KE   kinetic energy. Measured in fpe.
lawful vs. legal   Lawful is what is right to do, in a moral or libertarian sense. Legal is what is permitted to do by government. (See "unlawful.")
lp/mm   line pair per millimeter. Used to measure NVD resolution. The higher the better. Any value above 45 lp/mm is quite good.
locktime   The amount of time between the trigger's release of the sear and the firing pin's strike of the primer. Faster is better, as there's less movement of the shooter and target. The Remington 788, for example, is renowned for its fast locktime, whereas the Mauser 96s and Lee-Enfields are much slower. Electrically-primed cases (which have no locktime, practically speaking) are common in cannon shells and may someday be reliable enough for shoulder-fired rifles.
"loophole"   PolSpeak for paperwork-free, no-permission-needed, private, intra-State gun transfers—all protected by the 2nd Amendment.
M80   U.S. .308 ball.   Non-matchgrade (2½-3MOA) 147gr ammo. This is "spray & pray" stuff for M60 machineguns.
M91   Mauser 1891.   Beautiful old Mausers made for Argentina. While only 45,000cup actions, their 7.65 Argentine is a good round.
M96   Mauser 1896. A refinement of the M93 and M94 actions, made by the Swedes for their 6.5x55. The last pre-M98 Mauser bolt-action design; much better than the M91 action. It is cock-on-closing and doesn't have the third locking lug of the M98. A good 45,000cup action, though

not quite suitable for .308 level pressure. They can be converted to cock-on-opening for about Ø25.

M98   **Mauser 1898.** The last, and best, German Mauser action.

M118   **U.S. .308 Match.** 173gr 1¼MOA ammo. Good stuff, though not the equal of the ¾MOA Fed 168gr Match (or comparable handloads).

M193   **U.S. 55gr .223 ball.** It's been replaced with 62gr M855. 2MOA.

M855   **U.S. 62gr .223 ball.** A copy of the Belgian SS109 ball. 2MOA.

mag   Abbreviation for a gun's magazine.

magazine   A gun's ammo container. Can be detachable. Not a "clip."

malf   **malfunction.** A failure to feed, fire, extract, or eject. Not a "jam" (which is something you spread on toast).

Magnum   A cartridge of greater case capacity (and thus power) than earlier standards in the same caliber. Manufacturers include Dakota, H&H, Imperial, Lapua, Norma, Remington, STW, Weatherby, and Winchester. The Imperial and Dakota mags are beltless.

MBR   **main battle rifle.** A .308 semi-auto battle rifle.

ME   **muzzle energy.** The measure of fpe at muzzle—distance 0.

MG   **machinegun.** A full-auto firearm (*e.g.,* M1919, M2, etc.).

militia   All adult male citizens of gun-bearing age (18-45y/o) who constitute the backbone of a nation's defense. The organized militia is the National Guard, and the unorganized militia is the rest of us.

In modern PolSpeak, however, militia means any peaceable group of armed people who didn't vote for Clinton. The militia movement in general is falsely linked to *"hate crimes"* and domestic terrorism.

MOA   **Minute Of Angle,** which is exactly 1.047" at 100yds, though rounded down to 1". At 400yds: 1MOA is 4", ½MOA is 2", etc.

MPBR   **maximum point blank range.** A hunter's system of zeroing his rifle to eliminate holdover/holdunder estimations. Since the heart/lungs vital zone area of a deer is about 10" in diameter, an MPBR zero is one in which a bullet will neither rise nor fall more than 5" at some maximum distance, to hit inside a 10" circle with a center hold. The higher the MV, the longer the MPBR. Most MPBRs are about 225-350yds. While the MPBR system is unsuitable for long distance work, it is good for those hunting within 350yds without BDC scopes and rangefinders.

MV   **muzzle velocity.** The measure of fps at muzzle—distance 0.

NC   **non-corrosive.** Modern (*i.e.,* post-1950s) primers.

ND   **negligent discharge.** Causing a gun to fire unintentionally.

Neu Jersey   The Fascist State of New Jersey.

NFA34 *National Firearms Act of 1934.* The first serious federal gun law, passed by FDR's Congress. It mandated a national registry and oppressive taxation of automatic weapons and short rifles and shotguns. The camel's nose under the tent. Greatly expanded by *GCA68.*

NICBC **National Instant Criminal Background Check.** Mandated by the Brady Act, this overpriced computerized system is certainly not "instant." Purchases are now logged to SSN, and records are kept even though the law requires their destruction. NICBC is really the beginning of a national registry of firearms owners. A Bad Thing.

The DoJ and Clinton have claimed that the NICBC system has denied guns to 69,000- *"hundreds of thousands of felons, fugitives, and stalkers."* This is not true; it is a lie! (If it were true, then where are the hundreds of thousands of prosecutions for Brady Act violations?) Instead, the GAO found that about half of all refusals stemmed from paperwork problems and traffic violations.

NICS   National Instant Check System. This is the official (though improper) name for the above NICBC, and used (I believe) to incorporate future additional denial (*i.e.,* "nix") criteria (*e.g.,* tax-evaders, political dissidents, etc.). *"It's not just for criminals anymore!"*

NIJ   National Institute of Justice.

nm   nanometer. A billionth of a meter. Used to measure ranges of energy frequency, such as light. Lasers of 630-680nm are visible red (635nm being the brightest); lasers of 710-850nm are infrared (IR) and invisible to the human eye (seen only through NVDs).

NM   National Match. Moderate target-grade military rifles. These will usually shoot 1-1½MOA, without compromising reliability.

NVD   night vision device. Soon to be outlawed for us. Get one *now*.

OAL   overall length

OEM   original equipment manufactured. Stock stuff.

Old Duffer   A gun show codger. An affectionate, not pejorative term.

overbore   A cartridge (usually Magnum) which gives high velocities through its inefficiently high powder charge (*e.g.,* the .300 Phoenix). These calibers usually burn out their barrels very quickly (w/i 1000rds).

parallax   The tendency for scope reticles to shift and change impact point if the shooter moves his head. Consistent cheekweld is vital with scopes above 10X.

Patriots   Americans who love their country, but not their government.

"Patriots"   PolSpeak for potential *"terrorists"* or *"hate criminals."*

penetrate   When a bullet goes through only one side of its target.

perforate   When a bullet goes though both sides, leaving an exit wound. Also called an "in and out."

PM   preventive maintenance. Routine cleaning and replacement of worn parts to avoid malfunctions in the field. Some guns need little PM (*e.g.,* AKs and Glocks), while some need more (*e.g.,* AR15s).

POA   point-of-aim. Where you aim (versus POI).

POI   point-of-impact. Where the bullet strikes. Check POA vs. POI.

PolSpeak   A false pejorative applied to innocuous people, things, and activities. Different religious beliefs are *"cults,"* gun shows are *"illegal* *arms bazaars,"* etc. We must fight and win the battle for the metaphor.

pre-1899   Guns made pre-1899 are not *"firearms"* under Title 18, and therefore can be purchased without a Form 4473. See Chapter 21.

presentation   To draw a handgun from its holster.

QC   **quality control.**

QD   **quick detachable,** as in mags and mounts (sling and scope).

Rainy Decade   My term for a reoccurrence of 1773-83. Likely to happen, at least in certain areas (such as the South and West).

Raufoss   A .50BMG bullet containing a pyrotechnically initiated explosive and incendiary, also with a tungsten carbide penetrator. Called "Greentip" by the SEALs. The most destructive .50BMG round. Ø12-25.

rd   **round.** One loaded cartridge. Can also mean a bullet enroute.

reticle   The "crosshairs" in a rifle scope. Mil-Dot is the way to go.

RKBA   **Right to Keep and Bear Arms.**

RM   **Remington Magnum.** In .222, 6.5/7/8mm, .350, .416, and .44.

Rules 1-4   The overlapping safety rules popularized by Jeff Cooper.

SA   **single action.**   A trigger pull merely releases the already-cocked hammer; it cannot (as in DA) cock the hammer first. The Colt 1911 is a SA semi-automatic.

"Saturday Night Special"   A rascist term (from "N✱gger Town Saturday Night) used by gunphobes to describe inexpensive handguns. Also elitist, as if self-defense should be possible only for the wealthy.

SAW   **squad automatic weapon.**   An individually-carried MG, usually in an *"assault rifle"* cartridge.

SBT   **spitzer boattail.**   A long-distance, lead-tipped hunting bullet (*e.g.*, Sierra GameKing). Regular spitzers have a flat base.

SD   **sectional density.** The ratio of a bullet's weight in pounds to the square of its diameter in inches. Bullets of the same shape but with higher SD retain their velocity and energy better.

select-fire   Guns which can fire both semi-auto and full-auto.

semi-auto   A self-loading firearm which fires once per trigger pull.

SGN   Shotgun News.   Trimonthly display/classified ad digest for dealers and enthusiasts. Indispensable! 36 issues for only Ø29.

sight radius   The inch distance between the front and rear sights. The longer the radius, the more accurate the gun.

"sniper rifle"   PolSpeak for any rifle with a scope. The anti-gun pols are finally realizing the awesome capability of scoped, high-powered rifles, which make the AK47 look puny by comparison. As I predicted in 1998, this pejorative term is becoming a gunphobe buzzphrase (like *"cult," "compound," "Patriot," "militia," "Saturday Night specials," "assault weapons"* and *"cop killer bullets"*).

squib   A low-powered round. Used for indoor practicing.

Can also mean an unintentionally *powderless* round. When fired, the primer lodges the bullet mid-barrel. Firing a normal round behind this will often blow up the barrel and cause injury. If you ever feel or hear a squib round, cease fire immediately and check the bore!

"stockpile"   To store any quantity of Politically Incorrect items.

stopping power   The ability to hit a target's vital area with incapcitating fire within 2 seconds.

Sturmgewehr assault rifle.   Abbreviated StG. Legend has it that Hitler himself coined the term for the StG44, the archetypical assault rifle. This is a select-fire carbine in an intermediate caliber with QD mags. Now the world's combat long gun and favored over MBRs.

system   A particular gun (*e.g.,* Colt 1911, FAL, etc.) and its operating system, ergonomics, etc. Similar to "platform" or "OS" in computerese.

TANSTAAFL   *"There ain't no such thing as a free lunch."* From Robert A. Heinlein's *The Moon Is A Harsh Mistress.* A catch phrase and motto of many hip Libertarians.

training   The programming of subconscious athletic memory through physical exercise at the range. One trains by doing, not by reading. *"Training is to guns what location is to real estate."*

"Tupperware® Parties for Criminals"   PolSpeak for gun shows.

twist   A bore's spiral lands giving a bullet its spin, and thus directional stability and lift. Twist rate is described in turn/inches (1:9", etc.). The heavier the bullet, the faster the twist is needed to stabilize it.

unlawful vs. illegal   Unlawful is morally wrong (*malum in se*). Illegal is artificially wrong (*malum prohibitum*) because the government says so.

"unlicensed dealer"   Very recent PolSpeak for a private seller. This 2nd Amendment right is now decried as a *"loophole"* in the law. The term is quite honestly an oxymoron.

USG   United States Government.

USSA   United Socialist States of Amerika. A bitter pun on USSR.

victim disarmament.   *"gun control"*

VPC   Violence Policy Center.   A particularly vile freedom-hating group which still mouths the lie that the 2nd Amendment protects only state militias. They are working to ban handguns, *"assault rifles,"* and .50BMG target rifles. Masters of Insidious Metaphors. Home of the Specious Argument. A really noisome bunch. Life-long gunphobe Josh Sugarmann is their Executive Director. (www.vpc.org)

working   A cartridge or gun used mostly for hunting, pest control, etc.

WM   Winchester Magnum. In .264, .300, .338, and .458.

zero   To sight in a gun at a known distance (*e.g.,* 100, 300, MPBR).

zero-hold   An optical sight mount's ability to retain its zero. ZH.

>   **continuous** means ZH while the mount is attached to the gun.

>   **repeat** means ZH after detachment and reattachment.

ZH   zero-hold.

SAFETY & HANDLING

THE FOUR BASIC SAFETY RULES

There is no such thing as an "accidental discharge." There is a cause for every action, and **guns do not "go off" by themselves.** They must be loaded and fired by a human. When the shooter is untrained or careless—*then* occurs an ND (negligent discharge).

Rule 1
All guns are always loaded.

In your mind, there is no such thing as an "unloaded" gun. You *never* handle a gun differently because it's "unloaded."

Whenever you pick up a gun—even if you're alone and the only one handling it; even if you personally just disassembled it moments ago—*check the chamber.* You could have forgotten loading it, or somebody could have loaded/unloaded it without your knowledge. Have *firsthand* knowledge of its condition *every* time you pick up a gun! Make this a *perfect* habit, which you will later unthinkingly perform even if you are drousy, drunk, disoriented, injured, or distracted.

Rule 2
Never let your muzzle cover anything you don't want to destroy.

Do wave your muzzle past people. If somebody can see even a *crescent* of your muzzle, then you're being unsafe.

Rule 3
Keep your finger off the trigger until your sights are on the target.

Resting your finger on the trigger is one of the hardest habits to break. Your trigger finger should feel "at home" indexed straight on "armrest" of the frame.

One of General Patton's principles was that mistakes should be *paid for* instantly. Does a hot stove ever postpone burning you? Similarly, gun safety violations should be safely "painful." Make a pact with your family and shooting buddies that anybody catching you violate Rule 3 (or *any* Rule, for that matter) immediately gets a Ø20 bill. Safety violations should be *rarely* made, and *only* in the initial training.

Rule 4
Be sure of your target and what's beyond it.
One father, untrained and nervous, shot a suspected intruder hiding in the closet. It was his 16 y/o stepdaughter, skipping school. This was no "accident"—this was *negligence.*

GUN SAFETY AND CHILDREN

Thanks to safety programs like the NRA's Eddie Eagle, negligent fatalities of children 0-14 y/o have fallen from 550 in 1975 to 200 in 1995. This is nearly zero, considering the 40,000,000 gunowning homes (though even one is too many). With the exception of toddlers, I believe in gunproofing children, *not* childproofing guns (which can't be reasonably done to readily accessible defensive guns). With proper safety education, guns are no more risky in your household than are gas stoves, solvents, or steak knives. Do the following:

Demonstrate the destructive power of gun to children
They need to see firsthand how powerful guns are, instead of having false impressions made through TV. Shoot a can of soda or watermelon with a high-velocity hollowpoint.

No toy guns allowed
Toy guns which are "safe" to point at others create very stubborn bad habits. Guns are serious tools requiring awesome responsibility, and toy guns only dilute this vital issue. Take your children shooting often, and they'll never miss toy guns.

If a gun is unexpectedly found, don't touch it
The child should know to leave it alone and tell an adult. Praise the child effusively for doing this.

Family guns are *always* available for inspection
Eliminate the "forbidden fruit" syndrome of your guns. Face it, kids love to snoop around when their parents are away.

I did, and you did. (The hideous taste of that dictionary-sized bar of chocolate always perplexed me.) Therefore, let's make the desk drawer .38 and the closet shotgun no big deal.

Make an absolute promise to your children that, *with your supervision*, they may look at and handle *any* of the family guns *at any time, if they ask first.* You promise that you will drop what you're doing, day or night, and handle the gun together. **You will do this cheerfully, *without fail*.** Boston sez: Never break a promise to a child.

Once children are a little older and have proven their safe handling and responsibility, they may handle and/or shoot their guns without your supervision, but with prior permission. (In some States, children must have on their person your written permission, or they must be accompanied by you.)

Once they're in, say, junior high school, they may use their own guns as freely as their bicycles.

Once they're 18, take them to a good shooting school.

CONDITION OF WEAPON

Knowing these Conditions will not only help you understand firearms, but they're necessary for common communication (instead of saying *"loaded"* or *"unloaded"*). There are four variables involved (chamber, magazine, hammer, and safety), and these Conditions elegantly cover their relationships.

Zero
Loaded chamber. Cocked hammer or striker. Safety disengaged (*off*). (This would *only* be used during live fire.)

One
Loaded chamber. Cocked hammer or striker. Safety engaged (*on*). (This is how SAs should reside in their holsters. *"Cocked and locked."*)

Two (this is sort of "Condition 1" for DAs and Glocks)
Loaded chamber. Hammer down. Safety off. (Pulling trigger overcomes safeties in Glocks and DAs.)

Three
Empty chamber. Loaded magazine in gun. (Fine for drawer storage, but do *not* carry in Three. It's too slow!)

Four
Empty chamber. No magazine in gun. (Long-term storage Condition.)

RANGE COMMANDS

If you ever attend a quality shooting school or class, here are some common commands you'll hear at the range.

Index!	Straighten out trigger finger on frame.
Muzzle!	Adjust muzzle to safe direction.
Make Ready!	**From firing line only!**: load, chamber and engage safety: ready to fire.
Fire!	**From firing line only!**: Only on command. Draw or raise from Ready.
Front Sight!	You've lost the front sight. Reacquire focus.
Ready!	Keep muscle tension, down-hinge arms. Muzzle pointed 45° down. (Condition "Burnt Orange.")
Make Safe!	Reengage safety of loaded gun. Prepared to fire from Ready, or holster.
Unload!	**From firing line only!**: Drop magazine. Clear and check chamber.
Holster!	Preceded by *Make Ready!* or *Make Safe!* or *Unload!* command.
Sling!	Preceded by *Make Ready* or *Make Safe!* or *Unload!* command.

Range clear; Go Forward and Tape your targets.
                Only on command.

System check

This means ascertaining the loaded status of a gun. First, check the mag for capacity, and give it a *Tap-Tug*. Then, check the chamber for a round. (Avoid the archaic and perilous "press check" on 1911s. Keep your finger away from the muzzle!)

Loading

First, check the magazine for rounds (or insert it if necessary). Next, slightly open the action to inspect the chamber. If it is already loaded, then close the action and engage the safety if you wish. If it is not loaded, then continue to open the action fully, then release it (letting the recoil spring do its job).

Some people check the chamber first, then the mag. To me, this is backwards, as it requires a second slide rack if you need a new mag. Deal with the mag first, then the chamber.

Unloading

First, remove the magazine and hold it with your gun pinky. Then, *smartly* rack the action to extract/eject the live round. Do not slowly eject the round into your palm, as it can be accidentally set off by striking the ejector (it's happened in Glocks) or by impacting a high primer. Vigorously rack the slide to clear the chamber, and *then* pick up the ejected round.

Clearing malfunctions

Stop saying *"My gun jammed!"* First of all, jam is found only on toast. Equipment either functions or it *malfunctions*. Secondly, we need to be specific; what *kind* of malfunction? The firing cycle of any firearm is simple and sequential:

feed	(inserting a round from the magazine into the chamber)
fire	(mechanical action causing ignition of round)
extract	(removal of case from the chamber)
eject	(removal of case from the entire firearm)

Failures can occur at any phase, and fixing them must be ingrained in your subconscious to be performed *automatically* without conscious thought. The more reliable your weapon (*e.g.,* Glocks), the more you must practice malfunction drills.

Failure to feed (also called a Class 1 malfunction)

This is almost always the fault of either the magazine (empty, not fully seated, missing, or faulty) or the ammo (case deformed or too long). Sometimes it's just a dirty or faulty gun (*i.e.,* weak hammer spring or broken firing pin).

Usually the magazine was not fully seated. In tactically exigent situations, the first thing to attempt is the *Tap-Rack-Bang*. *Tap* forcefully the mag into the weapon to seat it fully. (With the *Tap* goes a *Tug*, to ensure a seated mag.) *Rack* the bolt or slide to charge a round into the chamber. *Bang* to fire the weapon. (Some instructors call this "attempt-to-fire.") *Tap-Rack-Bang*s take less than a second with practice, and should be practiced with dummy rounds slyly mixed with your range ammo to surprise yourself.

Failure to fire

This is either an ammo or gun problem. Usually it's bad ammo (bad, high, inverted, or missing primer). When under fire, *Tap-Rack-Bang*. When not under fire, eject the round after waiting out a potential hangfire for 30 seconds.

If an abnormal sound or sensation was felt upon the trigger pull, *cease firing* as it probably was a squib load. This is when a powderless round was nevertheless fired by the primer, lodging the bullet mid-barrel. Check your barrel!

Failure to extract (also called a Class 3 malfunction)

Usually it's because of a double feed, but sometimes a case sticks in the chamber, or a case rim rips off, or an extractor breaks. So, a round remains in the chamber with a second round pressed hard from behind. Because your gun's two most powerful springs (recoil and magazine) are working against each other, this takes much time to fix (versus a failure to fire).

If you've opted to fix it, yell to your partner *"Cover me!"* and drop behind cover (or at least lower your target profile by sitting, squatting, kneeling, etc.). Because this will take several seconds to fix, you can also transition to another gun.

Then, *Look-Lock-Drop-Rack-Rack-Rack-Tap-Rack-Bang*. A failure to extract will first be evidenced by a failure to fire with no hammer drop (as with a normal failure to fire from a bad round or empty chamber), so have a *Look*. Your gun will show you the problem. Then, *Lock* back the action, *Drop* the mag (hold it with your gun hand pinky), *Rack* vigorously 3X to clear, and *Tap-Rack-Bang*. While racking the action, inspect what's going on! (Keep your peripheral vision on the fight.)

Some instructors teach to *discard* the mag (as it could have caused the malfunction) with "drop" and insert a new mag. This is probably good advice with combat rifles (especially with the AR15, which is prone to mag problems).

Failure to eject

These are called "stovepipes" because of the case being caught between the boltface and the ejection port. This usually happens because of a bolt/slide which failed to recoil all the way back to its stop before returning forward. Anything which diminishes recoil force (*e.g.*, a too-gently held gun, which occurs often with the lightweight Glocks) or impedes bolt/slide movement (dirt, sludge, a rubbing thumb, etc.) can cause a stovepipe. The solution is usually a *Tap-Rack-Bang*.

SafetyOn—a fantastic interactive teaching CD

If you'd like more instruction in the basics on how guns work, care, handling, safety, defense, etc.—get this amazing CD which uses 3D and virtual reality! (www.SafetyOn.com)

SELF-DEFENSE & THE LAW

WHEN & WHY TO SHOOT

When to shoot

Lethal force is valid *only* against a *reasonably* perceived *imminent* and *grievous* threat. The jury must agree that your assailant had the capability, opportunity, and obvious intent to imminently cause you at least grievous bodily harm (GBH, in law talk). Let's discuss those three elements:

capability

The attacker must have the power to cause GBH or death, because either of his being armed, or through his disparity of force (*e.g.*, a 260lb man against a 110lb woman) or skill (*e.g.*, the attacker was known to be a trained martial artist).

Women can much more easily prove the "disparity of force" element, as even an unarmed man has sufficient strength to cause injury.

opportunity

The attacker must be capable of causing *imminent* (*i.e.*, immediately or nearly so) injury. He must be within range. You cannot shoot, for example, an unarmed dirtbag from across the street because he yelled out that he was going to kill you.

Since any average male can close 21' of distance within 1½ seconds, such would likely be considered by any reasonable jury as within range. 1½ seconds, incidentally, is not much time to draw and accurately fire your handgun. It can be done, but only with good training and much practice (and then, probably only from a belt holster, as deep concealment rigs take 2-4 seconds).

jeopardy
The attacker must behave in such a manner that a reasonably prudent juror would fear for his/her life.

Why to shoot
You shoot to *stop*—not to kill. Any kill is *incidental*, unless the *only* way to stop his lethal actions was to kill.

YOU *CANNOT* SHOOT...

to defend property
In most States, you cannot shoot a burglar just because he's leaving with your stereo. There is no jeopardy. (In some States, however, *any* intruder caught in your home—especially at night—can be *assumed* deadly and thus shot.)

The only exception I know of this is in cases of attempted arson (as a fire's spread can be uncontrollable).

when there is *no* threat of GBH or death
Such threat may appear, disappear, and reappear. *While* it is *not* present (including its temporary disappearance), you may not use lethal force. If you get in a fight with only one equal opponent, you cannot shoot him (unless the fight *really* gets bad and your life becomes in danger).

when you're being verbally abused
Although the courts have recognized that *"fighting words"* can create a quasi-automatic reaction, such will not excuse your employment of deadly force.

to stop a fleeing, unarmed criminal
This is generally true *unless* his escape will reasonably allow him to cause imminent GBH or death. Such can be a very close call, and I wouldn't even consider it unless the guy is running rampant with an Uzi or something.

WHEN IT'S *INADVISABLE* TO SHOOT

While you *may* defend the life of somebody else (including a stranger), you should think long and hard about it. First of all, you must be sure that an apparently violent incident with obvious assailants is *exactly* that. If you mistake the scene and shoot the victim, well...

Is a stranger's life worth the risk?

Secondly, you might conclude that the risk of defending a stranger is too great. One very respected shooting instructor has done precisely that. Clint Smith's policy is that unless he or a loved one were under attack, he would hold his fire. Any stranger (or mere acquaintance) would not be defended. To him, nobody but a loved one is worth risking the liability for a stray round. Meaning, for example, he would *not* have shot Hennard at the Luby's Cafeteria in Killeen to save the patrons. (He would have taken cover with a view to exit the building at first opportunity.) This is a very stringent policy, and one that I personally have some qualms with (though I can easily understand his point). I'll be chewing on it for some time, and suggest that you do, too.

YOUR LIABILITY

Once you let a round go, you're responsible for any injury it causes, even in the most hellacious of firefights. (Rule 4 applies even then!) Inadvertently kill somebody's kid and the parents will not care in the least that you were defending yourself and are very, very sorry. They will sue you down to your socks.

Prepare your financial and asset structure

As I explained in Chapter 18 of *Bulletproof Privacy*, there is no compelling reason to own property in your personal capacity. In fact, it is overwhelmingly compelling *not* to! What you don't own cannot be taken from you.

There are two main types of title (ownership): legal and equitable. Legal title means that it's yours on *paper*, but you have no right to convey it. (Your mortgaged home is a prime example. A college trustfund is another.)

Further, there is a difference between ownership and control. Ideally, you want to own nothing, and control everything. While ownership by its very nature usually includes control, the two can be separated with the use of a trust. A trust has full title to assets, but allows your usage of them (control). Thus you have the functional enjoyment of ownership (*i.e.*, control), without the liability. Will Rogers caught the essence of it when he quipped:

> *A trust is an accomplice who holds the stolen goods while the police search you.*

Naturally, I can't get into the mechanics of trust formation in this book, as the subject is quite involved. But you should do something, if only to create a Nevada corporation in which to place your home.

❖ 4

TACTICS
& TRAINING

The Bureau of Justice's national average states that I have a 1-in-4 chance of being a victim of violent crime in my lifetime. The risk conferred by living in a major population center...— where index felonies (rape, robbery, homicide, aggravated assault, etc.) number 200 a day—increases my chances of being a predator's lunch snack to 1-in-9 annually.
   — Mark F. Twight, "Eat or Be Eaten"
   S.W.A.T., March 2000 (p.60)

A human being is the most dangerous animal in the world as it alone has the ability to strike a deadly blow at a distance.
   — Timothy J. Mullin, *Round Guns—Square Guns* (2000)

According to FSU professor Gary Kleck's fine book *Point Blank: Guns and Violence in America*, defenders actually fired their gun in fewer than one out of four cases. Moreover, resistance with a gun was *the best* tactic to avoid injuries. Below are the percentages of those defenders who *were* injured:

12.1%	resisted with a gun
27.3%	did not resist in any way
29.5%	resisted with a knife
52.1%	resisted with bare hands

Those who resisted with a gun (the best tactic) were injured *less than half the time* of those who offered no resistance! So, if you'd like to survive these perilous times, you should learn how to fight with a handgun.

Why listen to *me*?

Though I am an occasional shooting instructor, I do not claim to be a working professional in the shooting industry. I am not a Jeff Cooper, Clint Smith, Bill Rogers, or Louis Awerbuck. I have neither the extensive military and/or police experience of these men, nor their years of instruction.

So, what? Did you learn to drive from *Al Unser*? My point is this: the personal instruction from bonafide experts is very expensive. Although not even 1% of gunowners will ever get to a shooting academy, there's no reason why much of that training cannot "trickle down" from civilian alumni.

Of all our prestigious shooting schools combined, probably less than 25,000 civilian Americans have enjoyed such training. That's 25,000 out of *75,000,000* gunowners, or one in 3,000. Most of them went to only one or two classes. I've been to more than six, for pistol, shotgun, and rifle. I'd guess that only 5,000 civilians have been to at least six Ø750+ courses. That's one in only *15,000* gunowners.

I always shoot in the top 10% of my class, much to the dismay of the SWAT, SEAL, and SF guys. (At fifteen, with pimples and braces, I won a local pistol competition with my Colt Trooper .357 Magnum. You can imagine how ecstatic the cops and highway patrolmen were.) Therefore, it seems fair to say that I'm a very well trained and practiced civilian and layman. Outside the military and police fraternities, few Americans have my firearms experience. I discuss all this, not to brag, but to back up my position of mild authority.

My dogma is fairly orthodox shooting doctrine. Shooting is more of a science than an art, and what has been so far discovered to work, *works*. If you learn and practice the basics, you'll get smooth, and with smoothness comes speed.

THE THREE KINDS OF PEOPLE

There are only three kinds of people:

predators (*i.e.*, those who cannibalize their own species)   **alpha**

prey (*i.e.*, those who allow themselves to be eaten)   **beta**

those who refuse to be either (*i.e.*, an armed libertarian)   **gamma**

If you're not predatorial (the first prerequisite of gamma), yet don't have the will or training to defend yourself, then you are by default *prey*. As the harshly accurate saying goes:

There are no victims, only volunteers.

So that you do *not* become prey, you must embrace at least a little bit of the Warrior spirit.

Mothers defending their offspring can exhibit terrifying ferociousness, but they must be trained to become ferocious when protecting *themselves*. Men generally do not seem to have this deeply ingrained programming, or if they do, they allow it to be weeded out through socialization. To be a *complete* man, he must retain a healthy portion of his innate savagery.

THE WARRIOR SPIRIT

Of every One-Hundred men, Ten shouldn't even be there,
Eighty are nothing but targets,
Nine are real fighters...
We are lucky to have them...They make the battle.
Ah, but the One, One of them is a Warrior...
and He will bring the others back.
　　　— Hericletus (*circa* 500 B.C.)

It is no accident that the quintessential Warrior is a 1% kind of man. If any society were entirely made up of Warriors, then combat (most of it merely for the combat's sake) would be incessant. Therefore, the Warrior is a rare and strong spice only sparingly sprinkled in the proletarian stew of humanity.

Only 10% have any degree of Warrior spirit, and the remaining 90% must rely on their Warriors for defense. Apparently, this is how it should be, just as not everyone is cut out to be an entrepreneur. Nevertheless, we must all *occasionally* be Warriors. There are two basic concepts you need to grasp early:

At some point in our lives, we *all* must fight. It's part of being human.
Every fight has its own unique distance, and thus its own needs.

At some point in our lives, we *all* must fight

Every creature is alternately predator or prey. When you're prey, you must defend yourself. This is called fighting. Part of being alive means *staying* alive. A Warrior is, first, merely somebody who refuses to be prey by mastering the offensive-defensive. (Secondarily, they become—whether for good or for evil—predators by mastering the offensive-offensive, but such is beyond the scope of this chapter.)

In gun classes I tell my students that they are not learning how to shoot—they are learning how to *fight*. Gunhandling and shooting are only *incidental* to this particular martial art.

All fights have their own distance

Since you are reading this overtly Warrior book, I presume that you are also among that 10%. It is a "blade profile" that all Warriors are born with, but it's also an edge that must be sharpened, and then honed. There are many ways to work your edge, and all of them valid in their own right. Becoming a *pistolero* is one of them. Learning to grapple is another, and so is the Filipino art of stick fighting.

Think of it this way: Each different martial art hones ½" of your edge. How much of your edge do you want to be sharp? If you're trained only in sniping, a kung fu guy will beat you by getting close. If you're trained only in judo, a gunfighter will beat you by staying 10yds away.

What's vital to grasp conceptually is that the main reason for different martial arts is for their different *distances*. (Bruce Lee was one of the first to understand this and then "cross-pollinated" his training.) The *distance* of the threat determines the weapon and tactics. For example, with guided missiles, you can fight your enemy from thousands of miles away. With a sniper rifle, up to a half mile away. With a .308 battle rifle, up to a third mile away. With a handgun, up to 100yds. With a throwing spear, up to several yards. With a stick, up to a yard. Anything closer than stick or knife ranges is reduced to feet and hands, then knees and elbows, and then your body itself (as in wrestling). Since you have no idea how far away your threat will be, you should be able to fight from 0 to at least 25yds. (When your threat is past 25yds, you can likely run and escape.)

Handgun limits

Every weapon is a specialized one. There is *no* universal weapon. Handguns are specialized for 2-25yds. Anything farther than 25yds becomes difficult to hit (and the bullet's energy drops off rapidly). Anything closer than 2yds, and you're now within contact range in just half a second. Within 1yd, your handgun becomes actually more of a *disadvantage* (as you shift from the offensive-defensive to the *defensive*-defensive in order not to lose your gun to your attacker). The longer range the weapon, the less its effectiveness at close range—and vice versa.

Learn hand-to-hand!

Thus, you should first learn how to fight at 0-1yds. A simple (but competent) array of blocks, strikes, punches, kicks, holds, etc. will fend off 95+% of your potential assailants, thus giving you the distance needed to get your handgun into play.

I make this point because gun people often have an unrealistic sense of confidence. Just because you can fight well with a handgun is no reason to be cocky. Any decent knifefighter can get within range and remove the nose from your face before you can even clear leather. You must learn some hand-to-hand techniques so that you'll be able to maintain and increase your range (and thus your advantage of delivering incapacitating energy from a distance, which is the whole *point* of a gun).

Begin with Grover's *Combatives* videos from Paladin.

The Warrior's fighting skills are distance irrelevant

The *consummate* Warrior, however, can fight and win no matter what the range of his opponent. The *entire* length of his edge has been sharpened, and he spends the rest of his life honing it. **Becoming a Warrior is a *process,* not a destination. You never arrive; you're always *getting* there.** There are *always* portions of your blade which will need work, at least in contrast with the rest of your edge. (Any bodybuilder understands this. As soon as his back and shoulders are in shape, his legs will then need work to catch up, and then his chest, etc.)

In fact, a black belt doesn't mean "expert," it means "qualified beginner." The best martial artists—those universally known as Masters—think of themselves as merely advanced *students.* (Guro Dan Inosanto comes to mind, obviously. When learning a new art, he dons a white belt like a novice and goes through class from the beginning, like a novice. His humility and his dedication to learning have combined to make him one of the world's most capable and respected martial artists.)

We all can learn from each other

Recently, at a martial arts camping weekend, I was the student of a most accomplished *escrima* stick fighter. The next day, he was *my* student in how to shoot a Glock and AR15 (which are outlawed in his native Philippines). He was easy to teach, because his mindset was one of a *student*, not master. (The masters become so only because they're the best students.)

Americans are the world's best gunfighters because we *can* keep and bear arms. Filipinos fight the best with sticks and edged weapons because that's all they've been *allowed* to own. Orientals fight the best with hands and feet because they were not allowed to own even sticks or edged weapons. So, add the Oriental open hand skills (0-1yds) to the Filipino knife and stick skills (1-2yds) to our firearm skills (2-800yds) and you've covered the entire continuum of visible range combat.

I say all this so that you don't get complacent just because you've learned how to fight with a handgun and a rifle. I once heard of a wealthy man who attended every class at Orange Gunsite, and became proficient at arms. He then had the chance to expand his training at another fine gun school, but refused since he *"already"* knew how to shoot. Nobody knows *everything* there is to know about shooting, and any honest instructor (or student) will admit that. (That's why the Navy SEALs, Marine Force Recons, and Army Special Forces train *everywhere*. They are always looking for just *one* small improvement or just *one* new technique, which could, in an odd situation, be *precisely* the one needed to win the fight.)

There is no "best" way to fight

Karate is not "better" than judo, or vice versa. Each merely sharpens a particular small area of the Warrior's blade. The kenpo braggart can get waxed by a Brazilian grappler.

In *every* fight you risk being (even momentarily) on your *opponent's* terms. That's why you must have *absorbed* his terms in order to *deny* him his terms. When you've made his terms yours, you force him to fight on *your* terms (as he no longer has any uniquely his own). *That* is why you cross-train!

There is no "best" school

Thunder Ranch is not "better" than Gunsite, or vice versa; a good student will learn something valuable from *both* of them.

So, when you hear somebody loudly defending his style as the "best" you'll know that he is a narrow-minded braggart and Warrior-wannabe. True Warriors are humble and attentive to new things. They know that since there is no "best," anybody they meet could be *better*. Thus, they are keen to learn in training *why* he's better, rather than experience it in a *fight* and have it be perhaps the last thing they *ever* learn.

YOUR THREAT

There are two solid rules regarding your Bad Guy(s):

Nobody can tell you what your threat will *look* like.

Even though it is most *likely* that your Bad Guy will be a 22.3 years old Black or Hispanic who is 5'9" tall, if you train exclusively for such an expectation you will one day be very surprised when some 48 year old white guy has a knife to your throat.

Even if a *known* person just threatened to kill you in 10 minutes, he could arrive in disguise or with accomplices. As Mark Twight remarked in his fine *S.W.A.T.* article, *"The smart predator fulfills no stereotypes and respects no boundaries."*

Nobody can tell what it will *take* to win your fight.

Yes, well-placed rounds from a .45 will *probably* do it. Yes, a well-placed 12 gauge slug will *probably* do it, and, yes, a round of .308 to his head will *probably* do it. But, "probably" is not 100%. In every one of the above cases, there has been at least *one* example of a Bad Guy who not only lived, but continued to fight! The human body (especially when amped up on drugs or adrenaline) can absorb incredible punishment. It is an adroit, well-armored, strong, and highly adaptive combat chassis.

What will it take to win? **Whatever it *takes* to win!** Even most gunfights occur within 7yds/4 seconds/4rds during low-light conditions, you should have many weapons and tactics at your disposal, especially hand-to-hand combat skills.

target indicators—some are always present:
sound

While you are sleeping, your subconscious mind is a marvelous guard dog. Its filtering process will ignore loud noises if they are part of your household, yet will instantly awake you because of any soft sound which shouldn't be there. Trust it. Stay quiet and wait it out.

movement (deletes camouflage)

What do animals do when they're scared? Freeze up. Most movement is seen by your peripheral vision on the sides of your eyes (which contain rods). In fact, if you want to look for something, do not stare directly at it, but a bit off to the side. Stay still and wait it out.

reflection/shine

The time length of this is likely to be short rather than long, so be ready to act quickly.

contrast

Camouflage is designed to minimize contrast, and can be quite effective. If it is, then other indicators must alert you.

outline

A bit of foliage on your head and shoulders does wonders for breaking up your outline.

smell

While this is a pretty rare indicator, it can happen. In Thomas Harris's *Hannibal*, the escaped Dr. Lecter was warned of an attacker by his goatlike body odor.

"sixth sense"

That "funny feeling" can be from one of two sources: one of your five senses which you have not consciously identified, or an actual sixth sense in the supernatural realm. Many hunters and professional soldiers (especially snipers) have remarked how important it is during a stalk to *not* directly stare or even *think* hard about your quarry, else he will often sense it. While nobody can adequately explain it, this phenomenon has been noticed by so many people that its truth cannot be questioned.

LEVELS OF ALERTNESS

There is a progression of alertness which we classify by increasingly darker colors. Learning the color codes and their concepts will help you stay alive in this dangerous world.

White

Unalert and unaware. This is a separation of the conscious and subconscious mind (*i.e.*, daydreaming). Drivers in car accidents often remark, *"He came out of nowhere."* This is White.

White may be fine when you're at home with loved ones, but you should *never* be in White in public (a condition which is called "food"). If you look or act like food, you'll be eaten.

Yellow

Alert and aware—focused and conscious of any potential problem. *"I might have to shoot some Bad Guy today."*

Nobody can tell you what your Bad Guy (or Girl) will look like, where they'll come from, or what they'll be armed with. *Statistically,* it will be a minority male(s) in his early twenties, however it could be a 53 year old Asian woman with a cane.

Orange

Heightened Yellow. You now have a *specific potential* problem. *"I might have to shoot that Bad Guy in a few seconds!"* Ask yourself, *"What is my objective? What are my alternatives?"*

If you're with somebody, immediately get their attention. (Indicate the Bad Guy and say *"Orange."*) Generally, your partner should then move to cover so that you both form a wide "Y" with your Bad Guy at the base. (If your partner is not armed, then get him/her to cover.)

Forewarned is forearmed, and the sooner you go to Orange on some creep, the better. See your threat before his sees his opportunity. Since reaction time is .25 seconds for most people (.20 if you're *really* quick), you are already behind the curve once he goes for his weapon or begins to rush you. You need time, and distance equals time (as Einstein proved). If you can't increase your distance, then at least *maintain* it.

Assailants can sense your Orange, and this usually is enough to make them bypass you for "Food in White." Once, in a Phoenix convenience store, I went "Burnt Orange" on two suspicious-looking dudes wearing trench coats (in July!) who were obviously casing the place. They saw me with my holstered Glock, glanced at each other, and hurriedly left.

Red   You now have a specific problem to solve.

It is no longer a *potential* problem, it is about happen.

You have a willingness to fight if required, and are holding at your "mental trigger." You may have drawn your gun, you may have discreetly placed your hand on it, or you may be ready to effect a full drawstroke. You may or may not have warned them about your imminent fire. Whichever (every situation is unique, and thus demands its own unique tactics), you are willing/able to deliver effective fire within 3 seconds.

The nature of self-defense is that it is necessarily *reactive* rather than proactive. Under the law, you must wait until you are attacked or until he begins to attack. (While the doctrine of "pre-emptive" self-defense *is* recognized, it's a heavy burden of proof and you'd better have some friendly witnesses.)

Remember to take some deep breaths, because your life may suck in just a few seconds. Be scanning for other Bad

Guys, be looking for cover, be thinking about your background (Rule 4). Move to the best tactical location. Mentally rehearse your drawstroke and movements. Tell yourself, *"Front sight. Press. Front sight."*

Black

You *are* engaging and will do exactly as trained through subconscious action ("viewing from above"). It's another separation of the conscious and unconscious mind. If you have *no* training, then *nothing* is exactly what you will do. *"Training is to fighting what location is to real estate."* You are in the fight. Whoever has the most training, practice, and *will* generally prevails. (Sometimes luck plays a significant part, too.)

Nobody can tell you *what* it will take to win your fight. That's why it is important to train with different weapons (including impact, edged, and bare hands). Keep your mind working, and use every advantage possible.

Always Cheat. Always Win. (Every fight is strictly Win or Lose. If you *win*, then you did it *right*.)

The only dirty fight is the one you *lose*.

The Gift of Fear, by Gavin de Becker

You may have already heard about or read this book. I personally have very strong mixed feelings about it, which I'll explain in detail. First, I'll discuss what I *like* about the book, and then I'll address my objections.

Survival signals relating to new people

How can you accurately tell if a stranger who offers to help you is a Good Guy or a Bad Guy? When should you properly go into Condition Orange? Gavin de Becker lists several survival signals that we should understand and heed.

forced teaming

When the stranger uses *"we"* and *"us"* and *"our"* he is likely trying to get you to think of him as a kind of partner.

> *Sharing a predicament, like being stuck in a stalled elevator or arriving simultaneously at a just-closed store, will understandably move people around social boundaries. But forced teaming is not about coincidence; it is intentional and directed, and it is one of the most sophisticated manipulations. The detectable signal of forced*

teaming is the projection of a shared purpose or experience where none exists: "Both of "; "We're some team"; "How are we going to handle this?"; "Now we've done it," etc. (p.64)

So, when you start hearing that you're suddenly in partnership with a total stranger, your antennae should go up. Mentally step back and begin to view the scene in objective context.

charm and niceness

Charm is another overrated ability. Note that I called it an ability, not an inherent feature of one's personality. Charm is almost always a directed instrument, which, like rapport building, has motive. To charm is to compel, to control by allure or attraction. Think of charm as a verb, not a trait. If you consciously tell yourself, "This person is trying to charm me," as opposed to "This person is charming," you'll be able to see around it. Most often, when you see what's behind the charm, it won't be sinister, but other times you'll be glad you looked.

Trust, formerly earned through actions, is now purchased with sleight of hand, and sleight of words. (p.66-7)

too many details

When people are telling the truth, they don't feel doubted, so they don't feel the need for additional support in the form of details. When people lie, however, even if what they sound credible to you, it doesn't sound credible to them, so they keep talking.

Each detail may be only a small tack he throws on the road, but together they can stop a truck. The defense is to remain consciously aware of the context in which details are offered.

Context is always apparent at the start of an interaction and usually apparent at the end of one, but too many details can make us lose sight of it.

A good exercise is to occasionally remind yourself of where you are and what your relationship is to the people around you. With a date who stays beyond his welcome, for example, no matter how jokey or charming he may be, a woman can keep herself focused on context simply by thinking, "I have asked him to leave twice." The defense for too many details is simple: Bring the context into conscious thought. (p.68-70)

typecasting

Another strategy...is called typecasting. A man labels a woman in some slightly critical way, hoping she'll feel compelled to prove that his opinion is not accurate. "You're probably too snobbish to talk to the likes of me," a man might say, and the woman will cast off the mantle of "snob" by talking to him.

Typecasting always involves a slight insult, and usually one that is easy to refute. But since it is the response itself that the typecaster seeks, the defense is silence, acting as if the words weren't even spoken. If you engage, you can win the point, but you might lose something greater. (p.70)

Another possible defense is agreeing with the insult to end the conversation. *"You're right; I am too snobbish. Good-bye."*

loan sharking

If the stranger's motive is not right, he will perform a favor or courtesy in order to place you in his debt. The "interest" he has in mind could be quite expensive.

the unsolicited promise

The unsolicited promise is one of the most reliable signals because it is nearly always of questionable motive. Promises are used to convince us of an intention, but they are not guarantees.

Here's the defense: When someone says "I promise," [think to yourself] *"You're right, I am hesitant about trusting you, and maybe with good reason. Thank you for pointing it out."* (p.72)

discounting the word *"no"*

Declining to hear "no" is a signal that someone is either seeking control or refusing to relinquish it.

*The worst response when someone fails to accept "no" is to give ever-weakening refusals and then give in. Another common response that serves the criminal is to negotiate ("I really appreciate your offer, but let me try to do it on my own first.") **Negotiations are about possibilities,** and providing access to someone who makes you apprehensive is not a possibility you want to keep on the agenda. **I encourage people to remember that "no" is a complete sentence.***

[T]he woman who turns toward [an uncomfortably persistent stranger], *raises her hands to the Stop position, and say directly, "I don't want your help," is less likely to be his victim.* (p.74)

If suddenly and inexplicably fearful—*trust it!*

This is the basic message of the book, and I couldn't agree more. Your subconscious mind processes all of your sensory input, and signals your consciousness when something deserves your attention. Often, this signal will be a sudden strong fear rather than a specific thought, idea, or instruction. This fear differs from a general anxiety. Anxiety is usually 24/7 and unfounded, whereas real fear is sharp, earnest, and *valid*.

The fear is not sent to explain all the detail; it is sent to get your own *attention*. It is a headline, not a documentary report. Its purpose is to get you to "read" further. Do so!

Immediately go to Condition Orange, regain your focus, look for threats, and look for exits. Begin at once to improve your tactical situation by: moving to the light, reducing your vulnerability by getting next to a wall, getting your hand on your gun (if not discreetly drawing it and concealing your hand inside your coat pocket, a newspaper, etc.), communicating your fear to your partner, etc. If no *obvious* threat can be perceived, yet the fear persists, leave the area immediately! Don't try to rationalize it by thinking *"Oh, I'm just being silly; it's probably nothing."*

If you perceive a *specific* threat, then get tactical. Increase your distance, look for accomplices, focus on your breathing, seek your exits. Stay cool and work your problem! If you go to Condition Red, mentally rehearse a smooth drawstroke, and tell yourself *"Front sight! Press! Front sight!"*

The Gift of Fear should be read by any adult who has ever had a sudden and inexplicable fear (which is all of us). This is, however, a very qualified recommendation as the book is extremely negative regarding the rightful use of firearms for protection. As a young boy, the author was traumatized by a shooting incident, and appears to never have gotten over it:

> *Before I was thirteen, I saw a man shot, I saw another beaten and kicked to unconsciousness, I saw a friend struck near lethally in the face and head with a steel rod, I saw my mother become a heroin addict, I saw my sister beaten, and I was myself a veteran of beatings that had been going on for more than half my life.* (p.48)

I suggest that his damaged psyche still has much to work out.

The Gift of Fear is a *very* gunphobic book

While the book contains much excellent information illustrated by relevant stories, its good work is tragically marred by its anti-self-defense position. In fact, his bladder on the subject holds only as long as page 7, wherein he releases a stream of USA versus Japan gun deaths statistics.

America is not, thank God!, Japan

Japan, that 20th Century example of nonviolence. de Becker conveniently fails to mention that it was *Japan* who treated us to the Rape of Nanking, Pearl Harbor, the Bataan Death March, *kamikaze* attacks, and brutal torture of Allied POWs. He somehow neglects to explain Japan's total lack of civil rights—that you are guilty until proven innocent, that you may be held without a lawyer and questioned for days, that the police need no warrant to ransack a suspect's home. Of *course* Japan has little street crime! (Neither did Nazi Germany...)

Americans are not the obedient, unquestioning *automata* that the Japanese are. *We* explicitly recognize our right to own and carry arms in our Constitution; *we* proclaim to the world that we are a free people, and will fight to stay that way. *We* know that only slaves are forbidden to own guns, and give a mirthless chuckle when we hear about Japanese tourists by the thousands who book flights to Hawaii just so they can pay hundreds of dollars to shoot a .22LR. We shake our heads at Japan's replica "gun" industry and those who eagerly pay as much for a toy *model* of a Glock as a *real* Glock costs over here.

As de Becker is so fond of comparing us to foreign countries, I'm curious why he didn't mention that Swiss men keep their full-auto rifles at home, without any criminal use. (Perhaps it wouldn't serve to justify his own fear of guns?)

Given the overwhelming body of evidence and true life stories supporting armed self-defense, de Becker's attitude is inexcusable. He has undoubtedly scared many readers away from owning a handgun and training with it, and this is a disservice of the ugliest order. (Because of this, he may have helped to *create* more victims than counseled.)

the author exudes self-importance

de Becker also detracts from a potentially fine work by subtly aggrandizing himself with borderline shameless name-dropping. He lards his book with ceaseless mentions of dignitaries in distress, waiting helicopters, Gulfstream jets, Michelle Pfeiffer, armored limousines, Senate committees, secret government installations, coast-to-coast important activity, Cher, being on *60 Minutes*, etc., etc. You get the idea.

From reading his book, one can easily infer that de Becker as a boy had his "nose pressed against the glass" and calculatingly insinuated himself into a position serving the "entertainment" elite he so adored:

> [I was] *running at eleven years old alongside a limousine, clamoring with other fans to get a glimpse of Elizabeth Taylor and Richard Burton,* [and then within eight years I was] *inside that limousine working for the famous couple...* (p.22)

(Just *what* an unknown 19 year-old kid could have offered Taylor and Burton is beyond me, but he figured out something.)

Guns for the elite and their bodyguards, but *not* for you!

de Becker has no problem with his *own* company's agents being armed, but guns are too dangerous for *you*! (If he is truly so upset that guns *"send a piece of lead into a person's flesh like a rocket"* then why let his own employees carry them?)

The gunowner stories de Becker describes are disgusting. They all pertain to untrained and/or wimpy people who botch their lethal emergencies and thus make guns look worthless. Not *one* incident of capable and successful self-defense with a gun is mentioned (much less detailed) in this book, even though such occur in America up to 5,500 times every day! (A book you should get on this subject is *The Best Defense: True Stories of Intended Victims Who Defended Themselves with a Firearm*, by Robert Waters. Call 888-439-2665.)

For example, on page 391 he described one gunowner who awoke to take some asthma medicine, grabbed her .38 by mistake and shot herself in the face. (This is hardly common.)

On page 351, Bill McKenna, a physician, comes home from dinner with his two little girls (to find the living room light on, the cat inexplicably outside, and an unfamiliar car cooling off near his driveway). They go inside, and go to bed. Later, Bill is awakened by a noise downstairs which scares him. He makes a *"quick walk around...to be sure that everything was all right,"* and returns to bed. Thirty minutes later, he's again awakened by another noise—the sound of an intruder breathing. Bill turned on the light, *"and there was this guy standing in the middle of the room with my gun in his hand and our CD player under his arm."* He held Bill and his daughters at gunpoint for an hour while he agonized *"over the most difficult decision of my life"* (killing the family). Fortunately, they were not murdered:

> The intruder not only left, but he left the CD player. He did the family another favor too: He took the gun, which now won't be available to some more dangerous intruder in the future. (Bill is not replacing it.)

The obvious message here is that household guns for self-defense are not only worthless, but *dangerous*, as your intruder will just take it from you anyway. This is vile, sickening, liberal pap. The *real* moral of that story is that Bill did *everything* wrong and he should be deeply embarrassed for himself.

Bill's tactical mistakes were many. First, he comes home and ignores all the screaming clues that somebody is *in* his house. (Anybody with good training or common sense would have written down the license plate and VIN, and gone to a neighbor to phone the police. He would *never* have gone inside!)

Next, Bill hears a noise downstairs, but sloughs off this danger signal, too. (I mean *really*—his girls are upstairs asleep yet he doesn't *thoroughly* check things out with a handgun and flashlight?) **Then, he goes back upstairs, and falls asleep!** (His gun is likely on the nightstand, and his bedroom door is probably unlocked.) Finally, he allows himself and his two preschool daughters to be held at gunpoint (by his own gun!) for an hour while their lives teeter-totter with death. After such a gross compounding of so many mistakes, this moron is lucky/blessed to be alive! He did *everything* wrong.

Bill, you are the poster child for Condition White. You bought a gun thinking that the mere ownership of it would make you safe. No gun could have made up for your shocking lack of alertness, common sense (your *cat* knew to stay outside!), training, and courage. Your wife Linda should be ashamed of your actions. You *failed* as a man, as a husband, and as a father. *You* put yourself and your daughters in harm's way by going inside, *you* failed to properly clear your home after a danger signal woke you up, *you* allowed an intruder to take your own gun, *you* nearly lost your lives, and then *you let him get away*—with your own gun!

Oh, but it's O.K. since your gun *"now won't be available to some more dangerous intruder in the future."*

Bill, you've *armed* a *criminal!* Do you think that he will merely keep it at home for self-protection? No, he will more likely be carrying it *with* him during his future burglaries! You think that just because he let you and your little girls live that he's nonviolent? Well if that's true, then why was his *not* killing you all *"the most difficult decision"* he ever made? (Do the math here: A nonviolent man would have had *no* decision to make, much less *"the most difficult"* one in his life. He'd have just left.)

The *next* time your intruder gets startled by a homeowner (perhaps one without small children to tug at his sense of mercy), he may use your own gun to murder. And that murder will be on *you*. If not for *your* catastrophically poor responses, your intruder *could* have been behind bars (or dead).

If Bill had recognized his mistakes and learned from them, then I wouldn't have been so harsh. But since he is *not* replacing his gun, he evidently decided that "guns aren't the answer" and likely repeats his slanted story to all. And with a gunphobic megaphone such as de Becker, thousands of people are clucking, *"Yeah, maybe I shouldn't own a gun"* instead of realizing that Bill allowed and contributed to his own ordeal.

"Only those with unresolved anxieties carry guns"

On page 353, de Becker discusses a middle-aged man from Florida who got a concealed carry license: *"Because if some guy walks into a restaurant and opens fire, like happened at Luby's in Texas, I want to be in a position to save lives."* de Becker slyly scoffs at this with fatuous argumentation, and then takes an incredibly cheap shot:

> [H]*is anxiety wasn't caused by fear of death—if it were, he would shed the excess forty pounds likely to bring on a heart attack.*

(*I.e.,* he's just a dumb, fat guy who foolishly carries a gun.)

> *His anxiety is caused by fear of people, and by the belief that he cannot predict violence. Anxiety, unlike real fear, is always caused by uncertainty.*

Here we come to his core theory: According to de Becker, violence can always be predicted, so you can avoid or walk away from violent people. Private citizens who carry guns have not honed their inherent ability of prediction, and are thus living in needless and harmful anxiety. (If they'd only read de Becker's book, they wouldn't have to own a gun!)

Often, it *is* true that violence can be predicted. That's why we have a Condition Orange. It is also true that once detected by our fear sensors, a Condition Orange focus can often be avoided. It's happened to all of us, by receiving a "bad feeling" about somebody and not sticking around to find out why. So, on this point, I agree with de Becker.

However,* violence cannot *always* be predicted!** Take the above man from Florida who cited the Luby's Cafeteria incident. Hennard drove his truck through the plate-glass window, jumped out, and began firing. **Who could have predicted *that? Handguns are carried by rational and responsible people for precisely those lethal emergencies which can happen *without* any (or sufficient) warning.

Heeding one's own natural sense of fear is only *part* of the self-defense continuum. Being able to *resist* one's rapist or murderer with force in the form of a handgun is the *rest* of it. Learning some punches and kicks at an IMPACT class for women (800-345-5425) can help, but statistics prove that having a handgun is the *best* weapon for self-defense. By dissuading the reader to own and train with statistically the most effective tool for self-defense, Gavin de Becker does a great injustice to Americans, and to *women* in particular.

But, having been a victim of gun violence himself at 10 years old, de Becker cannot exorcise his own firearm demons.

crime is a *software*, not hardware (*i.e.*, guns) problem

Many people, including children, own or have access to guns, yet somehow they never turn to violence. Since there are 240 million guns in the hands of 75-80 million gunowners, it is obvious that crime is not a hardware problem (else there'd be several times as many gun-related assaults). Rather, crime is a *software* problem—*i.e.*, people with bad "programming."

His Chapter 12 deals with horrifically criminal youths, every example of whom were deeply immersed in very dark music (*i.e.*, heavy-metal or death metal, such as Slayer or Judas Priest). Yet, de Becker sloughs off the correlation with:

> *The content of the media products matter, but the amount may matter more, whether it is watching television too much, playing video games too much, listening to too much rock music, **or for that matter listening to too much classical music.*** (p.262)

(Yeah, these Bach and Handel crazies are becoming a real menace. I no longer feel safe in the classical music room at the record store, and just last week a stalker followed me home from the symphony, eerily whistling Beethoven's 5th. I'm going to find some peace at that Ozzy Osbourne concert tonight!)

Since Gavin de Becker operates a professional security service for our entertainment industry "royalty," his refusal to admit the influence (if not triggering factors) that violent movies, music, and games exhibit over children is predictable:

> *The range of things people might do with any product makes it next to impossible to foresee all risks.* (p.258)

Naturally, he has to blame something else besides the death message of satanic music, such as *"our huge harvest of handguns"* and our *"armed and often angry countrymen."*

> *I, for one, do not accept the avoidable risks posed by your products. As a potential victim, I do not sign on to any implied agreement with Colt or Smith & Wesson or Ruger, and I hold you entirely accountable for your failure to build in child-safe and other locking features that would clearly and predictably reduce deaths.*

Colt and S&W and Ruger have *never* urged their customers to rape women or murder police officers, but heavy metal bands and rap groups can do so *without* responsibility? **How about**

some consumer product safety standards for *them?* de Becker argues that media products are not *"proven and intended to affect the perceptions and behavior"* of the consumer. (This reminds me of how the cigarette companies used to deny, perfectly deadpan, that smoking caused cancer.) If parents and schoolteachers are not training our children to use drugs, speak filthily, copulate promiscuously, and sneer at all things good and honorable—then who *is?* The "entertainment" industry, **who *else?*** If de Becker *truly* believed in promoting a healthy environment for children to grow up in, he would on principle refuse to taint himself with (much less *protect*) people who pump out poisonous excrement in the forms of images, sounds, and messages.

consumer safety standards for guns is *"gun control"*

de Becker embraces that newest insidious rationale for victim disarmament—making guns "safe" for children:

> For some people, banning handguns is the psychological equivalent of government-imposed castration (a rather bitchy Freudian dig), so let me be clear: I am not challenging our **so-called** right to bear arms (in whose name, by the way, more Americans have died at home than at war).
>
> ...I propose that we hold gun manufacturers to the same product-liability standards we require for every other consumer product. Imagine if caustic drain opener were sold in easy-pour, flip-top, pistol-grip dispensers made attractive to children by the endorsement of celebrities.... (Puhleeze!)

I don't need to use a bottle of *Drano* within a few seconds to save my life; I might have to with my handgun.

the tired fig leaf of trigger locks to protect the children

A household firearm must be *readily* accessible in case of a lethal emergency. If you cannot draw, aim, and accurately fire it within 3-5 seconds, it will not be of much protective value.

Yet, de Becker insists that you keep a combination lock behind the trigger. O.K., try it yourself to see if *you* can unlock your gun and dry fire it on target within 5 seconds. You won't be able to. If you cannot do so even while awake in the middle of the afternoon, what makes you think that you will do it in the middle of the night, drowsy and scared?

> Some gun owners explain that they needn't lock their weapons because they don't have children. Well, other people do have children, and they will visit your home one day. The plumber who

answers your weekend emergency will bring along his bored nine-year-old son, and he will find your gun. (p.391)

This highly specious example requires the plumber *not* to have trained his boy in both manners (*i.e.,* not to snoop in customers' homes) and gun safety. Further, it requires the homeowner to leave his gun out in plain view/reach, *and* to allow a stranger's child to wander around the house unsupervised. (This is precisely the kind of vexing "reasoning" with which de Becker argues his fatuous gunphobic case throughout the book.)

With the exception of toddlers, one doesn't "childproof" guns, *one gunproofs children.* But that would require training our children in gun safety and handling, which would instill skill and responsibility with guns, and *gosh!*, we can't have *that!*

de Becker can first set a proper example by requiring his *own* armed agents to put trigger locks on *their* handguns, so if an assailant disarmed one of them, the gun would be harmless.

de Becker's child profiling scheme—Mosaic 2000

Without parental consent, Mosaic 2000 profiles children for violence. We are not told how the data is analyzed, stored, distributed, or acted upon. Now, that's scary! (Kelly Patricia O'Meara wrote a fine article on this: www.insightmag.com.)

de Becker has a vested interest in victim disarmament

If people can be convinced to *not* provide for their own protection, then they will have to turn to surrogates, *i.e.,* the police and private security agencies (de Becker's own industry).

One quick aside: What are the odds that de Becker himself is licensed by the State of California to carry a handgun? (Pretty good, I'd say.) Even if he is not, I'd bet that he keeps a gun at home and usually travels with an armed escort.

Hollywood hypocrites

Carrie Fisher, one of de Becker's pals and Victory Over Violence colleagues, remarked that *"television exposes children to behavior that man spent centuries protecting them from."*

Yes, but I seem to recall in *The Blues Brothers* Carrie Fisher playing a deranged stalker who destroyed a hotel building with high-explosives, blew up a sleeping neighborhood with a four-barreled bazooka, and wantonly fired a full-auto M16 in public. (The irony here is way over de Becker's head.)

I suspect that the *main* reason why Hollywood becomes so morally narcissistic is because, deep down, they know their careers generally have soiled the human experience. (Charlton

Heston often rails against Hollywood's glorification of perversion, and is despised for it. Fortunately, Heston is noble enough and rich enough not to care. Very much worth reading is his 12/97 NRA chairmanship acceptance speech, and Hollywood's hysterical reaction to it, at www.vpc.org.)

One moment they laughingly scorn decency, and the next they're mouthing its platitudes. (Sam Kinison once brilliantly remarked *"Rock stars against drugs is like Christians against Christ."*) Hollywood's efforts to *feel* good and *look* good while *doing* good stem in large part from their need to atone for the damage they've wrought.

Taking this theory to its logical conclusion, one could even allege a Hegelian motivation: To create (or feed) problems in order to effect their own "solution," and thus remake society in their own image—all under the guise of doing "good." Very sick.

In summary, read *The Gift of Fear*, but only very carefully

I found my copy at a garage sale for 50¢ and definitely got my money's worth. You likely will, too.

Now, let's talk about guns and tactics.

WEAPON RELIABILITY

First, you must gain *firsthand* knowledge that your particular gun is *100%* reliable with its particular mags and ammo. If it's not, then wouldn't you rather find out in practice, rather than on the street when attacked? While this seems obvious, you'd be amazed at how many gunowners mistakenly presume that their weapon system will function.

I would not use any weapon that has not been fired at least 500 times to take the rough edges off the working parts, but...after you break it in by firing 500 rounds, you should not have any weapon-related malfunction more than once every 2,000 rounds.

— Timothy J. Mullin, *Handbook of Handguns* (2001)

This is very sound advice. Furthermore, you must extensively test your duty gun with its duty ammo, especially if you're using an expensive hollow-point load (*e.g.*, MagSafe, CorBon, etc.) **Only your life is at stake.** Don't *assume* your gun is reliable with particular mags and ammo. Test to make sure!

Don't assume that POA will equal POI. Find out! You'd be amazed at the difference in POI between dissimilar ammo (especially between light and heavy bullets).

TACTICS—AN OVERVIEW

*Singularly, it isn't the gun alone that provides protection in violent times. It is your whole security posture. **Depth of security is the answer.** The gun provides a last-line defense. **If a gunfight occurs, there was a gap somewhere in the security plan.***
— Jim Grover, *Street Smarts, Firearms, and Personal Security*

No book can fully discuss tactics or train your muscle memory, so go to several gun schools and learn tactics firsthand. In the meantime, I'll cover the basics—not so much to teach, but to perhaps show you what you *don't* know.

Education is the transfer of intellectual knowledge.
Training is the programming of automatic physical response.

The "Survival Chain"
mindset + attitude + tactics + gear = SURVIVAL!

As many successful fighters will tell you, gear is irrelevant if you don't have the first three elements sorted out.

Most people have the *willingness* to fight if threatened, but will they fight in *time* and will they fight *well*?

Finally, the best example of this is *not* to get into a fight.

The Force Continuum

I want you to always remember that a firearm is the *last* line of defense, to be used only when less extreme measures either were not available or did not work. Jim Grover explains this "force continuum" well in his excellent *Street Smarts, Firearms, and Personal Security* (www.paladin-press.com):

You should arm yourself for an escalation of violence in order to meet lower levels of violence with the appropriate-level countermeasure. You wouldn't counter a drunk's persistent pushing with a .38. You should likewise make sure your personal defensive system is redundant in case of failure of any component. For example, you should never consider carrying only a firearm; it's too restrictive. You should always carry a less-than-lethal weapon on your person as well as your legally concealed handgun. The highest probability is that you will have to use, in diminishing frequency, guile and wit, your less-than-lethal weapon, your hands and combative skills, and lastly a firearm. (p.185)

guile, with, verbal warnings, sly escape

If you did not exercise sufficient awareness to let you avoid a threat, then you should first try using your mind and your mouth to get you out of trouble.

less-than-lethal weapons

OC pepper spray, quickly accessible and properly deployed, can end many aggressive scenarios. Any LLW must be concealable, effective, easy to use under duress, hard to use against you if dropped, and legal.

hand-to-hand combat

As I explained earlier, a simple but effective array of martial arts moves can get you out of trouble. Remember, your goal is not to utterly "whip his ass"—your only goal is to escape unharmed. Put him down hard and good, and get out of there!

firearms

Most confrontations do not warrant lethal force, and thus can/should be handled by the above three measures. Only when you have *no other choice* than to deploy a firearm should you ever do so. This is sound advice tactically, morally, and legally.

M & M & M

MAXIMIZE your distance to the threat

Whether on the street or clearing a corner, maximize your distance. If the enemy is in range, so are *you!*

MINIMIZE yourself as a target

If you can get smaller (either by getting down or getting back), so do. If you can move to cover, do so.

MUZZLE always between you and the threat

Your muzzle leads the way always! Use that "third eye."

Dogma vs. dogma

Folks, there are endless arguments over which shooting stance is superior, which flashlight technique is better, etc. It's now the 21st Century, and there is nothing really new in shooting technieques. Guns and gear continue to slowly evolve, but the basics of a good shooting grip, drawstroke, trigger work, and sight picture are eternal constants.

Look, what works for *you*...works for *you*. Stick with it.

I really don't care to argue—I prefer to practice. (p.200)
     If you have truly acid-tested your shooting methods under pressure, while moving, at night, under heavy cardiovascular exertion, when seated, walking, climbing in and out of cars, etc., and printed acceptable hits, ***don't change anything.*** *"If it's not broken, don't fix it."** But make darn sure you have in fact acid-tested your methods and that you shot to an acceptable, reasonable, realistic speed and accuracy standard* ***when you didn't control the cue.*** (p.190)
     — Jim Grover, *Street Smarts, Firearms, and Personal Security*

DEFENDING YOUR HOME

When a strong man, fully armed, guards his own palace, his goods are in peace.
     Luke 11:21 (NKJV)

Much thought and planning should be put into doing this right, since home is where your loved ones are. It's also where you live. Statisically, you'll spend 50% of your time at home, 33% at work, and 17% moving on foot or in vehicles. The very first thing to learn is the vital concept of security layers:

[Y]*ou* [should] *have developed the three layers of security around your house. (Layer one is projecting security to observable areas beyond your property line. Layer two is covering with lights, denying areas to conceal, and limiting access to that area from the border of the public property up to and including the skin of your dwelling. Layer three is the safe room inside your house.) This demonstrates a good overlap of security measures that are redundant, mutually supporting, offer good early warning, and are passive. This is good depth.* (p.186)
     A gun cannot provide depth. It is the last line of defense...
     — Jim Grover, *Street Smarts, Firearms, and Personal Security*

The three most likely scenarios
Compromised Burglar

     You return home and an intruder is inside. There will likely be sufficient clues to warn you of this before you enter, such as lights being inexplicably on or off, indoors pets being outside, a strange car on the street, your dogs barking, movement inside, or even just a "funny feeling."
     Now, you must either clear your home, or have the police do it for you. I would generally call the police and let them do

their job, unless the situation demanded your quick action. If you feel that you *must* clear your home, Grover recommends:

> *First, if you definitely hear someone crashing about, I suggest you do four things: account for loved ones inside the house, move them to a designated safe room, call the police, and move to a barricaded position between the criminal and your safe room, saying these three things: "You're in my house. I've called the police. I have a gun."*
>
> *Only the most intent criminal would continue toward you at this point. Only someone who is intoxicted or otherwise impaired would lack the judgment to get the hell out. Only the most unreasonable man would choose to confront you. In my opinion, you have gone a long way to passing the "reasonable man" test (i.e., the jury, if you're ever tried) if you follow these steps.*

—Jim Grover, *Street Smarts, Firearms, and Personal Security*

Home Invasion

These involve multiple intruders employing a dynamic entry. It is a very high-speed and terrifying experience. While it may sometimes begin with an unexpected knock at the door, don't count on it. Unless you are wearing your handgun or have instant access to it, you'll have to run to the nearest weapon.

Stealth Intruder

On pages 4/15-17, I recount such a case. The stealth intruder scenario is a bad one. Waking up to find an armed Bad Guy standing over your bed is anyone's worst nightmare. Only because you didn't secure your perimeter and have any early warning systems can some guy sneak up on you. To win this scenario, you'll have to stay calm, think quickly, and look for the earliest opportunity to regain control.

Securing the perimeter

Security is accomplished by layers. First, you would lock your driveway gate, if you had one. Next, you would close and lock all doors and windows (even the upstairs ones). Then, you would lock off the sleeping areas from the rest of the house. Finally, you would deadbolt your bedroom door.

Early warning systems

These exist to wake you up and get you into Condition Orange. Situational awareness is often situational dominance. Do not allow yourself to ever become surprised by stealth!

dogs

Dogs can be the best early warning system, especially if they are made to sleep outside your bedroom. For the most possible warning, have dogs both inside and outside the house.

Although you doglovers won't enjoy hearing this, your life is more valuable than your dogs'. They are expendable in true lethal emergencies.

security system

This can be as simple or as elaborate as you can afford. Anything is better than nothing. I would at least have sensors on the downstairs doors and windows, with a bedroom control.

door jam with battery alarm

This is an inexpensive but invaluable device which can be used both at home and in hotel rooms. They not only help block the door, but will shriek an alarm when triggered.

portable infrared motion detectors

Another worthy system, and inexpensive. Smaller than a paperback book, they can be placed anywhere with variable sensitivity. (I take them camping and set them up by my tent.)

Home preparation

Working tactics out with your family in advance is most important. Discuss all of the "what ifs" and plan your responses. Involve *every* family member, and assign them appropriate and performable duties.

have codes with family and best friends

There may come a time when a loved one is under some kind of threat or surveillance and cannot speak freely. You should work out certain warning words or phrases in advance.

The first code word or phrase should be to alert the listener that something is gravely wrong. (For example, calling somebody "James" instead of "Jim.")

Then, the specific warning should be communicated with a code phrase. Some examples of warnings with their code phrases might be:

Warning	Code phrase
"I'm being held at gun/knife point."	"Have you heard from Ted?"
"Come home immediately, with stealth."	"The dog is sick again."
"Abort errand immediately, without questions!"	"The water bill is still too high."
"Do not go to home or office. Danger!"	"Oh, Sylvia called yesterday."
"Am under duress; do opposite of what I say."	"I had to let the maid go."
"Call police immediately."	"Please bring home Chinese."

Obviously, such code phrases will work only if there's no Ted or Sylvia, you have no dog, there's never a problem with the water bill, you have no maid, and the entire household hates Chinese food. Obviously, you'll have to compose them as a joint effort, but you get the picture. Be sure to practice them often so that nobody remains clueless during an emergency, blathering on about *"Chinese food? You hate Chinese food!"*

Some sort of acknowledgment/answer code is also important. For example, you could use $ amounts to express minutes. When your wife says *"The dog is sick again"* (*i.e.,* *"Come home immediately, with stealth"*), you can reply *"The last vet bill was only $15"*—meaning that you'll be there in 15 minutes.

Whatever code phrases you devise, they must sound innocuous at *both* ends of the conversation else the Bad Guys may suspect that it's a code.

create a safe room for family members

One particular bedroom or large closet could be dedicated as the safe room. During an attack on the home, vulnerable non-fighting members should be secured there.

It should have no windows and only one solid door (with a peephole, and secured by two quality deadbolts). Inside would be guns and ammo, food, water, flashlights fire extinguishers, first-aid kits, gas masks, OC pepper spray, body armor, two-way radios, AM/FM radio, police scanner, and a battery-charged cell phone (which can be had for only Ø100/year including the phone) with a list of phone numbers. (An alternate power supply such a large computer APS is a good idea.) The door, hinges, and walls should be strengthened to withstand a determined and lengthy (*i.e.,* over 30 minutes) attack.

The Terminator OC pepper spray "booby trap" is a device is remote triggered either mechanically or electrically and fills an entire room with OC pepper spray in just seconds. (The gas clears out in about 3 hours.) Excellent for the hallway leading to the safe room, or for uninhabited rooms, such as garages, offices, sheds, etc. They are Ø56 each ppd. from Revel Technology (610-582-1730; www.stopthecrime.com).

An escape route (*i.e.,* tunnel, false wall or floor, roof hatch, etc.) might be structurally feasible, and is recommended.

the bedroom sanctuary

One venerable shooting instructor designed his house to be fairly impenetrable. There are cleverly disguised gunports with overlapping fields of fire (similar to a Vauban Star). The walls can withstand small arms fire, and is fireproof.

The master bedroom can be reached only by going down a dedicated hallway, and there is a wrought iron gate with deadbolt lock to shut off that hallway from the house. Every night, when the couple retires, they lock the gate behind them. Even if an intruder gets through, he will wake up the homeowners long before and thus find himself at the end of a spotlit hallway/"fatal funnel." In short, an night attack on *this* couple would be nothing more than an elaborate form of suicide. No intruder could ever sneak up on this pair whilst sleeping.

Home guns and gear

If you have only one defensive handgun, then it must accompany you throughout the home. That means...

you must *wear* your handgun at home!

Your three handgun classes at Thunder Ranch will mean nothing if an intruder comes through the kitchen door and you left your Les Bauer 1911A1 upstairs.

Since concealment would rarely be an issue, you can wear it on a belt holster. This is also makes perfect tactical sense, as drawing from such is about the fastest of all carry options.

the bedroom handgun

If you can afford a second handgun, it should be dedicated and specialized for this room (where you spend ⅓ of your life), because if you ever need to use it, it will almost guaranteed to be during the *night*. Therefore, it should have:

an attached Sure-Fire flashlight with flip-out red (or IR) filter
tritium sights (I like the Ashley Outdoors sights)
a longer-than-normal barrel (to reduce muzzle flash, *e.g.,* Glock 24L)
an extended magazine (*i.e.,* containing, say, 20rds)
frangible ammo if you're concerned about "overpenetration"

While such may seem excessive, it's the right tool for the job. Since you won't be wearing it, the extra weight from the light, barrel, and mag won't matter. (I consider an attached Sure-Fire to be a *must*, as you can't risk fumbling around for one.)

the bathroom handgun

I recommend a quality stainless-steel (to resist bathroom humidity) revolver (which can remain loaded for years without stressing any springs). Frangible ammo is probably the best choice for most homes, given the short distances and thin walls.

home shotguns

The defensive 12 gauge pump described in Chapter 20 will serve fine. Again, an attached Sure-Fire flashlight is vital. Any #7½ skeet load will perform well within 15yds.

home rifles

A dedicated CQB AR15A3 is probably just the ticket. Such has a 16" Bushmaster Dissipator upper, Redi-Mag, and Sure-Fire flashlight system. (All described in Chapter 16.) Contrary to popular misbelief, .223 does not overpenetrate because the bullet (55gr or 62gr) quickly shatters upon impact.

Other possible choices (especially in urban areas) would be a .357 Mag Marlin lever-action, or an M1 Carbine—both of which are lightweight and easy recoiling for smaller family members, yet with JHP ammo have fine stopping power (*i.e.*, about 900fpe) within 50yds.

It should be stored loaded and in Condition 1. Why not Condition 3? Because you'd have to chamber the first round, which takes time and makes noise—either/both might be tactically risky. It should be very quickly and quietly accessible (perhaps inside your bedroom closet, in a rack above the door).

Those who live in the country should always keep a rifle with them when outdoors. Remember, a handgun is merely a tool you use to fight your way back to your rifle (which you shouldn't have left behind in the first place). Being on the "back 40" with only a *handgun* against a threatening bear or lion, or several Bad Guys will make quite an impression on you.

Home tactics

Don't be naked!

If you are [naked] stalking through your house, pistol in hand,...you are putting yourself at both a physical and psychological advantage. You should at minimum put on your shoes, pants, and shirt. The fact that you are fully clothed will avoid the psychological disadvantage you would feel at being naked. The shoes will avoid injuries to your feet by reason of stumbling or broken glass that may be present. If your threat level is very high, you might want to consider obtaining a ballistic vest,...sewn into a dark-colored undershirt. Slipping into it before you search the house would, no doubt, give you real peace of mind...

— Timothy J. Mullin, *Handbook of Handguns* (2001)

Never answer the door unarmed, even if it's somebody you know (as they could be being held at gunpoint by an intruder). Armed means gun in hand, or at least with your hand on it while holstered. Yes, I realize that this sounds "weird" and that many of your friends will call you "paranoid," but your goal is to stay alive. Being able to *instantly* repel boarders is part of that. There are often very few warnings to an assault, and if a Bad Guy succeeds in surprising you at the front door, then you will have no time to run to your bedroom or safe for your gun.

the "uniform" for clearing your house

This is a very specific and important job, and you must properly dress for the occasion. By already knowing your home better than your intruder, you can further increase your advantage over him with specialized gear.

quiet shoes, dark pants, and bulletproof vest (in a dark shirt)
Your confidence will be greatly enhanced by this attire.

night vision goggles in a handsfree headmount (*e.g.,* ITT PVS-7B)
Your intruder won't likely have them and being able to see and stalk him in the dark is an incalculable edge. The ITT goggles even have a built-in IR floodlight.

very bright flashlight (*i.e.,* Sure-Fire 9P) with flip-out red (or IR) filter
If you can't pay for night vision goggles, then at least have a red filter (which is the least harmful to your night eyes).

Peltor sound-amplifying ear muffs
These will greatly increase your hearing sense.

handcuffs or cable ties
Once you catch your intruder, he must be restrained. These should also be attached to your vest.

Motorla Talk-About radio (to converse with hidden family members)
This should be clipped (not Velcroed) onto your vest. A handsfree earphone speaker/mike is preferred.

work out your defensive plan in advance

Those who are co-defenders should know their places and duties. Those who are to hide should know exactly *where* to go, and *when* to come out. Leave nothing to chance, and practice at least once a month.

DEFENSIVE SHOOTING

the Combat Triad

To win a gunfight, you must have sufficiently developed all three "legs" of the Combat Triad:

gunhandling

Includes safety, drawstroke, firing grip, stance, being able to move and shoot, clearing malfunctions, etc.—*when you do not control the startle cue.*

marksmanship

Being able to make accurate shot placement under stress.

mindset

Having the commitment to train and the will to win comes from the Warrior spirit.

Weapon retention

This is much too rarely taught to civilians, but is a *vital* part of your training. Too many citizens (and cops) have had their guns taken away from them, and if you allow it you will very likely be shot with your own gun. 70% of all officers shot were shot with their own gun—and of those who *lost* their gun, 97% of them were shot and 16% of them died.

So, lose your gun and you have a 1 in 6 chance of paying for it with your very life. Pretty sobering, eh?

For a training "gun" get an Ø18 air pistol Glock 17-clone from CTD (#SOFT-951). These are life-sized and quite realistic, and at only 18 bucks it can be knocked around without worry.

retaining the handgun while still holstered

The most common technique here is, when you first feel somebody's hand on your gun from behind, to *immediately* grab his wrist *with your weak hand.* At the same time, give him a reverse strike with your strong elbow.

retaining the handgun *after* you've drawn it

First of all, keep or increase your distance to your threat. Once he gets within grappling range, the dynamics of the fight have changed to *his* advantage.

Once his hand is on your gun, your first priority is to keep the muzzle pointed *away* from you (and preferably at *him*). If at any time you *can* shoot him (he must not have pulled your gun's slide out of battery), *do so!* If you cannot shoot him, then you must cause him to release your weapon. There are a myriad of martial arts techniques for this, and I advise some actual *dojo* work to learn them. (You can also bring a knife or backup handgun into action.)

Any guns carried in Condition 2 (*i.e.,* Glocks, DAs, and DAOs) are *very* dangerous to lose as the Bad Guy has no safety to disengage—he need only pull the trigger. So, if you carry one of these, you've got even more impetus to learn weapon retention than does your buddy with a single-action 1911A1.

Keep your gun hand free!

Learn to carry items, open doors, etc. with your *weak* hand. This keeps your gun hand free to instantly draw and fire if necessary. If, however, your lifestyle requires your gun hand to be often preoccupied, then you must practice "busy hands" drills (wherein you immediately drop whatever you're carrying, eggs or a baby, after your startle cue).

Experienced bodyguards, for example, *never* carry packages or briefcases for their clients (although some clients really complain about this). If you and your wife are in public, and you're armed and she's not, then discuss the concept of your not occupying your gun hand with packages. (It'll take *quite* a lady to understand this, but such would likely be armed, anyway!)

The "tachypyschia" effect

Sudden and severe stress causes dramatic changes in the brain and body, which will affect you during a fight. Modern shooting instructors understand these and have developed techniques to minimize their effects.

fine hand/finger movements

Under severe stress fine dexterity evaporates. You will not be able to thread a needle, or sign your name. (You likely won't be able to operate your trigger lock, either.) Thus, we substitute large, coarse sweeping movements for precise ones.

critical decision-making ability

There is little time for conscious decisions; only muscle memory unleashed by your subconscious can win the fight. You must program your athletic memory with *one simple way* to load, clear malfunctions, change shooting positions, move behind cover, transition weapons, etc. Keep your techniques few, your responses simple, and your movement fluid.

memory
In a gunfight, you will *not* remember how many rounds you fired. You will shoot until you win the fight or until your gun is empty (and then you will immediately reload, and keep firing). Shooting your gun dry is not a sin; it's just evidence that you're in a fight.

tunnel vision
When you're in Condition Black, your whole world shrinks to the diameter of your front sight. While that is fine for fast tactical hits, you must program yourself to Scan and Search after putting down a particular Bad Guy. He may have accomplices, and it helps to shake off tunnel vision. Move your head, and track your muzzle with your eyes! (This is called the "third eye" principle.)

auditory exclusion
During a gunfight your concentration will be so intense that your shots will sound like muffled door slamming, and you will not easily hear your partner's commands. Such "tunnel hearing" is a component of tunnel vision, and can be minimized with loud verbalization to your threat and to your partner.

general muscle tightening
This will be intense, and can easily cause you to miss (if your stance and grip are not correct).
Rule 3 (*"Keep your finger off the trigger until your sights are on the target."*) is *vital* during severe stress, as sympathetic muscle tightening can cause you to inadvertently pull the trigger. (As soon as you no longer have a specific target, your trigger finger *must* immediately index on the frame.)

time-space distortions
Within seconds of going to Red, your endocrinology changes dramatically. Your body releases huge amounts of "Fight or Flight" fluids: adrenaline (for extraordinary energy), cortisol (to increase blood clotting), lactic acid (to warm up your muscles), two heart stimulants and three painkillers. Your heart rate will double. All this has *profound* effects on your sensory input, and your recollection of that input.
Events will seem to happen more slowly (because your mind just went into high gear), and objects will appear closer

than they really are. This explains why "eyewitness" testimony is often so faulty, and emphasizes the point of *never* discussing your shooting incident with *anybody* but your lawyer. It will take 3-4 hours for your blood chemistry to return to normal after such an adrenaline dump, so keep your mouth shut.

Shot placement is better than caliber

Would you rather miss with a .44 Magnum or hit with a .22LR? **Shot placement is *the* most important part of defending your life with a firearm.** I'd rather hit squarely with "only" a 9mm than wing him with a .45. To win the fight your bullets *must* damage vital organs, and not even a 1300fps 155gr 10mm CorBon will make up for poor shot placement.

Skill is better than equipment

When you're arguing about which caliber or bullet is superior, you're not shooting! **Your *trigger* time should be much greater than your *tongue* time.** Quit placing so much emphasis on mere equipment (an American trait) and begin to hone your *skills*. A good man with fair equipment will beat a fair man with great equipment—count on it! Get to the range often and work on your drawstroke and shot placement.

Front sight! Press! Front sight!

Front sight is *everything*. In Condition Black, nothing else in the universe exists but your front sight. Lose your front sight, and you'll likely lose the fight. You're going to be scared sh*tless—so what? *Anybody* would be. Focus on that front sight, press the trigger, and pick up your front sight again.

If you miss, pick up your front sight! As Clint Smith says, *"The sights are always aligned! You are not aligned!"*

Plan "A" Response—shots to the torso

The torso is the center of mass and the quickest area to hit. The torso contains the *energy* center of the threat. Most schools teach 2 shots, while others teach 3 (as it gives 50% more energy). I would vary your practice with 2-4 shots. While accurate, powerful rounds to the body will *usually* stop the fight, you're not interested in *probabilities*—you are concentrating on what *is* or is *not* stopping him. **Always change a *losing* game.** If torso hits aren't working, then go to Plan B:

Plan "B" Response—the headshot

Shots to the torso did not work. Maybe he's got a bulletproof vest. Maybe he's high on PCP or your MagSafe rounds don't impress him. *Whatever.* It doesn't *matter!* **Just recognize that** *"A" isn't working.* *Always* **change a** *losing* **game.** Move to the *control* center—the head. Front sight at the base of his nose, press, front sight. Make this shot count. If this doesn't work (it probably glanced off his skull), then go to Plan C:

Plan "C" Response—shots to the pelvis, A, B

Torso and headshots missed and/or did not work. You will be stunned and amazed—this is natural. **Don't analyze** *why,* **just recognize the noneffect and change your game plan.** *Keep fighting!* Now attack the *mobility* center, the pelvis. Anchor him to stop his advance, and deal with him while he's on the ground, going back to the torso and head.

Plan C really means to shoot *everything* that is available, *while* it is available, until something *else* becomes available. If he moves behind partial cover (*e.g.,* a car) with only his feet exposed, then shoot his feet.

Incidentally, my 1998 discussion of all this was termed *"gruesome"* by a libertarian organization's alleged gun expert, and they accordingly refused to carry the first edition of this book. You should have read my letter in reply. Mere intellectual comprehension of Liberty only goes so far. At some point, one needs the *courage* to enact it, and the general lack of such in Libertarian/Objectivist circles is the biggest bone of contention I have with them. (Read my Introduction to Claire Wolfe's *101 More Things To Do 'Till The Revolution* for an expanded soliloquy on this subject. I also touch on this in Chapter 19.)

Reloading your gun during a fight

If exchanging prolonged fire, you *will* shoot your gun dry. Ammo is only helpful when fired at hostile targets, and as long as they're hostile, you *will* fire. Fire long enough and you *will* run dry. This is no sin. Simply reload and continue fighting. (The doctrine of counting rounds while not spilling your martini on your tuxedo is *crap.* Ask any experienced gunfighter.)

How many mags should you carry? That's up to you: how *long* do you want to be able to fight? Ammo equals time in the fight. How much time/ammo will it take? Who knows? Some fights are ended in 0 rounds, some in 1, some in 39. (I'd carry as many mags as you can comfortably conceal and carry.)

Remember, you have the rest of your life to solve your problem. How long you live depends on how quickly you solve it.

The empty reload

You're in a fight. Your bolt/slide locks back after your last round. *First*, grab a full mag. (*Never* dump an empty mag before having a grip on the full mag!) Next, dump your empty mag *while* you move your full mag up to the gun. Finally, insert (Tap-Tug) the mag, and release the bolt/slide. An excellent empty reload time is 1½ seconds. You can do this with practice.

The tactical reload

When you're behind cover *and* there's a lull in the fight, a tactical reload is called for. *First*, grab your full mag. While holding onto the full mag with 2-3 fingers of your weak hand, pull out the less-full mag with the other fingers and replace it with the full mag—while still holding on to the less-full mag. (This will take practice, and it varies from gun to gun. Willem DaFoe in *Platoon* demonstrated a fine tac reload of his M16.)

Do *not* put the less-full mag in your mag pouch—that's where *full* mags go. Put it in your pocket or down your shirt where you can retrieve it later as it still contains *some* ammo.

Tactics in low-light conditions

As 70% of lethal confrontations occur in conditions of low, altered, or failing light, you must have the proper equipment (tritium night sights and a Sure-Fire flashlight) and training to effectively fight and win. There are techniques to tactilely discern your weapon's condition, hold your flashlight with your weak hand (the Harries and Rogers techniques), and shoot and move. The only way to learn all this is to attend gun school.

Transitioning from primary to secondary gun

If there's no time to clear or reload your rifle in a fight, then you must transition to your handgun. Since you don't want to drop your rifle and have it picked up by a hostile (who just *might* get it back into operation against you), you must somehow *retain* your rifle while drawing and firing your handgun. There are two general ways to retain your rifle—by holding onto it with your weak hand, or by using the sling. (However you do it, beware the hot barrel!)

holding onto it with your weak hand
Simply clutching it by the handguard to your chest muzzle up is the quickest transition hold. The obvious downside is that you must shoot one-handed.

using the sling
If you need *both* hands free, then slinging it over your neck, muzzle-up in the "scramble carry" is very quick.

Those with tactical slings can simply release the rifle.

Thunder Ranch teaches the sling dangle (muzzle down) on the weak elbow crook, but the swinging rifle makes accurate pistol shot placement more difficult.

If you've got the time and cover, sling the rifle across your body. This is very secure, but takes the most time. There are two techniques, Gizzi (across the back) and Fleischmann (across the front), both of which are shown in Gabriel Suarez's *The Tactical Rifle* (Paladin Press).

Clearing a building
You come home late at night and notice through the window an intruder inside. Call the police—that's what they're *paid* for! If calling or waiting for the police is not practical, then you'll have to clear your home alone. If clearing with a partner, *communicate*. One of you is the team leader; the other a subordinate member.

In a multistory building, work *up* if possible (it's easier to clear most stairwells going up). **Lead with your muzzle— where your eyes are looking your muzzle is pointing.** Make sure that your presence is not announced by sound and shadow. Clear as you go, leaving no uncleared areas behind you. You look in closets, behind doors and furniture, under beds —everywhere a potential threat could be hiding.

Also, try to herd the intruder towards an avenue of escape. Your goal is not to shoot him, but to make him flee. Finally, once you've called the police, don't startle them when they have arrived. They could mistake you for the intruder!

corners
Negotiating corners is the main task. Standing as far away from a corner as possible (so that an intruder cannot

easily grab your gun), you "pie slice" your way around, about 20°
at a time. At the *final* slice, *very* quickly peek (fire if necessary),
and duck back. Use different heights to increase surprise.

Taking prisoners

If you discover an intruder, don't look at the face—look at
the *hands*. **Hands, *hands*, *hands*.** Only *hands* can hurt you.
An intruder hand with a weapon, even if not pointed at you, is a
threat. If the intruder even so much as *moves* his hands in a
manner consistent with reaching for a weapon, shoot him. He
needn't have been actually armed—the law only requires that a
reasonable person would have *believed* that he was armed and
posed an imminent grievous threat.

Take charge!

Your commands must be clear and forceful, giving him no
time to think tactically. As I fully explain in Chapter 22, use
foul language if necessary, as that's often the only thing he will
understand. (He's a dirtbag, remember?)

He must comply *immediately* or be shot. *"Do it now!"*
He's unlawfully in your home and *you* are in control. Never
retreat from this high moral and tactical ground. His actions
must *diminish* his tactical position, or you are justified in
shooting him. Stalling, moving closer, pleading, hiding his
hands or inching them towards his coat—all of these are danger
signals to you. If he is not obeying you, then he's planning to
overcome you. *"Do it now or I'll shoot!"*

If you *can't* see his hands

Command him to raise his hands and turn around. Then,
command him to slowly lie on the floor (knees to elbows to stomach), and to place his arms behind his back, palms outward.

Now, you must restrain. Get a knee or foot on his neck or
back, and then secure his wrists (with handcuffs, cable ties,
tape, or cellophane wrap), followed by his ankles.

If he speaks, *command him* to shut up. At this moment,
you don't care *what* he has to *say*, only what he is able to *do*.
When he's safely in custody (*i.e.*, hands secured behind his back,
ankles bound, and lying face down), *then* you can listen to his
"wrong house" story, if you want to.

After he is restrained

Basically, keep him covered while you dial 911. (The next
chapter goes into full detail on all this.)

IN YOUR CAR

Most assassination attempts occur while the target is in the car, and 90% of them are successful. In a way, this is somewhat ironic as a car offers excellent mobility and fair ballistic protection (at least from handguns and carbines).

When we're driving it is very easy to slip in Condition White, not just about attackers, but about traffic. Have you ever been on a trip and suddenly wondered where the last 20 miles went? You were in Condition White, daydreaming. While that's fine for helping the trip to go faster, it may someday exact a horrible balloon payment in the form of your life.

Keep your car perfectly maintained!

Your goal is to avoid trouble, and then to be able to get out of it. Clogged fuel filters, bald tires, and tempermental starters are just begging for trouble. Unless you are an excellent and devoted mechanic of your own vehicles, get yourself under a pro.

And guys, this applies *double* to your lady's car. Most women are not mechanically inclined, so any breakdown will be *much* more inconvenient, if not dangerous, to them.

Have certain things in your car

Have a cell phone

Merely picking up the phone and pantomiming an urgent conversation will scare off many opportunistic creeps. If you must call in, then at least already have their license plate.

If you can't afford a cell phone, then at least get a CB.

Have a powerful spotlight

These can deliver a million candlepower beam, and all from your cigarette lighter! If ever chased at night, simply blind the driver just before a tight curve. (I had to resort to such one time, and it was instantly effective. It also sufficiently illuminated the driver's face, which I later identified from a high-school yearbook. The driver's dad happened to be a local police sergeant, who straightened out his boy *real* quick.)

Be appropriately armed

If you spend much time in the car, then you need to have some heavier car weapons than your handgun. You may need to shoot through some car's door, and only a long gun will do. I would recommend a .30 caliber rifle (an inexpensive .303 Lee-Enfield carbine would be perfect) or 12 gauge shotgun (even a break open double would be fine) with 000 buck or slugs. I wouldn't necessarily risk traveling with your H&K91 or FAL, unless it's an Ø800 post-ban and you can spare the loss from any theft or confiscation. (By the way, do not rely on a .223 for anti-vehicular combat. It just doesn't perforate as a .308 will.)

Securing it in a discreet yet accessible location will take some ingenuity, but if you're bright enough to be one of my readers then you'll no doubt figure out something.

Stay in Condition Yellow

When you pass or are passed by other cars, make eye contact with the drivers. Maintain a sense for your environment so that you can't be easily surprised. Keep track of any cars which seem to be on too identical a route.

Use your mirrors. If your windshield rearview mirror has a blind spot, add one of the convex panoramic clip-ons. (They take some getting used to, but they're amazing!)

Watch your attitude!

Don't stare at, challenge, or gesture at the creeps. Don't take the bait; don't throw down the gauntlet. Your goal is to get home safely to your loved one.

Watch your ingress and egress

Getting in and out of your car are the most vulnerable times. In high risk areas, I would try to have my hand already on my gun (say, in a pocket, newspaper, paper bag, etc.).

Don't become distracted with your destination or with your shopping when getting in/out of your car. Stay in Yellow!

Always think tactically

If you're stopping at multi-lane intersection next to another car, and that car has a front seat passenger, then pull up on their driver side (which limits the effectiveness of the passenger who can't easily shoot past his driver).

Conversely, if the driver is alone, pull up on his right side (which denies him the use of his driver side window as a convenient firing port). Yes, he may have electric windows (but he may not, or they may be broken), but even still he must fire with his right arm straight and unsupported through the passenger window, which is much more difficult than through his driver side window (where he can brace his arm against the sill or even his left upper arm).

While the tactical advantage is admittedly slight in both cases, you are seeking *every* advantage possible. Some gain you "pennies" and some gain you hundreds of dollars. Never pass up a chance to add to your "tactical account."

Always maintain an "out"

Never let yourself become boxed in. When stopping behind a car, stay back enough so that you can see its tires on the pavement. That will give you enough room to move around in case it stalls or it's part of a trap. If you're stopped and you notice cars suspiciously pulling up on both sides, drive away!

Don't be shy, either. Even if you have to cut somebody off or briefly drive down a one-way street, get out of there!

Write down license plate numbers often

Have a dashboard notepad and pen. If any car in traffic is acting weird or menacing, immediately get their plate before any action starts. Also notate the make, model, color, and any distinguishing characteristics (as you won't likely remember later). You can call it in if necessary, or, if you're injured, at least the information will likely be found and followed up on.

If somebody seems to be following you home, call the police or friend and relay the info. Whether you win or lose any subsequent fight, at least some investigative leads will survive.

If you think you're being followed...

Do *not* lead them to your home or office. Get into a residential area and take several random turns. If they follow, the odds are against mere coincidence. Don't stop to see if they will drive past you—keep them *behind* you and stay moving. Call a friend or the police for interception. (This could be done at stop sign, where you stop and your friend blocks them from behind.)

If a fender-bender or traffic stop feels hinky

A common ploy of carjackers is to bump the target car from behind. The owner gets out all concerned for her car, and has forgotten all about her personal safety. You don't have to get out; you don't even have to stick around! Tell the other driver to meet you at the police station and drive out of there.

If you're ever pulled over by an unmarked vehicle with a plainclothes "cop"—*beware*. It could very well be a ruse, even if he shows you a badge. Refuse to get out and ask that he radio for a marked patrol unit. Any *bonafide* officer will do so without fuss. If there's a fuss, then tell him to meet you at the police station, but no matter how much he blusters do *not* leave your car!

Don't be afraid to be bold

If Bad Guys are at the window, do not hesitate. They have done this often, and won't *expect* instant action on your part.

Ram them, scrape them against a parked car, back over them. Do what ever it takes to get out of harm's way. Don't be afraid to run a red light or even drive down a sidewalk. If you've left yourself an out, then all these maneuvers will be possible.

Passengers should be on the floor, or firing

They should be the picture of either defense or offense. Either get them on the floorboard, or have them put some lead in the attackers. There's no in-between. (At night, they should be wielding that powerful spotlight.)

As long as your car is mobile, stay *moving*

Even if the tires are flat or the radiator is spewing, as long as your car can still drive, keep driving! In large cities, several blocks can put you into an entirely new (and possibly safer) neighborhood. That next couple of miles or even 100yds may be all you need to reach safety or have the attackers finally peel off.

Your *car* can be replaced—you *cannot* be...

Have *no* qualms about battering your way through any obstacle. Your car has *thousands* of times more kinetic energy than any firearm. Use it! What's a car—*any* car—compared to your life? (Any car too valuable to trade for your life is one that belongs in a museum and not on the road.)

TEAM TACTICS

Thunder Ranch, by the way, has a very fine team tactics course (held only once or twice a year) with lots of indoors work and lots of shooting. You even get some vehicle firing time.

There was an excellent article by Max Joseph in *Guns & Weapons for Law Enforcement*, which I'll paraphrase here.

Advantages of a two-man team

coverage

One man can barely dominate 180°, and he certainly cannot handle 360°. Two men can advance with the rear covered.

coordinated fire

fire superiority	(you've doubled your accurate fire to your threat)
converging fire	(this forces your threat to fight in a "V")
covering fire	(vital for retreat or advance)
flanking fire	(one gives covering fire, the other moves to flank)
mobile fire	(one drives, the other shoots)

teamwork

The whole is greater than the sum of the parts.

consolidation

You're able to share equipment and magazines.

morale

Would you rather fight alone, or with a trained buddy?

Communication

For efficiency, you'll need command and control (C&C). An SOP is vital so that you both share the same language (which should include both voice and hand signals). Remember, during any fight you will suffer auditory exclusion, so you must *really* yell out to your partner. Make *sure* he understood you.

"Loading!"

This tells your partner that you're reloading. Wait until he confirms with *"Covering!"* While reloading, keep your muzzle on your threat area.

"Covering!"

The acknowledgment to *"Loading!"* and *"Cover me!"* and *"Stoppage!"* You must now cover your buddy's sector of fire.

"Cover me!"
You need covering fire to mask your movement. Wait until you've heard *"Covering!"*

"Moving!"
Communicates that you are moving and may cross into your partner's field of fire.

"Stoppage!"
Lets your partner know that you've got a problem and you're temporarily out of the fight (thus he has no backup). I wouldn't holler this during a *Tap-Rack-Bang* to clear a failure to feed, but I *certainly* would sound off to clear a double-feed.

"I'm hit!"
Lets your buddy know that he needs to cover and evacuate you. It remains your responsibility to cover your sector.

In order to confuse the enemy, you may want to substitute some code words. Using another language would serve well.

TRAINING

Body and spirit I surrendered whole
To harsh instructors—and received a soul.
— Rudyard Kipling, "The Wonder," *Epitaphs* (1919)

Train hard. Fight easy.
—Roman Legion maxim

Gun school—*"learning, then forgetting"*
[S]*tatistics reveal that police suffer from a stunning lack of training and competence with firearms. According to the national average, police hit their target **18%** of the time during violent confrontations. Individual locales vary: The LAPD's percentage is the highest in the nation (30%) while New York's is the lowest (11%).*

*In comparison, graduates of schools such as Gunsite, Range-master, Yavapai Firearms, Thunder Ranch, etc. who were involved in shootings subsequent to their classes hit **with 85-100%** of their shots fired in defense of life.*
— Mark F. Twight, "Eat or Be Eaten"
S.W.A.T., March 2000 (p.61)

Until you've been to a good shooting academy, you can't appreciate what you *don't* know about defensive firearm handling. Punching holes in 25yd paper may make you a fine target shot, but what can it teach you about empty reloads, clearing malfunctions, the use of cover, or moving?

Long-term muscle memory of these techniques requires *3,000* repetitions, which is infeasible from any course, but these schools *can* imprint your *short-term* athletic memory (which takes only 300 repetitions). The remaining 2,700 repetitions you'll be able to practice at home on your own—and that's the *goal* of gun school; teaching quality skills to the point of mature self-sufficiency. (Unlearning and replacing a bad habit takes *10,000* repetitions.)

Learn the techniques and ingrain them forever so that you can "forget" (consciously). Do you have to remember how to catch a ball? No, you've learned and "forgotten" it. You just *do* it. Defensive gun handling must be *just* as ingrained, or else you'll *lose* the fight, and maybe your *life*. **In any crisis you'll only do what's already been** *imprinted* **on your** *subconscious.* No imprint means a "nothing" response.

While there are now a couple of dozen schools, I recommend the following as the best currently available. (Any school not mentioned is welcome to have me evaluate them through one of their courses.)

Thunder Ranch

HCR 1, Box 53, Mountain Home, **Texas** 78058
830-640-3138/3183fax   www.thunderranchinc.com

Thunder Ranch offers extensive courses in all small arms on a 900ac. ranch in the Texas Hill Country (NW of Kerrville). Facilities and instructors are excellent. TR was founded and is operated by Clint Smith (of the ITC road shows). Clint has a very good "no-ego" approach to his training, and is interested only in what *works* (versus some precious dogma regarding Weaver vs. Isosceles, or 9mm versus .45).

I recommend starting with Defensive Handgun 1 and Urban Rifle 1. Each are 5-day courses costing about Ø950.

The five onsite cabins at Ø70/day are convenient and well-equipped, or you can even camp out at TR in your tent or RV. Fly to San Antonio or Austin and rent a car. Ship your ammo to TR ahead of time (include 200 extra rounds).

Although I do not believe in attending only *one* school, if you could attend *only* one school, make it Thunder Ranch.

Gunsite Training Center

2900 W. Gunsite Rd., Paulden, **Arizona** 86334

520-636-4565　　　　　　　　　　　www.gunsite.com

Originally founded by Jeff Cooper as the American Pistol Institute, Buz Mills bought it from Rich Gee in 1999. Under Operations Manager Col. Bob Young, the quality of instruction and facilities (many of them new) is excellent. Owner Mills and his staff are also fervently and unabashedly pro-RKBA.

Jeff and Janelle Cooper still live onsite at the Sconce and graciously welcom "Family Members" of Orange (*i.e.*, pre-1993, and post-1999) Gunsite and new friends.

Yavapai Firearms Academy

P.O. Box 27290, Prescott Valley, **Arizona** 86312

928-772-8262　　　　　　　　　　　www.yfainc.com

You'll like no-nonsense Louis Awerbuck, renowned for his excellent shotgun courses. Louis teaches by doing, unlike many instructors. Paladin Press sells his video and books.

Bill Rogers School of Weaponcraft

1736 St. John's Bluff Rd., Jacksonville, Florida 32246

904-642-7810　　　　　　　　　www.rogers-shootingschool.com

A champion *pistolero*, holster designer for Safariland, and inventor of the Rogers Sure-Fire Flashlight Technique, Bill is a relaxed, easygoing instructor who personally demonstrates every drill. Catering primarily to the military, he fortunately offers four pistol classes each year to civilians.

His Ellijay, **Georgia** range is quite innovative—all head shots. Each shooting lane has seven pneumatically-operated/computer-controlled steel plates at ranges from 7 to 25 yards. They pop up at random and remain for as little as ½ second. Speedy, exciting stuff! You *will* learn your front sight. Unless you've gone through other intermediate-level courses at Thunder Ranch, etc., and have done *lots* of dry fire practice, start with the basic class. I recommend the Ø700 class with room-and-board deal.

Judging a shooting instructor

The instructor does not have to impress me; he has to teach me. I do not have to impress the instructor; I have to learn what he is trying to teach me.

If the instructor does not give the reason for accomplishing a task a specific way, the student should be asking the following question: "Why?"

— Jim Crews, *From Behind the Line* (2001), p.1

First of all, you want somebody without a gargantuan ego. Any instructor who is all about *"I-me-mine"* will have gaping holes in his doctrine simple because he pyschologically disinclined to be the student and learn from others. The best teachers are always, first, the best students (*e.g.,* Dan Inosanto).

Secondly, you want an instructor who has attended several classes from at least two or three schools. As no school or guru has all the answers, cross-training is vital to round out an instructor's knowledge and teaching ability.

Thirdly, it is important (though not absolutely necessary) that you instructor has had some *active* military and/or police service, preferably with actual combat or gunfight experience.

Lastly, your instructor should generally have a favorable reputation amongs his colleagues. If over one in four surveyed have misgivings about the person, then beware. Truly high quality people are know as such by all.

Jim Grover recommends these qualities to look for:

Patient. Articulate. Knowledgeable. Personable. Honest. Self-secure (not threatened). Successfull. Published. Busy. Current (still going and going). Experienced. Steady (not melodramatic).

Training books

Want to learn something new? Read an old book.
— Jim Grover, *Street Smarts, Fireams, and Personal Security*

Although any martial art training is much more a physical than mental exercise, well-written books by quality instructors can save you a lot of training time. I personally have nearly 100 self-defense books in my library, and have gleaned something worth the cover price from every one. One tip or observation found in only book could be the one needed to save your life someday. As Clint Smith is fond of saying, *"You have the rest of your life to solve your problem. How long you live depends on how well you do it."*

Jim Crews
P.O. Box 556, Stevensville, Montana 59870
602-549-7389   www.marksman.com   crews@sprynet.com

Some good books for the beginner (especially regarding handgun and carbine) are by Jim Crews, a "weapons handling skills instructor." His doctrine is no-nonsense and thorough, and there is nothing of any significant note with which I have yet to find any disagreement. His *Some Of The Answer* series, and his *From Behind The Line* (which is a guide for shooting instructors) are concise and well-organized, as well as replete with all necessary photographs in a lay-flat sprial-bound workdbook format. I highly recommend them.

Training videos

These are good for those who can't get to a school, or to introduce novices to defensive gunhandling. Go in with some shooting buddies and get the collection. Then, go out and *train*. A portable 12VDC TV/VCR unit which can run off your car's cigarette lighter will allow you to watch your tapes at the range, and then immediately practice what was just shown.

I like Jim Grover's four-part handgun series from Paladin Press. Grover is a very practical and no-nonsense guy, and there's little of his doctrine or techniques that I disagree with. The videos total 230 minutes and retail for Ø125 (#10010833). His book from Paladin Press, *Street Smarts, Fireams, and Personal Security*, is highly recommended, as you know.)

Thunder Ranch (www.thunderranchinc.com) and Gunsite Training Center (www.gunsite.com) now offer their own videos, and, as expected, they're uniformly excellent.

PRACTICE

Advanced techniques are the basics mastered.
— from the 17th Century Samurai Code

Practice doesn't make perfect. Only perfect practice makes perfect.
— any good instructor of anything

As I've urged earlier, get to Thunder Ranch (or some near equivalent) *immediately*. The training is priceless. A superb firearm in untrained hands is almost worthless. If you can't get to school, then at least get some videos.

Test your guns and zero them *now*, while it's still not a problem to shoot. Later on, you may not *have* a hassle-free location, or the time, or the ammo. Get squared away *now*.

Finally, you must orient yourself towards practicing precisely those drills which you *hate*. **Murphy is alive and well,** and he *will* find the *one* area which you have avoided training for (such as weak-hand malfunction clearing).

dry practice

I can't stress to you enough how essential regular dry practice is to not only maintaining your skill, but *increasing* it.

There is a way to develop a high level of skill without firing a single shot. It is called dry practice. Dry practice is the effort a student puts forth off the range, at home, with an <u>unloaded</u> firearm. Dry practice allows you to execute perfect repetitions of all gun handling manipulations without the distracting muzzle blast or recoil. Remember that shooting is a motor skill, and that motor skills are enhanced through repetition. Dry practice allows you to perform an unlimited number of perfect repetitions. This will, in turn, yield impressive results at the range, as well as in stressful situations on the street.

Live fire is an important but minor part of the training. Each shot fired programs a subconscious imprint into the nervous system. If the shot is fired with perfect coordination and attention to basics, this is fine. If the shot is "thrown away," you've just programmed yourself to throw shots away. Look at live fire as a mere validation of your dry practice. The daily dry practice is the training; the occasional live-firing drill is the final exam. I have found that too much shooting actually makes officers poor shots.

— Gabriel Suarez, *The Tactical Rifle* (1999), p.19

Instructor Bill Rogers made the excellent point that although dry practice cannot train you for live fire muzzle control during multiple shots, it *will* train you to place that *first* shot perfectly.

Dry practice may also become extremely valuable in future times when either ammunition is short, or live fire practice becomes difficult (due to regulatory restrictions).

Pick a wall with nothing/nobody behind it for your dry practice wall. Tape up a full-color Bad Guy target. Completely unload your weapon and place the ammo and mags outside the door. Work slowly and smoothly at first, until the speed grows. Do this for about 10-15 minutes, then announce to yourself, *"I have completed tonight's dry fire practice."* Avoid the temptation to dry practice outside this room and its protocol, especially after you've just cleaned your gun. Don't invite an ND!

Do this at least three times a week, and you'll stay sharp. Recently, I got "too busy" for dry practice and let it slide for weeks. Then, when I got on the range, I was shocked at how poor my first several shots were! No matter how good your skills are, they *will* degrade without practice. Even the sharpest razor will dull over time.

timer

A good timer is necessary to replicate the urgency involved in a real shooting, and to measure your skill progression. The Pro-Tech II is probably the best, followed by the PACT.

target stands

A great new target stand from MTM (Ø13.50; 937-890-7461; www.mtmcase-guard.com) is the Jammit, which stakes into the ground and holds your target a full 3' off the ground. They weigh only 2lbs and can be stuck anywhere for mobile range practice. (Carry some in your car so you can practice out in the country any time.)

targets

Targets should be as realistic as possible, meaning no bullseye target for tactical simulation. Use cardboard torso targets, preferably with an armed bad guy on them (you can stencil on a pistol or knife). Draping the targets with old T-shirts (10-25¢ from the thrift store) greatly increases realism.

The best paper target in my opinion is the Anatomy Man, which was designed in conjunction with medical history of many fatal shootings. The target itself is the statistical average of 5'9". The scores represent deca-percentages of one shot stops. A brain or spine shot (a 10) should *generally* stop a Bad Guy 100% of the time. A heart shot is 90% stopper, since sufficient blood pressure can remain for him to continue fighting for many seconds. Lungs get a 7, and other vital organs get a 5. The training goal is to get 10 or more points in no more than 2 seconds. This is a realistic and challenging goal! (If you discover a source for these excellent targets, please let me know.)

The "Tactical Ted" is probably the best target for most uses. A realistic torso/head made of a resilient plastic (which will take many cumulative bullets) contains a bowling pin to approximate the "A" zone. Ø140 or so.

Sierra Metals (800-400-6634) offers an electrically-driven dynamic Train-Fire Target System.

barricades, walls, vehicles, etc.

Life is generally replete with brick wall corners, phone booths, trashcans, furniture, vehicles, etc. You must train yourself to successfully engage your threats amongst all of them. Also, many obstacles are actually forms of cover. Train to use them effectively! (A refrigerator carboard box is great for this.)

ONE-HANDED SHOOTING

According one PD's statistics, in about 12% of exchanged gunfire were officers wounded in the hand, arm, or shoulder. In a way, this is not too surprising as the Bad Guys were probably focusing on the officers' gun and thus often hit the strong limb.

We were given two arms and hands, but the weak side is rarely trained to the point of competent autonomy. So, if our strong side is ever disabled we will have a problem. The text-book case on this is Miami shootout. In fact, nearly *everybody* ended up shooting one-handed by the end of the fight.

On 11 April 1986, three Miami FBI agents found that out when Bad Guy Platt wounded their hands and arms. The only reason that they survived that horrific gunfight is because Platt, his own strong side disabled, thought that he had killed Agent Mireles with three shots from his weak hand. Fortunately, Platt had never practiced such, and he missed all three. The severely wounded Mireles, with only his strong arm working, managed to brain Platt as he was fleeing in an FBI car.

Had the FBI agents been trained and practiced in one-hand shooting and reloading, the results would have been quite different.

position of holster

Most professionals carry their handgun in a strong side belt holster (whether inside or outside the pants) just behind the hip. Not only is this a fine position for both concealment and draw speed, it will allow your weak hand to reach behind your back and draw.

strong hand

First, practice shooting, reloading, and clearing malfunctions with your strong hand.

shooting

Face your threat squarely, and extend your arm almost fully. Your arm will naturally want to cock inside about 45°, and that's O.K.—it will provide better stability.

Firmly hold onto the gun and smoothly work the trigger. *Front sight! Press! Front sight!*

reloading

First, dump your old mag. If it will not drop free, then catch the floorplate on something hard and pull it out.

Next, you must place your gun somewhere while you grab a new mag and insert it. Such places could be your holster, between your knees/legs (watch your muzzle!), or if kneeling inside your knee (with muzzle pointed to the outside). Personally, I prefer the holster method because it's the most secure, and allows full mobility. I really *dislike* the behind-the-knee method because of its inherent muzzle unsafety and its required kneeling position.

Insert the mag, and *Tap* the floorplate against your leg. Don't forget to *Tug*.

clearing a failure-to-fire

It will still require a *Tap-Rack-Bang*. First, tap the mag floorplate on your leg or knee. Then, stick the rear sight on your belt, pants pocket opening, holster, or boot heel and smartly rack the slide all the way open and let it go.

clearing a double-feed

The process *Lock-Drop-Rack-Rack-Rack-Tap-Rack-Bang* also doesn't change. Catch the rear sight against something to rack open the slide while you use your index finger to push up the slide lock. Then, use your index finger to push the mag catch. Rack 3X, place the gun somewhere while you grab and insert a mag, rack it to chamber a round, and fire.

It's not a "fun" drill to practice, but it could save your life!

weak hand

If you thought it was difficult and clumsy with the strong hand, wait till you try it with your southpaw! Though the process is the same, the difficulty level at least doubles.

If your holster is *not* worn behind your strong side hip, you'll need to turn the gun around for a weak hand grip. This can be done by either halfway removing the gun from its holster and turning it while still inside, or by drawing from the holster and rolling the gun 180° across your stomach. (I prefer the holster method.)

Also, when you fire weak-handed you must be sure to have a firm shooting grip for a stable firing platform, else the slide will easily short-cycle (giving you a stovepipe or a double-feed). This is especially true with any polymer frame gun, such as the Glock, H&K USP, etc.

Equipment recommendations for one-handed

Areas which would never be used in normal two-handed firing are not only used, but stressed, during slide racking.

belt

The belt obviously must be stiff to perform well for slide racking. A thick leather belt works fine, but the best is probably the Instructor belt from Wilderness (602-242-4945).

holster

Here is where the Kydex® holsters *really* shine. They are the best for one-handed slide racking. The leather holsters do O.K., and then nylon ones are nearly worthless.

rear sight

As long as the sight is steel with a 90° face, it'll work fine. Glocks come with a plastic rear sight (which, as well as the front sight, should *not* be plastic), and it gets roughed up pretty easily during these drills. Most tritium rear sights are acceptable replacements in this regard.

11 APRIL 1986 "MIAMI MASSACRE"

This incident—the "O.K. Corral of the 20th Century"—is well worth serious study. It demonstrated good and bad tactics.

Michael Platt and William Matix met in the Army, and became a duo of murder, mayhem, and robbery along Miami's South Dixie Highway. Banks, armored cars, and unwary folks in remote areas were all victims. One man was shot three times and left for dead as Platt and Matix took his black 1979 Monte Carlo. The owner Colazzo survived to describe his attackers, and the police and FBI were on the lookout for his car.

Still using the same stolen Monte Carlo in their old criminal haunts, Platt and Matix met an FBI rolling stakeout on the morning of 11 April 1986. The FBI botched a felony carstop within a neighborhood. It all came down at 12201 SW 82nd Ave.

Five FBI unmarked cars and 8 agents with 12 loaded guns faced Platt and Matix with two .357s, a pump 12ga, and a Ruger Mini-14. The Bad Guys were outgunned 3:1, and outmanned 4:1. The gunfight lasted about 4 minutes and 140 rounds. To kill Platt and Matix, two agents died, and five were wounded.

Lessons learned from "Miami Massacre"

There's nothing like a gunfight to find out if your training techniques really work.
— Louis Awerbuck, *SWAT* Magazine (Dec.2001, p.78)

A detailed overview of the gunfight can be found in Massad Ayoob's *The Ayoob Files: The Book*. He interviewed two of the survivors, McNeill and Mireles, and has apparently retold the incident fairly. (Also, John Ross's *Unintended Consequences* has a similar, but less flattering, take on the events.)

Let me say that although I have been critical of past FBI actions (*e.g.*, Ruby Ridge, Waco, Richard Jewell, etc.) and have little faith in their commitment to upholding the Bill of Rights, they were totally correct to have gone after the evil Platt and Matix. Those eight FBI agents involved in that gunfight were brave men, and Mireles is a real hero in my view. I deeply regret that agents Gorgan and Dove lost their lives, and that five other agents were wounded (three of them severely).

My respect notwithstanding, all eight FBI agents commited grievous tactical errors which contributed to (if not caused outright) their own injuries and deaths. However unpleasant it is to state this, facts are stubborn things.

Furthermore, the FBI glossed over this, claiming that their agents were *"outgunned."* (In the two autobiographies written by Oliver "Buck" Revell and Danny "Doc" Coulson, neither even so much as *mentioned* the event! I consider this an outrageous affront to their eight brave brethren.) Instead of focussing on their then-archaic training and tactics, the FBI blamed the tragedy on the poor stopping power of the 9mm. Such is typical of the Bureau's historic myopic pride and arrogance. It got their people killed and crippled.

So, the FBI concluded that if only they'd had 10mm handguns throwing 180gr bullets at 950fps, Miami would have ended differently. *If* Manauzzi and Hanlon had kept theirs holstered before crashing, *if* Gorgan had been wearing contacts or secured eyeglasses, *if* everyone had been wearing bulletproof vests, *if* somebody had thought to have brought along a *rifle, if, if, if*...then, *maybe*, their use of 10mm might have made a diff.

Let's review what can be learned about that horrific day. Some may call this "Monday morning quarterbacking" but I disagree. The lessons are many, obvious, and important.

	GOOD prep/tactics	BAD prep/tactics
Platt	750+rds weekly practice deployed the only rifle in gunfight had spare mags for Mini-14 had a secondary handgun excellent use of cover/shadows kept moving; always on attack disabled/killed 6 of 8 agents kept fighting even critically wounded	no weakhand practice it was only a .223 vs. a .308 did not have enough of them it was a revolver vs. semi-auto no bulletproof vest or earplugs blew out Matix's eardrums failed to kill Mireles point blank got hit 12 times and died
Matix	750+rds weekly practice had a secondary handgun hit Arrantia once	no bulletproof vest or earplugs it was a revolver, vs. semi-auto little tactical support of Platt got hit 6 times and died
FBI Mireles	had secondary gun incredible willpower and bravery always used his front sights killed Platt and Matix	it was a S&W 686 revolver poor use of cover--> McNeill got weak arm disabled
FBI McNeill	only agent to don a bulletproof vest made one hit on Matix	2½" 5-shot S&W 66 primary no secondary gun got wounded/disabled
FBI Risner	15-shot semi-auto had a spare mag good use of cover and distance had a secondary gun made 1-2 hits on Platt from 40yds only agent unwounded	it was a 9mm, vs. a .45 had only one spare mag no bulletproof vest it was a 5-shot S&W 60 never attacked failed to drive/outflank
FBI Arrantia		no bulletproof vest S&W revolver primary spare rounds in glovebox never attacked forward got wounded
FBI Manauzzi		no bulletproof vest S&W revolver primary no secondary gun lost S&W from lap in crash left Rem. 870 in back seat severely wounded
FBI Hanlon	had a secondary gun good, consistent use of cover	no bulletproof vest S&W revolver primary lost unsecured gun in crash it was a 5-shot S&W 36 failed to flank behind tree severly wounded/ crippled
FBI Grogan	very competent shooter 15-shot S&W 459 bravely returned fire, albeit blindly	no bulletproof vest it was a 9mm, vs. .45 failed to secure eyeglasses fired nearly 20 shots, w/no hits fired w/o cover, got killed
FBI Dove	very competent shooter 15-shot S&W 459 made 1 hit on Platt	no bulletproof vest it was a 9mm, vs. .45 had only one spare mag 1 hit out of 29 shots failed to flank behind tree inattention during reload, got killed

Training and practice pays off

Platt and Matix trained 750-1500rds/week, and it showed (particularly in the case of Platt). Dove got a torso hit on Platt.

Lack of training and practice results in injury/death

Apparently, nobody trained for one-handed shooting (and reloading), and Platt, Mireles, McNeill, and Hanlon had to resort to such. The agents apparently also had never trained for team tactics, and thus did not work to outflank Platt and Matix.

Sloppiness, laziness, and pride invite Murphy

Manauzzi and Hanlon not securing their handguns, and losing them in the crash. Only McNeill bothered to don his bulletproof vest, even though the agents *knew* that Platt and Matix were professional criminals using .357s, .45s, and .223s.

Vision/visibility is paramount

McNeill had previously lost his right eye vision in a shooting incident, and shouldn't have been on the rolling stakeout at all. Grogan didn't secure his eyeglasses, and they got knocked off, rendering him effectively blind. Both paid for it.

There was much dust in the air from six cars crashing and skidding to a stop. Either by accident or tactical design Platt remained in the tree shadows, while the agents were all in the sun trying to get a bead on Platt through the dusty shadows.

All spare ammo got used

Dove died with his S&W 459's slide locked back, after emptying two 14rd mags. Risner emptied both mags of his 459. Arrantia emptied his revolver and was frantically searching the glovebox for ammo. Platt went through all his Mini-14 mags.

All secondary weapons got used

Platt, Matix, Mireles, Hanlon, and Risner had secondary guns. All five used them.

Revolvers are poor primary and secondary handguns

They hold only 5-6rds, are slow to reload with two hands, and nearly impossible to reload with one hand (as McNeill learned). Also, 2½" snubbies are pretty worthless after 15yds.

9mm is not a reliable manstopper

Platt early on took a 9mm Silvertip under the armpit, severing the pulmonary artery—a mortal wound. Killing, however, is not *incapacitating* as he yet fought hard and well for nearly 4 minutes before finally dying from Mireles's fusillade.

Hands/arms got disabled

Platt (2x, gun arm), Mireles (weak arm), McNeill (gun hand), and Hanlon (gun arm) all suffered such. Dove's S&W 459 took a hit in the slide before he died from Platt's .223.

A semi-auto long gun was a huge advantage to Platt

Long guns are easier to hit with during great stress. Except for the meager and sporadic covering fire by Matix's shotgun (which lightly wounded Arrantia), Platt did all of the killing and nearly all of the wounding. He singlehandedly removed 6 of the 8 agents from the fight, and severely compromised a 7th (Mireles). Mireles described the loud report of Platt's Mini-14 as a *"psychologically devastating ka-boom."*

.223 fire wounded more often than killed

Although hit in his gun hand McNeill managed to reload 2rds in his revolver before taking a second .223 round in the neck. Manauzzi was only slightly wounded. Mireles, his weak arm splayed open, not only remained in the fight, but won it.

Use of a semi-auto .308 would have been *decisive*

Mireles would have died, rather than merely having his left arm *"peeled back like a banana."* McNeill would have also likely died, versus merely his gun hand being wounded. Manauzzi would have likely been at least severely injured, versus moderately injured. Arrantia's wound would have likely taken him out of the fight. Risner would have had much less effective cover from behind his car, and might have taken some hits.

Platt would have probably killed 4 of the 8, severely wounding 3 others—leaving only Risner available to return fire (who also might have been wounded from behind his car).

If passenger Platt had begun firing .308 AP through his rear window at the following FBI cars, *and* if Matix had also been armed with the same (instead of a shotgun), the morning would have ended *much* more badly than it did.

Those who moved and shot, more often got their hits

Under Matix's covering fire, Platt consistently moved towards the agents, and thus was not only harder to hit, but he took the fight *to* his opponents. He did this twice (to shoot Hanlon, Grogan, and Dove; and then to fire 3 shots at Mireles).

Mireles (a former Marine) finally abandoned cover (the only agent to have done so) and brained the pair.

Hanlon and/or Dove could/should have moved to their right behind the large tree for cover flanking of Platt.

Instead of waiting for clear shots from across the street, Risner could/should have (after the fight went on past 1-2 minutes) gotten in his car with Arrantia and simply driven *behind* Platt and Matix to surround them.

Willpower and bravery made *all* the difference

Both Platt and Mireles demonstrated great resolve and courage, and were the "stars" of the fight. Everybody else was more or less filler to the drama.

Luck/chance/providence also played a big part

Mireles's left arm blocking a .223 chest hit. Risner's disabling hit on Platt's gun arm (which ended his killing). Risner not getting hit at all. Nobody in the neighborhood getting hit by one of the 140 stray rounds.

That Platt and Matix were not both armed with HK91s.

FINAL CHAPTER THOUGHTS

Recognize your need for quality training

Mere gun ownership is not gun handling skill.

Find superb instructors and pay for quality training

Quality costs time and money. Spend both freely.

Keep up your edge with regular dry-fire practice

It's free, it's easy, and it's vital to maintain your skill.

Mix up/vary your live practice to anticipate Murphy

Always use startle cues (*e.g.*, from a timer or a buddy). Load up many dummy rounds and mix with your live ammo to realistically practice failure-to-fire drills. Frequently change targets, distances, angles, scenarios, and other variables.

Share your skills

Bring friends and family up to your level, and beyond.

Practice with your buddies

Team tactics cannot be honed by yourself.

Never stop learning!

AFTER THE
SMOKE CLEARS...

You've just properly and successfully defended yourself with a gun. The Bad Guy is down. Be *very* careful now. While the physical peril may be over, the legal peril is just beginning.

Stay or flee?

Even though self-defense is your most basic human right, any incidence of such *can* be treated as a homicide (especially in areas where private gun ownership is forbidden or highly restricted). Moreover, if you *leave* the scene of such an incident, it *will* be treated as an unsolved homicide. ("Acceptable" reasons for fleeing could include fear for your life from other assailants, or that you went to call 911. These should be kept in mind after any shooting, and not merely when flight is being seriously considered.)

If you've successfully fled, then your next decision will be whether or not to report the shooting at *all*. This is obviously a monumental, life-changing decision (even if you pull it off), so you'd better first think it through conceptually.

Thus, if a self-protective exodus is at all possible for any peaceable gunowner, then some cold carry precautions must be taken beforehand. Most "respectable" gun authors will not write about such, but I feel that this topic *should* be discussed given the outrageous prosecution of ordinary Americans whose only "crime" was exercising their constitutional right by "illegally" carrying a gun and using it for self-defense.

"I'M OUTTA HERE!"

It may be useful for our lady to be able to rapidly dispose of her weapon after an attack when leaving the area and if the weapon is not to come back to haunt her, a cold weapon devoid of all prints, naturally may prove useful. For example, in New York City, if our hypothetical shooter shoots her assailant and then reports it to the police, she is very likely to be charged with felony-murder for killing the "scum-bag" who attacked her.
— Timothy J. Mullin, *Handbook of Handguns* (2001)

It is important to note that the following information is provided solely for your academic consideration. I am not recommending that anyone flee the scene of a justifiable homicide, much less plan their life and equipment for such fleeing. In fact, after reviewing the precautions such a flight will require, most of you will properly conclude that it's far too involved and risky to succeed—and that's my point here. Call 911; don't flee.

Finally, I certainly am *not* discussing this to educate criminals, and such information won't be of any practical use to them. The really professional Bad Guys already know all about it, and the criminally unskilled won't be able to pull it off.

(So, how do *I* know about all this? I'm currently writing my novel, so I researched the cold carry scenario for fictional purposes.)

Whether or not to remain

The only scenario where fleeing would seem tempting is where your life was still in danger from other potential assailants. Then, yes, get out of there! Once you've arrived at a safe place, you will then wonder if you should make that call. *"What if the police don't believe that I was in fear of my life, and retort with a murder charge?"* Yes, that's possible (if not probable). What should you do? I don't know—remember, I'm just an author chatting about hypothetical situations!

Watching *Bonfire of the Vanities* or *The Player* or *Body Heat* is quite instructive, especially on how suspicious cops conduct their interrogations. If you don't envision yourself being able to handle such a grilling, then your options are rather limited.

How to screw up, *big* time? Emulate Bernhard Goetz!

Goetz of NYC was assaulted in 1981 by three youths. He subsequently applied for a gun permit, and was denied (natch). On 22 December 1984 he was accosted by four youths, this time on the subway. They were armed with screwdrivers (don't laugh; such can be weapons, especially when you're outnumbered 4-1), and "asked" him for five dollars. He drew his (unlicensed) gun and shot all four, including one a second time.

While I believe that Goetz had a valid fear for his life in that subway (the four punks were clearly menacing), he botched it in nearly every way possible. He was consistently his own worst enemy. First, he shot an already downed punk a *second* time (when Goetz was no longer in danger), saying *"You don't look so bad. Here's another."* Then, he *confessed* a week later. But what *really* did him in was telling the police how much he enjoyed causing his four to suffer:

> *I wanted to kill those guys, I wanted to maim those guys, I wanted to make them suffer in every way I could. If I had more bullets I would have shot 'em all, again and again...I was gonna gouge one of the guys' eyes out with my keys afterwards. You can't understand this. I know you can't understand this. That's fine.*

Goetz came across as unhinged. (Maybe he was.)

Finally, he didn't even have the sense to *move* out of state (if not the country) until the whole mess had died down. An NYC jury eventually convicted him of illegal gun possession. He was sentenced to six months in jail, appealed, and wound up with a full year. If it weren't for the City's disgust with rampant crime, Goetz would have been convicted of manslaughter.

Still, it's possible...

Your odds of making it home free greatly increase after 72 hours. *If* you didn't leave any direct evidence at the scene, and *if* you competently ditched your gun, and *if* your whereabouts then cannot be quickly ascertained, and *if* you successfully disappear for at least three days thereafter, *then* the odds *begin* to swing in your favor.

Finally, if you can keep your mouth *completely* shut for the *rest* of your life (*especially* to your spouse), then your secret will likely die with you. But, you'll have many, many moments of sudden and severe stress for the rest of life; the gnawing fear of being arrested will never go away. (You may even one day feel the overwhelming urge to "confess" your deed. This happens regularly with fugitives after many years, even when they've been successful at it. The stress gets to them.)

In *Unintended Consequences* is a story about how five Sicilian heavies tackled a mob assassin, shot him twice before television cameras, and escaped prosecution. Even though all five of them tested positive for nitrates, none of them spoke so much as one word, and the gun had been covered with friction tape. The police couldn't prove that the victim hadn't accidentally shot himself, and released all five after 20 hours of fruitless interrogation. They were never charged.

The lessons of the Columbo shooting are clear and uncomplicated:

1. Eyewitness testimony is the least reliable in court, even when the actions are filmed. There can always be multiple explanations for what someone saw.

2. Forensic evidence is much harder to refute, but it can be completely neutralized with a little foresight.

3. You pick the time and place for action if you want to succeed—don't let someone else dictate the terms.

4. Never talk to the police. Ever. About anything. You will only give them rope to make a noose for you. This is just as important to remember when you are completely innocent. Open your mouth and a case may get built on some fragment of your testimony, and you will take the fall for someone who was smart enough to keep his mouth shut.

Keep these lessons firmly in mind. They will serve you well in all circumstances, including the times when you've done nothing.

— John Ross, *Unintended Consequences* (1996), p.719

Cold gun preparation

Such preparation is *crucial*. After the smoke clears, you will have no time or mental clarity to undo any mistakes. In fact, you'll probably make more mistakes than you undo.

A true story

There was an interesting case back in the 1960s of a gold-digging conman who seduced wealthy older women for their money. Eventually, he turned to murder. He took his widow-ladyfriend to the Swiss alps, shot her in the head with a 9mm Browning Hi-Power, and dumped her body in an alpine ravine.

The body was found the following spring by hunters, and identified. The fatal bullet was recovered and testing confirmed that it had been fired from a Browning Hi-Power. (The spent casing was never found.) Since the dirtbag's California registration records indicated that he indeed owned such a gun, it was tested for a ballistic match which showed that the bullet had *not* been fired from that barrel. Not satisfied, the police contacted FN in Belgium who confirmed that the barrel had proofmarks of a *later* series than the gun and thus was *not* the gun's original barrel. Although this was still not sufficient probable cause to arrest (much less to convict), it did tell the police that they likely had the right guy (who was the last person seen with the poor victim). The murderer, an incredibly slippery fellow, nearly escaped the country, but was caught and convicted on a conspiracy charge.

When I read the book about this, it occurred to me that the guy had thought it out *backwards*. He *should* have used the gun with the *replacement* barrel, destroyed it, and then re-installed the original barrel. (As long as there were no linkable purchase records on the replacement barrel, this would have likely ended the matter.) Such is the proper setup for any cold carry gun.

cartridge choice is critical

Taking the barrel change concept even further, one could install a different caliber barrel, such as a .357SIG barrel in a .40S&W gun, or a .400 CorBon barrel in a 1911A1. (Although ballistic testing would very probably show that the bullet was fired from a .357SIG vs. 9mm barrel, such *initial* confusion over which caliber of gun to look for could work to one's advantage.) Unfortunately, most of these different caliber drop-in barrels are made of stainless steel, which is very difficult to torch.

all ammo should be loaded with gloves

While you can likely take your gun with you and deal with it later, you probably will *not* have the time or presence of mind to pick up your casings. Even if you *do*, remembering how many rounds you fired and then finding *all* of them is surprisingly unlikely. Even during training, firing to save your life is incredibly stressful and disorienting. You may not even remember whether he was right- or left-handed (don't even think about planting a weapon in his hands!), or what he was wearing. Thus, the less one has to deal with post-event, the better. Scrounging around a dark alley for your brass takes too much time and will just leave more clues (*e.g.*, fingerprints, shoeprints, inadvertently dropped personal items, etc.).

So, you should have loaded your ammo with gloves to avoid leaving prints on the brass. Even though a fired case goes through incredible heat and pressure, and violent extraction, your fingerprints could nevertheless remain (especially if they had been "etched" on by sweat salts, gun oil, etc.).

If you've already loaded your mags with bare hands, you should unload them and wipe off the rounds with a solvent. Then, reload them using surgical gloves. (There is a variety of these which are made with something other than powdered latex. While more expensive, they won't leave telltale powdered residue, or irritate those with sensitive skin. Medical and nursing supply houses carry them.)

Even totally devoid of prints, the casings will still very likely tell the investigators which gun fired them. Glocks, for example, make a unique primer dent from their striker, which is immediately identifiable on the scene by any average detective.

avoiding fingerprints on the gun

Applying friction tape to the gun's entire surface would prevent any fingerprinting. However, if you ever got caught with such a treated gun (which would resemble an assassin's weapon), the police would rightfully be unquenchably suspicious. So, perhaps carrying a taped gun isn't a great idea.

A bead-blasted gun then Parkerized would provide a texture and finish very resistant to fingerprinting. Plastic framed pistols with textured surface print very poorly, but such texture gets rubbed smooth rather quickly (which *will* then take a print).

Thus, you can't really rely on your gun to not have at least *one* incriminating fingerprint. The only thing you can do is wipe it down, which must be done *very* methodically and carefully. (Most people will *not* be able to do this perfectly.) One idea is to dip it in oil, which cannot be wiped off with wiping the prints.

the ideal cold carry gun

It should not eject its casings, as such provide the most ballistic evidence (usually even more than bullets). Thus, a *revolver* is preferred. (Other possibilities are single-shot weapons, whether handguns or long guns.)

It would have no registration, repair, or pawnshop records linkable to the owner. Thus, it would not have been purchased from an FFL, or from a local gun show (where the owner is known), or from anybody acquainted with the owner.

This is especially important for owners of post-1998 HKs, S&Ws, and Glocks. A fired bullet and casing is kept, and the unique striations are digitized as the gun's ballistic fingerprint.

At least these three (and perhaps Ruger) have been doing this with new guns since at least 1999. (This comes from a highly credible, well-informed source inside the gun industry.)

There would be no linkable purchase records of the ammo or anything related to the gun (*e.g.,* spare barrels and parts).

The owner would not have any spare ammo for the gun on his/her premises. There would be no spent casings from this gun on his/her premises, or at the local gun range.

Nobody (not even your spouse or best friend) could know that you own such a gun.

It would be fingerprint-proof (*e.g.,* covered in friction tape). The internals would have been wiped before reassembly.

It would provide no bullet ballistic matching to its bore, so sabot rounds would be the best ammo from a rifled barrel. (The plastic sabot parts in several pieces from the bullet, and will not likely be found. The absence of rifling on the bullet will, of course, immediately cause *great* concern for the investigators. Their wariness and dedication will increase several fold, as the use of sabot rounds is *very* rare.) Any smoothbore, however, would also work well as it has no rifling to striate the bullet. Or, one could use shotshell loads (though they have less power).

As I earlier mentioned, creating the perfect cold-carry handgun for self-defense is very involved. And, I haven't even begun to describe what it would take to properly *dispose* of it!

Disposing of a cold-carry gun

Any gunowner may be reluctant to part with a Ø600 gun which has been carried for years, and that's understandable. However, Ø600 is an incredibly cheap price to pay to avoid an erroneous conviction for murder or manslaughter. Ø600 won't even buy two hours of a good criminal defense attorney.

Face it, any gun used in a justifiable homicide is *gone*, one way or another. Either it's seized for evidence and kept for months (or forever), or it must be disposed of if the user flees the scene. Either way, it's gone, and it must it must be considered expendable. (This is why any person serious about their self-defense should own at least *two* unpapered handguns. One for carry, and the other held in reserve as a possible replacement.)

destruction

In any crime, the perpetrator leaves something *behind* and takes something *with* him. What's left behind in *every* shooting is the bullet, and there's no avoiding that. Other items can also include the casing (if fired from a semi-auto), footprints, fingerprints, tire tracks, DNA samples (hair, skin, saliva, blood), and personal items (*e.g.*, something could have dropped from the shooter's pocket, etc.).

What might be *taken* with the shooter could be site soil on the shoes, DNA samples from the aggressor, or the aggressor's prints if he touched any of your articles.

As this is not a "how-to" discussion on successfully fleeing such a scene, only gun-related residue will be described. Semi-auto gun parts in bold mark the bullet (which will be recovered and analyzed), while the rest mark the casing (which can be retrieved by the shooter, but don't count on it).

magazine	(mag follower and lip scratches on casing)
frame	(feed ramp scratches on bullet and casing)
barrel	(bore striations on bullet; chamber marks on casing)
bolt face	(impressions on case head)
firing pin	(indentation on primer cup)
extractor	(scratches on case head)
ejector	(leaves marks on casing)

All of these parts, except for the frame and magazine, are in the slide. So, destroying the slide is your first priority.

Puddling the parts with an acetylene torch is the best way to go. While the metal can be identified through neutron activation analysis as being from a certain manufacturer and model, no particular *gun* could ever be IDed from such a blob (assuming it were ever found).

One author recommends placing the barrel on some railroad tracks, to be squashed as a penny. This is much more risky as the barrel could be found before the train arrives, or the train could do an incomplete job. He also suggested scoring the bore with a stainless steel brush, scrubbing the bolt face with emery paper, and replacing the firing pin, extractor, and ejector. While such *may* suffice (though I wouldn't chance it), the peace of mind that can come *only* from torching and ditching the metal is worth the effort.

Start with the barrel, and puddle it. (Stainless steel barrels are *very* difficult to melt, and thus are not recommended for cold carry guns.) Then, do the bolt face, firing pin, extractor, and ejector. Then the slide, frame, and magazine.

Should you keep "safe" parts like the mag spring and floorplate, the expensive tritium sights, the custom grips, etc.? If you've got other guns for these parts, *maybe*. Still, it's probably better not to be greedy. Torch everything. That way, there's not even a *theoretical* chance of linkage. (Theoretical has a way of becoming actual. Risk nothing.)

disposal

If your escape is failing and detention seems imminent, then you will have no time to destroy the gun. A quick disposal is all that you can do.

First, you've got to *perfectly* wipe off all prints (this includes the magazine). Good luck.

Second, you must *very* quickly choose a place to ditch the gun where it won't likely (if ever) be found for at least several days (until after the heat has died down). There are two schools of thought on this: temporary disposal (until you can later reclaim it for destruction), or "permanent" disposal (*e.g.*, dropping the disassembled parts in a *very* deep body of water).

I say "permanent" because only torching is truly permanent—every other form of disposal can theoretically be undone. For example, actor Woody Harrelson's father shot a federal judge and then dumped the rifle off a causeway into shallow (*i.e.*, less than 50 feet) water. A passing motorist happened to see this and directed the police divers to the spot, where it was quickly found. Harrelson was properly convicted.

One rather clever example of "permanent" disposal was in a movie where a guy went to a truck stop, disassembled his gun and tossed the individual parts on top of different trailers. Such semis would later head down their unique roads to unique destinations, with many of the parts falling off on the way to who knows where. This was elegant and effective.

Other "permanent" disposals are sprinkling the parts in *different* public trashcans, storm drains, or deep water.

In short, do not convince yourself to *keep* the gun. Get rid of it as quickly and as permanently as possible. It's the one link that you can't afford to have on the planet. Make it go away.

evidence from the shooter

He/she *will* have nitrate residue on the hands (especially if a revolver was used), so a plausible explanation for that must be invented (*e.g.*, he/she was plinking in the woods that day).

There must be an alibi for the shooter's whereabouts during the event. Getting others to support such is *highly* risky as it brings in new people to something best kept to yourself.

Creating an alibi will be nearly impossible if evidence can reliably place you in the area at the time. For example, if you just left a bar where many people know you and were attacked in the parking lot, such a scene would *not* be one to flee from. Other evidence could be credit card receipts from neighborhood stores, phone calls made nearby, a parking ticket (this is how spree killer "Son of Sam" was eventually caught), or even security cameras never seen. If the scene seems hinky to any good investigator, he might dig up something incriminating. (Worse yet, he could decide that you did it and frame you.)

If all this seems overwhelming, you're right!

That's the moral of the story. It takes specialized tools, experience, and cool planning. The odds are against you.

Let's face it; you're not cut out for this kind of thing!

Criminals have a better practical chance of getting away with such flight because they have prior experience (you don't), they can plan for it (whereas you got surprised, and thus retrospectively left many inadvertent clues). They have the immediate support of the criminal underworld (you don't). They are ruthless (you are just an average person), they feel no guilt (you will, at least in the form of doubt), they can much more easily construct a "verifiable" alibi (your business partner or spouse won't eagerly *"go along"* with you on this), and they are very experienced in enduring police interrogations (you're not). As Mickey Rourke opined in the movie *Body Heat*:

> *In any decent crime, there are 50 ways to f*ck up. If you think of 25 of them, you're a genius. My advice is...don't do it.*

And that's my generic advice, too. *Don't do it.* Since we are talking about *technically* (though not morally) getting away with murder, you are more likely than not to get caught.

STAY AND DIAL 911

> *It is presumed that you have exhausted all avenues of escape and have been forced by the threat of deadly physical force to your life or the life of another by resorting to the use of your skills and weapon system to resolve the situation.* (at 87)
> — Jim Crews, *Some Of The Answer, Urban Carbine* (2001)

Forcefully demand verbal compliance

Yelling *"Get back!"* may indeed stop the aggression. Even if it does not, it bolsters your case of self-defense.

Front Sight! Press! Front Sight! (repeat as necessary)
Get...your...hits. Nothing matters but making good hits. You make successive hits until the threat is no longer threatening. As Clint Smith says, *"Shoot what is available, while it is available, until something else becomes available."*

Move, preferably to cover
Immediately following a shooting, you don't know if he is down, much less incapcitated and out of the fight. Relocate at *once,* to cover if you can.

Perform a threat assessment
Go to the Ready position (which provides a greater field of view, and helps to shake off tunnel vision), and Search & Scan for additional threats. The fight is not over just because you've fired—it's over once you've cleared the area for any threat.

Restore your weapon to its highest possible readiness
If you have a spare mag, then perform a tactical reload and systems check. If no spare mag, then do a systems check. Do this from behind cover, maximizing your distance from the assailant.

Check for an additional orifices
Hint: You were born with seven.

Keeping him behind your front sight, disarm the assailant
Even if he's clearly dead, disarm him. (Many apparently dead perps have shockingly "come alive" to surprise the victim.) If the weapon is still in his hand, step *hard* on his wrist and disarm him. If the weapon is on the floor, kick it away from him behind you. Leave it behind you, and don't touch it, if possible. If you can safely do so, cuff, tie, or tape his hands behind his back and leave him face down. Also, secure his ankles if possible.

Keeping him behind your front sight, call 911
You only wanted to stop his aggressive actions, not kill him. Now that the fight's over, get him medical help. Call 911, and say, *"I need an ambulance at____. An armed intruder has just been shot in self-defense. I'm the homeowner, and I'm wearing a ____ shirt and ____ pants."* That's it, nothing more. You should sound reasonably upset, yet not hysterical. No "iceman" tone, please—it'll freak out the jury later.

Keeping him behind your front sight, call your lawyer

First, you should achieve offer/acceptance of a retainer, in order to establish an attorney/client relationship.

Tell him *exactly* what happened. Most likely he will instruct you to respectfully remain silent until he arrives. Hopefully, he can come over right away. Take pictures if you can.

Do not try to tamper with the scene!

Don't try to put his prints on his weapon, and certainly do *not* try to plant a weapon *on* him. Above all, do not drag him in from outside to change your story! Forensic investigators are extremely competent at reconstructing together a scene, and your actions will very likely be discovered, which will severely impugn a righteous shooting.

Keeping him behind your front sight, wait for the police

The police will be very edgy when they arrive. Watch your muzzle! Once they have driven up, holster your handgun and calmly (with your empty hands in full view) identify yourself.

NEVER TALK OR EXPLAIN YOUR ACTIONS TO POLICE!!

Shooting the wrong person at the wrong time of year with the wrong reporting officer and the wrong prosecutor can result in your being in big trouble and your statements may harm you considerably. Only recently in my home town a man was attacked. If he would have kept his mouth shut, I feel certain he would have walked. Instead, he talked and faced a murder charge and lawsuit. So, no matter how much you want to explain yourself, KEEP QUIET!

— Timothy J. Mullin, *Handbook of Handguns* (2001)

They will naturally ask you what happened, and you will naturally want to talk about it. ***Don't!*** Simply say that you were in fear of your life, and your attorney instructed to remain silent until he arrives. If they badger you for a statement, reply that you are very upset right now and wish to consult with your attorney first. Then, clam up.

The reason for this is simple: Silence cannot be used against you in American courts, and it cannot be misquoted.

Moreover, your stress and adrenaline will grossly distort your memory of the events, and will *not* be a reliable witness on your own behalf. (It will take 3-4 hours for your blood chemistry to normalize.) You won't remember which hand his weapon was in, what he was wearing, or how many shots you fired. Any misstatement could create a criminal case against you.

After police have left, write down exactly what happened

This is for your *own* records. Details will float into your memory over the next days and weeks. Revise your notes. I'd enter it in an encrypted computer file.

Don't discuss the incident until the legal matter is over

If it was a righteous shooting and you were in lawful possession of the gun, then you're probably home free. Don't blow it by throwing a party, or mouthing off to the reporters. Let your lawyer do *all* the talking for you.

Long after the incident, keep your mouth shut!!!

Do *not*: brag about your marksmanship and the effectiveness of your defensive loads, gloat on how his chest cavity looked like goo, complain how law-abiding citizens are sick of scumbag criminals, or marvel at how calm you felt and that only wimps go through that "post-operational-trauma" stuff.

You were *terrified* for your own life, you were *forced* to defend yourself, you didn't *want* to shoot him, and you're *very upset* over having taken another's life. That's your attitude.

If the DA wants to prosecute, don't fool around

Get the best defense attorney you can find. If the prosecution seems especially petty and vicious, contact the NRA and GOA for legal help. Just in case they later search your home, I'd clear it of most guns, and *all* gun-related receipts, books, magazines, etc. If it seems likely that you'll be convicted of a felony, then *sell* your guns as they'll be taken away from you, anyway.

Massad Ayoob of the Lethal Force Institute is a widely acclaimed expert witness. His description of a jury is good to contemplate, *"A jury is a twelve-headed creature with an I.Q. of at least 1,200 and as much as 500 years of experience, with 12 simultaneous bullsh*t detectors in operation."*

Everything you do must seem prudent and reasonable to a jury later. Think through how your life and actions may come across to them. Above all, keep your mouth shut!

WOMEN & GUNS

❖ 6

Statistically, women have a 50% chance of being a victim of violent crime by age thirty. This predatory environment is the result of too many men abdicating their duty to protect women against society's nastier elements. I don't mean that women *cannot* protect themselves. My point is this: **Why should they *have* to?** They shouldn't *have* to any more than they should have to change their own oil. **Yes, they *can* do it—but they shouldn't *have* to, and there's a *difference*.**

Ladies, you are *much* finer creatures than we are. You are too precious and lovely for such crude tasks. Let *us* change the flat tires, put out the forest fires, and defend the borders.

Rabid "feminists" (*i.e.*, the men-hating kind) are no doubt shrieking at this point. *"We're liberated!"* they bellow. *"We don't need men to protect us!"* Technically, they're right—they don't. But that's not the issue.

"Women who seek equality with men lack ambition." Be careful what you ask for. In Russia, men and women *are* equal. The Socialist State recognizes only *"citizens"* and women join men in *all* the grimy chores. Women fix sewer pipes and change truck transmissions along with the men. And they *look* like men because of it. Civilization, random beauty, and elegance have died there—and *that's* the vital issue. Women *can* do a man's job, but men *can't* do a woman's job. It's just not in us.

Jeff Cooper wrote, *"Men are here to protect women, and women are here to civilize men."* When women are consumed with a myriad of coarse chores which men should bear, they have little time, energy, or inclination to civilize men. My other point is this: **Women can more easily protect themselves than men can self-civilize.**

"So?" Well, when men are *not* civilized, society becomes a beer-swilling trailer-park. Left to our own canine devices, men will regress to the raunchy raconteurs and methane dispensers we are at heart. While often dissatisfied with men, women don't realize that *they themselves* are the solution. **Men don't make men, *women* do. Women determine the quality of men.** As Louise told Thelma, *"You get what you settle for."* If women would quit having the children of oafs and morons, then they'd die off. Women are the *lifeguards* of the gene pool, and they should start choosing *quality* mates, as critters have always done. (Women have been debased so as to give oafs better odds. The question is, *why* have women *allowed* their debasement?)

Ladies! Do not speak to, date, sleep with, or marry a hopelessly substandard male. Don't encourage him with the slightest of smiles. He shouldn't exist—so treat him that way. **Above all, do *not* have his children!** If he can't catch an introspective clue, then let him die alone—let his shoddy genes be lost forever. Do not feel sorry for him. **This is not cruelty—this is *quality control.*** *You're* responsible because men will sleep with almost *anybody*. We're the seed-sowers and it's not in us to be *picky*. You're the child-bearers, so you *have* to be selective.

When women refuse to civilize men, men become Al Bundy from *Married With Children*. Why? Because inside *every* man is a *potential* Al Bundy, and it's women's duty to ensure that he never sees the light of day. Although men *can*, with rare and great effort, single-handedly keep their own "Al" locked up, what's the *point* if women no longer seem to *care*?

Believe me, we can *tell* if women care. They don't, and they're reaping the cruel justice of getting the lazy, irresponsible worms they deserve. Ignore genuine courtesy, honor, and responsibility in men—and women get prissy, whining, amoral cowards. Fill up a nation with such males, then a country is left with only bi-gender women, and the predators begin to take over. Courting Darth Vader, the feminized society then cries for a hyper-masculine police state to restore order. When gentlemen are gone, government thugs fill the vacuum. This trend has been accelerating in America since the late 1960s:

> *There was a time even in my remembrance when American men were manly, heads of their houses, and respected by their wives and children. They were rugged and hard-nosed and not swathed in a soft pink jello. A thief was a thief to them, and not a "disadvantaged, underprivileged, culturally deprived" weakling. I've seen men*

beat up other men who attempted to snatch a woman's purse on the public streets, or who kicked a dog or punched a child....

*When men are unmanned, spiritually if not physically, then a country becomes depraved, weak, degenerate, feeble of spirit, dependent, guideless, sick. **Such a country can never resist authoritarian despots, tyrannies, the men on horseback, Communism.** Our Presidents are always talking about our image abroad. I have news for them. Our "image" is a surrogate Mama, in an apron, with a baby's bottle in his hand. Surrogate Mama to a laughing and contemptuous world! Bottle-feeder to ravenous "infants" to proclaim themselves heads of some obscure state in some backyard continent!*

That is our image abroad. Does it make a nice picture to you? Then do something about it. Start in your own house, and then with your own local government. Unseat your emasculators in Washington. Drive them from your schools and your courts. Proclaim to the world again—and again—that you will stand for no more nonsense, and that our flag is to be honored wherever it flies over any embassy; that you have power and are quite willing to use it, in the name of freedom and justice, tempered only slightly by masculine mercy.

Then, perhaps, America will be honorably feared and respected, and peace might really come to a mad and disordered world. The center that "cannot hold" might tighten and become iron and invincible, and Doomsday thus averted. (p.100-101)

***Remember this: The strongest sign of decay of a nation is the feminization of men and the masculinization of women....The decay and ruin of a nation always has lain in the hands of its women.** So does its life and strength, its reverence for beauty, its mercy and kindness. And above all, its men.* (p.116-117)

— Taylor Caldwell; *On Growing Up Tough* (1971)

Men *will* be responsible, honorable, and even heroic—*if* women encourage and respect us for it. We *need* it, for we cannot forever run on our own meager batteries. (Granted, no man is emasculated without his assent, but we cannot fight the relentless onslaught on manhood without women's help.) A dime's worth of respect and approval from ladies gets a *dollar's* worth of effort from us. Men are the draft animals of the human race, and we work cheaply. (We're built that way and don't mind shouldering the yoke of human existence.) But we *do* need at least that dime, and we're getting pennies.

Ladies are not silly froth. Gentlemen are not brainless brutes. We were made to complement each other. But, until men are respected for their manhood so they that clean up our streets, American women, sadly, should daily carry a handgun.

HANDGUNS

Self-defense is not merely our legal right but our moral duty; because women are more vulnerable than men, their need and obligation to defend themselves is even greater than that of men.
— Dr. Thomas S. Szasz,
    Professor of Psychiatry, Syracuse University

The decision for a woman to go armed is a major one for most women. It is not just a matter of purchasing a weapon and training to become competent in its use. It is a change in her life-style and outlook on life. No longer will she be at the mercy of those who are physically stronger or more violent. She will be in a position to control her own destiny and go where she wishes knowing that she can depend on her own resources alone to see her through any developing crisis. This does not mean she should be foolhardy or go into areas where trouble is likely and could be avoided. What it means is that if all of the best laid plans go astray, she has a choice <u>not</u> to become another victim. This for many is a radical change in outlook on life. To be able to really accomplish this means that she will have to make certain adjustments in her life-style, clothing, and behavior patterns. ALL the firearms training in the world and best in equipment mean nothing if the weapon is not available in times of crises in the hands of someone who had adopted the proper mental outlook so as to allow her to utilize the training and equipment.

We will assume that the female shooter will be adequately trained before carrying a weapon. It is highly irresponsible to merely show someone how a weapon works and then to send her out armed on the street. The workings of the weapon must be carefully explained... [She] must learn how to shoot it under street conditions...and understand the legal limitations on the use of force. Lastly, [she] must be trained to respond to typical street-type encounters and <u>want</u> to be able to defend herself. She must realize the importance of her weapon and appreciate the critical role it plays in her life. In my experience, all but this last point are easy enough to achieve if you try hard enough, are patient, and utilize good training techniques and equipment.

The last point, what I call mental conditioning, is the hardest, It is very hard to convince many people that the only thing standing between them and serious harm is their weapon, that they must carry it with them at <u>ALL</u> times from now on. **It is <u>not</u> just an emergency situation but will be part of her life-style forever.** *Any other approach will lead to the weapon not being available at the right time. Once a person realizes this, no problem is encountered with leaving the weapon behind, but getting people to realize this is very difficult.*
— Timothy Mullin; *Round Guns—Square Guns* (2000)

A high-quality, reliable, concealable, and powerful handgun is essential for women. Without its daily presence (and the training to use it) women are at the mercy of random chance. I've trained dozens of ladies with their first handgun, and they constantly remark how much more confident they feel being armed. One friend had nearly given up hiking in the forest next to her home because she had once walked into a camp of dirtbags. Now, she hikes whenever she wants to, as is her right.

Which *kind* of handgun—a semi-auto or a revolver?

Semi-autos are usually more powerful, hold more rounds, are quicker to reload, and are more concealable. They do, however, require a bit more training and practice. Good semi-autos run from Ø325-550 (although there are a few quality bargains under Ø300).

If you cannot or will not spend the extra time and money for a semi-auto, then a revolver (*e.g.*, a S&W .38 Special or Taurus .44 Special) will suffice. Good revolvers run from Ø250-450.

Regardless which you choose, have a handgun.

Avoid the tiny *"cute"* guns—*"cute"* won't save your life!

Again, my rule: Carry the *largest* pistol you can *conceal*, in the *most powerful* cartridge you can *handle*. When I mean "handle" I mean *comfortably and confidently so*. While any handgun may seem intimidating at first, don't choose a tiny .25 because it's *"cute."* (Your handgun must be sufficiently powerful to stop an assailant. *"Cute"* won't do it.)

A *too*-powerful handgun, however, defeats the purpose. Unless you *enjoy* shooting your pistol, you won't train with it often enough (if at all), and regular training is vital. If you're not well-trained with it, you won't carry it, and your pistol must be *with* you to do its job.

The cartridge: not too small—not too big

For semi-autos, I recommend the .40S&W cartridge. If the .40 is *too* stout for you, then go 9x19 (or even 9x18 Makarov, or .380). **Any cartridge is better than *none* at all.** (Besides, with practice you'll probably be able to later work up to the .40, or even .45.) First rule of any gunfight: **Have A Gun.**

In revolvers, I recommend the .44 Special (if you can handle it), or, if not, the .38 Special.

Any good indoor gunrange will have various handguns to rent. Go with a teacher friend (preferably one who has attended Thunder Ranch, etc.) and try out different handguns. Among the models I list later on, choose one that feels *best* to you, as personal affinity is very important.

I guarantee you that at least *one* of them will seem particularly comfortable. As long as it's sufficiently reliable and powerful, then whatever it is will be a fine choice for *you*. (Don't worry if it's not a Glock. You won't hurt my feelings.)

Q: *"How much should I pay?"*
A: As much as your life is worth.

A quality handgun is a tool designed to save your life in a lethal emergency. So, how much is your *life* worth? For example, Ø150 will buy you a very decent Makarov in 9x18, but Ø500 gets you a Glock in .40 or .45. That Ø350 difference you paid for a Glock (or SIG or Colt or HK) could make *all* the difference. If I *had* to carry a Makarov, well, I'd make do, *but* my life deserves better. So should yours.

There's an important conceptual difference between how much one can pay versus how much one can *afford*. While you might technically be able to pay for a month at the Paris Ritz, *affording* it is likely another matter. *Pay* for the most reliable, highest quality handgun—*not* for merely what you can afford. We're talking about saving lives here.

Let me put it another way: If your spouse needed a complicated surgery to survive, wouldn't you seek out the *best* such surgeon in the *world*? What's the point of saving money at the local hospital if the operation fails?

Seek out the *best* handgun for yourself. The few hundred dollars you "save" in lesser guns and gear just isn't worth it. There are many things in life you should *never* skimp on, and tools for self-defense are at the top of that list.

Quality goods you pay for *once*. Crappy goods cost you forever. As Karl Welcher of Leica wisely quipped:

> *Expensive is when the product is not worth the money.*

Semi-autos
Which cartridge?

I'll start with handguns in the most powerful common cartridge (the .45), and work down to the .22LR. (For many reasons, I despise centerfire semi-autos by Ruger or S&W. They are not pro-2nd Amendment, and their products are often inferior.) I will recommend smaller framed handguns, which will fit your hands better and conceal more easily.

.45   Glock 30, Para-Ord 10, Springfield V-10, Colt Officer's ACP, and AMT Backup. In .45 ammo I recommend CorBon 185gr.

.40   Glock 23 or 27, SIG P229, H&K USP40 Compact, Astra (A70 or A75), Kahr K40, or Kel-Tec P40. In .40 ammo I recommend Cor-Bon 135gr or 155gr.

.357 SIG   Glock 32 or 33, and the SIG P229.

9x19   Glock 19 or 26, SIG (P228 or P239), AMT Backup, H&K USP9 Compact, Astra (A70 or A75), Kahr K9, or Kel-Tec P11. In 9x19 ammo I recommend CorBon 115gr +P.

9x18   Makarov (the East German, Bulgarian, or Russian models are identical except for the quality of their polishing), and CZ.

.380   SIG (P230SL or P232SL), Walther (PP, PPK, or PPK/S), AMT Backup, Sphinx AT380M, Makarov, Colt (Mustang or Pony), CZ83.

.32   Seecamp LWS32, NAA Guardian, Kel-Tec, or Beretta Tomcat. (Avoid the Autauga! It malfunctions often.) In .32 ammo I recommend Glaser Blue Safety Slugs. They're screamers.

.25   Forsake this for at least a .32 (which has twice the energy), and is no larger a pistol (if you choose a Seecamp, NAA, or Kel-Tec).

.22LR   Beretta 21A, or *German* Walther TPH.

If possible, choose a stainless steel model over blue (the steel resists corrosion better). Don't stray from my picks, as they're all fine guns, and there's something there to please any lady.

If you want a quick recommendation, go for a subcompact Glock—either the G27 (it's a .40S&W) or the G26 (it's a 9mm). I prefer the G27 as the .40 is a more effective fightstopper than 9mm. If a .40 is too stout, then get the 9mm G26. Not only are Glocks very simple to operate, they work, *period.*

The stainless Kahr 9mms and .40s are also excellent and highly concealable handguns, with a very smooth DAO trigger.

Revolvers

The choices are much simpler: a S&W or Taurus snub-nose (.38 Special, .357 Magnum, or .44 Special) with a shrouded or concealed hammer, preferably in stainless steel. (Revolvers have no mechanical feeding cycle, so they will function with any bullet shape, such as wadcutters or wide-mouth hollowpoints.)

I would only recommend a revolver *if* you do not have the extra time and/or money for a quality semi-auto. Although a

S&W 640 is a good gun (and it's certainly better than having no gun at *all*), I'd feel *much* better if you had a Glock or a Kahr. They hold twice the ammo, and are quicker to reload.

How to daily carry your handgun

Even though there are 24 open-carry states, few gunowners (especially women) wear their sidearms in belt holsters. It's just too startling for most areas. So, you'll have to conceal carry, which requires specialized gear.

Experiment with many different conceal carry methods. Basically, there is on-body (*e.g.,* fanny pack, or hidden holster) and off-body (*e.g.,* a gun purse). Both styles have their pros and cons. Something to keep in mind is the better the concealment, the *slower* the draw. You'll have to decide on the right compromise between concealment vs. speed.

conceal carry holsters

I like IWB (inside waistband) holsters. They are quick draw, and need only to be covered by an untucked blouse, vest, sweater, or jacket.

ThunderWear or the PagerPal (from CTD; 888-625-3848) are *not* quick draw rigs, but provide *great* concealment. They require loose fitting slacks or skirt.

An inside-the-thigh holster under a dress will work fine for the smaller handguns. Buxom women can bra-conceal, though this is quite slow on the draw.

on-body conceal gear

These are items you wear vs. carry. Many common articles are now made for handguns, such as fanny packs, and even *faux* pagers (for the .32 Seecamp). Or, a simple jacket pocket will work. The ActionPac (Ø54ppd; 800-472-2388; www.action-direct.com) under a T-shirt is great for jogging, etc.

off-body conceal gear

These are items you carry. There are many choices: purses, daytimers, soft attachés, and cell phone cases. Their advantage is that they'll go with most any wardrobe. The downsides to off-body carry is that you and your gun can become more easily separated, and its draw speed is much slower.

In an evening dress, for example, your only carry option is probably a purse (with a very small handgun, such as a .32 Kel-Tec). A business suit, on the other hand, would permit carry of a much larger purse (or daytimer holster, etc.)

Since draw speed is slower, you must practice more and keep even more alert (to give yourself ample time to draw). If you're purse carrying your gun and ever feel threatened, get your hand on your gun at once (if not draw and hold it behind your purse). There's no quicker draw than when your gun is already in your hand!

Some gun purse manufacturers are: Anderson (888-778-5725), Conceal 'N Draw (800-444-7090), Coronado (800-283-9509), Galco (800-874-2526), GML (800-345-BAGS), Not Justa Bag (405-376-2929), and Old World Leather (503-655-2837).

So, which is *best*?

There is no "best." It all depends on your situation, which is dynamic. You will need two or three methods in order to carry all the time. I'd recommend on *and* off-body carry methods: An ActionPac (or fanny pack) and IWB holster for on-body, and a purse or daytimer for off-body.

Don't forget a *belt* holster and mag pouch for shooting school and open-carry opportunities (*e.g.*, being in the country). Mad Dog Tactical gear (520-772-3021) is the best.

Handgun practice ammo

Any quality FMJ (full metal jacket, which means a copper shell without a hollow-point). At gun shows you should buy it 500-1,000rds at a time for 12-17¢/rd (versus 20-30¢/rd at the store in a 50rd box). If you can't get to a gun show, then pick up a copy of the *Shotgun News* and have some shipped to you UPS. This bargain ammo is called "factory reloads" which means professionally reloaded from once-fired brass. Don't worry—this ammo is quite safe and reliable. Always have at *least* 500rds of FMJ for practice. I know that sounds like a lot, but you can easily go through such in just a few afternoons.

Handgun defensive ammo

Regular FMJ ammo is the most reliable (in semi-autos), but these bullets do not expand or break up, which reduces their stopping power. Such is the price of 100% reliability.

Some sort of hollow-point (*if* your semi-auto will function with them 100%) or frangible bullet is often the preferred choice. Whichever defensive ammo you choose, it is *vital* that you run a few mags worth through your gun to make certain that it feeds and functions *100%*. (If it doesn't, then try another kind.) Don't *assume* that it will function 100%—*know* firsthand! Only your life depends on it. (When in doubt, stick with FMJ.)

Training with your handgun

If you can't get to Thunder Ranch, etc., then at least go through a local concealed-carry course. These are weekend courses at gunranges for Ø80-100 which will teach you the basics of safe and effective gun handling. (You don't have to get the CHL afterwards if you don't want to.) Or, you might be fortunate enough to know a shooting academy alumnus who can teach you. It's not difficult or grueling stuff; just a few hours and 200rds will give you the basics.

Frequently I teach basic and intermediate courses in handgun and rifle for my readers. In addition to travel expenses, I charge Ø100 per day per student, with a six student class minimum. You provide the range (preferably on secluded private property, and not on a public range), and I supply the targets, materials, etc. Contact me through Javelin Press.

Regarding husbands and boyfriends as instructors, that depends on his own weapons expertise *and* how well you two do in the Teacher/Student scenario. Many men turn into their fathers and get too bossy. Many women turn into daughters and get too sensitive. If a session is not working out with your man, then politely tell him and find a professional instructor.

Practicing with your handgun

Any unpracticed skill *will* erode over time. Get good training to imprint your short-term athletic memory (which takes 300 repetitions), and then *practice* a lot in your first six months to imprint your *long*-term athletic memory (which takes 3,000 repetitions). A weekend course won't turn you into a proficient handgunner if you don't work to increase your skill.

Since *un*training *bad* habits and replacing them with good ones takes *10,000* repetitions, I prefer to teach utter novices versus intermediates (who already have habits, some bad).

Find a gunrange you like (outdoors is better since it's much quieter than indoors), and go there at least twice a month. Dryfire practice several times a week, if not every night. Keep your presentation, front sight acquisition, and trigger press crisp and second nature.

SHOTGUNS

Chapter 20 applies equally to women. You might, however, prefer the lighter recoiling 20 gauge (which is nearly as effective as the 12 gauge within 25yds), although most women can master a 12 with proper training. The Remington 870 and Winchester 1300 Defender pump shotguns are excellent for home defense. (Call 928-772-8262 for a Yavapai Firearms Academy course; Louis Awerbuck is truly gifted at teaching shotgun work.)

Skeet, clays, and trap shooting are fun sports, with many women involved. The over/under barrel shotguns are rather expensive, but that's to be expected from the "polo" of shooting.

RIFLES

In my experience, women naturally shoot rifles better than pistols. They just seem to "resonate" better with them. As long as you don't start out with an overly powerful cartridge with scary recoil, you'll enjoy shooting rifles. Start with a .22LR to learn the technique and bolster your confidence, then go to a .223 AR15. Handling the bigger rifles is merely something to work up to, and one simply stops where one feels comfortable. Again, with proper training, most women can enjoy the .308 class of rifle power, which truly suffices for most needs. (If you can't do it with a .308, then you probably can't do it, period.)

Rifles are very specialized tools, so there are many different kinds. While some rifles are very versatile, you'll likely need at least two, if not three, to round out your battery.

Defensive rifles

For *indoor* defense, a shotgun (with #7½ birdshot) or a handgun is a better choice (given a rifle's penetration through walls). For a *rural* environment, however, the rifle is king.

Battle carbine (.223) vs. battle rifle (.308)

Yeah, a .308 FAL is marvelous, but a lightweight, easy recoiling AR15 is a better choice for most women. It's better to hit with a BB gun than to miss with a cannon, and the .223 is no BB gun. Besides, the AR15 is easy to work with, and after women struggle with the stupid controls of an AK, they kiss the AR15.

(So do the men.) For a semi-auto battle carbine, get an AR15. (Lefty ladies should also give the very reliable Daewoo a try.) The older A1s are nearly a pound lighter than the A2s, which some ladies really appreciate. (This is what I got for my mom, and she loves it.) However, A1s are nearly always pre-ban and thus Ø300-500 more expensive than post-ban A2s. For those on a *real* budget, a Ø250 Russian SKS is an unbeatable bargain.

Lever-action

If a Ø750-900 AR15 is too expensive, or you don't want a semi-auto, then the "mere" lever-action .30-30 will usually solve your problem. Most women like the Western look and feel of lever-actions. Being more rugged and easier to load, the Marlin is a better choice than the Winchester 94. A used .30-30 Marlin goes for Ø175-235. This is a good deer hunting rifle, a good car rifle, and a good ranch rifle. Since the .30-30 is only a 250yd round, no scope is necessary. I'd simply replace the original rear sight with a Williams peep sight for Ø40. You also might want to have the rear stock trimmed down a bit, and a Pachmayr Decelerator recoil pad installed.

A *real* sweetheart is the Marlin Model 1894 .44 Magnum. The 1894 is a bit smaller and handier rifle than the .30-30, and recoils less. You'll pay about Ø275 for a decent used one. The .44 Magnum was originally a revolver round, so it doesn't have the energy or range of a true rifle round (such as the .30-30). Still, within 100yds, it'll do most anything you could ask of it. These are fairly common at gun shows for Ø250-325. With a 20" barrel it holds 10+1 (versus 6+1 in the .30-30). The 16¼" barrel "Limited" holds 7+1 and is as handy as an umbrella. (The Winchester equivalent is the "Trapper.") I absolutely *love* mine. (Although the "Limited" edition rifles are few in numbers, any decent gunsmith could shorten a regular 1894. Take 4" off the barrel and 1" off the stock, and the pup would measure out at only 32" overall, with a pound's weight savings. Cost for this work would be under Ø100. I'd strip off the stock varnish, stain medium-dark Danish walnut, and then treat with tung oil. Such would make an excellent travel rifle, car or airplane.)

Either of the above, the .30-30 or the .44 Mag, would be an excellent first rifle for any lady. The design is over 100 hundred years old, and it works very well. Also, there's just something irresistibly charming about an American lever-action.

If you want a lever-action in a more powerful cartridge than the .30-30, then get a Browning BLR in .308. The BLR is very accurate, has a 4rd detachable mag, and scopes well. This is an excellent and handy 400yd rifle for hunting and defense. My mom likes hers very much, by the way. (The BLR would also make an excellent Scout rifle platform.)

Scoped bolt-action

First, let's talk cartridge. You want something powerful, accurate, and *common*. The .308 is ideal. It's quite effective, yet not a beast to shoot. Some women will think so and want a less powerful caliber, such as the .243. Since cartridges can be handloaded to more docile velocities, there's no reason to prefer a .243 over a .308. Get a .308, have some lighter ammo loaded for you, and it'll recoil as easy as a .243. Then, after practice, you can shoot the full power loads and enjoy what a .308 can accomplish. My point is this: A .308 can be downloaded to the recoil of a .243, but a .243's bullets top out at only 100gr.

Which .308 bolt-action rifle? The stainless steel Remington Model 7 is a favorite, but just about *any* Winchester, Savage (these are *highly* underrated), or Remington will be fine. I'd go stainless with synthetic stock if possible, unless you want blued steel and wood stock. (You might need an inch or so removed from the stock. As a test, put the butt in the crook of your arm. You should be able to easily reach the trigger.) Don't skimp on the scope—get a nice Leupold 3-9X. Quality guns are a lifetime purchase, so expect to pay for that quality. Guns are *not* the things to save money on.

Hunting rifles

The .30-30 (use the 170gr bullets) is fine for 200yd deer and 75yd elk, but is too weak for longer shots. The .44 Magnum is *positively* limited to 100yd deer and 50yd elk—don't exceed!

The .308 is great for 400yd deer/250yd elk. If you need *more* power than a .308, then the .30-06 or 7mmRM is probably the most you'll want to shoot.

Author Ragnar Benson's wife shoots 1MOA groups at 800yds with a .300 Win Mag, so there *are* exceptions. If you can handle *and enjoy* the big Magnums, then you're beyond needing *my* advice on the matter. Safari in Alaska or Africa and bag some big game. (Send photos.)

DEFENSIVE TACTICS—*BRIEFLY*

Don't be in Condition White!

This is unalert and unaware. The only place for Condition White is at home, when you're inside with the doors locked.

Stay alert and aware—Condition Yellow

Most assaults (and car "accidents") could have been *avoided* if the victim was in Condition Yellow at the time. A potential threat *anticipated* is a threat *halved.* When a lethal emergency arrives, you'll have *at most* only 3 seconds to draw and fire your handgun, and that's *not* enough time to go from Condition White directly to Black. Start from Yellow.

During a specific threat go to Condition Orange

When some creep is following you on the street, don't be shy. Immediately grip your handgun and draw it, discreetly if you can. If the situation is *beyond* such discretion, then draw it openly and get out of there. Don't be shy—your *life* is at stake!

Never let any Condition Orange focus get within two car lengths of you. An athletic man can cover 20' in only 1½ seconds. Distance equals time, and you want as much time— therefore distance—as possible. It will take you (after much training and practice) 2-4 seconds to draw from your purse, get your front sight focus, and hit your Bad Guy. That means you must keep him at least three car lengths away in order to have sufficient time. If that's not possible, then try to either increase the distance, or put a car between you and him.

If he *advances* on you, back up and maintain distance while drawing your handgun. **If he's a good guy, *he will stop*. If he *doesn't*, then he is a *Bad* Guy.**

Condition Red—holding at the "mental trigger"

If he *continues* to advance on you even though he sees that you're armed, then he is not "lost." He doesn't need a quarter for the phone. A *fight* is imminent. He *will* harm you if you *let* him. He will rape you and throw your dead, disgraced body in the nearest dumpster—*if* you *let* him. Will you? Never!

Condition Black—you're now in the fight!

Shoot him. Shoot him *repeatedly* until he *drops.* Do not listen to what he says. Heed not the innocent smile. Anybody advancing on an obviously scared and armed woman is a scumbag who should be shot *immediately.* If there's time for a verbal warning and you remember to give it, fine. If not, oh well. His seeing your handgun was warning enough.

A word about "warning shots"—*Don't*. A warning shot is a *purposeful miss*, and you *didn't* get trained to *miss*. Anytime you contradict your imprinted muscle memory, your *conscious* mind has to orchestrate the contradiction—before, during, and after. **There's *no time*.** The conscious mind is *too slow* and you *won't* be able to engage your subconscious training quickly enough to get your hits. Regardless of that, a warning shot wastes a round, and sends that bullet who knows where. Finally, legally speaking, you may not brandish or point a gun at a nonthreat. Conversely, if he's perceived as a lethal threat, then why aren't you *stopping* him? You *don't* shoot him, or you *do*. Tactically and legally, warning shots are a *big* mistake.

"What about just wounding him in the leg?" First of all, neither you nor I are *that* good a shot to reliably hit a thin, moving target as the leg. And even if we *were*, a leg shot is not a reliable stopper. Studies of police shootings have proven this. No defensive academy trains for "mercy" shots. *Listen to me:* this dirtbag is about to rape/kill you, you're scared sh*tless, and you need to stop his actions *immediately*. Body and head-shots only! Don't get fancy. **Have no mercy but for *yourself*.** Somebody *should* have dropped this sick creep in his socks years ago, but didn't. Now it's up to *you*. Shoot him and *live*.

Get *ugly* with a rapist!

In her excellent book *Armed & Female,* Paxton Quigley visited California State Peniteniary at San Quentin to interview convicted rapists for their thoughts on armed women. One insight seemed particularly useful:

> *Dennis Raymond advises a woman to **use foul language** when she confronts an assailant. "These guys are all used to hearing bad talk. We've been talking bad all our lives. We don't know any other way to talk, **so if they don't hear bad talk, they don't understand.** And you got to yell it.** We have been yelled at all our lives, too— cops, mothers, jail guards, and tough guys all yell. You got to yell if you are pointing a gun at someone. He'll listen."*

What Raymond was describing was the *language and culture* of the criminal world. Foul language *is* their language. You're on *their* streets where they practice *their* culture, so you've got to speak (*i.e.,* yell) *their* language. Your assailant is from "another country" so he thinks differently from you.

What's important to you (*i.e.*, life, family, etc.) is not important to him. He is more vicious and ruthless than you can ever imagine. To get through to him you must get angry and loud and nasty in his own *lingua franca*. *That* he will understand!

First of all, a very loud and forceful *"Get the f*ck back!"* makes yourself clearly understood by speaking the native tongue. Secondly, it takes command of the situation by your *not* acting like a *victim* (which is naturally expected of you).

Although demanding "verbal compliance" is taught by many gun schools, incorporating profanity is not, and that's a mistake. I teach it in my classes as I believe in training students with as much realism as possible. A rapist will not accost you with *"Oh, Miss, I do regret the inconveniece, but I need a few minutes of your time in that alley, else I'll inflict pain on you."* You do not calmly draw your gun and reply, *"That is totally unacceptable, and I refuse. Be on your way or I'll shoot."*

What you do in training is what you'll do in real life, and I try to give my students *every* possible edge. Yelling and screaming profanity is part of it. If the fear and anger of an attack are not approximated in class, then you are training under a different emotional state than you will feel on the street and it will cause you some dissonance if you're ever assaulted.

It's a nasty scene, and you've got to get nasty right back. Yes, I realize that ladies (and gentlemen) do not use such language and that you are uncomfortable doing so, but your *life* is worth yelling something coarse. When a female student just isn't getting into the forceful verbal compliance aspect of the course, whispering in her ear something like *"Do what I say bitch, or I'll cut you bad!"* usually gets her attention.

Actually, instant and deafening outrage can be more effective than a weapon. Carrying a gun, by itself, does not assure you of surviving an attack. You must also exude raw will and savagery, which is often more terrifying than the weapon itself. It's all about which side of "Fight or Flight" are you on. You cannot defend if you're in flight (*i.e.*, overwhelming fear). In order to summon your courage, you have to get *mad*, and dredging up some really nasty language will help. Profanity is the language of anger. Express it!

Civility and gentility during a lethal emergency will put you in the *grave*. If you want to wash your mouth out with soap later, fine. (At least you'll be *alive* to do so.)

By the way, if all this offends you—well, get over it. I'm talking about saving *lives* here, so hold off on that letter to justify your ethereal thinking. On the battlefield George Washington was known to swear quite a blue streak, and every drill instructor at boot camp uses blistering language. In these cases, profanity was used for the sake of emphasis, not vulgarity. I discuss all this not to be vulgar, but to stress upon you the gritty reality of the street.

To win, you must get *mad* and get *ugly*, and you must do it *immediately*. The *only* woman to have escaped a horrible death from serial rapist/murderer Ted Bundy was Carolyn daRonch, who fought like a *wildcat*. My mom was once stalked, so she removed her high-heel shoes and threatened to sink them into his head if he didn't go away. (He went away.) A Vietnam vet and martial artist friend of mine once told me, *"In the dance of death you can either lead or follow."* There is only Fight or Flight. You can only Win or Lose—Live or Die. Which is it going to be? You're going to *fight*, mean and dirty!

Think of it from the *rapist's* point of view: He was expecting an easy victim, and *now* all of a sudden, without warning, he's got this volcanically pissed off, armed, *crazy* woman screaming obscenities at him! There is sort of *zero* incentive to hang around, and that is sort of the whole idea.

Do *whatever* it takes to save your life, even if it means briefly becoming real ugly. You'll have the rest of your life to get over it, which certainly beats the alternative.

LADIES' RESOURCES

Armed & Female by Paxton Quigley is a great introduction to gun ownership for women. An ex-liberal and *"gun control"* advocate, Ms. Quigley is one of women's champions. Then, join the Gunowners of America and get involved as a woman.

Second Amendment Sisters

This is a superb organization (www.sas-aim.org). Click on and join up! (Tell 'em Boston sent you!)

◆ 7

COMBAT RIFLE HISTORY

*There is probably no other country that, like Switzerland, gives the soldier his weapon to keep in the home. The Swiss always has his rifle at hand. It belongs to the furnishings of his home. ...That corresponds to ancient Swiss tradition. ...the Swiss soldier lives in constant companionship with his rifle. He knows what that means. With this rifle, he is liable every hour, if the country calls, to defend his hearth, his home, his family, his birthplace. **The weapon is to him a pledge and sign of honor and freedom. The Swiss does not part with his rifle.***

— President Phillipp Etter, at a June 1939 shooting festival

There was no holocaust on Swiss soil. *Swiss Jews served in the militia side by side with their fellow citizens, and kept rifles in their homes just like everyone else. It is hard to believe that there could have been a holocaust had the Jews of Germany, Poland, and France had the same privilege.*

— Stephen P. Halbrook, *Target Switzerland: Swiss Armed Neutrality in World War II* (1998)

The modern battle SLR of the mid-20th Century was many years in the making, requiring brass cased ammunition (1860s), smokeless powder (1886), scientific advances in metallurgy and ballistics (1890-1905), and overcoming the inertia of ruling military and poltical leaders (eternally ongoing). And that was just to produce the modern smokeless turnbolt repeater!

19th CENTURY DEVELOPMENT

Until 1886, the Germans' M71/84 rifle and its 11.15x60R blackpowder round was world's best battle rifle. It threw a flat-pointed 385gr slug at 1380fpe, for 1580fpe. Zeroed at 100yds, it would drop 24" by 200. The rest of the world were also using a .43 caliber slug: the .43 Spanish, the Dutch 11mm Beaumont, the 11mm French Gras, and the 11mm Belgian Comblain. Our rifle was the Model 1873 .45-70, which was 11.43mm (.458). The Swiss, always a tad offbeat, used a 10.4mm (.41 Swiss).

In 1886 the French made the quantum leap to smokeless powder repeating rifles. Although the 8rd tube mag Lebel rifle was no treasure, the new 8x50R threw a 198gr bullet at the then-astounding 2349fps (for 2427fpe), nearly *double* the velocity of the German 11.15x60R. Overnight, the world's rifles were obsolete. The German High Command, fearing a French attack in retaliation of their 1871 defeat, went into a frenzy. You see, back in the late 1800s, the world's arms race was between the then superpowers of Germany and France.

When a French deserter sold his stolen Lebel rifle to the Germans for 20,000 Marks, the Germans immediately tried to reverse-engineer the secret of the smokeless *Poudre B* (which had been secretly procured from Russia for 5,000 Marks a kilo —about $9,260 a pound).

By the 1890s, the world was hurriedly rearming themselves with their first smokeless rifles. Early designs were the German Gewehr 88 (1888), the Lee-Metford (1888), the Swiss Schmidt-Rubin (1889), the Danish Krag (1889), the Italian Mannlicher-Carcano (1891), the Russian Mosin-Nagant (1891), the U.S. Krag (1892), the Swedish Mauser (1894), and the Japanese Arisaka (1897).

Still, the cartridges first used were generally heavy 180+gr cylindro-ogival bullets. Then the Spanish picked up Paul Mauser's long range spitzer 7x57 in the M93 rifle (the M92 renamed), and proceeded to give our boys (armed with new, but obsolete, .30-40 Krags) hell in 1898 Cuba. Boer commandos in South Africa (excellent riflemen) also used the 7x57 against the British with great effect. After that, the world rushed to replace its First Generation smokeless ammo with spitzer ammo (which required chamber work and rear sight recalibration).

From there, the rest was merely refinement. Second (and pretty much final) Generation rifles were the German M98, the Springfield 1903, the M1917, and the No.4 MkI Lee-Enfield.

BOLT-ACTION MILITARY

The World War I pilot in his biplane would be no match for the F-18 pilot, but the Pattern 14 Enfield-equipped [WWI] soldier may very well easily kill the soldier of the late 1990s armed with an M16A2 rifle. Certainly, the fighters in Afghanistan showed that their Enfields were equal to Soviet AK-74 rifles—and served as an example for all of us who are confronted with oppressive governments that seek to limit our ability to acquire current-issue military weapons.
— Timothy J. Mullin; *Testing the War Weapons*, p. 419

So, if you're "stuck" with, for example, an Enfield, don't despair. It's a fine 500yd gun, and deadly in the right hands.

These rifles are powerful, rugged, battle-proven, cartridge common, and modern bargains. While I wouldn't field with one *over* a modern battle SLR (which has better controls and semi-auto cyclic rate) or a countersniper rifle (which is 3-8X more accurate), these old workhorses are very capable out to 500yds and will handle combat conditions. (Many of the older rifles, such as the Swedish M94s, are zeroed for 300M, and thus need a higher front sight for a proper 100M zero.)

While I can't cover every single historical example, I will discuss those commonly available to us in 2000 (which is about 90% of them). Here are the more common models, in roughly chronological order. Model year means its year of *introduction* (*i.e., first* year of manufacture) and not necessarily the year when a specific rifle was made (it was usually later).

Until 1892, rifles generally had a 5rd straight-line mag which protruded beyond the bottom of the stock. (The Lee-Metford and Krag were the exceptions.) Until Mauser figured out with the M92 that staggered rounds would not only work, but shortened the mag to be flush with the stock, early rifles such as the Mannlicher, Carcano, Mauser M88-91, and Mosin-Nagant had the straight-line mags. They're easy to spot in gun show rifle racks, and if you learn to distinguish the unique shapes you'll be able to immediately and specifically ID them (which will really impress the Old Duffer behind the table).

Lee-Enfield No.4 Mk. I and II   (.303, .308)
History
From 1888 until declared obselete in April 1992, the Lee-Enfield in one form or another well served Great Britain for over 100 years (a record likely to remain unbroken). Inventor James Lee gave us the first box mag way back in 1879. The Lee-Enfield's short bolt throw is *twice* as fast as the M98's, and headspace is easily maintained by swapping out bolt heads. Rugged and accurate, many experts consider it the finest bolt-action battle rifle, and I'd be hard pressed to disagree. It certainly has advantages over the Mauser M98 and its clones (*e.g.*, our 03A3, which is a bit overrated, though very good).

The .303 British   (174/2400 for 2226fpe)
The .303 is 90% as powerful as the .308 (60,000 dead Soviets in Afghanistan can't be "all wrong"), and is adequate for any North American game. Ammo is available from all the major manufacturers.

Speer 150gr spitzers max loaded with 46.2gr of R15 will give 2755fps for 2529fpe (very nearly .308 energy), but your cases won't last long given the spongy Lee bolt.

Today
For our purposes, the real modern advantage of the Lee-Enfield is good .30 caliber power in a 10rd detachable box mag rifle for only Ø100. I don't readily add new cartridges to my battery, but the Lee is so rugged and affordable. Stick with the No. 4 Mk. Is and Mk. IIs. (The older No. 1s are serviceable shooters, but pretty crude.) Cut the barrel down to 18" and remove as much wood as possible to create a 7½lb carbine. Have several; they're great as vehicle rifles (if confiscated or stolen, you're out a whopping Ø100). It's surprisingly accurate; I can consistently hit man-size boulders up to 500yds offhand.

When folks catch on to these Ø100 rugged, powerful rifles with their 10rd box mags, they'll at last be cleaned out. (While prices have edged up a bit since 1998, you can still easily find a nice one for under Ø125.) Go to Springfield Sporters for parts.

Indian Lee-Enfields in .308
Having tried a few since 1998, I have come to view these 12rd mag-fed rifles as solid and serviceable. The Indians used better steel to beef up the Enfield action to .308 strength. At dealer cost of Ø70 (2A No.1 Mk.III; full length) to Ø160 (No. 7;

carbine length with 20½" barrel), they are a better bargain than the Spanish FR8 .308s were a few years ago at Ø140. As long as you pick out a nice one, it will provide good value. I'd choose the No. 7 carbine, which is much more handy.

Krag-Jorgensen (.30-40 Krag, 6.5x55 Swede)

I've got an unabashed crush on this funky 1890s rifle with butter-smooth action and hinged box mag. Designed in Norway by Capt. Ole Krag and Erik Jorgensen, it was very expensive to manufacture, and slow to reload (no stripper clips). Only Denmark, the U.S., and Norway ever adopted it, and they quickly replaced it with some variation/clone of the Mauser M98 (which is a much stronger action). U.S. Krags abound at gun shows, and you might try one out. It's a great first rifle to show a young boy 19th Century craftsmanship. Either the .30-40 or 6.5x55 are fine deer cartridges. Rifles <#152,670 are pre-1899.

U.S. Krag (.30-40 Krag; 220/2000 for 1955fpe)

This was our first smokeless military rifle, adopted in 1892, with rifles being delivered in late 1894. It fought in the Spanish-American War, the Phillipine Insurrection, and the Boxer Rebellion in China. Obsolete the day it was designed, we replaced it in 1903 with the excellent Springfield 03. Original condition U.S. Krags are worth Ø500+, however most sadly were sporterized long ago. The most common is the Model 1898 (263,000), though only 5,000 carbines of 1898 were made.

For us, the Krag is really just a fun game or collector's rifle. The .30-40 is adequate for deer and 200yd elk. I enjoyed a nicely sporterized one for years, but got tired of stocking its unique ammo. When loaded to its potential, the .30-40 is between the .300 Savage and .308 in power, which is quite ample.

The 45,000cup action can be rebarreled to .444 Marlin (1:16" twist) for a fantastic brush rifle for deer, bear, or boar.

Norwegian Krag (6.5x55; 139/2700 for 2352fpe)

Chambered for 6.5x55 Swede, this is a fine deer rifle and a very nice foreign treasure. They were made from 1894 until the early 1930s. I've only seen three for private sale: an original military model (Ø800), and two sporterized carbines (Ø300). They often have a flattened, checkered bolt handle knob, which is the quickest way to distinguish them amongst the U.S. Krags. No parts interchange between the Norwegian and U.S.

Krags. The Norwegian models are considered a bit stronger, since its bolt guide rib acts as a second locking lug.

Danish Krag   **(8x58R;   237/1985 for 2074fpe)**
Th 8x58R cartridge is practically unavailable here, so I'd pass on a Danish Krag. (It could be rebarreled to .444 Marlin, if you run across a non-original bargain.)

Mosin-Nagant M91/30   (7.62x54R)
History
Russian-made in the late 19th Century, the problem was that not enough of them could be cranked out for WWI. (For awhile, we sold them lever action Winchester M1895s in 7.62x54R!) The M91 model was modernized in 1930, creating the M91/30 which was the Red Army's main rifle in WWII. Weight was 9.6lbs, length a whopping 51.6", barrel length 31.5".

The 7.62x54R   **(185/2680 for 2951fpe)**
The 7.62x54R is no slouch (equal to the .30-06, and not a funky 7.5 or 7.7mm), and ammo abounds (although most of it is corrosive, except for Czech Sellier & Bellot). I prefer a 7.62x54R over a .303, as it's more powerful and bullet selection is better.

Today
These run from Ø46 (Burns Bros.) to Ø170 (Tapco, delivered direct as it's pre-1899 manufacture, except to Chicago, NJ, and NYC). A real workhorse and piece of history. Yours could have fought in Stalingrad! Many other nations used the Mosin (*e.g.,* Bulgaria, N. Korea, Romania, Hungary, Czechoslovakia).
The Finnish M39 is probably the nicest and Burns Bros. has them for Ø180. Less than 11,000 were stamped SkY for the Civil Guard, and these rifles command a premium.
Post-war carbines are the M44s. Russian and Polish versions are available from SOG (Ø55). These (and the Bulgarian M91/59s) make *great* truck and cabin rifles!

Mauser M1889, 1890, and 1891
But for minor features, these rifles are identical. All but the M88 were chambered for Paul Mauser's second cartridge, the 7.65x53, an excellent round giving 155/2810 for 2718fpe (nearly equal to the .30-06). While all these rifles are fine examples of Mauser's early work, they are inferior to his later designs (*i.e.,* the M92 through M98).

[Soon, the Mausers M88-91] *began to show some design and construction faults: The small spring extractor, with its narrow hook, proved unreliable; the magazine charger clip and clip guide, on the receiver bridge, proved faulty; the detachable box magazines were often lost and, because the magazine projected below the stock line, the rifles were not always easily carried. The trigger could be pulled regardless of the position of the bolt; the threaded connection between the striker rod and cocking piece often presented an assembly problem; the action had too many parts and needed simplifying. Double loading was possible—that is, unless the bolt was fully closed and locked after chambering each cartridge, the bolt could be opened without extracting and ejecting the chambered cartridge and the next round would jam behind it on reclosing the bolt.*
    — Frank de Haas; *Bolt Action Rifles* (1984), p. 25

It's a 112 year old design, and a crucial chapter of rifle history. For a shooting rifle, I'd much rather have a later Mauser (*i.e.,* M93-98), but the pre-M93s make fascinating collectibles. They are beautiful examples of Old World late-19th Century quality. Everything is well machined from fine steel, and polished. Even the trigger guards are a work of art; no stampings. Such rifles couldn't be made today for under Ø1,500, so you can understand why I'm so excited about these Ø70-175 bargains!

Belgian M89
    Three barrel lengths were made: 30.7", 21.7", and 15.8". The FN plant alone made some 275,000 of them from 1889 to 1925. Unnecessarily, they had a barrel jacket to center the muzzle, until the M89/36 model (a 1936 retrofit of earlier rifles).

Turkish M90
    Mauser made 280,000 of these rifles with 29.1" barrel (and no jacket). Few are seen today. Spain also adopted the same rifle, called the Spanish M91 (which had a small spring built into the right bolt lug, to prevent double loading).

Argentine M91
History
    This was one of Mauser's first popular export models, made primarily for Argentina (and much of South America; *e.g.,* Peru, Colombia, Bolivia, and Ecuador). These are lovely old rifles made by Loewe in Berlin in two barrel lengths: 29.1" rifle (180,000) and 17.6" carbine (30,000). It has a 5rd mag, and a 400M-2000M flipup sight. Because of the M91's popularity, we call its cartridge the 7.65x53 Argentine today.

The 7.65x53   **(155/2810 for 2718fpe)**

The NC/BE 7.65x53 round is available for Ø180/1000 from SAMCO (Belgian-made BE/NC in 1978). The .311-.312" bullet for .303 British is considered correct. Cases can be made from .30-06 cases and forming dies. Berdan cases can be decapped with the right tool and Euro 5.5mm primers are available. (I'd simply buy some Norma boxer-primed cases.)

Today

A large hoard of Argentine M91s was released in 1998-99, and these were quickly snapped up by shooters and collectors alike. While most had their distinctive Argentine crest ground off before export (and these sell for about Ø70-100), a few have their crest intact. Some of these are matching numbered in 95% condition and fetch Ø175 (which is a *steal,* all things considered). A fine shootable curio or beater rifle (if already in beater condition; don't rough up a nice one!). Prices are edging upwards, so hurry. Six times as many rifles were made than carbines, so I'd probably look for a carbine.

If you find a beater rifle or action and want to rebarrel it to something more common, many 45,000cup choices exist: .250 Savage, .257 Roberts (the 7x57 necked down), 6.5x55 (my first choice), 7x57, .300 Savage, and .35 Remington, among others.

Mauser Models 93 and 95

These were Mauser's 2nd Gen rifles, with huge design improvements (especially to the extractor and magazine) over the M88-91 series. The M93 and M95s are usually fine shooters.

The bolt has a guide rib to eliminate binding. The M88 extractor was totally redesigned in the M92 to a long, non-rotating version attached to the bolt body by a collar. From the magazine to the chamber, the round was always under the extractor hook, which utterly prevented double loading. Such was copied by Springfield, Arisaka, Winchester, Ruger, and many others. This extractor is also the strongest.

The wing safety looks the same, but is actually a 3-position control. With the rifle shouldered, "Fire" is 9-o'clock, "Safe"/unlocked bolt (for unloading) is 12-o'clock, and "Safe"/locked bolt is 3-o'clock. While not the fastest to operate, the safety was solid and versatile. (Its concept was retained in a modified form by Winchester and Ruger, and is considered optimum by most experts.)

The magazine of the Spanish M93 featured a flush, staggered-row system, now the standard on most bolt-action rifles.

But for a few small differences, the M93-96s are identical. The M93 and 95 were made for Spain in 7x57; the M94 and 96 (variants on the M93 and 95) were made for Sweden in 6.5x55.

Mauser M93 and M95 (7x57)

These rifles are the ones which faced Teddy Roosevelt's Rough Riders in Cuba back in 1898. The 29.1" barrel rifle weighed about 9lbs; the short rifle had a 21.8" barrel and weighed 8.3lbs. (The M95 is pretty much the same rifle, and often a cavalry carbine with 17.6" barrel weighing 7.5lbs.) Twist was 1-8.8" and bores were deeply throated for the 173gr.

While many were made in Germany (Loewe, 250,000; Mauser, 30,000), most were made in Spain (Oviedo or Cataluna) and are not of the same superb quality. All Spanish-made rifles have a left receiver oblong-shaped gas vent hole. Also, it seems that Spanish-made rifles have square-back mag followers (a last shot hold-open device), while the German- and Belgian-made rifles have a rounded edge. Although the Spanish rifles are not junky, I'd certainly hold out for a German one.

Turkish M93 and M93/38

Rawles ("Mr. Pre-1899") recommends these for several reasons: quality (they were made by Oberndorf), strength (they were re-heat treated in 1938 for their 8x57 conversion), affordability (from J&G and Sarco), and mainly for their pre-1899 *"antique"* (*i.e.*, *GCA68* non-firearm; FFL exempt) status as all were made by 1897 (and, according to the BATF, this status is not voided by sporterizing, rechambering, or rebarreling).

Chilean M95

Some Mauser orders in 7x57 for the Orange Free State, Africa ("OVS" on the left receiver ring) got cancelled, so they were engraved with the Chilean crest and sold to Chile. A fairly rare rifle (all had the 29.1" barrel), and all German-made.

These have a safety cutout just behind the bolt handle root to halt or retard rearward movement of the bolt in case the lugs failed. Also, these rifles had no thumb notch cut into the left receiver wall. These two features made this rifle a bit stronger.

Other M93s and 95s
These include the Brazilian M94 (7x57; Loewe and FN), the Orange Free State (7x57; Mauser), and the M95s for Mexico, Uruguay, and Persia (Iran).

The 7x57   **(142/2700 for 2299fpe)**
Except for the Turkish M93, all the M93s and 95s were in the excellent 7x57 (anticipating .308 muzzle energy, but with better BCs). It is still quite common, and a fine performer (especially on deer). It's also a better caliber which can be reloaded (boxer-primed 7.65x54 cases are uncommon).

Today
While no longer commonly available (they got snapped up quickly), you occasionally see them at gun shows. My favorite is the Chilean/OVS M95 made by Mauser.

I also like the M95 Spanish Carbine model with its turned down bolt handle and short 17.6" barrel. If you run across an original Spanish Mauser in 7x57 (not one rebarreled to .308 and sporterized), it will make a very pleasing collectible.

Swede Mauser M94, M96, M38, M41B (6.5x55)
Because of minor design improvements and outstanding Swedish steel, these are the best of the 2nd Gen Mausers. Made from 1895 until 1944, these are the most accurate and finest quality of *all* military turnbolts. If a Swedish Mauser didn't shoot within 1½MOA, it was rebarreled or rejected.

A distinguishing feature of all Swedish Mausers is the upright checkered projection on the striker end (which is a graspable decocker). Except for the earliest M94s, they also had two gas escape holes in the bolt.

M94 Carbine   (1894-1925; 115,000 made)
12,185 were made by Mauser in 1895 and 1896. Being pre-1899, they are non-firearm antiques. (Such a non-FFL gun firing wooden training bullets, lethal at short range but with little penetration, might be *just* the thing, legally/tactically, for urban shut-ins.) *Carl Gufafs Stads Gevärsfaktori* of Sweden began production in 1898 (until 1925).

It came with a 300M-1600M rear sight. (So astounded were the world's militaries with the flat trajectories of the first smokeless rounds that they figured a 300M zero was proper, not anticipating the shortened combat ranges of future wars.)

The first M94 was a Carbine with a 17.7" barrel for an overall length of just 37.4". It weighed only 7.3lbs. Intended for the cavalry, it thoughtfully featured a turned-down bolt handle. Later M94s kept their turned-down bolt handle, but copied the M96's deep thumb notch, guide rib, and gas vents. M94s did not have cleaning rods.

M96   (1898-1925; 515,000 made)

This was Sweden's quintessential long-barreled rifle. Weight was 8.8lbs, length 49.5", barrel length 29.1". Other differences from the earliest M94s were the deep thumb notch, bolt guide rib, and gas escape holes. All M96s have straight bolt handles. Some 515,000 were made (40,000 at Oberndorf, Germany; 475,000 at the Carl Gustafs factory in Sweden) from 1898-1925. Only 3,100 pre-1899 M96s exist (all Carl Gustafs).

M96s with SA or SkY proofs were used by Finland against the Soviet invaders, and are more desirable rifles.

M96/38   (1938-40; 30,000 made)

Not to be confused with the M38 (as Samco does in their ads), this was an M96 with a 23.6" barrel. Only 30,000 were so converted, and they kept their straight bolt handle. A buttstock brass plaque displayed holdovers for the new 139gr spitzer bullet and its 100M zero. Oberndorfs are more rare than Gustafs.

M38 Short Rifle   (1941-44; 60,000 made)

Realizing the M96's 29" barrel to be unnecessarily clumsy, the M1938 had a 23.1" tube and turned-down bolt handle. A 100M rear sight was standard. All 60,000 of the M38s were built by *Husqvarna Vapenfabriks Aktiebolag* between 1941-44, and kept in service until 1978.

They are rather scarce, and you'll easily pay Ø250-300 for one. Of the 804,000 Swedish Mausers made, only 90,000 of them were M38s and M96/38s (*i.e.*, only 1 in 9).

M41B Sniper Rifle   (1941-43; 5,300 made)

This was simply a particularly accurate M96 with one of three scopes: a German ZF Ajack 4x90 m/41 (until 1942), or a Swedish AGA 3x65 m/42 or m/44. Also standard was a turned-down bolt handle (to clear the scope). The M41B would shoot 1MOA, and was likely the most accurate WWII-era rifle. Only 5,300 M41Bs were made in 1941-43 (from all three arsenals).

In 1967-68, these were sold, with original scope and mount, for just Ø70! *Groan.* Sarco has them now for Ø1,200.

Parts, accessories, info

Lots of original stuff is still available (mostly from Sarco), so you might as well make your Swedish Mauser happy.

blank firing adapter Made to disintegrate wooden training bullets (which were lethal up to 25yds). Requires a threaded muzzle. Sarco; Ø13. Samco sells the wooden bullets.

flash suppressor Only Ø11.50 from Sarco. Requires a threaded muzzle. Word on the street is that these 3¾" long suppressors were not for the Mausers, but for .308-modified AG42 spotting rifles coaxially mounted to their 90mm recoilless gun. Muzzle threads are identical, so they'll fit fine. (Could also be an inexpensive flash suppressor for other .308s?)

muzzle cap For threaded muzzles. Sarco; Ø6. (Drill hole to make bore guide.)

bore guide For threaded muzzles. Protects muzzle from rod during cleaning.

front sight hood Original issue for all M96 and M38s. Sarco; Ø10.

M96 sights Original leaf sight, either leaf/slider, or entire assembly. From Sarco.

high front sight To zero your M94 or M96 at 100yds. Sarco; Ø13.

cleaning rod Specify M96 or M38. Ø5.95 and Ø6.50, respectively, from Sarco.

cleaning rod ext. To adapt USA cleaning jags and brushes. Sarco; Ø6.50.

bayonet Many folks sell these for about Ø25. A nice addition.

scabbard lock Keeps scabbard on blade for bayonet practice. Sarco; Ø2.50.

bayonet frogs For the M96 bayonet. Sarco; Ø5.

rear sight hood Stamped steel, snaps over rear sight assembly.

leather sling Original issue "M1353" for M96, M38, and AG42s. Sarco; Ø7, 3/Ø20.

Carbine barrels New condition, 17.7", no sights or bases. Sarco; Ø34.50, 3/Ø100.

brass cleaning rod 30", wooden handle, two patch slots, Swedish marked. Sarco; Ø15.

oil can A cute little double-chambered unit; one for oil, one for bore solvent.

M96 stock set All wood and metal furniture. Sarco; Ø21.50.

ammo bandoleer Heavy leather cartridge belt. Its five pockets hold several stripper clips of 6.5x55. Brass buckle. Ø15-20. Great decorative item, too.

stripper clips Since the 6.5x55's case head is .007" wider, .308 clips won't work. Very nice quality and scarce, and they're not cheap. Samco had these at one time.

Parts sources

For original and aftermarket parts/accessories, try:

Mark Hoffman	540-885-6555	kramhoff@vaix.net
Ellison's	607-527-8321	www.lightlink.com/cralyn/rifles.html
Gun Parts Inc.	914-679-5849	
Springfield Sporters	412-254-2626	
Sarco	908-647-3800	

For good Mauser info (*e.g.,* on rear sight graduations):

http://weber.u.washington.edu/~basiji/swedeFAQ.html

The Swedish Mauser Rifles, Kehaya & Poyer; North Cape Publ. (800-745-9714)
    A very detailed (text and photos) book, and a "must" for any collector.

Neutrality Through Marksmanship, Doug Bowser, from Sarco

"What's the deal with the brass disc on the buttstock?"

The smallest pie segment indicates the bore's condition. If the barrel was new (or like new), then no triangular stamp. If Condition 1 were stamped, it meant only very minor wear. If 2 were stamped, then some wear but decent condition. If 3, then the bore had considerable wear and/or permanent rust/pitting, and was replaced at the next inspection.

The second pie segment indicates throat diameter with an inner and outer row of numbers (which were a consecutive series from 6.49 to 6.55mm).

inner row	**9** (6.49)	**0** (6.50)	**1** (6.51)	
outer row	**2** (6.52)	**3** (6.53)	**4** (6.54)	**5** (6.55)

Later discs had a wider range, 6.46 to 6.59mm, represented by the inner row (6,7,8,9,0) and the outer row (1,2,3,4,5,6,7,8,9). When a throat measured 6.59mm, it was removed from service.

The 180° segment *Torpedam Överslag Str* noted the decimeter (3.9") POI change at 100M from the 139gr spitzers. (This system was changed in 1941 to the buttstock range chart.)

Finally, each time the rifle was returned to the armory for inspection, it was stamped with a Swedish crown on the stock underside, just behind the trigger guard.

The 6.5x55   (139/2750 for 2335fpe)

As the Norwegians and Swedes stipulated a 6.5mm bullet, their joint team designed the 6.5x55. Like the 7x57, it was also a huge success. Instead of merely necking down the superb 7x57, it had a 55mm case so that other rifles could not be misloaded with the wrong ammo. The case also had a wider head (.480" versus .473") and was thus too fat to chamber in a 7x57.

The excellent 6.5x55 Swede is great for all deer (and Bad Guys). Barrel twist was a fast 1:7.9", so 130-140gr bullets are the proper fodder. Since the original weight was 156gr, handloads with the droolingly fine 155gr Sierra MatchKing at 2500fps will be sufficiently stabilized.

Avoid **Danish surplus ammo!** It was designed for Danish Krags, and leads badly. (Headstamps are: V146, 48, HA.)

Avoid **PMC ammo!** Quality control is spotty, and one hot load of 139/*3004* for 2786fpe has already destroyed one M96.

Today

Only available in quantity since 1993. In 1994 these were being *given* away for only Ø80. You should pick up a WWI M94 or WWII M38 Carbine for Ø170-200. **The last lots arrived in 1998 and sold quickly.** (Folks at last caught on to how lovely these Swedish rifles are, and prices have gone up Ø50-80 since 1998!) Compared to 11,500,000 German K98s, the Swedes made only 804,000 Mausers. As Doug Bowser in *Neutrality through Marksmanship* (an excellent book from Sarco) put it, *"Although...not rare, we will be wondering where they all went in about 5 to 10 years."* (We're *already* wondering.)

Parts abound, and you can convert your gun to cock-on-opening. Get a RamLine synthetic stock to save the original wood stock from wear. A nonoriginal gun is prime meat for an Ashley Scout conversion. Even at Ø200, a Swedish Mauser can't be beat: The 6.5x55 is a jewel, you can't find equivalent quality for less than Ø1,500, and they will shoot 2MOA on a bad day. A conceptual bargain at any price under Ø500. *Hurry.*

My first *shooting* choice would be the M38 (as it's already got the short 23.1" barrel, turned-down bolt handle, and 100M rear sight). Second choice would be an M94 Carbine, preferably one made before 1899. For the best full-length collector rifle, choose an M96 (one made before 1915 when they all had walnut stocks, instead of beech), and hold out for one in *pristine* condition. (I have an unissued, *perfect* 1914 M96 that I bought for Ø140 back in 1996. What a treasure!)

Husqvarna manufactured a small portion of the Swedish Mausers, and these sell at somewhat of a premium.

If your rifle has mis-matching parts numbers
Email David Basiji (basiji@u.washington.edu) who is collecting names of those needing/supplying particular 3-digit serial numbered parts. (Note: Such number-restored rifles would *not* be "all original" guns, and should not be so misrepresented.)

Steyr M95   (8x56R)
History
Now *here* is a marvelous piece of 19th Century machinery! Tired of turnbolts? Well, the Steyr M95 is a *straight*-pull bolt with rotary locking. The official rifle of the Austro-Hungarian empire until 1914. The other notable straight-pull bolt rifles were Switzerland's Schmidt-Rubins (M1889, M1911, and K31).

Length was 39.4", barrel length 19", weight 7.9lbs.

The 8x56R   (208 at 2280 for 2402fpe)
The round gives 95% the energy of a .308. Speer and Hormady offer the correct .321" bullet, for those who wish to reload.

SOG sells ammo boxes of 10rds for just Ø1.50. That's just 15¢ per round, and loaded in 5rd stripper clips! (It's allegedly NC, but I'm skeptical. Most of the 8x56R I've seen is C/BE 1938 Nazi in original boxes. I'd treat *all* 8x56R ammo as if corrosive.)

Today
SOG has M95s for just Ø80 (add Ø10 for handpicked). This a *"curio and relic"* firearm, which can be directly ordered

by licensed C&R collectors (who are not required to have an FFL or storefront). If you're tired of turnbolts and want something unique, then a Steyr M95 oughta do it! (Be sure to stock up on lots of ammo for this old boy, or rebarrel to 7.62x54R.)

Some M95s are in the infinitely more common 8x57: the Greek M95/24, and the Yugoslav M95M (a post-WWII conversion with 23.2" barrel), for example. Such rifles would obviously be much easier to feed, and with NC ammo.

Mauser 98

History

An 1898 improvement on the M93-96s, the Mauser brothers created perhaps *the* best turnbolt ever. It is very simple, with only 10 parts. Only the P17 and the Arisaka, with 7 and 6 parts respectively, are simpler—and they're M98-based, anyway. (The MAS36 has only 5 parts, but no safety, which is "cheating.") The bolt is cock-on-opening.

Except for its longish lock time and slow safety, there is really nothing about the M98 to dislike. Strong (with its third locking lug) and smooth, it is today copied by FN, Winchester, Ruger, and many others.

The 8x57   (154/2880 for 2837fpe)

This is a good round, though the stubby 8mm/.323 bullet really doesn't have the BC for a very flat trajectory.

The pre-1898 bullet is 7.9x57J (a .318 caliber), which was quickly replaced with the 7.92x57 bullet of .323 caliber. Older rifles and drillings use the former, so be sure to check.

Today

Made for nearly every European and South American country, there are literally millions of these excellent war rifles around. While most M98s are in 7x57 or 8x57, the boltface is the same as the .308/.30-06 and new barrels are widely available. Any made by DWM, Loewe, Mauser, FN, Steyr, or CZ between 1920-1943, or post-WWII are fine. (Pre-1920 rifles are often a little soft, and the 1944-45 rifles are quite rough.) Springfield Sporters has plenty of M98 parts.

Argentine 1908 and 1909   (7.65x54)

These were made by DWM and Loewe in the 1920s, and the quality is *superb*. The caliber is the nice 7.65x54 Argentine, which has the same boltface as our .308/.30-06. The 1908 usually has a blind mag, while the more desirable 1909 has a mag floorplate. The actions are highly sought after to make custom rifles, although I would never tamper with a nice original gun.

Mexican M1910

Made at *Fabrica Nacional de Armas* in Mexico City, and based on the 1902 Mauser. These are small ring M98s and perfect actions to add the .308 barrel of your choice. J&G occasionally has them for Ø180.

Modelo 1912 (7x57)   Modelo 1912-61 (.308)

Made in Austria by Steyr for Colombia, and many were re-bored in 1961 to .308. A very nice quality .308 rifle for Ø170, and great for an Ashley Scout conversion.

SOG had these Mausers in .308 for only Ø100, which was great deal (and better made than the FR8). As I predicted in 1998, they went quickly. They now fetch Ø175+ gun shows.

Czech M1922 (8x57)   VZ24 (8x57)

SOG has the M22 for just Ø70. It has the Turkish crest, straight bolt handle, and 29" barrel. Made in Czechoslovakia.

Burns Bros. sells the pre-WWII VZ24 for Ø70-90, depending on condition. It sports the attractive Czech lion crest. Chamber ream to 8-06, or throw on .30-06 barrel and you've a bargain rugged rifle made by the BRNO factory in the 1920s.

FN Modelo 30 (Colombia), Modelo 1935 (Peru)   (.30-06)

Made in Belgium for Peru in the late 1930s. Lovely rifles with their checkered triggers and bottom-flattened bolt handles. The Peruvian crest is gorgeous. (All .30-06 FNs have a small cutout in the front receiver ring, and if in original .30-06 the buttstock will be stamped *Cal. .30.*) The Belgian Army dumped theirs in the 1950s for the FN49.

I once briefly had an all matching number (including the stock) gun without import stamp, but couldn't quite afford to keep it at the time. It would have made a nice companion to that 95% U.S. M1917 I let go. *Groan.*

Spanish FR8 M98   (.308)

If an additional caliber is totally out of the question, then the Spanish Mauser FR8 in .308 is a decent bargain. They're Spanish M98 actions with an 18" barrel and flash suppressor. Though most are a little rough, some are quite nice with *excellent* bores. They won't accept M14 stripper clips unless you widen the receiver ears. Back in 1994 the gun shows had *scads* of them, but they've long since been snapped up. Don't despair, as you'll find one for about Ø225 if you're diligent enough.

The front sight is often too short, resulting in a POI up to 20" high at 100, so you'll have to raise it up with a tool. Remove the bayonet attachment. Stone the sear, as the trigger is quite poor. If you've more time than Ø, the FR8 tarts up nicely. Consider a Tasco 4X scope (a 3-9X is wasted on these rifles). The Ashley Scout conversion would also work nicely on an FR8.

Avoid the sporterized Spanish and Chilean *M96* .308. They've been rebarreled to .308, but the M96 action doesn't have the third locking lug of the M98 and is really only a 45,000cup action (the .308 runs to 52,000cup). While I *might* trust a *Swedish* M96 in .308, I wouldn't trust a Spanish one.

Belgian FN, 1950s   (.30-06)
I once had a very nice 1952 in original .30-06 which I found for only Ø225. Since the rifle was quite accurate at 1½MOA with iron sights, I added a Timney trigger and a forward-mounted Burris 2¾X scope (to test Jeff Cooper's Scout rifle concept). This created a very sweet package (fed by stripper clips, since the scope wasn't covering up the action). With scope it shot ¾MOA and was extremely well-balanced and handy.

I took it out one afternoon with R.H., who set up a clay pigeon at 100 and bragged that he'd hit it first. Not finding out first what rifle he brought, I foolishly agreed. He then uncased his tack-driving .22-250 Ruger No. 1 with a Leupold 3-9X scope. *"Hey, that's hardly fair!,"* I whined. He replied, *"You shoot what you brought, and I'll shoot what I brought!"* (He wasn't a fan of the Scout rifle concept.) Well, that cheesed me off pretty good so I blasted the clay pigeon with a snap shot while he was just shouldering his Ruger. *"Ooo...kay,"* he said, and that was that.

FN also produced a contract run of M98ks in .308 for Israel in the early 1950s, before they adopted the FAL. SOG has these fine rifles for just Ø170. This is a home-run, folks.

Springfield 03A3   (.30-06)
After the 7x57 M93s made their impressive showing in Cuba, we dumped the Krag and basically copied the M98 (to such a degree that we had to pay over Ø500,000 in patent royalites to Mauser). Some improvements: magazine cutoff to allow single loading on top of a full mag; graspable cocking piece to restrike a hard primer. Con: two-piece firing pin.

M1903 actions numbering higher than 800,000 (Springfield) and 285,507 (Rock Island) received the double heat treatment and are stronger than the often brittle "low numbered" actions. All 03A3 actions, however, were double heat treated.

The Springfield was a very good military bolt-action, and they sporterize nicely with many available accessories. Mine shoots ¾MOA. While I wouldn't alter one that was in *very* good original condition, anything less is ripe. You'll pay Ø150-300 for a non-collector grade. Go to Springfield Sporters for parts.

Schmidt-Rubin M1911, K31 (7.5x55 Swiss)

These are beautiful old straight-pull bolt actions. Only the Swiss would choose such an expensively-machined rifle as their battle rifle. The cammed bolt is a work of art. Even though the cartridge (designed by Maj. Eduard Rubin, an excellent ballistician who pioneered the slim rimless case) is very uncommon (you'll have to reload for it), a Schmidt-Rubin is a joy to own. (The M1889s use the older non-spitzer bullet, and are not as strong. Stay with the M1911 or the K31.)

The M1911 (weight 9.8lbs, length 51.3", barrel 30.8") had a longer bolt throw than the K31 (weight 8.8lbs; 43.5", barrel 25.7"). The K31s (528,180 made from 1931-1946) were replaced in 1957 by the StG57s, and are now being surplused off for only Ø140 (Sarco). While rebarreling them is not really a viable option (there's too much headspace gunsmithing involved), the K31 tempts me still. What a fun Scout rifle *that* would make!

U.S. M1917 (P17)   (.30-06)

This is a U.S. WWI Mauser-style .30-06 designed from the P14 .303 British. 2,266,000 were delivered. The Springfield 03 was more labor intensive to produce, and twice as many M1917s served in US hands than 03s. It was *exceptionally* well made and finished. These are very good rifles, and Sgt. Alvin York used his to great effect on 8 October 1918.

Extremely rugged (using the bolt handle root as a third locking lug), 2½MOA accurate with great aperture sights, I'd take one over an 03A3 any day! Weight was 9.6lbs, length 46", barrel length 26". Winchesters and Remingtons are superior to the Eddystones (whose receivers are known for cracking).

Because of Britain's post-WWI gun control, the populace had allowed themselves to be cleaned out of rifles by 1939. When WWII broke out and Hitler's invasion of the British Isles was imminent, Churchill frantically begged us to sell them our WWI M1917s to arm their militia Home Guard (which could then release the Lee-Enfields to the army, who had left theirs at Dunkirk). By August 1940, we had sent them about 500,000.

Because, however, of its rear sight protective bridge and dogleg bolt handle, the M1917 is considered a tad homely. Converted sporters are Ø175+, and original rifles now begin at about Ø375 (Winchester get Ø100+ premium).

The ejector's leaf spring often breaks (Christy's Gun Works has a replacement *coil* spring). Also, you might consider converting yours in only 2 minutes to cock-on-*opening* with a Ø15 M1917 Speed Lock (which also reduces locktime by 72%; from Sarco). Those two items rectified, the M1917 is just about perfect. Springfield Sporters (724-254-2626) has other spare parts. Many M1917s have been sporterized, as their strong action and long mag body are very suitable for .300WM, .338WM, .35 Whelen, .458WM, and other powerful cartridges.

MAS36/51 (7.5x54 French)

The French just *can't* accept anybody else's proven design; only their own *unproven* weird design will do! To simplify manufacture, the MAS36 located its locking lugs to the *rear* of the bolt, and then turned its bolt handle *forward*. Furthermore, the gun has no safety. An ungainly but rugged pre-WWII rifle, it was the last bolt-action adopted by a major power (I'm using the term "major power" in its widest possible latitude).

Now being imported in original 7.5x54 and rechambered in 7.62x51 (the barrel has been set back about ¼"). For Ø110 dealer cost, you may want to try out one of these funky rifles.

Arisaka Type 38 and 99   (6.5x50, 7.7x58)

The Type 99 (1939) in 7.7x58 is basically the same rifle as the Type 38 (1905) in 6.5x50 but for its different cartridge.

This Japanese rifle is an M98 derivative with a *very* strong action well suited for rebarreling. A true story illustrates this well: Some guy sells his .30-06 Arisaka to a gun shop because it kicked too hard. Upon closer examination, somebody

noticed that it had merely been *rechambered* from its 6.5x50—a
.264. (The guilty "gunsmith" no doubt assumed that it was a
Type 99 in 7.7mm/.311, thus able to take a .308 caliber bullet.)
Sending a .308 bullet down a .264 bore sort of explains the stout
recoil, but it never bothered the Arisaka. *That's* strong! If an
Arisaka done right drops into your hands in the right chambering at the right price, then consider taking it home.

Madsen M47   (.30-06)

Just 5,000 were manufactured by Denmark for post-
WWII Colombia, these are well made and uncommon rifles.
Weight was 8.5lbs., length 43.3", with 23.4" barrel. They use
rear locking lugs, similar to the MAS36. It was the last turnbolt
MBR. Tidewater (757-425-2827) and Century have them.

Until recently, neither I nor "R.H." had ever seen one. I
found one at a flea market in 99% condition for next to nothing—*heh!* (If you ever run across one, snap it up immediately!
You'll have a very rare and interesting rifle.)

EARLY SEMI-AUTO BATTLE RIFLES

Battle rifles are full-sized and full-powered (*i.e.*, at least
2300fpe from the 6.5x55) rifles. Until the 1930s, they were bolt-
action (*e.g.*, Krag, Mauser M93 through M98, Mosin-Nagant,
Lee-Enfield, Swiss K11, etc.). After Paul Mauser's Model 1898
(and the many copies thereof: the 03 Springfield, P14 and
M1917, Arisaka, etc.), these rifles had by 1930 largely reached
their technological zenith for ruggedness, power, and accuracy.
Being manually operated, however, they did *not* give a high volume of fire. This would be addressed with the SLR.

1st Gen MBRs   (M1, SVT40, AG42, G43, FN49)

By the late-1930s the trend was to field the same powerful
(*i.e.*, 2300+fpe) WWI cartridges (*e.g.*, .30-06, 7.62x54R, 6.5x55,
and 8x57) in *self-loading* rifles (first used in WWII).   The
American M1 Garand (which rightfully beat out the Pedersen
Rifle and M1941 Johnson), Soviet SVT38/40, Swedish AG42,
G43, and FN49 are the obvious examples. All of the above (save
the G43) required numerous and complicated machining operations, but such was only natural in 1st Gen designs.

Such early battle rifles were robust and served well, but had only a 5-10rd mag capacity and were slow to reload (as they had no quick detachable mags and were fed by stripper clips).

2nd Gen MBRs   (FG42, MAS49, M14, vz52)

These rifles were distinguished by their 10-20rd QD mags and (usually) select-fire capability. The first example was the *Fallschirmjägergewehr* 42, a select-fire, design-amalgam 8x57 with detachable 20rd mag. Only 7,000 of the fascinating FG42 were made, and few survived WWII. Other 2nd Gen MBRs were the MAS49, M14, and vz52.

3rd Gen MBRs   (FAL, G3, SG57)

By the early 1950s Britain and Belgium were developing the first *3rd* Gen MBR (based on the FN49), the FAL, in their experimental 7x43 (a shortened .30-06 case, necked down to .284). In 1953 we had adopted the 7.62x51 round and arm-twisted the British into also accepting it, even though they were locked into their own 7x43. With the promise that we would choose the FAL, the British and Belgians redesigned it to take the 7.62x51. Typically, we reneged and adopted our own M14 (an M1 Garand with 20rd quick-detachable mag), even though field tests slightly favored the FAL. Britain stuck with the FAL.

The rest of the NATO allies soon followed .308 suit and the West rushed to rearm with new 3rd Gen MBRs. Most avoided the M14 and chose either the Belgian FAL (93 countries) or the German G3 (designed in Spain by WWII Mauser engineers and made by Heckler & Koch or under license, and adopted by over 50 countries).

A quick aside about 6-7mm bullets

Buried during the late-1950s was the nascent development of truly intermediate rifle cartridges in ballistically superior 6mm (*e.g.*, our 6x53 SAW; 105/2800 for 1828fpe) and 7mm (*e.g.*, the Brits' .280 Enfield; 140/2415 for 1814fpe). The drawback with .30 caliber bullets is that their ballistic coefficient (BC) does not exceed .530 until bullet weight is at least 190gr, which is too heavy to enjoy high velocities (and thus flatter trajectories) from a 51mm long case. A BC of .535 can be had in just a 168gr 7mm bullet, and in a *140gr* 6.5mm bullet.

The Europeans increasingly realized the advantage to a lighter, smaller caliber bullet, as they gradually experimented with such:

7.90mm	(8x57)	1888
7.70mm	(.303)	1888
7.65mm	(7.65x53)	1889
7.00mm	(7x57)	1892
6.50mm	(6.5x55)	1894

Since M118 ball is just 147gr, why not throw that weight in a *much* more streamlined 7mm or 6.5mm? I am trying to revive this superb concept with my .264 Boston, which would marry a new 2100fpe 140gr 6.5mm (or 120gr .257) cartridge with 5th Gen battle carbine technology.

4th Gen MBRs, and the end of .308 MBR development
Following the FAL and H&K91, less than ten more years of MBR development were left to produce the last of the breed, the 4th Gen AR10. This was a marked advancement in materials and ergonomics which paved the way for the M16. By the mid-1960s the trend had clearly turned toward battle carbines (as you can see by the declining numbers of new battle rifles).

Battle Rifle Development
1st Gen	M1 Garand, M1941, SVT38/40, AG42, G43, FN49
2nd Gen	FG42, M14, MAS44/49, vz52, BM59
3rd Gen	FAL, SG57, G3/HK91, Galil
4th Gen	AR10

Since the original AR10 (and its modern revivals), there has been no new further development in battle rifles, such as an AUG or SIG or G36 in .308. While the modern SR25 and AR10 are good guns, they are marketed to civilians and lack the military-level of ruggedness an MBR demands.

SURPLUS SEMI-AUTO MBRs

Explaining the pleasure of collecting excellent-condition examples of the astonishing engineering feats that are the firearms of the 19th and early 20th centuries—each with a story to tell, many having miraculously survived actual combat—to the gunhater would be like trying to explain the pleasure of accumulating a complete set of autographed first editions of your favorite author...to an illiterate savage, incapable of viewing their pages as anything but toilet paper or kindling. (at 366)
    — Vin Suprynowicz; *Send in the Waco Killers* (1999)

Here's a summary of the *commonly* available foreign semi-autos on the surplus market. Many have either sold out or have been shut off since 11/90 from import, so act quickly.

After Vin Suprynowicz's review of the 1998 edition of this book wherein he misunderstood (inexplicably, given his above quote) that I had *"recommended"* the Tokarev SVT40, I should emphasize that the below are *not* to be considered as primary defensive choices (although the M1 and FN49 would suffice, and perhaps the AG42B). Would many of them do in a pinch if you had no other option? Certainly, but that's not the point!

I list them because I'm interested in *all* smokeless powder military rifles for both their history and machinery, and assume that you are too! Today's market selection of hitherto now museum items is truly quite amazing. Until recently it was inconceivable to own, for example, a Simonov SKS—much less one for Ø275! These are authentic foreign rifles often in NRA Very Good to Excellent condition, many of which have been through a war. So, to me, picking up a Ø400 AG42B Ljungman in its highly desirable 6.5x55 Swede (to go with an 1898 Norwegian Krag) is a real no-brainer. But, hey, that's *me*. Your mileage may vary.

The below list does not mention every WWII and post-war rifle; only the ones generally available to us now (which constitutes about *85%* of them—remarkable!). It's a great time for us! (Note: Underlined rifles are also BATF *"curios or relics."*)

M1 Garand   (.30-06   USA, 1936-57)

John Garand, the brilliant gun designer at Springfield Armory, gave our WWII troops his superb M1. Robust, .30-06 powerful, fairly accurate, and extremely reliable, the M1 had a real edge over the Germans' slow Mauser M98k. 6,034,000 were made, and even the Germans and Japanese even made copies (visit the musuem in Cody, Wyoming to see a Jap gun).

Notable design qualities were the simple and rugged gas-operated action, the trigger (copied in many later weapons, such as the AKs), and safety. Its sights were also very good. Weight was 9.5lbs, overall length 43.5", barrel length 24".

M1 design flaws were excessive weight and length, inability to partially reload the 8rd clip (which had to be shot empty and ejected), the *Ching!* sound of clip ejection, and lack of a detachable mag (inexcusable given existing 20rd BAR mags). It should at least have had a 10rd mag fed by stripper clips (as had the FN49). Finally, it was also complicated and expensive to manufacture with its many machining operations.

If you can't afford an M1A, then a Garand would be a fine alternate rifle. With practice, it is *not* as heavy or slow to load, as I opined in 2000. Since we made so many of them, they're easy to find (though no longer cheap). You can still get one for Ø450 from the Civilian Marksmanship Program (419-635-2141). Gun show rifles of WWII/Korea vintage run Ø500+.

Sniper models, the M1C (all S.A., and within #s 3,200,000 to 3,800,000) and M1D (beware of fakes) were produced in very limited numbers in 1944. These extremely rare and desirable M1s have largely been melted down by the Clinton administration—yet another example of his 2nd Amendment treason. (They *should* have been sold back to the original owners, the American people, for up to Ø2,000 apiece!)

I cannot recommend the newly offered M1 from Federal Arms Corp. made up on sucky modern receivers with surplus parts. Stick with an original M1. (Springfield Armory WWII serial #s are 410,000 to 3,880,000.) FAC also sells a nice parts kit with fine bores for only Ø140. Have *lots* of clips (they're 25-75¢ in quantity)!

Tanker Garand

This modern rework by Springfield Armory was offered also in .308, which is much cheaper to shoot. Basically, the original 24" barrel was bobbed off to 18". Weight was 8.8lbs, length 37.5". Accuracy was pretty good at 2-2½MOA.

Tokarev SVT40 (7.62x54R USSR, 1939-45)

The "M1 Garand of Russia." Weight was 8.5lbs, length 48.3", with 24" barrel. While they were a bit too lightly made (especially for full-auto) and are sensitive to dirt and grease build up, they were of comparatively fine quality, and good shooters. They were until recently museum pieces over here, and now fetch Ø450+. (I rarely see them at shows anymore.)

Sellier & Bellot 7.62x54R brass cased, boxer primed ammo goes for Ø40/100, and BE/NC for Ø145/500. Stripper clips are Ø17/10. Given the .308/7.62 caliber bullets, the SVT40 are easily reloadable. Numrich has 10rd mags for Ø55.

AG42B Ljungman (6.5x55   Sweden, 1942-62)
History

This was hurriedly designed after the Nazi invasion of Norway to give Swedish troops (one per squad) semi-auto firepower. The *Automatiskt Gevär* 42 was delivered to the field in less than a year after the Erik Eklund's first drawings were laid down—an astounding feat. Naturally, shortcomings arose from such haste, but they were resolved in 1953 with the B model retrofit (*i.e.,* trigger, front sight, gas tube, and magazine). Weight was 10.4lbs, length 47.8", barrel 24.5".

It uses a gas tube (no piston) and Tokarev SVT40/FAL-style bolt and carrier (with no exposed handle, eliminating its receiver clearance and dirt entry). With its 10rd detachable mag (though normal loading is done with stripper clips), excellent trigger, and quick adjustable 100-700M rear sight (100-600M for the older round nose bullets), and standard muzzle brake, the Ljungman is fine shooter and probably the most accurate of any service-grade semi-auto. (The gas tube, however, can foul. Spray clean with CRC aerosol brake cleaner.)

The Danish copied the Ljungman in 1949. Commercially offered in 7x57, .308, .30-06 and 8x57, the Madsen is, sadly, nearly never seen here. A .30-06 Madsen would be *trés chic*.

In 1959 the Swedish government converted ten AG42Bs to 7.62x51. Seven of these FM59s are in European collections, and the other three were for sale by Sarco for Ø8,650. Gee.

The 6x5x55   (139/2750 for 2335fpe)

You've already learned about this round from the bit on Swedish Mausers. The only bulk distributor of it is Samco (305-593-9782) which offers NC/BE Hirtenberger 139gr FMJ (38.9¢/rd). Boxer brass is not cheap, but Midway, etc. have it. Lubing the action with moly grease instead of oil will reduce common case neck damage.

Today

Funky and 1½MOA accurate—the Ljungman is one of my favorite historic SLRs. They were originally imported for Ø145, but today go for Ø400 (and are scarce, as their happy owners rarely part with them). I've seen only seven for sale, ever.

Springfield Sporters (412-254-2626) has most Ljungman parts (including Ø40 barrels, Ø8 blank firing devices, and Ø7 night sights w/leather case). Sarco sells the original maintenance kit for only Ø25 and original leather sling for Ø7.

Walther G43   (8x57   Nazi Germany, 1943-45)

Over 500,000 of the "Nazi Garand" were made. Replacing the complex Walther G41(W), this Tokarev-style gas-operated rifle has a 10rd detachable mag. Weight was 9.6lbs, length 44", with a 22" barrel. As a wartime measure the gun is very poorly finished, but functioning did not suffer. A scope mount dovetail was standard, so most G43s were made into very good sniper models and fielded by capable riflemen. (The Czechs kept theirs for years after the war.)

The G43 is a very unique and interesting rifle for Ø1,200. You can even get original mags for Ø60. Gun Parts has parts.

In 1954, the Itajuba Arsenal of Brazil copied a few G43s in .30-06, and about 50 of them made it over here. (I may know of one for sale, and it's mint. Bidding starts at Ø2,000. Email me.)

Simonov SKS   (7.62x39   USSR, 1946-55)

History

Sergei Simonov shrunk down his WWII mammoth 14.5mm PTRS anti-tank rifle (994/3200 for *22,607*fpe, which is *73%* more powerful than that pansy .50BMG, in case you were wondering) around the new 7.62x39 cartridge. The action was similar to the Tokarev SVT40.

The SKS is a very rugged rifle of no-frills design with a 10rd fixed mag. Weight was 9.5lbs, length 34.6", barrel 16.3". It saw a bit of action on the Eastern Front, but the post-WWII arrival of the AK47 relegated the dowdy SKS to home guard use. The milled SKS is 2MOA more accurate than the stamped steel AK47, and makes a great trunk rifle.

The 7.62x39   (123/2340 for 1485fpe)

For its <300M design parameters, it does the job, though the .223 (especially in the 62gr SS109/M855 loading) is a far superior combat round.

Today

These Soviet rifles from the 1950s are nicely milled and make the rough-hewn ChiCom Type 56 versions look like crap. As it's BATF-classifed *"curio or relic"* it can retain its nasty bayonet. Ø275 at any gun show, for now. Folks, this represents one of today's greatest gun bargains. You'll regret not getting one.

If you can't find/afford a Russian model, the newly imported Romanian SKS for Ø180 dealer is pretty good, too.

FN49

(7x57, 7.65x54, .308, .30-06, 8x57   1950-58)

History

Also known as the Saive, SAFN49, or ABL49. Designed by D.J. Saive (quite accurately the "John C. Garand" of Belgium) and manufactured by FN until its "son" arrived, the FAL. Weight was 9.5lb, length 44", barrel length 23.3", twist 1-10".

After the Nazi invasion of Belgium, Saive fled to England and worked on his pre-WWII design from there. The resulting FN49 was too expensively-made for post-war needs (as were all 1st Gen MBRs). It used a tilting bolt similar to the Simonov and Tokarev system, but was devoloped independently. The trigger was a clone of the simple Browning Auto-5 shotgun, which FN had been making for more than 40 years. It had a 10rd box mag.

A narrow 1949-53 window existed before the debut of the 7.62x51, and the sole SLR then was the M1 (only in .30-06). FN cannily offered their FN49 (the equal of the Garand) in all the metric MBR calibers (thus avoiding an army's switch to .30-06). It proved to be fine marketing as the FN49 was sold to Egypt (37,641; 8x57), and to most of South America such as Brazil, (.30-06), Venezuela (8,003; 7x57), Colombia (.30-06), and Argentina (5,541; 7.65x53). Belgium dumped their .30-06 M1935 M98s and Garands, and bought 125,072 FN49s in .30-06.

Other countries that bought the FN49 in .30-06 were Luxembourg, the Belgian Congo, and Indonesia. Although only eight nations adoped the FN49, one must recall that the post-WWII world was awash in free surplus weapons (most of them donated by the USA). The fact that it sold at *all* despite its high cost speaks very highly of the FN49. Just 176,267 were made.

Ammo

Choose your flavor, but most common FN49s are in 8x57.

Today

The FN49 was blooded in Korea by Belgian troops, and it did very well. Truly, the M1 Garand has nothing on it. A rugged and accurate rifle, the FN49 makes a very nice collectible and very fieldable battle rifle.

In 1988, they were just Ø126 dealer. The Luxembourg .30-06 is the choicest model, though rarely seen for sale. Ø700.

In 1995 new .30-06 barrels were sold for just Ø100, so I picked up an affordable Egyptian model to convert from its 8x57. Once sold out, these barrels are now again available.

Today, SOG has Egyptian 49s for Ø350 (these are parts guns; identify as such by their plastic buttplates). New 8x57 barrels (in the white) are still available from Sarco for only Ø35. And, as you probably know, 8x57 is very cheap these days. Since all FN49s were made in Belgium, the quality of the Egyptian model is not suspect. (It does, however, have that baked-on paint finish, which the British call "stoving." This can be stripped down to the Parkerizing.)

My second favorite after the Luxembourg .30-06 is the 7x57 Venezuelan rifle. These are usually in lovely condition.

.308 FN49

In 1995 a few hundred of the rare 2,200 Argentine Naval FN49s (in arsenal-rebarreled *.308* w/20rd detachable mag) were imported for Ø400. (The original 20rd mag was converted to 10rd, to comply with the *"Crime Bill,"* and the muzzle caps were welded on, which no doubt affects accuracy. For optimum accuracy, have a gunsmith remove the cap, turn down the threads, and cryo-relieve the stresses.) These rare .308s are scarce today, but I sometimes see one. (In the 1960s, FN sold .308 conversion kits. Perhaps a small hoard will surface?)

Odds and ends

Its weak part is the 2-piece firing pin, so have a few spares. As the FN49 is 2½MOA accurate, you might want to procure a scope mount for it (the best is the original Echo/C. Herkner mounts of the 1950s, made in Boise for FN), which fits in the left side receiver. (B-Square makes one; 800-433-2902.)

You should locate an original bayonet, which are nearly identical to an M98's but for a larger muzzle ring. The least common (but most desirable) is the 15" Model 1924/49 Long Export (versus the more common 9" Model 1949 Short Export). (Much of this info was excerpted from *The SAFN49 Battle Rifle* by Joe Poyer; www.northcapepubs.com; 800-745-9714.)

MAS49/56   (7.5x54   France, 1951-65)

History

Not a bad rifle, though Gallic weird. Weight is 8.6lbs, length 39.8", barrel 20.5". The trigger is lousy, but the sights are great. The French seem to love direct gas impingement, which they further used in the FA-MAS. (MAS means *Manufacture d'Armes de Saint Etienne*.) These are tough and handy carbines, in an effective caliber.

The 7.5x54   **(139/2700 for 2251fpe)**

Same energy as the 6.5x55, but not quite as flat shooting. Also, the French (out of stupid Gallic pride) just *had* to avoid the 7.62x51 NATO when it became available in 1953, even though a mere rebarreling would have ushered them into the 1950s.

Today

I bought one of these in .308 for Ø275 with the goal of sending it out for the FAL mag Ø100 conversion. A French "FAL" for only Ø375! The trouble was, it was plagued with failures to extract due to a mistimed gas system (which is fixable; visit a test article on www.jpfo.org to learn how.)

It's an offbeat and rugged little beast, and would make a great car rifle. Burns Bros. and Classic Arms (800-383-8011) wholesales them new/unissued for Ø230. Parts, however, are nearly impossible to procure.

Sarco sells orginal sniper scopes in excellent condition with mount, tool, manual, and carrying case for just Ø250.

vz52   (7.62x45, 7.62x39   Czech., 1952-59)

A fantastically over-engineered rifle and great Ø85 curio (although prices have inexplicably climbed to Ø175+ recently). Most are beaters. Weight was 9.0lbs, length 40", barrel 20.5".

Nevertheless, the 7.62x45 round (130/2440 for 1719fpe) is pretty neat. (Necked down to 6mm/.243 to throw a .527BC Sierra 107gr at 2700fps, it would've been the *perfect* battle carbine round, and very flat shooting.) It's still fairly available (in unreloadable Berdan steel case). Federal Arms (612-780-8780) sells 7.62x39 chamber conversion kits for Ø35.

SIG SG57   (7.5x55   Switzerland, 1957-1980)

Called the 510-4 or AMT over here, it's a highly refined, accurate, and odd piece of work. With its roller-locked delayed blowback op system and fluted chamber, it's sort of a Swiss HK. Way too long (43.5"), heavy (12.4lbs), and with poor ergonomics. While I can list dozens of more enticing guns for the Ø3,000+, you'd surely be the first on your block. DSA sells the parts kits for both 7.5mm and .308 guns (Ø300 and Ø400).

Hakim   (8x57   Egypt, 1960s)

With Swedish engineering help, the Egyptians configured the Ljungman to 8x57. The Hakim has a 7-position gas regulator (clockwise to close—the 7 o'clock generally works best; Tapco sells the tool for 99¢). Fashion a case bumper around the operating handle from rubber auto hose. A Hakim can be had for <Ø300 (though prices are climbing) and is a competitor to the 8x57 FN-49 for Ø400. The 25rd mags for the MG13 can be fitted with little trouble (only Ø10 from Omega; 520-889-8895).

Rasheed   (7.62x39   Egypt, 1960s)

After the Egyptians saw the Soviet SKS, they downsized the Hakim to create the Rasheed in 7.62x39. (It's also often spelled "Rashid.") With a 10rd mag, Hakim-style gas regulator, and folding bayonet, only 8,500 were ever made. It's the only Ljungman-style rifle with a bolt handle. The Rasheed is more accurate than the SKS, but the springs wear out rather quickly. In 1988 these rare rifles could be had for only Ø100. Hunter's Lodge (800-533-8540) wholesaled in 1998 the *very* last lot at Ø440, and they today fetch up to Ø550. Sarco sells the *original* web sling for only Ø8.50. Unique, and cheap to feed!

Dragunov   (7.62x54R   USSR 1963-)

The Commies' sniper rifle. The Soviet SVD (*Samozaryad-naya Vintovka Dragunova*) has a 24.5" barrel of 1:10" twist, and with its short-stroke gas system will give ¾-1MOA with 200gr match ammo. (When fed machine-gun ball ammo, then any Dragunov will give only 2MOA at best.) The 4x PSO-1 (*Pristel Snaipersky Optichesky*) scope *looks* a bit dumpy, but is actually a good piece of kit with fine 1300m BDC and excellent zero hold.

The Yugoslavian M76 is usually found in 7.92x57, and rarely in 7.62x51. Probably the nicest of Dragunov variants, though I haven't seen one in several years.

The Romanian Romak-3 in 7.62x54R is only Ø800 dealer, and is a decent rifle when fed sniper grade NC 180gr ammo from S&B (which will give 1MOA). It uses the long-stroke gas piston of the RPK, has an auto hold-open, and two-stage trigger. (I had one for a few months and enjoyed it, but could not justify owning yet another rifle caliber. Simple, rugged, accurate.)

The pre-ban Chinese Norinco NDM-86 is now available from CDNN in 7.62x51, but for a whopping Ø1,700 dealer (as only 1,000 made it to the USA).

If you simply must have a Dragunov-type rifle, simply buy a Romak-3 for half the coin and feed it 8¢/rd 8x57 surplus ammo (after shooting, immediately use Windex in the gas system and barrel to neutralize the corrosive primer salts).

RISE OF THE BATTLE CARBINE

"What's the diff between battle rifles and carbines?"
Battle rifles are full-sized and full power; battle carbines (a.k.a. "assault rifles") are carbines in lesser cartridges.

The cartridges
During WWII, reduced combat ranges under 300M (and the decline of soldier marksmanship) led to some deep rethinking. The reasoning went: *"If soldiers do not often shoot past 300M, then why make them carry such powerful ammo?"*

This led to the development of "intermediate" cartridges between pistol and rifle (*i.e.,* between the .45ACP and .30-06, the 7.63x25 and 7.62x54R, and the 9x19 and 8x57). Instead of 8x57/.30-06-class muzzle energy of 2900fpe (or even 6.5x55 Swede-class energy of 2300fpe, which is still quite ample), it was decided that a mere 900-1500fpe would be adequate. We came up with the .30 Carbine (952fpe), the Germans the 8x33 (1229fpe), and the Soviets the 7.62x39 (1485fpe).

Shorter and lighter rifles (*i.e.,* carbines) were then designed *around* these new intermediate cartridges.

The guns
These weapons filled a niche between submachine guns (*e.g.,* the Thompson, the PPSh-41, and the MP40) and MBRs (bolt and self-loading). Since the Nazis created the archetypical assault rifle in the MP43 (later renamed the StG44), we'll look to them for the definition:

❶ Carbine (*i.e.,* short overall and barrel length).
❷ Fires an intermediate-powered cartridge.
❸ Select-fire capability.
❹ Uses a high-capacity quick detachable magazine.
❺ Fires from a closed bolt (unlike most submachine guns).

The German MP43/StG44 was designed to increase the firepower of soldiers against the Soviet hordes on the Eastern Front (who were armed with the 71rd drum PPSh41s). By all accounts, it was quite effective.

Still, the first carbine to meet the above criteria *wasn't* the MP43, it was (depending on if you consider its cartridge of nearly carbine level) an *American* rifle in service in 1942—the M1 Carbine. The German MP43/StG44, however, was clearly the *archetype* for most post-WWII assault rifles (*e.g.,* the AK47).

M1 Carbine

History

Designed to provide rear echelon and support troops more gun than a Colt 1911A1 .45ACP, this was a light and handy carbine with a Garand-style op system and QD mag. Weight was 5½lbs, length 35.7" with an 18" barrel. As Tim Mullin pointed out in *Testing the War Weapons*, the M1 Carbine (especially the select-fire M2 version) *could* be classified as the world's first *actual* assault rifle (beating the MP43 by a year).

The diminutive M1 Carbine was generally a big hit with the troops, who liked its light weight and good handling. Granted, it was no .30-06 M1 Garand, but if its limited range were kept in mind, the Carbine was quite capable.

The .30 Carbine

NYPD Stakeout Squad Jim Cirillo (veteran of 17 gunfights) said that *when loaded with soft-point ammo* the M1 Carbine was the most effective manstopper in urban situations (where targets are well within 50yds). With softpoint ballistics of 110/1975 for 952fpe (which are 74% of a .357 Magnum fired from a rifle at 125/2150 for 1283fpe), Cirillo's real-world experience shouldn't be all that surprising.

Still, they *should* have created a rimless 10x45 (at 200gr/2000fps for 1777fpe, nearly twice the .30 Carbine's fpe) and designed the M1 Carbine around *that*. A detachable 20rd mag, auto-rimmed 10x45 Carbine would have *really* been the thing out to 200yds. (For "**10mm Boston**" concept's sake, I'm going to straightwall a 7.62x45 case to seat a 10mm bullet.)

Today

So, after considering these two favorable opinions, I'm going to cut the M1 Carbine some new slack. While I always liked the *rifle* itself (it's got a fine safety and mag release, and great sights), its unique cartridge never blew my dress up, so I unfairly dismissed the rifle. In fact, I think I'll keep my eyes open for one (a real WWII model, and not a civilian Universal clone). Prices on nice combat guns begin at Ø500, but what a lovely little piece of history!

Actually, for city/apartment/trailer park dwellers, an M1 Carbine just might be the ideal home defense rifle (within 50yds). It's got good short-range stopping power without overpenetration, *and* it's light enough for even children, ladies, and the elderly to use. The 30rd mags often malf, so test yours (and have plenty of 15rd mags.) IAI (www.isrealiarms.com) makes their very fine new M888 for Ø599 retail, and its 2-2½MOA is quite accurate for a Carbine (3-5MOA is typical of the military models with their looser chambers).

While there is a firm which converts the M1 Carbine to .44 Auto Mag and .45 Win Mag (cool!), the softer civilian guns often couldn't handle the extra power and they occasionally blow up. *Cuidado.* (I'd rather buy a Ø275 used .44 Mag Marlin 1894.)

While these M1 Carbines *are* fine little rifles and great fun to shoot, the cartridge is truly limited to within 50yds. The Ø325 detachable mag SKS is nearly as much fun, and is a better field weapon for less money.

MP44/StG44

The new cartridge

Before WWII, the Germans had learned in the 1936 Spanish invasion that 90% of a soldier's shots were at targets within 300M, so why should he have to lug around a long-barreled M98 and its heavy 8x57mm ammo? Since the 9mm MP40 subgun was anemic past 50M, an intermediate round was designed—the 8x33, or 8mm *Kurz* (Short). The short case threw a 123gr bullet at 2120fps for 1229fpe (89% of a .223 and 83% of a 7.62x39). While 1229fpe from a rifle couldn't be called *powerful* by any means, it was nonetheless nearly a third more powerful than the .30 Carbine.

The new *Sturmgewehr*

This cartridge was fired by a totally new class of weapon, the gas-operated MP43 (later called the StG44, as Hitler personally named it the *Sturmgewehr*, or "assault rifle"). Highly controllable in full-auto (its 11.5lb weight certainly helped), yet effective out to 300M. Overall length was 37" and barrel length was 16.5". It had a number of innovative features, such as the above-barrel gas piston (for straight line stock design), left side bolt handle, dust cover, separate trigger group, and push-through select-fire control. Although it cost 14 *Reichsmarks* more than the Kar98k, it took only 14 hours to make, as it had much less complicated machining. (The Mauser StG45, father of the HK roller-locked delayed-blowback action and stamped steel design, would take only half as long as *that*, but the war ended before production could begin.)

The *Wehrmacht* and *Waffen SS* loved it, although it had been introduced far too late in the Eastern Front to make any real difference in WWII. StG44s are still found in Africa, and the now-defunct East Germany used to make ammo for it up until the 1980s. Your dad, uncle, or grandpa who served in the ETO of WWII just might have brought one back, and it could still be in some attic footlocker. *Viel Glück!* If you've just *gotta* have one, then get a Ø795 dummy gun from IMA.

The *Sturmgewehr* concept takes off

The assault rifle/battle carbine concept was firmly grasped by the USSR, which bypassed altogether powerful 2nd-4th Gen MBRs and armed their empire with 7.62x39 AK47s. Since the Commies enjoyed nearly inexhaustible supplies of troops for the meat grinder, they could afford to employ "human wave" tactics.

The Nazis and the Soviets started the trend, and by the 1960s the West rushed to downsize into "mouse guns" and are now using the 5.56x45—a caliber considered by responsible hunters as unsuitable for even whitetail deer. (The new combat doctrine favored merely wounding the enemy over killing him, which is why lesser cartridges were deemed sufficient. They forgot about having to shoot through cover.)

The fine .308 battle rifles of the 1950s-60s (*e.g.*, the FAL, M14, HK) had but a ten year reign and were sadly dismissed by the transition to 5.56x45 (which prevented the promising 4th Gen AR10 from even getting off the ground). Ironically, the Second and Third world countries aligned with the West ended up with better rifles, since they retained their FALs and G3s (being unable to afford M16s).

Battle Carbine Development

1st Gen	(cartridge)	M1 Carbine, StG44, SKS
2nd Gen	(QD mag)	AK47
3rd Gen	(materials)	M16, AR18, Daewoo, M63
4th Gen	(bullpup)	EM2, FA-MAS, L80, M17, AUG
5th Gen	(materials, ambi, modularity)	AUG, SIG550, G36
6th Gen	(NVD/thermal sights, caseless rds, bullpup)	G11

THE FUTURE

The trend is clearly towards modularity (*i.e.*, the same receiver being easily convertible to carbine, rifle, or SAW—a concept pioneered by Eugene Stoner and his M63), optical sights (*e.g.*, the AUG), NVD sights (*e.g.*, the G36), and the continued development of lightweight materials (such as ceramics and carbon fiber). Also, ambidextrous controls will be standard on the battle carbine of the 2010s (the G36 is the archetype here).

By 2010 I expect an operational marriage between night vision and thermal imaging sight systems into a rugged field unit weighing less than a kilo (2.2lbs). Won't *that* be something? Caseless round ammunition could become affordable by 2015, thanks to the pioneering work of HK and its G11.

Parting thoughts on battle carbines

Battle carbines/cartridges *do* have their proper realm (*e.g.*, CQB, urban fighting, perimeter defense, etc.), but one must always keep in mind their significant limitations: They cannot penetrate much cover and their effective range is only 200-300 yards. In my opinion, the M1 Carbine concept was the right idea (*i.e.*, an intermediate-powered carbine for *support* troops), but the Nazis and Soviets (and then everybody else) took underpowered carbines *way* too far by equipping entire armies with them. I'm glad that battle carbines (the modern equivalent to the Roman short sword) were invented, however, they need to be put back in their "place" and kept there.

For the purposes of Freedom, battle carbines are *not* our long gun answer. In our dilemma, "less" is not "more." Why field with the same rifle power level as our enemy? As we'll soon learn in this book, accurate .30 caliber firepower (whether from scoped bolt guns, or from MBRs) will be the only effective long-gun answer.

In our dilemma, only "more" than the .223 can ever be enough. Translation: Get a .308.

MAKE SURE YOU DON'T PAY THE PRICE OF "GUN CONTROL" AS THESE UNARMED VICTIMS DID

PERPETRATOR GOVERNMENT	DATE	TARGET	# MURDERED (ESTIMATED)	PERMIT OR REGISTRATION REQUIRED	DATE OF "GUN CONTROL" LAW	SOURCE DOCUMENT
Ottoman Turkey	1915-1917	Armenians	1–1.5 million	yes	1866 1911	Art. 166, Penal Code Art. 166, Penal Code
Soviet Union*	1929-1953	Anti Communists Anti-Stalinists	20 million	yes	1929	Art. 182, Penal Code
Nazi Germany** & Occupied Europe	1933-1945	Jews, Gypsies, Anti-Nazis	13 million	yes	1928 1938	Law on Firearms & Ammunition, April 12 Weapons Law, March 18
China*	1949-1952 1957-1960 1966-1976	Anti-Communists Rural Populations Pro-Reform Group	20 million	yes	1935 1957	Arts. 186-7, Penal Code Art. 9, Security Law, Oct. 22
Guatemala	1960-1981	Maya Indians	100,000	yes	1871 1964	Decree 36, Nov. 25 Decree 283, Oct. 27
Uganda	1971-1979	Christians Political Rivals	300,000	yes	1955 1970	Firearms Ordinance Firearms Act
Cambodia	1975-1979	Educated Persons	1 million	yes	1956	Arts. 322-8, Penal Code
Rwanda	1994	Tutsi	800,000	yes	1964	Law of 21 November 1964 on the Control of Firearms
		Total Victims:	57 million			

* The law(s) mentioned are part of an older and/or wider body of law on and regulation of private firearms ownership.
** For a complete translation of these laws, including regulations specifically banning Jews from owning any weapons and a side-by-side comparison of the Nazi Weapons Law with the U.S. Gun Control Act of 1968, see *"Gun Control": Gateway to Tyranny,* J.E. Simkin & A. Zelman, 1992; available from JPFO

©1994 JPFO

MODERN COMBAT SEMI-AUTO RIFLES

Combat rifles were not designed for plinking, although they are great fun for such. They were not designed for target shooting or for deer hunting, although many can suffice. Rugged, powerful, and self-loading, military rifles were designed to incapacitate and kill men in great numbers and at great distances. When Bad Guys appear suddenly and singly at close range, a pistol will usually solve your problem. When they appear at greater numbers or greater distances, only a battle rifle will do. Lethal emergencies vary, and so do the tools necessary to solve them. Owning combat rifles is no cause for shame, for lethally aggressive men deserve to be shot (and shot *well*).

One very possible lethal emergency for country folk is an attack by a pickup truck full of marauders. A quality combat rifle, along with the will and training to use it, is the best tool to solve your problem. City dwellers during severe civil unrest (*e.g.*, the L.A. riots) could take to their rooftops with combat rifles to protect their homes from hordes of looters and arsonists.

Another possible lethal situation is the armed assault on peaceable (though politically incorrect) American gunowners by government thugs dressed in Nazi *SS* black. They probably will be carrying one of three long guns: an H&K MP5 9mm subgun, an M16A3, or a Remington 700 sniper rifle in .308. It is essential that your entire family be equipped/trained with combat rifles to counter this likelihood. (The dress rehearsals were Ruby Ridge and Waco.) As Jeff Cooper put it in *Art Of The Rifle*,

Pick up a rifle and you change instantly from a subject to a citizen.

The politicians know full well that you won't *like* what they've got planned for you. They know that they've squeezed us into corner and we're as mad as hell about it. They also know that we'll eventually say *"Enough!"* and fight back —and this *terrifies* them. Whenever they see a picture of an AK47 or AR15, they envision it wielded at themselves. These are "evil" guns to our "leaders" for the simple reason that they expect to face the muzzle of one some day enroute to the noose.

If they *really* knew anything about guns, they'd have tried to confiscate all the scoped hunting rifles. They are, however, getting around to this. Recall the proposed ban on *"cop killer ammunition"* able to pierce bulletproof vests? Such means, practically speaking, nearly *all* rifle cartridges given their high velocities. (Say *bye-bye* to your .30-30, your .30-06, etc. Heck, even a .22LR will perforate most vests.)

So, if you *truly* cherish your residual liberties, then you simply must have a battle rifle. Wars are not won with pistols, any more than homes are built with Leatherman tools.

Every government can become genocidal. Your best life-preserver is personal ownership of a military-type semi-automatic rifle.
— Jay Simkin

First, I'll cover the six general designs of self-loading, mag fed, semi-auto combat rifles (battle and carbine):

AK (including the SKS variants)
Garand (M1, M1 Carbine, M14/M1A, and the Ruger Mini-14)
FAL
HK
AR15 (and South Korean Daewoo)
bullpups (AUG, FA-MAS, L85A1, Bushmaster M17)

Later, in Chapters 10 and 11, I'll thoroughly discuss and compare .308 battle rifles and .223 battle carbines.

WHAT ABOUT FULL-AUTOS?

At 600 rounds per minute, how many minutes can you carry?
— Douglas P. Bell

As Clint Smith of Thunder Ranch puts it, *"They only turn money into noise."* I rather agree. Tactically, "spray and pray" full-auto stuff is wasteful of ammo and your rounds/KIA ratio goes way up. In WWI the ratio was 10,000, in WWII 25,000, Korea 50,000, and in Vietnam it was over *100,000* rounds/KIA. Folks, firepower is *hits* per minute—*not* rounds per minute. Snipers in all of these wars averaged *1.5*rds per confirmed kill.

This aside, lawful Title II *NFA34* weapons are Ø2,000+, not to mention the Ø200 BATF tax stamp, the fingerprinting, the 4-6 month wait, etc. Finally, Title II owners can expect their 200,000 lawful weapons to be confiscated within 10 years. Do you *really* think that the feds will continue to allow Americans to own M16s, .30-06 BARs, .50BMG M2s, and 20mm Solothurns? No matter that only *two* of these registered weapons has *ever* been used in a crime since the *NFA* began in 1934 (in both instances by police officers, I understand). "They" cannot allow us to retain this kind of weaponry.

While finding (or converting) unregistered full-auto stuff is apparently easy enough, the risk is too steep. You'll have to store it away from home. Finding a remote place to practice without being turned in is a real hassle. Getting caught with it is a felony, and you'll lose your 2nd Amendment rights (what little are still recognized.) It's more trouble than it's worth.

COMBAT RIFLE CRITERIA

A superior combat rifle must:

❶ Function flawlessly in combat conditions.
❷ Deliver high-energy projectiles.
❸ Deliver them accurately.
❹ Handle well.
❺ Reload quickly.
❻ Field-strip easily.

❶ FLAWLESS FUNCTIONING

If the rifle is not 100% (*i.e.,* 99.9999%) reliable, then its accuracy and power are rather moot. It must work—*period*. Reliability and ruggedness are the most important qualities of a battle rifle. For example, much though I dislike some of the controls of the HK and Galil, they are stone reliable rifles and must be given their due.

➋ DELIVER HIGH-ENERGY BULLETS

The cartridge must have sufficient energy to incapacitate the enemy, often after having to perforate cover, foliage, or the target's own web gear and flak vest. As I'll amply explain later, the .308 is far superior to the .223 in this regard.

➌ ACCURACY

Firepower is *hits* per minute, not rounds (*i.e.,* misses) per minute. In my view, the *minimum* acceptable accuracy for a battle rifle is 4MOA (*e.g.,* 20" at 500yds). Anything worse than begins to really reduce effective range.

➍ ERGONOMICS, ➎ RELOADING

A combat rifle is simply a specialized hand tool. It is held and operated by human hands, and a good ergonomic design is vital. Some rifles have better controls than others. As I'll soon explain, the AR15 generally has the best (with the FAL being a close second), and the AK47 has the worst.

A combat rifle's controls are the bolt handle, the bolt stop/release (if any), the safety, the mag release, the trigger, and the sights. How they are laid out and how they work is crucial. Remember, if you have to resort to firing a combat rifle at somebody, then things must be pretty serious. You need every edge possible, especially since motor skills degrade under stress. You need a rifle that works *with* you, not against you.

Right-handed vs. left-handed controls

I'd give my right arm to be ambidextrous.
    — unknown

The strong (also called "primary" or "gun") hand holds the rifle and pulls the trigger. *Ideally,* it should also thumb the safety and index finger the mag release.

Your weak (also called "secondary" or "support") hand steadies the rifle at the handguard and reloads. *Ideally,* it should operate the bolt handle and mag release.

A good design allows your hands to work in concert *with* each other. The strong hand holds and fires the rifle, while the weak hand loads, reloads, unloads, and clears malfunctions. As 89% of shooters are right-handed, rifles properly designed for them is the *second*-best conceptual goal. (Perfect ergonomic ambidexterity is quite problematic, although the HK G36 nearly qualifies with its left-or-right side bolt handle.) Bullpups cannot be fired from the left shoulder because of their right side ejection port (lefties must learn to fire them opposite shoulder).

Ironically enough, certain combat rifles *do* work very well for lefties. It is the *older* generation rifles of the 1930s and 1940s such as the M1 Garand (and its derivatives, such as the M14, M1A, Mini-14, and Mini-30) and the AK47 which have their bolt handle mistakenly placed on the *right* side (happily operated by a lefty's weak/secondary/support hand). Except for the AK, they also have ambidextrous *center*-mounted safeties and mag releases—the ergonomic total of which makes for a, functionally speaking, left-handed gun. (Note: While the center-mounted mag release is tolerable enough, I personally don't care much for the Garand-style trigger guard safety, which to be disengaged requires the trigger finger to *enter* the guard barely in front of the trigger of a Condition 1 weapon. Try it with gloves! A much larger trigger guard would have greatly lessened the potential hazard of this otherwise clever design.)

So, the lefty has available a fine *ergonomic* choice of decent (though not superior) combat rifles in *all* the standard flavors: .223 (Mini-14 and AK47), 5.45x39 (AK74), 7.62x39 (Mini-30 and AK47), .308 (M14/M1A), and .30-06 (M1 Garand). Of these four, I'd favor the M1A, which is rugged, powerful, reliable, and accurate. Affordable parts are available, which is very important. (Downside: Mags are Ø40+.)

However, the more properly a combat rifle is designed for *right*-handers (*e.g.*, the AR15, FAL, and HK), the naturally more difficult their smooth operation is for lefties. It's no coincidence that these rifles are 1950s and 1960s designs (derived from the fine WWII StG44 carbine with left-side bolt handle) which reflect long-awaited advances in ergonomics (for righties, at least). However, just because a modern rifle has an ergonomic edge over the M1A or AK, doesn't mean that you should automatically choose it. Ergonomics must be contrasted against reliability and accuracy, which are more important.

The obvious next wave in ergonomic development is true ambidexterity (*e.g.,* HK's new G36, a.k.a. the SL8-1). In the meantime, lefties with deep pockets can adapt certain rifles (*e.g.,* the AR15) with left-handed controls, including even the upper (*e.g.,* the "Southpaw" AR15 from DPMS). While this won't result in a perfect lefty AR, at least you 11% of the shooting population are at last beginning to be *heard.*

Reloading

Since combat rifles are reloaded often, the next three controls are very important. When you're reloading under fire, speed is everything. The difference between, for example, an AR15 (2 seconds) and an AK (4-6 seconds) is crucial. In a firefight a *lot* can happen in those extra 2-4 seconds an AK needs.

Bolt handle (ideally, a weak-hand control)

This control is probably the most operated of all. It is used to load/unload, and to clear malfs. **It *must* be easily accessible and hand friendly under coarse, hurried exertion.** Examples: most accessible is the FAL (left-side front-receiver), instead of HK (handguard), or AR (rear-receiver); least accessible is the AK (you must with your left hand reach *under* a long 30rd mag, or turn it 90° right-side up). Most hand friendly is the FAL (fat and round); least hand friendly the AK (thin and sharp); moderate is the AR (drawbar catch is thin and serrated —consider adding a tac latch from QP).

Right side or left side bolt handle?

As a weak-hand control, a bolt handle should be on the left. Unfortunately, only the AR15, FAL, and HK are so set up. The Garand, AK, and Daewoo systems require the left hand to work from *underneath* the rifle—an awkward concept. (The Galil at least has a top-manipulated bolt handle, which is the best of the AK variants.)

Mag release button (right-hand control)

While your left hand is moving a new mag up, the right hand should be pressing the mag release, which should gravity-drop the empty mag. Only the AR15 and the Daewoo are set up correctly. (So is the little M1 Carbine, but it's not in a real rifle cartridge. Some FAL and HK variants also have this release.)

All other combat rifles require the *left* hand to operate the release. This is a faulty design as the left hand is *already* busy holding a new mag. (*Never* dump the old mag before gripping a new one.) Therefore, specialized techniques are necessary for successful "double-duty" of the left hand.

Leisurely tactical reloads behind cover during a lull in the fight present no problem for any combat rifle, however, when an empty load is demanded, the AR15 and Daewoo are best.

Bolt lock/release button (left-hand control)

The bolt should lock back after the last round. After some practice, you'll feel the sensory difference and automatically know to change mags and release the bolt. (Neither the AK nor the HK have automatic hold-opens. The AR15 and Daewoo do, and the bolt release button is properly placed on the left side.) Once the new mag is inserted, the left hand then trips the bolt release to charge the chamber, and smoothly moves up to the forestock. The FAL has a proper left-hand bolt stop/release, though not a right-side mag release. The AR15 is better still.

The HK bolt can lock back in an MP40-style notch and is slapped forward by the left hand enroute to the forestock.

The SKS bolt does lock back, but has no release button.

The AK is by far the worst offender. Since it has no bolt lock, you won't know you've run dry until pull #31 goes *"click!"* Now, you've got a terrifying 4-6 seconds of empty gun panic while the AK's crappy ergonomics become obvious. The left hand must (after changing mags) go underneath the rifle to rack the bolt, then return to the forestock. How 1947. Atrocious. (Commie engineers ignored vital *human* factors in their designs, which mirrors Communism's *anti*-human stance.)

Safety (right-hand control)

The AR15, HK, FAL, and Galil have *thumb*-operated safeties. The Garand systems require the trigger finger. The AK is atrocious; the right hand cannot simultaneously retain a shooting grip and operate the safety.

Overview

While this discussion has probably awakened you to the necessity of well-designed controls, you can't fully appreciate this until you train with different rifles and *personally* learn their differences. While the AK is cheap and utterly reliable, its controls are *abysmal*. While the AR15 is expensive, complex, and a touch finicky, its controls are just about perfect.

If you want a bargain rifle to blast away with on weekends, then the Chinese MAK-90 is your toy. But, if you're *serious* about your combat rifle, then you'll choose an AR15 or M1A or FAL. Superior controls are vital to staying alive. If I've convinced you of this point, then get to Thunder Ranch *ASAP* for Urban Rifle 1. Until you've been to gun school, you can't appreciate what you don't know. Go now, while you *can*.

❻ FIELD-STRIPPING

Battle rifles are heavily used tools in adverse condtions, and must be maintainable in the field. Modularity (*i.e.,* a system comprising sub-systems) makes repair easy—merely swap out a trigger group or bolt. No tools should be needed to field-strip a rifle (the HK and AUG are brilliant in this regard).

MARKSMANSHIP

Rifle marksmanship is a civilian attribute which is alien to the military environment. It must be introduced into the military by force and can be kept in the military only by ongoing active measures, else it will be eradicated and replaced by equipment familiarity.
    — 14th Iron Law of Marksmanship

How are we doing with rifle marksmanship? By Viet-Nam, wasn't everything beyond 200 meters abandoned to crew-served weapons?
    During Viet-Nam, troops pulled back from the line for R&R were tested to reveal that they could on average pump out 300 rounds a minute at a target 50 meters away at a rifle range, and they would average making one hit per minute. During the American Revolution, the enemy (British) advised their officers that even at over 200 yards the American riflemen will hit with his first shot, so officers should conduct themselves accordingly. Also, that these riflemen could reach as far as 300 yards.
    As flintlock riflemen can pump out a maximum of only four rounds per minute, it is obvious that the Viet-Nam troopers have 75 times the firepower (i.e., cyclic rate) of the flintlock riflemen of the Revolution. This is in terms of muzzle statistics. In terms of target statistics, the flintlock shooter has four times the firepower of the M16 user because [he] has the skill to make every shot a hit and the M16 user [cannot hit more than once per minute within 50M].

The military does not teach rifle marksmanship. It teaches equipment familiarity. Despite what the officer corps thinks, learning to shoot a rifle is not like learning to drive a car. Instead, it is like learning to play the violin. You can have coherent-appearing results after equipment familiarity training, but to get the real results you must keep plodding on. The equipment familiarity learning curve comes up quick, but then the rifle marksmanship continuation of the curve rises very slowly,...by shooting one careful shot at a time, carefully inspecting the result [and the cause].

— Darryl Davis, "On The Subject of Marksmanship...,"
MILITARY, February 1998, p.18-19

We have lost the concept of riflery (which won the Revolutionary War). In order to win the next one, we must become riflemen again. I'm not talking about benchrest target practice. I mean being able to hit a Bad Guy offhand at 300yds with a .308.

FEATURES & SPECIFICATIONS

After two generations of practical history with mag-fed, semi-auto, combat rifles, we have come to learn what *works* and what is *necessary*—so there is no need to reinvent the square wheel. Read and heed the below.

barrels

Barrel length means bullet velocity, which means energy. Unless a rifle was *particularly* needed for indoors CQB or for frequent deployment from vehicles, there's usually no good reason to shorten barrel length under 20", and certainly not under 16". This is especially true for .308s, which really should have at least a 19" barrel (if not 20") to avoid excessive muzzle blast, and to maintain high muzzle velocities.

The .223, however, can tolerate a 16" barrel without much additional muzzle blast, although muzzle velocity (of 3250fps from a 20") is reduced to 3000fps. Since the .223's energy is much more conditional than the .308 on *velocity* than its flyweight bullets, and since its terminal ballistics of bullet fragmentation *depend* upon velocities of at least 2800fps, that loss of 250fps shortens the *hyper*-effective (*i.e.*, multiple wound channels from bullet shattering) range from 150yds to 75yds.

Moral: Stick with the rifle's *full* length barrel unless there are highly compelling reasons to require a shorter tube.

flash suppressor

This is a *must* as 70% of defensive shooting is done in conditions of low/altered/failing light. The muzzle flash plume *without* a suppressor can be up to *2 feet* and is quite blinding. Available for FAL- and AR-type muzzle threads is the Smith Vortex suppressor (order from QP). It's *the* best, eliminating 99% of the flash. (Avoid theØ25 copies; their softer steel splays open with firing). QP also offers the Phantom, which doesn't catch on foliage (or break a tang) as the Vortex can.

pistol grip

This is a great improvement over the straight stock, especially in heavier .308 rifles. A pistol grip adds to the rifle's handling and sense of balance. Important, though not crucial.

magazines

Affordable quality mags are a key issue, as you should have *at least* 20 mags for each combat rifle. 30-50 mags are even better. Why so *many?* Because mags are "consumables." They fail, they get lost, and they are discarded in a firefight. You'll need lots of spares. (Remember, without its mag a semi-auto is just a single-shot.)

The most rugged mags are for the HK and AK, followed by the M14 and the FAL. The flimsy AR mags have the most problems, so I recommend having *30% more* of them.

sling

Every rifle (and shotgun) *must* have a sling, which is used more for *carrying* than for shooting steadiness. Remember, a pistol is what you use to fight your way *back* to your *rifle,* which you probably left behind because it didn't have a sling.

> *The sling is to a rifle what the holster is to a pistol. If you have a sling, chances are you will keep the rifle with you.* If there is no sling present, you will set the rifle down. When you are at the absolutely farthest point away from the rifle that you can possibly get, you'll need it.
> — Clint Smith, Founder/Director of Thunder Ranch

For your combat rifle, the simpler the better. G.I. 1¼" webbing works fine. At the *forestock* end there should be no excess sling, as this end and its keeper are not to be adjusted. Adjustment of sling length is to be done solely at the *buttstock* loop. Holding your rifle muzzle down, adjust sling for about 8-10" of parallel-to-ground buttstock slack. (More slack might be required for larger shooters or for thicker winter clothing.)

Through both keepers, loop the sling to the outside *away* from the rifle, and then leave enough length to loop *back over and through* the keeper in reverse. This secures the sling from pulling through a keeper. (Remember *Diehard* McLane's MP5 sling pulling through in the elevator shaft?)

I'm testing *The Claw* from Quake Industries (406-388-3411), which is made of a nonslipping rubbery material. While it is a bit heavier, it certainly doesn't roll off my shoulder easily. (It needs to have 1¼" webbing, not merely 1".) Also, its swivels are made of Zytel and thus very quiet. So far, so good.

iron sights

As Clint Smith is also fond of saying, *"Two weeks after the Balloon goes up, iron sights will rule the world."* Meaning, there's a natural entropy to Buck Rogers combat technology—things just have a way of devolving to their simplest state. Laser target designators and illuminated reticles are great—*while* they work. Moral: *Keep It Simple, Stupid.* Make sure your combat rifle has iron sights, that they're zeroed for all duty ammo, and that you can use them well.

tritium sights

These glow in the dark so you can pick up your sights. Tritium is a radioactive isotope of hydrogen with a half-life of 12.26 years. (They once used Promethium 147, but its half-life was only 2.6 years.) Effective life of tritium sights are 5-10 years. (They're the one gun part you can't stock up on!) The gas is housed in a tough sapphire crystal, and even if it breaks, the amount of radioactivity is less than a chest X-ray.

optical sights

[Mil-spec quality tactical scopes] *are not cheap, but they are, in my opinion, worth it. The optical or scope sight has advantages over iron sights that may make the difference in low light, in situations where the visibility of iron sights is diminished, or where visual identification of a small, obscured target is desired.* (at 60)
— Gabriel Suarez; *The Tactical Rifle* (1999)

The Ø700 Elcan 3.4X scope from Canada is superb. It mounts zero-hold/QD on flattop uppers, has an A2-style rear sight dial for quick 300-800yds elevation changes (available for 5.56 or 7.62), and its tritium post is replaceable. (Keep the iron sight carry handle with you!)

The ACOGs are also highly regarded and rugged optical sights which either mount on flattops or AR carry handles. QP sells them all, along with their mounts (AR15 carry handle channel, or Weaver/Picatinny rail). ACOGs are best for CQB.

The Israeli Army likes the C-More for their M16s. While it's battery powered, you can use the iron sights when the batteries go or if the unit fails. Ø345 from Dillon.

U.S. Optics has a full range of very high quality Mil-Spec optics, with phenomenal lenses.

light

Tactically/morally/legally, you cannot shoot at what you cannot see and identify, and 70% of defensive shooting is done in non-daylight conditions. Every defensive rifle and shotgun should have an *attached* flashlight. If you don't believe me, then stay at the firing range after dusk and try to hit your target without one. Sure-Fire lights from Laser Products are the *only* way to go, and since the 6P and 9P have 1" bodies, scope rings can attach them to any Weaver rail.

miscellaneous recommendations

Your combat rifle should have a self-contained cleaning kit and rod (not just for cleaning, but to remove a stuck case), and misc. spare parts (*e.g.,* firing pin, extractor, front sight, etc.), broken case extractor, oil, ear plugs, and mag charger. If possible, attach a last-ditch spare mag (to perhaps the buttstock or handguard). If your rifle's buttstock does not have a compartment (*e.g.,* the FAL), then perhaps a laced/Velcroed-on buttpouch could hold these items.

Testing the War Weapons

After *Boston on Guns & Courage*, I ran across *Testing the War Weapons* by Timothy Mullin and learned much from it. A former infantryman and U.S. Marshal, and friend/colleague of *Unintended Consequences* author John Ross, Mullin tested 100 of the world's most notable combat rifles. Some important considerations which I had in 1998 overlooked or glossed over are:

❶ Quality of the rifle's trigger remains very important.
❷ The handguard *must* have adequate heat protection.
❸ The rifle *must* self-contain a cleaning rod and tool kit.
❹ The rifle should feel *"alive"* in one's hands.
❺ The most famous rifles are not always the *best* rifles.
❻ French weapons really weren't all *that* bad!

COMBAT RIFLE CARTRIDGES

Let's compare the three common combat cartridges. I didn't have figures for U.S. military ball past 500, so the .223 and .308 below are Federal Match (69gr/.223 and 168gr/.308) from Major Plaster's *The Ultimate Sniper*. The .308FM shoots almost as flat as NATO M118 Match, while the 55 and 62gr .223 ball shoot flatter than the 69gr FM (though with not as good energy retention). Nonetheless, this table is very illuminating.

Ballistic Comparison: .223 vs. 7.62x39 vs. .308 (in yards)

velocity	Muzzle	100	200	300	400	600	800	1,000
5.45x39	2950							
.223 (69gr)	3000	2720	2460	2210	1980	1560	1240	1060
7.62x39	2340	2080	1836	1606	1388	1051		
.308 (168gr)	2600	2420	2240	2070	1910	1610	1360	1170

energy	Muzzle	100	200	300	400	600	800	1,000
5.45x39	1045							
.223	1380	1134	925	750	600	375	235	170
7.62x39	1485	1172	913	699	522	299		
.308	2520	2180	1870	1600	1355	970	690	510

trajectory"		100	200	300	400	600	800	1,000
5.45x39								
.223		zero	-3.2	-12.2	-28.3	-89	-207	-405
7.62x39		zero	-7.6	-29.2	-72.0	-145		
.308		zero	-4.5	-15.9	-35.5	-105	-228	-421

WHAT ABOUT THE 7.62x39?

The 7.62x39
While the 7.62x39 has a *bit* more energy than the .223 (unnoticeable by the recipient, I'm sure) out to 181yds, the .223 with its higher BC catches up, shoots flatter, and is easier to procure. Granted, the 69gr BT Fed Match will *not* (because of its lower MV) shoot quite as flat as the 55 and 62gr ball, but this rough comparison is still helpful.

The 7.62x39, with its low velocity and stubby 123gr bullet, quickly runs out of gas past 400yds. The overall round is inefficient, trading length for fatness, thus increasing magazine height for no good reason. Yes, the 7.62x39 meets its <300M design parameters (which were flawed, as were the .223's).

The Czech 7.62x45
If you're going to have a case head width of 11.35mm, then you might as well increase the length for more case capacity, which would make a nice sort of ".308 Lite." The Czechs did exactly that in the 1950s to make their 7.62x45 giving 130/2440 for 1626fpe. (The renowned Rhodesian guerrilla tracker David Scott-Donelan remarked that the 7.62x45 was an excellent combat round.) Had this case been necked down to .257 to give 120/2550 for 1699fpe, it would have been a *much* better ballistic choice (given the .257's superior BC and SD), with even more reliable feeding. But, I digress.

7.62x39 vs. .223?
So, for North American use, I *highly* recommend the .223 over the 7.62x39. You should train with cheaper 55gr (*e.g.*, the accurate Malasian, South African, or Venezuelan ball) and save your 62gr SS109/M855 for that Rainy Decade.

Battle carbines in 7.62x39
The *only* way I'd choose 7.62x39 over .223 is if I had a *lot* of people to equip on a *very* tight budget.

First choice
The 16"bbl SKS Sporter which uses AK mags (except for the drums, and even these will work with a bit of mag well whittling). Although I'm getting ahead of Chapter 11, with its superior ergonomics and accuracy the SKS/AK mag whipped its AK47 cousin (which had no advantage in weight, ruggedness, or

reliability). While I knew that I favored the SKS/AK-mag over the AK, I was surprised to see how much the AK lost out by. The SKS/AK goes for about Ø325; Ø100 less than the Maadi AK. For Ø70 you can get a Chinese 4X scope/rings/see-through mount, which will increase the effective range out to 400yds (assuming at least a 4MOA gun). 30rd mags are still under Ø10, and you should have at *least* 12 per rifle, carried in the 4 mag pouches. Be sure to invest in the complete spare parts kit for Ø35. Having an extra barrel, set of sights, and trigger group is a good idea. If you're really fond of it, then send it out for Parkerizing, as the Chinese steel rusts easily.

If a Ø325 AK-mag SKS is too expensive, then get the 10rd fixed mag version for Ø175 (no, they're not Ø100 any more!). Attach a new 20 fixed mag (the 30rd is too tall) and feed it with stripper clipped ammo. Spend an extra Ø75 for the high quality Russian SKS, if you can.

Second choice

The newly imported pistol grip Romanian for Ø230 dealer is reliable and 3MOA accurate (with better ammo). (The Bulgarian AK is O.K., too.) Granted, I'd love a pre-ban Hungarian or Russian AK, but will not spend the Ø1,000+.

7.62x39 ammo

Good-quality Russian ammo (NC/Berdan) can still be had by the case (*i.e.*, 1000rds) for about 8¢/rd, and I'd *hurry*. While boxer primed 7.62x39 exists in good quantity now, considering the cheap Russian stuff, why reload? (This goes for .223, too.) By the way, Wolf 7.62x39 is quite inaccurate, although their 5.45x39 and 7.62x54R is pretty good.

You'll need 5,000rds for training and practice, and another 5,000rds for the field. Who *wants* to reload 10,000rds per rifle, anyway? You're spending a lot of time without saving any real money. Simply stock up while you can. Surplus can *always* be sold later. **There's no such thing as *too* much ammo.** Spend *lots* of time and ammo in training—that's what ammo is *for*!

WHAT ABOUT THE 5.45x39?

This was very cleverly done. The Russian .221 bullet is a 52gr VLD (very low drag) with high BC and lots of SD (sectional density, for penetration). Instead of relying upon a downrange 2800+fps for bullet shattering, the 5.45 is designed to yaw (*i.e.*, tumble "head-over-heels") during terminal ballistics. This is done by making the 54gr bullet with a cone air pocket, which moves the center of gravity aft, behind the center of pressure. Upon impact, the base of the bullet swings around, causing a greater wound channel. Insidious stuff. So, for 16% less bullet weight and 8% less round weight than our M193 5.56x45, the Russian 5.45x39 provides the same lethality out to 300yds.

There is a trade-off, however. Because of lead core and air pocket variances, the bullet is not as gyroscopically stable as an FMJ bullet. Hence, accuracy can suffer, and some ammo is only 5MOA. (A better approach was the MK VII .303 Enfield bullet, which used aluminum in the forward third. CG was moved aft without sacrificing stability.)

Still, the 5.45x39 cannot compare with M855/SS109 62gr .223, and barely matches the M193 55gr.

Non-corrosive steel case ammo from Wolf abounds at Ø100/1000. This is 60gr stuff thrown at 2950fps (1156fpe), and it is quite accurate (2MOA) out of my Romanian AK74.

5.45x39 rifles

Romanian AK74s are Ø240 dealer, and are better rifles than the average AK. They have a decent two-stage trigger, and improved bolt handle (it's slightly angled up and is easier to manipulate). Accuracy at 2MOA is superb for an AK. (I astounded a friend of mine by routinely hitting, offhand with iron sights, a bathtub-sized boulder at a confirmed 800m.)

While I would not recommend that anybody field with an AK74 unless they've tons of ammo and dozens of mags, it *is* a capable carbine out to 300. The composite/steel mags are quite hardy, but weigh 0.52lbs, so carry most of your ammo in stripper clips. 30rd mags are only Ø6-10, depending on how many and from whom.

I would not recommend the AK74 muzzle brake due to the horrific muzzle blast and basketball-sized flash signature.

Since the Commie hordes have converted (or are now converting) from AK47 to the AK74, and since we don't know what the future might bring, having such a rifle might not be a bad idea. As my AK74 is so accurate (for an AK), I'm keeping it for training and will treat it to an excellent I.O.R. Valdada 4X M2 scope. (My AKs in 7.62x39 I've sold off. 6MOA never did it for me.)

.223 OR NOT .223?

*The .223 round is a marginal performer against humans. Al-though it offers certain advantages over handgun rounds or shotgun rounds, **you must be careful to not expect too much.** (p.40)*
— Gabriel Suarez; *The Tactical Rifle* (1999)

The large wound cavity of the 55gr is produced by bullet *fragmentation* (usually at the cannelure), which occurs only if impact velocity is at least 2800fps. Such velocities may be expected only within 150yds (for 20" barrels) and within 75yds for 16" barrels. At farther ranges, no bullet fragmentation will occur and the round's lethality (marginal at best) is significantly reduced.

The .223 is also a poor penetrator, which is good or bad depending on its intended use. You'll be surprised to learn that the 9mm, .40S&W, and .45ACP better perforate walls, car doors, and windshields. The .223 simply breaks up too easily (it was *designed* to fragment without *Geneva Convention*-prohibited hollowpoint construction).

The 55gr M193 round

This was the original bullet for the 5.56x45. Since it was designed for a slower twist of 1:12", many folks have discovered an accuracy reduction of 20-30% when using M193 in barrels with a mere 1:9" twist (and even more in Colt 1:7" barrels).

The 62gr SS109/M855 round

The .223 is, regardless of loading, very flat shooting, though has meager energy to deliver past 400yds.

The 62gr steel core bullet (decided on in 1985) is a substantial improvement in lethality and long range perforation. It also retains its energy better than the 55gr.

I've heard that the new Russian 62gr ammo made by the JSC Barnaul Machine and Tool Plant is 2MOA stuff, and costs less than Ø150/1000rds.

55gr vs. 62gr.

If you've got a modern A2 or A3 rifle (*i.e.,* with 1:7" or 1:9" twist), then train with 55gr (because it's much cheaper) but field with 62gr (because it's more effective).

A1 rifles with 1:12" twist can use only 55gr bullets. (The slow twist will *not* stabilize the 62gr. and you'll get 12" groups at 100yds. *"Honey, is it me, or the ammo?"*)

Higher bullet weights than 62gr?
If the 62gr load is better than the 55gr, then why not a 75 or 80gr bullet in the same .223 caliber?

Moreover, necking up the .223 case to seat a 100gr 6mm Sierra BTSP (.430BC/.242SD) still falls within the 2.250" COL mag restriction. The 6x45, while not as flat shooting as the .223, much better retains longer range energy. (What the 5.56x45 *should* have been was a 100gr 6x*48*.)

.223 conclusion

I used to *pooh-pooh* the .223 in favor of the .308 (and I still do to an extent), however, I'm now more accepting of the .223 than I was. Out to 300yds the .223 is *fairly* capable—assuming you won't be shooting in strong wind or through heavy cover.

.223 vs. .308
ammo/mag weight

1000rds	weight	space
5.45x39	34lbs	5x12x9½"
.223	40lbs	6x13½x13½"
7.62x39	45lbs	12¾x9x10"
.308	60lbs	7x16½x15"
.30-06	62lbs	7x18x15"

While an FAL is only 2½lbs heavier than an AR15, .308 ammo and mags take up *1½ times* more weight and *3 times* more carrying space than the .223. For example, an AR15 30rd mag pouch holding three mags will hold just two .308 20rd mags. An Eagle tactical vest will hold *12* AR15 30rd mags, versus only 6/20rd .308 mags. **A .308 bullet *alone* is heavier than an entire *round* of .223.** For a long patrol, humping an FAL, 10 loaded 20rd mags, and 200 extra rounds in stripper clips is *work*. The same 400 rounds in a AR15's system would weigh *20lbs* less, and 20lbs either way on a long patrol means a *lot*.

Put another way, a battle load of 10k (22lbs) in different systems (*i.e.,* rifle, mags, and ammo) would be:

FAL	7.62x51	9 mags	20rd @	180rds
AK47	7.62x39	7 mags	30rd @	210rds
AKM	7.62x39	8 mags	30rd @	240rds
AK74	5.45x39	12 mags	30rd @	360rds
AR15	5.56x45	15 mags	30rd @	450rds

Q: Is the .308 *worth* it?
A: *Yes*.

Performance: .223 vs. .308

*No responsible deer hunter would shoot an animal at 300 yards with [a .223 or 7.62x39], and I find it odd that they are considered suitable for a human—the most dangerous animal on earth (because only a human can inflict injuries from a distance). I do not believe we need to take bear cartridges to war, **but we do need to take white-tail cartridges, at least**.* (Hear, hear! BTP)
— Timothy J. Mullin; *Testing the War Weapons*, p. 410

It's just extra comforting having a .308 over a .223. The .308 is effective out to 600yds, and, in *very* capable hands and rifle, out to 900. Many have survived torso (and even head) shots with the .223, but the .308 seems to put 'em down for good. The fact that *any* FBI agents survived that 11 April 1986 Florida gunfight is largely because Bad Guys Platt and Matix fortunately used a .223 (Mini-14) instead of a .308.

Test medium	.223	.308
concrete at 100yds	1.4"	4"
¼" boiler plate steel	100yds	300yds
door of '68 Dodge	300yds (barely)	400yds (easily)

[Because they use .22 caliber battle carbines and not .308 battle rifles], infantry squads of both the East and the West will no longer be able to rely on small arms for engaging barricaded targets in urban areas and will have to rely instead on grenades, rockets, and crew-served weapons.
— Andy Tillman, *"Test-Fire Report: The AK-74"*

.308—The *winner*!

As you see, round weight *does* correlate to performance. Yeah, the .308 round *is* 1½ times as heavy, but it gives 2-3 times the *energy* (depending on range). While a .223 weighs much less, you'll have to give your targets more rounds to drop 'em than you would with a .308. TANSTAAFL, folks.

If I were somehow limited to only one of the two, then I'd choose the .308. You'll pay more in Ø and sweat, but it's truly an *awesome* cartridge. Besides, never forget that your enemy will have at best a mere 7.62x39, 5.45x39, or .223. Finally, they will have grenades, rockets, and crew-served weapons. We won't, so we will have to perforate their cover the "old-fashioned" WWI/WWII/Korea way: with a full-power .30 cartridge.

Since rifles are for neutralizing long-distance threats, choose the .308 over the .223. Although the .223 will sometimes (and even often) suffice, it's in all honesty limited to 300yds through light cover, while a .308 will go through 12" of tree, or drop a Bad Guy out to 800yds. You can sportingly hunt deer and elk with a .308, but not with a .223. **Get a .308 first.**

If you can't decide, then own *both* and choose when you need to. I'd routinely carry an AR15 on long patrols, but if a heavy scene were anticipated then I'd swap for a .308. (Granted, if I *knew* that I would *not* also have swap access to a .308, then I'd probably field with an M1A or FAL.)

Or, use the .223 for indoors defense, and the .308 for outdoors.

Another option is to carry an AR15 and backpack a lightweight, scoped .308 bolt with 40-60 Match grade rounds.

❖ 10

RATING THE
BATTLE RIFLES

Battle carbines/calibers *do* have their place (*e.g.*, CQB, urban fighting, perimeter defense, etc.), but one must always keep in mind their significant limitations. To wit: they cannot perforate much cover, and *effective* range is only 200-300 yards.

Take the .308 (or .30-06 or .303 or 8x57), however. It *will* strike an incapacitating blow as far as its shooter can hit with iron sights (*i.e.*, about 600 yards). It *will* perforate much battlefield cover, including trees and light steel. As a Vietnam vet friend remarked, *"There's no hiding from a .308!"* Amen.

It's been widely known for a long time that wars are not won by pistols. What we're now realizing is that wars are not won by even battle carbines. Afghanistan provided the perfect example: Guerrillas with "antiquated" bolt-action .303s fought off Soviet invaders armed with modern full-auto .22s (AK74s in 5.45x39), jet fighter-bombers, and helicopter gunships.

*Whatever rifle you have is fine—**as long as you can outshoot your opponent. The best way to do that is to be "at home" at 300-500 yards, and engage your opponent where his** [battle carbine] **fire is relatively ineffective.***

One of your best strategies is to get together with at least one or two others and shoot together. Practice primary and alternate targets [target assignment], and work out SOPs—like fire one mag and move to a designated spot and fire a second mag. Avoid doubling up on a target unless you consider it extra-valuable to take out fast! Work out a strategy for teams working together, but physically independent. Figure out how to be flexible with two teams—how they can be mutually supportive. You'll figure out that two riflemen working as a team are worth as much as 8 or 10 individual uncoordinated riflemen. The future will not belong to the loners, and not to the hiders, **but to those who are riflemen**, and who can work together to double or triple not only their effectiveness on the target, but also their protective factor.

One, **become a rifleman**—be able to keep all your shots in one inch at 25yds, and know your sight settings out to 500 yards. **Two, link up with at least two other people; encourage them to become rifle-trained, and shoot together!** Three, spread the word about shooting as a tradition and the need to pass it on to the next generation...

Every shot fired in this country to better your shooting skills, to make yourself more valuable as a potential defender of the Constitution, is a shot fired for freedom.

— *Fred's*, 1 February 2000, *The Shotgun News*, p.77

Moral: **While you can defend your *home* with a .223, your *Liberty* can be preserved only by a .308.** Whichever battle rifle you prefer—M1, M1A, FAL, or HK91—*get one now*! Training with your own honest-to-God main battle rifle should be the first priority of every professed lover of freedom. Get one today, even if you have to sell your AR15 to do it.

EMAIL TO "FRED"

Halfway through writing this chapter, I sent the below email to "Fred" of Fred's M14 Stocks (www.fredsm14stock.com). He has a great column in *The Shotgun News* (usually on p.71), which every American gunowner should regularly read. The below was partially printed in Volume 55, Issue 19, page 71 (55/19/71):

Fred,

Nice reply to DRP, the AK47 fan. I have recently wrung out a milled receiver Bulgarian AK, which "treated" me to 6MOA/100yds with Russian Wolf FMJ. In fact, the gun seemed to like only Lapua FMJ (4MOA—oooooh!), but who's going to feed steak to a junkyard dog? Handloading for an AK is worse still. Because of the dent/crease/cut the AK puts on its cases (like ringing a tree), reloading for it is like taking a Bic lighter in for repair! (Why bother?!) In short, the AK47 (regardless of mfg; stamped or milled receiver) is not a viable long-gun past 150yds. THAT'S why they're called CARBINES, folks!

Your explanation of how picking the wrong rifle will set too low a standard for marksmanship was spot on. Pick a real RIFLE instead.

Hitting with power is what counts. The AK47 does neither at rifle ranges—and while the AR15A2 can hit, it has little power.

Boys, give up your carbine toys for a real Man's weapon—a .308 battle rifle.

As to which battle rifle, my opinion (hardening into a conviction) has been changing since 8/2000 when "Boston's Gun Bible" came out. As a hint, I sold my AR10A4 (dirty gas system, mere O.K. accuracy, vicious muzzle blast, part/mag scarcity). My field opinion of the 91 (especially the modern clones) has worsened, although I'm still endeared to the genuine HK rifle. So, guess who owns more M1s and M1As these days?

M1A vs. the FAL? Can't say right now, but know that the M14/M1A has gone up quite a few points in the new competition. The more I shoot it, the more I like it. (This goes also equal with the M1 Garand—especially a quality Springfield Armory version in .308, which you can afford to feed.)

In short, I have recently de-emphasized two areas: Ergonomics (slightly), and Affordability (greatly). As you so well explained, "Cost will not matter when it comes to defending yourself, your family or your freedom. Effectiveness is the criteria, and the M1A, for the Rifleman, is more effective than the AK." Yeah, FAL mags are $5-10 vs. $40-50 for M1A mags, but this has become much less a big deal to me lately.

Finally, I now much more emphasize Reliability. I recently wrung out a DSA FAL (the best FAL made today, if not ever), which on two occasions left a bullet in the throat during manual extraction of the last round. Powder spilled inside the action, gumming up the fully retracted bolt carrier inside the receiver (preventing its break open because of the rattail). After several times striking the butt on the ground, the carrier inched forward enough to half-way hinge open the receiver. I then used a cleaning rod (from an M1A, as the FAL didn't have one...) to push the carrier forward, disassemble, remove bullet, and clean.

Moral: Had this malf happened in an M1A, I could have simply broken down the gun with the bolt retracted. Your harping on the necessity of positive chambering now makes much more sense in my own recent Real World...

With practice, I am, as Fred says, gravitating towards the most effective rifle(s?). Stay tuned—and meanwhile, get to the range and practice! As I like to say, "Ammo turns money into skill. I'd rather have 900rds of skill and 100rds of ammo than 1,000rds of ammo and no skill."

Yours for dry powder!
Boston T. Party
(author of "Boston's Gun Bible"; www.javelinpress.com)

In the 1998 *Boston on Guns & Courage* I painted with too broad a brush, so I got nitty-gritty in 2000 for *Boston's Gun Bible*. Since then, however, after *much* more battle rifle testing and subsequent reflection, I have reorganized/expanded this material into four simple, logical categories: Reliability (38%), Usability (24%), Combat Accuracy (34%), and Affordability (4%). Within these I have ranked many new areas (*e.g.,* within Combat Accuracy *13* criteria relate to sights alone).

A major motivation for all this was the polite urging of several readers and colleagues (in particular, "Fred" of Fred's M14 Stocks) to give the M14 a fairer shake against the FAL. In his excellent *Shotgun News* column, Fred even went so far as to urge his customers to buy the first edition *Boston's Gun Bible* which would become rare because of its erroneous preference of the FAL over the M14. Well, gee, *that* got my attention! You see, Fred is one of many excellent North Carolina *Riflemen* (*i.e.,* they can, from *field* positions, hit a man-sized target out to 500yds) who shoot monthly matches at the renowned Riverside Gun Club. Thus, I felt obligated to carefully weigh the man's conviction on the M14's superiority. To do that, I shot (under timed pressure) thousands of rounds through several M1As and FALs, as well as through the M1 and HK91.

On the range

The primary crucible was the Riverside Gun Club 25 Meter "200/300 Speed Shoot" Target. In this fun/exciting/useful drill, two identical 8½"x11" paper targets (each containing four small silhouettes; two simulated at 200yds and two at 300yds) are set landscape side-by-side at 25m/82'. From the firing line, these silhouettes simulate 20" silhouettes at 200 and 300yds. (Remember, it's an MOA thing; a 1" wide target at 25yds equals a 20" wide target at 500yds.) You must hit all eight within 60 seconds from ready prone. More difficult still is to make your hits from standing, kneeling, squatting, or sitting. (A hit is scored when at least the centerline of the bullet touches the target.) While this drill cannot test Real World target detection, rear sight manipulation, etc., it *is* a very fine drill which any Rifleman can practice in only 82 feet.

For any decent Rifleman, making these 8 hits from ready prone within 60 seconds is pretty easy. Doing it within *30* seconds, however, is more of a challenge!

You can pick up any misses if you have a spotter. Since I usually shot solo (my friends all have day jobs), I simply gave each silhouette one round, and counted only those drills with 8 hits. While I won't disclose the results right now, suffice to say that I was greatly surprised by the disparity in hit-making capability amongst the M1, M14, FAL, HK91, and AR10. (One carbine—a nice Bulgarian milled AK with Wolf ammo—couldn't ever make more than 5 out of 8 hits, due to its poor handling, sights, and trigger.)

As far as timing the drill, I began with the rifle slung African style (weak side; muzzle down). I hit my watch's timer button, and then unslung and went into "Rice Paddy Prone" (*i.e.,* Military Squat). On my 8th shot, I stopped the clock. (Manipulating the stopwatch took about 1½ seconds, so subtract that from my times to achieve actual drill time.)

With any battle rifle I could make 7 hits out of 8 rounds under 30 seconds. Shooting it *clean*, however, was much more challenging, as one round was nearly always *just* outside. For the longest time, I could only shoot it clean with either an M1 or an M14. *Finally,* I cleaned it with an HK91 and FAL—but with an M1 Garand I waxed the drill in just 20.08 seconds, on the very first afternoon! Sights and trigger, folks.

After thousands of rounds in the 200/300 Speed Shoot, I have come to *really* appreciate quality sights and trigger, as well as follow-up shot controlability (none of which the HK91 have; all of which the M1/M14 do). So, I apologize for not emphasizing Effectiveness over Ergonomics in the 2000 edition. Also, I placed *much* more weight on Affordability than it deserved, instead of shamelessly urging you to buy the best—cost regardless.

The criteria
This revised chapter explains the *63* criteria I used to rate the controls, features, and specifications of combat rifles. (In 2000, I employed "only" 35 criteria, and just 10 in 1998.) A scale of 0-10 was used for the unweighted score.

10	Exceptional			
9	Extremely Good		4	Poor
8	Very Good		3	Very Poor
7	Good		2	Extremely Poor
6	Fair		1	Worst Possible
5	Just Tolerable		0	Nonexistent

Many items were weighted (2 to 5 times) because of their relative importance. While scoring from 0-10 was easy, deciding whether or not to weight something—and if so, by how much—was highly subjective work. This was also where any subconscious bias would try to surface.

x2   reciprocating bolt handle, parts/mag availability, mag weight, handguard heatshielding, bolt stop, lefty ergonomics, overall handling, rear sight visibility/adjustability/ruggedness, scope base (battle rifles), recoil

x3   gas system, action exposure, design complexity, parts breakage, weight, bolt handle location & feel, mag-to-gun dynamics, sight radius, front sight visibility/ruggedness, rear sight visibility/precision

x4   action hygiene, reliability of feeding and ejection, overall ruggedness, mag ruggedness, front sight precision, trigger, target accuracy (battle rifles)

x5   reliability of firing and extraction

Several criteria were weighted differently for battle rifles vs. battle carbines, such as barrel length, scope base, and accuracy. (I'll explain why as we get to them.)

As to my credentials to judge these rifles, have I carried *each one* for days and shot thousands of rounds through them? Yes, I have. So, given my focussed experience in/study of them, my evaluation should have some palpable merit, even though unanimous agreement on my weighting and scores is impossible. Although I am still prone to certain biases, I *did* try to be fair point-by-point, and I think that shows up.

Also, understand that there is a high degree of *relativity* involved here. For example, a score of 10 was often given for the being the best of the bunch, or the best that is currently *realized* (though not necessarily the best *conceptually*). Can a battle rifle weigh less than an M14? Sure, but so far none do.

While there shouldn't be much squabbling over individual scores, the *weights* given (or not) are admittedly more speculative. Even with all the weights turned "off" (*i.e.,* all set at 1), the 1st, 2nd, and 3rd place order did not change, which indicates a solid and unbiased analysis.

Write me with your comments, and I'll consider them. However, do *not* pester me just because you think that the SKS is *the* combat rifle to own (simply because it's the only one *you* can afford), or that a carbine can do a rifle's work past 200yds.

RELIABILITY   (38% of total)

The first subcategory discussed is the Op System, following by Design Ruggedness.

Op System (58% of category)

This is the *heart* of the rifle, and determines if it will function in adverse conditions.

gas system   (x3)

Because the roller-locked delayed-blowback HK totally dispenses with any gas system, it is the most simple and most reliable, and thus received a 10.

The AR180 gas-piston systems (AUG, M17S, M96, G36) are the best of the bunch (and not obviously improvable) and got 10s.

The AK gas-piston systems (SKS, Galil, Daewoo), and the FAL got 9s.

The 1930s technology M1 got an 8, but the "Product Improved" M14 got a 9 (as did the Mini-14). The gas-tube AR is a 5-Just Tolerable.

gas regulator

Is gas port pressure adjustable to compensate for varying ammo, temperatures, and action fouling? If so, by how many positions? Clearly, the FAL is the king of the hill here with its 14-position regulator, which earned it a 10. The M96 has a 6-position regulator (8-Very Good), while the Daewoo and SIG550 have a 4-position regulator (7-Good).

Rifles which self-compensated for these varying conditions without a gas regulator, such as the delayed-blowback HK, got a 10.

The M14 has an elegant gas expansion/cut-off system which is self-regulating and compensates not only for fouling, but even for a rusted piston. A 10.

Mere gas on/off switches (for grenade launching, not for gas regulating), such as the M1 (which hasn't the M14's superior system), got a zero (as well as those rifles with nothing at all).

If your conditions include hot and dirty climates using different ammo and with little chance for PM, then you'll likely appreciate a gas regulator. Otherwise, it's not that crucial of a feature (which is why is was not weighted).

action hygiene   (x4)

Does the op system vent gas into the action (*i.e.,* does it sh✳t where it eats)? Such fouling *greatly* reduces the number of rounds which can be fired between mandatory cleanings. For example, an AR will need a thorough cleaning by 400rds at minimum, and by 1,000rds at most—while an AK can easily go 2,000+rds, and the AR180-type gas systems more than even that.

With its op rod, the M1 and M14 vent *no* gas into the action. The AR180-type systems (AUG, M17S, M96, G36) also vent no gas, and thus also got 10s.

While the FAL and AK were fairly clean, some gas can't help but escape past the piston, so they got a 7-Good.

The HK's fluted chamber gets filthy, and thus deserves a 3. So does the gas-tube AR (which truly fouls its own receiver nest).

action exposure   (x3)

A rifle should not be designed so as to encourage dirt, sand, vegetation, mud, etc. to get inside its action via the bolt handle slot and ejection port.

The AR15 not only protects its bolt and carrier, it also has an ejection port cover which can be closed shut between firings—a 10.

If it has a dustcover (AK), then it got a 7. Add a point for an 8 if it has a nonreciprocating bolt handle (FAL, HK), which slightly reduces exposure. The SIG550 has a neoprene lip for its bolt handle root, so I gave it an 8 also.

The SKS gets a 5, as the bolt carrier moderately protects the action.

If the bolt or bolt carrier is totally exposed on top and has holes for dirt entry (M1/M14, Mini-14), then it got a 3.

reciprocating bolt handle   (x2)

If the bolt handle is actually attached to the bolt or bolt carrier (M1/M14, Mini-14, SKS, AK, Galil, Daewoo, AUG, SIG550) to provide positive chambering when required, then it got a 10. The AR15 has a forward assist to somewhat increase positive chambering, so I gave it a 4. If the handle is non-reciprocating (FAL, HK, AR10, M17S, M96, G36), then it got a zero.

I've come to recently appreciate this feature, especially when checking the chamber of a dirty gun. Positive chambering can be difficult without it!

reliability: feeding   (x4)
reliability: firing   (x5)
reliability: extraction   (x5)
reliability: ejection   (x4)

Reliability is *the* most important criterion! Will your rifle *work* any time, all the time—period? Reliability is more important than accuracy or ergonomics. What point is there to an accurate or well-handling rifle if it doesn't *work*? I'd take a 6MOA AK47 which functioned 100% over a ¾MOA AR15 which double-fed every mag. (At least with that AK I could fight out to 250m.)

Instead of scoring reliability as a whole (as I did in 1998 and 2000), for greater clarity and accuracy I broke it down into the 4 stages of the operating cycle. I consider firing and extraction each to be worth a weight of 5, as the shooter can't accomplish these functions himself. (On the other hand, he *could*, if required, feed and eject without the rifle's total cooperation.)

The roller-locked delayed-blowback **HK91** *works* and got all **10s**.

Scoring an **8.3** overall was the **M14** with solid 8s and 9s.

The **M1** got an overall **7.8** (as it doesn't feed quite as reliably as the M14).

The **FAL** got an overall **7.7**, which had only 7-Good feeding.

AR15s got a **6.8** overall. Some AR fans will howl about this low score, demanding at least an 8-Very Good since modern ARs are very reliable with regular PM (*i.e.,* cleaning every 400rds). While I can see their point, I thought a 6.8 was stringently accurate, even though mine operates as an 8.5+.

The **AR10** got a **5.3** overall. It does not feed a fully-topped off 20rd mag (only 19rds or less will work), and recent rifles are plagued with malfunctions.

Design Ruggedness (42% of category)

This contemplates the rifle holistically, as an "organism" and what it takes to keep it healthy.

working parts placement

The reason why I scored this separately is that a buttstock is a potential impact weapon, and the rifle can become nonfunctional if any working parts there are damaged. If you take a round in the stock, will it kill your rifle? Working parts should be up front (which also allows for buttstock storage or a folding stock).

If all working parts are *forward* of the buttstock (M1, M14, AK), then it got a 10. (Because of the small buffer in the buttstock, I gave the HK a 6.) If there is a buffer spring needlessly housed in the stock, then it got a 1 (AR) or a 2 (FAL).

design complexity (x2)

How many total parts are there? Lots, as in the FAL's 143? Is the rifle made up of a bushel of pins, springs, and ball detents (AR; 119 parts)? Is it moderately complex (HK91; 92 parts), or is the rifle simplicity itself (M14; 61 parts)? Granted, some of the counts may be off by a half dozen parts (due to conflicting lists), but this will still serve as a useful comparison.

Using the M14's 61 total parts as a 90% standard, I divided the other guns into the theoretical goal of 55 parts to achieve a useful ratio which neatly becomes its score when multiplied by 10 (and rounded to the nearest integer). The AR, for example, gets a 5 (55/119 = .462 x 10 = 4.62). The scoring turned out well, I think—the M14 gets a deserved 9, the HK a 6, and the FAL a 4.

For contrast, the third column assumes the M14's 61 parts to be an unbeatable standard. Also, I threw in some oddball rifles (FN49, SVT40) just for fun. As you can see, the older systems are generally more simple.

	# of parts	55 / #	61 / #
M14	61	.900	1.000
M1	62	.887	.984
SVT40	64	.859	.953
FN49	70	.786	.871
SKS	70	.786	.871
AK	75	.733	.813
HK91	92	.598	.663
AR	119	.462	.512
FAL	143	.385	.427

parts breakage   (x3)

Is the rifle known for occasional parts breakage (*e.g.,* M1 op rod and spring), or is the thing a rock (HK, AK)? Scoring this is unavoidably somewhat anecdotal as *Consumer Reports* doesn't yet cover battle rifles and carbines. Thus, I had to rely upon my personal experience, plus the general consensus amongst Riflemen.

fieldstripping   (x2)

Once something breaks, how easy is it to replace in the field? Is the system totally modular (HK, M96), or is the trigger group built in the lower (FAL)? Does the bolt disassemble easily (AR, HK), or does it need a tool (M1/M14)?

This category also contemplates ease of cleaning and lubricating. Can you run a rod from chamber-to-muzzle, or not (M1/M14)? How easy is it to remove fouling? Is lubrication easy (FAL) or a chore (M1/M14)?

parts availability   (x2)

Governments don't have to care about this, but *we* will in the future when spare parts are restricted (or outlawed). What will you do when QP, Numrich, Sarco, etc. have been legislated out of existence? Stock up now!

overall ruggedness   (x4)

Combat rifles should *not* be built like a Swiss watch! They must survive all unintentional abuse, and most intentional abuse. Milled steel rifles (M1/M14, SIG550, Galil) are generally more rugged than stamped steel rifles (AK, HK), which are generally more rugged than aluminum (AR, Daewoo). Synthetics (G36, Pro-Ord Carbon 15), however, are now rivalling steel.

Anyway, how to score this? Actual service history and subjective feel.

handguard ruggedness

A 10 to the SIG550. 9s to the HK, AUG, M17S, and G36. 8 to the FAL. 7s to the M1/M14 and AR.

buttstock ruggedness

I'd have to give a 10 to the SIG550, and 9s to the HK and M1/M14. 8s to the FAL and AUG. 7 to the AK. 6s to the Daewoo and M96. A 5 to the AR.

mag ruggedness   (x4)

If the mag doesn't work, then you have a really nice single-shot. In combat, mags suffer brutal treatment, so they can't be flimsy (*e.g.,* like AR15 mags). Most failures to feed are mag-related, so mag ruggedness is crucial.

mag availability   (x2)

Yeah, the .308 Galil is a rugged gun, but where can you find mags? A battle rifle's semi-auto advantage is negated without plentiful mags. Keep in mind that mag supplies change constantly as hoards are discovered/depleted.

I gave 8s to the M1 and to the FAL, a 7 to the HK (which continues to improve), a 6 to the M14, and a 5 to the AR10 (which uses M14 mags).

USABILITY   (24% of total)

This will encompass Static Handling and Controls.

Static handling (45% of category)

weight   (x3)

A couple pounds either way makes a *big* difference in extended portability. **Battle Rifles:** At 8.7lbs, the M14 was the lightest, and thus got the 9-Extremely Good. (Since I believe that an 8¼lb MBR is possible, 8.7lbs did not rate a 10-Exceptional.) A point was subtracted for each additional ½lb above 9lbs.

Battle Carbines: Since the M1 Carbine at 5½lbs was the lightest, it formed the standard (even though it wasn't included in the chart). For each additional ½lb, a point was subtracted. 9lb carbines (the heaviest) thus got a 3—the pigs.

mag weight   (x2)

In case you didn't know, mags can be heavy! Yes, mag ruggedness is usually at the expense of mag weight, but we must nevertheless discuss weight (here is where M1 clips shine!). The M1 notwithstanding, the lightest battle rifle mags are the aluminum FAL's. Heaviest mags are the steel HK's.

length overall   (x2)

The *NFA34* decreed that no long gun may measure less than 26" overall. **Battle Rifles:** At 38.8" the Galil was the shortest and got the 10. Subtract a point for each additional inch. The M14 at 44¼" was the worst and got a 5.

Battle Carbines: Since the M17S was the shortest at 30", it got the 10. Subtract a point for each additional 2". A 9 was given for 32", an 8 for 34", a 7 for 36", a 6 for 38", and a 5 for 40" (which is the longest battle carbines get).

barrel length   (x2 for Battle Carbines)

Longer barrels tend to have less muzzle flash, and take longer to heatup. Increased barrel length, however, increases rifle overall length, although this is not a factor in bullpup rifles (which is their chief advantage). If a particular rifle were available in different barrel length (*e.g.,* 16" and 20"), I assumed 20" for equality's sake, and adjusted its weight and length.

Battle Carbines: So weighted because increased barrel length directly means increased velocity, which in a .223 determines its hyper-lethality (caused by 2800+fps bullet shattering). Since 16" is the shortest legal barrel length, the scoring began there at 1, and add a point for each additional ½" until 9 (for 20" barrels). A 10 was for any barrel over 20".

Battle Rifles: The .308's lethality is ample regardless of a 200fps loss from an 16" vs. 20" barrel. Thus, this factor is not weighted here. I gave the M1 and M14 the 10 because of their 24" and 22" barrels (any longer barrel in a .308 gives little meaningful velocity gain), and then subtracted a point for each inch less than 22".

handguard length

Unless you're keen on fighting in asbestos gloves, the less barrel exposed, the better. (You don't have to trust me on this—go ahead, *touch* it!)

handguard heatshielding   (x2)

This is an overlooked consideration by novices. Start spending serious time with your battle rifle and you'll gain a new appreciation for a well-shielded handguard (usually found in modern designs). If you doubt me, go shoot an M17S or StG58 for several mags and write me once the blisters have healed.

handguard fit/feel

Since you'll be gripping the thing for many hours, it really should be at least tolerably comfortable.

buttstock fit/feel

This must not be too long (too short is preferable, especially for winter clothes), and it must have a good fit. I subtracted 1-2 points each for poor cheekweld (HK), slippery or narrow buttplate (HK), or excessive length.

pistol grip fit/feel

First, the rifle should have one in order that the shooting hand can more easily maintain control of the rifle (especially during reloading and malfunction clearances). (The M1/M14, SKS, and Mini-14 do not, and thus are at a disadvantage against the FAL, HK, AR, etc.) Second, it should be comfortable and provide correct trigger finger length of pull.

butstock and pistol grip storage

A combat rifle should self-contain its own cleaning rod and tools, plus small spare parts (*e.g.,* firing pin, extractor, springs, etc.). In 2000 I ranked these separately, but have combined them in order to reduce their scoring weight.

Pistol grip storage is necessary if there's no buttstock storage. Only the Galil, AR, and M96 have both.

Controls (55% of category)

charging handle location   (x3)

The weak hand (*i.e.,* left hand for 89% of shooters) runs the rifle, remember? Thus, my preference is left side of the receiver, such as the FAL. The highest I rated any right side handle was a 7 (M1/M14).

charging handle feel   (x3)

It must be comfortably shaped/sized, else your hand will cringe (if not get hurt). The FAL knob handle (not the folding version) was the best (a 10), followed by 8s to the M1/M14. When the AR has a TacLatch, I'd give it a 7; otherwise, the OEM latch gets a 5-Just Tolerable. 2-Extremely Poor to the HK91. The AK47 was the 1-Worst Possible, although the Romanian AK74 gets a 3.

bolt stop   (x2)

At its best, this comprises *three* functions: a manual hold-open (used to clear double-feeds), an automatic (*i.e.,* last shot) hold-open (used for fastest empty reloading), and a bolt release (also needed for fastest empty reloading). Only the FAL, AR15, Daewoo, M17S, and SIG are so equipped. The other guns have varying combinations, and were scored according to utility:

	Manual H-O	Auto H-O	Release	
0				(AK)
2	✔			(HK)
4		✔		(M1, SKS, M96)
5		✔	✔	
6	✔	✔		(M14)
7-10	✔	✔	✔	(FAL, AR15, SIG)

Those with manual/auto hold-opens *and* a separate release button were scored 7-10, according to ergonomics.

I consider an auto hold-open the absolute combat minimum, and the lack of such in the HK is criminal.

safety

Ergonomics and quietness were the pertinent factors here. Good Rule 3 trigger finger discipline can mitigate a poor safety control (by not needing it!).

The AR has the best safety, hands down. The inch FAL (L1A1) follows a close second (9).

mag catch   (x2)

Since empty reloads are very common in rifle fights, a quickly reached and easily operated mag catch becomes important in the heat of battle—thus x2.

The AR has indisputably the best mag catch (10). The metric FAL's catch can be pushed by a right trigger finger (7). The HK button requires a bit of a stretch (5), but the aftermarket paddle release (Ø50) gets an 8, so I bumped up the overall score to a 6-Fair. The M14 catch is small, but centrally located, so it got a 7-Good. The M1 has a left-side clip ejection button (4).

mag to gun   (x3)

Considers the ease and speed of this important manipulation. Quickest and most fluid are the straight-up types (AR, HK) over the nose-in-rock-backs.

A 10 to the AR, 8 to the HK, 8 to the FAL (best of the nose-ins with its helpful receiver bridge), 7 to the M14 (sometimes fussy), and a 5 to the clip-fed M1.

lefty ergonomics   (x2)

Since 11% of shooters are left-handed, and since right-handed shooters may have their strong side disabled in a fight, lefty ergonomics are important. Ambi accessories are also contemplated here.

overall handling   (x2)

Rates the "feel" of a rifle. Does it feel "alive" in your hands, or like a club? While bad (*i.e.,* only 6-Decent) handling can be nearly forgotten over time (until you happen to wield something better!), handling nonetheless deserves to be double weighted.

COMBAT ACCURACY (34%)

Contemplates not merely target accuracy, but *combat* accuracy (*i.e.,* hits under time and pressure against indistinct and moving targets). Many elements affect accuracy, such as bolt lockup, handling, sights, trigger, recoil, and muzzle blast. Rifles strong in all those elements (M1, M14) hit very well, while rifles with weaker elements (AK, HK) require *much* more work from the shooter.

Sights (65% of category)

Until you shoot your rifle a *lot,* you just can't appreciate how important the sights really are. Good vs. poor sight radius and front sight visibility are not apparent at the gun show—only at the gun range. (The HK91 is a good example of this.)

Rifles with OEM optical sights (AUG) were scored for ruggedness, reticle design, and speed of target acquisition. The AUG proved that combat optical sights were viable, and such are becoming the wave of the future. Still, I prefer my rifles to have OEM iron sights (at least for emergency backup).

sight radius   (x3)

The longer the better as it reduces the MOA of movement and sight slop, thus increasing shooting precision. 1MOA of movement from an M1 is 0.0081", versus only 0.0064" from a FAL (which has 6" shorter sight radius), and 0.0043" from an AK74. The M1 is *twice* as forgiving of muzzle waver than the AK74.

The WWI US M1917 .30/06 (Sgt. Alvin York's rifle) has a sight radius of 31¾"! Little wonder that the M1917 (generally known as the P17 Enfield) is notoriously accurate. Eighty years ago, gun makers really knew how to design a *rifle*.

The hands-down winner is the M1 with a whopping 28". The M14 is basically tied with its M1 dad with a 27" radius (by wisely avoiding the design shortcut of placing the sight on the gas block), which helps to explain the M14's superb combat accuracy. A score of 10 to both of these rifles. We'll use the M14's 27" as the 10-Exceptional, and deduct a point for each 2½" less.

8-Very Good to HK91 and Mini-14 (both 22½"), and to the FAL (22"). The AR (20") and Daewoo (19½") got a 7-Good. The AK and SKS at just 14¾" got a score of 5. *Very* short sight radiuses under 10" (M17S; 4¾") got hammered.

sight offset

The lower the better. 1" is a 10, and deduct a point for each additional ¼".

The M1/M14 both boast a mere 1" offset. Can't be any less! A 10.

The metric FAL, HK91, and AK have a 2" offset to score a 6-Fair.

The AR has a towering 2½" offset to score a 4-Very Poor. (If the AR had a left-side charging handle, offset could have been reduced by ½".)

front sight visibility   (x3)

If you cannot easily focus on your front sight (*i.e.,* it's obscured, damaged, or of poor size/shape), *then you will not easily hit your Bad Guy.* Deservedly triple weighted. In my opinion, the best visibility is a *wing* protected (not hood, which obscures vision) *square* post (not rounded, which picks up glare).

front sight adjustability

In my view, a front sight should be easily adjustable for elevation zero without a tool (other than a bullet tip), which allows the rear sight to easily incorporate a BDC for range. I view the AR as ideal (plus, it offers good vertical range), so it got the 10. Deduct 2 points each for short vertical range, any adjustment tool requirement, and for blades (which require 180˚ turns).

The FAL is adjustable for elevation zero. The metric FAL uses a wheel (heights 1-4) turned by a bullet tip (I give this a 8 due to its very limited vertical range), while the inch FAL uses a threaded blade with set screw (I give this a 6).

M1/M14 front sights are adjustable only for windage zero, and rely upon the rear sight for elevation zero. While this is certainly a workable system, it is not my first design choice (the front sight block can loosen and shift, and the elevation knob must be index realigned for zero). 7-Good.

Some front sights are adjustable for elevation *and* windage zero (AK, SIG), which requires a special tool, and also unnecessarily complicates the sight. It permits, however, a simple and rugged rear sight. 5-Just Tolerable.

Front sights with utterly no adjustment for zero (HK, Mini-14, M17S) must rely upon the rear sight for such, which is a real flaw in my opinion.

front sight precision   (x4)

Only with experience does a Rifleman appreciate how important this is to making the hits. The front sight must be evenly square with very sharp corners. A poor quality post leads to a mushy sight picture, and misses. Round posts (AR15A1, metric FAL, SKS, AK) are too often maddeningly indistinct from glare. Also, the front sight's hood or ears should prevent glare.

It is essential that the post width not be excessive (AK) else hits past 250m will be quite difficult.

The sight must be precise. The NM M14 sight, for example, is 0.062" ± 0.005" wide. The corners cannot excede 0.003" radius. *That* is precise!

What's really helpful is when the post equals some particularly useful width at a known distance, thus serving as a ranging device. That 0.062" post width is 8MOA, which corresponds to about 20" (width of military silhouette paper target) at 250yds (which is "battlesight zero"/MPBR for the M14)—if the Bad Guy is no thinner than your front sight, then use a center hold and drop him! I rate the standard M1/M14 front post a 9, and the NM post a 10.

The standard AR15A2 (not A1) square post is also very good, getting a 9.

The HK91 blade post is flat and razor sharp. A 9.

The inch FAL with thin blade is worth an 8, while the metric FAL (fat rounded post) gets only a 5. Since most FALs are metric, the overall score is a 6-Fair. A target-quality square post would *really* help either FAL.

front sight protection   (x3)

When your rifle falls over the front sight is much more vulnerable than the rear. Thus, it must be protected by winged ears (M1) or ringed hood (HK).

rear sight visibility   (x3)

An aperture (*i.e.,* "peep") is *much* preferred over a notched blade (AK) for better target and front sight acquisition. I like a "ghost ring" (Jeff Cooper's term, now colloquial) which blocks very little downrange terrain.

rear sight readability   (x2)

How easily can you read—from a cheekweld—the range numerals, especially when the light is poor or the rifle is dirty?

rear sight adjustability   (x2)

The rear sight should be adjustable for windage zero, and for various combat ranges (in increments of 25-50yds) out to at least 500m in battle carbines and 800m in battle rifles.

If the front sight is elevation adjustable, then the rear sight is free to incorporate a BDC. The obvious standard here is the AR, which has range settings for 300m, 400m, 500m, 600m in the flat-top uppers, and out to 700m and 800m in the A2s. There are also several MOA clicks between the 100m-even settings so that odd distance hits (*e.g.,* at 475m) can be made.

rear sight precision   (x3)

This sight must provide precise zero and range adjustments during combat conditions. It must have nice and tight clicks, not slot and screw (HK). It must move with no slop, as only 0.004-8" can mean 1MOA.

rear sight ruggedness   (x2)

While not as crucial as the front sight (a good Rifleman can still hit out to 200m without a rear sight), the rear sight must be rugged yet remain quickly adjustable for low light conditions and varying ranges. Unfortunately, precise adjustability and ruggedness are somewhat mutually exclusive.

tritium sight

While only the Galil and SIG have OEM tritiums, aftermarket sights exist for a few other rifles (AR, HK) and such were considered. *Replaceable* sights (OEM or not) got a 10; nonreplaceable sights got a 6-Fair.

scope base   (x2 for Battle Rifles)

Combat optics and mounts have greatly improved since WWII, and are appropriate (if not required) in many situations. Optics are also preferred by older Riflemen (*i.e.,* those over 40) whose eyesight has deteriorated enough to hamper the effective use of iron sights.

Some rifles have built-in rails (AR flattop, M17S, AUG, SIG, G36), some have add-on rails (Daewoo), some have replaceable railed-dustcovers (FAL), and others have detachable bases (Mini-14, M14, HK, Galil). Ruggedness and zero hold (continuous and repeat) are usually best to worst in that order.

Battle Rifles: Double weighted given the .308's greater effective range.

Accuracy Miscellaneous (35% of category)

bolt and carrier

How does the bolt lock up? If it locks into the *barrel* (which is the most accurate, and also allows for the use of non-steel receivers) as with the Stoner rotary bolts (AR, M96, AUG, M17S, G36), then I gave it a 10. The WWII M1941 Johnson .30/06 was the first rotary bolt battle rifle, something that Eugene Stoner wisely picked up for his Armalite designs (his best being the AR180).

The HK locks into a barrel extension, so I gave it an 8.

Those bolts, however, which lock into the *receiver* (M1/M14, FAL) are not as precise and accurate and got a score of 7-Good. Granted, some M14s can be tuned to give 1MOA, however, the *potentiality* of its accuracy is limited partly because of its bolt-receiver lockup. ARs have an inherently more accurate action (¾MOA), and it shows in competitions. (Since I did not weight this criterion, let's not have you M14 High Power shooters freak out.)

To some readers this may not seem fair as certain rifles with receiver lockup are every bit as accurate as the barrel lockup rifles. This fact notwithstanding, it is inherently more accurate to place the locking lug raceway in the *barrel* rather than in the receiver. Eliminating the receiver from the lockup equation also makes accurizing much easier.

trigger pull   (x4)

I can't stress enough how important a quality trigger pull is to accuracy. Deservedly weighted a 4. Triggers should be 2-stage, with a 4-6lb letoff. Consistently fine triggers are historically found on all Swiss service rifles, from the Schmidt-Rubins, to the SG57, to the SIG550. The Swiss are *Riflemen,* and it shows in their equipment. In fact, I'm holding a beautiful Schmidt-Rubin K31 right now, which I've never even fired. It's a joy to own just for the trigger!

Folks, there's *no* excuse today for battle rifles to have less than 7-Good triggers (HK), especially since the M1 showed us how back in 1937!

My favorite battle rifle trigger is found on the M1/M14. Not only is the trigger group a superb piece of engineering (with only a 13 parts, and easily tunable), the quality of pull is excellent even from rack-grade rifles. These rifles are a pleasure to shoot because of the 2-stage trigger alone. A 9.

Next best is the AR. Although a single stage, it is easily replaced with a NM 2-stage version. I give it an 8-Very Good.

The FAL has a 7-Good trigger at *best,* and often a 4-Poor, and you'll never know what to expect from a random gun. (I've seen an Imbel FAL with a better trigger than a DSA FAL costing twice as much!) Most sad of all, the FAL trigger (a creepy 2-stage) is very difficult to tune. On average it gets a 5-Just Tolerable.

The HK has an intentionally heavy pull (for safety in drop tests) which could have easily been avoided with a Glock-type trigger safety. Not only is it very heavy, it's got lots of creep. This is a difficult trigger to shoot accurately with, and it's lucky to get a 4-Poor.

target accuracy   (x3 for Battle Carbines   x4 for Battle Rifles)

Measures accuracy under ideal conditions, and is less affected by poor sights and trigger. Target accuracy from a bench is the gun's best possible accuracy, which is significantly reduced in combat under time and pressure. While target grade accuracy (*i.e.,* under 1MOA) cannot be demanded of rugged/reliable combat rifles, there's no reason why 2MOA cannot be.

If 95% of combat ranges were not <300M, then accuracy would have been weighted a 5. Since MBRs have greater effective ranges, weight is 4 for them.

1MOA got a 10. Subtract a point for each additional ½MOA. 3MOA rates a 5-Just Tolerable (adding to which another 1MOA for less stable field positions gives 4MOA combat accuracy). 5½MOA is a 1-Worst Possible.

In determining individual scores, I had to rely upon what seemed to be the *average* system performance, not one specific gun test. Thus, it is with a fair degree of certainty that an AR15 is generally an 1½MOA gun and the AK is generally a 5MOA gun. (Yes, I know that some AR15s and AKs both shoot 3MOA, but such are the exception rather than the rule.) All battle carbines but the SKS, AK, and Mini-14 got at least a 7-Good, and usually an 8-Very Good.

All the battle rifles I shot but the AR10 gave 1½MOA with good FMJ, thus earning a 9-Extremely Good.

muzzle blast

Generally, I prefer *not* to use a muzzle brake. I'll put up with a bit of muzzle climb in order to avoid the extra/excessive muzzle blast from a brake. (I'm thinking of the AR10 here.)

Least (nearly unnoticeable, really) muzzle blast were from the M1(24" bare tube) and M14 (22" tube with flash suppressor). 10s to the pair!

recoil   (x2 for Battle Rifles)

Fighting with a jackhammer of a .308 is not much fun, and once flinching begins to rear its ugly head, your accuracy can easily be chopped in half. And I'm not even mentioning follow-up shot controlability.

The easiest recoiling battle rifles by far are the M1/M14. Either can truly be shot all day without undue fatigue.

time for 8 hits at simulated 200/300yds   (x3)

This was shot on the Riverside (N.C.) Gun Club's 25 Meter 200/300yd Speed Shoot. The drill measures the utility of the rifle as a *package* (*i.e.,* sling, handling, ergonomics, safety, sights, trigger, muzzle blast, and recoil). The only significant criteria not covered here were mag changing and malfunction clearance.

The three Springfield Armory M1As all had normal sights and triggers, except for one "Loaded" model with NM barrel/sights.

The FAL was a post-ban Imbel gun, one of the few which has been utterly malfless (although of average accuracy). I also tried a DSA FAL, but it shot abysmally low (even with a #1 post, the lowest made).

The 91 was a genuine HK rifle, which was *extremely* accurate. Its tactical chest-carry sling sped up the times by at least 1-1½ seconds. Of the six modern clones I tested—3 Hesse and 3 CETMEs—only *one* (a Hesse) functioned without a hitch *and* had aligned sights.

So, how to score this drill? Figuring on 18 seconds to be the theoretically quickest time, let's divide 180 by the rifle's average time.

	M1	**M1A**	**FAL**	**HK91**	**AR10**
best	20.08	25.38	24.44	22.77	
average	21.57	28.34	26.98	24.46	
spread	1.49	2.96	2.54	1.69	
score	**8.34**	**6.35**	**6.67**	**7.36**	**6.67**

Since this drill began from a slung position, the short M1 Tanker and HK had an advantage over the longer M14 and FAL. Next, a sharp front sight (all but FAL) really sped up the hits. Also, those rifles with an accuracy edge (M1 Tanker, HK) simply made easier hits.

I had sold off my AR10A4 before this test, but I recall it equaled the FAL.

Granted, my own skill level and rifle resonance greatly influenced these results, but such could not be avoided. Your mileage will vary, so try out all four battle rifles yourself and discover which rifle which *hits best* for *you*.

AFFORDABILITY (4%)

The remaining criteria below relate solely to private citizens (who have to suffer gun restrictions and spend their own money). While these factors are crucial to *us*, such would be largely insignificant (or even irrelevant) to *governments*. They neither spend *their* own money nor are bound by their own laws.

After deep reflection, I now admit that I overemphasized Affordability in 2000. As "Fred" sagely put it, *"Cost will not matter when it comes to defending yourself, your family or your freedom.* **Effectiveness is the** [criterion]..." Amen to that, brother! Thus, only mag price is still weighted, and only double at that. (Actually, Affordability doesn't change the rankings one bit, as it did in 2000.)

Sure, it'd be just peachy to have a SIG550, but who could afford the Ø8,000 gun and Ø100 mags? I'd also love to own an AUG (at least for a season), but spending Ø2,500 on a mere .223 is a mental hurdle I just cannot clear. (Good. Perhaps my "gun disease" is abating.)

Granted, quality costs money but most of these ridiculously high prices are due to the artificial premium of the *law*. If it weren't for the Import Ban of 1990 and the *"Crime Bill"* of 1994, you and I could own Ø1,200 SIG550s and AUGs. Belgian FALs would be Ø1,500. You get the idea.

Thus, the trick is to choose a quality rifle which somehow doesn't cost the Earth. In .308 battle rifles with a legal flash suppressor, a new Springfield Armory "Loaded" M1A with National Match sights and barrel is a bargain at about Ø1,400. Used "plain-Jane" M1As can still be found for Ø975-1,100 (only a few hundred more than the cookie dough-soft Chinese M14 clones). Holding out for a Ø2,500 pre-ban FAL is just silly. By the time you ever find a *private* sale model (I've seen 4 in my life), you'll have wasted all that time (and money) for possible training. Get an M1A or a DSA FAL *today* and get to work!

I'd *like* to recommend an affordable post-ban HK91 clone, but their general quality is very spotty. Oh, they'll *work*—they just won't *hit* due to unaligned sights (*e.g.,* CETME). I haven't yet tried the newer Portugese guns, however.

Some rifles are often available in pre-ban form (AR), some are *rarely* available in pre-ban form (Daewoo), and some were imported/introduced only after the 9/1994 *"Crime Bill"* (M96, AR10, G36). And then, there are the parts kit guns.

So, instead of mixing OEM apples with clone post-ban oranges (as I did in 2000), they are scored separately. Ø500 or less got a 10, subtracting a point for each additional Ø250. Ø750 a 9, Ø1000 an 8, Ø1250 a 7, Ø1500 a 6, Ø1750 a 5, Ø2000 a 4, and so on. Current (*i.e.,* 2002) prices (which can vary $\pm$ 10%) for nice used guns:

OEM rifle price
If you want the genuine article, then you'll have to pay for it.

WWII/Korean M1 Garand	Ø750	9-Extremely Good
Springfield Armory M1A	Ø1,100	8-Very Good
DSA SA-58 FAL	Ø1,500	6-Fair
HK91	Ø2,000	4-Poor
ArmaLite AR10A4	Ø1,250	7-Good

clone rifle price
O.K., so it's *not* important to own the genuine article? Well, that's your choice, but you're generally much better off spending the extra dough.

Century Arms Intl. M1	Ø450	10-Exceptional
Polytech M14	Ø500	10-Exceptional
Imbel FAL	Ø750	9-Extremely Good
Hesse 91	Ø500	10-Exceptional
Eagle Arms AR10	Ø1,000	8-Very Good

With the exception of the new AR10 by Eagle Arms (ArmaLite "Lite"), I've tried them all. Would I routinely trust my life to them? With the possible exception of an Imbel FAL, nope. The CAI M1s are crap, the Norinco/PolyTech M14s need a Ø500 heat-treat and bolt replacement from Smith Enterprises (which finishes out to be a very fine forged-receiver gun), and the Hesse 91s are very often (2:3 odds) problem guns.

DSA recently came out with StG58 (Steyr) parts kit guns (on DSA receivers). These are likely very good rifles for the Ø1,000.

brass reloadability
Governments don't have to care about this, but *we* will in the future when reloading components are restricted (or outlawed).

parts price
You should be stocking up on spare parts for a lifetime, *now!*

mag price   (x2)
<Ø10 got a 10, subtracting a point for each additional Ø10 in price.

Battle Rifles: The real bargain is M1 Garand clips at 40-50¢ each (a buck if you're spendy). That means you can load 40rds for as little as Ø2! Even a FAL will cost you Ø10 for the same 40rds in two Ø5 mags.

Battle Carbines: When .223 rifles could be adapted to accept AR15 mags, I so calculated. (OEM mag scores were figured in the first percentages.)

BATTLE RIFLE RANKING

These rankings will differ greatly from those made in 2000, but such is merely the result of much more comparative field experience performed in 2001 and 2002. Below each overall score are the subcategory scores.

Reliability   (38% of total)

As I mentioned earlier, Reliability is the most crucial thing in a battle rifle. As long as it *works*, a good Rifleman can compensate for poor accuracy or ergonomics.

❶ **HK91   84.5% (448/530)**
op system 82.6%   design strength 87.3%

This comes as little surprise. However the critics denounce the HK91, even they must admit that the rifle *works*. No other rifle came close to matching the 91's brute reliability. It also does not break—*ever*—and can be neglected with little risk of failure. (I mean, the *Mexican* Army carries them, if that tells you anything!)

I'd own one for my End-Of-The-World battle rifle.

❷ **M14   80.9% (429/530)**
op system 82.3%   design strength 79.1%
The M14 is a very reliable and rugged rifle. Its only real weakness is its exposed action, however, such can largely be negated by a conscientious Rifleman.

❸ **M1   79.1% (419/530)**
op system 76.8%   design strength 82.3%
M14 remarks also apply here. The M1, because of its gas system and clip feeding, isn't *quite* as reliable as its M14 "son," but if you take care of your Garand it will rarely let you down.

❹ **FAL   77.0% (408/530)**
op system 77.7%   design strength 75.9%
Nearly tied with the M1. Feeding is the FAL's weakest point (though it still rated an 8-Very Good). The bolt carrier, however, can easily be modified into reciprocating the charging handle, which would significantly ease failure-to-feed clearances. Generally a very reliable rifle—outside desert conditions (as the Israelis quickly found out).

❺ **AR10   52.8% (280/530)**
op system 49.0%   design strength 58.2%
In 2000 I rated its reliability as a 7-Good, but have learned since then that I was a tad generous. Feeding and extraction malfunctions are now known to be fairly common, and ejection is a real weak point.

ArmaLite's "Hear-No-Malfs" attitude isn't helping, either. One Thunder Ranch student's AR10 suffered from such bad bolt carrier-receiver galling that he had to complete the class with a loaner Romanian AK. All this a shame, since the .223 AR15 has grown to become a fairly reliable system (if you stay on top of PM every 400rds).

Usability   (24% of total)

Static (*i.e.*, weight, length, etc.) and dynamic (*i.e.*, controls) ergonomics were scored here.

❶ **AR10   82.7% (273/330)**
static 83.3%   dynamic 82.3%
This comes as no surprise. Being the most modern of MBRs, the AR10 has the best furniture and ergonomics. Such, however, does *not* make up for a pathetic 51.7% reliability!

❷ **FAL   77.3% (255/330)**
           static 74.7%   dynamic 79.4%

For righties at least, the FAL is very easy to use. The metric FAL has the better mag catch and bolt handle, but the inch FAL has the better safety. (Get a metric gun and install an L1A1 safety, and a DSA auto hold-open.)

❸ **M14   71.8% (237/330)**
           static 70.0%   dynamic 73.3%

Perfectly serviceable, though not brilliant. With practice, its right-side charging handle is no real handicap, nor is the mag catch. I'm dislike the cramped safety, but that can replaced with a safety from a winter trigger kit.

After much more recent time with the M14, I've found it more ergonomic than I thought in 1998 and 2000.

❹ **M1   64.8% (214/330)**
           static 68.0%   dynamic 62.2%

It's a little heavier than the M14, and not as well heat-shielded. Manipulating the 8rd clips takes some finesse, although quick and competent empty reloading is possible with sufficient practice. 65.5% is halfway between Fair and Good, and such is also my subjective opinion. The M1 handles well enough—but no better—to do its job.

❺ **HK91   59.7% (197/330)**
           static 70.7%   dynamic 50.6%

Ah, the German step-child of rifle ergonomics! With FAL-level of controls, the 91 would have totaled 1042 points for a solid 3rd place finishing—and that's *with* its crappy sights and trigger! Likewise, with *AR10*-level ergonomics (and such was certainly possible by Heckler & Koch in the late 1950s), it would have been just 10 points shy of beating the M14 for 1st!

Combat Accuracy   (34% of total)

This was the most developed new section of my latest testing. How well as rifle *hits* is the "proof of the pudding." Before 2001, I hadn't shot the battle rifles against each other under time and pressure, and doing so was *quite* illuminating.

❶ M1   80.4% (370/460)
        sights 75.3%   misc. 90.0%
    Recall that the M1 used here was a tackdriving Tanker
.308 with a 17.6" barrel. It was lighter, handier, and more accurate than any full size .30/06 Garand could be. So, was this *fair*?
Yes, I think so. First, to compete with the other battle rifles, the M1 had to also be in .308 as surplus .30/06 ammo is neither ubiquitous nor a bargain (at 21¢/rd). Second, if it's going to
have a .308 barrel, why choose a 24" when something about 20"
is the better choice? All in all, a .308 Tanker Garand is precisely
the flavor of M1 best suited for the 21st Century Rifleman. Besides, it was only Ø750 and has become a personal favorite.

❷ M14   79.4% (365/460)
        sights 75.7%   misc. 86.3%
    With its fine sights, trigger, and accuracy, the M14 is rifle
one can *very* easily hit with! In fact, it's very hard to miss with
an M14, especially at 400+yds. Even though the sights are basically a 65 year-old design, they still perform very well today.

❸ AR10   77.8% (358/460)
        sights 83.7%   misc. 66.9%
    Most AR10s are 1½MOA accurate, but not notably reli-
able. (Mine was just the opposite. Go figure.) Still, the system
is generally renowned for fine accuracy, and has the best battle
rifle sights in the business (83.7% vs. the M14's 75.7%), no matter what M14 devotees claim to the contrary.

❹ FAL   68.0% (313/460)
        sights 65.3%   misc. 73.1%
    Now *this* surprised me! I had expected a score much
closer to the M14's, not 11% below. The fat, rounded front sight
post, very mediocre rear sight, and the mushy trigger pull combined to do in the FAL with a 68.0%. Although the FAL has fine
target accuracy, it is noticeably more difficult to hit with in the
field. Unfortunately, that's just one of those lessons you can
learn only by testing a rifle in its natural environment.
    That I shot the 200/300 Speed Shoot about 1 second faster
with the FAL than the M14 was no doubt a reflection of the
FAL's superior ergonomics and handling, as well as my then
greater field experience with the FAL. After more practice with
the M14, I believe that my times would equal those of the FAL.

❺ **HK91**   **65.7% (302/460)**
         sights 66.0%   **misc. 65.1%**

Although the 91's sights scored 66.0% (edging out the FAL by 0.7%), its abysmal trigger really sunk the rifle into last place. Such was wholly unnecessary, as improved sights and trigger are absurdedly easy to implement.

When Germans are right about something, they are brilliantly correct. When they're *wrong*, nobody is more wrong...

Well, how did I manage to place 2nd in the Speed Shoot with an average time as fast or faster than the best times of the FAL and M14? As I earlier explained, the tactical chest-carry sling really sped up shoulder welds. The HK91's razor-sharp front sight also helped to make the hits, not to mention that the rifle itself was incredibly accurate. Finally, it just goes to show you how an experienced Rifleman can overcome a poor trigger pull and stout recoil.

Affordability   (4% of total)

Since including or excluding this did not change the rankings at all, Affordability proved informative only. Get the best battle rifle for *you*, cost be damned! You only have to buy it *once*. Nobody ever regrets having chosen top quality.

❶ 93.3% M1
❷ 78.3% FAL
❸ 68.3% M14
❹ 65.0% HK91
❺ 63.3% AR10

Overall Score

There was a 8.9% difference between 1st and 5th Place; a C+ versus a D+. Only 3.6% separated 1st and 3rd. So, you can understand why my favorites since 1998 and 2000 have been different from 2002 (which is final, given the extensive T&E I've done). Drumroll, please! This is the moment we've all been waiting for! In reverse order, here is Boston's latest and final pick for best overall battle rifle:

❺ **AR10**   **68.8% (949/1380)**

With its 1st in Usability and near tie for 3rd in Combat Accuracy, the AR10 was poised to take 1st overall but for its *last* place in Reliability.

Had the AR10 shown just 70% overall reliability (as I gave it in 2000), it would have (with 1046 points) beaten the FAL. Had it matched the FAL's reliability (75.5%), it would have been within 2 points overall of the M14.

I simply cannot recommend the AR10 for any role.

❹ HK91   71.5% (986/1380)

Last in Usability and Combat Accuracy, the HK91 simply falls short in everything but brute ruggedness and reliability. A good Rifleman could make do with a 91, but he wouldn't *enjoy* it. Personally, I'd scope my HK91 and store it at the cabin.

❸ FAL   74.1% (1023/1380)

4th in Reliability, 2nd in Usability, and 4th in Combat Accuracy—the FAL, while a very solid and capable system, just couldn't *quite* equal or edge out the M14 or M1. It was only 4.2% behind the M14. (Only 50 more points (out of 1380) would have put the FAL in 1st Place; that's how close it was between the FAL and the M14.)

With a reciprocating bolt handle (+24 points) and M14-quality sights and trigger (+42 points), the FAL would have had 1089 points for a 78.9% 1st Place.

If you have an FAL with a 7-Good trigger that you can hit well with, then there's probably no compelling need to switch to an M14. But, you should give the M14 a try; you never know...

❷ M1   76.9% (1055/1380)

Another surprise was how well the M1 acquitted itself: 3rd in Reliability, 4th in Usability, and 1st in Combat Accuracy. If the 8rd clips don't bother you, then the venerable M1 could be the battle rifle for you (especially if you're on a tight budget). Although the M1 can't compete with the 20rd mag-fed rifles in cyclic rate, this is not *ipso facto* a huge detriment unless facing human wave attacks. A calm and focussed M1 Rifleman can get the job done just about as well as with an M14. It's a similar comparison to the .30/06 vs. .308 debate: if you can't do it with a .308 then a .30/06 won't make any difference. Thus, if you can't do it with an M1, then an M14 won't turn you into a Rifleman.

Get a nice (though non-collectible) Korean War Springfield Armory rifle (they have the last mods and are of the best quality), and throw a cryo-treated Krieger .308 barrel on it. There's just something inexplicably special about a Garand!

❶ M14   77.7% (1072/1380)

2nd in Reliability, 3rd in Usability, and 2nd in Combat Accuracy—the M14 is the most *consistently* capable .308 battle rifle available today. In no area did it ever rate less than 70%, unlike the other four rifles. While the M1 and the FAL are also excellent all-around choices, the M14 is just a little bit better. Until 1994, it was my favorite, but then I scampered down other paths (*i.e.*, FAL, AR10, HK91). While I still like my FAL and HK91, I feel most confident with my M14—and it's what I have come to *enjoy* shooting the most.

Fred at Fred's M14 Stocks and Vin Suprynowicz—you guys were right! (Pause while I finish my meal of crow.)

Why the M14 won

Something just became obvious to me here. The M14 won for two basic reasons:

The M14 is about the *best* it can be.

The M1, FAL, HK91, and AR10 are *not*.

I don't mean that the M14 is the best that a battle rifle can be; I mean that it's the best an *M14* can be. Looking it over, I can't see any glaring design faults or shortcomings. As "Fred" puts it, the rifle *"has no vices."* The M14 is quite simply Good to Excellent in *everything*. Even its weakest area (Usability/Ergonomics) isn't really all *that* weak at 71.8%.

On the other hand, the M1, FAL, HK91, and AR10 all fall below 70% in at least one major area:

M1	65.5%	Usability		
FAL	68.0%	Combat Accuracy		
HK91	59.7%	Usability	65.7%	Combat Accuracy
AR10	51.7%	Reliability		

I pointed out how the FAL, HK91, or AR10 (1950s designs) could have easily beat the M14 (basically a pre-WWII system) if only a bit more design thought and consideration had been invested. All three are fine systems in their own right, but they simply fell short just shy of the finish line.

The M1 and M14 were better at being themselves than were the FAL, HK91, and AR10. This is how two Model Ts won against three Model As.

Regardless of all this discussion, I heartily urge you to try the M1, M14, FAL, and HK91 as only *6.1%* separated 1st from 4th Place. (The AR10 is not worthy of real consideration.) I have amply explained my 1st choice; now it's *your* turn to find the battle rifle which hits best for *you*. If you don't have the time, money, opportunity, or inclination to test them all, then just get an M14 (especially if you're a lefty) and be done with it.

ANOTHER WAY TO COMPARE

Instead of coldly ranking some 63 criteria of these battle rifles, let's simply compare them amongst different *roles*. I've come up with the six below, although there are certainly others:

Home

If the rifle is carried at all, it will be only for perimeter or neighborhood defense. It probably won't be shot very often, and rarely during extended battles. Count on excellent parts and gunsmithing support from home and gun industry. Affordability is most important here vs. the other roles.

Best Home Battle Rifle: **M1** (a fine Kalifornia MBR)

Basic Field (under moderate conditions)

Contemplates fielding from a ranch, farm, or base camp for wide area patrols. Rifle must carry well, and be rugged and reliable. Good parts and gunsmithing support from base.

Best Light Field Battle Rifles: **M14** or **FAL**

Heavy Field (under filthy conditions)

Total guerrilla conditions. Rifle ruggedness and reliability are paramount. Little or no parts/gunsmithing support from nomadic base camps.

Best Heavy Field Battle Rifle: **HK91**

Counter-sniper

Requires an inherently accurate system with excellent scope base, trigger, and barrel length (*i.e.,* 21" minimum for best velocity). Recoil must be mild, to avoid stressing the optics.

Best Counter-sniper Battle Rifles: **AR10(T)** or **M14**

Night

Must be readily adaptable to IR scope and/or laser target designator. Requires a flash suppressor and lengthy barrel.

Best Night Battle Rifle: **M14**

"Road Warrior"

Imagines utterly no parts/gunsmithing support in a post-apocalyptic world. Ruggedness and reliability are crucial.

Best "Road Warrior" Battle Rifle: **HK91**

Role comparison

★★★ Excellent   ★★ Good   ★ Fair   — Poor

	home	basic field	heavy field	counter sniper	night	"Road Warrior"
M1	★★★	★★	★	—	—	★
M14	★★	★★★	★★	★★★	★★★	★★
FAL	★★	★★★	★★	★★	★★	★★
HK91	★★	★★	★★★	★	★	★★★
AR10	★	★	—	★★★	—	—

So, what does this tell us? It confirms the results of the hair-splitting analysis—that the M14 (with 15 stars out of 18 possible) is still the most versatilely capable battle rifle of the bunch. It does everything at least well, and half superbly (being first or tied for first).

The second best rifle, the FAL, got 12 stars. The HK91 came in third with 11 stars. Fourth was the M1 with 7 stars, and fifth was the AR10 with 5 stars. (In this comparison, the FAL and M1 switched former 4th and 2nd place positions, reflecting the FAL's greater role versatility. Also, the HK91, because of its rugged reliability, moved the AR10 into last place.)

Conclusions

In general you should lean heavily towards the M14 and secondarily towards the FAL. If you expect *very* serious conditions for a *very* long time, then get an HK91. An M1 shines brightest for home and light field duty (ejected clips are not easily picked up during heavy battles).

So, think about *how* and *where* you will likely most use your battle rifle, and choose the most appropriate one.

Why did it take me so long to pick the M1A?

My first M1A was an inaccurate Bush rifle. My first FAL experience was with a lovely Belgian gun. And, I simply had a crush on the AR10 for several years. Today, after thousands of rounds of testing, I have earned a new and better perspective. Rifle to rifle (out-of-the-box) the M1A barely edges out the FAL.

Final comments on your .308 battle rifle

Remember, this is a *generalist's* rifle. It was designed to do everything at least pretty well. Is it the best CQB rifle? No, but it will certainly suffice. Is it a countersniper rifle? No, but it will do a fine job out to 600, and in the right hands out to 800. If I could own just one rifle—heck, just one *gun*—it would be an M14 or FAL or HK91. **They have the greatest versatility of any firearm.** Think of them like excellent midrange stereo speakers; they're neither woofers nor tweeters, but they sound pretty damn good for a single speaker.

Yes, you *may* need a CBQ carbine, so get an AR15A3 or an accurate/tarted up Romanian AK. Yes, you *may* need a tactical .308, so get a nice bolt gun with a fine scope. But, the M14/FAL/HK91 overlap well into those two categories, so begin here and then branch out to other systems if necessary. You can field carry only one rifle, so make it the one with the fewest compromises.

If your battle rifle can shoot ¾-1¼MOA, then it will be accurate enough for 6" groups out to 500-800yds. Do not accept iron sight FMJ groups larger than 4MOA—find a better rifle.

I'd acquire a *lifetime* supply of spare parts (*e.g.*, two or three sets of: bolts, sights, firing pins, extractors, ejectors, trigger groups, hammer springs, pins, etc.), an extra barrel or two, *30+* mags, and at least 10,000rds of boxer-primed ammo. Then, I'd get to Thunder Ranch (830-640-3138) *immediately* for Urban Rifle 1 and 2.

Why so *many* parts? Because I doubt I'll be able to order them in the year 2020, that's why. I mean, with the evil march of firearm industry lawsuits and increasing citizen disarmament measures, do you *honestly* expect in twenty years to be able to call up DSA, Fulton, or QP and order parts for your rifle—when *"assault weapons"* long since have been *outlawed*?

SOME RIFLEMAN PARTING WORDS

This is my rifle. There are many like it, but this one is mine. My rifle is my best friend. It is my life. I must master it as I must master my life. My rifle, without me, is useless. Without my rifle, I am useless. I must fire my rifle true. I must shoot straighter than my enemy who is trying to kill me. I must shoot him before he shoots me. I will...

My rifle and myself know that what counts in this war is not the rounds we fire, the noise of our burst, nor the smoke we make. We know that it is hits that count. We will hit...

My rifle is human, even as I, because it is my life. Thus, I will learn it as a brother. I will learn its weaknesses, its strength, its parts, its accessories, its sights, and its barrel. I will ever guard it against the ravages of weather and damage as I will ever guard my legs, my arms, my eyes, and my heart against damage. I will keep my rifle clean and ready, even as I am clean and ready. We will become part of each other. We will...

Before God I swear this creed. My rifle and myself are the defenders of my country. We are the masters of our enemy. We are the saviors of my life.

So be it, until victory is America's and there is no enemy, but Peace!

— *My Rifle: The Creed of a United States Marine* (1944),
by Major General William H. Rupertus, USMC

Whichever rifle you choose, you must *train* with it! Soon, hard, and often. In a rifle fight, I'd rather have an HK91 with 5,000rds of training behind me than a new M14 which I'd never fired. Merely owning a rifle no more makes you a Rifleman than owning a piano makes you a pianist. Whichever battle rifle happens to be the best for you, *it will not do if you will not do.* **Never love equipment more than training!** Pick up the phone and order at least 2,000rds of quality 7.62x51 FMJ today!

Call up "Fred" at Fred's M14 Stocks (800-979-2144; www.fredsm14stocks.com) and order his excellent *Guide To Becoming A Rifleman* and 25 Meter AQT targets, as well as his 3-year collection of columns (all for Ø24 + Ø6 S&H).

A rifleman is a man who can make first-round hits at unknown ranges, under unknown conditions, on demand and against the clock.

— Jeff Cooper

Riflemen are made, not born, and it takes a while. Right now battle rifles are legal and available, surplus 7.62x51 at 15¢/rd is the cheapest it's ever been, and training hasn't been restricted or outlawed. *Any of that could change next month!* (Ammo has dried up a bit since 9/11.)

You have an historic chance *now* to obtain the rifle, ammo, and experience required to become a Rifleman. The time to do so is *before* the next Lexington and Concord, not when the Redcoats have begun to march down your road. I'm not kidding about all this, folks. Get to work on becoming a Rifleman. If we have learned anything from history, it is that liberty can be preserved or restored only with a *rifle*. It takes considerable skill to use one well, and such skill comes *only* from proper training.

Start...training...*now*.

Handguns are *not* the priority; you can train with them anywhere and good instructors abound. Martial arts can wait; you can train in your garage without even your neighbors knowing. Training with battle rifles, however, is noisy, expensive, dramatic—not to mention becoming socially unacceptable and legally vulnerable. Furthermore, quality instructors are scarce. That's why you must start *today*. Next month may be too late. If this book convinces you of anything, then I hope it is that. Become a Rifleman and all else will fall in line.

A tidy anecdote from that race of Riflemen, the Swiss:

> ...*Kaiser Wilhelm made a state visit to Switzerland shortly before the Great War. After reviewing an honor guard of Swiss soldiers he stopped to compliment their non-com on the men's soldierly appearance. Half-jokingly he asked the old Sergeant-Major what would little Switzerland do if Imperial Germany invaded them with a force twice as strong. The gray haired Sergeant thought for a moment before answering:* **"Then, Your Excellency, we would all have to fire our rifles twice!"**
> — Paul Scarlata; *The Shotgun News Treasury 2000,* p. 46

Now *that's* the spirit!

Here's another anecdote from a Rifleman—a Finnish veteran of the 1939-40 Russian war—who just didn't understand the mindset of his sensitive, touchy-feely interviewer:

Q: *"You saw a lot of infantry action?"*
A: *"Much."*

Q: *"Did you ever engage in a firefight?"*
A: *"Often."*

Q: *"Did you ever have occasion to shoot at a human being?"*
A: *"Yes, several times."*

Q: *"Did you find this difficult?"*
A: *"Yes. You see they tended to duck, to get behind cover, and to run in a zigzag."*

How I wish I could have seen the interviewer's face!

	weight	M1	M14	FAL	HK91	AR10
RELIABILITY (38%)						
Op System (58% of 38%)						
gas system	3	8	9	9	10	5
gas regulator	1	0	10	10	10	0
action hygiene	4	10	10	8	3	3
action exposure	3	3	3	8	8	10
recip. bolt handle	2	10	10	0	0	0
reliability: feeding	4	7	8	8	10	6
reliability: firing	5	9	8	8	10	6
reliability: extraction	5	8	9	8	10	5
reliability: ejection	4	8	8	9	10	4
Design Ruggedness (42% of 38%)						
working parts placement	1	10	10	2	6	1
design complexity	2	9	9	4	6	5
parts breakage	3	6	7	9	10	7
fieldstripping	2	7	7	9	10	8
parts availability	2	8	7	8	6	3
overall ruggedness	4	8	8	8	10	5
handguard ruggedness	1	8	8	8	9	7
buttstock ruggedness	1	9	9	8	9	5
mag ruggedness	4	10	9	8	10	8
mag availability	2	8	6	8	7	5
RELIABILITY SCORES:	530	419	429	408	448	280
		79.1%	80.9%	77.0%	84.5%	52.8%
		M1	M14	FAL	HK91	AR10

	weight	M1	M14	FAL	HK91	AR10
USABILITY (24%)						
Static Handling (45%)						
weight	3	7	9	8	7	8
mag weight	2	10	8	9	6	8
length overall	2	5	5	6	9	7
barrel length	1	10	10	9	6	8
handguard length	1	10	9	8	9	8
handguard heatshielding	2	4	5	8	9	9
handguard fit/feel	1	9	9	9	7	9
buttstock fit/feel	1	8	8	7	6	9
pistol grip fit/feel	1	0	0	7	9	10
stock/pistol grip storage	1	6	6	2	0	9
Controls (55% of 24%)						
charging handle location	3	7	7	10	5	8
charging handle feel	3	8	8	10	2	5
bolt hold open & release	2	4	6	7	2	10
safety	1	6	6	7	8	10
mag catch	2	4	7	7	7	10
mag to gun dynamics	3	5	7	8	8	9
lefty ergonomics	2	8	9	3	3	7
overall handling	2	7	8	9	7	9
USABILITY SCORES:	330	214	237	255	197	273
		64.8%	71.8%	77.3%	59.7%	82.7%
		M1	M1A	FAL	HK91	AR10

COMBAT ACCURACY (34%)	weight	M1	M14	FAL	HK91	AR10
Sights (65% of 34%)						
sight radius	3	10	10	8	8	7
sight offset	1	10	10	6	6	4
front sight visibility	3	9	9	8	6	9
front sight adjustability	1	7	7	7	0	10
front sight precision	4	9	9	6	9	9
front sight protection	3	8	7	9	10	8
rear sight visibility	3	7	7	8	4	10
rear sight readability	2	4	4	7	10	8
rear sight adjustability	2	7	7	4	3	9
rear sight precision	3	9	9	4	4	7
rear sight ruggedness	2	5	5	4	4	7
tritium sight	1	0	0	0	10	10
scope base	2	6	8	9	8	10
Accuracy Misc. (35%)						
bolt and carrier	1	7	7	7	8	10
trigger pull	4	9	9	5	4	8
target accuracy	4	9	9	9	9	7
muzzle blast	2	10	10	9	7	3
recoil	2	10	10	8	4	6
8 hits at 200/300yds	3	8	6	7	7	6

COMBAT ACCURACY SCORES:	460	370	365	313	302	358
		80.4%	79.4%	68.0%	65.7%	77.8%
		M1	M14	FAL	HK91	AR10

AFFORDABILITY (4%)	weight	M1	M14	FAL	HK91	AR10
OEM rifle price	1	9	8	6	4	7
clone rifle price	1	10	10	9	10	8
brass reloadability	1	9	9	4	6	9
parts price	1	8	4	8	5	6
mag price	2	10	5	10	7	4

AFFORDABILITY SCORES:	60	56	41	47	39	38
		93.3%	68.3%	78.3%	65.0%	63.3%

TOTAL RIFLE SCORES		M1	M14	FAL	HK91	AR10
(OMITTING AFFORDABILITY):	1320	1003	1031	976	947	911
		76.0%	78.1%	73.9%	71.7%	69.0%

TOTAL RIFLE SCORES		M1	M14	FAL	HK91	AR10
(INCL. AFFORDABILITY):	1380	1059	1072	1023	986	949
		76.7%	77.7%	74.1%	71.5%	68.8%

RELIABILITY/TOTAL	38%
USABILITY/TOTAL	24%
COMBAT ACCURACY/TOTAL	33%
AFFORDABILITY/TOTAL	4%

11

M1 GARAND
& M14 (M1A™)

The M1 Rifle is the greatest battle implement ever devised.
— Lt. Gen. George S. Patton, Jr., 26 January 1945

As you learned in the chapter *Rating the Battle Rifles*, the M14-type system has at last become my pick of battle rifle. It does everything well, and most things *very* well. Having been derived from its battle-tested/proven M1 "father", it has no glaring faults. Although I still nevertheless enjoy my FAL (and would field with it without reservation), the M14 slightly edges out the FAL in every aspect but ergonomics. Even the M1 Garand remains a perfectly viable battle rifle for many applications, especially if you build a very accurate milspec gun in .308.

This chapter will discuss just about everything you need to know about the M1 Garand and M14-type rifles (which includes the M1A™ made by Springfield Armory, Inc.® in Illinois, vs. the National Armory in Springfield, Mass. of M1/M14 fame).

10	Exceptional
9	Extremely Good
8	Very Good
7	Good
6	Fair
5	Just Tolerable
4	Poor
3	Very Poor
2	Extremely Poor
1	Worst Possible
0	Nonexistent

M1/M14 RELIABILITY   (38% of total)

M1/M14 Op System (58% of category)

M1/M14 gas system   (x3)   **Score: 8/9**

The 1930s technology M1 Garand uses an op rod which is blasted directly rearward by gas pressure. While generally very reliable, it is fairly violent in action (as there was no inherent gas cutoff) and many earlier version op rods eventually broke under the strain. I scored it an 8.

The M14 has a far superior system. With the goal of reducing the force and heat applied to the op rod, the gas cylinder was moved back 8" and a hollow gas tappet was employed as an intermediary to deliver kinetic energy to the op rod. Upon firing, gas pressurizes the hollow tappet, pushing it rearward (moving the vent out of alignment with the gas port, shutting off gas flow), quickly forcing it back 1½" to strike the op rod. Once the tappet has done so, its travel lines uncovers the gas cylinder's exhaust port to relieve the excess pressure. The system enjoys all the pressure it needs to strike the op rod, but no more (as in the M1). Very elegant—a 9.

> *Though the two main European military rifles for* [the .308], *the German G3...and the Belgium FN/FAL are excellent rifles, one cannot go wrong with the M14 or its civilian version, the M1A. This is without doubt the finest general purpose main battle rifle ever developed. ...*[I]*t cannot, from a design and function standpoint, be easily improved upon.* (p.402)
>
> *Compared to other systems, this uses less velocity in making the rifle function; is more consistent; and is much more tolerant of slow burning powders and of changes in port pressure and ambient temperatures.* (p.403)
>
> — *Any Shot You Want* (1996)

M1/M14 gas regulator   **Score: 0/10**

The M1 (which does not enjoy the M14's superior gas system), got a zero. Under conditions of heavy rain, or due to great neglect or abuse, it was known to freeze or corrode shut.

The M14 has a gas expansion/cut-off system which is self-regulating and compensates not only for fouling, but even for a totally rusted-shut gas piston. Firing just one round of FMJ will free any carbonized or rusted piston, and the rifle will function perfectly thereafter. Hence, no gas regulator is necessary. (My thanks to Fred of Fred's M14 Stocks for setting me straight on this point.) A 10.

M1/M14 action hygiene   **(x4)**   **Score: 10/10**
  No gas is vented into the action. This eliminates any action fouling and *greatly* increases reliability between cleanings.

M1/M14 action exposure   **(x3)**   **Score: 3/3**
  The bolt is totally exposed on top and has several holes for entry of dirt, sand, mud, water, etc. The largest and most egregious is the huge gap behind the bolt's right side underneath the rear sight bridge. The shooter must take care not to dump foreign material in there which will gum up the trigger group.

M1/M14 reciprocating bolt handle   **(x2)**   **Score: 10/10**

M1/M14 reliability: feeding   **(x4)**   **Score: 7/8**
  The M1 doesn't feed *quite* as reliably as the M14

M1/M14 reliability: firing   **(x5)**   **Score: 9/8**
  The trigger group is superb:

In most weapons, the firing pin blow is either directly or indirectly caused by a compressed spring and the energy in the spring usually decreases as the firing pin moves forward. Thus, when the spring becomes fatigued, the impact on the primer is materially reduced and the result may be hangfires or misfires. In the Garand firing mechanism, the construction which controls the hammer is such that the leverage is increased as the hammer nears the point of impact, which tends to reduce the load on the sear, cause the the trigger to pull easily, and increase the load on the firing pin at the time of firing, helping to prevent the extrusion of the primer into the firing pin hole.
  — Beretta Arms Co., *Maintenance of the U.S. Rifle Garand*

The *only* reason why I did not score the M1A™ firing reliability a 9 like the M1, is that it is somewhat prone to receiver stretching, which increases the chances of failures-to-fire. (This is *guaranteed* to occur in the cookie-dough soft Chinese M14 clones.) It happened to a used Springfield Armory® .308 M1 Garand of mine, which after 2,000rds, suddenly became plagued with chronic hangfires and failures-to-fire (*i.e.,* 1-4rds per *clip*) with the particular FMJ I had stockpiled. I tried various firing pins, bolts, and trigger groups (and all combinations thereof), and nothing helped. Finally, I took it in to Ron Smith of Smith Enterprise who determined that the investment cast receiver had stretched *just enough* (about 0.005") to produce the failures. (I'll discuss investment cast vs. forged receivers later in this chapter.) While the rifle functioned with other ammo (of which I had little), the "handwriting on the wall" was clear. I reluctantly sold the gun, which had been a real favorite.

Check headspace and firing pin protrusion before buying!

M1/M14 reliability: extraction   (x5)   Score: 8/9
Because of the M1's violent op rod movement, stripped case heads can occur from tight or dirty chambers. The M14's gas system is much less violent, which solves that problem.

M1/M14 reliability: ejection   (x4)   Score: 8/8
The ejector is a spring-powered post contained in the bolt, which works quite well, but not *quite* as well as a fixed ejector (such as found in the FAL and HK91). Failures to fully eject occasionally show up in rifles with steel scope mounts.

Overall, the **M1** got an **8.1**, with its slight weakness in feeding and extraction relative to the M14. Scoring an **8.3** overall was the **M14** with solid 8s and 9s. (In truth, good M1s with good PM operate at an 8.5-9, and similar M14s at 9-9.5.)

M1/M14 Design Ruggedness (42%)
M1/M14 working parts placement   Score: 10/10
All working parts are *forward* of the buttstock.

M1/M14 design complexity   (x2)   Score: 9/9
Using the M14's 61 total parts as a 90% standard, I divided the other guns into the theoretical goal of 55 parts to achieve a useful ratio. For contrast, the third column assumes the M14's 61 parts to be an unbeatable standard.

	# of parts	55 / #	61 / #
M14	61	.900	1.000
M1	62	.887	.984
SVT40	64	.859	.953
FN49	70	.786	.871
SKS	70	.786	.871
AK	75	.733	.813
HK91	92	.598	.663
AR	119	.462	.512
FAL	143	.385	.427

M1/M14 parts breakage   (x3)   Score: 6/7
The M1 must be kept *very* well-greased else you'll bend an an op rod or snap a spring. (Make sure that your op rod has that hemicircle relief cut!)

The M14 is not nearly as prone to such during poor lubrication, but the risk is still there.

M1/M14 fieldstripping   (x2)   Score: 7/7
The M1/M14 is a rather mixed bag. I love its fine modular trigger group, and the rifle's brilliantly-easy disassembly, but breaking down its bolt takes strength, finesse, and a small screwdriver. (If you work on them a lot at home, then get the special tool.) Also, a tool is needed to open up the gas system. Cleaning the rifle is not difficult, but I do find it AR-tedious. The action must be lubed, not oiled. Thus, it got only a 7-Good. Full lubrication details are explained later in this chapter.

M1/M14 parts availability   (x2)   Score: 8/7
M1 parts abound, but some M14 parts (*e.g.,* op rods!) are more difficult to find. For both rifles, check *Shotgun News* for:

Amherst Depot	941-475-2020	www.amherst-depot.com
Fred's M14 Stocks	800-979-2144	www.fredsm14stocks.com
Fulton Armory	800-878-9485	www.fulton-armory.com
Sarco, Inc.	908-647-3800	www.sarcoinc.com
Dupage Trading Co.	630-739-5768	www.dupagetrading.com
CMP	888-267-0796	www.odcmp.com

M1/M14 overall ruggedness   (x4)   Score: 8/8
Thoroughly tested in WWII/Korea (M1), and Vietnam (M14). By Korea, the troops thought the M1 Garand was just about perfect as is, and they were right!

M1/M14 handguard ruggedness   Score: 8/8
Very Good.

M1/M14 buttstock ruggedness   Score: 9/9
Designed when buttstocks were known be used in combat as impact weapons.

M1/M14 mag ruggedness   (x4)   Score: 10/9
The most rugged mags are the M1 (it's a blind mag, remember?). The M14 mag is almost as rugged as the HK91's.

M1/M14 mag availability   (x2)   Score: 8/6
M1 *en bloc* 8rd clips are available everywhere and are unaffected by federal *"gun control"* legislation (so far, so stock up!).

M14 mags, however, are the most difficult to find amongst battle rifles—now even more so than HK91 mags (which is a reversal from the 1980s).

M1/M14 USABILITY   (24% of total)

M1/M14 Static handling (45% of category)

M1/M14 weight   (x3)   Score: 7/9

At 8.7lbs with synthetic (not wood) stock, the M14 is the lightest, and thus got the 9-Extremely Good. (Since I believe that an 8¼lb MBR is possible, 8.7lbs did not rate a 10-Exceptional.) The 10lb M1 Garand is about average.

M1/M14 mag weight   (x2)   Score: 10/8

Here is where M1 clips shine! 5 clips containing 40rds weigh much less than any two 20rd mags. On a separate note, M1 clips may be kept loaded forever without weakening, which is obviously not the case with spring-powered magazines.

M1/M14 length overall   (x2)   Score: 5/5

The M1 is 43.6" long, and the M14 (with 22" barrel and its flash suppressor) is 44.3" long. Thus, they got the lowest scores. Unless you expect a lot of urban warfare and house clearing, a 44" long MBR shouldn't pose much of a problem.

M1/M14 barrel length   Score: 10/10

I gave the M1 and M14 the 10 because of their 24" and 22" barrels (any longer barrel in a .308 gives little meaningful velocity gain).

M1/M14 handguard length   Score: 10/9

The M1 is king (10), followed by the M14.

M1/M14 handguard heatshielding   (x2)   Score: 4/5

A 5 to the M14. (Increased ventilation and/or better heatshielding would raise this to a 7 or 8.) The unshielded wooden M1 furniture gets hot really quickly, and rates a 4.

M1/M14 handguard fit/feel   Score: 9/9

Both rifles are superb in this respect.

M1/M14 buttstock fit/feel   Score: 8/8

The slippery steel buttplates (likely an unavoidable adjunct of their buttstock compartments) cost the 2 points.

M1/M14 pistol grip fit/feel   Score: 0/0

In the 1930s, rifles simply did not have pistol grips, so the M1 never a chance for this feature. Such were contemplated only later for select-fire guns (*e.g.,* MP40, FG42, MP44, etc.), and only the squad automatic M14A1 had a pistol grip. (I once

saw an M14A1 stock—with all the metal fittings!—for only
Ø150, but I had just spent Ø200 on a minty 1942 M38 Swedish
Mauser. The stock sold in the 10 minutes it took me to round up
the cash. *Arrrgh!*)

Lack of a pistol grip in the M14 slows down shouldering
and malfunction clearances, and really hurt the rifle's ranking
here. An AR-quality pistol grip (10 points) would have put the
M14 only 6 points behind the FAL (2nd place here) in Usability.

McMillan makes a fiberglass pistol grip stock (#M2A),
which is used on the Marines' DMR of the 26th MEU.

M1/M14 butstock and pistol grip storage   Score: 6/6
The M1 and M14 both have excellent buttstock compartments, but no pistol grip, so they got a 6.

M1/M14 Controls (55% of category)
M1/M14 charging handle location   (x3)   Score: 7/7
The M1/M14 handle is mistakenly on the right side, but
works surprisingly well from a shooting grip, so I gave it a 7.

M1/M14 charging handle feel   (x3)   Score: 8/8
The handle is wide, nicely curved, and fairly smooth.

M1/M14 bolt stop   (x2)   Score: 4/6

	Manual H-O	Auto H-O	Release	
4		✔		(M1)
6	✔	✔		(M14)

Since the M1's internal mag cannot be easily topped off (unless
you've installed the Holbrook "Thumb Saver", discussed later),
the lack of a manual H/O is, on its own, rather moot.

As the M14 can be quickly charged from the righthand
shooting grip (or even underneath the rifle by the left hand), the
lack of a bolt release is less an issue than I thought in 2000.

If you can find a Smith Enterprise bolt stop, *buy* it! It's a
great improvement over the tiny original control.

M1/M14 safety   Score: 6/6
*...[T]he M1's trigger is among the safest in the world, and the simple
act of snapping the safety on does three things. It grips and holds
the hammer so that it cannot move. At the same time, it cams it totally out of engagement with the sear and blocks the forward movement of the sear, which of course stops the rearward movement of
the trigger, as the two are connected.*

— Roy Baumgardner, *Precision Shooting With The M1
Garand* (2000), p.65

The M1/M14 safety, while mechanically brilliant and simple, should have been placed *forward* of the trigger guard for easier manipulation (especially when wearing gloves). I don't much like its ergonomics (and it's a bit noisy), so it got a 6.

Perhaps a clever machinist could adapt the front of the safety with a perpendicular tab (about 1¼" wide) which could be manipulated by either index finger (gloved, or not) forward of the trigger guard. (This done, I'd raise the score to a 9 or 10.)

Or, install the M14 safety from the winter trigger. (As merely stamped steel, somebody oughta start making these.)

M1/M14 mag catch   (x2)   Score: 4/7

The M1 has a left-side clip ejection button (4). The M14 catch is small, but centrally-located (7).

M1/M14 mag to gun   (x3)   Score: 5/7

A 5 to the clip-fed M1 (watch your thumb!), and 7 to the M14 (a nose-in-rock-back variant which is sometimes fussy).

M1/M14 lefty ergonomics   (x2)   Score: 8/9

The M1 (8) and M14 (9) are the most naturally ambi battle rifles. A lefthanded buddy just got his first M1A, and loves it.

M1/M14 overall handling   (x2)   Score: 7/8

Balance is pretty good, but the rifles' length and lack of a pistol grip (and the M1's weight) detracted from the score.

M1/M14 COMBAT ACCURACY (34%)

M1/M14 Sights (65% of category)

M1/M14 sight radius   (x3)   Score: 10/10

The hands-down winner is the M1 with a whopping 28". The M14 is tied with its dad with a 27" radius (by wisely avoiding the design shortcut of placing the sight on the gas block), which helps to explain the M14's superb combat accuracy.

M1/M14 sight offset   Score: 10/10

The M1/M14 boast a mere 1" offset, which is really about the lowest possible.

M1/M14 front sight visibility   (x3)   Score: 9/9

A wing-protected blade, which is very clear.

M1/M14 front sight adjustability   **Score: 7/7**
M1/M14 front sights are adjustable only for windage zero, and rely upon the rear sight for elevation zero. While this is a workable system, it is not my first design choice. The front sight block can loosen and shift (it happened on my M1), and the elevation knob must be index realigned for zero.

M1/M14 front sight precision   (x4)   Score: 9/9
The M1/M14 front sight is very sharp. The NM sight is 0.062" + 0.005" wide, and the corners cannot excede a radius of 0.003". *That* is precise!
Furthermore, the sight was designed as a ranging device. That 0.062" post width is 8MOA, which corresponds to about 20" (width of military silhouette paper target) at 250yds.
I rate the standard front sight a 9, and the NM sight a 10.

M1/M14 front sight protection   (x3)   Score: 8/7
The M1/M14 have winged ears, though the sight block can shift in its dovetail. (If your shots begin to increasingly string horizontally, this is likely why.) Since the M1 block is much thicker and uses a larger set screw, it got an 8 to the M14's 7.

M1/M14 rear sight visibility   (x3)   Score: 7/7
A nice aperture is found on the M1/M14, though at 0.074" it is a bit too small for CQB/low light, so I gave it a 7.
The hooded NM sight is available in two aperture sizes: 0.0520" (#7781282) and 0.0595" (#7791113).

M1/M14 rear sight readability   (x2)   Score: 4/4
The M1/M14 elevation knob unfortunately uses very small and lightly stamped numerals. Also, a larger diameter knob would have eliminated the unnecessary overlapping of markings. I gave it a 4-Poor. (My M1 Tanker Garand had a knob from a BM59, which I found superior.) Brighten up those numerals with some orange or yellow paint, and/or paint a line across the drum for your 250m/275yd battlesight zero (BSZ).

M1/M14 rear sight adjustability   (x2)   Score: 7/7
The M1/M14 rear sight is quite good with MOA elevation increases per click, but a bit tedious to zero because the elevation knob must be unscrewed and reindexed. (Proper tightening of the windage knob pinion takes practice.) Range dialing requires the tiny elevation knob to be *carefully* clicked (as it's very easy to overdo it). The M1 is calibrated for yards (out to 1200), and the M14/M1A is calibrated for meters (out to 1100).

M1/M14 rear sight precision   (x3)   Score: 9/9

The M1/M14 rear sight is quite precise (especially the NM ½MOA version with its 64tpi). A 9 to the standard sight, and a 10 to the NM sight. BDC precision is superb. (Once I lased a bathtub-sized boulder at 800m, dialed up the sight and began spanking the hapless rock immediately.)

M1/M14 rear sight ruggedness   (x2)   Score: 5/5

The M1/M14 aperture is not fully protected and should have had higher and thicker ears (as on the WWI US M1917 .30/06). Also, the fine splines (especially on the NM sight) are prone to running, jumping, and slack movement:

> The problem with the M14 sight is that taking on or off a click some-times doesn't: Put on a click of wind and shoot another round into the same (uncorrected) place. Puzzle that for a moment, give an-other click in the same direction and all of a sudden get two and find yourself out the other side of the target. The rear sight can also "run," that is, move elevation on its own. These sight problems are usually fitting problems, and sometimes parts problems, but fre-quently are due to shooters loosening up the knobs too much to make them easy to turn. **The combination of correct adjustment, true parts, and a skilled hand can make an M14 sight reliable**, and I have one that's downright solid, but suffice it to say that you better have mapped out its sight movement before taking a new M14 to the line. (pp.273 and 274)
> — Glenn D. Zediker, *The Competitive AR15* (1999)

Although a simple (only *8* parts!) and clever sight (especially having been designed in the 1930s, and honed throughout WWII), it is not without its problems.

M1/M14 tritium sight   Score: 0/0

New for 2004: 24/7 tritium stripe set! www.xssights.com

M1/M14 scope base   (x2 for Battle Rifles)   Score: 6/8

Satisfactory M1 mounts exist, but stick with iron sights. For your M14, Smith Enterprise is the *only* way to go! (Other steel copies may *seem* the equal, but don't have the hardness.)

M1/M14 Accuracy Miscellaneous (35%)

M1/M14 bolt and carrier   Score: 7/7

The M1/M14 bolt locks into the *receiver* and is not as pre-cise and accurate as the AR-type barrel lockup. Granted, some M14s can be tuned to give 1MOA, however, the *potentiality* of its accuracy is limited partly because of its bolt-receiver lockup. ARs have an inherently more accurate action (¾MOA), and it shows in competitions. (Since I did not weight this criterion, let's not have you M14 High Power shooters freak out.)

M1/M14 trigger pull   (x4)   Score: 9/9

My favorite MBR trigger is found on the M1/M14. Not only is the trigger group a superb piece of engineering (with only 13 parts, and easily tunable), the quality of pull (4½-5½lbs) is excellent even from rack-grade rifles. These rifles are a pleasure to shoot because of the 2-stage trigger alone.

M1/M14 target accuracy   (x4 for Battle Rifles)   Score: 9/9

Easily tunable to 1½MOA without hindering reliability.

M1/M14 muzzle blast   Score: 10/10

Least (nearly unnoticeable, really) muzzle blast were from the M1 (24" bare tube) and M14 (22" tube with flash suppressor). 10s to the pair! (That 17.6" .308 Tanker M1 with Smith brake, however, had a healthy amount blast and would score a 5-Just Tolerable.)

M1/M14 recoil   (x2 for Battle Rifles)   Score: 10/10

The easiest recoiling battle rifles by far. Either can truly be shot all day without undue fatigue.

M1/M14 time for 8 hits at simulated 200/300yds (x3)   Score: 8/6

The M1 Garand I tested was a *very* accurate Springfield Armory® .308 Tanker. It had a 17.6" Match barrel (very barky, but the Smith muzzle brake worked superbly), and a lovely trigger job. It handled as easily as an umbrella, and hit almost automatically! (I also had WWII and Korean War M1s at my disposal, but not enough .30/06 ammo for a proper test. Their times would probably have been about 25-26 seconds.)

Two Springfield Armory® M1As had normal sights and triggers, and one "Loaded" model had NM barrel/sights.

Figuring on 18 seconds to be the theoretically quickest time, let's divide 180 by the rifle's average time.

	M1	M14	FAL	HK91	AR10
best	20.08	25.38	24.44	22.77	
average	21.57	28.34	26.98	24.46	
spread	1.49	2.96	2.54	1.69	
score	**8.34**	**6.35**	**6.67**	**7.36**	**6.67**

Since this drill began from a slung position, the short M1 Tanker had an advantage over the longer M1As. That Smith muzzle brake reduced muzzle jump by at least 50%, making successive shots *very* fast. Thus, the Tanker had all the advantages of short handiness, crisp front sight, accuracy, and little muzzle jump—and it paid off with an average time a second faster than the nearest rifle's *best* time!

While the M1As were accurate and easy to shoot, their extra length increased time to first shot, and muzzle jump slowed down successive shots. Although one could add an efficient muzzle brake, I prefer to leave the flash suppressor intact. In my opinion, lack of muzzle flash is much more tactically important on a *semi*-auto than any muzzle brake.

M1/M14 AFFORDABILITY (4%)

M1/M14 OEM rifle price   Score: 9/8
If you want the genuine article, then you'll have to pay for it.

WWII/Korean M1 Garand	Ø750	9-Extremely Good
Springfield Armory M1A™	Ø1,100	8-Very Good

M1/M14 clone rifle price   Score: 10/10
O.K., so it's *not* important to own the genuine article? Well, that's your choice, but you're generally much better off spending the extra dough.

Century Arms Intl. M1	Ø450	10-Exceptional
Polytech M14 clone	Ø500	10-Exceptional

The trick is to choose a quality rifle which somehow doesn't cost the Earth. Don't let the siren call of a bargain lure you: the CAI M1s generally have crappy receivers, and the Polytech M14s need a Ø500 heat-treat and bolt replacement from Smith Enterprise (which finishes out as a nice forged-receiver gun).

Pay for quality. A new Springfield Armory® "Loaded" M1A with National Match sights/barrel is a Ø1,300 bargain. Used "plain-Jane" M1As can still be found for Ø975-1,100 (only a few hundred more than the Polytech M14 clones).

M1/M14 brass reloadability   Score: 9/9
These systems are very gentle on brass.

M1/M14 parts price   Score: 8/4
M1 Garand parts are quite affordable (as 4X as many M1s were made than M14s).

Some M14 parts are very pricey (*e.g.*, retail Ø150 trigger groups, Ø200 op rods). Join a gun club affiliated with the CMP and order them respectively for Ø35 and Ø50.

M1/M14 mag price   (x2)   **Score: 10/5**
The real bargain is M1 Garand clips at 40-50¢ each (a buck if you're spendy). That means you can load 40rds for as little as Ø2! Even a FAL will cost you Ø10 for the same 40rds. Fred tells me that M1 clips are drying up, so buy plenty now.

Genuine M14 surplus parkerized mags are Ø40-50. Avoid the modern, blued steel Ø15 copies (which will malf/wear out).

This concludes the 63 criteria evaluation. The winner, as you know, was the M14/M1A, which beat out the FAL by 3.6%.

BATTLE RIFLE RANKING
M1/M14 Reliability   (38% of total)
❷ **M14**   **80.9% (429/530)**
op system 82.3%   design strength 79.1%
The M14 is a very reliable and rugged rifle. Its only real weakness is its exposed action and several orifices, however, such can be largely negated by a conscientious Rifleman.

❸ **M1**   **79.1% (413/530)**
op system 76.8%   design strength 82.3%
M14 remarks also apply here. The M1, because of its gas system, clip feeding, and no bolt roller isn't *quite* as reliable as its M14 "son," but if you take care of your Garand it will rarely let you down. As I'll explain shortly, the Korean-era rifles are about 10% more reliable than the WWII-era rifles.

M1/M14 Usability   (24% of total)
❸ **M14**   **71.8% (237/330)**
static 70.0%   dynamic 73.3%
Perfectly serviceable, though not brilliant. With practice, its right-side charging handle is no real handicap, nor is the mag catch. I'm still not in love with the safety, however.

After much more recent time with the M14, I've found it more ergonomic than I thought in 1998 and 2000.

❹ **M1**   **64.8% (214/330)**
static 68.0%   dynamic 62.2%
It's a little heavier than the M14, and not as well heat-shielded. Manipulating the 8rd clips takes some finesse, al-

though quick and competent empty reloading is possible with sufficient practice. 65.5% is halfway between Fair and Good, and such is also my subjective opinion. The M1 handles well enough—but no better—to do its job.

M1/M14 Combat Accuracy   (34% of total)

❶ M1   80.4% (370/460)
                sights 75.3%   misc. 90.0%

Recall that the M1 used here was a tackdriving Tanker .308 with a 17.6" barrel. It was lighter, handier, and more accurate than any full size .30/06 Garand could be. So, was this *fair*?

Yes, I think so. First, to compete with the other battle rifles, the M1 had to also be in .308 as surplus .30/06 ammo is neither ubiquitous nor a bargain (at 21¢/rd). Second, if it's going to have a .308 barrel, why choose a 24" when something closer to 19" is better? All in all, a .308 "Tanker" Garand is precisely the flavor of M1 best suited for the 21st Century Rifleman. Besides, it was only Ø750 and has become a personal favorite.

If, however, we were considering a surplus M1 in .30/06, then the M14/M1A would clearly be superior in accuracy.

❷ M14   79.4% (365/460)
                sights 75.7%   misc. 86.3%

With its fine sights, trigger, and accuracy, the M14 is rifle one can *very* easily hit with! In fact, it's very hard to miss with an M14 (versus a FAL). Even though the sights are basically a 65 year-old design, they still perform very well today.

M1/M14 Affordability   (4% of total)

❶   93.3% M1
❸   68.3% M14

M1/M14 Overall Score

❶ M14   77.7% (1072/1380)

2nd in Reliability, 3rd in Usability, and 2nd in Combat Accuracy—the M14 is the most *consistently* capable .308 battle rifle available today. In no area did it ever rate less than 70%, unlike the other four rifles. While the M1 and the FAL are also excellent all-around choices, the M14 is just a little bit better. Until 1994, it was my favorite, but then I scampered down other paths (*i.e.*, FAL, AR10, HK91). While I still really like my FAL

and HK91, I feel most confident with my M14—and it's what I have come to *enjoy* shooting the most.
Fred at Fred's M14 Stocks—you were right all along! (Pause while I finish my meal of crow.)

❷ **M1   76.7% (1059/1380)**
Another surprise was how well the M1 acquitted itself: 3rd in Reliability, 4th in Usability, and 1st in Combat Accuracy. If the 8rd clips don't bother you, then the venerable M1 could be the battle rifle for you (especially if you're on a tight budget). Although the M1 can't compete with the 20rd mag-fed rifles in cyclic rate, this is not *ipso facto* a huge detriment unless facing human wave attacks. A calm and focussed M1 Rifleman can get the job done just about as well as with an M14. It's a similar comparison to the .308 vs. .30/06 debate: if you can't do it with a .308 then a .30/06 won't make any difference. Thus, if you can't do it with an M1, then an M14 won't turn you into a Rifleman.

The Garand made second place on my list, tying with the FAL... But remember the '14 is an improvement of the the battle-tested M1, correcting its major fault—the en bloc 8-rd clip. Say you are attacking, and you've [already] fired 4 rounds. You have a moment, and maybe you want to top up your ammo. About impossible with the Garand. You gotta eject the clip, usually spilling the 4 rounds in the dirt, losing 'em. Remember, dust, noise, confusion, excitement, fingers shaking, etc. And every clip you fire in combat is, usually, a lost clip, unless you make a point of stopping and searching for it on the ground. Heck, why not go ahead and police up your brass for reloading! Sooner or later, you're gonna run out of clips. And while Garand clips are cheap—for the moment—how about that .308; much cheaper and easier to find than surplus 30-06. Stock up!
On paper and in real life, the M1A wins a rapid fire fight with a Garand, as the Garand shooter has to reload twice before the '1A shooter has to reload once.
— Fred of Fred's M14 Stocks, *Shotgun News* (56/3/71)

Get a nice (though non-collectible) 1950s Springfield Armory rifle (they have the last mods and are of the best quality), and throw a good .308 barrel on it. There's just something inexplicably special about a Garand!

Why did I take so long to favor the M14?

My very first M1A was a gorgeous Bush rifle (with 18" barrel) in a woodland camo synthetic stock. It was, heartbreakingly, a 4MOA gun—which soured me on M1As (and the M14 system in general) for 5 years. I then started seriously dating an FAL (and actually got engaged). Meanwhile, however, I had a torrid affair with a sexy-but-bipolar AR10, plus occasional flings with the Rubinesque-but-ever-willing HK91 (and all her cheap slutty clones). Whenever the FAL, AR10, and HK91 somehow displeased me, I'd phone up the M1A and take her out to dinner and a movie. Her patience and steadfastness finally won me over, especially after my DSA FAL fiancée began to behave erratically. In 2001 I at last married the long-suffering M1A, with the proviso that I may keep FAL and HK91 concubines. She doesn't really mind, for she knows that she's #1 with me and that if I *had* to choose just one woman, it would be her.

THE M1 GARAND (1936-1957)

*...I realize now why I so cherish the M1, the BAR,... We can't retain these men and their vigor, spirit, and stories forever. We can honor what they accomplished, once we understand the real forces involved (the terror, the desperation), but before this book has gone through a couple of printings, many more of them will be gone. **This hardware we collect and shoot was American, reliable, powerful, fast.** The only full-power, semiautomatic standard infantry rifle in the world, it was conceived by a brilliant Canadian and produced daily by factories in New England, advancing American infantrymen and their tactics into levels of flexibility and mobility far ahead of the rest of the world.* (at ix)

What we are trying to preserve is a legacy, and not just a legacy of violence, by any means. There's a manufacturing legacy, a design legacy, a service legacy, a training legacy, a shooting legacy—in the end, not much about war, and virtually nothing about crime. (at xiii)
— Jim Thompson, *The Classic M1 Garand* (2001)

The U.S. Army in WWI, with the revelation of the BAR, figured out the wisdom of "fire and maneuver" versus the static European tactic of basing infantry around the machine gun. Hence, our military asked for a semi-automatic battle rifle to spread cyclic firepower out to the level of the individual soldier. (This concept would be even further extended in Korea with the select-fire M1 Carbine and M14, and in Vietnam with the M16.)

What our troops fortunately got from the beginning of WWII was the M1, thanks to the persistent genius of John C. Garand. The more I study the mechanical ingenuity of the M1, such as the trigger group, rear sight, and feeding mechanism, the more in awe I become. Moreover, the rifle simply has a "presence" about it. It's solid, competent—and oh, so *American.*

The fire and maneuver concept, and the M1, were amply proven. The USSR scrambled to emulate both with their SVT40, while the Germans belatedly brought out the FG42, the G43, and the MP44. In fact, the Germans experimented with a carbon copy of the M1, called the *Selbstladegewehr 251 (a).* Even the Japanese made 200 copies, which had a tangent rear sight and 10rd mag fed by stripper clips. (The Buffalo Bill Museum in Cody has one of only ten still existing. *Trés* cool!)

But, the USA got there first, and got there best.

Just in case you're interested, 1939 procurement price of the M1 was about Ø92, which was *three* times the amount of the 03A3 Springfield bolt-action it replaced. Back in 1939, Ø92 was *big* money! So, don't whine about paying Ø700+ for a really nice Garand 63 years later as it's relatively a better bargain today!

It's only been since 1985 that M1s have filtered down to civilian hands in any numbers. We are very fortunate indeed to enjoy them today. I urge you to get your hands on one soon!

WWII M1s versus Korean-era M1s

The [WWII] *M1 Garand may be the typical, "definitive," and most common M1 Garand, but the postwar (i.e., 1950s) rifles are unquestionably the best, and for very simple reasons: they're newer and have therefore been knocked around less; they were made without the pressure of an ongoing "hot" war; and they reflect all the technological and safety improvements of 16 years' research, experience, and progress.*

— Jim Thompson, *The Complete M1 Garand* (1998), p.98

Honed in WWII

During WWII, only Springfield Armory (SA) and Winchester Repeating Arms (WRA) made the M1, which went through literally *dozens* of upgrades throughout its life. Virtually every part was continually improved by SA (which was our National Armory, and not operated for profit as was Winchester). The rear sight was finalized only after the third redesign. The first WWII receiver of around 1940-41 was drawing sheet version -2. The last WWII receiver of 1945 was a -35.

Winchester, however, was notorious for using earlier pattern parts (to use up inventory and save money) long after several upgrades. (For example, they were still using -13 receivers in 1945.) Also, Winchester's overall quality—though always satisfactory—was not up to par with Springfield Armory's (especially in machining and finishing).

The M1 was a difficult rifle to produce, requiring nearly 1,000 machining operations. Even still, the Springfield National Armory by January 1944 was producing nearly 4,000 rifles *per day*, and Winchester 500/day. Over *four million* were made during WWII—a *stupendous* feat, especially given the M1's consistent quality throughout the war. (Our wartime manufacturing base by 1944 was so tremendous, that the USA's output was *half* of the entire world's production. Wow.)

If you want a *shooter* WWII M1, then choose a later one made by SA (the last number was about 3888000). For example, my first Garand was a 3.57 million numbered gun made in February 1945 (which had the last/best WWII mods) with a 1953 barrel. It was a great WWII-era shooter, although not extremely collectible. Collectors usually prefer the Winchester M1s (the last number was about 1640000).

Post-WWII M1 Garands (1952-57) are superior

The issue [M1] rifle has performed adequately in Korea and is regarded by troops with a liking amounting to affection. This is true of all forces, Army and Marines alike. They have found that it stands up ruggedly against the most extreme tests by terrain, weather, and rough handling. They want the weapon left as it is now, and they have no suggestions as to how it might be changed for the better.
— Brigadier General S.L.A. Marshall

Post-WWII manufacturers were Springfield Armory (SA), Harrington & Richardson (HRA), and International Harvester Corp. (IHC). As U.S. troops in Korea fought primarily with rebuilt WWII rifles, few of these post-WWII production M1s actually saw combat (hence their very often nice and original condition). Below is a guide on serial number block ranges for the post-WWII M1 Garands.

Springfield Armory	4200001—4399999	1952-54
International Harvester Corp	4400000—4660000	1953-54
Harrington & Richardson	4660001—4800000	1953-54
	4800001—4999999	unassigned
Springfield Armory	5000000—5000500	8/1952 NATO
International Harvester Corp.	5000501—5278245	1954-56
Springfield Armory	5278246—5488246	1954-55
Harrington & Richardson	5488247—5793847	1954-56
Springfield Armory	5793848—6099905	1955-57

Within the above are the invariable subgroups which are interesting to collectors. (One example are IHC receivers of

4440000-4445000, 4638XXX-4660000, and 5198034-5213034 having been produced by Springfield Armory. These will also have SA heat lots on the right front receiver leg.)

So, my advice is to first get a 1950s surplus shooter before you embark on collecting WWII M1s (which is a very tricky business frought with guns of dubious originality).

7.62x51 NATO U.S. Navy M1s

In 1957 the U.S. Navy had little economic choice but to convert their M1s to the new NATO caliber 7.62x51 (.308). At first, a chamber bushing was inserted, and the rifle was designated the Mk.2, Mod 0. These barrels were dated <1957.

Once it was discovered that this bushing worked loose, the Navy bought 30,000 7.62x51 barrels from SA in 1965-66. These barrels were marked "SA 11686514-SS (month)-XX (year) - MO61." These rebarreled M1s (converted from the bushing Mod 0's) became the Mk.2, Mod 1, and are good .308 M1s.

Good M1s

Get a surplus Springfield Armory or HRA M1

I picked up for just Ø500 a very nice CMP gun made in June 1954 by SA, with original barrel (excellent bore) and op rod. (The stock, sights, and bolt are WWII-era, however.) The gun simply reeks quality from 50' away, and the gray phosphate finish is flawless. While I *could* restore it to 1954 condition, I think I'll rebarrel it in .308 and keep my 1943 M1 as original.

Harrington & Richardson Arms made late-spec M1s from 1953-57, and all were of superb quality.

Other fine manufacturers: Beretta (PB), Breda (BMP)

Beretta made forged-receiver M1s of post-WWII configuration into the early 1970s, and most of these were originally barreled for 7.62x51. (Springfield Armory® imported many of them in the 1980s.) Made on Winchester machinery, Beretta M1s were the best fitted and finished Garands ever made. These are usually fairly expensive due to market pressure from both shooters and collectors. (I'm looking for an original gun in 7.62x51. That'd be really dandy.)

Good post-1985 imports: Sherwood/Samco, Arl Ord, SPR

Sherwood/Samco brought in a nice batch of M1s (including some M1Cs and M1Ds without glass) used by several European countries. Usually in very nice condition.

Arlington Ordance imported some very nice WWII M1s, often still in original condition (or easily restorable to such).

Springfield Sporters (SPR SP) M1s came from Colombia (including some Berettas), and most have excellent barrels. These are excellent candidates for creating your .308 Garand.

Civilian Marksmanship Program (CMP)

Promotes firearms safety training and rifle practice for all qualified American citizens with special emphasis on youth. Operates through a network of affiliated shooting clubs and associations offering firearms safety training and marksmanship courses and the opportunity for continued practice and competition. Created by the U.S. Congress (to replace the Army's Division of Civilian Marksmanship), the original purpose was to to provide civilians an opportunity to learn and practice so they would be skilled marksmen if later called to serve the U.S. military.

The Civilian Marksmanship Program offers M1s to members of NRA-sanctioned shooting clubs. (For Ø20 you can join the Riverside Gun Club, POB 335, Ramseur, N.C. 27316.) You may buy 5/year Ø500 "Service Grade" M1s and 2/year Ø400 "Danish Issue" M1s. The CMP also allows you to buy 2 of each inventoried part per fiscal year (which is a great deal for M14 trigger groups and op rods and Ø35 and Ø50!).

POB 576, Pt. Clinton, OH 43452   888-267-0796   www.odcmp.com

As far as the condition of M1 you'll get, it's a crapshoot. Quality varies widely (although there are no true junkers), but you will generally get a fairly decent gun. The two CMP guns I have (1943 SA, 1954 SA) I bought used from their owners, so I had the opportunity to thoroughly inspect them beforehand. Generally, CMP M1s have been extensively rebuilt, reworked, and modified, so your chance of getting a collectible is nil.

Less-than-good M1s

International Harvester (IHC)

International Harvester (that's right, the *tractor* manufacturer) rifles were known for spotty quality control. Even though SA made quite a few receivers for IHC, the rest of the parts of such rifles were still IHC manufactured, so beware. Although they are not *bad* rifles, why even go there (unless you're an M1 collector) when you can easily find a SA or HRA gun?

Avoid remils!

These receivers were rewelded from scrapped/torched receivers. Quality varies, but look for a "bump" in the ridge line of the clip ejector access area, or in the op rod's track on the receiver's right side. (Same goes for remilled M14 receivers.)

Imports to avoid: Blue Sky, Federal Ordnance

Blue Sky imported from South Korea, and most have worn barrels and crude refinishings. Good source of rare parts.

Fed Ord M1s came from the Philippines, and many were pitted from the humidity. Ugly, but decent shooters.

Avoid the new Century Arms Intl. (CAI) parts guns

Although the Danish parts are very good, the CAI receiver (cast in Spain, and machined and finished here by Caspian Arms) just plain sucks on average. I once bought a used receiver for only Ø110 to build up a .308 gun, and it was a warped kludge. Unless you can thoroughly test your Ø400 "bargain", you should simply hold out for a *real* milspec forged M1 for just Ø200-300 more. (You never regret having bought top quality.)

Interstate Arms Corp.   800-243-3006

From the Australian Lithgow arsenal. These are advertized in *Shotgun News* as being milspec receivers, but this is not accurate as they are cast, not forged. Completed with genuine surplus parts (made by Beretta, which were superb) and a new American walnut stock, they purport to be the *"very best"* M1 Garand available today. I handled one at SHOT 2002, and the bolt somehow got locked open. *Hmmmm.*

For the Ø730 retail price you can get into a surplus 1950s Springfield Armory or H&R M1 in 90+% condition—*and* enjoy the historical/collectible aspect.

What about the modern M1s from Springfield Armory®?

These have serial numbers of 7,000,000+, in contrast with the last of the Springfield National Armory M1s made in 1957 in the low 6,000,000 range. Since they are investment cast receivers, they are *not* true milspec forged guns. As you can get a *real* .30/06 M1 for the same money, the only M1 lure that Springfield Armory® has is perhaps one of their .308 "Tanker" Garands. I had one, and loved it, until it shat the bed on me.

Although *most* of them are good guns, why take a chance when there are genuine milspec M1s for the same money?

Inspecting the seller's M1

Garand shopping requires a bit of specialized knowledge (if not experience), so I'd recommend showing any prospective rifle to an expert you trust (especially if you're looking for a collector-grade M1). Also, I strongly recommend that you invest in an M1 library, which will save you much grief and money. Meanwhile, here are some tips.

Remove the M1 action from its stock

You're looking for several things: A lack of rust under the rear of the receiver. A sound op rod and action spring. A properly cut-relieved op rod. Parts and barrel which are series matching (if seeking a collectible rifle), and of proper post-WWII origin (*e.g.*, prefixes of "55", "65", and for the op rod "77"). Original USGI parts versus import copies (*e.g.,* Taiwanese hammers).

Remove the op spring and test the bolt for smooth lockup and release. Do this by tilting the action 60° from horizontal. A good action will engage/disengage by such gravity alone.

If any seller objects to any of this, then pass on the gun.

Check the throat erosion!

A borelight will only show you the bore, which although may indeed be sharp and bright says nothing about the condition of the *throat.* An absolute "must have" is a throat erosion gauge (TEG) from Brownells (#022-101-030; Ø54). The higher the number, the worse the erosion. Reading from 0-10, think of each number as 10% of barrel life gone. In military barrels, look for a reading of 2.5 (Excellent) to 3.5 (Good). 4 is Fair. 5 is Poor, and 8-10 is Unusable. (Civilian barrels have larger throats, and hence a reading of 4 or 5 is still likely a nice barrel.)

You *will* learn of the rifle's headspace, either at the gun show before you buy it, or at the range after you've bought it. I'ts cheaper to find out before you buy...

Check the firing pin protrusion

Minimum is 0.044" and max is 0.059".

Check the muzzle tolerance

Carry with you a dummy round of FMJ and nose it into the muzzle. There should be at least ⅛" of bullet showing pas the case neck. If not, then the barrel's shot out (regardless of how sharp and shiny it looks!). I learned this the hard way on a Blue Sky import which took forever to get rid of!

Shooting your M1 Garand
en bloc 8-rd clips

Stick with parkerized steel military surplus clips. You should have at least 200-400 of these, preferably all loaded up. Clips usually sell at guns shows for 50-75¢, but I've often snapped up a batch for 3-4/Ø1. The best quantity deal I've seen is from Gun Parts Corp. for 1,150 (#547160; Ø335; 29¢ each) and 1,950 (#547170; Ø498; 26¢ each), plus freight.

Does it have a cut relieved op rod?

Before shooting an unfamiliar M1, see that its op rod has that relief cut radius at the junction of the arm and hook section of the handle. **If not, *do not fire!*** Such unrelieved op rods *will* break, taking out your eye (or killing a lefty). No joke.

Uncut op rods are worth good money to collectors, who wish to restore their nonshooting M1s to original status.

Reloading for your M1 Garand

Never use any powder faster than IMR3031, or slower than IMR4320! (That means no IMR4350 or IMR4831, even though they are great .30/06 powders for a bolt gun.) Such will give you feeding problems and eventually damage your M1! One of the best powders is IMR4895. I also like IMR4064 (very good for any .308, too), VARGET, and AA2520.

Best bullet weight for accuracy is 165-180gr.

Use grease, not oil!

For any semi-auto rifle, oil is not a lubricant. It's merely a transient slippery substance which will quickly leave the premises, and you'll bend or snap an op rod. Use grease, and *often*—every 200-500rds. White lubriplate works very well, and has the added advantage of turning dark to cue you to change it.

The bargain lube is high-temperature wheel bearing grease for just Ø2.50/pound at any auto parts store. Any name brand will do fine. MDS/graphite stuff is great.

I prefer to use a superior grease which is certified for CV joints (if it will lube *CV joints*, it will lube *anything*), such as Valvoline's semi-synthetic *DuraBlend* (which offers low/high temperature protection from -54° to 400°F). A 1lb tub for Ø3.50 will easily last the life of the rifle.

Get a full cleaning kit from Sierra Supply (970-259-1822; www.sierra-supply.com) plus an M14 oiler, and fill the smaller chamber with *DuraBlend*. (Fill the larger chamber with CLP.)

Areas to lube on the M1/M14:
  bolt lugs
  top rear of the bolt (where shiny)
  op rod track, op rod guide
  bottom of barrel where op rod touches

Lightly oil the op rod spring, and ½ drop of oil on the ejector plunger. Savvy owners also *yearly* lube the top of the hammer (where shiny), hammer/trigger pins, and the rear sight internals, which reduces slack movement and eases adjustability.

Loading the clips

If your M1 is finicky (*e.g.*, giving "7th round jams"), then try loading the clips so that the top round is on the right. (This also makes feeding the clips into the magazine easier for righthanded shooters.)

To feed the rifle, place your thumb just behind the cartridge shoulder, and not on/near the case head.

How to adjust the M1/M14 rear sight

There are only 8 parts to the sight, but sometimes simple devices ironically require more intelligence from the user.

Adjusting knob tension

If your M1/M14 does not have a Type 3 sight, replace it.

The *right* knob is the windage knob, and its center screw adjusts the sight's overall tension of both knobs on their respective splines. If this tension is too loose, then the sight will run and jump and have a wandering zero. If it's too tight, then the sight will be difficult to adjust with your fingers (and never use pliers on the knob, else you'll crack it).

So, you should first adjust this tension. Raise the aperture to its full height, and then drop it down 2 clicks. Next, wrap your support hand around the stock behind the trigger guard, with your thumb on the aperture applying downward pressure. If the aperture moves, then increase tension by turning the screw clockwise one click at a time until the aperture no longer moves. (Your combination tool has the proper screwdriver.)

That accomplished, it's time to zero your rifle.

Zeroing your rifle

The *left* knob is the elevation knob. The M1 is calibrated for yards (up to 1200), and the M14/M1A is in meters (up to 1100, unless it has an M1 knob). Each click changes elevation

1MOA (or, if you have a National Match sight, ½MOA). This knob has a flat-head locking screw, which we'll discuss shortly. To zero at 100yds (or 100m in the case of the M14/M1A), turn the elevation knob clockwise (*i.e.,* towards you), bringing the aperture all the way down. Next, from that bottom position, move it back up 8 clicks. Fire 5rds at 100yds/100m, and adjust elevation (and also windage) as necessary. If you must adjust elevation, add or subtract in your mind how many clicks to/from the 8 you already did from the bottom. Write this number down on a piece of duct tape placed under the hinged buttplate. That way you will always be able to recreate your 100y/100m zero if the elevation knob ever slips loose. (Most rifles will be within, either way, 1-2 clicks of the 8 from the bottom.)

Indexing the elevation knob to your zeroed distance

Once point-of-aim (POA) equals point-of-impact (POI), you will then need to index the knob's 100yd/100m line with the sight base witness mark. (Although the other distances are numerically marked, the 100 is merely a line in between the "2" and "12".) When the elevation knob's locking screw is loosened, it allows the knob to freely turn without moving the aperture. *Tightly* holding the knob with padded pliers, loosen the locking screw. That done, next apply lateral pressure on the aperture with your thumb (to prevent it from moving, and thus changing your zero) and set the elevation knob to the 100yd/100m mark. Do not allow the aperture to move during this indexing! Finally, retighten the locking screw while again holding the elevation knob with padded pliers. Again, do not allow the aperture to move. It usually takes people a couple of tries to get it right, but since you've already figured out how many clicks up from bottom is your 100yd/100m zero, nothing is lost in the learning curve. If you unintentionally move the aperture, simply start all over by moving it back down to the bottom and then come up that necessary number of clicks for your 100yd/100m zero.

If you don't have access to a 100yd/100m range, you can do almost as well at 25 (which also corresponds to 200). Simply zero at 25, and then reset the elevation knob to 200. This will put you on paper until you can confirm zero at long range.

A quick word about windage

You'll notice that the front sight is adjustable for windage. Why, since the rear sight is also windage adjustable? Because having *both* sights windage adjustable gives you twice the range of adjustment in case something is screwy with your gun (such as out-of-time or bent barrel, or broken sight).

For your initial zero, start *both* sights at their precise center. If windage adjustment is necessary from there, then move the *front* sight (don't adjust the rear sight) in the opposite direction that you want the impact to move. (Remember, it takes only the width of a human hair to shift POI ½MOA.) Once you're zeroed for windage, the front sight should be LocTite set *wherever* it needs to be to correspond with a centered rear sight, and *forgotten*. (You should also scribe the base the precise location of the front sight. That way, if the sight ever came loose, you could always retighten it where it was.) The reason for setting the front sight in relation to the rear (rather than vice versa) is that you are free to occasionally adjust the *rear* sight in the field for varying conditions (such as a high wind), yet still be able to return to windage "home" (*i.e.,* right in the center).

Make sense?

In truth, most rifles will have good barrel timing (and thus near-perfect sight alignment), so all this is largely academic. Nevertheless, this kind of thing *is* what you pay me for...

Each click changes windage 1MOA.

A word about your battlesight zero

Your "battlesight zero" (BSZ) is 250m/275yds, which is usually 2 clicks up from 200. (3 clicks up from 200 will put you at 300.) Once you've actually confirmed this BSZ on the firing range (and only your *life* depends on it!), paint a line across the elevation knob and sight base. This will allow you to instantly return to BSZ. In case you don't recall, a center hold on your Bad Guy from BSZ will drop him from 0-300yds/m. (Think of BSZ as MPBR.) Only if he is farther than 300 (and you'll know this because he is thinner than your 8MOA front sight post, which means 20" at 250yds) will you have to click up or hold over. We'll cover this thoroughly in Chapter 19.

It's also a good idea to notate on that duct tape the number of clicks from bottom it takes to reach BSZ.

That's it; you're done! Assuming that you stick with the same ammo, you should never have to re-zero your rifle again.

Shooting beyond BSZ

Remember that each click in elevation changes impact by 1MOA. The farther the bullet travels, the quicker it drops, and the more clicks you need between equal incremental distances. While it takes only 3 clicks to move from 200 to 300 and from

300 to 400, it takes 4 clicks to move from 400 to 500, and 5 clicks from 500 to 600. (A chart is provided in Chapter 19.)

In a sense, the rear sight was designed like an older scope without an internal BDC, whereby a click equals some amount of MOA. While there is nothing grossly wrong with this (and it makes for a more simply constructed rear sight), I personally would have prefered that the elevation be graduated in 50m (or even 25m) increments (as in BDC scopes). That way, the shooter would not have to (as in the M1/M14 sight) figure out how many clicks up from 500m he needs to hit at 550m.

The *ideal*, in my opinion, is a big, fat elevation wheel with very large and clear numerals. The BDC would be built-in, and all you'd have to do is accurately judge the distance and then dial it up. Basically, what I'm asking for is a tangent sight's parabola applied to an elevation wheel.

The Swedish AG42B Ljungman 100-700m rear sight is the earliest example of this, albeit in mere 100m increments. Much more preferable would have been 50m increments out to 500m, and then 25m increments thereafter. But I really can't bitch *too* much about it, given how revolutionary the rifle truly was, and how quickly it was fielded after design conception.

The AR15A2 rear sight had *partially* the right idea (in its big, fat knob with large and clear numerals), but did *not* provide for an *equal* number of clicks between 300m, 400m, 500, and 600m (which correspond to 6, 8, and 10 ½MOA clicks). There is no doubt that the AR15A2 sight *could* have been designed with a progressive ballistic cam to account for increasing trajectory.

Hey, did I ever mention that I am an idealist?   ;-)

Cleaning your M1
To clean the gas cylinder

Once your M1 becomes sluggish, the fault usually lies with a dirty/corroded gas cylinder. Open it up and scrape out the gorp. Dry thoroughly. *Very* lightly oil (one drop of oil on the pinky will do it) the piston head and cylinder wall.

M14 gas cylinders require only yearly cleaning at most.

If using corrosive ammo (*Shame!*)

After following your final shot, flush out the bore and gas cylinder with some ammonia-based window cleaner to neutralize the primer salts. Then, clean thoroughly with solvent.

Even still, you'll never get it all. I urge you *not* to use corrosive ammo in gas-operated guns (especially those which are difficult to clean, such as the SVT40 and Hakim).

Be sure to clean and degrease the chamber

The chamber collects a lot of brass debris and powder fragments which must be removed. Use a chamber cleaning brush with a patch over it, followed by the brush alone, and patched brush. The chamber must be spotless and free of oil (to prevent "hydraulic adhesion"-related failures-to-extract).

Do not routinely degrease an M1/M14

Just wipe off the old lube and apply the new. It's better to leave old lube in the nooks and crannies (where it will provide some lubrication), rather than leaving a spot bone dry if you happen to miss it during new lubrication.

Accurizing your M1 Garand

An excellent book by a real M1 enthusiast is *Precision Shooting With The M1 Garand* by Roy Baumgardner. Many of the below tips I gleaned from it. (Many also apply to the M14.)

M1/M14:   Try different ammo

All rifles will show some kind of bias for/against particular ammo. Vary its diet to discover what it likes.

M1/M14:   Install a "Type 3" rear sight

This third iteration of sight had the last and best locking system. If your M1/M14 has a Type 1 or Type 2, swap it out.

M1/M14:   Install National Match (NM) front and rear sight

The front sight is more precise, and the rear sight has a hooded aperture and ½MOA adjustability.

M1/M14:   Rubber band around aperture/windage knob

This removes play in both directions, up/down and lateral. A human hair is 0.003-0.004" and that's about ½MOA. Any slop will translate to minute-of-Roseanne's butt accuracy.

M1:   Tighten up gas cylinder

This was designed to stay a bit loose because of the corrosive ammo and foul weather conditions. It was made to be removable, so that the soldiers could clean out any rust or corrosion. Since, however, the front sight dovetails in the gas block, such slop degrades accuracy.

There are a couple of fixes: Slightly peen the three barrel splines to snug up the gas cylinder contact.   Or, try different gas cylinder locks (the "figure-8" shaped part that screws on the barrel forward of the gas cylinder) for one with a tighter fit.   Use a proper hourglass wrench to support the gas cylinder while tightening the plug, else you'll misalign the thing.

M1:   Tighten the stacking swivel in the forward position

Since you won't likely be stacking your M1, swing the swivel facing the muzzle (which is its natural orientation under the stress of recoil) and LocTite it down.

M1/M14:   Neco Moly on trigger group bearing surfaces

This is *the* stuff to use on any military trigger.   From QP.

M1/M14:   Smith Enterprise hardened 4140 trigger pin kit

For just Ø13.60 you can replace the sloppy factory pins and achieve a more consistent trigger pull.   From Brownells (#851-000-018).   M14/M1A pins are Ø22.48 (#851-000-019).

M1/M14:   Have trigger tuned to a crisp 4½lb letoff

www.smithenterprise.com can do this work.

M1/M14:   Secure the handguard

[Glue it] *into the front band with epoxy or high temp silicone. Before you actually glue it, check to see that it does not touch the stock anywhere—if it does, file it down so there is at least a sixteenth inch of clearance all along the margin between the handguard and the stock. Likewise make sure there is similar clearance between the rear of the handguard and the receiver. When the rifle heats up, sometimes the rear of the handguard will forced back into the receiver, changing barrel dynamics and opening up your group. A simple modification, well-worth doing.*

— *Fred's Guide to Becomeing A Rifleman,* p.11

M1/M14:   Install a synthetic stock

Although the M1's wood stock is handsome, wood warps and breaks. Accuracy suffers. Brownells has two stocks:

DPMS reddish/brown polypropylene	(#231-001-000; Ø127)
Bell & Carlson black fiberglass/Kevlar	(#137-100-001: Ø198)

I've seen the DPMS stock and its color and quality seemed a bit to be desired.   I'd go with the Bell & Carlson.   MPI has an M1 polymer stock (www.mpistocks.com; Ø259).   www.ramline.com offers their M1 stock in black, Wood-Tech, or RealTree.

For M14 stocks, visit www.fredsm14stocks.com.

M1/M14:   Bed the stock
This will often shrink groups by 1-3MOA. You can DIY (be patient, follow the instructions), or send it to a gunsmith.

M1/M14:   Try a new barrel, and have it cryo-treated
If none of the above seems to work, then a new barrel is probably called for (see recommendations below).

300 Below (217-423-3070) can stress-relieve your new barrel, and this will often cut groups by 1MOA, as well as extending barrel life.

M1/M14:   Keep fingers *off* the op rod while shooting
You'll avoid inexplicable flyers this way.

Storing your M1 Garand
Remove the trigger group (store with hammer down) to avoid compressing the wood stock. Lightly oil the bore and gas cylinder. Remove the gas plug and op rod, clean the gas cylinder thoroughly, lightly oil, and leave it open to air out.

M1 Garand modifications
Holbrook "Thumb Saver" device
This new device stops automatic bolt closure when a full clip is loaded. The clip will latch but the bolt will not release until the op-rod handle is pulled and released, like an M14!

After the last round is fired, the bolt will lock back but the empty clip will not eject until the clip release button on the receiver is pushed. No more lost clips!

A standard GI clip can be attached into the receiver and 1 through 8 single rounds may then be loaded into the clip while it is in the receiver.

This device is a direct replacement for the USGI operating rod catch and has been thoroughly tested!

The basic rifle is not modified and may be converted back to USGI configuration in minutes!

— John Holbrook (360-671-8522; holbrj@aol.com)

2015 24ᵗʰ St., #57, Bellingham, Wash. 98225 (Ø45ppd.)

This is a fine addition to any shooter Garand. John has sold over 2,000 devices in the past 2 years, and owners love 'em. I have one in my .308 M1, and it works great.

Smith Vortex (#PN-3003) and muzzle brake (#PN-3002)
The Vortex flash suppressor totally elimates all flash signature, and the muzzle brake really reduces muzzle flip

(without drastically increasing overpressure). Too bad we can't have both in the same attachment, so, you'll have to pick one. Order directly from www.smithenterprise.com.

.308 conversion

A very fine replacement barrel in .308 is just Ø141-226 (not including installation costs). Assuming a savings of at least 5¢/rd over the .30/06 ammo, such will pay for itself in 2,800-4,520rds. Since you'll *easily* get 12,000rds from a well cared for barrel, a .308 barrel will save you Ø374-425 in the long run before it's eventually used up. *"But, Honey, the more I shoot it the more money we make!"* (Let me know if this works...)

milspec 6-groove (1:10" twist)	(Gun Parts Corp. #532580; Ø141)
Wilson Arms 4-groove (1:12" twist)	(Brownells #983-002-124; Ø175)
Fulton Armory standard milspec	(Fulton Armory; Ø175)
Douglas/Barnett heavy 4-groove (1:10" twist)	(Brownells #086-001-427; Ø226)
Douglas/Barnett heavy 6-groove (1:10" twist)	(Brownells #086-001-627; Ø226)
Smith Enterprise tanker 4-groove (1:10" twist)	(Smith Enterprise; Ø275)
Krieger (1:10, 11, 12" twist)	(www.kriegerbarrels.com; Ø325)

Which barrel should you get? The best overall barrel values for the average shooter are probably those from Wilson Arms and Fulton Armory (Jim Thompson's pick, and he gets NM results) for Ø175. Although the Douglas Premium barrels contoured by Barnett are very nice, they are quite thick and heavy and thus require hogging out the handguards. Krieger barrels are renowned for their accuracy, and they now offer normal thickness barrel in stainless or chrome moly.

The gas port must be enlarged from 5/64 (0.07813") to 0.100"-0.1065". Most .308 M1 barrels are the full 24", but I see no reason for such when 18-20" makes for a very handy gun without too much loss of muzzle velocity.

Ron Smith at Smith Enterprise (480-964-1818; www.smithenterprise.com) specializes in .308 Garand tanker conversions, so chat with him first. Tell him Boston sent you.

www.kriegerbarrels.com also offers rebarreling services.

How about a Scout M1 Garand?

This would seem to really make a .308 Tanker M1 come alive. Such would be a dandy hiking or car rifle (especially in Occupied Territory where *"assault rifles"* are banned, such as Kalifornia, etc.), in my opinion.

Brownells has the base (#100-000-136; Ø90), which requires the barrel to be drilled and tapped.

M1 accessories

5rd hunting clips
Gun Parts Corp.; #546280; Ø3.65, or 5/Ø13.

winter trigger
Gun Parts Corp.; #548810; Ø7.80.

sight covers
The best are from Brownells (#100-000-323; Ø10).

sling
OD canvas or M1907 leather are correct for the M1.

10 pocket belt pouch
Originals may often be found at gun shows for under Ø50, or you can get a quality replica from Gun Parts or Sarco.

bayonet
Genuine WWII M1 bayonets and M7 scabbards have gotten pretty pricey lately (*i.e.,* Ø60-100 for the pair). (The 1950s Danish bayonet/scabbard is a fine M1 copy for just Ø35.) The shortened M1905E1 10" bayonets cost about the same, too. And you'll *really* pay for a 16" M1905 with original scabbard.

The Korean-era M5 knife/bayonet and M8A1 scabbard can be found for just Ø44 (Gun Parts Corp.; #546060).

leather scabbard
A very nice treat for your Garand is a leather scabbard. Original ones with brass (or painted steel) charging handle covers can be found at shows in various condition/completion for Ø20-175. I paid just Ø45 for my 1942 Boyt, though Ø100 is average.

Quality replicas with straps and hardware are from I.M.A. (www.ima-usa.com; #MU1612; Ø90) Hold out for USGI.

folding stock   Ø245 (www.reesesurplus.com)
Transforms a .308 Tanker M1 into a compact travel rifle.

M1 parts/tools

With your M1
Pins (firing, trigger, hammer), extractor (& plunger), ejector, combo tool/chamber brush, front sight allen screw/wrench, broken shell extractor, grease lube.

M1 parts/tools at home
The above, plus a front sight (& screw), complete rear sight, follower/op rod springs, op rod, op rod catch, bullet guide,

clip ejector, stock, complete bolt, gas port drill bits (#46 and "P" bits), gas cylinder, and gas cylinder plug. A fine Danish parts kit from CAI is a good deal for the Ø190.

Brownells Pro-Spring Kit (#080-665-900-M1-900; Ø27).

Boyds sells a very nice walnut stock for just Ø75 (605-996-5011; www.boydboys.com).

Brownells (retail prices are rounded up) has your tools:

M1/M14 bolt disassembly tool	#080-818-000	Ø60
M1/M14 trigger group assm. fixture	#784-100-014	Ø61
M1/M14 handguard clip pliers	#093-200-050	Ø25
.308/.30/06 throat erosion gauge	#022-101-030	Ø54
.30/06 headspace GO gauge	#319-306-049	Ø20
.30/06 headspace NO-GO gauge	#319-306-055	Ø20
.30/06 headspace FIELD gauge	#319-306-058	Ø20
.308 headspace gauge kit	#079-308-000	Ø187

If you plan on replacing barrels, then you'll need the below:

M1 bolt timing block	#812-001-001	Ø37
M1/M14 action wrench/head	#080-800-114	Ø80
M1/M14 barrel timing gauges	#093-200-010	Ø72

Building an M1 Garand library

GCA Newsletter, Garand Collector's Association
P.O. Box 181, Richmond, Kentucky 40475

Garand Stand Report, G.S. Publications
P.O. Box 34005, Houston, Texas 77234-4005

The M1 Garand of World War Two
The M1 Garand: Post World War Two, Scott Duff

M1 Garand: 1936 to 1957, Joe Poyer

Rifle, National Matches, United States Army Weapons & Munitions

The M1 Rifle, National Rifle Association Publications

Book of the Garand, Maj. Gen. Julian S. Hatcher

Know Your M1 Garands, E.J. Hoffschmidt

The Complete M1 Garand—A Guide for the Shooter and Collector
The Classic M1 Garand—An Ongoing Legacy, Jim Thompson
Paladin Press

Precision Shooting With The M1 Garand, Roy Baumgardner
Order from Militia of Montana.

THE M14 (1957-1963) & M1A™

Towards the end of WWII, the U.S. Army asked the Springfield National Armory to develop a mag-fed, select-fire version of the M1 Garand—sort of an American FG42. The goal was to replace the M1 Carbine, the M1, and the BAR with one rifle. This result, the T20E2 was completed by summer of 1945. It used a gas expansion/cut off system (U.S. Patent #1,907,163; Joseph C. White) and incorporated the 20rd mag from the BAR, but was exhausting to fire on full-auto (as one might expect).

The M1's inventor, John C. Garand, honed the T20E2 into what became the test rifle T44, which would compete against the British EM-2, the Belgian FAL, and the T47 (a falling block version of the M1). In December 1952 the T48 (FAL) handily won the first of two U.S. Army trials. The EM-2 and T47 were dropped from future testing, and orders were given to further develop the T44 (M14) and T48 (FAL) for a final test in 1956.

The prospective adoption of a *foreign* rifle alarmed the Army Ordnance Corps, so they redoubled their efforts to ensure the success of the T44 (M14). Springfield National Armory stretched the truth by claiming that the M14 would be cheaper to produce than the FAL as they could use M1 Garand tooling, and that training would be simpler (partially true). So, the M14 was adopted on 1 May 1957.

Basically an M1 Garand in .308 with a 20rd mag, the M14 was a fine rifle, and a worthy successor to its father. Weight was 8.7lbs, overall length 44", barrel length 22". The M14A1 had a pistol grip and bipod for SAW duty (though it was too light and had no quick-change barrel).

Deliveries (after startup difficulties relating to funding) finally began in July 1959. Four companies manufactured the M14: Springfield Armory, Winchester, H&R, and TRW (Thompson, Ramo, Woolridge). SA, WRA, and HRA (in particular) had teething problems, but TRW (being an aircraft firm) consistently made the finest M14s from the start.

The M14 saw its first combat in 1961 Vietnam. The full-auto fire reduced the M14's reliability, and there were accuracy problems (related to both the ammunition and the manufacturers' quality control). Since John Garand had not been consulted during the final stages of the M14's development, the rifle did not end up as robust and reliable as it could have been.

Meanwhile, Eugene Stoner's new rifle, the AR15, was being stalled by the M14 loyalists within the Ordnance Department (who were later discovered by the IG to have rigged the tests against the AR15 in favor of the M14).

Secretary of Defense McNamara ordered a full investigation, and learned of the trials' duplicity. This, and the M14's reliability/accuracy problems, clinched the matter. On 23 January 1963 McNamara announced termination of further procurement of the M14 after the intial contract had been fulfilled. He then began ordering the M16 in 1965, and closed down the Springfield National Armory on 30 April 1968 (which had been opened in 1794 by George Washington). The M14 was our "Standard A" rifle until only 1 January 1968, and was withdrawn from service before it had even fully been issued to the Army. It was our shortest lived combat rifle in history.

1,380,346 were made from 1957 to 1963. Only 20-50K are left in U.S. inventories today. First, the USG gave away about 450,000 M14s as free Excess Defense Articles. Then, even though storage cost only a buck/year per rifle, they destroyed 750,000 M14s by 1996. Finally, Klinton *gave away* 90,000 M14s to Estonia, Latvia, and Lithuania in 1998-99. I consider all this a criminal offense against the American taxpayers!

Israel used M14s until adopting their excellent Galil. The M21 variant was a good sniper rifle used to great effect in Vietnam, serving until this day in modified form. The 26th Marine Expeditionary Unit (SOC) has their Designated Marksman Rifle (DMR) in Afghanistan, and SEALs still use the M14 for certain missions. Delta operators used them in Somalia with Aimpoints (read/see *Blackhawk Down*).

The special forces community is quickly distancing itself from the 5.56 (fresh reports of terrs still in the fight after taking 2rds to the *head*, or 4+rds to the body), and embracing the 7.62. An eventual FAL system is likely (although M14s and HK91s are in current use). As I predicted, the .308 battle rifle is making a come-back. Robinson should design their M96 in .308, as should ArmaLite in their AR180B. Combat rifle technology ceased in the 1950s for the .308, and we've since learned that the .223 round is not a manstopper (*Duh!*). The future will be found in the 7.62x51 past, and it's about time.

Forged receivers (new info for 2004!)

Milspec means *"Forging shall be of 8620 steel, heat treated..."*, not investment cast. Steel is either poured into a a mold (cast), or beaten/crushed into shape (forged). Cast steel produces a non-defined grain structure, and has more bubbles than forged, hence has about half the tensile strength. When you shoot a forged M14, it rings like a bell, instead of the investment cast *clunk*. All military M1s and M14s were forged. Very few civilian M14 manufacturers (*e.g.*, Smith Enterprise) ever made forged receivers.

New hammer forged semi-auto M14s from LRB Arms

In the 2002 printing I discussed the now defunct M-K Specialties (which stupidly assembled rifles with M14 full-auto parts and got busted by the BATF!). Fortunately, a new company has stepped up to the plate, with the steely guidance of "Mr. M14" Ron Smith (www.smithenterprise.com).

Receivers (only) are $669 dealer/$899 retail. Have Ron Smith build up a complete rifle for you with his 18" Wilson barrel, direct-connect Vortex, gas block sight, and tuned trigger.

LRB Arms, 245-06 Jericho Turnpike; Bellerose, NY 11001
516-327-9061   www.lrbarms.com

Why have an investment cast M1A, when you can have a modern forged M14 with all the Smith Enterprise goodies? Once I test an LRB M14SA, I'll post results on www.javelinpress.com.

What about the Chinese M14-clones?

Polytech is a subsidiary of the People's Liberation Army. Norinco (North China Industries) is a collection of 150 separate factories under a marketing agreement as a subsidiary of the Ministry of Ordnance Industries. Either way, ChiCom generals are getting rich from American gun buyers. (It's an odd world.)

Some Chinese parts interchange with American guns: gas cylinder, bolt parts (but not bolt), rear sight group, trigger group, and buttplate. Numrich has some replacement parts.

The Chinese barrels are good. Chrome lined, but with metric threads for the flash suppressor, front sight, gas block.

U.S. barrels fit in Chinese receivers, but not vice versa.

If you are considering a Chinese M14, check the headspace! It absolutely must *not* bolt close on a NO-GO gauge!

The only reason to consider one of these rifles is that their receivers are made of forged steel, although left much too soft:

	Springfield Armory®	Polytech	Entréprise
receiver	50 Rockwell C	44	55-57
barrel	33	29	
bolt	58	44	
hammer	58	46	

Ron Smith of Smith Enterprise really praises the Chinese clones after he's heat-treated the receiver and machined it to accept milspec bolts. (He reports no difference between Norinco and Polytech, so I stand corrected). I recently picked up a like-new Polytech for just $550 (they're now $650-700). Ron charges $570 for the heat-treat, giving a core hardness of Rc 52-56, and surface hardness from the space-program "Mellanite" of Rc 60 (plus it is nearly impervious to rust and corrosion). Nobody else can do this kind of heat-treat but Ron. A forged M14 for $1,120!

I then swapped out the rear sight for a Type 3 M1, added a Springfield Armory Scout scope mount, and topped it off with a Burris 2-7x Ballistic Plex handgun scope. Very, very dandy.

Beware of cheap investment cast replacement parts

Many parts are investment cast. In this process, a mold is made of the original part and molten metal is poured into the mold under pressure to form the new part. Often, very little is done in the way of heat treating to relieve stress or properly harden the metal. This can be extremely important and even dangerous with parts such as hammers and sears which depend not only on a precision fit, but proper hardness for safe and effective functioning.

It is usually fairly easy to tell if a metal part was investment cast. Look for raised lines or "joins" where the parts of the mold were fitted together. Look also for rounded corners and edges. Machined parts usually have sharp, square edges—if edges were relieved or rounded, machining marks will usually show. Investment-cast parts will rarely show numbers, inspector's initials or other markings. If they are obscured, shallow, faint or appear abraded, they were molded in the metal and not stamped.

— Joe Poyer, *The M14-Type Rifle* (1997), p.24

Here is some generically fantastic advice about "bargains":

*It's unwise to pay too much...but it's worse to pay too little. When you pay too much, you lose a little money...that is all. **When you pay too little, you sometimes lose everything,** because the thing you bought was incapable of doing the thing it was bought to do.*

*The common law of business balance prohibits paying a little and getting a lot. It can't be done. If you deal with the lowest, it is well to add something for the risk you run. **And if you do that, you will have enough to pay for something better** [in the first place].*

— John Ruskin, from the Brownells catalog

Investment cast receivers (new info for 2004!)
How good is the cast M1A™ made by Springfield Armory®?

Early guns (*i.e.*, <#20,000): usually only fair. Recent guns (*i.e.*, >#140,000): often pretty poor. In between, generally good. Investment cast 8620 is not forged, and an M1A™ won't last as long as a forged M14. An OK way to *begin* your M14 experience, but if you're *truly* serious about battle rifles then you should eventually get into a forged receiver rifle (*e.g.*, LRB, or Smith Enterprise heat-treated Chinese M14), which will last you at least 75,000 rounds (just like a real M14).

I do not recommend current M1As. Internal finishing is now very rough, and I've seen *fake* TRW bolts (not forged as the originals, and with faux drawing numbers—*beware!*). To my way of thinking, cast bolts with fake TRW stampings is *fraud*. (Note: you can tell they're cast because of their orange peel surface and lack of heat-treat dimple. *Caveat emptor!*)

Smith Enterprise 480-964-1818 www.smithenterprise.com

Ron Smith is a 4th generation armorer and metallurgist, who specifies in quality heat treating. Although Ron's dad once made forged M14 receivers, today's are precision investment cast 8620 alloy steel with a double heat treat (overall 52-56; surface to 60 at a 0.0002" depth). He also offers many superbly made parts and accessories. Honest, no-B.S. parts and service.

He's getting fed up with whining civilians (who don't appreciate true quality) and stays busy with military contracts, so be professional when you deal with him. Take his advice and don't waste his time with any chatter. His prices may seem high, but you won't find higher quality. *Cry once, laugh forever.* We civilians are very fortunate to still enjoy his parts and service. The US Navy alone nearly absorbs all of his production, and we may soon lose him to military demands. So, I'd get your order in *immediately*. Have him build up an LRB forged gun his way, and you'll have a real treasure. Tell him Boston sent you.

Armscorp USA   410-247-6200

Investment cast 8620 alloy steel, and better made than S.A.'s M1A. The op rod rail is cut differently so that the bolt roller no longer slams back (as in original M14). The rail is 1/16th wider for extra strength. Uniformly high quality and finish. They build up into very nice Match rifles, often holding ⅔-1MOA at 300yds. That's superb accuracy from an M14.

www.sarcoinc.com (908-647-3800) has stripped receivers for Ø365, and bolted/barreled headspaced actions for Ø595.

Entréprise Arms 818-962-8712   www.enterprise.com
CNC milled from solid billets of cast 8620 alloy steel. Exterior hardened to 55-57 Rockwell C at a depth of 0.0002". Good reputation amongst Match gun builders.

Inspecting the seller's M14/M1A

M14 shopping requires a bit of specialized knowledge (if not experience), so I'd recommend showing any prospective rifle to an expert you trust. Also, I strongly recommend that you invest in an M14 library, which will save you much grief and money. Meanwhile, here are some *caveat emptor* tips:

Remove the M14 action from its stock

You're looking for several things: A lack of rust under the rear of the receiver. A sound op rod/spring. Original GI parts versus import copies (*e.g.,* Taiwanese hammers). Is the bolt face pitted? Is the rear sight loose? Does the safety function?

Remove the op spring and test the bolt for smooth lockup and release. Do this by tilting the action up to 60° from horizontal. A good action will engage/disengage by such gravity alone.

If any seller objects to any of this, then pass on the gun.

Check the throat erosion (as with the M1)

The single most important thing to check, as barrel replacement is the highest potential parts cost.

Check the firing pin protrusion (as with the M1)

Check the gas piston for free movement

One M1A I looked at was for sale by a small town cop. He didn't like it, and was selling it for an HK91-clone. When I asked him what problems he'd had with his M1A, he replied that the gas plug wouldn't stay in place unless he used LocTite. *Hmmmm.* (This was a new one on me.) What he had done was failed to insert the gas piston properly. The end which protrudes from the gas cylinder is shaped like a "D" so that the piston cannot rotate, thus always always keeping the port facing the bore. The guy dropped the piston in *backwards*,...and... was....stupefied...why...the...gas...plug...would...not....tighten... more...than...*half*way. (*"It's like something's blocking it!"*) So, he gooped in a bunch of LocTite on the plug's threads, half of which were exposed outside the cylinder! Not only that, he proceded to shoot the gun! (He remarked that it wasn't very accurate. Yeah, I'll bet not. How the rifle cycled at *all* I have utterly no idea.) M1s and M14s are not for the sloth of mind.

The cherry on top of this story is that, 10 months later, I noticed his ad selling his HK91-clone. Who knows how he goobered up *that* rifle as well! Folks, if you ever encounter such a gun cretin, pick up your skirt and *run*!

Lock open the action and tilt the muzzle up and down. You should hear the piston slide back and forth. If you do not, then it's probably corroded (or backwards, or missing!). Remove the gas plug and inspect the cylinder and piston.

Shooting the M14/M1A

Much/most of the M1 discussion also applies to the M14, including zeroing and adjusting the sights.

Use grease, not oil!

See the remarks under the M1 section.
CLP/BreakFree should be used on the bolt cam roller.

M14/M1A MODS, PARTS, & TOOLS

No rifle is perfect, and all can benefit from some simple modifications. Also, you'll want to be able to keep your battle rifle up and running for generations, so you'll need parts and tools for the long run.

The cost of such tools adds up (get a shop to order them wholesale for you, and split the cost amongst your buddies), but with spare barrels and other consumable parts you could see 50,000+rds from your battle rifle! Such a "Liberty's Tooth" will not likely be newly available during the Second American Revolution, so you must be able to keep your M14 (or M1, FAL, HK91) working until we win back our freedom!

M14/M1A modifications

Install a NM front sight, and perhaps a rear one as well (for the ½MOA adjustability). Either paint the elevation knob numerals, or replace with a BM59 knob. Replace OEM handguard with ventilated one. Buy 3 synthetic stocks from www.fredsm14stock.com and paint for winter, summer, and fall.

Brownells Pro-Spring Kit
These are superior springs (#080-665-900-M14-954; Ø27).

recoil buffer   www.buffertech.com   Ø15
A simple part which eliminates op rod/receiver battering.

sight covers
The best are from Brownells (#100-000-391; Ø10).

scope base
Since the receiver stripper clip ear is not all that vital (nor does such loading work very well, anyway), remove it and install a U.S. Tactical Systems Picatinny-rail scope base (#660-201P; Ø200) and rings (Keng's Firearms Specialty; 404-691-7611).

Wolff magazine springs
Wolff makes some of the best mag springs in the business (I use them in my Glocks). Their M14 springs are 5% more powerful, longer lasting, and will revive any tired mag (which are expensive and getting scarcer). 10/Ø56 (Brownells #969-000-066).

M14 accessories
5rd hunting mag   (Brownells #817-501-900; Ø25)

Smith Enterprise muzzle brake
Very effective device, which makes follow-up shots much easier.

M2 bipod
The bipod clamp encircles the gas cylinder as the gas cylinder lock. Chinese copies are Ø50, and USGI are Ø100.

M6 bayonet and M8A1 scabbard
If you have a pre-ban rifle, then *Joy!*, you can mount a bayonet.

Winter trigger
Even if you don't live in a cold climate, the winter safety has an extended tang which keeps your trigger finger out of the guard during disengagement. (Somebody oughta start making these.)

An interesting/infuriating "paperweight"
How about the demilled rear portion of genuine M14 receivers? They've got the rear sight ears, makers' mark, and serial number. 4 for only Ø17.95 from Dupage Trading Co. (630-739-5768; www.dupagetrading.com). Your choice of make.

The "interesting" aspect is a given. The "infuriating" aspect should also be a given to any enthusiast of American Liberty in general and the M14 in particular. I will keep one on my desk to maintain a perpetual burn over the firearm treason committed by "our" Government. Torching *750,000* M14s (which you and I *paid* for, damn it!), then giving what's left to the *Latvians*? *Treason*, folks. Thank you, Bill Klinton.

M14 parts/tools
with gun
Pins (firing, trigger, hammer), extractor (& plunger), ejector, combo tool/chamber brush, front sight allen screw/wrench, broken shell extractor, grease/oil container with *DuraBlend*.

at home
The above, plus a front sight (& screw), complete rear sight, op rods/springs, stock, complete bolt, gas piston/plug.

From Brownells (retail prices are rounded up):

M1/M14 bolt disassembly tool	#080-818-000	Ø60
M1/M14 trigger group assm. fixture	#784-100-014	Ø61
M1/M14 handguard clip pliers	#093-200-050	Ø25
.308/.30/06 throat erosion gauge	#022-101-030	Ø54
.308 headspace GO gauge	#319-308-630	Ø20
.308 headspace NO-GO gauge	#319-308-634	Ø20
.308 headspace FIELD gauge	#319-308-638	Ø20
.308 headspace gauge kit	#079-308-000	Ø187
M14 castle nut pliers	#553-014-001	Ø10
M14 gas piston drill bits	#054-114-000	Ø30
M14 gas cylinder "hourglass" wrench	#054-214-000	Ø30
M14 bolt roller greaser	#093-223-025	Ø 8
⅜" box wrench (for gas cylinder plug)	(from Snap-On or Sears)	

If you plan on replacing barrels, then you'll need the below:

M1 bolt timing block	#812-001-001	Ø37
M1/M14 barrel timing gauges	#093-200-010	Ø72
M1/M14 action wrench/head	#080-800-114	Ø80

M14 library
M14 Preventative Maintenance, from www.fredsm14stocks.com
M14 Owner's Guide, Scott Duff
M14 Shop Manual, Kuhnhausen
The M14-Type Rifle, Joe Poyer
M1/M1A Armorer's Course, AGI video (707-253-0462)

♦ 12

FAL / L1A1

The FAL is a *very* fine rifle—rugged, reliable, and accurate. I still sometimes find myself waffling between it and the M1A. The FAL's only real deficiencies are sights and trigger, which the M1A totally beats. Remember, only 49 points/3.6% separated the two rifles in my test. 3.6%. Big deal.

Lack of reciprocating bolt handle cost 20 points, and 52 points were lost in Combat Accuracy. Many of those 72 points *could* be made up. For example, if a DSA FAL owner improved his sights (or installed an I.O.R. 4x24 M2 scope on DSA mount), gave it a trigger job, made the charging handle reciprocating, and added a cleaning rod, he would then lack really nothing over the M14. In fact, he may even surpass it.

The FAL vs. M14 debate is *not* dead! Many dedicated FAL manufacturers, gunsmiths, and shooters are constantly improving the system. Although my test results favored the *average* M14 over the *average* FAL—a properly tricked-out DSA FAL would be hard (impossible?) to beat by a properly tricked-out M14. Such a comparison only *you* could make for yourself.

METRIC vs. INCH FALs

As 93 countries of the (generally) Free World at some point adopted the FAL and often produced them locally under license from FN, there are two main variants of metric and inch (as well as subvariants within both). Metric/inch pattern really describes the country of origin rather than parts dimensions, as most parts are interchangeable.

Metric FALs (Belgian, Austrian, Argentine)

More common than inch models. Most metric FALs will be the superb Austrian StG58 type, from whose blueprints DSA makes their fine FALs. The 1960s German G1 is very similar. There are other metric variants. Argentina and Brazil made some very nice FALs. Israeli guns are of good quality but have several parts uniquely different from other metric FALs, and many gunsmiths consider them somewhat of a pain.

Inch FALs (Australian, British, Canadian)

These are often called "ABC" FALs, which also include the Commonwealth guns (N.Z., India, etc.). Quality is satisfactory, but not up the level of Austrian metric FALs (which I prefer).

Scoring differences between metric and inch

Some parts between metric and inch FALs differ only to a gunsmith, while several (especially in Israeli guns) are easily discernible to the shooter and different enough to actually change the scoring:

	Metric	Inch
gas regulator	7 positions	11 positions
handguards	wood or steel	synthetic
pistol grip	hollow	solid tang
charging handle	knob	often folding
bolt hold-open	manual only	auto/manual
forward assist	Israeli only	N/A
front sight	round post	flat blade
rear sight	nonfolding	flip up

Since most of them are interchangeable, I gave these criteria the higher score of the two when possible.

10	Exceptional
9	Extremely Good
8	Very Good
7	Good
6	Fair
5	Just Tolerable
4	Poor
3	Very Poor
2	Extremely Poor
1	Worst Possible
0	Nonexistent

FAL RELIABILITY   (38% of total)

FAL Op System (58% of category)

FAL gas system   **(x3)**   Score: 9
  A long stroke gas piston, similar to the AK.

FAL gas regulator   Score: 10
  Clearly, the FAL is the king of the hill here with its 7- and 11-position regulator, which earned it a 10.
  Proper adjustment for semi-auto fire is to gradually close off the valve (*i.e.,* turn towards 0) until the bolt begins to short cycle, then open it back up a couple of notches. This ensures that only *just* enough gas gets to the piston, which reduces fouling. Blocking off the gas flow entirely will turn the FAL into a manually-operated single shot for either grenade launching without bolt clatter.
  Reduce bolt carrier battering with a Ø15 buffer from www.buffertech.com.

FAL action hygiene   **(x4)**   Score: 8
  While the FAL is very clean, some gas can't help but escape past the piston, so it got an 8.

FAL action exposure   **(x3)**   Score: 8
  The FAL has not only a dust cover, but also a nonreciprocating bolt handle which slightly reduces exposure. The ejection port has no AR-type cover.

FAL reciprocating bolt handle   **(x2)**   Score: 0
  Not OEM except on Israeli and heavy barrel Belgian FALOs . You can either install a bolt and bolt carrier from one of these, or mill out a 0.220" slot in the carrier's rail for the charging handle pawl.

FAL reliability: feeding   **(x4)**   Score: 8
  The recoil spring could be more robust.

FAL reliability: firing   **(x5)**   Score: 8
  Strong hammer spring and forgiving of headspace.

FAL reliability: extraction   **(x5)**   Score: 8
  I've had occasional extraction troubles in a few FALs, although I wouldn't say that this is a typical problem.

FAL reliability: ejection   **(x4)**   Score: 9
  Fixed ejectors are superior to the in-bolt types.

The FAL got an overall **8.2**, although many FALs operate in the 9.0-9.5 range. My Imbel FAL, for example, has had no malfunctions whatever in over 2000rds.

FAL Design Ruggedness (42% of category)

FAL working parts placement   Score: 2
Except for the pre-ban Para models, the buffer spring needlessly housed in the stock.

FAL design complexity   (x2)   Score: 4
The FAL has the most parts of any battle rifle.

	# of parts	55 / #	61 / #
M14	61	.900	1.000
M1	62	.887	.984
SVT40	64	.859	.953
FN49	70	.786	.871
SKS	70	.786	.871
AK	75	.733	.813
HK91	92	.598	.663
AR	119	.462	.512
FAL	**143**	**.385**	**.427**

FAL parts breakage   (x3)   Score: 9
The FAL is not known for breaking parts.

FAL fieldstripping   (x2)   Score: 9
The FAL is generally quite good. The rifle hinges open to drop out its bolt and carrier, and its gas piston is easily removable. The trigger group is not modular, although replacing individual parts is easy. The FAL is also very easy to clean.

Though not often a required procedure (unless you're swapping buttstocks), the buttstock-contained concentric recoil springs are a *real* pain to cram back in, so beware. Use a ¼" aluminum tent peg (the one with an eyelet).

A good video for the beginner on rebuilding the FAL is from AGI (800-797-0867; #122; Ø34 ppd.).

FAL parts availability   (x2)   Score: 8
Widely available in all the variants. Check DSA first. G1 partst kits are Ø130 from www.gunsnammo.com.

FAL overall ruggedness   (x4)   Score: 8
A very tough rifle. You'll have to work hard to break one!

FAL handguard ruggedness   Score: 8
Most handguards are either synthetic (DSA, Belgian, or Argentine) or steel (StG58), although a few are wood (Australian, German).

FAL buttstock ruggedness   Score: 8
Stout, and firmly attached to the receiver.

FAL mag ruggedness   (x4)   Score: 8
The Austrian steel mags are quite tough, and even the aluminum mags rate a 7.

FAL mag availability   (x2)   Score: 8
Fairly ubiquitous, and more common than M14 mags.

FAL USABILITY   (24% of total)

FAL Static handling (45% of category)

FAL weight   (x3)   Score: 8
The quintessential FAL (*i.e.,* DSA SA58 with 20" barrel) weighs 9.75lbs. This is nearly as heavy as an M1 or HK91.

DSA also offer two aluminum lower receiver 16¼" barreled carbines: one with full length handguards (8¼lbs) and one with short handguards (7¾lbs; with shorter sight radius).

FAL mag weight   (x2)   Score: 9
The lightest battle rifle mags are the aluminum FAL's.

FAL length overall   (x2)   Score: 6
At 43" the FAL is fairly limousine in length.
The DSA Carbines measure only 38¼' long, which is shorter than even a .308 Galil.

FAL barrel length   Score: 9
At 20", the FAL has a sufficiently lengthy tube.

FAL handguard length   Score: 8

FAL handguard heatshielding   (x2)   Score: 8
An 8 goes to the synthetic FAL (not steel StG58 hand-guards, which really heat up quickly!) DSA offers a fine synthetic replacement (#021-US; Ø60).

FAL handguard fit/feel   Score: 9
The synthetic handguards have great ergonomics.

FAL buttstock fit/feel   Score: 7
Cheekweld for optical sights is only fair.

FAL pistol grip fit/feel   Score: 7
The inch grip is blocky, but the metric grip is very good. There are a few aftermarket replacements available, and Ergo Grips (www.gunguide.com; 877-281-3783) has one which replicates the excellent HK91.

FAL butstock and pistol grip storage   Score: 2
FALs have no buttstock storage, but the metric (not inch) FAL has a cleaning bottle in its pistol grip.

FAL Controls (55% of category)
FAL charging handle location   (x3)   Score: 10
Correctly placed on the left side and forward of the bolt for easier operation. The best! (Most inch pattern rifles come with the folding paratrooper handle, which I do not prefer. Simply replace it with a metric round knob handle from DSA.)

FAL charging handle feel   (x3)   Score: 10
The FAL knob handle (not the inch folder) was the best.

FAL bolt stop   (x2)   Score: 7

	Manual H-O	Auto H-O	Release	
3	✔		✔	(metric FAL)
7	✔	✔	✔	(inch FAL)

Also correctly placed on the left, and just where the left thumb will be after loading a mag. Although a bit cramped behind the mag release button and requiring a downward pull (instead of an inward push as on the AR10), it's still very good.

Because of the bolt handle's rearward travel ending just above the bolt release button, the bolt can be retracted *and* locked back with only the left hand, something that no other rifle can boast. Superb.

Although most metric FALs have no auto hold open, DSA sells one (#053; Ø25). To install, use a blunt toothpick slave pin.

FAL safety   Score: 7
The inch FAL (L1A1) follows a close second (9) to the AR10, but the metric FAL is too small and tight (5), so the FAL got an average of 7-Good.

L1A1 inch safeties work in metric FALs with some fitting.

FAL mag catch   (x2)   Score: 7
The metric FAL's catch can be pushed by a right trigger finger, and the L1A1's catch is moderately ambidextrous.

FAL mag to gun   (x3)   Score: 8
With its helpful receiver bridge, the FAL is the best of the nose-in-rock-back types.
One quick aside: metric mags will also work in inch pattern, but inch won't work at all metric. Go metric.

FAL lefty ergonomics   (x2)   Score: 3
The FAL has awkward charging handles and mag catches for lefties, and no provision for ambi safeties.

FAL overall handling   (x2)   Score: 9
Superb balance and overall feel.

FAL COMBAT ACCURACY   (34%)

FAL Sights (65% of category)

FAL sight radius   (x3)   Score: 8
Very good at 22".

FAL sight offset   Score: 6
The metric FAL has a 2" offset.

FAL front sight visibility   (x3)   Score: 8
The metric FAL ears are a bit thick.

FAL front sight adjustability   Score: 7
The FAL is adjustable for elevation zero. The metric FAL uses a wheel (replacement in heights 1-4) turned by a bullet tip (I give this a 8 due to its very limited vertical range), while the inch FAL uses a threaded blade with set screw (I give this a 6).

FAL front sight precision   (x4)   Score: 6
The inch FAL with thin blade is worth an 8, while the metric FAL (fat rounded post) gets only a 5. Since most FALs are metric, the overall score is a 6-Fair. A target-quality square post (*e.g.,* an NM AR15) would *really* help either FAL.

FAL front sight protection   (x3)   Score: 7
A 9 to the metric FAL with its thick closed ears. The inch pattern ears are usually open and a bit thinner.

FAL rear sight visibility   (x3)   Score: 8
The FAL visibility is very good, almost a ghost ring.

FAL rear sight readability   (x2)   Score: 7
The ramp is stamped in large numerals.

FAL rear sight adjustability   (x2)   Score: 4
The FAL has a simple range ramp, with set-screws windage zero. There are no indents for ranges between the even-100m ranges, and a screwdriver is required to zero windage. Needlessly poor.

FAL rear sight precision   (x3)   Score: 4
The FAL has a wobbly ramped aperture adjustable from 200-600m. The windage adjustment needs a screwdriver, but at least has clicks. (The inch FALs have the floppy flip-up aperture blade.) The ramp wobble is at *least* 0.010" in either direction (1½MOA), which at 600yds is 9" (enough to miss a shot).

FAL rear sight ruggedness   (x2)   Score: 4
The sight block is robust, but the blade is unprotected.

FAL tritium sight   Score: 0

FAL scope base   (x2 for Battle Rifles)   Score: 9
Second place (after the flat-top AR10) goes to the DSA SA58 FAL mount (#620-A; Ø68; the *only* FAL mount which actually holds zero). Don't bother with any other!

FAL Accuracy Misc. (35% of category)
FAL bolt and carrier   Score: 7
Bolt locks on a locking shoulder in the lower receiver. Headspace is adjustable with 16 different locking shoulders.

FAL trigger pull   (x4)   Score: 5
The FAL has a 7-Good trigger at *best,* and often a 4-Poor, and you'll never know what to expect from a random gun. (My Imbel FAL has a better trigger than a DSA FAL costing twice as much!) Most sad of all, the FAL trigger (a creepy 2-stage) is very difficult to tune. "Gunplumber" Graham's Lesson 304 (www.arizonaresponsesystems) has instructions on how to attempt this yourself, but I'd simply send it out for the work.
On average it gets a 5-Just Tolerable.
www.ak47trigger.com is working on FAL trigger.

FAL target accuracy   (x4 for Battle Rifles)   Score: 9
A good FAL will shoot 1½MOA with accurate ammo.

FAL muzzle blast   Score: 9
The post-ban FAL's 20-21" bare barrel has little blast.

FAL recoil   (x2 for Battle Rifles)   Score: 8
8-Very Good to the FAL (especially due to its adjustable
gas regulator), although you feel the buffer action through the
buttstock. Not as comfy as an M14, but it beats the HK91!

FAL time for 8 hits at simulated 200/300yds (x3)   Score: 7
The FAL was a post-ban Imbel gun, one of the few clones
which has been utterly malfless (although of average accuracy).
I also tried a DSA FAL, but it mysteriously shot abysmally low
(even with a #1 post, the lowest made).

Figuring on 18 seconds to be the theoretically quickest
time, let's divide 180 by the rifle's average time.

	M1	M14	FAL	HK91	AR10
best	20.08	25.38	24.44	22.77	
average	21.57	28.34	26.98	24.46	
spread	1.49	2.96	2.54	1.69	
score	8.34	6.35	6.67	7.36	6.67

What hurt the Imbel FAL was its length, indistinct front sight,
mushy trigger pull, and 2½MOA accuracy. It got better times
than the M14, however, because of its pistol grip, and because
I'd had much more experience on the FAL than the M14. (That
is changing by the week.)

FAL AFFORDABILITY (4%)

FAL OEM rifle price   Score: 6
DSA SA58 FAL   Ø1,500   6-Fair

FAL clone rifle price   Score: 7
Imbel FAL   Ø750   9-Extremely Good

From my experience, Imbel FALs are very often (2:3 odds) problem guns (likely due to fitting by the importer). DSA offers a
StG58 (Steyr) parts kit guns on DSA receivers. These are likely
very good rifles for the Ø1,000.

FAL brass reloadability   Score: 4
The case neck gets pretty dinged up during ejection.

FAL parts price   Score: 8
All parts are reasonable, as well as barrels. Go DSA.

FAL mag price   (x2)   Score: 10
      In mag-fed battle rifles, how can you beat Ø5 FAL mags?
Any FAL owner without at least *20-30* of them is very foolish!

FAL RANKING

FAL Reliability   (38% of total)
❹ **FAL**   77.0% (408/530)
               op system 77.7%   design strength 75.9%
      About tied with the M1. Feeding is the FAL's weakest
point (though it still rated a 7-Good). The bolt carrier, however,
can easily be modified into reciprocating the charging handle,
which would significantly ease failure-to-feed clearances.
      Generally a very reliable rifle—outside desert conditions
(as the Israelis quickly found out).

FAL Usability   (24% of total)
❷ **FAL**   77.3% (255/330)
               static 74.7%   dynamic 79.4%
      For righties at least, the FAL is very easy to use. The met-
ric FAL has the better mag catch and bolt handle, but the inch
FAL has the better safety.

FAL Combat Accuracy   (34% of total)
❹ **FAL**   68.0% (313/460)
               sights 65.3%   misc. 73.1%
      Now *this* surprised me! I had expected a score much
closer to the M14's, not 11% below. The fat, rounded front sight
post, very mediocre rear sight, and the mushy trigger pull combined to do in the FAL with a 68.0%. Although the FAL has fine
target accuracy, it is noticeably more difficult to hit with in the
field. Unfortunately, that's just one of those lessons you can
learn only by testing a rifle in its natural environment.
      That I shot the 200/300 Speed Shoot about 1 second faster
with the FAL than the M14 was no doubt a reflection of the
FAL's superior ergonomics and handling, as well as my then
greater field experience with the FAL. After more practice with
the M14, I believe that my times would equal the FAL's.

FAL Affordability   (4% of total)

❷   78.3%   FAL

FAL Overall Score

Only 3.6% separated the 3rd place FAL from the 1st place M14. So, you can understand why my favorites since 1998 and 2000 have been different from 2002 (which is final, given the extensive T&E I've done).

I recommend the DSA FAL SA58 and ironing out its few deficiencies. Then, you'd have a battle rifle equal to or better than an M14.

❸   FAL   74.1% (1023/1380)

4th in Reliability, 2nd in Usability, and 4th in Combat Accuracy—the FAL, while a very solid and capable system, just couldn't *quite* equal or edge out the M14 or M1. It was only 3.6% behind the M14. Only 50 more points (out of 1380) would have put the FAL in 1st Place; that's how close it was between the FAL and the M14.

With a reciprocating bolt handle (+24 points) and M14-quality sights and trigger (+42 points), the FAL would have had 1081 points for a 78.9% 1st Place.

If you have an FAL with a 7-Good trigger that you can hit well with, then there's probably no compelling need to switch to an M14. But, you should also give the M14 a try, especially if you're a lefty. You never know...

THE FAL

Used at one time by *93* countries, most of the free world chose the *Fusil Automatique Leger* (Rifle Automatic Light). (When did *93 countries* ever agree on *anything*?) It's been utterly battle tested (*e.g.,* Vietnam, Africa, Northern Ireland, the Falklands, etc.) and has some very nice control features gleaned from the WWII German MP44. There are several military models:

50.00	Standard fixed stock model with 21" barrel. Most common.
50.41	HB (heavy barrel) FALO with bipod. Sort of a .308 BAR.
50.42	Same as the 50.41, but with wood buttstock.
50.63	Para, with folding stock and 18" barrel. Rare/expensive.
50.64	Para, with folding stock and 21" barrel. Rare/expensive.

Which FAL for me?

Ergonomics are excelled only by the AR10. The gas regulator valve is outstanding. Reliability is great and balance is good. For those wanting a *real* battle rifle in a *real* caliber, the FAL is about the equal of the M14. These days, there are four price ranges:

❶ Ø 600   used Century Arms hybrid with bad sporter stock

❷ Ø 700   new American upper/Steyr StG58 parts
               Imbel parts gun (*not* Hesse!)

❸ Ø1,595   new, totally American-made SA58 from DSA

❹ Ø2,300+ used pre-ban Belgian model

So, which should you buy? The most expensive one you can afford, probably. (Yeah, it's a lot of dough, but if you're *serious* about fighting with a battle rifle then just how important is that *jet ski*, anyway?) Let's discuss them one by one:

❶ used Century Arms hybrid with bad sporter stock

This 1994-1998 import hybrid (Brazilian metric upper on a Canadian inch lower) *was* a whopping deal at Ø400, but now fetch over Ø600 at shows. These "Frankenstein" FALs are of tolerable quality, though I never cared for its folding bolt handle or crappy thumbhole stock. As is, it's an imported post-ban rifle which cannot have a pistol grip or a flash suppressor. (You can order the original buttstock, pistol grip, and flash suppressor for only Ø15 (800-888-3006; #AX0M-23408), but *don't* get caught with these parts on this rifle, or under the same roof.)

The best plan for these rifles is to swap Century's thumbhole stock for a DSA "Dragunov" (#090-DI; Ø75), add the Ø99 American parts kit (reducing the 27 CFR import parts count to less than 10), and *then* you can legally add a flash suppressor. (Remember, on *domestic* post-ban semi-autos you can legally have a pistol grip *or* a flash suppressor, but not both.) Since total additional cost would be Ø190 (on top of a Ø600 used rifle), you'd have spent Ø790 for effectively a pre-import ban rifle.

❷ new American upper/Steyr StG58 parts on Imbel rcvr.

For Ø75 you can add a "Dragunov" stock to achieve a virtual pre-import ban rifle for Ø875. Is the extra Ø85 over Option ❶ worth it? Since you're getting a *new* American receiver and excellent Austrian Steyr parts, you bet! (Plus, you don't have to install the American parts kit yourself.)

I'd swap the steel handguards (too hot) for DSA's synthethic version, and the tiny safety for a Brit L1A1 version. Once done, you've got today's best FAL bargain. (I'd also buy another StG58 parts kit, or two, which the includes original flash suppressor. Barrel threads allow QP's FN-FAL Vortex.)

The Brazilian-made Imbel receiver is fine quality (forged steel), as Imbel is licensed by FN. An already-installed American parts kit avoids the import ban. Well-made and 1½MOA accurate.

Recall back in 1998 when Klinton signed an Executive Order banning for 120 days the importation of foreign semi-autos? Once it expired, Klinton made it permanent. No more imported *"assault rifle"* receivers.

❸ new, totally American-made SA58 from DSA

DSA (847-223-4770; www.dsarms.com) domestically manufactures (from Steyr blueprints and CNC equipment) their modern SA58 with pistol grip. Quality is outstanding, and probably better than original Belgian manufacture. Receivers are machined from a *forged* (not cast) 19lb billet of 4140 steel. (If only the M1A were forged!)

Regarding DSA's competition, their quality doesn't compare. Hesse Arms receivers are cast, and horribly so. Entreprisé, got caught misrepresenting the hardness of their receivers as RC45, when they tested at RC16. (They blamed it on their contractor.) Stick with DSA!

Which model? The 16¼"bbl Carbine loses 250fps for increased muzzle blast, so stick with the 21"bbl models. I'd pick the 21" medium contour barrel (it has the cooler synthetic handguard), and in stainless for an extra Ø50. Dealer cost is Ø1,200; retail Ø1,595. (The medium and bull barrels are cryo treated, which is well worth the extra price.)

Note: The medium and heavy contour barrels are target barrels and chamber cut for 168gr bullet ogive, and not the 147gr FMJ. You will occasionally pull an FMJ bullet during manual extraction. If you will shoot lots of FMJ in such barrels, then have a gunsmith slightly ream out the throat.

❹ used pre-ban Belgian model

If you've got the bucks for a genuine pre-ban, then go for it! They're lovely rifles, and quite the status symbol.

FAL MODS, PARTS, & TOOLS

FAL modifications

Reciprocating charging handle

Within the most forward left-side bolt carrier rail, mill out a 0.220" (+0.005") center slot for the bolt handle pawl. Now you have a reciprocating bolt handle! Test to make sure that the sliding charging handle cover (which now also reciprocates with the bolt carrier) does not bind up during firing.

Handguards

Install fiberglass or DSA phenolic resin handguards.

Sights

If your metric FAL has a fat front sight post, replace with a thinner one from DSA. Enlarge rear aperture (either by simply drilling it out, or drill & tap for a screw-in aperture).

Optics

Install a DSA scope base (#620-A; Ø68). It's see-through without optics, so just leave it on the gun. Any 1"/30mm tube scope (*e.g.,* Shepherd, IOR M2, etc.) will install nicely. Use DSA's QD see-thru rings (#VT-QD-H; Ø59).

The Ø700 Elcan works well on the FAL, but a more affordable (*i.e.,* only *half* the cost!) scope of equal quality and ruggedness is the I.O.R. M2 from DSA. (Both are discussed at length in the Chapter 18 *Combat Rifle Optics.*)

Also covered is the L2A2 SUIT (includes FAL mount).

DSA is worked with www.grsc.com/acog/html to design a low-profile mount for the ACOG. They took DSA's fine scope base and channeled it out to the same dimensions of the AR carry handle channel. Thus, an ACOG drops right in, retaining iron sight visibility. And, you don't need a chinweld for the ACOG. What a superb idea! This has to be the sweetest optics rig for an FAL. Such a system would be very hard to beat.

Get a trigger job

Visit www.arizonaresponsesystems.com for this and any other FAL gunsmithing.

FAL accessories
Tactical chest-carry sling
I became sold on such from my HK91. It is the *only* way to carry a battle rifle or carbine. The "Sling Thingy" from Schneider Machine (schneidermachine@hotmail.com) is a plate that fits between the rear receiver and stock which accepts a side-mounted sling.

DSA sells the fine slings from www.grsc.com. #656; Ø40.

Buttstock mag pouch
I firmly believe that every battle rifle should have an attached spare mag. Get a SpecOps pouch from DSA (#896; Ø25), which thoughtfully includes a ring for top-mounted slings.

Cleaning rod
Not stock with the FAL, and any battle rifle needs one (if only to extract stuck cases—it happened to me). The breakdown rods will fit in a sling-mounted pouch. Numrich Gun Parts.

FAL parts/tools with gun
Pins (firing, trigger, hammer), hammer spring assembly, extractor, rear sight ramp aperture.

FAL parts/tools at home
Different height front sights, spare bolt and carrier, barrels, ¼" aluminum tent stake (w/eye) for recoil spring removal. The below are all from DSA:

two piece extractor disassembly tool	#646	Ø25
front sight tool; Belgian, Austrian, Brazilian	#640	Ø15
front sight tool; L1A1	#640-A	Ø12
front sight tool; Israeli, Argentine (open ear)	#640-B	Ø 5
upper receiver wrench	#603	Ø60
gas regulator wrench	#641	Ø15

For a metric front sight tool, you can use a pair of straight snap-ring pliers in a pinch.

FAL sources
DSA, Inc.   847-277-7258   www.dsarms.com
DSA is to FALs what QP/Bushmaster is to ARs. They simply make the best FALs in the business. High quality parts, knowledgeable and helpful staff, and excellent customer

service. The folks at DSA like to *shoot*, and it shows. Their catalog has not one bogus or cheesy part or accessory.

Tell 'em Boston sent you!

Arizona Response Systems

623-873-1410   www.arizonaresponsesystems.com

I've personally found T. Mark "Gunplumber" Graham to be an abrasively arrogant young curmudgeon who is reluctant to accept any opinion not his own—*but*, he is a straight-forward/no-nonsense guy and his work is good. He also sells an informative FAL gunsmithing workbook (available on shareware) and video, both of which I highly recommend. Regarding the FAL, he has "Been-there/Done-that." If you want a parts gun built, send it to him, as he has ample experience with all variants and knows which works with what.

Use only email for questions—do *not* phone for advice:

> *I WILL NOT discuss any aspect of* [my] *workbook by voice telephone. Let me reiterate: DON'T CALL ME FOR HELP IN BUILDING YOUR GUN! We reserve voice communications for paying customers. You may request assistance by email. I'll be happy to assist you at my convenience, usually in a day or two.*

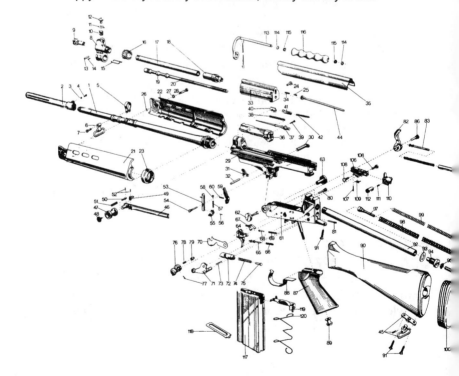

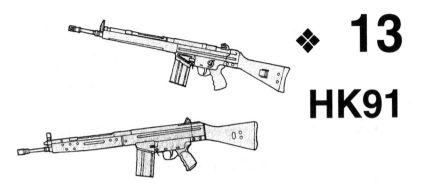

13

HK91

Designed by WWII Mauser engineers in post-war Spain at CETME (*Centro de Estudios Technicos de Materiales Especiales*, or Center for the Technical Studies of Special Matériel, a wonderfully bland moniker), they basically completed the work begun on the WWII StG45(M). The idea for a roller-locked delayed-blowback action (*e.g.*, MG42) was likely stolen from Polish engineer Eduard Stecke, who had patented it in 1937. (Another fine Polish design stolen by the Nazis was the Enigma encoding machine, sold in the 1930s for commercial use.) Making ingenuous use of pressed steel, welds, and plastics, the rifle was simpler and cheaper to manufacture than the FAL.

Heckler & Koch (which had formerly made *sewing machines*) took on production of the G3. (The G1 was the FN-FAL which Germany had actually adopted, but FN refused to license production to its recent invader. WWII had been over for just ten years.) The G3 has been picked up by over 50 countries, and many are still in service (*e.g.*, Mexico). In 7.62x51, if it's not an FAL, then it's a G3.

All HK rifles are typically German: high-quality, reliable, expensive, accurate, robust, and heavy. Shooters seem to either love or hate HKs (on a purely *personal* level, as they are very fine rifles). As for me, while I did not formerly resonate with HKs, after my research I recently bought my first genuine HK91. Although I still loathe the charging handle's placement and operation, I've been won over by the 91's simplicity, accuracy, and brute ruggedness. I have great confidence in the system with its surplus Hensoldt 4x scope. (The overly heavy and expensive HK93 in .223, however, I have utterly no affection for.)

10	Exceptional		
9	Extremely Good	4	Poor
8	Very Good	3	Very Poor
7	Good	2	Extremely Poor
6	Fair	1	Worst Possible
5	Just Tolerable	0	Nonexistent

HK91 RELIABILITY (38% of total)

HK91 Op System (58% of category)

HK91 gas system   (x3)   **Score: 10**

Because the roller-locked delayed-blowback HK totally dispenses with any gas system (both tube and piston), it is the most simple and most reliable, with fewer moving parts and less (perhaps no) sensitivity to ammo, but with stout recoil.

HK91 gas regulator   **Score: 10**

The delayed-blowback HK is self-compensating.

HK91 action hygiene   (x4)   **Score: 3**

The HK's fluted chamber gets absolutely filthy, not that seems to ever affect function.

HK91 action exposure   (x3)   **Score: 8**

The HK91 has not only a dust cover, but also a nonreciprocating bolt handle which slightly reduces exposure. The ejection port has no AR-type cover.

HK91 reciprocating bolt handle (x2)   **Score: 0**

Not OEM, and no way to adapt one.

HK91 reliability: feeding   (x4)   **Score: 10**

The recoil spring is strong, and feeding is flawless.

HK91 reliability: firing   (x5)   **Score: 10**

Very strong hammer spring and forgiving of headspace.

HK91 reliability: extraction   (x5)   **Score: 10**

The fluted chamber allows a layer of hot gas to separate the case from the chamber wall. The extractor is huge.

HK91 reliability: ejection   (x4)   **Score: 10**

Fixed ejectors are superior to the post-in-bolt types.

The roller-locked delayed-blowback HK91 *works* and got **10s** straight down the line. They are even more reliable than the extremely reliable AKs and Galils. The HK91 I tested even fired 100% of some foreign FMJ that the M1A and FAL could not light off (due to deeply set hard primers).

HK91 Design Ruggedness (42% of category)

HK91 working parts placement   Score: 6
Because of the small buffer in the buttstock, I gave it a 6.

HK91 design complexity   (x2)   Score: 6
The HK91 is of average modern complexity.

	# of parts	55/#	61/#
M14	61	.900	1.000
M1	62	.887	.984
SVT40	64	.859	.953
FN49	70	.786	.871
SKS	70	.786	.871
AK	75	.733	.813
HK91	**92**	**.598**	**.663**
AR	119	.462	.512
FAL	143	.385	.427

HK91 parts breakage   (x3)   Score: 10
Getting the only 10 was—surprise, surprise—the HK. The gun basically never breaks a thing!

HK91 fieldstripping   (x2)   Score: 10
The fieldstripping queen is the HK with its total modularity, simplicity, and tool-free disassembly. Hard to match, and probably impossible to beat! A 10.

A good video for the beginner on rebuilding the HK91 is from AGI (800-797-0867; Ø34 ppd.).

HK91 parts availability (x2)   Score: 6
Common enough (not that you'll need any). Generally available through HK-oriented dealers (*e.g.,* QP). Parts kits are Ø155-200. (Not that 91s ever *need* spare parts. My brother has never had to replace a *single* thing!)

HK91 overall ruggedness   (x4)   Score: 10
A brutally tough rifle. Seemingly impossible to break!

HK91 handguard ruggedness   Score: 9
Most handguards are synthetic and very tough, although a few are wood (Spanish CETME).

HK91 buttstock ruggedness   Score: 9
Stout, and firmly attached to the receiver.

HK91 mag ruggedness (x4)   Score: 10
The steel mags are the toughest MBR mag around, and even the aluminum mags rate an 8.

HK91 mag availability   (x2)   Score: 7
Fairly ubiquitous, and more common than M14 mags.

HK91 USABILITY   (24% of total)

HK91 Static handling (45% of category)

HK91 weight   (x3)   Score: 7
The HK91 weighs 10.3lbs. This is as heavy as an M1.

HK91 mag weight   (x2)   Score: 6
Since they're built like a bank vault, they are heavy.

HK91 length overall   (x2)   Score: 9
At 40.2" the HK91 is one of the shortest MBRs.

HK91 barrel length   Score: 6
At 17.75", the HK91 is rather too short, and loses 150fps.

HK91 handguard length   Score: 9

HK91 handguard heatshielding   (x2)   Score: 9
Assumes the fat, not slim, synthetic handguard.

HK91 handguard fit/feel   Score: 7
It's a bit blocky, but satisfactory.

HK91 buttstock fit/feel   Score: 6
Only Fair. It gives a poor cheekweld, and has a thin and slippery buttplate. Somebody should make a proper buttstock with an internal compartment.

HK91 pistol grip fit/feel   Score: 9
Ergo Grips (www.gunguide.com; 877-281-3783) has has excellent textured grip for the HK91.

HK91 buttstock and pistol grip storage   Score: 0
The HK has no storage of any kind, which was a needless oversight, especially since the buttstock hasn't the recoil spring.

HK91 Controls (55% of category)

HK91 charging handle location   (x3)   Score: 5
The handle should have been closer to the rifle's center of gravity (as in the FAL), thus it got a 5.

HK91 charging handle feel   **(x3)**   **Score: 2**

It's small, cornered, and must be unhinged. I hate it.

HK91 bolt stop   **(x2)**   **Score: 7**

Manual H-O	Auto H-O	Release
2	✔	(HK)

It can *manually* lock in an MP40-style forestock notch, and is bumped forward to release. In this sense, it does have an edge over the Galil (which hasn't even a manual hold-open), so I scored the HK91 a 2.

I consider an auto hold-open the absolute combat minimum, and the lack of such in the HK is criminal. The *Bundeswehr* specified its omission for fear of dirt entering the chamber. Today, however, their G36 has an auto hold-open (which may be disengaged by the soldier).

HK91 safety   **Score: 8**

The HK safety is fairly reachable and quiet.

HK91 mag catch   **(x2)**   **Score: 7**

The HK button requires a bit of a stretch (5) to reach with the trigger finger (hand must come off the grip). The quicker method is to use left hand middle finger underneath.

The aftermarket paddle release (Ø50) gets an 8, so I bumped up the overall score to a 7-Good. (An extended mag catch is sold by Federal Arms for Ø20.)

HK91 mag to gun   **(x3)**   **Score: 8**

Straight-up insertion as an AR. Smooth and quick. The mag *does* pop out on release, which is a Good Thing.

HK91 lefty ergonomics   **(x2)**   **Score: 3**

The HK91 has an awkward charging handle, and no provision for ambi safeties. The paddle mag catch mod is ambi.

HK91 overall handling   **(x2)**   **Score: 7**

Good (though not brilliant) balance and overall feel. While the engineers made a very tough and reliable rifle, they lost track of the *human* element. (For me, the charging handle and lack of bolt hold-open really compromises things.) With not much extra design work, the 91's ergonomics *could* have equaled the FAL's. Now *that* would have been a rifle!

HK91 COMBAT ACCURACY (34%)

HK91 Sights (65% of category)

HK91 sight radius (x3)   Score: 8
   Very good at 22½".

HK91 sight offset   Score: 6
   The metric HK91 has a 2" offset.

HK91 front sight visibility   (x3)   Score: 6
   The HK gets a mere 6-Fair due to the fat hood. Many vets sawed off the top 40% to convert the hood into ears, which really opens up the picture.

HK91 front sight adjustability   Score: 0
   Zero. Zilch. Nada.
   The CETME *is* elevation zero adjustable (as well as slightly adjustable for windage), but requires a tool (which also works in the FR8 bolt guns). (Ø11.50ppd.; DeGennaro, Box 349, Clarksville, NY 12041; 518-768-2922)

HK91 front sight precision (x4)   Score: 9
   The HK91 blade post is flat and razor sharp.

HK91 front sight protection   (x3)   Score: 10
   The HK ringed hood provides the most protection, though at the expense of some visibility.

HK91 rear sight visibility   (x3)   Score: 4
   The HK91 sports a crappy V-notch for 100m and *very* small apertures for 200-400m. Ugh. 4-Poor. No excuse for this!
   I tried out the 1200m rear sight (Ø175) which was OEM for the HK21E machine gun. Its aperture I had threaded for interchangeable hooded target apertures, such as 0.050", 0.093" (nearly ideal), and 0.125". This proved to be fruitless, as that sight is not properly cammed for either distance or increasing drop at long range. *Oh, well...*
   Somebody needs to make replacement drums with 0.075" apertures from 200-600m, and then I'd quit bitching about this.

HK91 rear sight readability (x2)   Score: 10
   The largest and clearest are found on the HK's drum.

HK91 rear sight adjustability   (x2)   Score: 3
   Inexplicably and inexcusably, the HK91 has no elevation zero adjustablity (front *or* rear!). Windage adjustability is quite meager, and requires a screwdriver. Range is limited to just

400m (in a .308!) in even-100m increments, although its range elevations are spot-on. 3-Very Poor.

The handsome wood stocked CETME rifle has no windage adjustment whatsoever, unless equipped with an HK91 rear sight, as on the later CETME parts guns.

The Hesse and CETME clones have severe POA vs. POI problems, which I'll discuss shortly.

HK91 rear sight precision   (x3)   Score: 4
The HK has a tight aperture drum (100-400m) but a Phillips set-screw windage zero (with no clicks, as has the FAL).

HK91 rear sight ruggedness   (x2)   Score: 4
The HK sight block is attached by only one small Phillips screw, and the drum is not protected at all. HK really hindered the 91 with such inexcusably bad sights!

HK91 tritium sight   Score: 10
Trijicon from Brownells (#892-401-002; Ø50). I believe that AO also makes one for the HK.

HK91 scope base   (x2 for Battle Rifles)   Score: 8
The genuine HK base (8) and ARMS copy (7) are both fine QD/ZH mounts.

The best optics deal today are the German surplus 4x Hensoldt (military Zeiss) or Karl Kaps G3 scopes on HK STANAG mount for only Ø375-480 (without/with case and acc.). They are rugged, clear, BDC'ed for 100-600m, and they are *accurate*. The one I tested was practically zeroed upon installation, and was dead on at all ranges. Really a superb piece of kit! Look up the *Shotgun News* ads for Wholesale Guns, AIM, and SOG.

HK91 Accuracy Misc. (35% of category)

HK91 bolt and carrier   Score: 8
The HK locks into a barrel extension, so I gave it an 8.

HK91 trigger pull   (x4)   Score: 4
The HK has an intentionally heavy pull (for Condition Zero safety in 12' drop tests) which could have easily been avoided with a heavy two-stage trigger. Not only is it very heavy, it's got lots of creep. (Note: The CETME has a better trigger, and being more similar to the M1/M14 trigger it's also easier to tune. It drops right in an HK91 with little trouble. This is worth a Ø130 parts kit.)

HK91 target accuracy   (x4 for Battle Rifles)   Score: 9
A good HK91 will shoot 1½MOA with accurate ammo.

HK91 muzzle blast   Score: 6
6-Fair to the HK91, as all the post-bans have brakes.

HK91 recoil   (x2 for Battle Rifles)   Score: 4
The HK91 gets a 4-Poor, and is brutal to shoot after 80rds or so. Ah, the price of a delayed-blowback .308! TANSTAAFL. (The wood buttstocked CETME with rubber buttplate is almost pleasant to shoot, and gets a 6.)

Install an aftermarket plastic buffer to eliminate bolt carrier/receiver battering, thus reducing felt recoil by about 20%, raising the score to a 5. Visit www.buffertech.com (#HK1; Ø15).

Installing a CETME buttstock with buffer would probably increase this score to 7-Good.

HK91 time for 8 hits at simulated 200/300yds   (x3)   Score: 7
The 91 tested was a genuine HK rifle, which was *extremely* accurate. Its tactical chest-carry sling sped up the times by at least 1-1½ seconds. Of the six modern clones I tested—3 Hesse and 3 CETMEs—only *one* (a Hesse) functioned without a hitch *and* had aligned sights.

Figuring on 18 seconds to be the theoretically quickest time, let's divide 180 by the rifle's average time.

	M1	M14	FAL	HK91	AR10
best	20.08	25.38	24.44	22.77	
average	21.57	28.34	26.98	24.46	
spread	1.49	2.96	2.54	1.69	
score	8.34	6.35	6.67	7.36	6.67

All this explains why the HK also did so surprisingly well. Its razor-sharp front sight was quickly focussed on, which largely overcame the dark rear sight aperture and heavy trigger. (Personally, I'm inclined to suspect that I was just a bit luckier with the HK, but one can never tell for sure.)

HK91 AFFORDABILITY   (4%)

HK91 OEM rifle price   Score: 4
HK91   Ø2,000   4-Poor

HK91 clone rifle price   Score: 10
Hesse 91   Ø500   10-Exceptional

I'd *like* to recommend an affordable post-ban HK91 clone, but their general quality is very spotty. Oh, they'll *work*—they just won't *hit* due to unaligned sights (*e.g.,* CETME).

I haven't yet tried the newer Portugese guns, however.

HK91 brass reloadability   Score: 6
The fluting ridges are pressed out in the sizing die.

HK91 parts price   Score: 5
Not cheap, but affordable if you look around. Fortunately, inexpensive parts kits abound. FAC has them for Ø155-200, and Inter-Ord (704-225-8843) sells kits with all new green furniture and green phosphate finish for Ø300.

HK91 mag price   (x2)   Score: 10
Recently available (Inter-Ord, 704-225-8843) for just Ø5, and these are HK and Rheinmetall mags! How can you beat Ø5 HK91 mags? Any HK91 owner without *20-30* is very foolish!

HK91 RANKING

HK91 Reliability   (38% of total)
❶ **HK91**   **84.5% (448/530)**
              op system 82.6%   design strength 87.3%

This comes as little surprise. However the critics denounce the HK91, even they must admit that the rifle *works*. No other rifle came close to matching the 91's brute reliability. It also does not break—*ever*—and can be neglected with little risk of failure. (I mean, the *Mexican* Army carries them, if that tells you anything!)

I now own one for my "End-Of-The-World" battle rifle.

HK91 Usability   (24% of total)
❺ **HK91**   **59.7% (197/330)**
              static 70.7%   dynamic 50.6%

Ah, the German step-child of rifle ergonomics! With FAL-level of controls, the 91 would have totaled 1042 points for a solid 3rd place finishing—and that's *with* its crappy sights and trigger! Likewise, with *AR10*-level ergonomics (and such was certainly possible by Heckler & Koch in the late 1950s), it would have been just 11 points shy of beating the M1A for 1st!

HK91 Combat Accuracy   (34% of total)

➎ **HK91**   **65.7% (302/460)**
      sights 66.0%   misc. 65.1%

Although the 91's sights scored 66.0% (edging out the FAL by 0.7%), its abysmal trigger really sunk the rifle into last place. Such was wholly unnecessary, as improved sights and trigger are absurdedly easy for a manufacturer to implement.

When the Germans are right about something, they are brilliantly correct.   When they're *wrong,* nobody is more wrong...

HK91 Affordability   (4% of total)

➍   65.0%   HK91

HK91 Overall Score

➍ **HK91**   **71.5% (986/1380)**

Last in Usability and Combat Accuracy, the HK91 simply falls short in everything but brute ruggedness and reliability. A good Rifleman could make do with a 91, but he wouldn't *love* it.

THE HK91

Mags are plentiful and currently Ø5 from Inter-Ord. Parts and accessories abound. It's the Mercedes Benz of battle rifles, and a little funky. The feeling of rugged quality is very strong and reassuring. It was employed by some 60 armies, about ⅔ as many as the FAL. Recoil is stout, and it *does* beat up brass, but the HK91 *works*—period.

Although I still prefer an M1A (better sights and trigger) or FAL (better ergonomics and parts/mag availability), I'm still happy with my HK91. If the ergonomics and recoil don't bother you, then a 91 is for you. It won't ever let you down.

Choosing your HK91

Since the clones are problematic, you'll have to spring Ø1,900 for an original pre-ban HK. (My brother bought his in 1984 for, *get this!*, only Ø400. Ah, to have a time machine...)

Absolutely avoid *aluminum* receiver clones!

These chunky guns have a built-in Picatinny rail, and will crack under extreme use/moderate abuse. Stick with steel!

Avoid the CETME clones

Many of the modern parts kit 91s (especially the Hesse and CETMEs) won't even hit paper at 100m due to chronic sight misalignment. Unadjusted, it is about 24MOA off to the left. (*With* the rear sight fully drifted over, POI is still 12" off!)

I spoke with Century Arms reps at SHOT 2002, and they claimed the problem was due to the vertically eccentric front sight post (which allows for some windage adjustment). If 1MOA equals 0.007", then 24MOA would be 0.168", and the post is not off-center by nearly *that* much.

While the post may slightly add to the problem, I maintain that this 24MOA error is due to 5-6° insufficient barrel tightening (which you should be able to eyeball at the gun show). Whether or not such can be remedied without overly shortening headspace is a question for Century and your gunsmith.

If you see a clone 91 for sale with a drifted over rear sight (or a buggered windage screwhead), then you probably know why it's for sale. **Always grill the seller about POA vs. POI!**

I've owned 3 of them (in the hopes of finding a good one for a car rifle) and they all had chronic sight misalignment. Only one CETME had an HK91 rear sight, and even it could not be sufficiently windage adjusted. Apparently word is getting out, as the wholesale price has plummeted to Ø368. If your 91 clone has chronic sight misalignment, either sell it or attach a combat-rugged 4x Hensoldt scope on the OEM HK mount currently available for only Ø375. (Personally, I'd send it down the road and get an M1A or FAL.)

This is a real shame, as the CETME is handsome, has a nice trigger pull, and functions flawlessly. If you still can't resist one, at least insist on test firing first.

Avoid the Hesse receiver parts guns

They are also prone to the POA/POI offset. I've found only one which shot straight. It was 2MOA accurate, too. But, that was a rarity. Test fire a Hesse before you buy!

HK91 MODS, PARTS, & TOOLS

HK91 modifications

Tactical chest-carry sling
I became sold on such from my HK91. It is the *only* way to carry a battle rifle or carbine. DSA sells a heavy 1½" nylon sling (#657L; Ø41) which is much better than the OEM canvas.

Paddle mag release
Ø50 aftermarket versions exist. Good for lefties.

CETME trigger group
Dropping in a CETME trigger group, or getting a trigger job, will really improve practical accuracy.

CETME buttstock
To reduce recoil, try the CETME buttstock (it has a rubber buttplate).

Recoil buffer   www.buffertech.com
This dampens about 15-20% of felt recoil. Only Ø15.

Open up front sight hood
Some owners like to saw off part of the front sight hood to make it into ears for better target area visibility. You may want to try this on your parts kit hood, and not destroy the HK part.

Trijicon tritium front sight post
From Brownells (#892-401-002; Ø50).

HK91 accessories

HK91 optics
Since the sights are poor and limited in range, but the rifle itself is very accurate, I'd treat the deserving 91 to some optics. Get one of the German surplus G3 scopes for only Ø360. (Since the HK91 barrel is only 17.7", it has 150fps less than a FAL or M1A, so the HK's 600+yd range capability is somewhat hampered—hence the *Bundeswehr*'s proper choice of the 4x Hensoldt with its 100-600m BDC.)

GG&G has a very low offset scope mount which I am keen to test with an I.O.R. M2 4x24mm

HK91 bipod
The thicker handguard is inletted for this, and it's a worthy accessory. Ø99 from www.cdnninvestmenst.com.

Mag cinch **www.buffertech.com**
 This connects two 20rd mags side-by-side. Great for a grab-and-go rifle. Only Ø20. Best I've seen.

Parts/tools with gun
 Pins (firing, trigger, hammer, buttstock, handguard), extractor, rear sight assembly, mag catch.

Parts/tools at home
 Perhaps an extra barrel, trigger group, and stock. I'd get a Ø130 CETME parts kit from *Shotgun News*, and call it done.

HK91 sources
DSA, Inc. **847-277-7258** **www.dsarms.com**
 High quality parts, knowledgeable and helpful staff, and excellent customer service. The folks at DSA like to *shoot*, and it shows. Their catalog has not one bogus or cheesy part or accessory. Tell 'em Boston sent you!

Arizona Response Systems
623-873-1410 www.arizonaresponsesystems.com
 Authorized HK refinishing center.

AR10

A *prima facie* alluring choice (because of its superior ergonomics and accuracy) is the modern ArmaLite AR10, which is an oversized AR15 in .308. It is not to be confused with the original AR10. The original AR10 was produced in 1955-61. Only 5,500 or so were made (and only 100 as semi-auto, now a Ø7,500 collector's item), and sold to Portugal, Burma, Nicaragua, Dutch NWM, and Sudan. Many Angolan mercs preferred it over the FAL or G3. Weight was 10.6lbs, and it had a 20" barrel. (ArmaLite is now making a semi-auto rendition of it, with central bolt handle and brown furniture. Cute.)

The Stoner SR-25 is much more expensive and a bit more accurate, but is *far* too finely tuned and fragile for battle rifle duty. The AR10 shoots just about as well for half the price, and preferred by High Power competition shooters (who often re-barrel theirs in 6.5-8.).

10	Exceptional
9	Extremely Good
8	Very Good
7	Good
6	Fair
5	Just Tolerable
4	Poor
3	Very Poor
2	Extremely Poor
1	Worst Possible
0	Nonexistent

AR10 RELIABILITY (38% of total)

AR10 Op System (58% of category)

AR10 gas system   (x3)   Score: 5

"It sh*ts where it eats!" according to my anti-AR friend "R.H." I, too, am not a big fan of direct gas impingment, but it's a tolerable enough system if you keep on top of PM. (A gas piston system would have *really* been nice.)

AR15s (which I *would* generally trust in the field) are *much* more reliable than modern AR10s (which I have come to *not* rely upon at all). Yes, many AR10 owners have (so far) had no problems with theirs, but I have heard of enough consistent trouble from AR10s (especially weak extraction and ejection, including chronic bolt carrier to receiver galling). Two guns (one with two different uppers, an A4 and a T) which visited Thunder Ranch in 2001 did not make it through class.

ArmaLite's "Hear-No-Malfs/See-No-Malfs" attitude isn't helping, either. I personally spoke to Mark Westrom about this at SHOT 2002, and he was naturally very defensive, calling my accusations *"unsubstantiated."*

AR10 gas regulator   Score: 0

None, and reliability suffers because of it.

AR10 action hygiene   (x4)   Score: 3

ARs are pigs, and the AR10 is dirty than its little brother.

AR10 action exposure (x3)   Score: 10

The AR10 has not only a dust cover, but also a nonreciprocating bolt handle which slightly reduces exposure.

AR10 reciprocating bolt handle (x2)   Score: 0

Not OEM, and no way to adapt one. It doesn't even have the AR15's forward assist.

AR10 reliability: feeding   (x4)   Score: 6

Only Fair, and never from a topped-off 20rd mag.

AR10 reliability: firing   (x5)   Score: 6

Only Fair. The hammer spring is too weak.

AR10 reliability: extraction   (x5)   Score: 5

Very weak. I had trouble with mine.

AR10 reliability: ejection   (x4)   Score: 4

Post-in-bolt type, which is pretty poor.

AR10 Design Ruggedness (42% of category)

AR10 working parts placement   Score: 1
   The buffer and spring are in the buttstock.

AR10 design complexity   (x2)   Score: 5
   The AR10 is of high complexity.

	# of parts	55/#	61/#
M14	61	.900	1.000
M1	62	.887	.984
SVT40	64	.859	.953
FN49	70	.786	.871
SKS	70	.786	.871
AK	75	.733	.813
HK91	92	.598	.663
AR	**119**	**.462**	**.512**
FAL	143	.385	.427

AR10 parts breakage   (x3)   Score: 7
   Gas rings, firing pins, extractors are parts to watch.

AR10 fieldstripping   (x2)   Score: 8
   Though complex, the AR is well thought out and strips
easily. The bolt and carrier remove quickly, and the bolt is
simple to break down. The trigger group is not modular, though
the parts are quite accessible. Easy enough, although the AR is
intricate.

AR10 parts availability   (x2)   Score: 3
   With ArmaLite's poor service, parts are largely unavail-
able. Happily, 60% of AR10 parts interchange with the AR15.
For those bolt parts that do not, get an ArmaLite Field Repair
Kit from Bob Swanson (520-721-4066; Ø95).

AR10 overall ruggedness   (x4)   Score: 5
   A 5 was harsh, but fair. This rifle should have been made
in steel, and would have scored an 8 to tie with the FAL.

AR10 handguard ruggedness   Score: 7
   Synthetic and tough.

AR10 buttstock ruggedness   Score: 5
   I gave it a 5 because it's not as rugged as it should be. If
you break it, your gun won't work since the buffer and spring
are (mistakenly) housed there. Remember, an MBR's buttstock
is also a potential *impact* weapon.

AR10 mag ruggedness   (x4)   Score: 8
While it uses M14 mags (which scored a 9), I dinged a point for the mag's spring-loaded bolt stop tab.

AR10 mag availability   (x2)   Score: 5
I dinged the score a point from the M14 mag's 7 because the ArmaLite followers are hard to procure. (OEM kits to convert the M14 mag are Ø47.)

AR10 USABILITY   (24% of total)
AR10 Static handling (45% of category)
AR10 weight   (x3)   Score: 8
At 9.8lbs, it's the second lightest of the bunch.

AR10 mag weight   (x2)   Score: 8
M14 mag weight.

AR10 length overall   (x2)   Score: 7
At 41" the AR10 is about average.

AR10 barrel length   Score: 8
At 20" this is good combination of length and handiness.

AR10 handguard length   Score: 8

AR10 handguard heatshielding   (x2)   Score: 9
Superb.

AR10 handguard fit/feel   Score: 9
Superb.

AR10 buttstock fit/feel   Score: 9
One of the best.

AR10 pistol grip fit/feel   Score: 10
Many choices. Try Ergo (www.gunguide.com; 877-281-3783). Get Ergo's Gapper.

AR10 buttstock and pistol grip storage   Score: 9
Good trap door and compartment. Could be roomier.
Get an A2 Stowaway Grip. The DPMS plug takes up too much internal room, and doesn't stay secured well.

AR10 Controls (55% of category)
AR10 charging handle location   (x3)   Score: 8
The rear drawbar is fairly handy.

AR10 charging handle feel   **(x3)**   Score: 5
    You might consider adding an AR15 tac lever (from QP).

AR10 bolt stop **(x2)**   Score: 10

	Manual H-O	Auto H-O	Release	
10	✔	✔	✔	(AR)

    Right where it should be. The best!

AR10 safety   Score: 10
    Right where it should be. The best!

AR10 mag catch   **(x2)**   Score: 10
    Right where it should be. The best!

AR10 mag to gun   **(x3)**   Score: 9
    Straight-up insertion. Smooth and quick. The mag's rear
tab knocked off a point from the AR15's 10.

AR10 lefty ergonomics (x2)   Score: 7
    With mods, pretty good.

AR10 overall handling **(x2)**   Score: 9
    Superb.

AR10 COMBAT ACCURACY (34%)

AR10 Sights (65% of category)

AR10 sight radius **(x3)**   Score: 7
    21".

AR10 sight offset   Score: 4
    2¾".

AR10 front sight visibility   **(x3)**   Score: 9
    Winged post is quite visible.

AR10 front sight adjustability   Score: 10
    Good elevation range for zeroing.

AR10 front sight precision (x4)   Score: 9
    One of the best.

AR10 front sight protection   **(x3)**   Score: 8
    Wings are strong, but aluminum.

AR10 rear sight visibility   **(x3)**   Score: 10
    Two apertures, one for CQB and one for 200m+. Perfect.

AR10 rear sight readability (x2)   Score: 8
Large, clear numerals readable from a cheekweld.

AR10 rear sight adjustability   (x2)   Score: 9
Dual aperture, and windage adjustable. A 300-800m BDC cam wheel is quick and accurate, with 1MOA clicks.

AR10 rear sight precision   (x3)   Score: 7
It has a bit of wobble when raised past 400m.

AR10 rear sight ruggedness   (x2)   Score: 7
While the AR aperture is well protected, the sight assembly is attached to the receiver by only one bolt and can be fairly easily damaged from impact. I would have scored this fine sight a 10 if it had more structural support than merely its vertical axis. The sight *will* break if hit only moderately hard.

AR10 tritium sight   Score: 10
AR15 front/rear tritium sights work perfectly. From QP.

AR10 scope base   (x2 for Battle Rifles)   Score: 10
Nothing beats a flattop AR. Solid, close tolerances, low offset, and *anything* will fit on it.

AR10 Accuracy Misc. (35% of category)
AR10 bolt and carrier   Score: 10
Bolt lugs lock into barrel. My ideal.

AR10 trigger pull   (x4)   Score: 8
Add a National Match two-stage. It's the best.

AR10 target accuracy   (x4 for Battle Rifles)   Score: 7
A good AR10 will shoot 1½MOA with accurate ammo, though mine did not. My AR10 was a 2½MOA gun (on its best day with Federal Premium!), thus barely getting a 7-Good. I was quite disappointed with it, however, your own AR10 mileage may vary as most AR10s are 1-1½MOA rifles (when they function).

AR10 muzzle blast   Score: 3
The braked AR10 gets a 3-Very Poor in my book, and I *tried* to ignore/accept it, believe me!

AR10 recoil   (x2 for Battle Rifles)   Score: 6
6-Fair to the AR10, which recoils more than you may expect even with its noisy muzzle brake. It falls between Pleasant and Unpleasant in my experience—something tolerated, but never loved.

AR10 time for 8 hits at simulated 200/300yds   (x3)   Score: 6
    Figuring on 18 seconds to be the theoretically quickest time, let's divide 180 by the rifle's average time.

	M1	M14	FAL	HK91	AR10
best	20.08	25.38	24.44	22.77	
average	21.57	28.34	26.98	24.46	
spread	1.49	2.96	2.54	1.69	
score	8.34	6.35	6.67	7.36	6.67

Although I had sold off my AR10A4 before this test, my recollection would score it even with my Imbel FAL.

AR10 AFFORDABILITY (4%)

AR10 OEM rifle price   Score: 7
    AR10   Ø1,400   7-Good

AR10 clone rifle price   Score: 8
    Eagle AR-10   Ø900   8-Very Good

AR10 brass reloadability   Score: 9
    Gentle and predictable ejection.

AR10 parts price   Score: 6
    The AR15 60% parts interchangeability saves the day.

AR10 mag price   (x2)   Score: 4
    A point was subtracted because of the extra work involved in drilling out the AR10 mag catch.
    OEM AR10 mags are Ø65+. ArmaLite no longer offers their 2-for-1 program (two M14 mags for one AR10 mag). Given how relatively simple it is to DIY, I wouldn't bother anyway.
    Burns Bros. sells 20rd Thermolds for Ø22 (they're Ø35 from CDNN). Steel GI mags are now Ø45+.

AR10 RANKING

AR10 Reliability   (38% of total)
❺ AR10   52.8% (280/530)
                 op system 49.0%   design strength 58.2%
    In 2000 I rated its reliability as a 7-Good, but have learned since then that I was a tad generous. Feeding and extraction

malfunctions are now known to be fairly common, and ejection is a real weak point.

ArmaLite's "Hear-No-Malfs" attitude isn't helping, either. One Thunder Ranch student's AR10 suffered from such bad bolt carrier-receiver galling that he had to complete the class with a loaner Romanian AK. All this a shame, since the .223 AR15 has grown to become a fairly reliable system (if you stay on top of PM every 400rds).

AR10 Usability   (24% of total)

❶ **AR10**   **82.7% (273/330)**
            static 83.3%   dynamic 82.3%

This comes as no surprise. Being the most modern of MBRs, the AR10 has the best furniture and ergonomics. Such, however, does *not* make up for a pathetic 51.7% reliability!

AR10 Combat Accuracy   (34% of total)

❸ **AR10**   **77.8% (358/460)**
            sights 83.7%   misc. 66.9%

Most AR10s are 1½MOA accurate, but not notably reliable. (Mine was just the opposite. Go figure.) Still, the system is generally renowned for fine accuracy, and has the best battle rifle sights in the business (83.7% vs. the M14's 75.7%), no matter what M14 devotees claim to the contrary.

AR10 Affordability   (4% of total)

❺ 63.3% AR10

AR10 Overall Score

❺ **AR10**   **68.8% (949/1380)**

With its 1st in Usability and near tie for 3rd in Combat Accuracy, the AR10 was poised to take 1st overall but for its *last* place in Reliability.

Had the AR10 shown just 70% overall reliability (as I gave it in 2000), it would have (with 1046 points) beaten the FAL. Had it matched the FAL's reliability (75.5%), it would have beaten the M14 by 4 points.

I simply cannot recommend the AR10 for any role.

Final comments on the AR10

If ArmaLite would just work out the AR10's bugs and fully stand behind the gun with DSA-quality support, then ArmaLite would have a dandy rifle. *C'mon Westrom!*

A pity that ArmaLite was *too* loyal to Eugene Stoner's gas impingment system. With a superior AR180 gas system (and perhaps a steel upper), the AR10 would have been absolutely unbeatable at an estimated 80.6% overall. If Mark Westrom ever built such an "AR11" (using HK91 mags, to boot!), I'd be the first in line!

If you have an accurate and *reliable* AR10 and you *love* it, then squirrel away a lifetime's supply of parts and keep it. I'd still have an M14 (which uses the same mags) just in case!

As for me, I'm officially *finished* with being the AR10's cheerleader. I sadly sold my A4 and won't replace it. *Sigh.*

IF YOU "MUST" HAVE AN AR10...

If I haven't persuaded you to buy an M1A or FAL or HK91, and you're still dead-set on getting an AR10, then at least let me reduce some of the damage of your faulty decision. The below has been lifted from the 2000 edition of this book, and is partially reprinted without cheer or enthusiasm.

Which AR10 to choose?

In general, I'd pick a *flattop* upper AR10 with a 20" barrel (not 16"). So, this means either an AR10(T) target, or the AR10A4. (A 20"bbl A2 model with fixed carry handle would also be acceptable, but I would miss the flattop upper of the A4.)

AR10(T)

This has a stainless 24"bbl and National Match two-stage trigger. With the right scope (*e.g.,* a Leupold tactical), it would make an excellent countersniper rifle out to 800yds, although it is too long and heavy to carry as a true battle rifle. Dealer cost is Ø1,495; retail is Ø1,995.

AR10A4

This model has a 20"bbl (add Ø100 for stainless), flattop upper, and weighs nearly a pound less than the (T). A good A4 will shoot at *least* 1½MOA, and sometimes ¾MOA (which is countersniper-grade accuracy out to 700yds). With stainless barrel, dealer cost is Ø1,095; retail is Ø1,425.

AR10 mags

Since original mags are Ø65+ and nearly impossible to procure from ArmaLite, you'll have to be resourceful elsewhere.

Adapting M14/M1A mags

The M14/M1A 20rd mags *can* be DIY-adapted to the AR10. First, test insert each mag for excessive mag well tightness (it should drop free when the mag release is depressed). Use a CD case front cover for the template, whose edge ridges will very nicely X and Y axis on an ArmaLite mag. (Index from the mag lips, not from the bottom.) Now, carefully carve out the template's mag catch hole. Then, dab some DieKote on the M1A mags, and scribe them from the template hole. Finally, cut out the hole on a drill press or mill, or by a steady hand and air grinder, Dremel tool, etc. Test each mag for fit and function, and file as needed. (Many thanks to my friend "R.H." for this procedural tip!)

Since the AR10's mag well is slotted for the M14 mag's rear locking tab, removing this tab is not required (unless you wish to replace the original follower with ArmaLite's, which trips the bolt stop). While these altered M14 mags *will* function without ArmaLite's follower, the bolt will lock behind the M14 mag follower (thus the mag won't gravity drop free). You must then retract the bolt ½" and engage the bolt stop *before* removing the mag (else the bolt will simply slam forward). In practice, this seems only a small annoyance. (For duty mags, you might *try* to order ArmaLite mag followers. Good luck!)

Burn Bros. sells the synthetic Thermold mags (which are much easier to adapt) for only Ø22. Steel M14 mags are now Ø45+ all of a sudden.

Iron sights for the flattop AR10A4

A reader friend of mine has a flattop AR10A4 and was desperately trying to obtain a front sight assembly and carry handle, so I went on a little quest for him. *Twurnt easy!*

AR10A4 detachable front sight assembly

Good luck finding an OEM part, although CFI (817-595-2485) *occasionally* has it (#EA5095; Ø75) and even the AR10A4 carry handle. Also, the front sight assembly for a Knight's SR25 Stoner will work (CFI; #98041; Ø125).

If you can't find a front sight base from CFI or somebody else, then you'll have to buy a barrel-mounted flip-up version from GG&G (www.gggaz.com; 520-748-7167). Their stuff is great, but pricey.

AR10A4 detachable carry handle

If CFI doesn't have the ArmaLite carry handle, then the one for the SR25 will work (CFI; #97079; Ø175).

While an AR15 carry handle *will* attach to the AR10A4 (a flattop is a flattop), the handle is over an inch too short (which looks weird), the aperture offset is too short to match the front sight, and the elevation adjustments will of course be off for .308 trajectory.

How to legally add an AR10 flash suppressor

While no modern AR10s exist in pre-ban form, you can replace the pistol grip and buttstock with a thumbhole stock (DPMS; #BS-30; Ø100) and thus use your one 18 USC § 921(30)(B) feature allowance for a Vortex.

AR10 parts

Their ad reads *"ArmaLite Lower Receivers Not For Sale."* Well, apparently neither are any of their *other* parts these days. *Beware:* It is nearly impossible to get stuff from ArmaLite, although that has improved a bit since 2000.

Furthermore, nobody else makes AR10 parts. Even though 60% of its parts (*e.g.,* trigger group, buttstock, rear sight internals) do interchange with the AR15, the 40% that do *not* (*e.g.*, bolt, bolt carrier, etc.) will be enough of a snag. While the ArmaLite catalog claims that the hammer and trigger pins are interchangeable, word on the street disagrees (The AR15 pins' O.D. allegedly are a mite too small).

If you ever see an ArmaLite AR10 Field Repair Kit (contains below parts in **bold**), jump all over it! It's got the non-interchangeable bolt parts that every AR10 owner should have. From there, AR15 part interchangeability will get an AR10 owner most of the way home. *Bon chance!*

As a service to all the afflicted AR10 owners, here is a list of AR10/AR15 parts interchangeability:

AR15 interchangeable

Handguard set, A2 round
Front sight post, A2
Front sight detent
Front sight spring
Front sight pin
Front sight swivel rivet
Front sight swivel
Front sight housing
Rear sight retaining pin
Rear sight helical elev. spring
Rear sight index set screw
Rear sight windage knob pin
Rear sight windage knob
Rear sight helical spring (3)
Rear sight ball bearing (3)
Rear sight windage screw
Rear sight aperture
Rear sight aperture spring
Rear sight standard base
Bolt carrier key screws
Bolt carrier key
Pistol grip
Pistol grip screw
Pistol grip screw washer
Takedown pin detent spring
Takedown pin detent
A2 buttstock screw
A2 buttstock
A2 buttstock spacer
Rear sling swivel
Rear sling swivel screw
Detent (takedown/pivot)
Detent spring (takedown/pivot)
Bolt stop pin
Bolt stop plunger
Bolt stop spring
Safety selector
Disconnector
Disconnector spring
Trigger (standard or NM)
Trigger spring
Hammer spring
Trigger guard pin
Trigger guard assembly
Buffer tube (a.k.a. receiver extension)
Buffer detent
Buffer detent spring

AR15 *non*-interchangeable

Barrel slip ring retaining ring
Barrel slip ring spring
Barrel slip ring
Barrel extension
Barrel extension index pin
Gas tube
Gas tube retaining pin
A4 detachable carry handle (too short)
Rear sight elevation index
Ejection port cover pin ret. clip
Ejection port cover pin
Ejection port cover spring
Ejection port cover
Charging handle
Upper and lower receivers
Firing pin (and AR10 spring)
Firing pin retaining pin
Bolt cam pin (could fatigue early)
Bolt carrier
Bolt
Extractor
Extractor pin
Extractor spring
Extractor spring plunger
Ejector
Ejector pin
Ejector spring
Gas rings
Lower receiver
Takedown pin (*i.e.*, rear)
Pivot pin (*i.e.*, front)
Buffer
Buffer spring
Bolt stop (could fatigue early)
Mag catch
Mag catch button
Mag catch spring
Hammer
Hammer/trigger pins (2)

There. That's all I've got to say about the AR10, and it's 12 pages that I'd rather have skipped, but thoroughness required their inclusion. Please, save yourself the bother, and buy another battle rifle. The AR10 just isn't presently a viable choice.

❖ 15
RATING THE BATTLE CARBINES

In this revision, I tested the SKS (with AK mag), Romanian AK74 (more accurate than the AK47), Mini-14, AR15A3, Robinson M96, Daewoo, Bushmaster M17S, and the AUG. These are the commonly available and/or affordable carbines. Thus, I did not test the following:

FAL	too rare and impracticable
HK93	too rare and impracticable
Galil	rare, expensive, and represented by the AK
SIG550	ultra rare, Ø8,000+, though a superb weapon
SL8-1	10rd post-ban; no parts support

Remember, this revision focuses on *battle rifles*, and I am not looking for ways to give ink to carbines (especially ones which few of us will ever see, much less own). Love your .223 Galil? Fine, it's a nice carbine—keep it. See, I'm not upset. A man carrying a .308 doesn't get upset over the small stuff. *Tee, hee.*

This will be a short chapter. In fact, I'll go ahead and ruin it for you right now by divulging the test results:

❶	AUG	85.0% (w/o Affordability)	82.6% (w/ Afford.)
❷	Daewoo	79.0%	78.6%
❸	AK74	77.9%	78.1%
❹	AR15	76.5%	76.4%
❺	SKS/AK	74.0%	74.7%
❻	M96	74.8%	74.5%
❼	M17S	69.5%	70.3%
❽	Mini-14	64.5%	64.5%

Big upset from my scores of 2000! The Daewoo beat the AR15? Yep. The *AK74* beat the AR? Tarted up, *yeah*. Wow.

I'd have liked to have tested ArmaLite's new AR-180B, which retails for a bargain Ø650 (assuming it shoots well). When I wring one out, I'll discuss it on www.javelinpress.com.

Instead of including six pages of 63 criteria analysis per eight carbines, I merely post the spreadsheet results. The AR15 and AK74, however, got their own chapters due to their ubiquity. The remaining six below did not, because:

AUG	Why pay Ø3,000+ for a *.223?*
Daewoo	*Very* nice guns, but we can't yet get *parts.*
M96	A decent gun, but accuracy is mediocre at best.
SKS/AK	Competent, rugged, dowdy gun out to 200m. Nuff said.
M17S	Great gas system, and well-made. Not fully developed.
Mini-14	For plinking only, and be gentle! I hate 'em...

Was I too hard on your favorite mouse gun? Well, *boo, hoo.* *"But these carbines are lighter and you can carry twice the ammo!"* **Yeah, and you'll *need* at least twice the ammo to put down your Bad Guys.** (Extending this silly argument, one should carry a Ruger 10/22 into battle with 5,000rds.)

As I wrote earlier, battle carbines/cartridges *do* have their place (*e.g.,* CQB, urban fighting, perimeter defense, etc.), but one must always keep in mind their significant limitations. To wit: they cannot penetrate much cover and their effective range is only 200yds—and even *that* is debatable due to the poor stopping power of the .223. If you spend your life primarily in urban areas, then a battle carbine *might* suffice, but don't expect too much from it. Unless you truly *cannot* tolerate the expense, weight, or recoil of a .308, I *implore* you to get a battle *rifle*.

I hope that you don't feel cheated by my short shrift of these carbines. If you need one, get an AR15A3 or an AK in .223. There's really nothing more necessary to say. I have neither the time nor inclination to further discuss these guns. I will not spend any more ink on weapons that fire an ineffective round.

10	Exceptional		
9	Extremely Good	4	Poor
8	Very Good	3	Very Poor
7	Good	2	Extremely Poor
6	Fair	1	Worst Possible
5	Just Tolerable	0	Nonexistent

	wt.	SKS	AK74	Mini	AR15	M96	DAE	M17	AUG
RELIABILITY									
Op System									
gas system	3	8	9	9	6	10	9	10	10
gas regulator	1	0	0	10	0	10	9	10	10
action hygiene	4	8	8	10	3	10	8	10	10
action exposure	3	6	7	3	10	9	9	10	10
recip. bolt handle	2	10	10	10	4	0	10	0	0
reliability: feed	4	9	10	7	7	9	10	9	10
reliability: fire	5	9	10	8	8	8	9	9	10
reliability: extrac	5	9	9	8	7	5	9	9	10
reliability: eject	4	9	10	7	8	7	9	9	10
Design Ruggedness									
working parts	1	10	10	10	1	10	10	10	10
design complexity	2	9	7	8	5	7	9	8	9
parts breakage	3	9	10	6	8	8	8	8	10
fieldstripping	2	9	8	8	8	9	8	9	10
parts availability	2	9	8	1	10	8	1	9	4
overall ruggedness	4	9	10	6	8	9	9	9	10
handguard ruggedness	1	8	8	7	8	9	8	9	8
buttstock ruggedness	1	8	8	6	7	8	8	9	8
mag ruggedness	4	10	10	5	5	5	5	5	9
mag availability	2	9	8	5	10	10	10	10	6
RELIABILITY SCORES:	530	457	473	371	361	411	443	452	480
		86.2%	89.2%	70.0%	68.1%	77.5%	83.6%	85.3%	90.6%
		SKS	AK74	Mini	AR15	M96	DAE	M17	AUG

	wt.	SKS	AK74	Mini	AR15	M96	DAE	M17	AUG
USABILITY									
Static Handling									
weight	3	4	7	8	6	2	7	5	5
mag weight	2	4	4	8	9	9	9	9	10
length overall	2	5	8	8	5	4	6	10	9
barrel length	2	9	2	5	9	9	9	10	9
handguard length	1	5	5	6	9	9	6	6	7
handguard heat	2	8	8	7	9	9	9	3	9
handguard fit/feel	1	7	8	8	9	8	8	4	8
buttstock fit/feel	1	7	7	6	9	8	7	5	9
pistol grip fit/feel	1	0	7	5	10	9	8	7	9
stock/grip storage	1	0	5	0	9	7	4	0	6
Controls									
handle location	3	7	7	7	5	10	7	7	10
handle feel	3	10	4	8	5	7	9	7	7
bolt hold open	2	4	2	6	10	4	10	10	6
safety	1	5	7	6	10	6	5	8	8
mag catch	2	6	8	6	10	8	9	7	8
mag to gun dynamics	3	6	7	6	10	10	10	8	8
lefty ergonomics	2	8	8	9	7	4	6	0	6
overall handling	2	6	7	6	9	8	9	6	8
USABILITY SCORES:	340	205	208	228	270	244	271	221	267
		60.3%	61.2%	67.1%	79.4%	71.8%	79.7%	65.0%	78.5%
		SKS	AK74	Mini	AR15	M96	DAE	M17	AUG

COMBAT ACCURACY	wt.	SKS	AK74	Mini	AR15	M96	DAE	M17	AUG
Sights									
sight radius	3	5	5	5	7	7	7	1	10
sight offset	1	6	6	9	4	4	4	5	6
fr. sight vis.	3	6	8	7	9	9	7	4	10
fr. sight adj.	1	10	8	0	10	10	0	0	9
fr. sight precision	4	8	8	7	9	9	7	4	8
fr. sight ruggedness	3	10	9	3	8	8	10	8	9
rear sight vis.	3	8	9	4	10	10	9	5	10
rear sight read.	2	7	7	5	8	5	7	10	10
rear sight adj.	2	6	6	5	9	4	5	0	9
rear sight precision	3	8	8	5	8	7	5	5	8
rear sight ruggednes	2	8	8	5	8	7	7	7	10
tritium sight	1	0	0	0	10	10	0	0	0
scope base	1	6	9	9	10	9	8	9	9
Accuracy Misc.									
bolt and carrier	1	7	7	7	10	10	10	10	10
trigger pull	4	6	10	8	8	7	9	4	4
target accuracy	3	6	8	5	9	3	9	8	9
muzzle blast	2	7	8	6	9	8	8	10	8
recoil	0	0	0	0	0	0	0	0	0
8 hits 200/300yds	0	0	0	0	0	0	0	0	0
COMBAT ACCURACY:	390	270	301	214	333	287	281	203	324
		69.2%	77.2%	54.9%	85.4%	73.6%	72.1%	52.1%	83.1%
		SKS	AK74	Mini	AR15	M96	DAE	M17	AUG

AFFORDABILITY	wt.	SKS	AK74	Mini	AR15	M96	DAE	M17	AUG
OEM rifle price	1	10	9	9	4	4	7	8	1
clone rifle price	1	10	9	9	10	4	7	8	1
brass reloadability	1	6	3	8	6	7	8	8	8
parts price	1	8	8	1	5	7	1	8	3
mag price	2	10	10	6	10	10	10	10	3
AFFORDABILITY:	60	54	49	39	45	42	43	52	19
		90.0%	81.7%	65.0%	75.0%	70.0%	71.7%	86.7%	31.7%

		SKS	AK74	Mini	AR15	M96	DAE	M17	AUG
TOTAL RIFLE SCORES									
(W/O AFFORDABILITY)	1260	932	982	813	964	942	995	876	1071
		74.0%	77.9%	64.5%	76.5%	74.8%	79.0%	69.5%	85.0%

		SKS	AK74	Mini	AR15	M96	DAE	M17	AUG
TOTAL RIFLE SCORES									
(W/ AFFORDABILITY)	1320	986	1031	852	1009	984	1038	928	1090
		74.7%	78.1%	64.5%	76.4%	74.5%	78.6%	70.3%	82.6%
		5	3	8	4	6	2	7	1

RELIABILITY/TOTAL	40%
USABILITY/TOTAL	26%
COMBAT ACCURACY/TOTA	30%
AFFORDABILITY/TOTAL	5%

The A1 (pre-1985)

This has the fragile triangular handguard, simple rear sight, and a thin barrel with 1:12" twist (suitable only for 55gr ammo, like M193 ball). 62gr bullets are *not* stabilized here.

The A1 got off to a poor start in Vietnam, primarily because of normal teething problems, insufficient cleaning by the troops, and an unforgiveable gunpowder change which caked up tremendously.

The A2 (1985 on)

This version has the rounded, stronger handguard and improved rear sight. The buttstock is ⅝" longer, which fits shooters better. It has a forward assist and a heavier barrel with at least a 1:9" twist for 62gr ammo (Colts have 1:7").

The modern A2 version can be called a "triumph of engineering over design" which works very well (if you clean them every 400rds). I didn't use to like ARs at all, but have grown convinced of their utility. Regardless of whether or not you choose an AR for your .223 battle carbine, you should certainly *train* with one as you may encounter them in the field.

The A3 (flattop w/carry handle)

Choose this, as it gives you the most sighting options.

10	Exceptional		
9	Extremely Good	4	Poor
8	Very Good	3	Very Poor
7	Good	2	Extremely Poor
6	Fair	1	Worst Possible
5	Just Tolerable	0	Nonexistent

AR15 RELIABILITY   (38% of total)

AR15 Op System (58% of category)

AR15 gas system   (x3)   Score: 6

"*It sh✳ts where it eats!*" according to my anti-AR friend "R.H." I, too, am not a big fan of direct gas impingment, but it's a tolerable enough system if you keep on top of PM.

A Daewoo gas piston system would have *really* been nice.

AR15 gas regulator   Score: 0

None, and it could use one when dirty.

AR15 action hygiene   (x4)   Score: 3

It's a pig.

AR15 action exposure (x3)   Score: 10

The standard. Probably impossible to beat.

AR15 reciprocating bolt handle (x2)   Score: 0

It has none, and this is a real drawback.

AR15 reliability: **feeding**   (x4)   Score: 8

Reliable only with mags loaded <2 from capacity.

AR15 reliability: **firing**   (x5)   Score: 8

Generally quite reliable, when the gun isn't filthy.

AR15 reliability: **extraction**   (x5)   Score: 7

An AR15 weak point, as there is no primary extraction. This is enhanced by the products from www.armforte.com.

AR15 reliability: **ejection**   (x4)   Score: 7

In-bolt ejector, and it's not terribly robust.

AR15 Design Ruggedness (42% of category)

AR15 working parts placement   Score: 1

The buffer and spring are housed in the buttstock.

AR15 design complexity   (x2)   Score: 5

About average these days.

AR15 parts breakage   (x3)   Score: 8

You'll eat up gas rings yearly, and the odd firing pin.

AR15 fieldstripping   (x2)   Score: 8

Easy enough, although the AR is intricate.

AR15 parts availability (x2)   Score: 10
  The best. Go to QP first.

AR15 overall ruggedness   (x4)   Score: 8
  This rifle should have been made in steel, and would have scored an 8.

AR15 handguard ruggedness   Score: 8
  The A2 handguards are pretty tough.

AR15 buttstock ruggedness   Score: 8
  Though it has good fit and feel, I gave it an 8 because it's not as rugged as it should be. If you break it, your gun won't work since the buffer and spring are (mistakenly) housed there. Remember, a combat rifle's buttstock is also a potential *impact* weapon. (For a rugged buttstock, think HK.)

AR15 mag ruggedness (x4)   Score: 5
  One of the AR's weakest links. The aluminum mags are flimsy and bend easily. Have lots of spares.

AR15 mag availability   (x2)   Score: 10
  Ubiquitous.

AR15 USABILITY   (24% of total)

AR15 Static handling (45% of category)

AR15 weight   (x3)   Score: 6
  At 7.6lbs, it's about average.

AR15 mag weight   (x2)   Score: 9
  At ¼lbs, AR mags are the lightest going.

AR15 length overall   (x2)   Score: 5
  At 39" the AR15 is one of the longest battle carbines.

AR15 barrel length   Score: 9
  At 20" this is good combination of length and handiness.

AR15 handguard length   Score: 9

AR15 handguard heatshielding   (x2)   Score: 9

AR15 handguard fit/feel   Score: 9

AR15 buttstock fit/feel   Score: 9

AR15 pistol grip fit/feel   Score: 10

Over a dozen choices. I like the Ergo Sure Grip (www.gunguide.com; 877-281-3783), and the Ø3 Gapper (which fills in the bottom space of the trigger guard).

AR15 buttstock and pistol grip storage   Score: 9

Good trap door and compartment. Could be roomier. Use the A2 Stowaway grip. (The DPMS plug falls out.)

AR15 Controls (55% of category)

AR15 charging handle location   (x3)   Score: 5

Should have been FAL-style.

AR15 charging handle feel   (x3)   Score: 5

OEM is small and will rip your hand on a sticky extraction. Get a TacLatch.

AR15 bolt stop (x2)   Score: 10

	Manual H-O	Auto H-O	Release
10	✔	✔	✔

Right where it should be. The best!

AR15 safety   Score: 10

Right where it should be. The best!

AR15 mag catch   (x2)   Score: 10

Right where it should be. The best!

AR15 mag to gun   (x3)   Score: 10

The receiver mag well should be flared a bit for easier insertion, though I'm just being picky.

AR15 lefty ergonomics (x2)   Score: 7/9

Drawbar is quasi-ambi, and an ambi safety and mag catch are sold by DPMS.

AR15 overall handling (x2)   Score: 9

AR15 COMBAT ACCURACY (34%)

AR15 Sights (65% of category)

AR15 sight radius   (x3)   Score: 7

20".

AR15 sight offset   Score: 4

2½".

AR15 front sight visibility   (x3)   Score: 9
   Winged post with superb visibility.

AR15 front sight adjustability   Score: 10
   Elevation zero adjustable.

AR15 front sight precision (x4)   Score: 9
   Square post is quite precise.

AR15 front sight protection   (x3)   Score: 8
   Wings protect very well.

AR15 rear sight visibility   (x3)   Score: 10
   Two apertures: one CQB, and other for >200m.

AR15 rear sight readability (x2)   Score: 8
   Large and clear numerals

AR15 rear sight adjustability   (x2)   Score: 9
   ½MOA clicks. 300-600m.

AR15 rear sight precision   (x3)   Score: 8
   Crisp movement, which holds well.

AR15 rear sight ruggedness   (x2)   Score: 8
   Secured by only one bolt, but nonetheless quite rugged.

AR15 tritium sight   Score: 10
   While not OEM, several aftermarket sights are sold.

AR15 scope base   Score: 10
   Nothing beats a flattop upper A3. Solid, close tolerances,
and anything will fit on it.

AR15 Accuracy Misc. (35% of category)
AR15 bolt and carrier   Score: 10
   The ideal for accuracy.

AR15 trigger pull   (x4)   Score: 8/10
   A very nice one-stage is OEM.
   Add a National Match two-stage. It's the best.

AR15 target accuracy (x3 for Battle Rifles)   Score: 9
   The best. Sub-MOA is not uncommon with good ammo.

AR15 muzzle blast   Score: 9

AR15 AFFORDABILITY (4%)

AR15 pre-ban rifle price   **Score: 4**
    Colt AR15   Ø1,200

AR15 post-ban rifle price   **Score: 10**
    Bushmaster   Ø700   10-Exceptional

AR15 brass reloadability   **Score: 6**
    Gentle and predictable ejection.

AR15 parts price   **Score: 5**
    Very affordable.

AR15 mag price   **(x2)**   **Score: 10**
    Milspec 30rd mags are still out there for Ø15, but most are
Ø25-35. Prices are steadily rising, so stock up now. (Remember
back in the 1980s when AR mags were Ø2 each? *Groan!*)

AR15 RANKING

AR15 Reliability   (38% of total)
❶ **AR15**   **68.1% (361/530)**
    Some ARs are almost AK-reliable, while some are fussy.

AR15 Usability   (24% of total)
❺ **AR15**   **79.4% (270/340)**
    Great ergonomics and handling.

AR15 Combat Accuracy   (34% of total)
❺ **AR15**   **85.4% (333/390)**
    1st in this category. Superb sights and inherent accuracy.

AR15 Affordability   (4% of total)
  ❹ 75.0% AR15

AR15 Overall Score
❹ **AR15**   **76.4% (1009/1320)**
    4th. Within 2.2% of the 2nd Place Daewoo.

Final comments on the AR15

It's 2002 and I have become less and less enamored with the .223 round, regardless of the carbine. Furthermore, I have become less and less enamored with the AR15. Used very hard and very often, you will scrape through its (thick) patina of reliability and ruggedness, and you *will* discover its faults.

Nevertheless, if you keep in mind what the .223 and the AR15 are good for, and don't often excede such, then the AR15 will serve you well. Every home likely needs one, at least for the lady of the house (who will not savor lugging around a .308).

AR15 MANUFACTURERS

The AR15 is made under license by over a dozen firms these days. I'll discuss the most common ones:

American Spirit   888-486-5487   www.gunkits.com

A newer (*i.e.,* post-1994) firm from Phoenix which makes only post-ban rifles. I've handled one of their ARs, and its quality seemed very good, though I didn't get to fire it.

ArmaLite

Their AR15s are much better than their AR10s. They don't sell their lowers, so you can't assemble an AR. Parts support is pretty scant. Pass. Get a Bushmaster or Colt or PWA.

Bushmaster

Probably my favorite. Bushmaster rifles are just as nice as Colts, but not as expensive. I like Bushmaster's Dissipator model with the 16" barrel and full-length stock (which uses the full sight radius of the fine A2 sights).

L063000 was the last pre-ban lower.

Colt

Fine quality, but Colt is *very* anal-retentive about gun legislation, and they go *far* out of their way to *over*comply.

Pre- and post-ban guns have different hinge pin diameters. (Colt upper to milspec lower needs bushings; Colt lower to milspec upper needs an offset pin. QP has both.) Also, their lowers have a special block to prevent full-auto conversion, which precludes certain bolt carriers and trigger group parts.

Colt will someday likely manufacture ARs and handguns only for Government. (There have been whispers of this for some time, and such trend has accelerated since 2000.) *Wimps.* Sam Colt must be spinning in his grave at 85,000rpm. Domestic manufacturers seem to be voluntarily reducing themselves to dedicated Government contractors. (Ruger will probably next stoop to such whoredom.)

DPMS
Very good quality with an awesome selection, including left-ejecting uppers and a pump-operated AR (not subject to the *"Crime Bill"*). Their array of accessories is also staggering.

Olympic Arms
Since they just *had* to make an AR15 pistol in 7.62x39, they single-handedly triggered a BATF ruling against imported steel-core ammo (the law forbids such in a pistol). Only one factory pistol using a rifle caliber made it also a pistol caliber, so 90% of the cheap Chinese ammo was cut off. The major ammo importers even offered to compensate Olympic's expected profit on the gun if they didn't manufacture it, but Olympic *refused!*

Moral: *Don't* buy a *new* AR15 from Olympic Arms. The older Olympic ARs were pretty crappy, but the 1990s models are tolerable (though not great).

Professional Ordnance 97S
They offer a *4.3*lb carbon fiber AR15 rifle. It feels as light as an umbrella. Length is 35" with a 16" barrel of 1:9" twist. Since the *"Crime Bill"* forbids only folding and telescoping buttstocks, Pro-Ord came up with a perfectly legal alternative: a *detachable* stock (which even has a cylindrical 1¼"x6" compartment inside). Once removed, the rifle packs into nearly any suitcase or bag. (A good travel rifle for airplane trips.) The collet-attached muzzle brake is quickly removable.

The P97S is a vast improvement on their Type 97 (which I did not generally recommend in 2000). It has some decent (if basic) iron sights, and an improved buffer, bolt carrier, and handguard. *Gun Tests* found it to be very reliable, and 1½MOA.

PWA (Pac-West Arms)
Pretty good in general. Upper/lower fit is a little loose and requires an Accuwedge (Ø5; QP). 35,222 was the last pre-ban.

AR15 COMPONENTS

Upper

While a carry handle A2 upper is fine, the flattop A3 lowers any additional sighting device about an inch—which aids accuracy and handling—and is a more solid mount. Besides, you'd also have the QD carry handle.

New Colt 20" (1:7" twist) barreled flattop uppers are Ø525 (Hoplite; 502-955-5014). The identical in Bushmaster (1:9") is the the same price (from QP). While there are "bargain" barreled uppers from Model 1 Sales (Ø375; 847-639-3192) and M&A (Ø395; 847-639-3192), I can't vouch for their quality. Spend the extra Ø130-150 to get a Colt or Bushmaster and thus never have to worry about it failing you after 3,000 rounds.

Barrel

length

Except for target-length barrels, civilian choices are 16" and 20". Both have their pros and cons. (Note: Regarding 16" barrels, I'm speaking only of the *Bushmaster* Dissipator models which enjoy full 20" A2 sight radius. Avoid the shorty handguard models with truncated sight radius.)

A 16" barrel really must be a pre-ban since its short length demands a Vortex flash suppressor. That aside, a 16" is much more handy for clearing buildings and CQB. Within 75m, you'll never miss its 200fps velocity sacrifice. Rear sight wheel maxes out at 600m, which is fine for the .223/16" combination.

One quick note on the 16" Dissipator: Make *sure* that it's an original Bushmaster and *not* a 20" barrel simply cut down. The reason why is that an AR gas port needs at least 4" of forward barrel to develop sufficient back pressure, else it won't cycle reliably (if at all). Bushmaster understands that, and uses a hidden gas block instead of the normal front sight base gas block. So, if considering a Dissipator-style upper, look through the handguard vents to verify the mid-barrel gas block. If the gas tube runs all the way to the front sight base, then it's a 20" barrel that's been cut for Dissipator appeal (not performance). *Caveat emptor!* (I speak from personal experience on this.)

A 20" barrel, while slightly more cumbersome, pays dividends in less muzzle flash, higher muzzle velocity (which increases hyper-effectiveness to 150yds), and better accuracy.

Also, a wider range of attachments can be fitted. Finally, post-ban 20" barrels do not permit all that much muzzle flash.

So, unless your AR is dedicated for in-house or CQB, you're probably better off choosing a 20" barrel.

twist

Unless you're shooting exclusively 62+gr bullets, I'd avoid the Colt barrels with their too fast **1:7"** twist (which was specified by the U.S. Army because of the extra-long M856 tracer). Although Colt barrels are of excellent quality, 55gr ball is often 1MOA less accurate with such a fast twist. Experiment.

The pre-1985 A1s with a **1:12"** twist will *not* sufficiently stabilize the 62gr (10-12MOA!), and are only suitable for 55gr. (providing the best accuracy for it, too).

A twist of **1:9"** is probably the best compromise for either military ball weight, the 55gr M193 ball or the 62gr U.S. M855/foreign SS109. (Know that 1:9" will *not* be fast enough for bullets heavier than 72gr, such as 75gr and 80gr.)

muzzle caps

They're only 50¢ and worth having to keep water, dirt, and bugs out of the bore. It can be shot off without harm (*i.e.,* to the gun; the cap's wasted) if you forget to remove it.

Flash suppressor

Install the Smith Vortex or Phantom (whose tangs are joined together at muzzle) suppressor from QP. Avoid the gun show generic Vortex copies; accept only a genuine Smith part.

Buttstock

The older A1s are ⅝" too short for some people, and the telescoping stocks are too flimsy, and neither have a storage compartment. Unless you wear heavy coats or tactical vests, the standard A2 is fine. Have a spare buttstock, buffer tube extension, buffer and spring, just in case you break a buttstock and/or its internals (which will shut down your AR).

Pistol grip

It's important for your shooting hand to fit well with the pistol grip, trigger, and safety. Grips can be either too small or too large, so you must experiment. I've tried most of them: the original A1, the A2, Pachmayr, Stock Option, Hogue, etc.

A2

It has that annoying ridge, and I've never much cared for it.

Pachmayr

Although comfy, it is Ø40, heavy, and moves your hand off the controls somewhat.

Hogue

This is quite a nice soft grip (made of Kraton). Good for CQB but not rugged enough for a field AR, in my opinion.

Ergo (800-216-1960)

They offer many options, and the Sure Grip (a rubberized H&K-style grip) is one of my favorites. Nice folks, too.

While you're on the phone with them, order a Ø3 **Gapper** for each of your ARs. This is a polyurethane plug for that sharp-edged space at the bottom/rear of the trigger guard. (No more torn up index finger on long patrols!). You'll love it.

Lone Star Stowaway

From QP (#56PT87SPG2; Ø13), this grip makes use of the wasted hollow space. QP also sells an H&K91-style grip (#ARG02; Ø25).

A1 grip

One Ø5 solution is the old A1 grip with a piece of bicycle tubing; it's OEM, thin, lightweight, and comfy (especially for smaller hands).

DPMS grip plug

It takes up too much internal room, and it pops out. Pass.

Finish

The stock finish is a long-lasting dark gray or black anodizing. The color, however, is too dark and monochromatic, and is easily distinguished from foliage or backgrounds.

BowFlage camo paint

Get a few different cans and camouflage your gun. Start with a light green or sand base, and then add snaky diagonal patterns with other colors. Don't get too ornate; less is more. The wider apart the pattern, the more effective it will be. The paint will rub off with handling; simply reapply. (Be sure to close your dustcover first, and don't paint over your tritium sights! Mags should be painted only *below* the mag well.)

Camouflage nylon tape
From CTD, this is an option for the furniture. I'm trying some out for durability, and so far it's been satisfactory.

Magazines
The mag is the AR's weakest link, so get at least 20 (as up to a third will fail). Government-contract issue 30rd only. (No civilian plastic mags from Eagle, etc.) While 30rd mags are still plentiful, they're now Ø25+. The green followers work the best according to all of my military contacts. (The Colt 20rd mags are the most reliable, in case you're wondering.)

Magpuls
These rubber endloops greatly assist mag extraction from pouches and tac vests. Black, OD, and sand. (877-4MAGPUL; www.magpul.com; about Ø4 each)

synthetic mags
Mil-spec synthetic mags are the Thermold (Canadian, good for cold weather; from R Guns for Ø21 or CDNN for Ø23) and the Orlite (Israeli, good for deserts; from J&G for Ø20). Thermold mags seem slightly superior. I'd use them just for training, and save your tested aluminum mags for duty.

drum mags
The large "90 Rounder" mags work O.K. and are still seen at gunshows. The Chinese 120rd drums don't work, *period.*

the C-Mag
The 100rd C-Mag works well, but is not terribly robust. If you live in the city and plan on staying, or fighting your way out, then get a C-Mag. Why a *100rd* mag? So you can stay in the fight *longer.* Even 30rd mags shoot empty quickly, and if you're trying to outrun the inner city hordes you'll kiss that C-Mag afterwards. "Omega Man" stuff? *You bet.* Pre-bans have dropped from Ø600 to Ø400 (800-588-9500), and the the Ø225 post-bans are sold only to cops and feds, darn it.

mag discipline
"How long can I keep mags loaded without ruining the springs?" I'd rotate them out every 6 months, though many experts insist that such isn't really necessary. Load to only 28rds—it's more reliable (less pressure on the bolt carrier's

underside) and it saves the spring. Get some 20rd mags for prone firing. Scratch an X on bad mags and cull them out.

mag loaders and holders

The Sally Speedloader (Ø20 from CTD) fits on your belt like an open mag well with catch to load mags by stripper clip.

QP sells a buttstock 20rd mag pouch (#TIMP; Ø26).

The Ø55 Redi-Mag with bolt stop (from Dillon) holds a second loaded mag right next to the gun's mag. Your mag release drops both mags. (C-Mags will not work with Redi-Mag.) One downside: Clearing Class 3 malfs causes you to drop the spare mag with the gun mag.

I prefer the Ø25 Mag Cinch from www.buffertech.com.

Or, you can cut some 2½" bicycle tube into four ½" wide bands to hold a third mag on top of the handguard.

Finally, QP sells a buttstock mag pouch for Ø26 (#TTMP). Now, your AR15 has up to 112 (*i.e.,* 4x28) rounds as its *grab-n-go* package. *112* rounds of .223 oughta do it. (Piling on all three extra mags is a bit much, but I discuss the possibility just in case this sort of thing really lights your fire.)

The "Rhodesian chest pouch" from Blackhawk is a fine piece of kit. Very comfortable, roomy, and out of the way.

Buy lots of G.I. 3-mag pouches for Ø3-5 each. They can be installed on packs and belts, and they'll even nicely hold 2-20rd .308 mags (M1A, FAL, H&K91, etc.). For an inexpensive carry rig, get a multi-holed 2" wide pistol belt (a new one with Fastex buckle; Ø10), a load-bearing suspenders (Ø15), and 4-8 of those 3-mag pouches (depending on weight). Now you can carry 12-24 AR15 mags (about* 360-720rds), or 8-16 .308 mags (about* 120-240rds).   * since mags aren't fully loaded to capacity

Sling

The simpler the better, and G.I. 1¼" webbing works fine. I also like chest-carry Giles tac slings (from Wilderness). QP sells side carry adapters (#NES-09K; Ø15) for such.

Iron sights

Rifles with 20" barrels have elevation adjustments out to 800yds; 16" barrels to 600yds. Therefore, the rear sight wheel will begin with either 8/3 or 6/3, and then continue to 4(00), 5(00), 6(00), and up to 8(00)/3 for 20" barrels. From 0-300yds, leave the wheel on 8/3 (or 6/3) and switch to the smaller aperture from 100+.

how to zero AR15 iron sights

To zero, set the rear sight at 8/3 (or 6/3) and leave it there, as elevation zero will be adjusted at the front sight. **To zero, always use the *small* rear sight aperture.** The larger aperture (for low-light conditions) can later be used without a change in point-of-impact. (If you mistakenly zero with the *large* aperture, your POI will be *high* with the small.)

For **A1/55gr**, zero at 25m, for a 375m BSZ.

For **A2/62gr**, zero at 25m, for a 300m BSZ.

For **A2/55gr**, zero at 42m, for a 250m BSZ.

The below chart will cover nearly every AR15. ("Short" and "full" refer to *sight* radius, *not* barrel length. A 16" barrel Dissipator has a full-length 20"A2 sight radius, compared to the 14¾" radius of the short handguard guns.)

A1 guns are marked in yards and have round front sight posts; A2 guns are marked in meters and have square posts.

Bullet impact change in inches per click at 25-50-100yds:

	A1 (55gr) (short)	A1 (full)	A2 (62gr) (short)	A2 (full)	
front	0.31"	0.25"	0.50"	0.30"	**25yds**
	0.62"	0.50"	1.00"	0.60"	**50yds**
	1.25"	1.00"	2.00"	1.20"	**100yds**
rear	0.31"	0.25"	0.20"	0.12"	**25yds**
	0.62"	0.50"	0.40"	0.24"	**50yds**
	1.25"	1.00"	0.79"	0.47"	**100yds**

(Xerox this table for your range box.) In case you're a metric kind of dude, a full length A2 front sight click moves impact 3.5cm at 100M, and a rear click moves impact 1.25cm at 100M.

Once windage has been zeroed, dab a bit of paint or nail polish on the dial to mark its setting, so you can return to it later if moved (even accidentally). A Testors Paint Marker pen (from any art shop or hobby store) works well.

Know that AR15s have a 2.5" *offset* between bore and front sight. From 0-3m, you will shoot 2.5" low, so you must *holdover* a bit to strike your target. For example, to correctly place a 3m headshot on the nose, you must aim at the hairline.

To about 46m (at which point the bullet has climbed to intersect that 2.5" above the boreline), some holdover (though quickly reducing) is required. Past that 46m intersection, the bullet travels 83m more to climb 1.8" *above* the sight line, and thenceforth begins to drop.

After you've zeroed at 25m or 42m, see where you are at 50 and 100m, and record it. You must know where your rifle prints at several distances within 300m. After 300, adjust your rear sight, which compensates for bullet drop up to 600 or 800m.

If you've a new rifle and no time or place to zero it, remove the upper, strip out the bolt carrier and bore sight to some object 50m away. Such will get you on the torso out to 100m.

Tritium sights

I *highly* recommend a tritium front sight (not rear), which dramatically facilitates night shooting. From QP (Hesco #ML31618; Ø65, or Trijicon #CP-25; Ø80), or NSC (#RIVFPG; Ø70; 888-256-0500). Trijicon has the edge on quality and comes with a 10-year guarantee (compared to 5). Keep the original front sight with your rifle as a spare.

The Trijicon sight free-wheels on top of its bottom post. First, adjust the *entire* part for elevation zero. Then, turn just the *top* half to face the tritium vial towards the rear. (If it were a *one*-piece part as some are, it would require 360° adjustments to keep the tritium facing the rear. A full circle of A2 front sight adjustment means *4 clicks*. At 1.2"/click at 100yds (2"/click for short-handguard A2s), this 4.8-8" per turn would be *far* too much change to get a proper zero. I learned this firsthand.)

If you install a tritium post on your AR, be sure to *re-zero* with *all* kinds of duty ammo (*i.e.,* 55 and 62gr bullets).

Optical sights   (see Chapter 18)

The AUG's 1.4X optical sight has proven the concept to be combat effective and rugged. AR15 owners have many superb optical sights to choose from. The best AR scopes are the Elcan, the ACOG, and the I.O.R. M2. The U.S. Optics SN-12 is also an excellent choice.

deciphering the bewildering array of mounts

While all mounts are "detachable" (*i.e.*, what goes on must by nature also be removable) they are usually not (unless specified) *quick* detachable (**QD**), which means without the use of tools. QD systems have throw levers (*e.g.*, ARMS#19) or large knobs (*e.g.*, Elcan) that are easily hand-operated.

While all mounts are "zero-hold" (**ZH**) in a *continuous* sense (*i.e.*, they'll retain their zero throughout its presence on the gun), they do *not* provide (unless specified) a *repeat* ZH, which means that zero will remain after the system has been detached and then reattached (even many times). Most QD systems are *ipso facto* ZH. (They'd *have* to be to be fieldworthy.)

Channel (*i.e.*, the carry handle channel) to flattop mounts are required on A1 or A2 model ARs. (The A3 is the flattop.) Most mounts are see-through, allowing use of the iron sights. Channel mounts are not repeat ZH, as the channel and handle hole are not precise enough.

Flattop "dedicated" means not QD or repeat ZH, although *continuous* ZH is a given. Use this when an optical sight is to be "permanently" mounted (*i.e.*, with little/no detachment).

QD/ZH mounts offer quick detachability *and* repeat ZH (the way to go for mutiple devices alternating on the same rail, or when optics are mounted in front of the rear sight).

Flattop to channel mounts allow the use of carry handle optics (*e.g.*, the Colt 3X-20 BDC scope, and certain ACOGs) on a flattop. The TA51 is dedicated and the ARMS#19A is QD/ZH.

Below is a table to explain what goes where. QP stock #s.

channel to flattop	flattop dedicated	flattop QD/ZH	flattop to channel
Aluminum (#RAY-002) Ø15	Mini-Risers (#YHM-226) Ø15@	ARMS#22 (#ARMS22) Ø90	TA51 (#TA51) Ø80
Kwik-Site (#KSN-M16) Ø50	ARMS#5 (#ARMS5) Ø60	ARMS#19 (#ARMS19) Ø140	ARMS#19A (#ARMS19A) Ø150 (QD/ZH)
ARMS#2 (#ARMS2) Ø60	Swan Sleeve (#ARMS38???) Ø150-180		
MK ARMS (#2693830) Ø90	Mark Brown (#MBC-03) Ø196		
ARMS#39A2 (#ARMS39) Ø125			

The QP catalog lists and describes all these mounts, and their customer reps will gladly help you further.

"Gee, these mounts are expensive!" Yeah, they *are*, but just how much is hitting your target *worth* to you? Miss your bad guy because of some Ø15 "bargain" mount and congratulate yourself on the Ø45 you saved—*if you live*. (When choosing a carry handle mount, I didn't even go for the very good Ø40 Ultralux over the Ø60 A.R.M.S. #2. Saving a whopping Ø20 just wasn't worth it to me.) **Get *rid* of cheap thinking, folks!** When it comes to guns and gear, get the *very* best and you'll never regret it. (Note: I didn't say the very best you could *afford*. Get the very best stuff, *period*. Save money elsewhere.)

DPMS has three-sided rail mounts for either carry handle (see-through, even!) or flattop ARs. Thus, you could attach a light on the left, scope on top, and laser on the right. Gee.

Light

I *highly* recommend the Sure-Fire Flashlight by Laser Products. CTD has the best price on 3V lithiums (Ø3.69; SF-CELL). With a shelf life of up to 10 years, stock up on dozens.

Although a handgun tactical light may easily be used with the support hand, such is not feasible on a long gun. (Yeah, Kurt Russel did it with a pump Ithaca in *The Thing*, but...) Experiment yourself if you wish, but I think you'll also conclude that the light *must be attached* to your long gun to be effective. There are several ways to do this.

Sure-Fire 6P and 9P

This 2-cell 6P light (CFI; Ø48) is considered the minimum for tactical usage. The 3-cell 9P is about 50% brighter than that. Since both lights have a 1" diameter tube body, any 1" scope ring will hold them. Then, simply attach to any Weaver rail. (More on this below.) Weight with mount is under 1lb.

Sure-Fire M500A (3 cell) and M500B (6 cell) systems

These high-power lights are built into the handguard (easily swapped out on your rifle). In fact, the lights are *so* bright (especially the M500B model) that they are a force in themselves, as you can tactically blind your Bad Guy. Just the thing for a perimeter defense rifle. Any rancher or farmer with an AR should get one. Weight is about 1lb. Ø400 retail.

The only thing I don't like about the M500 is the 2 o'clock position of the light. This is not what you want for clearing right hand corners. (Sort of like a righthander using the Harries flashlight technique.) The light should have been at 6 o'clock.

Light mounts
Sure-Fire Tactical Light and Mount   (QP; #678-SF; Ø278)
You get a 6P light, front sight base mount, and pressure switch. Well done, but a needlessly expensive way to go.

Yankee Hill Triple mount   (QP; #YHM-639; Ø70)
My personal favorite for a dedicated light. This fits on the barrel just forward the front sight base and offers left, right, and bottom rails. If right handed, then mount the light on the left side for support hand access. (The bottom rail is the theoretical best for a tactical light as there's no offset, which can be a problem for clearing corners. If mounted there, however, you will need a pressure switch as the off hand can't easily operate the light button.)

3Bucc LLP detachable mount   Ø40   www.3Bucc.com
What if you'd like to use your AR's Sure-Fire 6Z with your handgun? If it's bolted on, too bad! 3Bucc's solution was simple and clever: bolt the base onto the handguard, allowing the light to slip on/off the *base* without any tools. Fine quality, with excellent installation instructions. This is a very good piece of kit!
3Bucc also makes a fine selection of brasscatchers.

Laser gunsights
visible laser gunsights
No, I still do not care for these. Just after you've trained yourself to rely on them, they'll puke. Do not use them to replace your iron sights—only to *supplement* them if necessary.

infrared laser target designators
Any sufficiently advanced technology is indistinguishable from magic.
— Arthur C. Clarke

Seen only with NVDs, IR lasers are target designators, not illuminators. When used with ITT's PVS-7B night vision goggles or 6015 monocular, this system is just amazing. In near total darkness you can hit bad guys out to 200yds. Simply light him up with the IR laser and squeeze the trigger. (Using a hardened steel target will provide lots of exciting sparks.)

An IR laser gunsight has windage/elevation adjustment knobs; its specs sticker will read Class IIIb (5-50mW) at **710-905nm.** (The *visible* red lasers operate at *630-680*nm with often only 5 milliwatts of Class IIIa product power.) So, if you ever see a gunsight laser marked between 710-905nm, it *is* IR. Snap it up *immediately.* All Class IIIb lasers are quite capable of burning corneas, so take care not to blind anyone.

Good luck, however, *finding* an IR laser gunsight as they are not available to civilians, though I'm aware of no specific *legal* restriction. (The restriction is based on their eye hazardous +5mW output, rather than their IR transmission.)

IR lasers are sold to cops for about Ø700. You might try Laser Products for their Model L-74, or Laser Devices (2 Harris Ct., Monterrey, Ca. 93940). Insight Technology (603-626-4800) manufactures the excellent milspec AN/PAQ-4B IR laser gunsight which mounts to the AR15's front sight block.

"Will an IR filter convert a visible red laser to an IR laser?"

Nope, and here's why. A laser, any laser, emits a particular frequency of light and none other. A 635nm visible red light laser operates at 635nm and nothing else. A filter cannot change a 635nm wavelength into 710nm or 850nm, or anything in between. Bummer.

White light, on the other hand, incorporates wavelengths outside the visible spectrum, and therefore can be filtered to emit solely IR.

laser mounts

There are only three possibilities: upper receiver mount, handguard mount (Knight's), or barrel mount.

Upper mounts interfere with other sighting options, and require a long cord to the handguard switch.

The Knight's handguard rail system is excellent, though very expensive (Ø330) unless used for multiple attachments.

The Yankee Hill Triple Mount described earlier is the best choice. Your laser should be on the bottom rail (which is totally out of the way of *everything*) is aligned with the barrel, and allows for a conveniently short cord. If you're also mounting a Sure-Fire light to this mount, put it on the side (thus eliminating need for a second pressure switch).

Night vision scopes

NAIT (800-432-6248) offers the very nice Gen 2 and Gen 3 Python series scopes for Ø1,449 and Ø3,625 respectively.

Tools

I recommend the following from QP:

combination barrel wrench	(#223 WRENCH)
firing pin protrusion gauge	(#MMT-0005; Ø15)
go/no-go gauges	(Ø16@)
bolt carrier carbon scraper	(#MBC-002; Ø30)
gas tube wrench	(#MBC-001; Ø30)
A2 sight adjustment gauge	(#RAY-005; Ø8)
Dewey bore rod	(#DEWEY-100; Ø25)
muzzle rod guide	(#DEWEY-1100; Ø9)
breech rod guide	(#DEWEY-1000; Ø20)
drift punches	(#STA-PNCHSET; Ø20)
roll pin punches (which are designed for roll punches)	
vise blocks	(AMER-001; Ø15)
armorer's action block	(#PR-003; Ø39)
lower receiver block	(#PR-006; Ø30)

Brownells is also a fine source of gun tools and parts.

Ambi AR controls

Ambi controls are great not only for lefties, but for righties whose strong hand/arm has been disabled.

charging handle

I like the Ambi Tac Latch (QP; #ambi-tac; Ø20).

safety

From QP for Ø25 (#MMT-0007K).

Norgon mag release   703-455-0997

Drops in without tools.

AR accuracy

Without making a dedicated target rifle out of a combat weapon, your 1½-2MOA AR *can* be made into a ¾-1MOA rifle without compromising reliability and ruggedness. Assuming a quality 20" barrel (a 1:7" Colt is quite good), not much else is needed: DCM NM free float handguards/tubes, two-stage trigger, and ½ minute rear sight. Visit www.accuracyspeaks.com.

Absolutely *the* one book to get on AR15 accurizing is *The Competitive AR15—The Mouse That Roared* by Glen D. Zediker (ISBN 1-9626925-6-5). You'll learn as much, and likely more, than you ever wanted to know on tuning ARs. (From a publisher's standpoint, I can also commend it as a very well *packaged* book, which is always a rare treat these days.)

A quick aside on the shooting hobbyists

The above is about Service and Match *competition* rifles. Meaning, it's a *sports* book. I don't recall one word about empty reloads. Tactical lights and Redi-Mags are for loonies. While Zediker and his AR15 can outshoot me and mine at 300 and 600yds, take away his padded shooting jacket and gloves for a 100yd snapshot from a Condition 1 rifle slung in African carry. His disdain for tactical equipment and training might waver.

I'm a Big Boy and can absorb cheap shots. However, what really chapped my hide was that no ink was given to the *"Crime Bill"* or the 2nd Amendment. Nothing about how the late 1990s gun restrictions frighteningly mirror those of the 1760s (which the British tried to enforce just ten years later). Yes, I know that a gun sports book shouldn't be a political tract, but a simple paragraphical *obiter dictum* on Lexington and Concord seems obligatory in *any* military rifle book. **Benchrest hobbyists exist by virtue of the battle rifle, not vice-versa.**

If some sub-MOA weenie wants to wax on about chamber dimensions and powder drops, fine—he'll never hear a peep of protest from me. (One, he's still a shooter. Two, we all can benefit from his work.) He can even dismiss us tactical people as butt-crack Rambo types who can't shoot. (Admittedly, he *does* have a point there. Most focus *way* too much on their equipment and not enough on their shooting skills.) *However,* when said technoid ignores gunowners' current 2nd Amendment peril to the point of not even *mentioning* the NRA (much less the GOA or JPFO), my disgust boils over. I get the creepy impression that if all guns were ever outlawed, these guys would, without any fuss, quietly wander off to radio-controlled helicopters.

I'm not asking anything of the shooting hobbyists but some *perspective.* They're so wrapped up in a 0.015" world that they've totally missed the *macro* point of what privately-owned guns are *for*—Liberty's teeth. Enamored with tree bark dust, they are oblivious to the forest. And it pisses me off.

My FAL and AR15 have no *"sporting purpose"* and I'm not going to give them one. They exist as tools to disable those who would initiate force against me; those who would try to steal my God-given rights. I would not insult the magnificent purity of such weapons by attaching micrometer sights and handguard weights any sooner than I would make my Rottweiler wear a poodle sweater. To dilute a battle rifle is to dilute its *purpose,* and diluting a man's tools invariably dilutes the *man.*

The battle rifle black sheep are being picked off from the fringe, but the *Angora* sheep don't mind. (It's not happening to *their* respectable sport.) It is *far* too late to so wholeheartedly entertain such specialized luxuries as IPSC shooting at Liberty's exclusion. America has *75 million* gunowners. If they would each put in just 1% the effort of a Larry Pratt or an Aaron Zelman, we'd see the repeal of *Brady,* the *"Crime Bill,"* the 1990 import ban, and the *GCA68*—and maybe even the *NFA34.*

I don't expect the shooting hobbyists to become firebrands, but I *can* reasonably demand that they do *something* to defend our 2nd Amendment rights. Join the GOA and/or the JPFO. Contribute to a gun-rights political candidate. Even if you merely join the NRA, *do something!* Finish your dinner *before* you have dessert; finish homework *before* you play outside. *Then* I'll shut up about you guys.

(Here endeth the ranting.)

Universal AR15 recommendations
The important basics

In my humble opinion, *all* AR15s should have the following: tritium sights, a Sure-Fire 6P or 9P light (on either a Yankee Hill Triple mount, or a 3Bucc handguard mount), flash suppressor (Vortex or Phantom), sling, and spare mag holder (either a Redi-Mag, buttstock mag pouch, or handguard rubber bands cut from a 19" bicycle tube).

Thus, you will *see* your Bad Guy *and* your sights, suffer *no* muzzle flash, *and* have a spare mag attached to the rifle. Such an AR15 will be *very* capable of solving most <200M problems. Grab it and go, without thought or planning.

Miscellaneous suggestions

The Ø5 Accuwedge eliminates the upper/lower slop. Get the plastic box G.I. earplug container with its swivel lid, and paracord it *short* to the front sight rear base (leaving the barrel portion free to accept a bipod).

Spare parts with the AR15

The trapdoor, full-length A2 buttstock would have cleaning rod and gear, extra firing pins (they won't fit in the pistol grip), and a ½oz bottle of CLP.

The A2 Stowaway pistol grip would contain a spare bolt, original front sight, and field rebuild kit. Why a spare bolt *and* a field rebuild kit? In a hurry I'd simply swap bolts to get the rifle running, and then later I'd rebuild the bolt that malfed. (Also, even though the kit contains a firing pin, I like having a second extra just in case I pierce a primer, which often peens the firing pin tip enough for it to break later.)

Spare parts at home

As with my MBR, I'd own three sets of common spare parts (*e.g.,* mag catch, bolt stop, gas rings, bolt, sights, springs, pins, etc.), an extra barrel or two, *30+* mags (they get damaged easily), and at least 5,000rds of ammo.

My ideal CQB AR15

If I could build any (*i.e.,* non-*NFA*) AR15, it would be a Bushmaster 16" pre-ban Dissipator model, on an A3 flattop receiver, with Colt C-More sight. In addition to the setup described above, it'd also have a Redi-Mag, Sure-Fire M500A Flashlight, Ashley Tritium front sight, and a *tactical* sling. It would weigh, with two loaded mags, about 11½lbs.

I'm liking a lot the drawbar Tac Lever (QP; #1005-249-02; Ø20). I also like the ambi tac latch (QP; #ambi-tac; Ø20) which allows easier right hand operation. (What should be done is to *combine* the two.) A perimeter defense gun might enjoy an IR laser gunsight bottom-attached to a Yankee Hill Triple Mount. I'd be wearing PVS-7Bs, of course.

Remember, this is a specialized CQB carbine which would be too heavy for extended field use.

My ideal field AR15

Before you get this, get an MBR (*e.g.,* M1A, FAL, or HK91) first. *Then,* if you can afford it, get a field AR15.

I'd choose a 20" barrel Colt or Bushmaster A3 with an ACOG. It would not likely have any attached light or IR laser. (Basically, I'd keep it as light as possible because I'd be *carrying* the thing all day.) The Tac Lever might protrude too much for field carry. The entire rifle *certainly* would be painted with 2-4 colors of BowFlage. Bipod case containing a Zytel bipod atop the handguard.

AR goodies
bayonet

Don't laugh. A rifle-mounted bayonet in trained hands is a most deadly weapon. The original-issue M7 in an M8A1 scabbard is just Ø28 (Major Surplus; 800-441-8855).

brasscatcher   www.3Bucc.com

Great for target shooting. Base mounts inside the carry handle (using the bolt hole, which precludes a scope), and the brasscatcher slips on/off the base. Velcro closed bottom for easy emptying. Holds 70 .223 cases or 50 .308 cases. Available for many other rifles; see their website. Several color options.

faux M203 grenade launcher

It fires the 40x46R grenade at 235fps with a max range of 400M. It weighs 3lbs unloaded and 3½lbs loaded.

A left side lever unlocks the barrel, which then slides forward to extract/eject any fired casing. A new round is inserted, and the barrel is slid back. When engaged, the safety blocks the inside trigger guard, preventing the finger's entry.

There are two sights issued: a simple leaf sight (which uses the rifle's front sight, 50-250M in 50M increments), and a quadrant sight (which attaches to the rifle's carry handle; 50-400M in 25M increments).

Since I "can't" have a *"destructive device"* M203 grenade launcher, perhaps a 37mm flare launcher M203-wannabe would "suffice." They weigh 4½lbs. QP sells them for Ø200 (specify standard or heavy barrel). RPB (404-297-0907) also has them, and with all the accessories (*e.g.,* leaf and quadrant sights, 37mm→12ga adapters, reloadable 37mm casings, and bandoleers). This rig looks *quite* authentic, so be prepared for some real apprehension if you dare take it out in public (*i.e.,* the police will freak, and understandably so).

heavy barreled LMG upper

There were some Canadian heavy barrel LMG uppers around recently for about Ø600, which would, with a C-Mag, make a nice (semi-auto) "SAW" for fixed positions.

ArmForte Counterpoise primary recoil reduction system

Co-designed by one of the original M16/AR15 inventors, James Sullivan, and Mack Gwinn (of early Bushmaster rifle and pistol fame), this system reduces felt recoil by 50-80% (depending whether a semi- or full-auto rifle).

Consisting of an added 3oz weight to the bolt carrier and different buffer, the Counterpoise spreads out the normal recoil spike from 1/1000th to 1/10th of a second. (The system requires the gas port to be enlarged from .062 to .083".) Muzzle climb is all but eliminated and thus you don't lose your sight picture. The increase in full-auto control is reportedly quite amazing.

Coupled with the D-fender plastic "D" ring (a Ø13 part which fits around the extractor spring to increase the extractor's leverage four-fold), the system also greatly increases reliability in adverse conditions (especially when the rifle goes for 500+ rounds without a cleaning).

Sullivan and Gwinn are determined to improve on our longest serving military "A" rifle, the M16 (which just this year beat out the M1903 Springfield). For example, other tasty projects are self-regulating gas tubes and quick-change barrels. Visit www.armforte.com or call ArmForte at 207-884-8226. These guys are bringing the M16/AR15 into the 21st Century!

Miscellaneous AR warnings

There are a hundred possible additions to an AR, and only a dozen are worthy. Most stuff is just excrescent excrement.

Avoid titanium firing pins!!!

Titanium is a *reactive* metal in the same class as magnesium, and it *will* burn if hot enough. I'm now hearing stories about ruptured primers setting off titanium firing pins, which then utterly fuse inside the bolt (which prevents the bolt's removal from the carrier). Unfun. The risk is perhaps tolerable in a *target* rifle, but never in a combat weapon. (Stick with one and don't try to make a hybrid combat-target rifle.)

Avoid chromed bolt and carriers!

They are not reliable after several hundred rounds.

Avoid demilled M16 parts as AR15 substitute parts
Quality and tolerances will often be off.

No fragile/hollow telescoping stocks, please!
They won't hold up when you have to bang the butt on the ground during a difficult fail-to-extract malfunction. Also, these stocks have no compartment for a cleaning rod and kit. Finally, they rattle in the field.

Avoid the "shorty" Carbine handguard models!
These needlessly sacrifice 5¼" of sight radius and 200fps of muzzle velocity, and thus 75yds of hyper-lethality. They've less hand protection, too. Look, the only reason why the shorty handguards even exist at all is because feds and cops can use barrels <16" (for clearing out crowded elevators, presumably).

.223 AMMO
Generally, I would buy only brass case B/NC, and that which is *new* production. While professionally reloaded ammo is often (*i.e.*, 99.99%) reliable and good enough for training, you can't afford an ammo malf in a firefight.

55gr
Malaysian FMJ, my all-time favorite, no longer seems available. It was very accurate and hard-hitting chow!

I very much like the South African FMJ. J&G has it for Ø148.50/1000rds. The Czech S&B is also very good, and sold by J&G for the same price. (Both are B/NC.)

62gr
Military ammo will run about Ø250/1000rds, but it's a *much* better combat round than 55gr. (Canadian C77 FMJ shoots very well, *if* you can find it.)

Avoid steel-cased Russian stuff!
The lacquer coating has a higher lubricity and often misfeeds in ARs (especially those not Colt or Bushmaster). One fellow got a live round stuck between the top of the bolt and the receiver, and it took 15 minutes to extract. Unless you really dig double-feed malfunction drills, stick with brass case ammo.

Reloading for the AR15

With excellent South African (PMP) and Czech (Sellier and Bellot) boxer-primed ammo is running only 15¢/rd, I see no reason to reload for training ammo. You may, however, wish to load heavier target loads (up to 80gr will work from an AR mag).

bullets

55gr FMJ is really cheap these days, and just fine for training and plinking.

The Hornady 60gr HP shoots very accurately without the cost of a match-grade bullet.

The Sierra 69gr MatchKing is the favorite in that weight.

brass

Buy a bunch of primed Winchester cases for about 5¢ each. The brass is the strongest, the primers are the hardest, and size is the most consistent. A proven winner.

primers

To reduce the chance of slam fires, use hard primers like Winchester (and not the soft Federals). Another fine choice is the Remington 7½.

powder

Commercial reloaders of 55gr loads favor 748 or AA2230, both fairly fast powders. 748 particularly likes the 69gr Sierra (25.0gr in WW cases/primers is a good starting load). Other good choices in this range are the H335 and XMR2015.

For *heavier* bullets (*i.e.,* 65-80+gr), a slower burning powder is required. It's hard to beat IMR or H4895, which was the original powder for the .223 back in the 1950s. AA2520 (a ball powder) is a very good and predictable performer. Other favorites are RE15, VARGET, and VVN540.

CLEANING

AR15s can be rather fussy about needing to stay clean, and they certainly cannot be ignored (as can an AK or an HK). With the right tools and some practice, a thorough job can easily be done in 20 minutes, and this should be performed perhaps every 400rds or so (and at every 1000rds, to be sure).

cleaning tools

Some necessary items are a chamber brush (to adequately clean the lugs), a bolt carrier carbon scraper (from QP; #MBC-002; Ø30), and pipe cleaners. Use *bronze* bristle bore brushes (*never* stainless steel!), and buy *lots* of them (Sierra Supply; 970-259-1822) to be "demoted" every several cleanings to parts scrubbers. For jags, I prefer the stab variety, with patches cut to need from a roll.

the receiver

The cheapest and easiest way to remove all the carbon is with a Ø1.50 can of CRC brake cleaner (which does just as well as a Ø6 can of GunScrubber). Drain towards the rear, not through the bore. Also, do not use metal brushes in the scratchable aluminum receivers!

the bolt and carrier

Decarbonize well (this usually requires a bit of scrubbing), and make sure the gas ring gaps are evenly spaced. Take out the extractor and clean out any gunk underneath. Examine the firing pin tip for any peening, and replace if needed. Lube well.

the gas tube

Spritz some CRC through the gas tube, and swab out the bore. (Do *not* use pipe cleaners to clean the gas tube! Such will invariably jam inside. Besides, tubes do not—*cannot*—clog up with carbon as the pressures are too high.)

the bore

The best bore solvent is Kroil. It is a bore-harmless penetrating oil which really lifts away the filth. Use a 36" coated steel Dewey rod and Sinclair bore guide to protect the throat. (Never use ammonia-based solvents, such as Sweet's, in chrome-lined barrels.) Or, "cheat" with a BoreSnake.

A 12ga shotgun swab works well for chamber cleaning.

Clean the flash suppressor *before* your final bore patching, else you'll keep ending up with dirty patches.

what to lube

Liberally lube the buffer (and tube), and bolt/bolt carrier (where shiny) with BreakFree CLP. Friction Block oil is also great stuff. Don't forget to oil the front sight post's threads, which will rust over time. Do not oil the firing pin.

Neco Moly-Slide (from QP) is just amazing stuff for sliding surfaces and trigger parts.

AK74

Designed for peasant armies, and quite suitable for bandits and terrorists of all descriptions, the AK47 has never been one my favorites for us Americans. Why have a heavy, ungainly, grossly inaccurate *semi-auto* stamped-steel carbine?

Although the pre-ban Russian and Hungarian AK47s are nicely milled/finished guns of tolerable accuracy (*i.e.*, 3-4MOA), their Ø1,200+ price isn't justifiable. I even tried one of the new milled Bulgarian guns, but it shot 6+MOA with Wolf FMJ and I wasn't about to feed the thing its preferred Lapua diet at 50¢/rd! Filet mignon to a junkyard dog.

So, I was just about to eternally forswear AKs until I took a chance on a trade Romanian AK74. No, the "74" is not a typo; it's the AK47 chambered/modified for the 5.45x39 round (which generally duplicates the external and terminal ballistics of our M193 5.56x45). Since I got into this 30rd mag AK74 for only Ø300 (which is wholesale price, and they're no longer imported), I figured I had nothing to lose. (It had a two-stage trigger. Side-rail scope mount. East German mags were just Ø6-9, new in wrap. *Hmmm.*) In order to possibly find a decent one for training, I'd give the AK *one* last try.

I'm *very* glad that I did. The thing is a tack-driver! I'm talking 1½-2MOA with Wolf 60gr FMJ. Who ever *heard* of such a thing from a stamped-steel receiver AK? On a goof, I took aim at a bathtub-sized boulder at a lased distance of 791m (that's 865yds, or ½mile away, folks), ramped up the rear sight to 8, and began spanking it offhand. With an iron-sighted AK! My friends nearly collapsed in disbelief. (So did I.)

Not only am I keeping it, I'm tarting it up. Read on...

10	Exceptional		
9	Extremely Good	4	Poor
8	Very Good	3	Very Poor
7	Good	2	Extremely Poor
6	Fair	1	Worst Possible
5	Just Tolerable	0	Nonexistent

Where aftermarket mods exist (*e.g.*, rear sight, trigger, butt-stock, safety, etc.), a dual score is listed (*e.g.*, 6/9), and the higher score counted in the rankings. The point of this chapter is to test/compare a modernized AK to discover the limits of its improvement. I think you'll be surprised. I was.

AK74 RELIABILITY   (38% of total)

AK74 Op System (58% of category)

AK74 gas system   (x3)   Score: 9

An excellent gas-piston system. Because the gas piston is attached to the carrier, the bolt carrier-to-bolt weight ratio is 6:1 (in the AK47 it is 4.75:1), which greatly contributes to its reliability. (The piston-less AR suffers in this regard.)

AK74 gas regulator   Score: 0

Has none, but seemingly without detriment.

AK74 action hygiene   (x4)   Score: 8

The action stays pretty clean.

AK74 action exposure   (x3)   Score: 7

Dust cover really helps, but there is slot for the bolt handle root just above the trigger group. An engaged safety covers this up, but is impractical during a firefight.

AK74 reciprocating bolt handle   (x2)   Score: 10

AK74 reliability: feeding   (x4)   Score: 10

The recoil spring is strong, and feeding is flawless.

AK74 reliability: firing   (x5)   Score: 10

Fine fire-control system (copied from our M1 Garand).

AK74 reliability: extraction   (x5)   Score: 9

6:1 bolt carrier/bolt weight ratio. Although there is no primary extraction, the extractor itself is massive.

AK74 reliability: ejection   (x4)   Score: 10

Fixed ejector.

AK74 Design Ruggedness (42% of category)

AK74 working parts placement   **Score: 10**
   All working parts are forward of the buttstock.

AK74 design complexity   (x2)   **Score: 7**
   The AK74 is of good simplicity.

AK74 parts breakage   (x3)   **Score: 10**
   It basically never breaks a thing.

AK74 fieldstripping   (x2)   **Score: 8**
   Sublimely easy. The dust cover pops right off, the gas piston/bolt carrier/spring slide right out for simple removal. The bolt strips easily due to its less-is-more design. Not that this is often necessary, as AKs run without regular cleaning (although I'm *not* recommending laziness).
   Most AKs and SKSs have a cleaning rod under the barrel, and contain their (crude) tool kit in the buttstock.
   Trigger group is not modular, which cost it 2 points.

AK74 parts availability (x2)   **Score: 8**
   Not quite as ubiquitous as its SKS cousin. Inter-Ord sells parts kits for Ø130-170. Individual spare parts also abound (not that you'd need many).

AK74 overall ruggedness   (x4)   **Score: 10**
   A very tough rifle. You'll have to work hard to break one!

AK74 handguard ruggedness   **Score: 8**
   Very robust.

AK74 buttstock ruggedness   **Score: 8**
   Very robust.

AK74 mag ruggedness (x4)   **Score: 10**
   The rust-colored mags are glass-reinforced, polyethylene plastic which are molded in two parts and epoxied together. Very tough. (Paint them OD or brown for better camouflage.)
   There are also dark-brown and black ABS mags (mostly from Bulgaria), which would rate an 8 here.

AK74 mag availability   (x2)   **Score: 8**
   Inter-Ord. J&G. Sarco. RPB. Scour the *Shotgun News*.

AK74 USABILITY   (24% of total)

AK74 Static handling (45% of category)

AK74 weight   (x3)   Score: 7

    At 8.0lbs, the AK74 is fairly lightweight.

AK74 mag weight   (x2)   Score: 4

    ½lb vs. the ¼lb AR mag.

AK74 length overall   (x2)   Score: 8

    At 34.7" only the bullpup M17S and AUG are shorter.

AK74 barrel length   (x2)   Score: 2

    Only 16.3", which significantly reduces MV.

AK74 handguard length   Score: 5

AK74 handguard heatshielding   (x2)   Score: 8

AK74 handguard fit/feel   Score: 8

AK74 buttstock fit/feel   Score: 4/7

    The OEM thumbhole stock is pretty uncomfortable.
    Many variations exist (see the list at this chapter's end).

AK74 pistol grip fit/feel   Score: 3/7

AK74 buttstock and pistol grip storage   Score: 5

    No grip storage. Buttstock holds small cleaning kit.

AK74 Controls (55% of category)

AK74 charging handle location   (x3)   Score: 7

    Although the German MP44 correctly located the bolt handle on the left side, and Kalashnikov originally copied it, a Soviet general complained that it was visually distracting.

    Proper technique with the AK is to rack the bolt with the left thumb from *underneath* the rifle. While awkward and requiring practice, it's the best that can be done with such a poor design.

    Somebody oughta to start making left-side handles.

AK74 charging handle feel   (x3)   Score: 4

    On the AK47 the bolt handle is far too thin, and your left thumb will often get cut on the sharp-edged safety. A 1.

    The Romanian AK74, however, has its handle slightly tilted upwards (to clear the folding stock of the military AKs), which moves your thumb away from the safety.

AK74 bolt stop (x2)   Score: 0/2

Manual H-O	Auto H-O	Release	
0			(AK)
2	✔		(AK-modified)

Flash Distributing (970-249-0302) offers a modified safety with a manual hold-open notch. Only Ø20.

AK74 safety   Score: 4/7

It's abysmally located. It not be operated without the right hand releasing its shooting grip, and it's inexcusably noisy (just what a soldier wants on a patrol). To quiet it, wrap some monofilament line around the leg near the detent.

www.krebscustom.com sells an ergonomically-improved replacement safety with trigger finger tab for Ø50. Very nice.

AK74 mag catch   (x2)   Score: 6/8

Also abysmal. It cannot be correctly reached by the right index finger, and needs the left thumb.

Flash Distributing (970-249-0302) offers a modified mag catch which is reachable by the trigger finger. Only Ø20.

AK74 mag to gun   (x3)   Score: 7

A rugged design, but tedious to operate under stress. The mag's front corner is first inserted to (hopefully) catch the receiver notch, and then the mag is rocked back to the catch. While very securely holding the mag in place, all this takes considerable practice. During an empty reload, you should hit the mag catch with the new mag.

The AK74 is *much* easier to run than the AK47, probably due to the smooth finish of the synthetic mags.

AK74 lefty ergonomics (x2)   Score: 8

Left-handed shooters, however, will find the right side handle an unexpected bonus. (The SKS is even a little better.)

AK74 overall handling (x2)   Score: 7

With aftermarket safety, manual bolt hold-open, and mag catch, the AK74 begins to handle pretty well! With a left-side charging handle and auto hold-open, the AK would be fantastic.

AK74 COMBAT ACCURACY (34%)

AK74 Sights (65% of category)

AK74 sight radius (x3)   Score: 5
>   A very short 14¾".

AK74 sight offset   Score: 6
>   About average at 2"

AK74 front sight visibility   (x3)   Score: 8
>   Winged post. Not hooded as the SKS.

AK74 front sight adjustability   Score: 8
>   Zero adjustable for windage and elevation. Minus 2pts for the tool requirement. (Sarco; Ø13)

AK74 front sight precision (x4)   Score: 8
>   A fairly fat rounded post, though quite crisp. Not perfectly vertically eccentric, which affects windage.

AK74 front sight protection   (x3)   Score: 9
>   Steel (add a point over aluminum) wings.

AK74 rear sight visibility   (x3)   Score: 4/9
>   Notched ramp is OEM, and it sucks.
>   You *must* get the aperture replacement from Krebs Custom for Ø50 (www.krebscustom.com). It transforms the AK!

AK74 rear sight readability (x2)   Score: 7
>   Large/clear numerals, unreadable from cheekweld.

AK74 rear sight adjustability   (x2)   Score: 6
>   100-1000m in 100m increments. Not adjustable for zero.

AK74 rear sight precision   (x3)   Score: 8
>   Negligible slack/wobble. Solid elevation detents.

AK74 rear sight ruggedness   (x2)   Score: 8
>   Simple and rugged assembly.

AK74 tritium sight   Score: 0
>   None. That will change, given the simple threaded-post.

AK74 scope base   (x2 for Battle Rifles)   Score: 9
>   The side-rail mount is truly QD/ZH. Simple and very easy to use. Astonishingly effective.
>   The steel STANAG/Picatinny milspec mount from www.valdada.com is the best. Add an I.O.R. M2 4x24mm scope and you can make headshots out to 250m. No joke.

AK74 Accuracy Misc. (35% of category)

AK74 bolt and carrier   Score: 7

Bolt locks into receiver cam slots.

AK74 trigger pull   (x4)   Score: 4/10

Like the SKS, of the "soft" variety. Loooong creep! Ugh. The 2-stage trigger from www.ak47trigger.com provides an M1A-quality trigger pull. Drop in parts, and fully adjustable. Wow! This is simply the best Ø80 you can spend on an AK.

AK74 target accuracy (x4 for Battle Rifles)   Score: 8

With Wolf FMJBT (60gr/2952fps for 1161fpe), the AK74 shoots 1¾MOA at 100yds, and 7"/300yds (2.3MOA). Gee.

I don't know if the 7.62x39 Romanian SAR-1 is similarly accurate, but I'll find out and let you know on the website. I'd bet that the 5.56 VEPRs are quite accurate.

AK74 muzzle blast   Score: 8

This score assumes a bare barrel.

The superb Krebs Custom copy of the Soviet AK-103 muzzle brake greatly increases side blast, but eliminates rise/recoil.

AK74 AFFORDABILITY   (4%)

AK74 OEM rifle price   Score: 10

SAR-2 AK74   Ø350   10-Exceptional

Although the 30rd mag Romak-2 (SAR-2) has been banned from further importation, you might still find one from KY Imports (502-244-4400). Romanian 7.62x39 SAR-1s are Ø360.

Make sure that their AK accepts the 30rd mags, and not the new single-column 10rd mags.

AK74 brass reloadability   Score: 2

Upon ejection the case gets a serious dent from the port, and reloaded cases have successive ringed dents (which acts like a can opener). In short, don't bother reloading for any AK.

Since Wolf 60gr FMJ is only 9.8¢/rd, just buy a ton of it.

AK74 parts price   Score: 7

Most AK parts interchange with the AK74.

AK74 mag price   (x2)   Score: 9

Only Ø6-9. Best deal I've seen is from Sarco for Ø5.95 each, or for Ø22.95 for 4 mags with mag pouch and sling. RPB also has them for Ø5 @.

AK74 RANKING

AK74 Reliability   (38% of total)

❶ **AK74   89.2% (473/530)**
Only the AUG got a higher score (90.6%).

AK74 Usability   (24% of total)

❼ **AK74   61.2% (208/340)**
The mag catch and safety/hold-open mods significantly increased this score. The AK can be made tolerable.

AK74 Combat Accuracy   (34% of total)

❸ **AK74   77.2% (301/390)**
This accurate gun with rear sight and trigger mods makes for a very capable carbine.

AK74 Affordability   (4% of total)

❹ **81.7%   AK74**

AK74 Overall Score

❸ **AK74   78.1% (1031/1380)**
It beat out the AR15A3 by 2.7% for a 3rd Place finish. Wow.

Final comments on the AK74

By all means, you should spend a lot of trigger time behind an AK because you are likely to encounter one in the field someday (either as Billy Bob's MAK-90, or as some UN Bulgarian's AK.)

A VEPR or Romanian AK (for accuracy) in .223 (for ammo availability) are the best choices. Today, there is no compelling reason to have an AK in 7.62x39 (inaccurate ammo). The 5.45x39 round is a decent performer, but uncommon (and that will not improve in the future, unless we are overrun by former Warsaw Pact armies).

Get a .223 AK with plenty of mags, install all the mods I recommended, and you'll have a very reliable, accurate, and decent handling carbine.

AK47

History of development

Soviet tanker sergeant Mikhail Kalashnikov saw the genius of the gas piston MP44 and modified it with an M1 Garand-style bolt (with its twin lugs), trigger, and safety.

Instead of using expensive, heavy machined parts, the AK used cheap and light stamped steel. It uses a gas piston instead of a tube (*e.g.*, AG42, MAS49, and AR15). While generally not accurate (4-6MOA), it is *absolutely* reliable and can be field-stripped by a drunken monkey.

Its cartridge, the 7.62x39, was also an improvement over the German 8x33. Heavily tapered for easy extraction, it gives the 30 round magazines their distinctive "banana" shape. Physically, the AK is probably the most recognizable of any gun in history, a characteristic amply assisted by the sheer number in existence; some *50-100 million.*

The modern AK74 variant fires the 5.45x39, which is similar in external/terminal ballistics to our 55gr M193.

AK military variants

Nearly all AKs were/are made by Communist countries (USSR, Czechoslovakia, Hungary, East Germany, Bulgaria, Yugoslavia, and China). Egypt makes the Maadi (fairly crude, not that the AK requires Swiss manufacture). China and Romania also produce it in our .223, although mags are slightly more expensive and harder to find (although not onerous).

The Commie AK

The Hungarian AKs are probably the finest in quality, followed by the East German, USSR, Romanian, and Bulgarian. The Chinese clones (*e.g.*, MAK-90, NHM-91) are fairly shoddy and inaccurate, but they *do* work well—a testimony to the sound AK design.

The Finnish Valmet

This is a high-quality AK, beautifully made and accurate. Downside: The receiver is cast aluminum, price is Ø1,200-1,800, and the ergonomics suck.

The Israeli Galil

Never shy about co-opting a good design for themselves, the Israelis produce their own high-quality version of the AK in both .223 and .308. The bolt handle protrudes up top rather than to the right, so you can rack with the left hand from above (rather than from underneath). The best AK bolt handle.

The Galil has a milled steel receiver, a right thumb-operated safety (unique, except for the South African R4s). The folding stock is great, and a retractable bipod is standard. For the desert, the Galil is King.

YOUR AK

Pre-ban AKs

Since most pre-ban AKs never had a flash suppressor, there seems little point in spending the Ø1,200+ when modern pistol grip stocked USA AKs are available starting at Ø300.

Post-ban AKs

Romanian AK74

This is so far my favorite AK. Quite a value for the Ø280.

I'd like to fire their .223 gun to see if it is as accurate as their 5.45x39.

VEPR   (from Robinson Arms   www.robarm.com)

Russian parts on USA receivers. Available in 7.62x39 (1:10"), 5.45x39 (1:12"), or .223 (1:9"). Hammer-forged, chrome-lined barrels. Two-stage trigger. Modern fiber-reinforced thermoplastic furniture. Left-side scope rail.

Regarding the 5.45x39's 1:12" twist, this seems *way* too slow to stabilize a 0.990" long bullet, 56gr as it is. (The USSR rifles correctly had 1:7.7" twist.) I wouldn't expect much accuracy from a VEPR 5.45x39 carbine.

VEPR used to have a .308, which is alluring to me.

I've not fired any VEPR AK, but I've handled them and their quality seemed good.

Avoid the Egyptian Maadi ARM!

I tried one, and it was awful. The fire control parts were so crudely cast, that the gun would often fail to fire, or fire doubles! Accuracy was atrocious, as was fit and finish. A toad.

AK74 MODS, PARTS, & TOOLS

AK74 modifications

Tactical chest-carry sling

I became sold on such from my HK91. It is the *only* way to carry a battle rifle or carbine. DSA sells a heavy 1½" nylon sling (#658L; Ø42 for the Galil, which should work for the AK74) far superior to the OEM canvas.

Flash Distributing paddle mag release

POB 1187, Montrose, Co. 81401   970-249-0302

Only Ø20, and it installs in seconds. A must.

Red Star Arms trigger group

573-372-5684   www.ak47trigger.com

How would you like an M1/M14-quality 2-stage on an AK? Well, who wouldn't? EDM'd and CNC's from steel bar stock, you can have a 4-8lb pull, adjustable for either single or two stage. (I prefer 2-stage triggers in my battle rifles/carbines, but that's up to you). The drop-in parts are just Ø83.50ppd., and take about 30 minutes work if you've worked on your AK before. (I highly recommend a disassembly manual for this job. It's not difficult, but it is a tad tricky.)

Once installed, lube the hammer/sear bearing surfaces with Neco MolySlide (from QP). Then, use the supplied allen wrench to reduce the first stage travel, and then to reduce the second stage travel. Done correctly, you'll have a trigger equal to that of any M1A! Your buddies just won't believe it.

Krebs Custom can also do a very nice AK trigger job.

Krebs Custom aperture rear sight

847-487-7776   www.krebscustom.com

The OEM notched blade has *very* slow target acquisition and poor visibility. Ø50 and 2 minutes will give you a snag-free, very fast, M1-quality aperture with tangent ramp elevation. (This is similar to the WWII Arisaka rear sight.)

Replacement is easy. The front of the sight blade is under heavy spring pressure. Push it down with a fat punch and pull the blade out towards the rear. Remove the elevation slider, and replace on the Krebs blade (make sure that catch is on the correct side). Install in reverse (pushing down the spring plate makes it easier).

You won't believe how much the sight picture opens up! This mod, along with the above trigger group, gives the AK74 better sights and trigger than the FAL—which takes some getting used to. After installation, I spent 20 minutes dry firing the thing, and the next day shooting it. What a transformation!

Krebs Custom muzzle brake   www.krebscustom.com

This is a very nicely manufactured Soviet-style brake, which is extremely effective on an AK74. *Totally* eliminates muzzle rise and recoil. (You'll pay for it, however, in greatly increased muzzle blast and flash signature. Your choice.)

buttstock

Several firms offer USA-mfg. pistol grip stocks. (Note: stocks differ for milled vs. stamped receivers.)

Laser Sights   800-833-4780   www.appliedlaser.com
    Romanian-style stamped rcvr. stock w/pistol grip handguard   Ø60

RPB   800-858-0809
    FSE Krinkov stock (black anodized aluminum)   Ø60

Ace Ltd.   530-346-2492   www.riflestocks.com

AK74 accessories

AK74 optics

The I.O.R. M2 4x24mm is the way to go. Ø330 from DSA.

AK chest pouch   Ø14   Global Trades

Holds three 30rd mags, and small bits of gear.

AK74 sources

AK carbines

VEPR (Russian)	801-355-0401	www.robarms.com
Arsenal (Bulgarian)	888-539-2220	
KY Imports (Romanian)	502-244-4400	
Tennessee Guns (Roman.)	423-577-1939	
J&G (Romanian; Ø289)	928-445-9650	www.jgsales.com
SOG (Romanian; Ø280)	800-944-4867	www.southernohiogun.com
Wholesale Guns (Rom.)	631-234-7676	www.gunsnammo.com
Hesse (.223 w/AR mags)		www.cdnninvestments.com

AK parts

K-VAR	702-364-8880	www.k-varcorp.com
Global Trades	713-944-3351	gtc@flash.net
RPB	800-858-0809	

AK gunsmithing/custom work

| Richard Parker | 215-541-1099 | edendwellers@att.net |
| Marc Krebs | 847-487-7776 | www.krebscustom.com |

Parts/tools with gun

Firing pin, extractor. Maybe a spare bolt.

Parts/tools at home

Perhaps an extra barrel, trigger group, and stock. Front sight adjustment tool (Sarco; Ø13).

COMBAT RIFLE OPTICS

The purpose of sights is to *hit* your target. If your vision has deteriorated enough that you cannot effectively use iron sights at long range, or if you expect lots of low-light combat, then a quality optical sight is necessary for your battle rifle.

A word about "bargains"

Don't be lured by the Ø100 siren song of a bargain Tasco. These are decent scopes, but they are not *great* scopes. *"Buy cheap, buy twice. Only the rich can afford to buy twice."* Spend the money on great optics, rings, and mount—and enjoy it forever. Life is too short to waste on shoddy gear. Do it right the first time and move on. Although there are no certainties in life, and your Leupold may indeed fail before your Tasco—the *probability* is the other way around. Paying for top quality merely increases the odds in your favor. Do this consistently and the odds of equipment failure will be reduced to nearly zero.

Whenever my students express temptation to save a few bucks on a cheaper alternative for something important, I ask them, *"If the cheaper item were the same price as the expensive one, would you still be inclined to choose it?"* When they invariably answer in the negative, I ask them why not. *"Because the quality isn't the same."* Then I ask them, *"Oh, but isn't that what's important to you—quality?"* Sheepishly, they agree.

Expensive is when the product is not worth the money.
— Karl Welcher of Leica

DIFFERENT OPTICS
FOR DIFFERENT RIFLES

As battle rifles, battle carbines, and tactical rifles solve different (though occasionally overlapping) problems, their optics will be somewhat specialized.

Battle rifle optics (*e.g.,* I.O.R. 4x24 M2)

Optics must be very rugged and versatile. Rugged because a .308 MBR has hefty recoil and sees hard use. Versatile because the battle rifle will be employed for everything from CQB to precision work. Hence, it must have a quickly acquired aiming point, as well as rangefinding stadia lines and a BDC. The mount should be see-through in order to have immediate use of the iron sights.

Battle carbine optics (*e.g.,* ACOG)

Optics must be rugged, lightweight, and offer very fast target acquisition for CQB. A circle, dot, or triangle aiming point is the norm, and it should be illuminated at all times day or night (*e.g.,* ACOG "BAC" system with tritium). Distance stadia lines are nice (*e.g.,* ACOG), but not absolutely necessary (*e.g.,* the AUG's 5MOA "doughnut of death"). As in battle rifles, the mount should also be see-through.

Tactical rifle optics (*e.g.,* Leupold Mk 4® M3)

If you needed to make a 250yd headshot or 600yd bodyshot, this is the rifle you'd want. (Also called a "precision" or "countersniper" rifle.) Hence, it will have something like a 3-9x magnification scope with at least ½MOA adjustments (if not ¼MOA). The reticle will likely be Mil-Dot, and the scope will have a BDC. Some battle rifle optics make for very competent tactical applications, such as the Shepherd P2 and I.O.R. M2.

Because of the higher accuracy requirement, these rifles are often, if not usually, bolt-actions. But, not always. An M14 can make a fine tactical rifle if tuned to <1¼MOA accuracy.

While I have a lot of experience with and affinity for the Leupold Mk4 M3-10x, the I.O.R. Tactical 2½-10x42 and 4-12x50 scopes are quickly gaining my favor. Also, the Shepherd 310-P2 is very fast, very accurate, and very rugged.

RANGEFINDING & BDC

Most modern combat and tactical optics have a system to not only measure range, but to also compensate for bullet drop.

Rangefinding (RF)

RFs calculate unknown ranges based on some known dimension of the target (such as 5'7" height or 19" torso width), or by precise graduations of angular width (minutes-of-angle, or milliradians, both of which will be discussed shortly).

Range based on height/width of enemy soldier

In the first case, the underrated Soviet PSO-1 Dragunov scope from the 1960s used the 1.7m/5'7" average height of a soldier. Bracket him between two horizontal stadia lines, read the corresponding range below (from 200-1000m in 100m increments), dial in the range on the BDC and drop him. It was very innovative and remains an effective tool. The Romanian firm of I.O.R. Bucuresti has continued this concept in their superb M2 4x24mm scopes.

As the smart enemy is not known for his standing up, range based on torso width is becoming the preferred method. Whether standing, kneeling, squating, or prone, an enemy's torso (or at least shoulder) is invariably exposed. Torso widths are assumed to be 20" (same as a military silhouettte target).

Range estimation based on angular width

I once saw these 3" tall aliens. "Are you really that small?" I asked.
"No, we're actually very far away."
— Steven Wright

To the eye, something will appear twice as small at twice the distance, or 5x as small 5x as far. The effect is linear.

Just as an inch and a centimeter are two different ways to measure length (1" = 2.54cm), mils and minutes-of-angle (MOAs) are two ways of describing the same thing: the cone effect of distance (*i.e.*, angular width).

Minutes-of-angle (MOA)   (1.047" @ 100yds)

There are 360 degrees in a circle, and 60 minutes in each degree. Imagine a pie cut in 21,600 (60 x 360) slices. That's how many MOAs there are in a circle. 1MOA is a *very* thin "slice." *How* thin? Assuming pie slice with 100yd length (*i.e.*, 3600" radius), 1MOA would subtend (*i.e.*, cover) 1.047197551197", or 1.047". (π = 3.14159265359)

$$\frac{radius \times 2\pi}{21,600} = 1MOA \qquad \frac{3600" \times 6.28318530718}{21,600} = 1.047197551197"$$

Using the 26.75" M14 sight radius, 1MOA = 0.0077812". ((26.75" x 2π) / 21,600). If your M14 sight is off by just 8/1000th of an inch (*i.e.*, the thickness of two human hairs), your POI will be off 1.047" per 100yds. It is critical that sights (both iron and optical) must be manufactured to *very* close tolerances. (This is why I dislike the FAL's sloppy rear sight so much.)

At 200yds, 2.094"; 1000yds, 10.47"; etc. Conversationally, however, we round off that 1.047" and say that 1MOA is 1" at 100yds, 2" at 200yds, 5" at 500yds, etc. Although we're disregarding 4.7%, 1" per 100yds is still close enough for most purposes. (For you metric fans, 1MOA equals 2.908cm at 100m. Round up to 3cm.)

Using MOAs to calculate range

Most scopes and nearly all iron sight BDCs (*e.g.*, M1, M14, AR15) are graduated in MOAs. The Shepherd scopes use stadia lines of 1MOA. Here is how to use MOAs to calculate range:

$$\frac{(size\ of\ object\ in\ inches) \times 100}{size\ of\ object\ in\ MOAs} = range\ in\ yards$$

What is the MOA width of my front sight?

This is highly useful to know, as you can then employ your front sight as a ranging device for known target widths (such as 20" military silhouettes). To calculate front sight MOA width:

$$\frac{21600}{(sight\ radius" \times 2\pi)\ /\ front\ sight\ width"} = MOA$$

Let's calculate front sight MOA for the M14. Its sight radius is 26.75" and its National Match front sight width is 0.062":

$$\frac{21600}{(26.75" \times 6.28318)\ /\ 0.062"} = 7.9679MOA$$

So, the M14/M1A has an 8MOA width front sight (although many believe it's 7MOA). As we will shortly learn, this was not by accident. (To have been *exactly* 8MOA, width must be 0.06225", which is within the sight specs of +/- 0.0005".)

Using your front sight to calculate range

Let's say the 8MOA front sight on your M14 precisely covers a military silhouette target (which is 20" wide).

$$\frac{(20" \text{ torso}) \times 100}{8\text{MOA}} = 250\text{yds}$$

This is not by accident, either! 250yds is the battlesight zero (BSZ) for the 147gr/2600fps ballistics of 7.62x51 FMJ. BSZ was discussed in the M1/M14 chapter. If your front sight covers a 20" wide torso, the range matches the rifle's battlesight zero (BSZ) of 250yds. Center hold from 0-300yds and drop him. No holdover is needed. Pretty neat. (Perhaps, if I have time, I'll calculate the front sight MOAs for all the battle rifles...)

This will also work with optical sights if you know the MOA width of your reticle. For example, the TA11E ACOG has a chevron 5.53MOA wide at the bottom, which equals 20"/300m.

To convert yards into meters, divide by 1.09361

We arrive at that because there are 2.54cm/inch, and thus 91.44cm/yard. 100cm/91.44cm equals 1.09361.

Divide the M14 BSZ of 250yds by 1.09361 for 229m.

Mils (3.6" @ 100yds, or 36" @ 1000yds)
1mil = 3.438MOA (*not* 3.375MOA)

You may not have a cooperative enemy soldier to range on, but you could have another item of known dimension such as rifle length, doorway, vehicle, telephone pole, etc. So, the U.S. Marines developed a system in the 1970s using what are called milliradians, "mils".

A mil also measures angular width. A radian is an angle whose width of arc equals the length of its radius. Since a circle's circumference is 2π times the length of its radius, there are 2π (6.283) radians in a 360° circle. (In case you're interested, a radian is approximately 57.3°, because 360° / 6.283 = 57.296°. There are compelling geometric reasons for using radians instead of degrees, but that's for another time.) A mil (1/1000th of a 6.283 radian circle) is 1/6283th of a circle, which subtends exactly to a 1 yard arc at a 1000yd radius. Pretty cute, eh?

Note: Some authors/firms describe a mil as being 1/6400th of a circle, which is 3.375MOA. It is *not*. Plug in a 3600" radius and 3.6" arc width into the MOA sight formula, and you'll get 3.4377496MOA. (Not that it *really* matters, as the 0.063MOA difference between the two means just 0.63" @ 1000yds.)

One mil equals 3.438 MOA. (21,600 minutes divided by 6,283mils = 3.438MOAs per mil.) A mil is a fatter "slice" than a MOA. Artillerymen have been using mils for decades, as it's a fine way to measure the precise range of large objects (*e.g.*, buildings) at great distance (*e.g.*, several miles).

It can also be used to measure smaller targets (*i.e.*, enemy soldiers) at hundreds of yards:

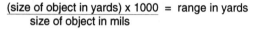

$$\frac{\text{(size of object in yards)} \times 1000}{\text{size of object in mils}} = \text{range in yards}$$

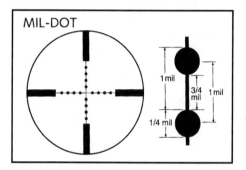

If a 6' man (2 yards) is 4mils in your scope, then you know that he is exactly 500yds away (2x1000/4 = 500). A mil is measured on the reticle as the distance between the *centers* of two neighboring Mil-Dots.

The Mil-Dots are ¼mil in diameter, and the space between them is ¾mil. (Some reticles use hash marks instead.)

Calculating yardage by target height" (inch vs. mil)

	12"	16"	18"	19"	20"	22"	24"	28"	32"	36"	48"	60"	66"	72"
.50	666	890	1000	1056	1112	1222	1334	1556	1778	2000	2668	3334	3666	4000
.75	444	593	666	704	741	815	889	1037	1185	1333	1778	2223	2444	2667
1.00	333	445	500	528	556	611	667	778	889	1000	1334	1667	1833	2000
1.25	266	355	400	423	445	489	534	622	711	800	1068	1334	1466	1600
1.50	222	296	333	352	371	407	445	519	593	667	890	1111	1222	1333
1.75	190	254	285	302	318	349	381	445	508	571	762	953	1047	1143
2.00	167	222	250	269	278	306	334	389	445	500	668	834	917	1000
2.25	148	197	222	235	247	272	296	346	395	444	592	741	815	889
2.50	133	178	200	211	222	244	267	311	356	400	534	667	733	800
2.75	121	161	182	192	202	222	243	283	323	364	486	606	667	727
3.00	111	148	167	176	185	204	222	259	296	333	444	556	611	667
3.25	102	137	154	163	171	188	205	239	273	308	410	513	564	615
3.50		127	143	151	159	175	191	222	254	286	382	476	524	571
3.75		118	133	141	148	163	178	207	237	267	366	445	489	533
4.00		111	125	132	139	153	167	195	222	250	334	417	458	500
4.25		104	118	125	131	144	157	183	209	235	314	392	431	471
4.50			111	118	124	136	148	173	197	222	296	370	407	445
4.75			105	111	117	128	140	164	187	210	280	351	386	421
5.00			100	106	111	122	133	156	178	200	266	333	367	400
5.25				105	116	127	148	169	190	254	318	349	381
5.50				101	111	121	141	162	182	242	303	333	364
5.75					106	116	135	155	174	232	290	319	348
6.00					102	111	130	148	167	222	278	306	333
6.25						107	124	142	160	214	267	293	320
6.50						103	120	137	154	206	256	282	308
6.75							115	132	148	198	247	272	296
7.00							111	127	143	191	238	262	286
8.00								111	125	167	208	229	250
9.00									111	148	185	203	222
10.00									100	133	167	183	200

So, if you know a dimension of something you can with Mil-Dots calculate its range. Or, if you know its range, its dimension. Very handy. It's not terribly quick to use, and requires a little chart table or calculator, but it's quite accurate. The I.O.R. 2.5-10x42mm and 4-14x50mm Tactical scopes use hash marks of ½, 1, and 5 mils (instead of dots). Someday, some scope manufacturer will offer a scope with stadia lines in *both* mils and MOAs (you heard it here first!).

MOA vs. mil

Personally, I prefer measuring angular width using MOA. The math is easier, and MOAs are 3.438x more precise. Mils make more sense for a .50BMG shooter ranging a vehicle.

My advice: learn both and it won't matter.

Ballistic drop compensator (BDC)

BDCs do not generally calculate unknown ranges. They merely compensate for bullet drop at a *known* range, and allow the shooter a proper holdover. There are two methods: mechanical or reticular.

Mechanical BDCs (*e.g.,* Elcan, I.O.R., Hensoldt)

The mechanical method requires that you dial in the desired range on the scope (which shifts reticle elevation), then reacquire your target. Although this work perfectly well, it's slower and it adds mechanical complexity to the scope.

Reticular BDCs (*e.g.,* ACOG, Shepherd)

Instead of shifting the reticle, why not simply use the bottom vertical leg of the reticle for necessary holdovers?

RF and BDC together

This is the concept behind the Trijicon ACOG and Shepherd scopes. In the ACOG, simply line up the 19" torso width of the target to the proper horizontal stadia line for the proper holdover, and use that crosshair as your aiming point. It's faster because it needs no finger manipulation and your eye never leaves the scope. It's simpler because no third mechanical turret is required.

Can it be any better than that? Yes, if you ask the folks at Shepherd Scopes, who use ranging circles in diameters of (depending on the application) 9", 18", or 24". Such is probably quicker to center a target than lining up a stadia line on a torso.

BATTLE RIFLE OPTICS

I have in mind several very nice scopes for your .308 MBR. With the exception of the ACOG, I actually own *all* the scopes discussed below. I have used them all extensively on HK91s, M1As, FALs, AR15s, AKs, and a SAKO bolt .308. (Hey, it's what you *pay* me for! Not that I'm complaining...)

Trijicon ACOG   www.trijicon.com

The Advanced Combat Optical Gunsight (which came out in 1989) is unique in that its aiming point is always illuminated. The ACOG was designed for the .223 M16 (and dozens of models exist for these carbines), there are just three models calibrated for .308 (and the TA11C and TA11E are identical but for donut vs. chevron reticle). ACOGs have a reticular BDC out to 800m:

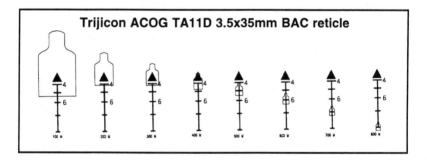

Trijicon ACOG TA11D 3.5x35mm BAC reticle

TA01B 4x32

Its reticle and 4x magnification more favor distance work than the below TA11C. Weight is 9.9oz. Retail price from DSA (#TA01B) is Ø610. ⅓MOA adjustment.

TA11E 3.5x35

This has Bindon Aiming Concept (BAC) dual illumination (using a fiber optic for daylight and tritium for night) and a chevron reticle. This is a larger scope than the TA01B, weighing 14oz. Retail price from DSA (#TA11E) is Ø825, reflecting the cost of the BAC (which is truly impressive). ¼MOA adjustment.

ACOG reticle and stadia lines

The **TA01B** has a tritium crosshair and distance stadia lines from 200-800m.

The **TA11E** has the BAC chevron red-glowing reticle (its base is 5.53MOA, which equals a 19" width at 300m). Horizontal stadia lines from 300-800m.

The **TA11C** is identical to the E, but for the CQB AUG-style donut reticle (measuring 4MOA O.D. and 2MOA I.D.).

I believe that the TA11E's chevron reticle is nearly as quick as the TA11C's donut, and is certainly more precise for the .308's long range capability.

Zeroing the ACOG

The TA01B adjusts in ⅓MOA increments, which, although seems very odd in a ¼ or ½MOA world, makes a lot of sense. ¼MOA is too fine for CQB work, and ½MOA becomes too coarse at ranges past 600yds. Upon reflection, ⅓MOA may be the illusive Goldilocks "just right" for most shooters, although it may be more difficult to mentally compute for some. Your call.

ACOG pros

Built like a tank. Great illumination. Extremely fast target acquisition. Simple, yet effective, reticle BDC.

ACOG cons

No diopter adjustment for shooter far/nearsightedness. No interchangeability of reticle or BDC. The BAC fiber optic is sensitive to DEET. They look a bit odd.

Final word on the ACOGs

Rugged, compact, lightweight, and dependable. The most optics in the smallest package. Great for military and police. The TA11E with its 2.4" eye relief and more precise chevron reticle would be my pick.

Elcan 7.62   www.elcan.com

Developed by Leitz in conjunction with Colt for the Canadian military flat-top M16A3s, the Elcan is a huge rugged beast of a scope with a built-in Picatinny QD/ZH mount (containing the windage/elevation adjustments and BDC). It sports Leica glass (which is as renowned as Zeiss or Schmidt & Bender).

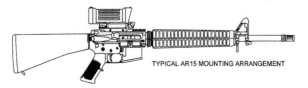

TYPICAL AR15 MOUNTING ARRANGEMENT

Elcan BDC
BDC is an AR-type 200-800m knob. I've used it on my FAL out to precisely 600m and 800m, and the BDC was spot on.

Elcan night vision
One really fine accessory is the Blackcat® Night Vision (www.elcan.com). Gen III or Gen III+, with at least 64 lp/mm, the unit simply attaches to the rear of the Elcan. This would make a dandy rig for a pre-ban (flash suppressor) flat-top AR15.

Elcan reticle and stadia lines

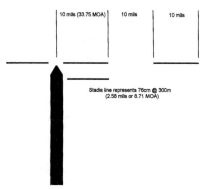

The reticle is a German-style picket post, which makes for very quick target acquisition. The triangle tip contains a replaceable tritium element. Since all adjustments are external, the reticle never moves and is thus much more rugged. I like it.

I don't, however, particularly care for the 10mil (34.38MOA) horizontal stadia lines or the ¼mil (0.8595MOA) clicks, but any dedicated Rifleman really should learn the mil system, anyway.

It has two parallel horizontal stadia lines representing a height of 76cm (30") at 300m (328y). This is 2.58mils (8.87MOA). Maybe it's a "Canadian thing," but I just don't get it. 8.87MOA? (Weird.) 30" at 300m? (Half-height of a 5' tall soldier? Will the Canadians be invaded by 7th graders?)

From my own calculations, the *width* of the post seems to be about 7.4MOA, which means 20" wide at a BSZ of about 250m/275yds. *Hmmm.* This is useful. (The Canadians at least got *this* right.) For example, if your Bad Guy is as thick as the reticle post, then leave your elevation on 300 and drop him with a center hold. If he's ¼ thinner, go to 400. If he's ⅓ thinner, 500. If he is ½ thinner, 600. (If ⅔ thinner, then he is at 900m, which is beyond the BDC's 800m capability.)

Zeroing the Elcan

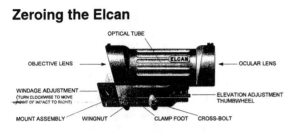

Setting the BDC on 400m will allow you to zero at 25m. Each clockwise windage click moves impact 0.86MOA to the right. To zero elevation, turn the knob to 200m (which is the silver zero lock), move the lock up to release the BDC for zero adjustment, and move back to the lower position to lock in changes. Each click to the right moves impact up 0.86MOA.

Elcan pros

Rugged, waterproof, fine optics, great BDC, built-in Picatinny mount, and NVD capability. It has emergency back-up iron sights (good probably out to 75yds).

Elcan cons

The Elcan's greatest faults are its 22½oz weight (over twice that of the ACOG TA01B) and 2.8" height (designed for flat-top M16A3s, it needs such offset). I don't care for 0.86MOA clicks (too large, and too odd). Mount is not see-through.

Since, however, it has an excellent BDC out to 800m and the 7.4MOA-wide reticle post coubles as a combat RF, the Elcan's funky 2.58/10mil stadia lines are no great loss. I'd have liked the BDC adjustable in 50m increments >300m (*e.g.,* M2).

It will *not* fit on an M14 mount, as its left-side tightening knobs interfere with the mount. (Besides, offset would be ridiculous). It is also far too high for the already tall HK91 scope mount. Hence, FAL and AR only.

At Ø700 retail (DSA; #EL-7.62), the Elcan is on the high end of average price.

Final word on the Elcan

It's a shame that they didn't incorporate a BDC reticle similar to the ACOG's. Even though I like the Elcan (and it will remain on my FAL), I bought mine (for my AR10) before the I.O.R. M2s were available. I likely would not buy an Elcan today as I can not mount it on *all* my MBRs. However, *if* one lands in your lap at a *great* price, you may want to give it a try. The Elcan is limited to a flat-top AR (superb rig for such), or an FAL with DSA mount (works very well, but offset is a bit high).

I.O.R. 4x24 M2 7.62   www.valdada.com

Industry Optico Romania (I.O.R.), the "Zeiss of Romania," has been manufacturing quality mil spec optics for over 60 years. The mil spec M2 is an improvement of the Soviet PSO-1 (*Pristel Snaypershy Optichesky*) scope found on the SVD (*Snayperskaya Vintovka Dragunova*), better known as the Dragunov. It is simple, rugged, easy to use, and has an excellent BDC based on range (not MOA). The glass is Schott Glasswerk with Zeiss T3 multi-coating (to eliminate glare and maximize light transmission), and the optics are superb. Dioptrical adjustment is -4/+4. The reticle is photo engraved on the glass, and thus is very crisp and rugged.

I.O.R. M2 BDC

From 100-1000m in 168gr .308. A nice touch is 50m clicks from 300m on. This is a true *range*-based BDC, rather than an MOA- or mil-based BDC with range numerals on the drum. It is extremely well-calibrated, as were the PSO-1 cousins.

I.O.R. M2 reticle and stadia lines

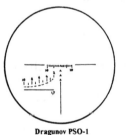

Dragunov PSO-1

PSO-1 style Chevron reticle, which is quick and precise. The stadia lines are 1.7m/5'7" in height for 200-1000m. The three narrow chevrons below the top chevron are for holdovers out to 1100m, 1200m, and 1300m (which are beyond the mechanical range of the BDC cam).

The entire reticle is red illuminated (7 positions of brightness) with a Ø3 lithium CR2032 battery available anywhere. *Very* nice! (Curiously, the .223 M2 has green illumination.) The 168gr BDC works for 147gr FMJ out to 600m, but after that you'll have to holdover a bit for the FMJ's lower BC.

Zeroing the I.O.R. M2

My scope did not come with zeroing instructions, and after I flubbed it up, I had to call Valdada for help. Turns out that the procedure was much easier than I'd thought. (Figures...)

If you're zeroing at 100m, set the elevation ring on 1, and the windage on 0. Both windage and elevation turrets have three screws. *Never touch the staked center screw!* (It connects directly to the reticle.) Using a quality hollow-ground flat head gunsmithing screwdriver (*e.g.*, Midway, Chapman, etc.), loosen the two outside screws only 2 turns; about halfway. *Do not remove the outside screws!* (Removal will prevent zeroing, and you'll likely lose a screw. I did.) Hold the ring, and turn the upper plate (it is under friction contact, so there are no clicks) to zero POI with POA. Once zeroed, retighten the two screws.

Loosening the upper plate's outside screws also allows the numeral ring to be reindexed without shifting the reticle (sort of like reindexing the elevation knob of the M1/M14). This is how I zeroed my M1A when I had only a 600m target which could be hit only with the elevation on 2(00m). (The mount had too much down angle.) I loosened the two plate screws, and held the plate from moving while I simply adjusted the ring from 2 to 6.

So, you can adjust the reticle (the upper plate) to match a numerical ring setting, or you can adjust a ring to match the reticle's position. Pretty slick.

I.O.R. M2 pros
Fog/shock/waterproof, great optics, illuminated reticle/stadia lines, fine BDC, clear knob markings, and excellent value (Ø330 from DSA). I like the removeable rubber eyepiece.

I.O.R. M2 cons
Some scopes (*e.g.*, ACOGs) use 19" widths, which I prefer as you can't always expect your Bad Guy to be fully standing. Windage clicks/marks are too large: 2.25MOA/4.50MOA. Eye relief is only 2" and I came to disenjoy my FAL's M2.

Final word on the I.O.R. M2
Until recently I was a huge fan of the M2. No longer, mainly because of Valdada's astonishing lack of customer support and poor attitude towards civilian customers. If you aren't LE or military, you will not be taken seriously by Valdada.

I personally know of two 6x Super M2s which quickly lost their illumination assembly through no fault of the shooters, but Valdada claimed "customer abuse" (which I assure you was *not* the case). One of those scopes, in my own presence, puked after just two hours on its M14 and 47 rounds of NATO ball!

While the optics are fantastic, woe be unto you if you ever need factory service. To me, it's just not worth it, sorry Valentin.

Instead, for Ø199 delivered, get a Burris 3-9x40mm Ballistic Plex Fullfield II with 200-600yd holdovers. Made in America, with a Forever Warranty, and no elevation knob twiddling. (For a special 6-page report on these scopes, send me a Ø20 bill.)

Hensoldt Optische Werke (Wetzlar) 4x24

These were used in the 1960s by the West German *Bundeswehr* on their FAL G1s and HK G3s. Hensoldt is military Zeiss, so the quality is naturally superb. BDC for 7.62x51 is 100-600m, and I can assure you that it's spot on at all ranges. The scope is compact and rugged, and the optics are very good. It comes with simple, yet clever, rubber lens caps (which I wish were available for other optics). Surplus condition will be Good-Very Good.

Hensoldt HK mount

For only Ø375 it also includes a mil spec HK91 STANAG QD/ZH mount (a Ø200+ value!), although a chinweld is required due to the tall offset. (GG&G offers a lowboy mount which reduces offset by ¾" at the expense of see-through iron sights. www.gggaz.com 520-748-7167) Mounted on my HK91, it required only 3 clicks of windage to zero—very impressive! This is the hot ticket for any of you with Hesse and CETME clones (assuming that your rifle works well).

If this scope is for another rifle besides the HK91 system, simply get an ARMS STANAG-to-Picatinny mount and the scope will attach perfectly.

As the HK91 does not scope as gracefully as an FAL, I will leave my Hensoldt on. Besides, it seems to "belong" there!

Hensoldt reticle

Classic German picket-post (which the Elcan copied), of a width that seems to be about 5MOA. Target acquisition is very fast with this reticle, though precision suffers a bit. Nevertheless, out to the scope's max BDC of 600m the reticle is just fine.

There are also some vertical stadia lines of unknown angular width (though I'd guess they're 5mil). No manual comes with the scope (unless you opt for the deal with the case and accessories, which were sold out when I ordered).

Hensoldt zeroing

Each click moves impact 2.5cm at 100m, which means 0.9" @ 100yds, or 0.8596MOA (which is ¼mil, as in the Elcan). Don't sweat this; merely round up to 1MOA. You'll be low only 0.16" per 100m, which is only 0.96" @ 600m. Big deal.

The disks can be reindexed after zeroing, which is similar to the elevation knob of the M1/M14.

Hensoldt availability

In mid-2001 I noticed several sources for this scope in *Shotgun News*, but it's now 3/2002 and only SOG seems to have them. HK91 owners (myself included) probably cleaned them out, and I don't blame them. Still, you might keep looking, as another batch may someday be imported. (I've seen a couple at gun shows, but for Ø500+ from sellers trying to make a buck.)

Shepherd P2   www.shepherdscopes.com

We've all seen Shepherd's full page ads in *Shotgun News* for years. (Since they never listed price, I assumed that they were too expensive for me. *Au contraire.*) My friend Fred at Fred's M14 Stocks raves about them and reminded me to test one. I met the wonderful Shepherd family at SHOT 2002 in Las Vegas, and had my first chance to look over their renowned products. These are very unique scopes, which need some explanation to convey what is different and superior about them.

Rule #1 is: "In order for a scope to lose its zero, something between the reticle and target must move."

Rule #2 is "In order to see what moved you need two reticles; each one to track the other."

The old type German scopes put the cross hair in the front focal plane. They hardly ever lost their zeros because the only thing between the reticle and the cross hair was the objective lens. The drawback was that the reticle magnified when zoomed and blocked out long range targets. Americans put the reticle in the rear focal plane where it would not magnify. The main drawback with this was that it put about three more lenses between the reticle and the target. The American system was then three times more likely to lose its zero. The American system was more convenient but the German system was more reliable.

®Shepherd gives you the best of both worlds with the drawbacks of neither. We use the front focal plane location for our rangefinding and bullet drop compensating circles. This gives us the German dependability and, when zoomed, the circles do not block the targets but instead frame them and give you instant target engagement on any power.

We then put the cross hair in the rear focal plane (where the Americans do) in order to get the benefits of a nonmagnifying reticle. This patented Dual Reticle System™ lets each reticle monitor the other and thus allows for: one shot zeroing in, "at a glance" verification of the original zero, and visual confirmation of windage and elevation adjustments before you shoot. The ®Shepherd is truly the

*most reliable of all and the only one to tell you if something is out of
zero before you shoot.*
— ®Shepherd Enterprises, Inc. 2002 Catalog

This is *very* ingenuous. One-shot zero, and confirmation of zero
without having to shoot! (Such makes great sense for those who
cannot often go to the range, or want a reliable travel rifle which
must have confirmable zero without shooting.)

Shepherd P2 reticle and stadia lines

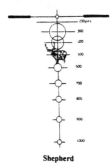

Shepherd

Crosshair with 18" (*i.e.*, torso width) ranging circles from 200-1000yds. (Hunting
scopes have 24" circles, and .22 scopes
have 9" circles for standing prairie dogs.)
All scopes are ordered for caliber and bullet weight, and mine was 150gr/.308 (as I
shoot more FMJ than 168gr MatchKings).

Vertical and horizontal stadia lines in
1MOA increments, which is highly usable
in the field. (Elcan, take note!)

Shepherd P2 pros

Its D.R.S.™ is the obvious highlight of a Shepherd. There
is nothing like it in any other optical sight. The reticular BDC is
very fast and surprisingly precise. It makes hits easy to get!

Shepherd P2 cons

The scope tube is 1", but 30mm is far superior. Some reticle illumination and tactical turret caps would have been nice.
50yd hash marks between 100yd increments >400yds would
help with those iffy long shots.

Final word on the Shepherd P2

Nice folks selling a superb product with a Lifetime Guarantee. Available only factory-direct.

L2A2 SUIT (Sight Unit Trilux)

These were used in the mid-1970s on L1A1 FALs and Israeli M16s. It's a very simple, rugged, combat 4x optic with
250m/450m BDC. The aiming point is an *inverted* pointer,
which doesn't obscure the target during holdovers. Comes with
a #357 lithium battery powered red illuminator (the milspec
SUITs had a tritium element which has long since decayed).

Weight is only 12oz, and the optics are quite good (86% light transmission). The focus is fixed, and windage/elevation adjustments are pretty basic, but remember that this was designed to be a very simple optic effective at typical combat ranges. You'll be able to quickly hit out to 450m, and that's good enough for most Riflemen.

DSA sells these with Inch pattern FAL mounts for just Ø200 (#TRI-L2A2), and with their SA58 mount for Ø260 (#TRI-MT-L2A2). Either way, the mounts are not see-through for the iron sights, but the scope removes quickly enough if needed. Condition was Surplus Very Good, with no lens scratches. Supplied with decent instructions/diagrams.

If you have a FAL, then the SUIT is the affordable way to go for good combat optics. I have a Ø400 Inch FAL I bought years ago, and my SUIT is going on that for a great truck rifle. DSA had less than 100 of them in 3/2002, so order quickly if you'd like one. It's a good sight, and quite a piece of history.

Comparing battle rifle scopes

Without getting into 20 criteria for a weighted Kepner-Trogue analysis, let's briefly compare some basic features:

Glass

This contemplates not only the quality of the lens and its coating, but its light transmission ability (which is also affected by objective lens diameter).

For example, although the Elcan's objective lens is only 28mm, its glass is made by *Leica* so the image is superb. Similarly, even though the I.O.R. M2's lens is only 24mm, the Schott glass with Zeiss T3 multi-coating rival any fine 40mm lens.

Reticle

Contemplates clarity and useability.

The ®Shepherd uses rangefinding circles to dispense with a BDC cam, while the ACOGs use stadia lines for 19" width. This is *much* quicker, as you don't have to look away from your target or disturb your cheekweld.

BDC

Mechanical cam (Elcan, I.O.R. M2, Hensoldt) versus reticular holdover (ACOG, Shepherd).

Ruggedness

All six scopes were quite rugged, but the ACOG, Elcan, and I.O.R. M2 were *extra* rugged.

Knobs/controls

These should be large, finger-friendly, and not require any tools. (If a tool is required, then it should be nothing more elaborate than a coin.)

The Elcan's AR-type elevation knob is very easy and fast to use, as was the Hensoldt's dial knob.

Weight

Obviously, lighter is better (as long as ruggedness is not sacrificed, which did not occur here). The ACOG at 9.9oz is the featherweight here, followed by the Hensoldt and the I.O.R M2.

The Elcan at 22½oz was the pig, but it includes the mount, so to be fair I needed to compare the other scopes with *their* steel rings attached. Thus, I added 4oz to the others, and used the ACOG at 13.9oz for the score of 10, subtracting a point for every additional 2oz.

	glass	reticle	RF/BDC	rugged	knobs	weight	TOTAL	
TA01B	8	8	10	10	7	10	**53**	2nd
TA11E	8	10	10	10	7	8	**53**	2nd
Elcan	9	8	8	10	7	6	**49**	5th
I.O.R. M2	9	9	9	10	9	9	**55**	1st
Hensoldt 4x	9	6	7	8	8	10	**48**	6th
Shepherd P2	8	9	10	8	8	7	**49**	5th

These are all very fine scopes. Only 2 points separated 1st from 3rd. If your MBR optic needs are more tactical, then pick the I.O.R. M2 or TA11E ACOG. If more CQB, then go with the donut reticle TA11C ACOG. If you use your MBR for hunting, then the Shepherd P2 would make a good all-around scope.

BATTLE CARBINE OPTICS

While most of the battle rifle optics will also do fine on an AR15, a battle carbine's job is different enough to require specialized optics. For example, since it will be more employed for CQB work, magnification above 4x is not only unnecessary but would actually hinder fast target acquisition.

Trijicon ACOG
Compact ACOGs for .223
These are CQB optics, and not really suitable for general carbine work past 300m. Hence, I will not fully describe them here. Nevertheless, I counted *48* models! Magnification/objective lens combinations are: 1.5x16, 1.5x24, 2x20, and 3x24. (Gee, if they'd only make one in 2x24, I'd buy it!) Each is available with choice of bases (ring vs. M16), reticle styles (dot, triangle, or crosshair), and reticle colors (amber or red).

Full-size Trijicon ACOGs for .223

	magn.	obj.	BAC?	reticle	misc.
TA11	3.5x	35mm	✔	2/4MOA red donut	
TA11B	3.5x	35mm	✔	circle/red chevron	
TA11D	3.5x	35mm	✔	4MOA red triangle	
TA11F	3.5x	35mm	✔	5.53MOA red chevron	flat-top adpt.
TA01	4x	32mm	–	crosshair	
TA01C	4x	32mm	–	cross/red center	
TA01NSN	4x	32mm	–	cross/yellow center	flat-top adpt.
TA31	4x	32mm	✔	2/4MOA red donut	
TA31A	4x	32mm	✔	4MOA red triangle	
TA31F	4x	32mm	✔	5.53MOA red chevron	flat-top adpt.
TA55	5.5x	50mm	✔	5.53MOA red chevron	

Which ACOG for me?

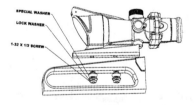

First of all, it must have the fiber optic BAC. No TA01s.

Secondly, I like the 3.5x35 **TA11s** for their 2.4" eye relief (necessary if you shoot with gas masks, goggles, or glasses) and ¼MOA adjustment. Also, the lower 3.5x is marginally better for CQB, but plenty strong for work <800m. Downside of the TA11s: they weigh 14oz vs. the 9.9oz TA31s. If the extra 4oz really matter, get a TA31 model.

ACOG reticle
As far as which reticle, that depends on the expected range of your Bad Guys. For more CQB stuff, the **TA11's** 2/4MOA red donut can't be beat for lightning-fast 0-200m work, yet it still has the 300-800m reticular BDC.

For 300m+, the **TA31F** with 5.53MOA chevron has stadia lines from 400-800m. (The **TA31A** with 4MOA triangle is also fine, but obscures more of the target than the chevron.)

ACOG pros
Probably the best overall optic for the AR15, whether carry-handle or flat-top. There's one to suit any shooter.

ACOG cons
None, really. Price and weird appearance.

Elcan .223
Designed for the M16, this is a perfectly capable optic. The ACOG, however, is lighter and quicker to use on target.

I.O.R. M2 4x24mm .223

Crosshair with center dot, which is clear, uncluttered, and very fast. I like it very much. (The dot seems about 2MOA.)

The BDC is simpler than its .308 brother, as 1.7m/5'7" height stadia lines are for 200, 400, 600, and 800m only. There is 7-position green illumination by CR2032 battery. This is a great carbine scope, especially for only Ø330 (DSA).

Leupold Mark 4® CQ/T™ 1-3x14mm
A combination red dot sight and variable power scope.

At 1x its 9MOA dot works like an Aimpoint.

At 3x its large red Circle Dot sight works like an ACOG TA11. The circle's diameter is 72MOA @ 100yds, which equates to 6' in height. The center dot is 3MOA.

Illumination in 10 positions, plus 2 NVD settings. Requires one AA battery, which will power the reticle for up to 7 hours of continuous use on the brightest setting.

Huge FoV: 84-117' @ 100yds. 2.8" eye relief.

Mounts to AR15 carry handle, or Picatinny rail. Weight without battery or mount is 17.5oz. Price from QP is Ø850.

I've handled the CQ/T, but have not fired it. Impressive quality (to be expected from Leupold), and very innovative (a sort of "ACOG Aimpoint"). Probably more suitable for police and military than for you or me.

U.S. Optics SN-12   www.usoptics.com

This is a relatively new optics firm, and the only one making its own lenses in-house. In fact, they manufacture everything themselves, and thus can/will provide custom optics.

The first thing you notice about one of their scopes is the weight. Their scopes are built like bank vaults. Tube thickness of the 7075-T6 forged aluminum is 0.125", which is generally *twice* that of most scopes.

The second thing you notice is the overwhelming sense of quality. Gorgeous machining. Hand knurled, not extruded grooves. Hand made/fitted parts. Beautifully precise clicks.

The U.S.M.C. has purchased the SN-12 for their M4s and M16s, and I don't blame them.

U.S. Optics SN-12 glass

Since the average human eye will resolve about 40 lp/mm, most optics manufacturers don't bother to exceed (or even match) such. Quality European and Japanese glass will sometimes resolve up to 40 lp/mm. U.S. Optics, however, has the capability to make lenses with *100* lp/mm resolution.

I handled an SN-12 at SHOT 2002, side-by-side with an ACOG. The superiority of the SN-12's glass was astounding. My first thought was that the ACOG's objective lens was dirty! It wasn't. I tell you, the SN-12's glass is *that* good (48 vs. 36 lp/mm). Real BMW vs. Buick stuff, and the Buick is a *good* car!

My eye still fantasizes about that glass.

U.S. Optics SN-12 reticle

A Circle Dot (3MOA) engraved on the objective lens.

U.S. Optics SN-12 BDC

Your choice of .223 or .308. Custom BDCs available.

U.S. Optics SN-12 pros

Unsurpassed quality, ruggedness, and available features (*e.g.*, reticles, diopters, BDCs, finishes, mounts, etc.).

The SN-12 is a lovely scope for either .223 or .308 combat rifle. Given its weight and optical quality, I put it on a .308.

U.S. Optics SN-12 cons

ØØØØ. Weight. I've heard persistently conflicting reports on their service (especially in regards to promptness).

Two inexpensive alternatives...
Buying cheap goods to save money is like stopping a clock to save time. (quoted from Brownells' *Gunsmith Kinks III*, p.418)
— Dave Wyer

O.K., I realize that not every AR15 owner can truly afford a Ø610 ACOG (much less a Ø1175 SN-12, the price of a pre-ban AR15!), even though they may really need optics.

Bushnell Turkey Scope (#71-1548)
This 1½-4½x-32mm scope retails for only Ø99. It has an AUG-type circle reticle (great for CQB) with internal crosshairs (for more precise aiming at distance). FoV/100yds is 46' (1.5x), eye relief is 3", exit pupil is 6.7mm. Length 11.7", weight 13.5oz. ¼MOA adjustments. Matte finish.

Overall quality is good, and the glass is surprisingly good, especially for the money. Given the .223's gentle recoil, this would make for an excellent low-cost scope for any budget AR.

Oh, is Ø99 still too much coin? Well, how about this:

Chinese copy of the Colt 3x20
This can be had for just Ø40 from Tasco (and many others; just scour the *Shotgun News*). It has an AR carry handle mount (see through), good optics, and an astonishingly accurate 100-500yd BDC (calibrated for 55gr, as the scope is a copy of Colt's optic for the 1:12" twist AR15A1).

I bought one on a dare for my AR15A2. Just last weekend I took it out for some long range work. Lasing a 500yd rock, I bumped up the BDC and took a shot. Bullseye! *Unzeroed,* and at 500yds! Gee. I think I'll leave it attached...

Who knows how much use/abuse the thing will take, but even if/when it fails, at least the rifle contains a 3x monocular. Lepers (from Tapco) also makes a 3-9x version for Ø75.

RED DOT OPTICS
Being a Thunder Ranch kinda dude who eschews battery-powered combat sights, it's taken me years to warm up to the idea of red dot optics. The Aimpoint Comp M2 XD, however, has given me great pause, however...

Aimpoint Comp M2 XD

This is actual U.S. Military Contract gear, and for good reason. Shock/drop/water/fogproof. 1x-36mm parallax-free objective lens. ¼MOA adjustments. 4MOA red dot has 6 daylight positions (1 extra bright) and 4 NVD positions. Battery life is 100-1000 average hours, and *10 years* on the lowest setting. (This was the most significant improvement over the earlier Comp M version.) NVD compatible. 30mm tube. 6.3oz.

From DSA for just Ø332 (#AIM-5040). (Note: The ML2 version has no NVD settings. Stick with the M2.)

TACTICAL RIFLE OPTICS

I haven't tested every tasty scope from Schmidt & Bender, Swarovski, Zeiss, U.S. Optics, Lightforce USA, etc. (There will not be a lemon from any of them, so you can relax.)

I do have, however, ample experience with Leupold's Mark 4 M1-16x and M3-10X scopes, and a bit with I.O.R.'s Tactical 2.5-10x-42mm. Either Leupold or I.O.R. can provide you with the quality optics you need for your precision rifle.

Shooting FMJ in a tactical rifle

Incidentally, I test fired the superb Malaysian 147gr FMJ in an M1A, HK91, Imbel FAL, and SAKO bolt-action, and the stuff was nearly as accurate as Federal Match! I'm talking within ½MOA difference (my buddies were amazed), although the FMJ threw a few more flyers than did the Fed 168gr. Although I don't recommend that you feed your tactical rifle MG ball ammo, it's good to discover beforehand how your rifle shoots it, just in case FMJ is all you have someday.

I.O.R. 2.5-10x-42mm Illuminated MP-8 reticle
www.valdada.com

This is dandy tactical scope, especially for the Ø699. Lenses by Schott Glasswerk of Germany (who also provide lenses for Schmidt & Bender).

I.O.R. 2.5-10x-42mm reticle

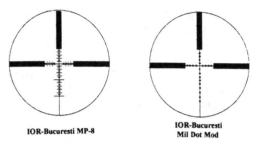

IOR-Bucuresti MP-8

IOR-Bucuresti
Mil Dot Mod

In this scope, you have choice of the V-Mark (similar to the M2's 1.7m/5'7" height stadia lines from 200-1000m), or the MP-8 (which has hash marks in ½mil gradients).

The MP-8 reticle is my preference. Very precise work can be done with it, and ½mils are easy to use. Spend Ø50 for the illuminated MP-8. It has 7-positions, and uses a common Ø3 CR2032 lithium battery.

I.O.R. 2.5-10x-42mm zeroing

½MOA adjustments. Magnum lock prevents shifting.

I.O.R. 2.5-10x-42mm pros

Fantastic optics, great ½mil-based illuminated reticle, rugged, and a great value at Ø699 (QP; #IOR-B-10x42-ILUM).

I.O.R. 2.5-10x-42mm cons

It has no BDC as does the Leupold Mk 4 M3. ½MOA adj.

Leupold Mark 4® M3-10x40mm

www.leupold.com

Developed in 1985 for the SEALs and used on the Army's M24 SWS, I've had one of these on my SAKO bolt-action .308 for years, and like it very much. With its 0.100" wall thickness (twice that of hunting scopes), it's one of the few scopes to withstand a .50BMG. Its Multicoat 4 is superb.

Leupold M3 BDC cams

Four pop-in cams are currently included:

.223	55gr	3200fps	100-500y
.308 Fed	168gr	2600fps	100-1000y
.30/06	180gr	2700fps	100-1000y
.300WM	190gr	2900fps	100-1200m

This makes for an extremely versatile scope which works for nearly any common tactical caliber/load. (My scope must be pretty old, as it also has a cam for .308 M118.)

Leupold M3 BDC

Range elevation is from 100-1000yds, with clicks being 1MOA-based. This is nearly identical to the M1 Garand sight:

		168/2600 .308 Fed **Leupold**	150/2750 .30/06 FMJ **M1 Garand**
100 →	200yds	2 clicks	2 clicks
200 →	300yds	3 clicks	3 clicks
300 →	400yds	3 clicks	4 clicks
400 →	500yds	4 clicks	4 clicks
500 →	600yds	5 clicks	4 clicks
600 →	700yds	5 clicks	5 clicks
700 →	800yds	6 clicks	6 clicks
800 →	900yds	6 clicks	6 clicks
900 →	1000yds	8 clicks	7 clicks
1000 →	1100yds		7 clicks
1100 →	1200yds		8 clicks

I personally would have preferred 25yd increments, but the 1MOA-based system works fine once you've learned it.

Leupold M3 reticle

Factory Mil-Dot.

Zeroing the Leupold M3

The focus knob is the left turret, which is perfect for right-handed shooters. Windage is ½MOA. Knobs can be reindexed to zero after sighting in.

Leupold M3 pros

A very high-quality scope from an excellent American manufacturer. Rugged (especially being fixed power), fine optics, easy to use. Fantastic service reputation.

Leupold M3 cons

FoV is very small. I don't care for the 1MOA elevataion adjustment, but that's just me. Also, the ½MOA clicks means 3" at 600yds, which gets a bit much for true precision work at long range. The Mil-Dot system requires some training.

Final word on the Leupold M3

This scope has been out since 1985, and it's now getting some real competition from the I.O.R. 2.5-10X-42mm Illuminated for Ø649 with MP-8 reticle (in ½mils).

Shepherd P2   www.shepherdscopes.com

One-shot zero, and confirmation of zero *without* having to shoot!

Shepherd P2 reticle and stadia lines

Crosshair with 18" (*i.e.*, torso width) ranging circles from 200-1000yds. (Hunting scopes have 24" circles, and .22 scopes have 9" circles for standing prairie dogs.) All scopes are ordered for caliber and bullet weight, and mine was 150gr/.308 (as I shoot more FMJ than 168gr MatchKings).

Vertical and horizontal stadia lines in 1MOA increments, which is highly usable in the field.

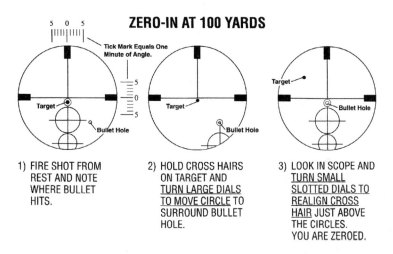

ZERO-IN AT 100 YARDS

1) FIRE SHOT FROM REST AND NOTE WHERE BULLET HITS.

2) HOLD CROSS HAIRS ON TARGET AND TURN LARGE DIALS TO MOVE CIRCLE TO SURROUND BULLET HOLE.

3) LOOK IN SCOPE AND TURN SMALL SLOTTED DIALS TO REALIGN CROSS HAIR JUST ABOVE THE CIRCLES. YOU ARE ZEROED.

Final word on the Shepherd P2

If your targets are consistently a specific diameter of 9", 18", or 24", then a Shepherd may be just the scope for you. It doesn't make for the best tactical scope, or the best battle rifle scope, or the best hunting scope—but the Shepherd is probably one of the best *all-around* scopes on the market. It will serve nearly any need quite well. A fine choice if you don't want a mechanical BDC or laser rangefinder, and am not keen on learning the Mil-Dot system.

Available only factory-direct in any caliber load you want.

Tactical rifle optics specs and features

	I.O.R.	Leupold M3	Shepherd
model #	2.5-10x	M3-10x	310-P2
body	6061-T6	6061-T6	an. alum.
glass	Schott	Leupold	Japan
diopter?	-4/+4	✔	✔
parallax?	✔	✔	✔
illuminated?	7-pos.	–	–
tritium?	unnec.	–	–
+NVD?	–	–	–
mount?	rings	rings	rings
tube	30mm	30mm	1"
reticle type	hash	Mil-Dot	cross/RF
stadia	½mil	–	18"/1MOA
wind. clicks	½MOA	½MOA	¼MOA
elev. clicks	½MOA	1MOA	¼MOA
reticle adj.	82MOA		
rangefinder	MOA	Mil-Dot	200-1000y
BDC cam?	–	100-1000y	unnecessary
BDC reticle?	–	–	18" circle
BDC gr	168	168	150 or 168
magn.	2.5-10x	10x	3-10x
obj. lens	42mm	40mm	40mm
exit mm	8mm	4mm	13mm (3x)
FoV/100y	34'	11'	42' (3x)
eye relief	3.5"	3.4"	3-3.5"
length	13.8"	13.1"	14"
weight alone	17oz	21oz	17oz
weight w/mnt.	21oz	25oz	21oz
retail	Ø699	Ø1130	Ø575
source	QP		Shepherd

RINGS & MOUNTS

First of all, do not be tempted by a pair of Ø10 Tasco aluminum rings! Pick the finest rings and mount you can find, not the finest you can "afford." I'd prefer an average scope in the finest mount over the finest scope in an average mount.

An average mount will fail you before an average scope.

Aluminum vs. steel

When in doubt, go with steel. Although aluminum *can* be very, very strong, only forged aircraft aluminum (*e.g.,* 7070-T6) is such (and is fine for aluminum AR15 receivers, etc.). I, however, prefer high-quality forged steel, such as 4140, 8620, etc.

Weaver vs. U.S. MIL-STD-1913 "Picatinny"

Very similar, but different. Weaver rings will fit in a Picatinny base, but Picatinny (which has thicker cross-bolts) will not normally fit in a Weaver base.

When there's a choice, go with the Picatinny (which is usually zero hold, and offers more sighting options, including *all* the military applications). Heavy duty tactical rings are almost always Picatinny.

Although Weaver rings will fit in a Picatinny base, free play is excessive (*i.e.,* 0.060"). Use Picatinny rings if you can.

Install HD "tactical" Picatinny rings and mount

Your rifle *will* fall over or be dropped at least once in its life. It *will* get banged up against a tree. Your rings and mount must be as strong as the rifle they're on, so pay a bit extra in money and weight and install tactical-grade stuff. (I've even seen scopes mounted with *three* pairs of steel rings.) Brownells has a great selection for any rifle.

Don't bother with the Ø99 cookie-dough soft aluminum M1A mount from Springfield Armory® (which will peen out in 500rds). While the U.S. Tactical Systems wire-EDM mount seems very well made, its heat-treat is sadly not up to snuff. **The *only* M1A/M14 scope mount to buy is the one from Smith Enterprise.** Yes, it's Ø200, but no other mount enjoys the double heat-treat "Mellanite" process with a surface hardness of Rc 60. Any other mount, including the very nice steel copies, will likely peen out their cam or screws after 1000rds.

For the Rem 700, Smith Enterprise makes a Picatinny tactical base machined from bar stock (8620, Rc 52-56), not to mention tactical rings (4140, Rc 35) with 12mm nuts. (Now *this* is what I'm talking about!) Retail price on the set? Ø310. Could you mount a scope on a Rem 700 for Ø50? Sure, but why would you *want* to? Spend the Ø310 *and you are done*!

U.S. Optics makes a very interesting system called the Mk.V. QD without tools, and absolutely ZH.

Granted, there are mounting systems between Ø50-310 which are perfectly satisfactory for most shooters, but I discuss an ultimate (and largely overkill) system to illustrate my point.

SCOPES & ACCESSORIES

misc. scopes		www.riflescopes.com
sunshade	killFlash	www.camouflage.com
	Lens Shade	www.lens-shade.com
polarizing filter	LSU	www.camouflage.com
lens caps	Butler Creek	
scope cover		www.scopecoat.com
Angle Cosine Indicator		www.snipertools.com

HOW TO MOUNT OPTICS

This is not Rocket Science, but there *is* a proper procedure to follow. Correctly done, it's a one-time affair.

Prepare the mount and rings
Thoroughly degrease the screw threads and ring walls
What remains lubricated *will* move over time, and this is sort of undesired in a scope mount. Simple Green works great for this without toxic fumes. Use Q-Tips for the screw holes.

Install the mount or base on the rifle
Will the serial number be obscured?
If so, then notate before installation. (I once bought a sporterized U.S. M1917 which was so affected.) You may wish to stamp or inscribe the serial number on a visible part of the receiver so that it could be quickly identified if stolen.

Lightly oil the mount's receiver footprint
Place a *very* light coat of oil on the receiver, but not enough oil to seep into the screw holes. (If the mount or base is also steel, do the same to its underside.) Place the mount or base on the rifle, and 242 Loctite (Blue) the screws per specs. (If you don't have Blue Loctite, you may substitute fingernail polish in a pinch. Do not, however, make a habit of this!)

Correct eye relief
Most scopes have an eye relief of at least 2". (Low magnification optics will have more.) You want the scope mounted to suit *your* natural cheekweld on *that* particular rifle. To accomplish this, there are two mechanical variances: scope within rings (a range of 1-2½"), and rings on mount (a range of 1-4"). Generally, if you place the rings midway between the lens bells and adjustment tower, you will still have enough range on the mount alone to achieve proper eye relief. Nevertheless, as you may need some scope-within-rings variance, keep the scope free in its rings for now.

Remove or sufficiently loosen the ring bases to freely move the scope/rings about the mount. Have a friend hold the scope/rings while you shoulder the rifle and assume a proper cheekweld for your iron sights. (If you shoot with eyeglasses or contact lenses, put them on beforehand.) Then have him place the scope/rings at the most rearward position on the mount, moving it forward one slot at a time until the image begins to darken at the circumference. Go back one slot. You're home.

This will give you maximum eye relief, which you want so as to avoid getting battered during recoil.

Ring-to-mount fit

Even in the Picatinny mounting system there will be at least 0.010" of longitudinal (*i.e.,* front and rear) play between the rings' cross-bolts and the mount rails. (In the Weaver system there will be a bit more.) Once you've determined the correct scope placement for proper eye relief, put the scope/rings in their appropriate slots.

Pay attention here: *before* you tighten the ring-base nuts, move the rings *forward* (*i.e.,* towards the muzzle) to take up the play. This sets the cross-bolts against the *rear* of the mount rails, which is where the scope would eventually move under recoil (as the rifle moves rearward). If, on the other hand, you had set the rings against the rear of the mount rails, that 0.010+" amount of play would be gradually shifted front to rear, likely changing the scope's POA (and thus the rifle's POI).

Loctite the ring-to-base nuts

Loosen only one nut at a time (the other remaining one stays tight to keep the whole rig firmly attached to the rifle), Blue Loctite, and torque to specs. (60 inch/pounds is about max for the most heavy duty of mounts. Lesser systems need less.)

Preparing the scope to be tightened in rings

Use a black marker to mark the rings' position on the scope, and then remove the scope from the rings (leaving the rings in the base or mount).

Wrap *one* layer of quality masking tape around the scope for each ring. This will not only prevent the scope shifting inside the rings, but will keep the scope body from becoming marred. (Another tip is to lightly coat the inside of the rings with Brownells with 600 grit carborundum flour.)

Leveling the scope inside the rings

O.K., you've got the base installed on the rifle, the proper eye relief achieved, the position of the scope in the rings, and the rings installed on the base. The last step is to tighten the rings without *any* canting of the scope. Only 6° of cant can add ½MOA of unwanted windage. That's 3" @ 600yds!

The only way to *perfectly* level a scope is to use a collimator. (Pick one from Brownells.) After leveling the scope, *partially* tighten the rings enough to firmly hold the scope.

The ScopLevel (800-200-7267) is a fine shooting aid:

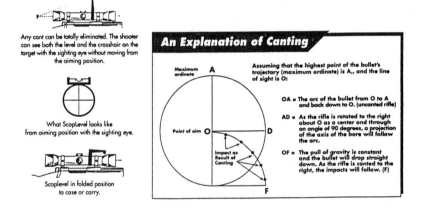

Any cant can be totally eliminated. The shooter can see both the level and the crosshair on the target with the sighting eye without moving from the aiming position.

What ScopLevel looks like from aiming position with the sighting eye.

Scoplevel in folded position to case or carry.

An Explanation of Canting

Assuming that the highest point of the bullet's trajectory (maximum ordinate) is A,, and the line of sight is O:

OA = The arc of the bullet from O to A and back down to O. (uncanted rifle)

AD = As the rifle is rotated to the right about O as a center and through an angle of 90 degrees, a projection of the axis of the bore will follow the arc.

OF = The pull of gravity is constant and the bullet will drop straight down. As the rifle is canted to the right, the impacts will follow. (F)

Maximum ordinate A

Point of aim O   D

Impact as Result of Canting

F

Fully tighten the rings on the scope

One ring screw at a time loosen, Blue Loctite, and retighten halfway. Once all have been done, tighten them the rest of the way in stages so that the split rings are evenly tightened over the scope body.

Note: The above assumes upper/lower split rings, not Weaver rings (these will turn the scope 2-5° during the final tightening, which is why I don't care for them).

Recheck the scope for reticle cant

If you did it right, then the scope *should* have remained level. If not, then loosen the rings and begin again.

Battle rifle optic specs and features

	TA01B	TA11E	Elcan	I.O.R. M2	Hensoldt	Shepherd
model #	TA01B	TA11E	7.62	M2 .308	G3	310-P2
body	7070-T6	7070-T6	an. alum.	6061-T6		anod. alum.
diopter?	—	—	—	-4/+4	—	✔
illuminated?	—	✔	—	✔-7 pos.	—	—
tritium?	✔	✔	✔	unnecessary	—	—
NVD?	—	—	✔	—	—	—
mount?	✔	✔	✔	rings	STANAG	rings
tube				30mm	30mm	1"
reticle type	cross	chevron	post	chevron/RF	post	cross
reticle MOA	—	5.53MOA	7.4MOA			
stadia	—	—	10mil	5'7"	5mil?	1MOA
click adj.	⅓MOA	¼MOA	0.86MOA	½MOA	0.86MOA	¼MOA
rangefinder	200-800m	200-800m	—	200-1000m	—	200-1000y
BDC cam?	—	—	200-800m	100-1000m	100-600m	—
BDC reticle?	200-800m	200-800m	—	1100-1300m	—	200-1000y
BDC gr.?	168	168	147	168	147	150 or 168
magn.	4x	3.5	3.4x	4x	4x	3-9x
obj. lens	32mm	35mm	28mm	24mm	24mm	40mm
exit mm	8mm	10mm	8.5mm	8mm	6mm	13mm (3x)
FoV/100y	37'	29'	42'	29'	29'	42" (3x)
eye relief	1.5"	2.4"	2.75"	3.15"	3"	3"
length	5.8"	8"	6.3"	8.75"	8.5"	14"
weight alone	9.9oz	14oz	—	12oz	10oz	17oz
weight w/mnt	13.9oz	18oz	22.5oz	16oz	14oz	21oz
retail	Ø610	Ø825	Ø700	Ø330	Ø375	Ø575
source	DSA	DSA	DSA	DSA	AIM	Shepherd

Battle carbine optic specs and features

	TA11	TA31F	Elcan	I.O.R. M2	CQ/T	SN-12
model #	TA11	TA31F	7.62	M2 .223	CQ/T	SN-12
body	7070-T6	7070-T6	an. alum.	6061-T6	an. alum.	7075-T6
diopter?	—	—	—	-4/+4	-2/+0.5	-3/+3.5
illuminated?	✔	✔	—	7 pos.	10 pos.	11 pos.
tritium?	✔	✔	✔	unnec.	unnec.	unnec.
+NVD?	—	—	✔	—	✔	✔
mount?	✔	✔	✔	rings	✔	✔
tube				30mm	30mm	35mm
reticle	donut	chevron	post	cross dot	circle dot	circle dot
reticle MOA	2/4MOA	5.53MOA	7MOA		3/9MOA	3MOA dot
stadia	19" wide	19" wide	10mils	5'7" tall	—	—
wind. clicks	¼MOA	⅓MOA	0.84MOA	½MOA	½MOA	custom
elev. clicks	¼MOA	⅓MOA	0.84MOA	100m	½MOA	custom
rangefinder	300-800m	300-800m	—	2,4,6,800m	—	—
BDC cam	—	—	200-800m	100-800m	—	.223/.308
BDC reticle?	300-800m	300-800m	—	—	—	—
BDC gr.?	55	55	55	62	62	62/168
magn.	3.5x	4x	3.4x	4x	1-3x	3.5x
obj. lens	35mm	32mm	28mm	24mm	14mm	24mm
exit mm	10mm	8mm	8.5mm	8mm	4mm	6.8mm
FoV/100y	29'	37'	42'	29'	84'/117'	42'
eye relief	2.4"	1.5"	2.75"	3.15"	2"/2.8"	4"
length	8"	5.8"	6.3"	8.75"	8.8"	7.5oz
weight	14oz	9.9oz	—	12oz	17.5oz	
weight w/mnt	18oz	13.9oz	22.5oz	16oz	21.5oz	26oz
retail	Ø750	Ø750	Ø700	Ø330	Ø850	Ø1175
source	DSA	DSA	DSA	DSA	QP	U.S. Optics

❖ 19

HOW TO BECOME
A RIFLEMAN

If you cannot, without fail, hit a dinner plate at 100yds with one shot, under field conditions, within 5 seconds—you're not yet a Rifleman. And until then, no oppressor will ever take you seriously.
— Boston T. Party, Rifleman

It is a fine thing to have ironed out one's philosophy and politics with the reading of Bastiat, Jefferson, Rand, Rothbard, and Hazlitt. Such is the proper intellectual basis for Americans. However, intellect is not action, and action is what wins freedom. Those who profess to love liberty must understand that such has usually been won only through the use of force. Force, albeit, in a self-defensive manner, but force nonetheless.

Reading *Atlas Shrugged* is a fine place to begin, but a sorry place to end. Do you really believe that we will turn a sufficient number of Americans into Libertarians or Objectivists?

"Maybe so, but I'd love to hear your backup plan!"

Writing your congresscritter may be worthwhile, but do you really believe that such will result in the repeal of the *National Firearms Act*, the *Gun Control Act*, the *Bank Secrecy Act*, and the *USA Patriot Act*?

"Maybe so, but I'd love to hear your backup plan!"

On the morning of 19 April 1775, the Minutemen of Concord did not stand around quoting Locke to the Redcoats. They did not exclaim to the British, *"No initiation of force!"* No, they *shot* them—well and often—all 24 miles back to Boston.

did not work. What *did* work? Their backup plan—the rifle. One schoolteacher, upon hearing of the 19 April fighting, calmly told his students, *"Deponite libros."* (*"Put down your books."*)

There's the soap box, the ballot box, the jury box, and the cartridge box—in that order. It's a progression, you see. Few Libertarians and Objectivists actually *have* a cartridge box. They have no backup plan if intellectual and political efforts are ever proven to have been for naught.

And they apparently don't like me harping on this. A large Randian bookseller passed on both *Hologram of Liberty* (which proved the likely ineffectiveness of political action) and *Boston on Guns & Courage.* And even when readers from as far away as Switzerland urged them to carry *Boston's Gun Bible*, they still refused (saying that they don't sell "how-to" books).

Folks, the 2015 USSA will let you read *The Fountainhead* all the way to the camps. **Mere intellect is *not* a threat.** However, intellect fused with arms, skill, and courage *is* a threat. We must face the unpleasant fact that a 2nd American Revolution is at least a distinct possibility. Thus, we must begin to prepare for that possibility—if only to render it unnecessary.

We don't need to read 900 pages of *On Socialism* by von Mises to understand that our rights are being destroyed. We don't need to read 1087 pages of *Atlas Shrugged* to comprehend that freedom is vanishing. What we need is the simple ferocity of any dog protecting its food bowl. It is inelegant, but is it ever effective! Americans have no ferocity, no teeth—and this former Rottweiler of a people is getting its food bowl picked clean by poodles and sparrows. Disgusting.

Massachusetts—the birthplace of Liberty—and you can't own a gun. You're forbidden to even carry a muzzleloader on Lexington Green to reenact 19 April 1775. Disgusting.

Oh, am I ranting again? You're damn right I am! We have sunk to such a putrid state of affairs all because Americans *who knew better* just didn't have the courage to hold onto their freedom. Libertarian Americans know best of all, and for them not to be armed and trained is...disgusting.

Oh, now I'm *really* ranting? Overstretching the hyperbole? Exaggerating the situation? Painting too grim a picture with too broad a brush? Well now, let's see. Here are a few current laws of the land, just in case you forgot (or became numb):

A national database of employed people.
"Health care crimes" with seizure of assets from doctor and patient.
The largest gun confiscation in American history.
An unconstitutional *ex post facto* law triggered by a misdemeanor.
Guns banned in ill-defined schoolzones, enforced by roadblocks.
Executive branch labeling various groups as "terrorist" without appeal.
A law authorizing secret trials with secret evidence for certain people.
A law requiring that your SSN be used on your driver's license.
A law requiring that your driver's license be encoded with your prints.
A national database to contain every detail from your doctor's office.

Apparently they dismantled the former East Germany and are reconstructing it over here. Still *believe* that we live in a "free country"? We are poised to become one of the most totalitarian nations ever to have existed. Why? **Because Americans will evidently put up with *anything*.**

Demand that you get a license before marrying? *Sure.*

Be forced to pay for the State indoctrination of your children in a dangerous and toxic government "school"? *Sure.*

Submit to random and intrusive roadblocks by thug cops (*"law enforcement officers"*) dressed like Rambo? *Sure.*

Allow a third to half of your wages to be extracted before you ever see your paycheck? *Sure.*

Endure for 8 years a morally-autistic President obviously guilty of perjury, obstruction of justice, subornation of perjury, and a dozen other crimes—just because the *economy* is strong? *Sure.*

Ordered to lock up your guns, even if it means that a parole-violating, pitchfork-wielding maniac kills two of your five children while a third runs next door to fetch an armed neighbor? *Sure.* (Merced, California on 23 August 2000.)

Prohibit commercial airline pilots from being armed to protect their planes and passengers from terrorists? *Sure.*

Hassle retired Marine General Joe Foss at airport security because his Medal of Honor might be used a weapon? *Sure.*

Still *believe* we live in a "free country"? Americans don't want to be free, they want to feel "safe." They want an eternal governmental parent so that they can remain eternal children.

There's just one problem. Some Americans are *adults* and will fight to enjoy their own adult lives as they see fit. It's called *freedom*, and some Americans still cherish it. Many of them know that the only thing which has ever *ultimately* preserved freedom is the rifle, and they are not going to give theirs up.

Rifles are *"liberty's teeth"* and the badge of the Freeman. If you don't own one—you are not fully committed to Liberty.

The unarmed man is not just defenseless, he is also contemptible.
— Machiavelli

Democrats are not the problem. Republicans and Libertarians are the problem. Republicans without the intellectual stamina to become Libertarians, and Libertarians without the physical courage to become Riflemen.

If you *do* own a rifle, but spend more time in your TV chair than at the gun range—you are not fully committed to Liberty. *Fully* committed to Liberty means knowing what it historically takes to win it. It means having that backup plan of last resort: the cartridge box and the will to effectively empty it.

And if you can't legally own a battle rifle in Occupied Territory (*e.g.,* L.A., N.Y.C.), then why on earth are you still *there*? Why live in *any* city or state which allows only declawed subjects? Why voluntarily live in such a prison? Read Chapter 34, pick a gunowners' state, and move there!

If you don't, well that's *your* choice. Just don't write me from Taxachusetts or Neu Jersey complaining about how bad things are there. Don't preach to me from Manhattan that my writings are suited for toothless trailer-park militiamen, when you have the stench of a coward.

My backup plan is my M14. Your backup plan can never be anything but endless, putrescent submission. I will die a single death, peaceful or valiant. You will die a dozen times each day, feeling every one. But, that was *your* choice, wuss.

WHY WE *ALL* MUST BE RIFLEMEN

...The average infantry soldier...has not been impressed sufficiently with his own potency and the effect of well-aimed, properly distributed...rifle fire.
— U.S. First Army Report, *"Tactical Lessons in Normandy"*

A Rifleman is a man *skilled* with his rifle. A soldier with a rifle is not *ipso facto* a Rifleman. (Remember Corporal Upham in *Saving Private Ryan?*) An army has only two kinds of troops: Riflemen and Cooks. *I.e.,* those who deliver accurate rifle fire (the point of the spear)—and everybody else (the spear's shaft).

Guess what? In the likely coming struggle (*i.e.,* AmRev2), we must *all* be Riflemen.

We have delegated—no, *relegated*—our eternal vigilance to others, and it has not worked. It has *never* worked in history. As the saying goes, *"If you want a job done right, do it yourself."* If *you* want to remain free, then *you* must be eternally vigilant. There is no effective surrogation. All it's done has been to wear out such fine men as Larry Pratt of GOA and Aaron Zelman of JPFO who are pulling *your* weight!

Liberty is not a cruise ship full of pampered passengers. **Liberty is a *man-of-war*, and we are all *crew*.**

You don't get to be a Cook in AmRev2. You don't get to throw Ø35 a year to the RKBA group of your choice and call it even. You don't get to stay in the car while others push. Stop being a Cook, and become a Rifleman. Get out of the kitchen and get to the gun range!

> *...anyone can be a rifleman. It really is a universal skill. And if you can be a rifleman, in the battle for freedom, you should be a rifleman. You have the time, and there is no excuse.*
>
> *No one has ever killed an enemy soldier with any of the following: a golf ball, a basketball, a baseball, a football, a hockey puck, a tennis ball, a soccer ball, a race car, a fishing pole. This has always been the task of a well-trained marksman.*
>
> — *Fred's Guide to Becoming a Rifleman*

Get a copy of *Fred's Guide to Becoming a Rifleman*

Ø16   800-979-2144   www.fredsm14stocks.com

A marvelous compendium, chock-filled with invaluable info and tips. Geared toward iron-sighted battle rifles in general, and the M14/M1A in particular, but highly useful for everybody regardless of his/her rifle. Fully explains natural point of aim (NPOA), sight picture, breathing, trigger work, and follow-through. Discusses practice drills, riflemen skills, equipment, political defense, tactics, and much more.

Includes several different copy-ready 25m targets (*e.g.,* the Riverside Gun Club 200/300yd Speed Shoot), as well as some buff AQT targets (I'll explain these shortly). Order today!

Build your Rifleman's library

Begin with this Army Field Manual, which is downloadable:

FM-7, Infantry Rifle Platoon & Squad
http://155.217.58.58/cgi-bin/atdl.dll/fm/7-8/toc.htm

Other fine titles (and videos) would include:

The Art of the Rifle, Jeff Cooper (Paladin Press)
The Military and Police Sniper, Mike Lau (Paladin Press)
The Ultimate Sniper, Maj. John Plaster (Paladin Press)
The Tactical Rifle, Gabriel Suarez (Paladin Press)
Camouflage and Concealment, David Scott-Donelan (Paladin)
Invisible Resistance to Tyranny, Jefferson Mack (Paladin)
books by Peter R. Senich (Paladin Press)
A Rifleman Went To War, McBride (Lancer Militaria)
The Great Anglo-Boer War, Byron Farwell
Shots Fired In Anger, John George
The Last Parallel, Martin Russ
novels by Stephen Hunter

Buy a real rifle

If all can truly afford (for now) is an SKS, well, O.K. Learn the basics and it will see you through out to 250m until you buy your M14 or FAL. But start saving money for a *real* MBR. Don't rest with merely a carbine, as an SKS or AK or AR15 cannot do a rifle's job (instantly incapacitate past 200m, or perforate battlefield cover). Remember, we will not have air and artillery support, and we must engage the enemy *beyond* the range of their 250m carbines. Only a .308 battle rifle will do.

At the rifle range

Learn to zero your rifle   (see Chapter 29)

The most important item of equipment that a rifleman can have in his possession in combat is a well-zeroed rifle.
— Unit Marksmanship Training Program of Instruction
Hot to Do It Guide, USAMU (1979), p.37

Your rifle is not zeroed until it is zeroed. Don't assume that POI equals POA, *find out at the range!* (As a bonus, you'll also discover if it functions reliably.) I can't think of any higher priority than to immediately zero a newly purchased defensive firearm.

The basics of zeroing are constant, although every gun is somewhat unique. Learn to zero your rifle! Then, learn to zero any *other* rifle you may have to fight with.

Use proper training targets

Shooting at bullseye targets from a bench just won't cut it. You need to practice from field positions on field targets, such as the Army Qualification Test (AQT) for a possible 250 points, or the NRA Highpower Rifle Course for a possible 500 points.

A good shooter the first time will shoot around 375 to 410 on the 500-point Highpower Rifle Course. On the 25m AQT, he will shoot 185 to 200 points maximum. Both courses require 10 rounds slow-fire standing, 10 shots in about a minute in a sitting and a prone stage, starting from standing, and with a mandatory mag change (it's easier than you think—but challenging), and a prone slow-fire of 20 rounds.

— *Fred's Guide to Becoming A Rifleman,* p.4

You make Rifleman by scoring at least 80% on these courses. Any score less and you're still a Cook, sorry. Keep at it! Fred's has these targets, as well as other innovative and fun targets in his *Guide*. Save the masters and copy off hundreds.

At the end of this chapter I've included reduced-size masters of the AQT. Enlarge pages 19 and 20 by 200%, and keep as your copy masters. (Copy an extra Stage 3 target to use for the slow-fire Stage 4.) Place the enlarged copies at 25m.

Most work can be done at 25yds

200, 300, 400, and 500yd targets can be simulated at just 25yds. Remember, it's an MOA thing: 1" at 25yds equals 4" at 100, 8" at 200, 12" at 300, 16" at 400, and 20" (the width of a military silhouette) at 500yds.

If your rifle's sight is graduated in meters, then simply train at 25m (25m is 27yds, or 82') to be on at 200m, 300m, etc.

If you can, with an iron-sighted rack-grade rifle firing surplus FMJ, hit 4 out of 5 shots a large postage stamp at 25yds, you'll be able to hit your Bad Guy out to 500. *That* is a Rifleman!

Once you've learned the basics at 25yds, go long range

The 25y/25m range can teach you everything but estimating range, practicing your rear sight come-ups, and doping the wind (that eternal devil, as Fred puts it). Have some steel targets (20" wide) made up and place at unknown ranges.

Know your M1/M14/M1A rear sight

M1s will be graduated in yards (up to 1200). Most M1As will be graduated in meters (up to 1100), although some will have an M1 yardage elevation knob (make sure that your team has the *same*, meters or yards). Meters are 9.4% farther than yards, not that it really makes any difference out to MBR 500yd range—especially when estimation of range can easily be off by that amount.

All M1/M14/M1A rear sights have 1MOA clicks, except for the NM versions which have ½MOA windage clicks (and an aperture hood which adjusts for ½MOA between the 1MOA elevation clicks).

from	to	NATO ball	168gr Match
100	200	3 MOA	2 MOA
200	300	3	2.5
300	400	4	3
400	500	4	3.5
500	600	5	4
600	700	5	4.5
700	800	6	5
800	900	8	5.5
900	1000	8	6

In the field
Target detection is the most difficult task

There must be training in difficult observation, which is needed for the offense. ...[O]nly 5% of the men can really see while observing.
— Col. Merrit A. Edson, C.O. 5th Marines
Medal of Honor winner

Teach the young fellows to look over the ground and look in the trees and to learn where the enemy probably will be.
— Master Gunnery Sgt. 1st Marine Div., Guadacanal 1942

Americans no longer typically have field and woods experience, as hunting and rural life peaked in 1920. It is no coincidence that Medal of Honor winner Sgt. Alvin York of WWI was a very accomplished hunter and superb Rifleman. (He was quite bowled over by his issue .30/06 M1917, which was a real upgrade from his squirrel gun.)

Your job as a rifleman involves target detection, range estimation, and firing an accurate shot—in that order of difficulty.
If you can't see [the target], you as a rifleman can still hit it (more on this later), but if you don't detect it, if you can't spot it, you'll never fire the shot at all.
— *Fred's Guide to Becoming a Rifleman*, p.9

Basically, you quickly sweep in successive pie slices from close to long range. Then, you repeat this process slowly with optics if you have them.

Rangefinding is the second most difficult task

A 275yd BSZ (this is very similar to MPBR) in an M14 means +3"/100, +5"/200, 0"/275, -3"/300, and -14"/400yds. Your first question upon seeing a Bad Guy should be, *"Is he within or beyond my battlesight zero?"*

As explained in the *Combat Rifle Optics* chapter, an 8MOA M1/M14 front sight equals 20" at 250yds. If your Bad Guy is no thinner than the sight post, then use your BSZ with a center hold and drop him. This will work out to 300yds.

Although battle rifle BSZ is 275yds, we Riflemen must often shoot much farther than that to keep the carbine-armed troops at distance. 400-500yd shots will be typical. When the Bad Guy is thinner than your front sight post, then you must range him (with a rangefinder, Mil-Dots, MOA scale, known range, etc.). Your front sight is actually a rangefinder!

For example, if he is exactly ¾ the width of your 8MOA front sight, then he is exactly 333yds away. (Remember, 20" x 100/6MOA size = 333yds.) Here is a chart to help you:

full width	250yds	BSZ (200 + 2 clicks)
¾ width	333yds	300 + 1 click
⅔ width	375yds	300 + 3 clicks
½ width	500yds	500
⅓ width	750yds	700 + 3 clicks
¼ width	1000yds	1000

Since this is obviously imprecise past 500yds, you should use co-ordinated fire from your teammates on such long-distance targets. Let's say you've spotted a Bad Guy who is ⅓ the width of your front sight, so you estimate his range at 750yds. Go up 3 clicks from "7". (On an M14 there are 6 clicks between 700 and 800.) Your two teammates should shoot 3 minutes high and low, meaning one should set his sight on 700 and the other at 800. Thus, you'll be putting ranged fire into him at 700, 750, and 800yds—and one of you are likely to hit him as your team is putting rounds out in three levels about 22½" apart (3MOA x 7.5), which covers a height of nearly 4' (22.5" x 2 = 45").

If, however, the entire team had set their sights at 750 and the actual range was only 700, then all shots would have gone 22.5" high, and just over his head.

If one of you has a laser rangefinder, then simply have the team set their sights on that calculation and fire.

Slant angle   (always compensate by aiming *low*)

Remember to compensate for any target angle declination. If shooting uphill or downhill (it doesn't matter which), the horizontal (*i.e.,* gravitational) distance is *less* than the air distance, and it is gravity which is pulling your bullet down.

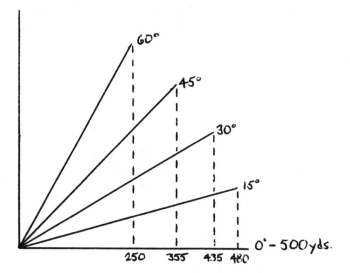

degrees	divide	multiply	subtract
10°	/1.02	x0.98	-2%
15°	/1.04	x0.96	-4%
20°	/1.06	x0.94	-6%
25°	/1.10	x0.91	-9%
30°	/1.15	x0.87	-13%
35°	/1.22	x0.82	-18%
40°	/1.31	x0.76	-24%
45°	/1.41	x0.71	-29%
50°	/1.56	x0.64	-36%
55°	/1.74	x0.57	-43%
60°	/2.00	x0.50	-50%

The effect is *not* linear. A 30° shot is not 2x the horizontal distance of a 60° shot, it is 1.74x the distance. I would photocopy and laminate this table, and tape it to your buttstock.

I have listed three different ways to calculate horizontal distance. Let's say you've spotted a 500yd target at an estimated 30°. Simply multiply 500yds by 0.87, or subtract 13% (whichever is easier for you), to get 435yds. Now set your scope or sight on 450yds and get your hit.

If you had mistakenly left your BDC on 500yds, you'd have been *11"* too high with a 168gr Federal Match BTHP.

In the field without a pocket calculator, subtracting % is probably the easiest. Or, you can round off the multiplication figures (*e.g.*, 30°'s 0.87 rounded up to 0.9, a discrepancy of just 15yds from a 500yd air distance, which is probably not enough to miss a Bad Guy).

Be forewarned, however, that the steeper the angle and/or the longer the shot, the more precise your math must be. I'd take a calculator (either pocket, or Casio watch) in the field.

How to calculate the slope? This is not easy to do by mere visual estimation. Remember in 2002 that I thought somebody should make scope-attached device for this? Now they have! Go to www.snipertools.com for their **Angle Cosine Indicator**. It's very well-made, easy to install, and simple to use. A must!

Why the 500yd range limit for Riflemen?

Shooting surplus FMJ through rack-grade M1, M1As, FALs, and HK91s, we can expect an average field accuracy of just 4MOA. Out to 500yds, we will group 20", which is as small or smaller than our Bad Guy. Past that, our groups begin to cone out larger than our target, and only luck or multiple shots will hit him. (At 1000yds, the group is 40"!)

Thus, beyond 500 the Rifleman's world is over, and the countersniper's world begins.

One rifle can nearly do it *all*

A very accurate M1A or FAL using 168gr Federal Match can easily group 2MOA, and thus with optics be quite deadly out to 800-900yds (which is firmly in countersniper territory). Thus, a man with just *one* rifle can effectively control all that he can see. A semi-auto .308 battle rifle can approach bolt-gun accuracy, but a bolt-gun with its 5rd mag can never approach the cyclic rate of a semi-auto.

Therefore, I'd probably choose a very accurate M1A or FAL in order to (generally) eliminate the need for a .308 bolt-gun, saving that Ø for a .338LM or .408CheyTac. Then, if I still had some rifle Ø left over, I'd consider a .308 bolt-gun.

Train regularly and often
The most deadly weapon on any battefield is the single well-aimed shot.
— Cpt. Jim Land, USMC, Sniper School Instructor
Vietnam 1966

Riflery is a martial art skill, and you must first grind that particular length of blade into an edge. You'll need a good instructor to get you properly started, and from there you can hone that edge into razor sharpness.

Teach others, and create new Riflemen
We have not been increasing our numbers as we need to. Culturally, battle riflery has been on the decline since Oklahoma City (a despicable act which unfairly tar-babied itself onto the militias). Handgun usage, however, is up after 9/11.

You must bring in at least 3 new Riflemen to the fold in the next 12 months. Take your prospects to the range, lend them your gear, devise some fun drills, and help them acquire their own rifle and ammo.

Train as a 3-man *team*
Experience has shown that in the absence of team training the fire of a group of riflemen in battle is poorly controlled and is haphazardly directed. **This fact remains true even where every individual in the group is an expert shot...**
— U.S. Army training manual, 1942

If I had to train my regiment over again, I would stress small group training and the training of the individual even more than we did...
— Col. Merrit A. Edson, C.O. 5th Marines
Medal of Honor winner

Three coordinated and efficient Riflemen (using .308 MBRs) are more effective than a full squad of enemy soldiers.

In March 1967, Marine Sgt. Carlos Hathcock (.30/06 Win 70 with 8x Unertl scope) and his spotter L.Cpl. Burke (iron-sighted M14) engaged an entire *company* of NVA at 500-800yds, and pinned them down for five days (with nighttime artillery illumination). They killed about *two-thirds* of the 150 enemy (who could never advance within range of their AK47s).

To train, set up three 1" square targets at 25m, give the team 10rds apiece, and require 8 hits/target in 30 seconds. That sort of thing. Fred's *Guide* has many other examples.

First Rule: Take No Unnecessary Risks
Remain undetected until your bullets hit the target.

Your mission is to harass, delay, and cause maximum casualties to the other side. If you are good enough, you can get several hits before the other side has time to react, thereby catching multiple targets unaware and undetected.

Once your position is revealed you will immediately relocate to another position 50 or 100 yards away,...

Now's when you <u>don't push your luck</u>. Better to get out and fall back to the next good position and wait for them to saddle up and come down the road again. Eventually they will put out scouts to walk ahead, and these will be "gimme" targets, until you've got them so demoralized they 1) stop for the night, 2) button up and ram their way down the road, or 3) call in fire support. By this time, you should be bugging out, satisfied with a job well done, not pushing your luck—there'll be other days...

Depending on the persistent stupidity, or the quickness of the other side, you will have fired as few as half-dozen rounds or as many as 25-40 rounds.

—*Fred's Guide to Becoming A Rifleman,* p.17

Get in physical shape!
Don't whine about your lack of freedom, when you have voluntarily reduced your *own* freedom of action with your beer gut, cigarette smoking, TV-dinner diet, and no exercise. Whenever I see some fat, wheezing toad I think to myself, *"Now <u>there</u> is somebody can't control his own body. How valuable can <u>his</u> <u>opinions</u> possibly be?"*

PT is not actually fun, but it *is* necessary. Whatever exercise regimen you choose, do it daily without fail, and begin to increase it once it becomes easy. We don't have to get into triathalonic shape, but you should be able to fast walk 2 miles with your rifle and gear. Anything less puts an irresponsible burden on your fellows.

FINAL THOUGHTS

The Rifleman concept is spreading!
I think that many folks are realizing the futility of further endless study of philosophy and politics. All of the good, basic groundwork has long since been done. Anything more at this point (when such is *years* away from being instituted), is mere intellectual masturbation. Thought is just a means to the end of

Action. We do not need another book on governmental inter-
vention in _____ (you fill in the blank). What we desperately need are people ready to challenge existing tyranny.
    We need to see some ferocity and resolve! One financial
and geopolitical newsletter author well understands this:

> *Warning: I may be one of the most militaristic writers you have en-*
> *countered. I want to see a world in which every adult holds copies*
> *of the Declaration of Independence and Bill of Rights in one hand,*
> ***and a rifle in the other.** I am sure that when this condition is*
> *achieved, 99% of all political and economic problems will go away.*
>
> —Richard Maybury, *Early Warning Report*, March 2002
>   800-509-5400

Notice that my friend Rick adroitly covered *both* bases: the
metaphysical and the physical. Well-thinking people with the
rifle means to resist organized tyranny. That says it *all!*

Become implacable foes of government supremacists!

    The days for polite argument are over. We need to be get-
ting in the faces of these government supremacists who blithely
demand our surrender. We need to become their implacable
foes. "Implacable" means not able to be *placated*.
    My friend Bob Glass (the owner of the former Paladin
Arms in Longmont, Colorado—one of the best gunstores I've
ever seen—and publisher of *The Partisan*) began the first
Tyranny Response Team. Whenever some gunphobe pol was
scheduled to speak, they would show up and loudly ask all those
embarrassing questions no pol wants to hear. With truth and
verve, the TRT would turn these socialist propaganda events
inside-out. And boy did the liberals ever howl about it later!
    When you see Charles Schumer on the plane, get in his
face about his deplorable stand on civil rights (*i.e.,* the 2nd
Amendment). Sarah Brady, McCain, Lieberman—get in their
faces and let them publicly know their statist politics are making implacable foes out of real people!
    When their sheeple minions blather their government
supremacist views in public, call them down. Recently, I was
enjoying a quiet restaurant dinner when two couples at the next
table began loudly lamenting what a rube our President George
W. Bush, Jr. is. *"Why, he can't even speak correctly! It's embar-*
rassing!" I put down my fork, turned to them, and icily replied,
"What I am embarrassed about is the 8-year regime of the Clin-
tonistas." I then proceeded to describe the moral desert of a
man who bombed a pharmaceutical factory in Sudan with

cruise missiles, just to divert public attention from Monica Lewinsky's testimony that same day. They responded (predictably) that *"what Clinton did with his genitals was his business"* (curious how Newt Gingrich was not allowed that tired, old excuse during the Dems hypocritical uproar over his affair). To make a long harangue short, I told them that Klinton was the Left's "Nixon"—and that at least we owned up to ours. I succeeded in making one couple *"uncomfortable"* enough to leave, and the remaining couple actually praised me for *"standing up"* for my views. *"It's nice to see that somebody is thinking!"* he complimented. Moral: Challenge these fools in public, let them meet the enemies they've created, and you'll run 'em off!

Why should we remain polite and docile to those who have ruined the American Dream with their institutionalized envy? They have *foes*, and we need to start *acting* like foes.

Get in their faces! Here's a letter from *Fred's* column in the *Shotgun News*. This is what needs to be said and heard:

> *I didn't used to be so blunt. For many years I have argued history, law, facts and logic with liberal gun-grabbers of my own country. I have come to conclusion that such arguments are useless exercises. In the end it always boils down to a conversation I once had with a child psychiatrist just before a "gun violence seminar."*
>
> *The psychiatrist announced boldly (he thought): "Well, I think ALL guns should be banned."*
>
> *"Really? I responded, "Do YOU have a gun?"*
>
> *"WWWWWWWWWell, NO!" he stammered, seeming as shocked as a lesbian would be if asked about male anatomy or Dracula if asked to hold a crucifix.*
>
> ***"Well, then," I smiled, "How do you propose to get mine then?" I asked.***
>
> *That one puzzled him, but only for a second: "Why, we'll pass a law and you'll have to turn them into the government."*
>
> *"Wrong, sport," I replied, "let me tell you how this works:* ***If you want my gun you're gonna have to kill me to get it. You're gonna have to kill my son. You're gonna have to kill my brother. You're gonna have to kill all my friends.*** *And if even 10% of American gun owners feel the way I do, you're gonna have to kill upwards of eight and half million people, and that doesn't count all the godless gungrabbers like you that we'll kill in righteous self-defense before we meet our Maker, and we intend to make that more than a one-to-one ratio, so you've got to ask yourself: 'Is it worth it?'"*
>
> *The psychiatrist, somewhat nonplussed by my vehemence, started backing up about half way through his oration and responded by stammering; "WWWWWWWhy you're paranoid!"*

I smiled and said softly, "Well, let's accept the expertness of that snap judgment, you being a psychiatrist and all. Let's say I'm paranoid," I offered. "Let's say I'm crazy." I winked at him. "I'm still armed to the teeth, that just complicates your problem, doesn't it?"

He turned to flee, but I hooked him with one last question: "Can you just do me one favor, sport?"

He turned, listening.

"Just do me this favor: you want my guns, YOU come get them. Have the courage of your convictions and YOU come get them. Don't send somebody else's son or daughter in federal service to come get them. YOU come get them. *And hey, I may even let you have 'em after I unload 'em."*

The psychiatrist, like me, was on the seminar panel, and he waited in the back of the room until I took a seat, and then found the chair as far away from me as could get.

— M.V., Alabama

Let these people hear that they are *bullies* for choosing violence to enact their statist views, and *cowards* for sending thugs in their place. **Make it personal, because it *is* personal.** Get the sweat beading out on their evil, pinched faces. Get their whiny voices quavering. Get their rat paws shaking in nervousness. Let them know that there are unpleasant *consequences* to their beliefs and actions. Make them *pay* for who they *are*.

So far, they aren't paying for it, and that's the problem. They are making *us* pay for our beliefs, aren't they? As Fred wrote, *"The best person to protect freedom is the guy in danger of losing his."* Begin standing up for your freedom. Quit rolling over for these fuzzy fascists, and start getting in their faces.

Here's a really radical idea...

Instead of sending strong letters to the gunphobe pols, why not send copies of your best targets? Photocopy and include the following note, and send anonymously:

"After 9/11, I have been going to my local gun range to practice with my semi-auto, full-capacity magazine handgun and military pattern rifle. You can count on me and my friends to defend America against all enemies, foreign and domestic. Please continue to support our Bill of Rights. Together we can stay free and proud! Sincerely, an armed American."

That should warm their little hearts, eh? Oh, and don't get me wrong, this isn't meant to be threatening in any way. You're simply demonstrating your skill and commitment to defending American liberties, and what politician could ever have a problem with that? **Homeland Security is a nation of *Riflemen*.**

"Oh, there's no point! We'd be fighting modern armies!"
Somebody call the *Waah*mbulance! You're forgetting one
crucial thing. Modern armies have no Riflemen! Today's troops
cannot shoot. Not even our troops can shoot.

*One of our weakest points...our deplorable marksmanship...poor fire
discipline, failure to zero weapons periodically and insufficient time
on ranges...*
— Cpt. Michael Ekman, Company Commander,
173rd Airborne Brigade, Vietnam, 1967

*Good soldiers shoot well. For many reasons (none good enough)
standards and knowledge of shooting in the Army have been declining for many years.* [BTP Note: Since WWI, actually.] *I want you to
join with me in a "crusade" to reinstate the traditional excellence of
the American soldier with his hand held weapon.*
— Commander, Army Marksmanship Training Unit, 1979

Where did this *"traditional excellence"* come from? From the
American's private possession of and training with his rifle. An
unintended consequence of *"gun control"* is that its enforcers
(who are drawn from the non-gunowning populace at large)
cannot shoot. The Europeans are the prime example of this,
and we are merrily following down their path.

Case in point: I personally know of an active-duty SEAL
who never even shot rabbits as a boy, and had a hard time doing
so recently with his issue M4A1 carbine. Not even our highly
trained operators are generally Riflemen (although there are
certainly a few exceptions).

Marines are supposed to be Riflemen first and foremost,
but their SOPMOD M4A1 does not have a back-up rear sight. If
their CompM2 or ACOG goes Tango Uniform, troops must dig
through their ruck for the carry handle during a firefight.

Our military is actually contemplating an over/under
.223/20mm long gun which fires "smart rounds" out to 1000yds.
Puhleeeeze. Gee, anything to avoid real rifle training, apparently. (At least the Marines have begged off on this stupid idea.)

Hmmmm. Perhaps the military's obsession with "smart"
weapons is a sly way of *purposely not giving the citizen soldier
any valuable rifle training* (which otherwise could be used in a
revolution). Thus, Joe Corporal is deadly only when in uniform
serving the Government, and harmless as Joe Salesman once
his enlistment is up. The "smarter" the gun, the less trained he
is as a future guerrilla. (I have a sneaking suspicion that some
Pentagon wonk figured this out in the 1980s.)

What the government supremacists do not realize...

We gunowners have a *culture*. Our terminology has even been embraced by the mother culture: *"Lock, stock, and barrel"*, *"bulls-eye"*, *"Lock and load"*, *"half-cocked"*, etc. **We know how to *shoot*. Our oppressors do not.**

We will we fighting for our culture. They will be fighting for reasons no more noble their government paycheck. Sure, they'll have air and arty and huge logistical support—but if just one of their blue-helmeted UN dragoons is within 500yds of a Rifleman's iron sights, he's going back to Belgium in a box.

And I haven't mentioned our scoped bolt-gun boys who can work out to at least 1000yds. Ever try to move troops around with an safety radius of *1000yds*? *500yds? It cannot be done.* Not from the ground, and not even from the air. The Afghans showed the Soviets this 25 years ago, and *we* are better Riflemen than they ever were.

The best defense is a well-directed fire from your own guns.
— Admiral Farragut

Modern armies have limited themselves to 250m carbines and 50m marksmanship. So, please—no more pants pissing!

The answer to fear is *confidence*.
Confidence comes from *skill*.
Skill comes from *training*.

It's really just that simple. You don't get skill from reading, because education is merely an intellectual transfer of information. You get skill by physical training. Get trained, and you'll stay alive and free.

Before 19 April 1775...General Gage ordered:

You will march with the corps of Grenadiers and Light Infantry put under your command with the utmost expediency and secrecy to Concord, where you will seize and destroy all of the artillery and ammunition, provisions, and other military items you can find...

After 19 April 1775...Lord Percy wrote in his diary:

Whoever looks upon [the militiamen] *as an irregular mob will find himself much mistaken. They have men amongst them who know very well what they are about.*

Heh! He got *that* right... So, are there *men* amongst you? Are there *Riflemen* amongst you? If so, send me and your favorite politician a copy of your best target! ☺¨

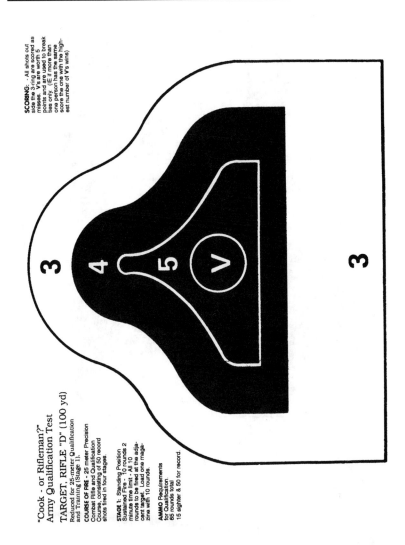

"Cook - or Rifleman?"
Army Qualification Test

TARGET, RIFLE "D" (100 yd)
Reduced for 25-meter Qualification
and Training (Stage 1).

COURSE OF FIRE - 25 meter Precision
Combat Rifle and Qualification
Course, consisting of 50 record
shots fired in four stages.

STAGE 1: Standing Position
Sustained Fire - 10 rounds 2
minute time limit - All 10
rounds to be fired at the adjacent target. Load one magazine with 10 rounds.

AMMO Requirements
for Qualification.
65 rounds total
15 sighter & 50 for record.

SCORING: - All shots out
side the 3-ring are scored as
misses. V's are worth 5
points and are used to break
ties only. (If more than
one person has the same
score the one with the highest number of V's wins)

Note: Enlarge this by 200% and shoot at 25m

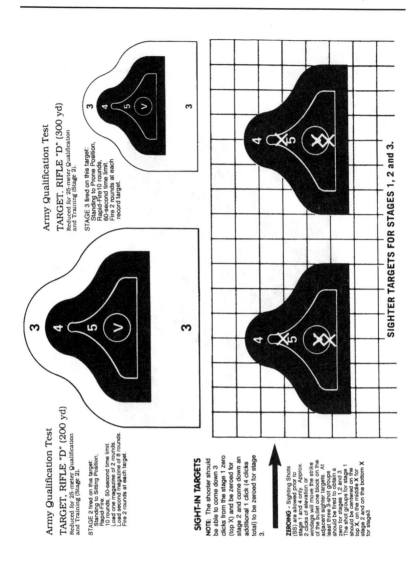

Army Qualification Test

TARGET, RIFLE "D" (300 yd)
Reduced for 25-meter Qualification
and Training (Stage 2).

STAGE 3 fired on this target:
Standing to Prone Position.
Rapid-Fire 10 rounds.
60-second time limit.
Fire 2 rounds at each
record target.

Army Qualification Test

TARGET, RIFLE "D" (200 yd)
Reduced for 25-meter Qualification
and Training (Stage 2).

STAGE 2 fired on this target:
Standing to Sitting Position,
Rapid-Fire.
10 rounds, 50-second time limit.
Load one magazine of 2 rounds.
Load second magazine of 8 rounds.
Fire 2 rounds at each target.

SIGHT-IN TARGETS

NOTE: The shooter should
be able to come down 3
clicks from the stage 1 zero
(top X) and be zeroed for
stage 2 and come down an
additional 1 click (4 clicks
total) to be zeroed for stage
3.

ZEROING - Sighting Shots
(SS) are allowed prior to
stage 1 and 4 only. Approx.
2 clicks of elevation or
windage will move the strike
of the bullet one block on the
adjacent sighter targets. At
least three 3-shot groups
should be fired to obtain a
zero for stages 1, 2 and 3.
The shot groups for stage 1
should be centered on the
top X, on the middle X for
stage 2 and on the bottom X
for stage3

SIGHTER TARGETS FOR STAGES 1, 2 and 3.

Note: Enlarge this by 200% and shoot at 25m

Shotguns are especially good for defense in urban environments, and certain kinds of hunting (birds and heavy brush game with slugs). Since these situations are not very common for me, I'm not into shotguns all that much. I prefer a rifle.

Pump vs. Auto?

The Remington 1100s and 1187s are no doubt fine shotguns, but a pump is more reliable and easier to clear malfunctions. With training and practice, a good shooter can hit *just* as quickly with a pump (*e.g.*, Kurt Russell in *The Thing*, even though he managed, without reloading, *11* shots from a 4+1 Ithaca). A good pump (*e.g.*, Rem 870) with a total of three barrels will handle anybody's shotgun needs. Finally, pump shotguns were not affected by the *"Crime Bill,"* but autos were.

An 18" barrel auto, however, *is* a good *car* shotgun as the driver can fire it one-handed. (The High-Standard Model 10B bullpup comes to mind here...) Alternate slugs and 00 buck.

Remington 870 Special Purpose (3" Mag; 20" Remchoke)

Use Federal Tactical 00 buck for attackers, and Brenneke slugs for barricades. Specialty rounds are DragonsBreath, flechettes, smoke, CS gas, etc. (800-870-2666).

For urban dwellers, such is *the* first line of defense. Condo bee-hivers should use only birdshot (#7½ is best) to avoid wiping out their neighbors just beyond the drywall.

While the Ithaca 37 and Mossberg M500 pumps are rugged, the Remington 870 is much easier to run. The Winchester 1300 Defender is also a very fine pump, and even less prone to malf than the 870, although barrel changing is not as convenient. Robar or Scattergun can nicely set up your gun.

A 20" barrel with Remchoke and ghost-ring rear sight, +3 mag tube extension, Choate pistol-grip full-length stock, forestock with Sure-Fire flashlight, tactical sling, and 6-shell Sidesaddle make for an awesome weapon. The two other barrels are a 28" vent-rib for hunting and a rifled slug barrel with iron sights. Pattern your load from 3-25yds.

I *highly* recommend Louis Awerbuck's Yavapai Firearms Academy (928-772-8262; Prescott Valley, Arizona) to maximize your effectiveness. (Get his books and videos from Paladin.)

Firearms for inmates of NYC, etc.

Tim Mullin recommends a percussion blackpowder shotgun, which is not a *"firearm"* according to federal gun laws. Even though such could be *purchased* legally out-of-State, legally *owning* it is likely not possible in Occupied Territory like NYC, but how much do value your life?

No.	12	11	10	9	8	7½	6	5	4
Actual Size	•	•	•	•	•	•	•	•	•	●
Diameter In Inches	.05	.06	.07	.08	.09	.095	.11	.12	.13	

No.	Air Rifle	BB	No. 4 Buck	No. 3 Buck	No. 1 Buck	No. 0 Buck	No. 00
Actual Size	●	●	●	●	●	●	●
Diameter In Inches	.175	.18	.24	.25	.30	.32	

BOLT-ACTION RIFLE CARTRIDGES

While a few cartridges (such as the .308) have been chambered in every kind of rifle (*i.e.*, lever, bolt, civilian semi-auto, and MBR), most fall within a specific class of rifle. The lever-action cartridges are usually venerable and rimmed. Bolt-action cartridges include both the lever and MBR cartridges, plus many dozens of others.

I wish to touch on the best *general* cartridges for American use (working and defense), as most of us cannot afford a dozen specialized rifles. We must first become proficient with a general-purpose, bolt-action, scoped rifle chambered in a common, effective round.

BEST GENERAL CARTRIDGES

Basically, we want to be able to kill elk out to 250yds, mule deer out to 400yds,, and Bad Guys out to 700. The cartridge must be accurate, tolerable if not comfortable, easy to reload, and *common*. While it's not a varmit or bear cartridge, it'll do either in a pinch from a good man and rifle. In short, this rifle/cartridge will do 90% of anything a bolt-action is expected to do. For *specialized* needs, you'll need *specialized* rifles, thus I ignore in this chapter the Magnum cartridges (including the new, impressive Short Magnums from Winchester and/or Remington in .270, 7mm, and .30). Underlined cartridges are the semifinalists.

.223   .22-250   .220 Swift

Throwing a 55gr pill at 3300-3700fps, these are varmit calibers *only*. I wouldn't dare hunt even whitetails with any .22 caliber, even though it's often done.

.243   6mm Rem.   .250 Savage   .257 Roberts

Throwing a 100gr at 3000fps, these are excellent varmit and whitetail deer cartridges, though a bit light for mulies, and decidedly unsportsmanlike to use on elk. The .243 (6-08) is the most widely available and renowned for its accuracy, but it and its ballistic brothers are too light for general purposes.

.260 Rem.   6.5x55 Swede   7x57   7-08

Now we're getting somewhere. Throwing a 140gr at 2700-2900fps, these are great for mule deer (and elk under 175yds). The ballistically excellent 6.5 and 7mm bullets are *very* efficient. Good for intermediate counter-sniper use, too.

The 6.5x55 Swede and 7x57 Mauser

These are excellent 1890s European military cartridges, giving good power with little recoil. However, they are long-action cases, and there are better cartridges (*e.g.*, the .30/06) for such actions. While I wouldn't buy a *modern* rifle in these two, I have an absolute crush on the Swedish military rifles in 6.5x55. In 7x57 I'd also probably be rather tempted by an M98 made in the 1920s by Loewe or DWM for a South American contract.

The .260 and 7-08

These two are factory manifestations of very popular wildcats: the .308 case necked down to 6.5 and 7mm. They are two of my favorite short-action cartridges. (Giving an extra 200fps, they are ballistically superior to the 6.5x55 and 7x57.) One of these is what we *should* have gone to in the 1950s, as their ballistics are *much* better than the stubby .308's. Bullets max out at 160gr for the 6.5mm and 175gr for the 7mm. These are good hunting rifle choices in countries which forbid military cartridges (*e.g.*, 7x57, .308, .30/06, 8x57, etc.).

.284   .270   .280

These give nearly identical performance—150/2900. The .284 is a short-action cartridge, while the .270 and .280 are long-action rounds derived from the .30/06 case. Maximum bullet weight for the .270 is 160gr; for the .284 and .280 (both 7mm) is 175gr. These are excellent for any 400yd deer, and great for elk and black bear within 250yds.

The .284 Winchester
Technically, I like the .284 a lot. It gives superb .280 ballistics from a *short*-action (which is stronger and ½lb lighter). It has a fat case (such provide better ignition and accuracy) with a rebated rim to .473 (the same bolt face as the .308/.30/06). For a light pack rifle in open deer country, a .284 can't be beat.

Finding a *rifle* in .284, however, is a problem. Only a few manufacturers ever made rifles in .284, and *nobody* does today. (A fine concept that didn't catch on in its day.) If desperate, you could get a rifle in 7-08 (it must have a 22-24" barrel), chamber ream it for .284 and widen the feed rails. This is a bit of work for an extra 200fps over the 7-08, but, hey, occasionally these projects have an irresistible (though rather illogical) appeal.

Because of its case capacity, short-action length, and common head width (not requiring any bolt face alteration), the .284 case is a real favorite with wildcat handloaders. It's been necked down to .22, .243 (6mm), .25 (a short-action .25-06), .264 (6.5mm; a superb round!), and .277 (a short-action .270). It's been necked up to .30 (a short-action .30/06), .338 (a very nice mid-caliber short-action round), .35 (a short-action .35 Whelen), .375, and .45 (the ".45 Professional"; a stout carbine round).

.270 and .280
Although you can find .280 rifles and ammo easily enough, only the .270 is *widely* available. While the .280 with its wider/heavier bullet selection is a better *ballistic* choice, the .270 of 1925 simply has 32 years on the .280. For all-around use on anything up to mule deer, the .270 really is hard to beat.

Personally, I'd rather have a .280, .30/06, or 7mmRM over the .270 as I like the heavier 175gr bullets for elk or black bear.

.303 British   .308   .30/06   8x57
Throwing a 180gr at 2550-2800fps, these martial four are powerful, accurate, and well-proven on the battlefield.

.303 British
Too bad the English didn't change it to rimless in the 1890s when the 7x57 Mauser showed us how. Not a *bad* round, but the rimmed case is a loading hassle. For somebody on an *extreme* budget, a surplus Lee-Enfield No.4 Mk.I for Ø80 can't

be beat. It's 90% the power of a .308, and will take elk or black bear within 200yds. Sierra offers a long overdue 174gr HPBT MatchKing. (Still, I'd save up for a .308 or .30/06.)

.308

The best post-WWII cartridge, giving 95% the power of a .30/06 in a short case. Every kind of rifle has been chambered for it, and it is still used by many armies. Supremely accurate, easy to reload, and cheap brass make the .308 very hard to beat.

.30/06

Inspired by the 7x57, this 1906 .30 caliber was a home run. It is *the* most popular centerfire cartridge in the world, and justifiably so. The .30/06 can be loaded with an astonishing range of bullets (from 80-220gr!), and will do about *anything*.

8x57 Mauser

The 8x57 was designed by a German commission for the *Gewehr 88*. (Paul Mauser counter-designed the 7.65x53 in protest.) The 8x57 is a good round (the 7x57 is better), but the .323 bullet reduces its long-range potential. There's no reason for a 8x57 unless you can't afford anything but a Mauser ac-tioned rifle—or unless you're a fan of G43s, FN49s, and Hakims.

.260, .270, 7-08, .284, .280, .308, or .30/06?

All of these are excellent general-purpose cartridges. Three give .308-class energy (2600fpe is certainly ample), and the other four give .30/06-class energy (which is 300fpe more than the .308). Of the entire seven, two shine slightly brighter than the others—one by its MBR usage and fine ballistics, and the other by its global ubiquity and a century of fine service.

.260 Remington (6.5-08)

Great, but uncommon. Fine for deer and bad guys, but a too light for elk and black bear as bullets top out at 160gr.

.270 Winchester (.277-06)

An excellent plains, mountain, or desert cartridge. *Very* flat shooting and very common, but bullets top out at just 160gr. (which is a consideration if you hunt elk or black bear).

7-08 Remington

More common than the .260, and bullets are available up to 175gr. It is flatter shooting than the .308, but it's still lacking 200fps on the .280. It's also not *quite* common enough.

.284 Winchester

While the .284 is superb and my *theoretical* ideal (giving long-action .280 ballistics from a short-action), it's just *not* common at all (brass is as expensive as the .45-70!).

.280 Remington (7-06)

The .280 is much more common than the .284 and has a better bullet selection than the .270, but it still shares one 7mm problem: bullets top out at 175gr, which isn't *quite* enough for brush hunting elk or bears. The Nosler Partition is a great 175gr bullet, but a 200gr .30 is better. (The .30-284 comes to mind here.) Also, the .280 isn't as common as .308 or .30/06.

And the finalists are...the .308 and .30/06

While I love the BC and SD of 7mm bullets and believe that a 185-190gr bullet is feasible, reality is a stubborn thing. I hate to dismiss the above excellent 7mms, but *realistically* it's between the .308 and .30/06 due to their unsurpassed availability, wide usage, versatility, and heavier bullet weights of 180gr (.308) and 220gr (.30/06).

.308 or .30/06?

For Bad Guy work out to 700yds either of these do well. Both are excellent rounds with very similar performance. Bullet weights range from 80 to at least 180gr, so these two have bullets to handle about anything. Which is better? It's a difficult choice, and one by no means clear cut.

.30/06 pros and cons vs. the .308

.30/06 pros

It has an average edge on velocity of 150fps over the .308. While not huge, it *does* give the .30/06 an indisputable 100yd/300fpe advantage. It also throws the higher BC 180-220gr bullets with adequate velocity, such being too heavy for the .308. It's probably a tad more common in very remote *Deliverance*-class areas. Jeff Cooper is fond of saying: *"If you can't do it with 180 at 2,700, then you probably can't do it."* He's talking about a .30/06 load of 180gr/2700fps.

The .30/06 can (with an inexpensive and removable chamber insert) adequately fire the .308 (although the bullet must jump ½" to the lands, which reduces accuracy by 1MOA).

.30/06 cons

There is no current U.S. military ball in .30/06. It is heavier and more expensive than .308 with only a moderate velocity advantage. Finally, the only MBRs ever chambered for it were the BAR, M1 Garand, M1941 Johnson, and FN49.

.308 pros and cons vs. the .30/06

.308 pros

It's an *extremely* efficient case, giving 95% the velocity of a .30/06 in a .479" shorter round. By most accounts, it is also a *tad* more accurate. It requires only a short-action, saving you ½lb in your bolt gun. Since you will *rarely* have a 600+yd shot during a routine patrol, the .308 is an excellent round for most threats. Brass is more plentiful. Best of all, modern battle rifles are chambered in .308 (7.62x51), so one cartridge can serve for both bolt and battle rifle. The .308 is a great round for intermediate distances and *can* be stretched out in *really* good hands. A wealth of sniper dope exists on the .308.

.308 cons

The .308 won't *quite* reach out there (*i.e.,* +600yds) like the .30/06, and 190-220 grainers are really too heavy for the case. The .308 is fine with 168-180gr out to 600yds, but is pretty much out of gas thereafter. (Yes, I *know* kills have been made at 900-1000yds with the .308, but that was by "excellent" shooters, who *would* have chosen at *least* a .30/06 had they known such a distant shot was likely.)

.308 commonality between bolt and MBRs

Regarding commonality of the battle-scavengeable 7.62x51 NATO—I say "fine," *to a point.* Pull up a chair.

First of all, the only U.S. military use of 7.62x51 is in M60 and MAG58 GPMGs (using M80 ball) and in sniper rifles. (I'm not envisioning being invaded by the Mexican Army with their G3s.) Thus, there won't be much 7.62x51 *to* scavenge.

Using military 7.62x51 M80 ball is O.K. out to 400yds, but it *isn't* accurate enough past that. (Most M80 groups only 3-4MOA. Foreign FMJ is worse, often up to 6MOA!). If your "very good" riflemen are using .308, they must carry their own matchgrade ammo, anyway. **My point is this:** For accurate,

400+yd work, M80 ball might as well be in *another* cartridge, so its commonality loses much of its *prima facie* advantage.

As M80 ball is unsuitable for "very good" riflemen who must train/equip with matchgrade ammo—why not simply field them with the more potent .30/06 or .300WM? If you're good enough to wring out a .30/06, why not *carry* one since you'll have to pack matchgrade ammo, *anyway*? For these reasons, I can't see why the .308 *must* be the cartridge of your "very good" bolt-action riflemen.

So, what's the answer—.308 or .30/06?

It depends on the situation. For example, if I *positively didn't need* the extra 150yds of the .30/06, *or* the cyclic rate of a battle rifle, *and* my field activities insisted on a lighter rifle, then I'd feel quite comfortable with a .308 bolt gun.

If, however, I envisioned some longer shots, then I'd field with at least a .30/06, which is clearly superior to the .308.

Other good bolt-gun cartridges

Regarding other fine cartridges, such as .250 Savage, .264WM, etc., their main drawback is relative scarcity of ammo versus the .308, etc. Sure, they're around *now*, but in 2023 it may like trying to find a box .256 Newton today. (This goes triple for the wildcats.) We've got to be able to *feed* these guns for many years. You might have to live off the ammo you've acquired within the next few years *for the rest of your life.*

Many of our elderly Patriots have a lifetime of field experience (hunting and warfare) and have settled on their rifle. If he's *really* good with it, so *what* if it's in 7x57? If a 400+yd man had a *choice* 400+yd rifle (whatever the cartridge) and was *really* dialed in with it, I wouldn't budge him out of it for a .308. A proven combination of man/rifle/cartridge is a "magical" thing and should *not* be broken up. **Remember, *hitting* is the only meaningful goal.** If he and his rifle are so well-bonded, you're nearly there already. (If it ain't broke, don't "fix" it! The only modifications *might* be a rust-resistant finish, a composite stock, and a *really* fine scope.) He needs at least 1,000rds of his pet load, and a complete spare parts kit. Then train him for counter-sniper work (with a ghillie suit, binoculars, rangefinders, etc.).

A SECOND OPINION

In the excellent book *Any Shot You Want* (available from www.a-squarecompany.com), the authors recommend the following cartridges/loads. They summarize by touting the 140gr .270 and the 165gr .30/06 as the best all-around hunting cartridges, and I certainly agree.

Eastern woods hunting

.257 Roberts, .25-06	117gr+
6.5x55	140-160gr
.270 Win	150gr
7mm-08, 7x57, .280 Rem., .284 Win.	140-160gr
.300 Savage, .308, .30/06	165 or 180gr
.30-30	170gr
.338-06	200-250gr
.35 Rem	200gr
.356 and .358 Win	200-250gr

Western plains, Eastern beanfields

.25-06	100gr
.270 Win	130gr
.280 Rem, .284 Win	140gr
.30/06	150gr

Mountains and horns

.25-06	100 or 117gr
6.5x55, 6.5-08, 6.5-06	140gr
.270, 280, .284	130 or 140gr
.30/06	165gr

All-around combination

6.5-06	140gr
.270	**140gr**
.280, .284	140gr
.30/06	**165gr**

Even after 60 years, the .270 Winchester is hard to beat. That is a bit much for eastern whitetails and western pronghorns, and maybe a bit light for a huge mule deer across a canyon, but the shooter who is willing to develop a good load, and really learn to shoot it, will shade the guy who owns a half a dozen rifles and is not really familiar with any of them. (p.216)
    — Any Shot You Want (1996)

A good Rifleman with a .270 or .30/06 could take any game he desired in the Lower 48.

I'd prefer the .30/06 for its greater bullet frontal area to better anchor large mule deer and elk. It's not quite as flat-shooting as the .270, but such is only really important >400yds, and it's unsportsmanlike to hunt at such distances, anyway.

❖ 22

BOLT-ACTION RIFLES

What a rifle delivers is highly-accurate power at long range. Compared to SLRs, bolt-actions are usually chambered in more powerful cartridges and are also much more accurate, therefore they far eclipse battle rifles when shooting at hard and far targets. Basically, your battle rifle is for threats up to 500yds, while your scoped bolt gun interdicts past 500yds.

Battle rifle vs. bolt-action rifle

If I thought that <200yd action against assailants was more likely than 400+yd shots, then I'd carry a .223 AR15A3.

If both concerns were *equally* likely, then I'd field with a *very* accurate .308 battle rifle. While I could stalk within countersniper range of my M1A, I could *not*, conversely, transform my turnbolt to a 20rd/semi-auto MBR. **If multiple bad guys are at *all* likely, then carry a *battle* rifle.**

Since I enjoy rifles and can afford them, I have bolt-actions in .308 *and* .30/06, and battle rifles in .223 *and* .308.

If I had to have only *one* centerfire rifle for all possible needs, it would likely be a very accurate .308 MBR (*i.e.,* M1A, FAL, or HK91) with rugged scope on a QD/ZH mount. Such a rifle could conceivably do just about anything (including 300yd headshots and 700yd bodyshots).

Those with limited budgets (or interest) would be adequately armed with a *very* accurate .308 battle rifle (skipping the AR15 and .308 bolt gun), *or* an AR15 and .30/06 bolt gun (skipping the .308 for the .30/06's extra range).

RIFLES

It's hard to really goof with *any* modern commercial rifle. In order of personal preference, I like the stainless Winchester 70 Classic, Sako, Savage, and Remington 700. I have at least one of each, so I know them well. The M77, 70, and 700 will constitute about 60% of all used bolt-actions at the gun shows.

Extremely expensive and "pretty" rifles would be the fine Colt-Sauer, Kleinguenther, and Weatherby.

Sako (pronounced "*sock*-o")

Made by the *Suojeluskuntain Ase-ja Konepaja Osakeyhtio* (Civil Guard Arms and Machine-shop Co., Ltd.—recently bought out by Beretta), these Finnish rifles are of extremely high quality and have an excellent integral scope mount receiver base (copied by Ruger). They are wisely made in three action families, .222, .308, and belted mags. Some experts do not care for the push-feed, and one friend had extractor problems with his beloved .30/06 (although such is uncommon), and made the painful decision to sell it.

Choose the older L-579 actions for .308, or the L-61 Finnbear for .30/06, over the modern AVI and AVII actions (which are more cheaply made—a sad sign of the times). If you plan on building a *choice* rifle, then you can't beat an older Sako action. My custom .308, for example, is a real jewel.

Sako makes very high-quality counter-sniper rifles in the TRG-21 (.308) and TRG-41 (.338LM), based on a superb action introduced in 1989 (with a 10rd QD box mag, no less!). ½MOA.

Other manufactures once used Sako actions: Model 52 J.C. Higgins (.222), the Colt Coltsman (.243 and .308), Browning (.22-250), and H&R Model 317 (.223). Howa of Japan copied the L-61 in their .30/06 Model FSD-43.

Savage 110

They are *quite* accurate and *very* competitively priced. In fact, they often outshoot rifles costing 2-3X the price. Furthermore, Savage is a *pro*-gun company (unlike Ruger, S&W, etc.) The bolthead completely encloses the case, and the action is quite strong and safe. In order to headspace at a minimal cost, Savage uses a barrel lock nut (instead of a shouldered barrel), so some folks object to the aesthetics. Personally, I've always thought that their bluing was weak (my combo .30-30/12ga. rusts at a harsh word), but Parkerizing is only Ø70 these days. That aside, these are excellent shooters at an affordable price. You should give one a try, as this is an underrated company offering very good rifles. I finally ran across a Savage Scout, and it shoots 2MOA with foreign military FMJ and ≤1½MOA with 168gr handloads. I'm keeping it!

Ruger M77II

This is similar to the pre-64 Winchester M70 (which is a commercial variant of the M98 Mauser). Besides the Mauser claw extractor, the M77II has many nice features. I like the slab-sided action which looks more modern and beds better than round actions. I like the Winchester 70-style three position safety (the older M77s have a Fire/Safe tang safety) which allows the safe operation of the bolt to load/unload.

What I *really* like is the integral base on the receiver, so screw-on mounts are not needed. Plus, steel rings come with each rifle, so you save a total of Ø30-60. The Sako-style mounting system is extremely rugged and keeps its zero very well.

Every Ruger I've had has been not only very accurate, but a *bargain*. Rugers are Ø50 cheaper than the 70 or 700 because their receivers are investment cast instead of machined. The M77's only downside is that its barrel shoots out a tad early, by 15,000rds. I'd get the stainless version and replace the cheesy, fluted, non QD-stud stock with a McMillan, etc.

One final comment, however: Sturm Ruger is no unabashed friend of the 2nd Amendment or gun shows. Try to steer yourself towards a Winchester or Savage.

Winchester 70

While the pre-64s (<700,000 serial #s) command a Ø550-800 price, they are not *quite* as accurate as the modern 70s. I don't care for the cheapy version made from 1964-1968 (700,000 to 866,000 serial #s). The post-68 model (>G866,000) is what you'll see most of these days, and it's a very good rifle for the money. A stainless model is now available. I think that the Win 70 is a little more rugged and handsome than the Remington 700, and I prefer the 70's safety and extractor.

The new "70 Classic" is a revived pre-64 action. It's a great rifle; very accurate with its hammer-forged barrel, and available in stainless. A bit pricey, but *well* worth it. A good choice for your .308 sniper rifle.

Remington 700BDL

While I favor the Ruger and Winchester over the Remington, such is more a matter of personal taste as there's nothing *really* wrong with the 700. It is the Army and USMC choice for their .308 sniper rifles, as well as for most SWAT teams. Winchester lost their lead in Vietnam when they stupidly replaced the pre-64 Model 70 with the inferior 1964-68 model, and the military snipers changed to the Remington 700. Today, the 700 over 70 stems more from post-Nam inertia than any difference in quality or performance (of which there's very little).

Model 7 carbine

This a 600 action with 19½" barrel in .223, .243 .260, 7-08, and .308. It is a very handy little field carbine (especially for youngsters and the ladies). It's also an ideal Scout rifle platform. Get a stainless steel model with synthetic stock.

Browning A-Bolt II with BOSS

This a quality rifle from Japan with a short bolt throw. I had one in .308 and liked it O.K., *"But Chuck, there just wasn't no love connection!"* It's funky and uncommon enough to give the owner difficulty in finding bases, stocks, triggers, etc. I'd go instead with a Savage, Winchester, or Remington.

The B.O.S.S.

The B.O.S.S. is muzzle brake tunable for each barrel's "sweet spot" of least vibration, which adds *significantly* to accuracy. The B.O.S.S. can be added to any rifle for Ø185. It *works*.

If on a *really* tight budget

Fortunately, high performance does not always require high dollars. The following rifles give very good accuracy and service for under Ø300 (and is sometimes *with* a scope, albeit this will undoubtedly be a Bushnell, Tasco, or old 4X Weaver). Still, such make good bargain rifles, or perfect truck rifles (I believe that every vehicle should have a dedicated .308 or .30/06).

(Realize that I'm not mentioning here all the bargain military rifles, such as the Lee-Enfields and Mausers, which were well covered in Chapter 6.)

Remington 721 (long-action) and 722 (short-action)

These are pre-700 actions, and *very* good values for the money (they are usually *extremely* accurate). The action, when introduced in 1948, was rightly hailed for its strength and safety. It was, with pedestrian features such as stamped floorplate and trigger guard, also a third less expensive than the Winchester Model 70.

These rifles are very similar to the models 600 and 660 carbines (now somewhat collectible). The 721 and 722 were discontinued in 1962, when the 700 came out. I haven't seen too many of them over the years, as most of them have probably been made into benchrest rifles for their inherent accuracy.

Remington 788

For the money, a 788 can't be beat. Because of their bargain finish and noisy QD mag, they were never very popular (made from 1967-1984). Target shooters, however, appreciate their incredibly fast lock-time and seek out 788s to make custom rifles. This is a no-frills rifle (*e.g.*, stamped trigger guard, beech stock, etc.), but for Ø200-250 it's a very good value.

Common chamberings are .223, .22-250, .243, 7-08, and .358. (The .223 rifle is very popular with varmit hunters.) Uncommon chamberings are .222, .222 Mag, .30-30, and .44 Mag. (The .30-30 rifle is pretty neat, as its box mag can be loaded with spitzers, thus significantly extending the range. The .44 Mag rifle is accurate and plain funky—and these sell at a premium.)

Savage 110

I'm now big fan of these affordable and accurate rifles. Their modern .308 Police version (with heavy barrel, black finish, composite stock, etc.) is quite a bargain which shoots very well. Their Savage Scout is also an accurate bargain.

In summary

If you want to study up on 20th Century turnbolt rifles (military and civilian), then a good book to start with is *Bolt Action Rifles* by Frank de Haas.

A good .308/.30/06 is probably the most rifle the average Patriot can accurately shoot and *afford* (usually about Ø500 with decent scope). In "good" hands at prone, it hits reliably (95%) out to 300yds. In "very good" hands, out to 500. Rarely will longer shots be expected, and rarely will greater than "very good" skill be available. A good .308/.30/06 will handle *most* rifle situations for *most* skilled Patriots, so it should be the general bolt-action arm of Liberty.

If Ø is no object, then get a modern Winchester 70 Classic or an older Sako (*i.e.,* L-579 or L-61). If you're on a budget, then get a Savage. If you somehow don't like the Savage, then get a Winchester 70 or Remington 700BDL or Ruger M77II.

stainless vs. blued steel

Go stainless if possible, as the steel and corrosion resistance are superior. The shiny finish will stand out in the field, so you'll need to camo it with anything from Bow-Flage paint to a full-boat Robar treatment.

synthetic vs. wood stock

Choose a synthetic stock when available, as such do not warp, shrink, or break as do wood stocks. Today, there are several good choices, beginning with Ram-Line's affordable stock (it's hollow and thus highly timpanic, so fill it in with polyurethane foam) to the fine stocks from McMillan, Brown Precision, or Bell & Carlson.

Choosing your level of accuracy

As with most things in life, you generally get what you pay for. For a non-Magnum/<700yd rifle, there are three levels of price/performance. Pareto's Law (also known as the 80/20 rule) is amply demonstrated here: **Level 1** rifles will give you 80% of Level 3 performance for 20% of the cost. **Level 2** gives 95% for 35-50% of the cost. **Level 3** gives 100% for 100%. Performance is just a matter of money—how much accuracy can you *afford*?

The question is probably more correctly posed inversely: how much accuracy can you afford *not to have*? If terrain and threat are limited to 400yds, then a Ø450 Level 1 rifle will suffice, but if you're living in flat country and expect Bad Guys with bolt guns, then you'd better get a Ø3,000 Level 3 rifle.

GENERAL-PURPOSE RIFLES OUT TO 400yds

Affordable, decent performance—Level 1

While these clearly are *not* sniper-grade rifles, they give fine performance (1½-2MOA) for *much* less money. They are remarkable weapons for Ø350-500 and will do 80% of anything ever asked of a bolt-action rifle. Several of these can be had for one Ø2,500-4,000 sniper rifle, so many "good" riflemen can be well-armed for no more than Ø500 apiece.

A good Tasco or Simmons 3-9X scope costs Ø200 less than Ø300 Leupold. These are decent scopes for the money, and your rifle will be capable out to 500yds.

For example, assuming a .308 throwing a 168gr Sierra MatchKing at 2700fps, if you zero your rifle at 275yds, you will be within 5" above or below line of sight out to 325yds. This is known as MPBR (maximum point blank range), meaning that you should be able to hit within a 10" circle out to 325 with a center hold. Exact holdovers for 300, 400, and 500yd shots are 2.3", 16.4", and 39.7" respectively. As it becomes nearly impossible to accurately holdover more than 36" (½ a man's height), such scopes limit your rifle to about 400yds.

For game, use the 165gr Sierra GameKing (a soft nosed MatchKing, no re-zeroing!), Nosler Partition, or Barnes X (if your rifle will shoot them accurately). Carry sub-caliber adapters (MCA; 907-248-4913; www.mcace.com) in .30 Carbine, .30 Tokarev (oughta be real zippy at 2000fps for 764fpe), and .32 ACP (this capable of quiet 50yd headshots), along with a broken shell extractor, firing pins, extractors, and ejectors.

The Jeff Cooper Scout rifle

His concept is a rifle capable of taking 400 kilos (880lbs) targets out to 400m in a package no more than 1m in length (39.36") or 3.5 kilos (7.7lbs).

Usually in .308, this rifle has a Leupold M8 2½X-28mm scope, barrel-mounted *in front* of the action. The advantage of this arrangement is that you keep *both* eyes open, track with your *weak* eye, and once you're about on target you then focus through your strong eye for the shot. Since the magnification is low, there's no significant image disparity between the eyes. It's *extremely* quick and *the* best bolt-action rifle sighting system for moving targets. In 1990 I visited (Orange) Gunsite and watched students in an API270 class *routinely* bust thrown clay pigeons with their .308s. Way impressive.

The Scout concept is lightweight, utterly handy, and well serves as a day-in/day-out general purpose rifle. Since the action is not covered by a receiver-mounted scope, the Scout is quick to reload (especially in a military bolt-action with stripper clips). I've seen some which even took M1A 20rd mags (Robar *used* to offer these, but Robbie told me that it's a huge pain).

If you don't want a 500+yd range .308 bolt gun (saving that work for a .30/06, 7mmRM, or .300WM), then a Scout .308 might be just the ticket.

Steyr Scout Rifle

Steyr Mannlicher unveiled their production Scout, a project shepherded by Jeff Cooper himself. It looks great and is quite accurate. It comes with a Leupold 2½X IER scope, and two 5rd mags (upgradable to 10rd mags). Price is a *very* Austrian Ø2,595. I owned one for a season, but mine was (oddly) not very accurate (and, no, it wasn't *me*) and suffered from the malfunction discussed below.

There has surfaced a quite frequent (*i.e.,* about 30% of rifles) failure-to-fire problem from light primer strikes (especially using military ball). It happened in my rifle (which would chamber a NO-GO gauge!), and in *Gun Tests'* rifle (1/02). The firing pin spring is too weak, and turning it down more than two notches makes the cock-on-opening action too stiff to easily open! As the barrel is pressed in the receiver through an extension, there is no feasible way to decrease headspace. Beware. (This is a shame, for I wanted this factory-produced concept to be an unqualified success.)

In 2001 I visited Jeff Cooper and his lovely wife Janelle to present them with a copy of *Boston's Gun Bible*. He found the page on the Steyr Scout in less than 30 seconds and at once took me to task for *"bantering about"* a statistic such as 30% (which he believed unsupported). Well, about 3 out of 10 Steyr Scouts I've shot or personally heard about from their owners have suffered from this problem. (Gun industry grapevine also supports the figure.) He countered that the matter really wasn't a problem as the owner could increase the firing pin weight and/or length, or increase the striker spring tension. I replied that such shouldn't be *necessary* on a Ø2,600 rifle with his name on it. Jeff maintained that *his* rifle is problem-free, and I'm sure that it is, as Steyr no doubt tested it *very* carefully before shipping it out to him. While I can understand Jeff's frustration (if not embarrassment) over Steyr's corner-cutting actions, it is the *shooter* who is really suffering here (who rightfully expects a problem-free rifle for that kind of money and hype).

It also peeves Jeff to no end that Steyr had the gall to recently offer the Scout in .223. I have to agree with him there...

As revolutionary and trick this rifle is, make sure that the one you're considering functions and shoots to your satisfaction *before* you buy it. If it does, then you'll enjoy the handiness, speed, and versatility of a Steyr Scout. *Caveat emptor!*

other "Scout" rifles

Other rifles suitable for the Scout treatment are the Marlin .45-70 lever-actions (with their great power and quick operation), the Lee-Enfield (with its short bolt throw and detachable 10rd mag), and the Remington Model 7 (it's already light and handy, and the Burris Scout scope mount uses the rear sight screw holes). I've made two inexpensive test Scouts (one from a 1952 FN M98 .30/06, and the other from a Lee-Enfield), and was very impressed with their performance.

Springfield Armory offers their M1A Scout—neat! It has an 18" barrel with an effective muzzle brake (though I wonder what its flash signature is like at night). With its forward-mounted scope rail and ability to also accept the standard mount (get the machined steel mount from Smith Enterprises, not Springfield Armory's soft aluminum), this rifle is *versatile*. CQB or counter-sniper, or anything in between. Reports of its accuracy, however, vary widely. One test saw a poor 2½MOA with factory match ammo (and 4MOA with 7.62 ball), yet *SOF*'s 12/01 article claims <1½MOA with its favorite ammo. As I now consider the M1A as the best .308 MBR, and as I like the Scout rifle concept, I should perhaps look for my own M1A Scout to test. If it shoots at least 2½MOA with quality FMJ, I'll keep it.

To "Scout" any military surplus Mauser M98, my friend Ashley Emerson invented a component package containing scope mount and ghost ring sights. Pick up a new surplus FN .308 or .30/06 barrel, a Timney trigger, RamLine synthetic stock, and Burris Scout scope. Send to any decent gunsmith to put together, and you have a very handy "Scout" rifle for as little as Ø650 (excluding labor). Brownells has the parts.

The *best* "Scout" bargain of all is the Savage Model 10FCM. Dropped in 2004, this 6.1lb (with no optics) rifle offers a 4rd QD mag, dual-pillared synthetic stock, QD sling swivels, 20" barrel, ghost ring rear/gold bead front sight, and a one-piece scout scope base. Simply mount a Burris Ballistic Plex handgun scope in Leupold QRW rings, a buttcuff pouch from Eagle, XS sights, and a sling, and you're about done. (Swap out the bolt head and firing pin for the magnum parts, which contain a more robust bolt head retaining pin.) Used, it is a *screaming* deal at Ø350—especially given how it will shoot as well as a Steyr without the functioning problems. I've had one for two years now, and love it. (It fires practice FMJ with *no* trouble.)

I've compiled an exhaustive 11-page report on my highly modified rifle with the Burris scope. I doubt anybody else has spent as much time and effort improving the Savage Scout, or wringing out the great potential of the Burris Ballistic Plex. (I would put this rifle against any Steyr Scout, any time.) For a Ø20 bill, this report is a whopping bargain! It contains *way* too much information to include here.

Every Scout rifle *affectionado* should have this report. Even though Savage has dropped their Scout model, such can be easily recreated by installing a 20" sporter barrel on a detachable mag Model 10. Meanwhile, we should all be pestering Joe deGrande at Savage Arms to reintroduce their Scout rifle!

OUT TO 700yds

Only accurate rifles are interesting.
 — Col. Townsend Whelen

Spending Ø1,200-1,500 for a Level 2 rifle

Your "very good" shooters deserve a bit more rifle. With this rifle, not only will they be effectively fielded, but they'll have a weapon on which to hone their skill—possibly emerging as "excellent" riflemen deserving 1000yd Magnums. This rifle *must* shoot at *least* ¾MOA to be effective out to 700yds.

Pay for a *very* good Ø350+ scope (with BDC, if possible): a Leupold VariXIII. If it doesn't have Mil-Dots, then send it to Premier Reticle (540-722-0601 for Ø100).

I recommend a *good* composite stock—professionally pillar-bedded and floated; a bead-blasted matte blue finish, Harris bipod, 3lb trigger, etc. **Don't skimp on this weapon. Pay for *quality* and get it *right*.**

Total cost will run Ø1,200 minimum, because of the glass. I know it's tempting to attach a cheaper scope—*don't!*—such suffices only for your "good" shooters. For *affordable* clarity and ruggedness, you can't beat a Leupold, and your "very good" riflemen deserve such. Lesser scopes tend to fog or lose their zero at the worst moments. Take my word on this! Excellent vs. average accuracy adds 200+yds to your effective range.

If it won't group tightly, try a Douglas or Shaw stainless barrel (recommend 1:10" twist for .30/06, and 1:11" for .308, unless you're going to shoot only the heavier bullets, and then 1:9" is preferred). This should turn it into at *least* a 1MOA rifle. This rifle will do 95% of whatever asked of a bolt gun.

Handloads

A good .30/06 load is the 168gr Sierra HPBT MatchKing atop 58gr of IMR4350 and CCI Mag primer, which gives an honest 2875fps. For ultra-long range or windy conditions, try the 190 or 200gr Sierra HPBT.

The .308 likes the 168gr Sierra atop 41.5gr of IMR4895 or 42.0gr of IMR4064 with a WW case/primer. If it won't shoot with these, then it ain't the load—you've got a dud of a rifle.

Dropping Ø2,000+ and doing it right—Level 3

From CFI (817-595-2485) is the superb .308 Steyr SSG PIIK with 20" barrel and 10x Hensoldt (military Zeiss) ZF500 scope (¼MOA clicks, 500M BDC w/Mil-Dot) for Ø1,995—which is a whopping bargain. GSI (800-821-3021) might still have the PII 26"bbl, 800M package. Robar makes a *very* nice Ruger M77II based .308 rifle with M1A mags (cool!). Practice thoroughly with your rifle past 400yds and become *awesome*.

700-1000yds—Level 4

Any decent .308 or .30/06 Level 1 rifle will, out of the box, hit pretty well out to 500yds. Accuracy out to 700yds, however, requires steeper expenditures in time and money for your Level 2 and 3 rifles. **If your ranges are past 700yds and you are**

an absolute dead shot ("excellent"), then go to one of the *common* Magnum cartridges (7mmRM or .300WM).

For 1000yd work, you'll need a Ø3,000+ **Level 4** rifle. Scopes, barrels (replaced every 2-4,000rds), etc. are more expensive. Also, handloading for this kind of extreme range is *highly* meticulous, demanding: precisely neck-turned brass (water weighted), deburred and uniformed flashholes, perfectly seated Federal Bench Rest primers, absolutely consistent powder weights, precise bullet seating depths, and dozens of hours of experimentation. You see, every rifle is an enigma and you must send many different loads down the barrel to discover *the tastiest* combination of bullet, bullet depth, brass, powder and primer. To achieve less than ¾MOA (which means hitting vs. missing past 700yds) requires an awesome Level 4 rifle with lovingly-made handloads; oh, plus just one other thing:

Choosing between the 7mm Rem. Mag and .300 Win. Mag

A 7mmRM throwing a sleek 175gr Sierra SBT (.533 BC; .310 SD) at 2900 makes for an ideal countersniper round at distances 200yds past the effective range of the .30/06. The Secret Service snipers use 7mmRM. The 7mmRM needs less bullet, powder, and recoil to do *nearly* the same job, with almost twice the barrel life of the .300WM.

For harder targets and/or windier conditions, the .300WM throwing a 200gr Sierra HPBT (.565 BC; .301 SD) at 2900 is far superior to the .30/06. Bullets identical, the .300WM throws *300*fps faster than the .30/06, with a 200yd down range velocity equal to .30/06 at the *muzzle*. It edges out the 7mmRM with 150 more ft/lbs at 1000. The U.S. military uses the .300WM, so it's well-sorted out ballistically with lots of field dope. *Police Sniper* by Craig Roberts discusses a *900yd* .300WM headshot. Wow. It's an awesome cartridge. If a .300WM won't solve your problem, then you're in *real* trouble.

Since the .300WM can send 200-220gr bullets (vs. only 175gr for the 7mmRM) and has 15% more case capacity, the .300WM is the Level 4 cartridge choice. (The 7mmRM does, however, make an excellent Level *3* cartridge.)

The .300 Weatherby, Dakota, and Imperial mags (not to mention the wildcat mags) are *very* hot, but you'd have to stock up on a lifetime's supply of brass and forsake all the .300WM data. Such isn't worth it for an extra 200fps. Besides, if the .300WM is too sissy for your needs, then a mere 200fps increase won't melt your butter, anyway. You'll need a Level *5* rifle.

1000-1500yds—Level 5

If the .300WM won't do it, then the seriousness of your situation is growing geometrically. You'll need one of these two: a .338-378 Weatherby or a .338 Lapua.

The awesome .375-50BMG (proportionally, a sort of gigantic 6mm-06, but sending a 350gr at over 3600fps) is probably more fittingly a Level 6 cartridge.

The long-range .338 cartridges

These are very powerful rifles with a supersonic range of 1500yds. (There's also the .408 Cheyenne Tactical.)

.338-378 Weatherby   (250/3200 for 5886fpe)

While .338-378 Weatherby has a velocity edge of 250fps over the .338 Lapua, it is *way* overbore and throat erosion happens quickly. (Since the throat erodes far sooner than the bore, Ashley Emerson merely turns back his slightly overlength barrel; a clever trick he can do 3-4X per barrel.)

.338 Lapua Mag (8.58x71)   (250/2950 for 4832fpe)

My personal preference. The .338 Lapua will do the same work without burning out barrels. Accuracy International's SM is Ø3,825, and the Dakota Arms T-76 goes for Ø4,250.

CLOSING COMMENTS

In short, to each according to his *ability*. Most of your people, **"decent"** riflemen (*Bronze* quality and 80% of your men), get carbines in .223 (or Commie 7.62), .30-30s, and .303s for effective ranges of 250yds.

Your **"good"** (*Silver*-16%) get a Ø500 Level 1 .308 and can reach out to 400yds. They can handle 80% of distant threats.

Your **"very good"** (*Gold*-3%) get Level 2 and 3 rifles which can reliably kill 700yd threats, 95% of your distant problems.

Perhaps one in ten "very good" riflemen can be honed into **"excellent"** (*Platinum*) and kill out to 1000yds, and he gets a Level 4 rifle, lots of gear, and a spotter.

The man behind the rifle

The rifle and ammunition are 2nd and 3rd to the ability of the *shooter*. A top man with average equipment will beat an average man with top equipment—*count on it*. Don't be lured into the old trap of spending all your money on weapons and gear. A Ø3,500 Level 4 rifle will not hit at 1000yds if *you* can't deliver at 500. You must *deserve* such a quality weapon by first learning to consistently outshoot Levels 1, 2, and 3 rifles.

Only when *your* accuracy equals a Level 3 rifle, *and* your tactical situation *demands* 1000yd capability, should you then go with an expensive Level 4 rifle. Be prepared, however, to spend Ø2,500+ for the rifle, Ø1,200 for the scope/rings/mount, and another Ø1,000+ for ammo and supplies. You'll need countersniper gear such as 1000yd laser range finder, spotting scope, notebook, ghillie suit, etc.

And finally, there's the training

Pay for quality training, while such is still legal, and *practice*. Past 700yds, wind is the crucial variable. Practice and log your shots. Work out the kinks, and acquire your data, endurance, and patience *beforehand*. You won't have the opportunity to play "catch up" when the Balloon Flies. Reading, thinking, and gun polishing alone won't do it. You've got to get out there, sweat, get dirty, and suffer the bugs. **The more you sweat in training, the less you'll bleed in battle.** There is no time for games. Get serious, or give your stuff to the *serious* man who has the mettle but not the gear.

❖ 23

.50BMG
TARGET RIFLES

1500+yds—Level 6, the .50BMG

This kind of distance work requires *big* bucks and *lots* of practice. My motto is, *"If you can't do it with 700 at 2,800, then you probably can't do it."* A .50BMG has a mere *13,075*fpe. This is more for busting up equipment than for countersniper work. Adopted in 1918, the awesome .50BMG round will certainly see its 100th year of military service, especially with all of its current interest, development, and planning. In fact, no other cartridge has had as many different bullets made for it.

".50BMGs are the 20mm Solothurns of today."

A .50 owner told me that at a gun show, and the analogy really hit home. Until the *GCA68*, there was *no* restriction on the private unlicensed ownership of cannons and mortars! Such were affordable and could be shipped right to your door through mail-order. The 14.5mm Soviet PTRS anti-tank rifle could be had for just Ø99.95, and threw a 994gr bullet at 3200, for 22,607fpe—about *twice* that of the .50BMG. Gee.

When you read *Unintended Consequences*, did you also groan when you learned of pre-*GCA68* Ø189.50 Swiss 20mm Solothurns and Ø99.95 Finnish Lahtis? How about 20mm ammo for just 75-99¢ a round? The WWII 20x138 threw a 2160gr shell at 2700fps for a muzzle energy of—are you sitting down?—**34,973fpe**. To put it in perspective, the 20mm cannon is to the .50BMG what the .308 is to the .30 Carbine. Imported

20mm cannon ammo was cut off in 1968, and today sells for a minimum of Ø30/round (if available).

Having a .50BMG rifle today is like having a 20mm Solothurn back in the 1960s. No special license is currently required, and if you find a *private* sale gun (rare, though not unheard of), the Government will never know that you own one. If you can't afford one, then pool together with some buddies and buy one together. With Leupold scope, ammo, and dies, you're looking at Ø4,500+. Three serious guys should be able to cough up Ø1,500+ each. (Then, don't tell *anybody* about it!)

If you can't afford even a partnership, then at least snap up some ammo while you can. Right now, AP, API, API-T, and phosphorus (blue tip) rounds are all available. Even Raufoss rounds can still be had at Ø20+ each. Once, however, ammo importation and retail sales are banned, a round of mere M8 API will go from Ø2 to at least Ø5 (and perhaps up to Ø10). Raufoss rounds won't be had for under Ø50, if you can find them. Moral: Buy now or cry later.

One reader/friend of mine recently asked me if he should make getting a .50 a priority. (He still has yet to even buy his FAL.) I replied that he could likely always find a battle rifle, but that the .50's days are probably numbered. (Besides, any good man bringing a .50 to the party will undoubtedly be loaned a battle rifle.)

The FCSA   435-527-9245   www.fcsa.com

Get in touch with the Fifty Caliber Shooters Association at POB 111, Monroe, UT 84754-0111. (Read my *Bulletproof Privacy* to understand aliases and mail drops. You do *not* want your real name and address to be in the files of FCSA! Someday, the feds will try to get their database in order to confiscate .50BMG target rifles from known shooters.)

The Complete .50-Caliber Sniper Course
—Hard Target Interdiction, **by Dean Michaelis (2000)**

This is a new 563 page book from Paladin Press, written by one of the pioneering .50BMG sniping instructors of the Army Special Forces. Michaelis has clearly *"Been There—Done That."* A highly instructive book. I'll quote from it extensively.

The military classifies the .50BMG in the "heavy" class of sniper rifles. The "light" class means up to 7.62x51. The "intermediate" class means anything larger than the 7.62x51 but smaller than the .50BMG (*e.g.,* .300WM and .338 Lapua Mag).

THE .50BMG (12.7x99) CARTRIDGE

Ammunition for the heavy-class of rifles is in many people's opinion the most exciting and dynamic subject of small arms development. No other class of weapons system that is hand-held or shoulder-fired has seen the kind of thought, insight, and drive that has gone into the development of the .50-caliber cartridge. (p.387)
— Dean Michaelis, *The Complete .50-Caliber Sniper Course*

A word about tracers
They shoot 4-6MOA flatter than normal bullets
This is for two reasons. One, as the tracer compound burns out, the round becomes lighter. Two, the heat escaping from the tracer round's base cleans up the turbulence, thus effectively raising the ballistic coefficient of the trailing edge.

Tracers work both ways
They illuminate a line between gun and target, and if seen by the enemy the shooter's position can be quickly known. Use only as spotting rounds when no enemy is nearby.

Current U.S. military .50BMG rounds
Good, basic information on all U.S. military small arms ammunition can be found in *TM43-0001-27*, dated April 1994. Entitled *Army Ammunition Data Sheets*, this unclassified doc covers .22LR up to 30mm cannon.

muzzle velocities
Velocities quoted are from the 45" barrel of the M2 HB. For shorter barrels such as the 29" Barrett, deduct 215fps. (Note: 29" is really too short for the .50BMG. A 34" barrel gives 141-197fps more, which nearly equals the 45" barrel MV.)

accuracy
MOAs quoted are from a twist of 1:15". If only 647-670gr bullets were fired, accuracy would be improved by about 20% if a slower twist of 1:18" were used.

color codes
In 1995, our military decided to worry about the ozone effect their bullet paint might have (rather ironic, wouldn't you agree?), and did away with the lacquer-based silver for a water-based white. Unfortunately, this white is still listed as "silver." (Foreign manufacturers, however, are not subject to our wise

and benevolent EPA, and still use the nasty, old silver paint.) So, when I say "silver," it could also mean "white" for post-1995 American military ammunition. Just so you know...

M33 Ball   (647/2950fps;   BC 0.680   2-3MOA)

Accuracy of this prior 1994 was pretty bad, but it's now been tightened to 3MOA (and sometimes 2MOA), which means 20-30" at 1000yds. This is satisfactory accuracy for equipment (though it has no AP or incendiary capabilities), but not accurate enough for Bad Guys past 500yds (as the human kill zone measures about 12"x18"). Government cost is Ø1.17/rd.

M17 Tracer (brown tip, with second knurled cannelure)

Commonly linked with M33 (1:4). This is a 618gr bullet at an MV of 2910fps. The 235gr of powder is either WC860 or IMR5010. Red tracer burnout range is 1600yds. The M17 is ballistically very similar to its companion M33 round.

The newer "Product Improved" (PI) M17 has a boattail, and thus smaller flame column, which reduces visibility (especially in daylight). Some troops are grumbling about this, and wish the old M17 flat-base tracer bullets were back.

M2 AP, Armor Piercing (black tip)

The 2MOA M2 AP is more accurate than M33 Ball. Major Plaster fired his AMAC with M2 at a 55gal drum 1250yds away and hit 70%, which is less than 2MOA.

It was corrosive, and discontinued in 1945 for the M8 API.

M8 API, Armor Piercing Incendiary (silver tip)
(648/2950fps;   BC 0.663   2MOA)

A 385gr steel penetrator is enclosed inside ample incendiary mix. API is the best value for the money, though not as destructive as Raufoss. It was generally corrosive until 1953.

M20 Armor Piercing Incendiary, Tracer (red/silver tip)

API-T is the tracer companion to the M8.

M903 Saboted Light Armor Piercing (SLAP)
(355/4000fps;   3MOA)

Sends a .30 caliber 355gr tungsten steel penetrator at 4000fps. Government cost is Ø7-12/rd. The sabot is amber. It requires a totally different twist to achieve even 3MOA, and thus is not very accurate in normal 1:15" twist barrels.

Important! M903 (and its tracer) is certified only for the M2 HB machinegun. Do *not* fire from any barrel fitted with a muzzle brake, compensator, or flash suppressor (unless you are *sure* that they are compatible).

M962 SLAP-Tracer

This is the tracer for the above M903 SLAP. Red sabot. It is also an in-bore, sub-caliber training round for the US Army's 105 and 120mm M1 Abrams tank guns, which ballistically simulates out to 1500M those tank rounds (costing Ø250-1,000@).

where to get the above military bullets/ammo

River Valley Ordnance (314-926-3076) sells pulled G.I. bullets for about 60¢/rd: M1 Incendiary, M2 AP, M8 API, M17 Tracer, and M20 API-T. (I'd get mostly M8 API.)

Mk 211, Mod-0 (green/white or silver tip)

(671/2950fps;   BC 0.649   1½-2MOA)

Its technical description is HEIAP (Hi-Explosive-Incendiary-Armor-Piercing). Developed in Norway, it is called the NM140. Here, we call it "Greentip" or "Raufoss" (the Norwegian firm's name, now RATEC).

Raufoss originated the Multi-Purpose concept of incendiary and explosive payloads in small caliber projectiles without requiring complex mechanical fuses. Raufoss provides good anti-personnel lethality (20 fragments on average), fire-starting, and light armor penetration against aircraft, missiles, and unarmored vehicles.

Our U.S. Navy became interested in Raufoss rounds back in the late 1970s, and procurement began in the early 1980s to replace the M8 API. Grade A rounds (similar to the Army's Grade R) are bulk-packed without links and used by SEAL snipers. Grade B (*i.e.,* the Army's Grade MG) rounds are not as accurate and thus relegated for M2 HB machinegun use. (When Raufoss is available in the civilian markets, it is probably Grade B stuff. Look for case scratches from the de-linking.)

the explosive

This is a PIE (Pyrotechnically Initiated Explosive) round which uses impact's crushing effect to set off the incendiary and zirconium compounds, which sets off the RDX Comp A-4 explosive. (The original RX51-PETN explosive was too sensitive.)

Since there is much less than ¼oz. (109.75gr) of explosive, Raufoss rounds are happily not *"destructive devices"* according to 26 § 5845(f)(D) of the *NFA34*. Translation: You *may* legally own them. (I was wrong about this in 1998.)

the penetrator

Its 215gr tungsten carbide penetrator zips through most light armor. (The Raufoss round is much more effective than the M8 API, though with very similar external ballistics.)

Who uses Raufoss?

The Navy uses Raufoss for all its ships as standard service M2 HB ammunition, and the SEALs use it exclusively. The other military branches, however, have it only on their war pallets. (Given the fine accuracy and superior destructiveness of Raufoss, however, I expect this will be rectified.)

they ain't cheap, but they're worth it...

When you can find Raufoss, it'll run you Ø12-25/rd (it costs the Government Ø9/rd). Fun stuff—buy all you can find! Raufoss is the most powerful load made for the most powerful firearm we may own without special license. (It is analogous to being back in 1967 and buying HEAT rounds for your 20mm, with the *GCA68* just around the corner.)

Any Raufoss round which seems to be Norwegian-made is generally Collector Grade, and should not be fired. (Trade it at a premium for shootable stuff.)

Beware the painted tip Raufoss scam!

Since M33 Ball is just Ø1.50/rd and Raufoss is at least Ø20 (when available), some unscrupulous folks out there have been known to paint up M33 and sell it as Raufoss. Since genuine Raufoss is often sloppily painted, you can't tell from the paint. (Generally, proper colors are green/silver or green/white, although several other valid colors exist on earlier rounds.)

M33 Ball, however, has two knurled cannelures (one for crimping, and the other above for identification), whereas Raufoss has only one cannelure (it is smooth and used for crimping). Thus, any alleged Raufoss round with a visible knurled cannelure is fake. (Headstamp is often Lake City, as in LC 86.)

Modern American-produced (by Olin) Raufoss headstamp is WCC. Norwegian-produced rounds (using brass from Holland, Canada, US, Spain, Belgium, and Greece) have a dozen possible headstamps, and several paint schemes. (A chart of all these is provided below.)

Identifying the various Raufoss rounds

Tip color	Headstamp	Country	Notes
Light green	EMZ 79	Norway	Raufoss NM140 **Dutch** case
Light green	IVI 84	Norway	Raufoss NM140 **Canadian** case
Light green	LC 81	Norway?	Raufoss NM140 **U.S.** case
Light green	RA----	Norway?	Raufoss NM140 **Raufoss** case
Light green	12,7x99 SB 44	Norway	Raufoss NM140 **Spanish** case
Dark green	WCC 84	US?	OLIN-license built NM140?
Yellow	WCC 85	US	OLIN/Winchester WALAP PIE
Green/Silver	50 FNB 91	Norway	Raufoss NM140A1 **FN** case
Green/Silver	HXP 89	Norway	Raufoss NM140A1 **Greek** case
Green/Silver	LC 92	Norway?	Raufoss NM140A1 **U.S.** case
Green/Silver	WCC 87	US?	OLIN-license built NM140A1?
Green/Red	RA----	Norway	Raufoss NM160 Tracer
Silver/Green	50 FNB 87	Belgium	FN design HEPI
Silver/Yellow	50 FNB 86	Belgium	Raufoss design APEI 169 from FN
Yellow/Silver	50 FNB 84	Belgium	Raufoss design APEI 169 from FN
Green/Silver	50 FNB 91	Norway	Raufoss NM140A1 **FN** case

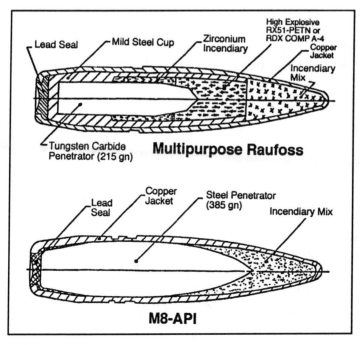

Multipurpose Raufoss

M8-API

Handloading for the .50BMG

Loading the .50BMG is not a recipe type of affair. After loading over 3500 rounds...through six different rifles over the past eight years, I concluded that a good loading manual for the .50BMG cannot exist. Why is this so? To put it succinctly, the range of variation in guns and components far exceeds that found in smaller arms.

— *op. cit.,* at 459

Things foolish handloaders get away with in lesser rounds (such as changing bullets within the same weight class without backing off the powder charge) can easily bring doom if done with the .50BMG. Remember, you've got the equivalent energy of four .30/06s going off *simultaneously!* 13,000 foot/lbs of muzzle energy is Righteous Stuff, and you must be reverent.

Reloading equipment

As of 5/2000, Natchez (www.natchezss2.com/50cal.html; 800-251-7839) offered the following deal: an RCBS AmmoMaster press set for 1½" dies, full length dies, shell holder, ram priming, and trim die—all for just Ø334.

Since you'll be loading only for one rifle, get a neck sizing die (Ø120). Natchez also sells primers, bullets, and powder. Other suppliers are Midway and Widener's (Johnson City, TN).

cases

New, unfired cases are available from PMC and IMI. Used brass goes for about Ø1 a case.

Case preparation requires much more time and money. Uniforming primer pockets, deburring flash holes, measuring case wall concentricity, turning casenecks, etc. all demand high-dollar tools from specialty suppliers.

primers

There are only two primers available: the RWS #8212, and the CCI #35. Primers for your .308 are just 1.7¢. Primers for the .50BMG cost *17¢.* (Have I now your attention?) Even though they're not even twice as large, they still cost ten times as much. Welcome to the world of the .50BMG.

powders

Oh, you're gonna love this:

One attribute of powder which we generally trust is the burning rate of the multitude of available powders. If we buy a can of IMR4350, for example, it will perform almost identically to any other can of IMR4350. This is because commercial powders for reloaders are

cannister grade powders...[which] must meet a specific criterion for burning rate.
Since variation occur from batch to batch, manufacturers store powder in countless lots [most of which are non-cannister grade.]
The essential message...is that most of the powders we are using for handloading the .50BMG are non-cannister grade powders. **Simply put, not all 5010s, 860s, and 870s are the same.**
— *op. cit.,* at 469

What this means is that powder charge weight will change significantly between powder lots, sometimes as much as between different kinds of powder!

A pound of powder can load only 30 rounds of .50BMG (at about 235gr); an 8lb keg will load 240 rounds. Thus, once you've experimented with a new lot of powder to achieve just the velocity and accuracy you want, you've used much of it up! Then, you're soon obligated to start all over again. The only safe thing to do is begin with very conservative starting charges and very carefully work up. By way of example is a recommended table. (Note: Do not rely on the following until you have read and understood the Michaelis book.)

[The below table can be used for any] *of the following powders which have similar burning rates: IMR5010 (AA5010, H5010), WC870 (T870, AA8700), WC860 (RVO57, T5020, AA8600), WC872, T5070, HC-30. Choose either the RWS or CCI primer and any bullet of nominal diameter (.510"). Any cartridge brass that has been trimmed to 3.91" or less and is free from cracks or corrosion will suffice.*
— *op. cit.,* at 462

Bullet Weight	Starting Charge	Expected MV, 29-32"
650 grains	210 grains	2700-2850 fps
700 grains	205 grains	2650-2800 fps
750 grains	200 grains	2600-2750 fps
800 grains	195 grains	2500-2650 fps
900 grains	185 grains	2350-2500 fps

commercial benchrest bullets

Thunderbird	800-535-2666	www.tbirdammo.com
Arizona Ammunition	623-516-9004	
AAA Ammunition	402-334-3389	www.aaa-ammo.com

Many excellent choices exist (especially in monolithic steel, brass, or bronze): Thunderbird Match, the Hornady 750gr HPBT (BC .860), the Dabco Bieber Bore Rider (BC .910), and the Barnes double ogive 700gr bronze with a 1.015BC.

Benchrest shooters routinely place 5 shots in a salad plate at 1000yds. (The current record is 3¼"!) Any of these bullets from an excellent rifle will print 85% in a 8'x10' panel 3000yds away. Translation: Parked enemy equipment riddled at *1¾ miles.*

important bullet info

There are three important ranges of velocities: supersonic, transonic, and subsonic. When a bullet's speed drops to about 1400fps, it enters the transonic range where its dynamic stability is markedly reduced (especially as it drops below the speed of sound, 1120fps, or Mach 1). Within the subsonic range, its drag coefficient increases dramatically, quite literally applying aerodynamic brakes to the bullet.

Thus, for long-range accuracy, a bullet is only accurate enough while its velocity remains *above* the transonic 1400fps. Although the downrange distance of this depends on many variables (*e.g.,* ammunition temperature, bullet BC, barometric pressure, temperature, MV, etc.), the .50BMG can generally remain supersonic (and thus accurate) out to 2000yds.

This does not necessarily mean, however, that our bullet is accurate from *muzzle* to 2000yds. In fact, it is almost assured that from 0-500yds our bullet will be rather *inaccurate,* and then mysteriously becoming accurate at about 500yds. The reason is that the bullet has "gone to sleep" at 500yds. Think of a top which has just been spun very hard. It takes a few seconds to sort itself out (*i.e.,* 0-500yds as it overcomes its muzzle-induced yaw), and then it "goes to sleep"—spinning without lateral movement (*i.e.,* fine accuracy from 500-2000yds). Finally, when rotational velocity falls off enough (*i.e.,* it falls to transonic velocity of 1400fps), the top begins to wobble and soon falls over.

To summarize, it's crucial to know two things about any potential bullet: At what distance does it "go to sleep," and at what distance does it become transonic. *Within* that range is where that bullet will be effectively accurate. Such can be modeled through the Ø5,000 PC-PRODAS computer program, or it can be learned at the range with much shooting. Either way, it'll be costly.

My point here is not academic. Such discussion is hardly required with a 600yd .308, but it's *vital* in understanding the external ballistics of the .50BMG (or the .338 Lapua Mag, for that matter). The .50BMG isn't just a bigger round; it's in a different and bigger *world.* The sooner you learn that from books, the less time and money you'll have to spend.

SHOOTING THE .50BMG

Yes, shooting a .50BMG at 1500yds is similar to a 600yd shot with a .308, but it's only similar. Do you know what a black belt in an Oriental martial art means? Not an expert, but a "qualified beginner." Being a .308 "black belt" only means that you're a qualified beginner with a .50BMG.

Support gear

Oh, you'll need *much* more than just the rifle! Total cost for a .50BMG hard target interdiction team that is serious about their business can easily run over Ø25,000.

anemometers

Judging the wind speed downrange is vital to making a long shot. These hand-held wind meters avoid the guesswork.

range-finder

The only laser range-finder that has the accuracy for .50BMG missions is the Leica Vector 1500 7x42. It's accurate out to 1500M, and can measure out to 2500M. Besides distance, it can figure vertical difference, azimuth, inclination, and differences between the above. It's quite a unit (which costs at least Ø4,000). Still, laser range-finders can be detected with inexpensive sensors.

Most heavy snipers prefer instead a passive theodolite (a surveying tool for measuring angles). The Leica TM-6 is a 6" model, and very accurate (*i.e.*, 1.6M at 1600M). The optics serve well as a spotting scope, and the system is NVD compatible. Cost is Ø3,000-5,000.

scientific calculator

As you'll soon see, a Ø30 Hewlett-Packard is worth its weight in gold. A fire mission can be figured in just minutes.

meteorological instruments

You'll need to measure air temperature, barometric pressure, and ammunition temperature. The Casio Triple Sensor watch can do it all. (Makes you glad you've lived this long, eh?)

hearing protector

The Peltor Electronic Hearing Protection amplifies speech and other soft sounds, while blanking out loud ones. An essential piece of kit, for any dedicated shooter.

Dope it (*i.e.*, do the ballistic calculations)

"Doping" the shot means measuring all the variables which influence external ballistics so that you can adjust your scope. After 500yds, many new such variables come into effect. In fact, it becomes so involved that scientific calculators chewing on 22 step calculations are required. (Truly, you're solving artillery equations!)

Meteorological (MET) conditions

When shooting to 1500yds you're not really shooting the bullet, but *lobbing* it in with a peak trajectory of *56* feet (assuming a 500yd zero). MET conditions play (not merely "can play") a *huge* difference at such ranges.

altitude	(supersonic velocities are lower at altitude)
barometric pressure	(when the pressure is up, bring sights up)
air temperature	(temperature up, sights down)
wind speed/direction	(bullet deflection must be precisely estimated)
ammo temperature	(each gain in 50fps raises impact 1MOA)

Environmental (ENV) conditions

Primarily, this has to do with the slope angle of the ground you're shooting across. Regardless if you are shooting uphill or downhill, you will shoot *high*. While this seems logical for downhill shooting, it seems paradoxical when shooting uphill. Uphill or downhill, the slant range is still shorter than the true range:

> The problem with slant range is compounded by the fact that the original range to the target *is* the actual amount of air between shooter and target. **The slant range is the range in relation to the amount of gravational force that the bullet will encounter on the way to the target.** If the shooter is higher or lower than the target, the slant range will always be shorter than the true range. It cannot be longer. True range is the long [er] range, and slant range will be the short [er] range.
>
> Remember, barometric pressure and air temperature would be corrected for [true range]...which is...the amount of true air between the shooter and the target. Winds are also based on true range.
>
> — *op. cit.,* at 110

If slant range is not calculated and added to the equation, you will shoot high (because you assumed that gravitational effect was more than it was). Only when there is *zero* slant angle to target will true range and slant range be equal (*i.e.,* air and gravity both affecting the bullet over an identical distance).

Another ENV condition (because it relates to true range) is spin drift. The 180,000RPM of gyroscopic precession your bullet left the muzzle with will, at one mile, cause it to drift about two feet! Obviously, this must be corrected for.

Dial it (*i.e.,* adjust your scope accordingly)

Here's where you'll wish you'd have remembered your geometry and trigonometry! Fortunately, a Ø30 pocket calculator will do it all for you. (Get an HP20S or a TI-30X. The edge goes to Hewlett-Packard with its 10 memory cells.)

Finally, is your target within supersonic burnout range? That is, will the bullet velocity still be at least 1125fps at target? If so, then you are good to shoot.

Dump it (*i.e.,* keep mouth open, and *squeeze*)

Assuming your calculations were perfect, and the scope properly corrected for the shot, you still must *make* the shot. There are several things trying to work against you:

The human factor

intimidation	(let's face it—the .50BMG can be scary!)
perceived recoil	(flinching is guaranteed)
overpressure	(you must shoot with mouth open)

.50BMG TARGET RIFLES

As you can see, I've saved the rifles themselves for last. I had you wade through all the prior discussion on ballistics and handloading so you would more appreciate just what is involved in owning a .50BMG target rifle. It is not merely a .30/06 that is four times the size. A .50BMG is in a world of it *own,* with its unique rules and precautions.

While I cannot list every available rifle and their test results, I can at least get you started on your shopping. For most entry-level shooters, I would recommend a single-shot rifle for under Ø3,000. With this, you can begin to learn the basics of .50BMG handloading (which must be approached with great care and reverence) and long-range shooting (which is more like running artillery equations). Crawl before you try to walk, and walk before you try to run. Underlined models are my favorites.

Semi-auto

These are generally Ø7,000 rifles, which trade off accuracy for cyclic rate. I would say that these are an unnecessary expense, unless you've got a real need for one (*e.g.*, interdiction of long-range moving targets).

semi-auto M2 HB   Ø6,900   503-429-5001
A fully-legal "Ma Deuce" belt-fed .50BMG! Gee. Wow. Cool.

Harris M96   Ø6,800   602-230-1414
More accurate (1MOA) than the Barrett.

Barrett M82A1 Ø6,750   www.barrettrifles.com   615-896-2938
Used by our military in the Persian Gulf. 2MOA accurate.

Barrett M82A2   www.barrettrifles.com   615-896-2938
A lighter version of the A1, and with some unique features.

Knight's Armament SR50
This was Eugene Stoner's last design. Poor ergonomics.

Pauza P50
Based on WWII Simonov (*i.e.,* SKS) design. Similar to Harris.

Bolt-action repeater (*i.e.,* mag fed)

These are Ø4,000+ rifles. If fairly quick follow-up shots are required, then you'll need at least one of these.

A.I. AW50 Ø11,820   www.accuracyinternational.com   423-482-0330
Probably the most accurate gun in this class.

AWT Black Arrow
This is a new offering from Greece with many good features.

American Arms M 2000 M/P   407-636-1943
10rd mag. Light for a repeater at 29½lbs. Very strong action.

EDM Arms Windrunner   (largely unavailable)
In competition with the Barret M95 for the USSOCOM heavy-rifle. Many innovative and high-end features. Krag-smooth bolt! ½MOA.

PGM Hectate II   516-277-6887
7rd mag. Weighs 29lbs. 1MOA claimed at 1000yds with M8 API.

State Arms Gun Corp   608-849-5800
Giant copy of the Rem. 700 action. O.K. accuracy (2MOA).

McMillan M88   www.mcmfamily.com   602-780-2115
An oversized Rem. 700. Fine action. *Extremely* accurate.

Robar RC50   Ø4,720   602-581-2648
Superb McMillan action, but better barrels than the M88.

Barrett M95   Ø4,650   www.barrettrifles.com   615-896-2938
5rd mag, 22½lbs, 29"bbl. Ordered for the USSOCOM heavy-rifle
contract. (see it at www.FirstDefense.com)

Single-shot bolt-action

These are very simple systems without even a magazine
(you remove the bolt and load the round in the face). While they
are not fast, they are quite accurate, lightweight, and easy to
maintain. Many of the below do not have a safety; as soon as it's
chambered, it's in Condition Zero. (This is not as risky as it may
seem. Just don't slam the bolt forward.)

AMAC 5100   Ø2,995   208-756-6810
Very accurate (¾MOA/1000yds) and an excellent value.
Used to great effect by the Afghans against the Russians.

ArmaLite AR50   Ø2,615   www.armalite.com
Great muzzle brake, 1¼MOA. 8lb. trigger.

Barrett M99   Ø3,100   www.barrettrifles.com   615-896-2938
Even Barrett has finally come out with a basic, no frills .50BMG.
This is lightweight and well-balanced. Many excellent features.

Redick Model 650   501-636-3188
One of the most rugged and accurate (½MOA).

Maadi-Griffin   Ø3,150+   www.maadigriffin.com   480-325-5623
Well-regarded, ¾MOA/1000yds accurate rifles.

L.A.R. Grizzly   Ø2,570   www.largrizzly.com   801-280-3505
Similar bullpup as the Maadi, but heavier built (and with a safety).

Rib Mountain Arms M92   605-957-4249
Very accurate and high quality custom rifle.

RMC Mfg.   Ø2,250-3,250   605-348-3736
I don't know anything about this rifle. Call them and find out.

Serbu BFG-50   Ø1,975   www.serbu.com   813-243-8899
Only 22lbs., 4lb. trigger, and ¾MOA.

State Arms Rebel   Ø2,250   www.statearms.com   608-849-5800
Excellent 3½lb. trigger pull, with ½MOA accuracy.

Scoping the .50BMG target rifle

Only two scopes are robust enough for the .50BMG:

Leupold Mark IV M1

This was the first scope suitable for the .50BMG, and it's still a real favorite. The 16x is adjustable to 75MOAs up/down, and is thus capable of 100 to 1500yd shooting. Some shooters prefer the 24x. Older scopes without Mil-Dots you should send to Premier Reticle.

If your used .50BMG target rifle comes with this scope, then keep it with confidence. If, however, you must buy a *new* scope, then I would recommend the Lightforce:

Lightforce 5.5-22x56 NXS   www.nightforceoptics.com

Designed specifically for the .50BMG, and endorsed by Kent Lamont, the well-known Class 3 and .50BMG shooter. The 6061-T6 aircraft aluminum 30mm tube is brutally strong (with the edge over Leupold, in my opinion), pressure-tested for 24hrs at 100' of water, and recoil-tested to +1,250Gs. 100MOA elevation/60MOA windage. ¼MOA clicks. Several reticles available. And, it's illuminated. Retail Ø1,334.

.50BMG MISCELLANEOUS

Alpec laser BoreSighter   www.alpec.com

It may be one thing in a .308 to throw a few sighting-in rounds downrange, but such is costly/noisy with a .50BMG. Why not at least get on paper with Alpec's fine product?

The laser unit (#8508) is housed in a solid brass case that fits a .223 chamber. This unit is then placed in a sleeve for the particular caliber of application (*e.g.,* .50BMG; #8520), and Alpec has sleeves for anything. A quality, worthwhile item!

Angle Cosine Indicator   www.snipertools.com

Remember my discussion of slant angle in Chapter 19 and how I wished for a device which could be mounted on the gun? Well, wish no more—it's been done! The ACI attaches to the scope tube at a 90° angle, allowing the shooter to read the value without disturbing his cheekweld.

Chamber Maid™   www.cjweapons.com

Flexible cleaning rod for any chamber. #CMB50. Neat!

OTHER RIFLES

.22LRs

These are *essential* for training, pest control, and small game hunting. You shouldn't be without a .22 rifle any more than a chef would be without a paring knife.

.22LR semi-auto takedowns

The advantage of a takedown is that it stores away easily in your backpack, trunk, boat, etc.

Charter Arms AR7

Some of these are O.K., but test fire them first as they often malf. I've collected a few over the years, but had to sort out a couple of real lemons. The buttstock doubles as the waterproof, floating carrying case—neat. The iron sights are poor; accuracy is only fair. They are not dovetailed for scope mounts. I'd pass on the AR7, generally—unless you find a *really* good one, and even then, delegate it to secondary/stash status. It's a shame they weren't better made and with decent sights.

Browning

This is a little jewel of a gallery rifle with its buttstock mag tube. They're collector items, however Norinco makes a decent copy (and even *these* are hard to find).

Marlin Papoose M70P

This is lot of rifle for 4lbs and Ø140. The Papoose disassembles into a package as short as your forearm and packs in its own little floating case. Attach a compact 4X scope and you'll have great little woods rifle. Headshot countersniping is possible out to 100yds with practice. Get some 15rd mags. Spend another Ø50 for the stainless M70PSS, and camo it with removable Bow-Flage paint.

If you can afford only *one* .22LR rifle, make it a Papoose. It's 90% as accurate as the Ruger 10/22, yet more versatile.

.22LR semi-auto full-size

While these aren't as handy as the takedowns, the full-size rifles hold more rounds and are a bit more accurate.

Ruger 10/22

This is one of the finest .22 autos, and fairly compact in a folding stock, though 1½lbs heavier than the Papoose. It is quite accurate and mag capacity runs from 10 to 50rds. Parts and accessories abound. A real staple in one's battery. You gotta have one. It can be found used for Ø120-150.

Marlin 60 tube mag

The Marlin 60 is just like the Papoose but with a 14-18rd tubular mag and fixed barrel. It single feeds .22 Shorts and Longs as well as Long Rifle; versatility which may be vital someday. It typically runs Ø70-90; a real bargain for nearly half the cost of a 10/22. Stock up on several and outfit younger kids, the elderly, and random guests. A barrage of .22LR from your random party guests will keep the marauders' heads down at a minimum, if not inflict some real injury.

Other .22LR rifles

Many other .22 semi-auto rifles exist (Sears, Savage, etc.) and most can be had for under Ø100. While these are often O.K., there's no reason to stray from the cheap and plentiful Marlin 60. Stick with a proven winner.

The Winchester and Rossi pumps are nice (tube mag and manual action means that you can use Shorts, Longs, and LR), but a bit uncommon.

Bolt-action .22s are curiously more expensive than the semi-auto Marlin 60, but are good for children to develop single shot accuracy and reliable bolt-action experience so useful with your centerfire bolt-actions. The Chipmunk (www.ChipmunkRifle.com) is a diminutive .22 for kids.

I prefer, however, lever-action .22s over bolt-actions. They usually have a capacious mag tube (vs. a small detachable mag), will feed .22 Shorts and Longs, and they are more fun to shoot. The Marlin 39 and the Browning BL-22 are superb rifles, and superior to the Winchester. These are very popular with their owners, so keep your eyes ajar at gun shows.

Scoping your .22LR

As I'm an accomplished shot, and a good .22LR has headshot potential out to 100yds, I prefer to scope my more accurate .22LRs. With any gun, hitting is the goal and shot placement is paramount—especially with a .22LR. A scope detracts little from the rifle's handiness, increases effective range by 50yds, and can quickly be removed if necessary. A small Ø35 4X is sufficient (Tasco, Simmons, Bushnell, Norinco, etc.). Don't forget a sling.

Closing thoughts on .22LR rifles

Every vehicle and *every* home should contain a .22 rifle and 1,000rds of ammo—for survival's sake, at least. Never be without a gun, even if it's a modest Ø70 .22LR. Such could easily feed you or save your life. (A woman alone at home, barricaded in the corner behind her bed, quietly waiting for the intruder to come to her, could easily repel an attack.) For less than Ø100 and a couple hours of practice, *anyone* could become proficient enough to prevail in such a defensive scenario. Those not willing to invest *so little* time and money are simply not serious about preserving their lives in these perilous times. **If you look like food, *you'll be eaten.***

Take at least basic steps for your own self-defense. Folks, stop whining for more police, or else we'll *get* a Police State.

SPEED & ACCURACY OF ACTIONS

From fastest to slowest actions, they are: auto, slide/pump, lever, bolt, and single. It's no coincidence that this order also corresponds to least-best to best accuracy. The looser the action type, the quicker and less accurate it is. You'll have to decide the right balance between speed and accuracy, and actions will differ 2-3X more in *speed* than accuracy.

An auto is more accurate than a single-shot is quick. Levers offer a good compromise, though a well-practiced bolt-action can be almost as fast but with better accuracy. Become proficient in operating *all* the different actions. What you're untrained for is exactly what you'll be forced to someday use.

SPORTING AUTOS

I'm not a big fan of these rifles. Granted, they cycle more quickly than bolt-actions, but somewhat at the expense of accuracy and reliability. The H&K SL7 in .308 is nice, but eccentric. Some of the Browning BARs are very accurate. I've taken a few deer with a Remington 7400 .243 and liked it, but I think I'll just stick with a bolt-action. If you've already got an *accurate* semi-auto that you like, keep it, but train with a turnbolt.

SPORTING PUMPS

The Remington 760 comes to mind. A friend of mine has one in .30-06 and can shoot 2½" 300yd groups, so they can be quite accurate. *Personally*, I just don't care for them (except for the "Shorty" from Germany, which has a pistol-grip actuated pump), but if *you* resonate with the slide-action rifles, then fine. They are ambidextrous, however, but so is a lever-action.

LEVER-ACTIONS

These are very handy, good for lefties, their ammo is available anywhere, and they travel well. Typically Ø175-250 (they've risen about Ø50 since 1998), they're still a great bargain and make fine car/truck rifles.

Winchester or Marlin?

While there's nothing actually *wrong* with the Winchester 94 (and the Rossi copies), I prefer the Marlin as it's more rugged and side ejects (which allows a top-mounted scope, if desired, though unnecessary in its 100-250yd calibers). To me, the 94 *seems* fragile, and I *really* don't like its loading gate and follower. Also, the Marlin has a decided edge on quality.

Marlin (.30-30, .357 Mag, .35 Rem., .44 Mag, .444, .45-70)

The **.30-30** (from 1895) can be found *anywhere* in the Americas. Although ballistically mild, if you don't expect too much from it, the .30-30 is still pretty effective and will do if *you* will do. It'll take deer up to 200yds and elk within 100yds. Choose the 170gr bullets over the 150gr. The Model 30AS is the no frills version of the Model 336. Used, they go for Ø175 to Ø250, depending on model and condition. I'd stock up on bargain Model 30ASs for trading *wampum*.

While the **.357 Magnum** rifles are pretty cute, you might as well get the same diminutive gun in .44 Magnum, unless your child or lady cannot take the extra recoil.

The **.35 Remington** is basically a necked-up .30-30 and a better brush caliber, though not nearly as common. (I'd choose a .30-30 instead.)

In **.44 Magnum**, this is a fun poodle-shooter out to 200. For deer, the .44 is limited in power and accuracy to only 100yds (4MOA with only 1,000fpe). Used, the Model 1894 is uncommon and folks want at least Ø250 (even though new wholesale is about Ø315). I found a used Marlin Limited (16¼"bbl; 7+1rds) and I absolutely love it. I added a Weaver aperture sight and a custom-made leather butt cuff holding 10rds. It is *sweet*. When I pull the rear stock off, it packs into any suitcase or bag.

The **.444 Marlin** (a .44 Magnum *Magnum*) is a fine round, but since the Marlin's 1-38" twist doesn't stabilize 300gr bullets well, 150yd elk is really about the most its 265gr load will handle. In truth, the .444 really *can't* compare with the .45-70.

For elk and bear country, Marlin offers the 1895SS in the stompy **.45-70**. This is *great* Scout rifle platform using the Ashley kit. The newer "Guide" guns have Ballard deep-cut rifling and are not as accurate as the MicroGroove rifling when using jacketed bullets. (Ballard rifling is, however, better for cast lead bullets.) I'd get an older model, cut the barrel to 17", and add a Pachmayr Decelerator pad. When handloaded at 40,000cup near its *real* potential (*far* beyond Springfield Trapdoor specs), the .45-70 can take all but the *big* bears. (You can load up to 50,000cup in the Browning 78 or Ruger No. 1 to approach within 300fps of .458WM velocities, though such isn't necessary but for griz.)

A final note on the Marlins: ***Don't dryfire them off safety.*** Their firing pin has no return spring and dryfiring will eventually break the pin. Have a couple of spares.

Other lever-actions

Without getting into all the old cowboy rifles (and their modern replicas) in .38-40, .44-40, and .45LC, here are some other fine lever guns.

Browning BLR

This lever-action in .22-250, .243, 7-08, .308, .270, .30-06 and 7mmRM with detachable mag (so it can use spitzers) is a good rifle, though you'll pay at least Ø475 for a nice one. (Pick a Belgian over a Japanese.) A good 6X scope does well here.

A .308 BLR would make a handy little Scout rifle.

Savage 99

This has a very strong action, can use spitzers in its rotary mag, and is generally well regarded—however, I didn't have much luck with the three .308s I've tried. Mine just weren't accurate enough. The tightest group I got was 2¼", and I won't keep a .308 which can't give me at least 1¾".

Besides, I prefer the exposed hammer of the BLR and Marlin, which I carry with a chambered round, hammer down, safety off. For a shot, I thumb back the hammer while I unsling, and this is a very fast technique—less than 3 seconds for a standing 100yd shot. A hammer-down BLR feels a bit more safe to me than a cocked/locked Savage.

Winchester 1895

This is a wonderful 100-year old design, now remanufactured. Theodore Roosevelt carried one in .405 (*"Big Medicine"*) on his African safari. Used .30-06 1895s go for Ø700-1,200 (the .30-40 models cost less), but if you've the spare coin for a unique and rugged rifle, then an 1895 may be just the thing.

New 1895s are about Ø700, and are even available in stainless steel (which is rather alluring).

Winchester 88

No longer made, the 88 was about the strongest of all the lever-actions and very accurate, but the trigger pull was lousy. For a great brush gun, get an 88 in .358 (.35-08).

Ruger M96/44

It holds only 4+1 (.44 Magnum), but has a very quick lever throw. The Marlin is a much more handsome rifle, has an exposed hammer, and holds 3 more rounds.

SINGLE-SHOT RIFLES

The World's most versatile rifle?

This could very well be Thompson/Center's Encore break-open single-shot. The two-piece rifle simply changes barrels by removing two forend screws and a barrel/frame hinge pin. Such might make the ultimate back-country pack rifle (three different barrels could do it all). Currently available Encore barrels (all 24" unless noted) are:

.223	
.22-250	(also available in 26" barrel)
.243	
.260	
.270	
.280	
7-08	
7mm Rem Mag	(also available in 26" barrel)
.308	
.30-06	
.300 Win Mag	(also available in 26" barrel)
.45-70	
20-gauge	(smoothbore, ventilated rib, with choke tubes)
209X50 muzzleloader	(240gr sabot at 2100fpe for 2351fpe)

RIFLES IN PISTOL CARTRIDGES

Except for the Marlin 1894 .44 Magnum (or perhaps the M1 Carbine for urban use), I don't much care for these. The 9mm/.45ACP Marlin Camp and Ruger 9mm/.40 carbines are fun to shoot *because they don't recoil*. **Little recoil means little muzzle energy.** You've got to *take* it in order to *give* it.

Besides, if you're going to pack a rifle and its weight, then you might as well have it in a *rifle* cartridge, even if it's only in .223. While a .44 Magnum comes alive from a 16+" barrel, the 9mm, 40S&W, and .45ACP do not. I'd even rather have a 12ga shotgun over a 9mm rifle.

Still, to be fair, a pistol-cartridge rifle can be just the gun for apartment or mobile home dwellers, or for those who haven't the physical strength for a "real" rifle. If a 9mm Marlin Camp Carbine is all you can afford and wield, then by all means own one! I'm not so much of a snob or a purist or a "he-man" to deny that *any* rifle is better than none at all.

RIFLES FOR ROUTINE TRAVEL

Don't get caught these days away from home without a handgun *and* a rifle. Remember, a handgun is only what you fight your way back to your *rifle*. If you travel often you might get caught in a strange city under sudden martial law or catastrophe. So you're in L.A., more riots break out, and you need your rifle but left it at home? *Uh, oh.* Handguns can serve within reason, but they *cannot* perform a rifle's duty.

Rifles for airplane trips
Battle carbines
A friend of mine has vowed to *never* get caught in a big city without a rifle. He has a pre-ban folding stock Chinese AK especially for his checked suitcase. (He paid only Ø300 for it in 1988, though it's worth Ø1,000+ today.) With it go nine 30rd mags (one for the rifle and the other eight in two 4-mag pouches already on their belt) and 270rds of ammo in stripper clips. This is a very capable set up, although he takes a *big* chance having an *"assault rifle"* in the wrong city or state.

Military bolt-actions
I've chosen a No.4 Mk.I Lee-Enfield for *my* travel duty. The barrel was shortened to 16¼" (¼" over legal minimum) and the buttstock cut down and thinned out. The whole thing is only 27" long (1" over legal minimum) and weighs 6lbs. For only Ø120 (which included the barrel and front sight work) I've got a dependable, accurate, powerful rifle with detachable 10rd box mag. With it go two extra mags, and 100rds in strippers. Being "only" a bolt-action, there will be much less hassle if caught with it vs. an *"assault rifle"* with nasty "banana clips."

M1 Garand
An M1 (especially a .308 Tanker) would also make for an excellent travel rifle. Even the 24" barreled M1 breaks down into 31" action and 29½" stock. Since the clips are not mags (thus integral to the gun), they can be kept loaded.

Lever-actions
Another fine traveling rifle is the Marlin .30-30 (or .44 Mag) lever-action. Its rear stock removes quickly, and ammo can be found anywhere. It's also the least "threatening" rifle of all to officials.

A Browning BLR .308 with a low-powered variable (*i.e.*, 1-4X, or 1½-5X) scope (*e.g.*, Leupold Vari-X III, Weaver V3) would be a very capable gun to fight your way back home.

Have good ammo pouches to carry 50-100rds.

Pistol cartridge rifles?

I would *not* choose a rifle in a *pistol* cartridge (*e.g.*, 9mm and .40S&W). They are just not powerful enough (except for the Marlin .44 Mag), and if you're going to pack the *weight* of a rifle you might as well enjoy the *power* of a rifle. I don't consider the .30 Carbine to be sufficiently powerful, even though it does perform well enough within 50yds. A *true* rifle cartridge will strike an incapacitating blow to at least 300yds.

It should takedown, or have a folding/removable stock

The point is to avoid having to transport them in an obvious rifle case. If the rifle is somehow short enough, then it can fit at least diagonally in most any hard suitcase. Be *anonymously* armed.

Packing tips

Use a hard suitcase with combination lock, which allows quick keyless access. Also take a small backpack for the *"Oh, sh*t!"* essentials. Don't forget tactical boots (dress shoes won't cut it) and pack a rugged vest or jacket to conceal your belt-holstered handgun, mag pouch, and Sure-Fire flashlight.

Checking in at the airport

By law, checked firearms must be unloaded (mags included, as they are considered part of the weapon), in a locked case, and declared to the counter agent (who will have you sign a tag attesting to their unloaded and locked status—no big deal). Ammo must be packed in their original containers, but plastic ammo boxes (CaseGuard, etc.) will do. All this is still perfectly legal—*unless* you're flying to an anti-gun city or state (*e.g.*, NYC, NJ, etc.). *"Assault rifles"* are generally illegal in all but the southern and western states. *Cuidado.* Know before you go.

After 9/11 and all the ridiculous airport hysteria, expect some hassle. (You might UPS your guns to yourself % a friend.)

Rifles for car trips

Use your air travel rifle

That .308 Lee-Enfield "Jungle Carbine" or .30-30 Marlin will serve just fine on a car trips.

A scoped bolt-action .308 or .30-06

This would also be a fine choice. I and many of my friends have a bargain Win 70, Rem 700, or Savage 110 for just this purpose. Although a bolt gun's cyclic rate and reloading speed cannot compare with an SLR, they are much less expensive and are not illegal in touchy areas (in case your car is ever searched).

Have at least 50rds of handloaded 165gr or 180gr Sierra GameKing with your rifle, along with a Lens Pen, broken shell extractor, and cleaning supplies.

What about a battle rifle?

If you have the money and nerve to pack one, then do so. A Ø700 post-ban H&K93 or FAL (since they are not expensive) would be preferred over any valuable pre-ban rifle. I would *not* recommend a .223 battle carbine, given that you might have to shoot through some Bad Guy's car. Only a .308 can do that.

Have also a .22LR rifle in your car

These are inexpensive and handy for pests, putting down injured animals, or for arming a passenger. A Ø75 Marlin 60 in a soft case with a few boxes of shells provides great utility.

Gun laws on the road

In some states (*e.g.*, Texas) you can drive around with a loaded, accessible long gun but *not* a handgun (unless licensed). In other states your rifle must be unloaded and locked in a case or in the trunk. **Know *before* you go.** (Chapter 34 is your basic guide on this.) When in Rome...

Watch out for those *"school zones"*

Although the *Gun-Free School Zones Act of 1991* (which prohibited in certain cases the knowing possession of a firearm within 1,000' of a *"school"*) was overturned by the Supreme Court in 1995 *U.S. v. Lopez* as an unconstitutional use of the interstate commerce power, Congress brazenly repassed the struck-down act in §657 of the 2,000 page DoD Appropriations Act of 1997. (See 5/8 and 9/18-19 of my *Hologram of Liberty*, and page 30/10 of this book.)

Thus, to avoid the possibility of an erroneous felony arrest, do not flagrantly violate the overturned, yet unlawfully resurrected congressional prohibition. While nobody to my knowledge has been arrested for this, it would be a fantastic test case which I don't think the Supreme Court could dodge.

RIFLE / SHOTGUN COMBINATIONS

In his *Survival Guns*, Mel Tappan praised the versatility of the Savage Model 24 over/under combo guns. I have some and like them very much. Made in .22LR/20ga, .22WMR/20ga, .223/20ga, and .30-30/12ga, they make excellent backpacking guns to handle most any game within 50yds. The shotgun barrel can throw a rifled slug for bigger game, although this is really not accurate enough past 50yds.

Their biggest drawbacks are poor sights and *abysmal* triggers—both of which can be addressed. I'd send it out for a rust-resistant finish (Parkerizing, Teflon, etc.), install an ammo butt cuff, sling, and good sights. Threading the barrel for a Remchoke is also very worthwhile.

For the shotgun barrel you can even get some rifle cartridge insert barrels (in .223, .30-30, .44 Magnum). O-ringed sealed inside your barrel, these aren't known for their accuracy but will work out to 75yds in a pinch. (MCA; www.mcace.com)

Smaller shotgun gauge inserts are also available. I pack many .410 shells and a few 20ga shells to save weight. With practice, a .410 will drop *nearly* as many birds as will a 20ga.

Within its limitations, the Savage 24 will accomplish much for one long gun. It's a good gun for a young boy to hone his skills with. It's also a good gun to break down and pack in the truck or camper. Used, they go for Ø175-250. The models in .22 Mag or .223 barrel are quite versatile, since they're much more powerful than the .22LR, but you can still shoot .22LR with inexpensive brass chamber inserts (from MCA).

BLACKPOWDER GUNS

A good man with "merely" a blackpowder rifle will challenge (or beat) an average man with better equipment. Even with my Glock I don't think I'd happily face a Colt Single Action-armed Clint Smith to a gunfight. **It's the *man*, not the gun.** The *man* (courage, intellect, stamina, alertness, etc.) is the weapon—his gun is merely a *tool*. A good man can kill with a rolled newspaper. A poor man can't kill with an FAL.

Blackpowder guns are either muzzleloaders or they fire cased rounds. The original blackpowder cartridges (*e.g.*, .45LC, .45-70) now loaded with smokeless powder could revert to homemade blackpowder in some future "Road Warrior" society.

There are two ways to go: replicas of antique rifles or modern designs in composite stocks, stainless steel, etc. For example, Ruger's modern 77/50 is pretty neat. It chamber loads two Pyrodex 50gr pellets, a cap, and plastic-flanged Black Belt Bullet to throw a 405gr bullet at 1348fps (1635fpe) and 2¾MOA at 100yds with very little smoke and fouling. This is near .45-70 ballistics from a 6½lb rifle with a 22" barrel—without the expensive brass and reloading of the .45-70. *Hmmm.*

Some of us may be reduced by circumstance to blackpowder, so know how to fight with them. On this note, I must mention that Clint Smith has designed an 1880s weapons class for Thunder Ranch. You get to clear the Tower with blackpowder guns, using oil lamps. Cool!

I'm still acquiring *modern* firearms and ammo. Perhaps when I've got some extra money and time I'll give one a try. I'm *not* discounting blackpowder; I'm just saying...*prioritize.*

Muzzleloaders

I've never gotten into muzzleloading, which seems to me more of a hobby than a practical shooting discipline. Comparatively, they're slow, inaccurate and cumbersome. Though I'm not utterly discouraging you from trying them, you should at least have aqcquired your primary guns beforehand.

One interesting advantage to muzzleloaders is that they are not considered *"firearms"* under the *GCA68* and are thus largely unregulated. You can even buy them through the mail!

AIR RIFLES

These are great for pest control and indoor practice. The Chinese models are very powerful and reasonably accurate for only Ø35-60. The German Feinwerkbau is the BMW of air rifles; beautiful and accurate for hundreds of Ø. I found a nice English Webley and Scott at a flea market for only Ø75. Whatever you buy, get thousands of pellets (target and hunting).

✦ 25

HANDGUNS

Let's make this clear: there's a huge difference between *being* (*i.e.,* caught) in a fight and *going* to a fight. If you *knew* in advance that you had to shoot a Bad Guy (*i.e., going* to a fight), you wouldn't pick a *handgun*, would you? No, you'd take a *rifle.*

A handgun is merely a weapon used to fight your way *back* to your *rifle*—which you shouldn't have left behind. Handguns are concealable weapons for sudden lethal emergencies. Defensive rounds (*e.g.,* MagSafe, Glaser, CorBon) from a powerful cartridge (*e.g.,* .40S&W or .45ACP) placed well will *usually* solve your problem. If not, then you need a rifle.

Handgun rounds are not very powerful and have only modest effect against human assailants. There's no hydrostatic shock (which requires 2000+fps velocities). You'll be interested to learn that *80%* of those shot with handguns survive the experience! As long as you understand the purpose and limitations of handguns, as long as you have a powerful and accurate rifle nearby, you won't expect too much of handguns and get yourself into an inappropriate tactical situation.

For these reasons, this book is admittedly *not* a handgun book. While I used to be *much* more interested in pistols, they somewhat bore me today. I've owned (or at least shot) nearly everything out there, and have become rather sold on the Glock. It works perfectly right out of the box. Install some tritium sights, stuff it full of CorBon, and go on with your life. (I have.) If you're sold on the 1911 or the SIG or the HK, that's fine, too. They are all excellent weapons, and although I am clearly a "Glockaholic," I'm not a complete snob, either.

My point being, there's no longer time to endlessly debate 9mm versus .45. Pick a quality, reliable gun you like in the most powerful cartridge you can handle, use reliable ammo, pay for the best training, dry fire daily, shoot weekly, and carry it every hour. If you do that, it won't really *matter* if it's a Glock or a Colt, a 9mm or a .45. Carry a good gun with you daily, have the skill to use it instantly—and you're 98% there.

Besides, handguns never won a war—only *rifles* win wars. Only *rifles* perforate bulletproof vests and combat web gear. If you want to spend Ø2,000 on a custom 1911, fine, but *if* such an expense *precludes* your buying and training with a .308 battle rifle, then your priorities are inverted. I'd rather spend that money on an M1A, even if it left me with a Makarov 9x18 pistol. With the Makarov I could fight my way back to my M1A; if you only have your fancy 1911, where can you fight *to* from there?

My point made, let's now discuss some handguns.

SEMI-AUTOS

These were not designed for plinking or hunting, but to quickly drop a lethal assailant in his tracks. Such a handgun must be utterly *reliable,* and sufficiently *powerful and accurate.* **Above all they must be *reliable.***

Semi-autos vs. Revolvers

While revolvers have their small place in a defensive battery, a good auto is the way to go. When autos weren't as reliable, then perhaps revolvers had the nod—but no longer. Autos are chambered for the excellent .40S&W and .45ACP, hold 8 to 16rds, and can be fully reloaded within 2 seconds with practice.

Which semi-auto cartridge?

This choice is crucial. You are delivering kinetic energy to a hostile, adrenalized, lethal assailant—and the goal is to stop his actions. Obviously, you want to give him as much KE as possible. As Clint Smith wisely counsels, *"No handgun is too small to conceal, and none is too large in a fight."*

Carry the *largest* reliable handgun you can *conceal,* in the *most* powerful cartridge you can *handle.*

.22LR   (40/1100 for 107fpe)
.25ACP   (50/750 for 62fpe)
Unless you can place shots with eyeball accuracy *without fail*, these cartridges will likely merely enrage your assailant. Granted, those shot by them often die, but only *hours* later, which is no consolation to you in that dark, terrifying alley. In truth, these guns are really practical only as a 3rd or 4th carry gun, and used to fight your way back to your main handgun.

While .22LR is only 2¢/rd vs. 20¢/rd for .25ACP, the centerfire .25 is a bit more reliable. If you choose one of these imps for a backup gun, you might get one in *each* cartridge, practice with the .22LR and carry the .25. (Still, I'd forgo them both for a micro .32ACP.)

7.62x25 Tokarev (74/1600 for 421fpe)
This is a zippy (*i.e.*, 1600+fps) Commie round which punches through many Kevlar vests. Bulgarian ammo is the hottest. Available in the CZ52 for Ø125. This is also interchangeable with the .30 Mauser (of C96 Broomhandle fame).

.32ACP   (72/875 for 122fpe)
.380ACP (9mm Short/9mm *Kurz*/9x17)   (95/900 for 171fpe)
These are popular in Europe, where all the *Gendarmie* have to do is wing a Bad Guy for him to give up. They are still too weak (unless perhaps using MagSafe or Glasers) to reliably drop a truly nasty dude. Choose the .380 over the .32 (which only makes sense in the 12oz micros, such as the Seecamp, Guardian, or Kel-Tec). .380s are a decent compromise for smaller shooters who can't handle a compact 9mm.

The modern Hungarian RK59 is basically a Walther clone with an alloy frame, and is a high-quality bargain.

9x18 Makarov   (95/1100 for 255fpe)
In between the .380 (9x17) and the 9mm Luger (9x19), the 9x18 is the most powerful round in a pocket blowback handgun. Why have it in .380 when you can have it in 9x18? I consider this Commie round to be the *absolute* defensive minimum. When loaded with MagSafe, this is a fairly capable cartridge, although I still prefer something more powerful.

Any of the East German, Russian, Bulgarian, or Chinese Makarov pistols are a fine choice, as well as the Hungarian or Czech CZ Walther-clones. (You should also buy a spare barrel in .380ACP, just in case 9x18 ammo ever dries up.)

9x19 Luger (115/1300 for 431fpe)

While the 9mm was once the only reasonable alternative to the .45ACP, it's not any longer because of the .40S&W. The 9mm, if loaded with *very* hot (1300+fps) 115gr Hornady XTPs or other zorchy defensive loads (MagSafe, Glaser, CorBon), can be quite deadly, however, standard FMJ is not very impressive.

Since most 9mm handguns are also offered in .40, there's no compelling reason to keep (much less *buy*) a 9mm for primary defense. If it comes in 9mm, it'll likely also come in .40, so why (unless you've weak wrists) have it in the lesser 9mm?

Yeah, more people have probably been killed with the 9x19 than any other handgun cartridge—so *what?* Before spears, knives, and bows were around, more people had been killed by rocks. Progress, folks. Unless, you can't handle more powerful cartridges or unless you've chosen it for a backup gun, there's little point for the 9x19 today.

If you're overseas, know that civilians often may *not* own military cartridges like the 9x19, so their guns are chambered in 9x21. (Wherever instituted, *"gun control"* is just plain silly.)

If you must carry a 9mm, then CorBon is your fodder. Their 115gr +P loads have given 92% one-shot stops.

.38 Super   (125/1275 for 451fpe)

Developed in the 1920s to perforate early body armor, Elliot Ness used 1911s and *Thompsons* (cool!) in .38 Super. While the ballistics are very respectable, it's a semi-rimmed case which gives irregular accuracy. A dying cartridge whose performance is exceeded by the .357 SIG.

.357 SIG   (125/1375 for 525fpe)

A 10mm case shortened to 22mm and necked down to 9mm, giving 125/1375—nearly duplicating a 4" .357 Magnum. Barrels for Glocks (only Ø75-90 from CTD) drop in the G22/23/27 models and use the same mags. Because its .355 bullet is feeding into a .40 chamber, the .357 SIG is known for malfunction-free feeding. Dies and factory ammo now exist. Best factory loads are the 125gr CorBon and Speer Gold Dot.

Stopping power *should* be excellent (*i.e.*, 90+% one shot stops), however, street data on this 1995 cartridge is still developing. The .357 SIG has a *lot* going for it. Stay tuned.

9x23 Winchester   (125/1500 for 625fpe)

This a 9mm "Magnum." While as hot as the .357 Mag, and with a 9mm's mag capacity, not many handguns are yet made for it. A Glock in 9x23 would be great, but since the *"Crime Bill"* mandates a 10rd mag, stay with the .40S&W or .357 SIG.

9x25 (125/1750 for 850fpe)

Jim Cirillo had Jarvis make a Glock barrel for this wildcat, and it's quite the deathray. It's ballistically similar to the .30 Carbine, which is (in JHP) quite an effective stopper within 50yds. With an MV of 1750fps, the Bad Guy will experience mild hydrostatic shock—which is exactly the point.

.40S&W (135/1300 for 507fpe, or 180/1100 for 484fpe)

Ballistically a "10mm Lite" (or a .41AE without the rebated rim). The .40 caliber bullet measures exactly between the 9mm (.355) and .45, and is a fine compromise between the 9mm's capacity and the .45's knockdown power. For example, the same sized mag will hold 15/9mm, 13/.40, or 10/.45.

Introduced in 1990, most badges now use the .40 (usually the Glock 22) so ammo is very common. Its real-world effectiveness (far superior to the 9mm and just as good as a hot .45ACP) has been well-proven by the police. (CorBon has a wonderful 135/1350 load with 96% one-shot stops. The 150gr penetrates a bit more with less fragmentation, and would be a fine winter choice given the heavier clothing of the season.)

The .40S&W is easily available outside North America (the 9x19 and .45ACP being *verboten* military rounds).

10mm (135/1450 for 630fpe, or 200/1200 for 640fpe)

Jeff Cooper's rule of thumb for a minimum defensive handgun cartridge is a 200gr .40 at 1000fps. He was instrumental in developing the 10x25 (200/1200, which is about 85% of .41 Magnum specs) and its original handgun, the Bren Ten. Since the Bren was a Ø1,000 handgun and mags became as scarce as hen's teeth, the 10mm nearly died on the vine until Colt came out with the Delta Elite in 1987. Once Glock introduced their Model 20, the 10mm's survival was assured.

The 10mm is the best stopper of any common auto cartridge; better than the .40 or even the .45ACP. Its 75yds downrange energy equals the muzzle energy of the .45ACP, just in case you're wondering. The 10mm is *stompy*. This does not come without a price, however, as it's a handful to control. It also needs at least a 5" barrel to make its muzzle velocity.

The 10mm also makes an excellent trail cartridge for those insisting on an auto over a revolver. Guitarist and hunting activist Ted Nugent carries a Glock 20 wherever he goes, ranch or city, and such is a fine choice. (He even concealed it onto the stage of *Politically Incorrect*, to the horror of liberal co-guest Donna Shalala who hugged him at show's end. *Heh!*)

.400 CorBon   (150/1350 for 607fpe, or 165/1300 for 619fpe)

A shortened .45 case (ACP or Win Mag) necked down to .40. Conceptually, it is the .357 SIG's big brother. 10mm energy from a G21 or Colt 1911A1 with a simple barrel change, although frame battering from excessive slide velocities is common unless you add a stiffer recoil spring. A better stopper than the .45ACP, with superior penetration and reliability (it's a bottleneck case). (Call CorBon at 800-626-7266.)

I'm wondering when somebody will neck down the 10mm case to 9mm, or even .32? A 115gr 9mm bullet at 1600fps, or a 72gr .32 bullet doing 2000fps would be very potent!

.40 Super   (165/1500 for 824fpe, or 200/1300 for 750fpe)

This is also a bottlenecked case very similar to the .400 CorBon, but slightly longer. The 155gr and 165gr loads statistically have given 98% one-shot stopping power. Basically, this is an autoloading .41 Magnum. (What dandy carbine caliber this would make!) I've got a Glock 21 that is just begging to be converted to .40 Super.

Although the 135gr at 1800fps for 971fpe is *trés* zappy at 97% one-shot stops, the bullet is really too light for good all-around penetration. The 200gr at 1300fps for 750fpe is "only" an 89% one-shot stopper. (I'd choose the 165gr load.)

.45ACP   (185/1153 for 546fpe, or 230/820 for 343fpe)

People shoot 9mms for the pistol, and .45s for the caliber.
— Jeff Cooper

Designed by John Browning in 1905 with a 230gr/820fps load, the .45 (11.25x23) has been historically proven an excellent stopper. While not noted for its penetration, neither is a brick, but either will put 'em down. I like the .45, except for its reduced mag capacity (the same sized mag will hold 3rds *more* in .40S&W). Since the *"Crime Bill"* stuck us with 10rd mags, many folks are now going back to the .45 since the higher potential mag capacities of the 9mm and .40 are moot (for new guns). If you can only have a 10rd mag, then it might as well be a .45! The Glock 30 is my favorite .45—11rds of concealable power.

Again, CorBon makes the chow of choice in their 185gr.

.45 Super (185/1300 for 694fpe, or 200/1200 for 640fpe)

This is made from .451 Detonics brass which has a much thicker case. Cut to .45ACP length, the .45 Super feeds and chambers in any .45ACP, but you will need a 35% stronger recoil spring. This hotter .45 will give you an extra 200fps, thus 10mm/.400 CorBon muzzle energy. Robar can set up your gun. It'd probably be cheaper to just get a .400 CorBon barrel, and the higher velocity .400 would have better penetration.

There are also other very hot .45 cartridges, such as the .450 SMC and the .460 Rowland (185/1550 for 987), but these are truly overkill and will wear out your gun pretty quickly.

The winners are...the .40S&W, 10mm, and .45ACP

Their one-shot stop performance is 94+%, many handguns are chambered for them, and ammo can be found anywhere. The .357 SIG, .400 CorBon. 40 Super, and .45 Super are *great* defensive rounds, but uncommon. (That will change.)

I did not include the 9mm, since the .40S&W is available in 80% of modern 9mm-class handguns. Why settle for a 400fpe cartridge when you can have *500*fpe from the same sized gun?

So, which *is* it—.40S&W, 10mm, or .45ACP?

This choice is by no means clear cut, as all three rounds are very fine stoppers. For me, one edges out the other two, but you may disagree based on your personal needs and opinion.

10mm

If I were carrying around a *full-size* handgun in a belt holster, and cartridge commonality with my other guns or with my buddies wasn't a big issue, then I'd wear a 10mm Glock 20 (not the shorter barreled G29, as I'll soon explain) stuffed with 155gr CorBons. I don't mind the 10mm's recoil—you've got to *take* it in order to *give* it—there's no getting around Newton's Law.

.45ACP

The .45ACP is also excellent (even with FMJ), although mag capacity suffers and few compact autos are available (*i.e.*, Glock 30 and 36, Detonics, ParaOrd P10, Colt Officer's ACP, AMT, and Star PD). The G30 probably would be my first choice (using 13+2rd G21 mags for spares).

.40S&W

I think the .40S&W is the most *efficient* cartridge as it delivers 93% of the .45's KE from a more compact round. This is usually quite ample since modern handgun technique demands 2+ shots to the body. If 2+ solid hits with a .40 won't do it, then it seems unlikely that using a .45 or 10mm would have made the difference. Therefore, I'd rather have the extra mag capacity of the .40 without the 10mm's recoil. The Glock 23 would be my top choice, with 15+2rd G22 mags for spares. (By the way, I've heard of reloaded .40 case head failures in Glocks, as the head isn't totally supported near the feed ramp).

I will also discuss handguns in 10mm and .45ACP, just in case you're already set on one of these fine cartridges.

Handgun practice ammo

Any quality FMJ (full metal jacket, which means a copper shell without a hollow-point). At gun shows you should buy it 500-1,000rds at a time for 12-17¢/rd, versus 20-30¢/rd at the store in a 50rd box. If you can't get to a gun show, then pick up a copy of the *Shotgun News* and have some shipped to you UPS. This affordable ammo is called "factory reloads" which means professionally reloaded from once-fired brass. Don't worry—this ammo is quite safe and reliable. Always have at *least* 500rds of FMJ for practice. I know that sounds like a lot, but you can easily go through such in just a few afternoons.

Handgun defensive ammo

Regular FMJ ammo is the most *reliable* (in semi-autos), but these bullets do not expand or break up, which reduces their stopping power. Many experts (notably Clint Smith) use only FMJ in their duty guns because of the reliability, and since FMJ is a poor fightstopper, these experts logically pick the .45 (which throws the biggest and heaviest FMJ bullet). This all makes cold, hard sense, and I would concur on behalf of most readers.

However, not everyone can or will carry a .45, and thus FMJ's effectiveness in 9mm or even .40 is much reduced. So, some sort of hollow-point (*if* your semi-auto will function with them 100%) or frangible bullet is often the preferred choice.

Whichever defensive ammo you choose, it is *vital* that you run a few mags worth through your gun to make certain that it feeds and functions *100%*. (If it doesn't, then try another kind.) Don't *assume* that it will function 100%—*know* firsthand! Only your life depends on it.

defensive hollowpoint rounds

There are many: CorBon, Speer Gold Dot, Golden Saber, Starfire, and Hydra-Shok to name a few. The best in my opinion is CorBon. Muzzle velocities are quite high, and the bullets expand very consistently. (Handloaders can nearly duplicate CorBon rounds with Hornady XTPs loaded to equal velocities. My friend "R.H." does so using a secret blend of powders, with amazing results.) Which weight? **When in doubt, pick the 2nd lightest.** (For example, in .40S&W this would be the 150gr, and in .45ACP the 185gr.) Although the lightest bullets often have the highest energy and the highest percentage of one-shot stops, they are really too light for general use (which may require greater penetration). If you anticipate having to shoot through thicker cover (*e.g.,* heavy clothing, barricades, automobiles, etc.), then choose the 2nd heaviest load in your caliber.

defensive frangible rounds

When shooting a lightly clothed attacker within 25yds, nothing stops better than a MagSafe. (Glaser comes close.)

However, these bullets are made to break up within a couple of inches, and thus are not suitable for penetrating heavy clothing or cover.

Furthermore, since these rounds employ hypervelocity to achieve their substantial energies, such quickly lose energy after 25-50yds as velocity falls off.

Also, due to their composition, accuracy of frangibles is not as good as solid core bullets. This may prove to be a real problem when trying to make a crucial headshot at 25yds.

Finally, at Ø3/rd, MagSafes and Glasers are too expensive to test for reliability and accuracy, much less to train with.

In summary, I would not recommend frangible rounds for anything but *indoor* urban defense. They are fine for apartment or condo dwellers, but not for outdoors. This conclusion differs somewhat from my 1998 edition's, but I've since then put much more study into the issue. Remember, I did not—and still do not—know everything about guns, thus my experience and knowledge remain evolutionary. (Two years from now, I may be wholeheartedly agreeing with Clint Smith and recommending only .45 FMJ due to its highest reliability.)

Single-action, double-action, or Glock?

Now that we've decided on one of three cartridges, which kind of trigger and safety operation is the best?

Single-action (SA)—Colt 1911, etc.

To fire your first shot (we're assuming a chambered round) you must either thumb cock the hammer from Condition 2, or drop the safety from Condition 1. In duty mode, carrying in Condition 1 is preferable, although proper training is essential. This is better than a DA from Condition 2 (because of the DA's longer first trigger pull).

Good SA handguns are the Colt 1911A1 (and quality clones like the Kimber, Springfield Armory, Para Ord, Argentine 1927 Sistema, Ballester-Molina), HK USP, Browning Hi-Power, Astra A70, Tokarev, Star M40 Firestar, SIG P210, Polish Radom (WWII), Swedish Lahti, Helwan Brigadier, and Star Model B.

Double-action (DA)—Beretta 92, etc.

Since the trigger will both cock and drop the hammer (thus the "double" action), a DA handgun may be ready-carried in Condition 2 and needs no thumb cocking or safety manipulation to fire your first shot.

This sounds real neat, *however*, that first trigger pull needs 10-15lbs of effort, and all successive shots are single-action pulls (since the slide cocks the hammer during its cycle). The SA pulls are only 4-6lbs. So what, you ask? Try to put two fast shots to the body from a DA sometime. You'll usually pull one of them off target because of the trigger effort difference. (The Daewoo DP51 minimizes this with its clever lightweight DA pull, but a disparity still remains. The DAO handguns like the Colt 2000 and some S&Ws were another try.)

While this can be overcome with *a lot* of practice (like *"swimming the English Channel without flippers"* according to Cooper), there's a much better way—the Glock.

Good DAs are Walthers, HKs, SIGs (220, 225, 226, 228, 229, 230, 232, 239), Beretta 92s (and Taurus clones, which are better than the Berettas), Astras (A75, A80, A90, A100), AMT Backup, Hungarian FEG FP9, Makarov, Daewoo DP51, Colt Double Eagle, and Browning BDA.

I think that S&W autos *suck*, although their 3rd Gen models are reportedly very reliable. (Still, after S&W's March 2000 sellout, why bother? Clint Smith of Thunder Ranch proposed that we get together and buy back that firm so steeped in American heritage, rather than merely bitch and boycott.)

The CZ75 and 97B (and quality clones, like the Tanfoglio TA90, EAA Witness, Beretta 92M9, Springfield P9, Taurus PT92/99 and PT52S, Jericho 941, etc.) are SA *and* DA. You can carry in either Condition 1 (cocked and locked in SA) or Condition 2 (hammer down, safety off, DA pull).

Avoid DAOs in general, except for the Seecamp and other quality micros (*e.g.,* Guardian, Kel-Tec).

Glock "Safe Action"

Gaston Glock, an Austrian engineer, made a quantum leap on several levels with his Glock 17 in 1981. Regarding the trigger system, there is no manual safety on the slide. A safety bar protrudes from the trigger face and is automatically pressed by the finger when pulling the trigger. Further pressure unlocks an internal safety, and the final pressure cocks the striker (there is no hammer) and then releases it.

This means that the chambered Glock is carried in sort of a Condition 2 and that a mere pull of the trigger will fire the handgun without any SA 1911-style safety manipulation. **The real beauty is that the first trigger pull is the *same* as the rest.** Until you've trained with a Glock you can't appreciate how superior this is to a DA, or even a SA.

Because the Glock has no manipulative SA safety, there's no safety to miss on the draw stroke or accidentally to thumb up when firing—and either can happen to the best of shooters. Because the Glock's trigger pull never changes (as do the DAs), you will shoot better in adrenalized conditions.

With the Glock, you must *flawlessly obey* Rule 3 discipline. (Rule 3 should be flawless with *any* weapon, but it's *especially* important with the Glock.)

S&W blatantly copied the Glock trigger/safety system for their crappy Sigmas. Gaston Glock sued for patent infringement. After realizing that Glock was *serious*, S&W settled for Ø3,000,000 and agreed to alter their Sigmas. Heh!

GLOCK

Not only is the Glock trigger/safety system the simplest and easiest to train with, Glocks are the most rugged and reliable of *any* auto handgun. (The factory has a G17 with over

*500,000*rds through it.) You can run over a Glock with a truck, dunk it in a swamp, drag it through the dirt, and it'll still work.

The Glock is made of just 33-34 parts (the Colt 1911 has 57 to nearly 80), and uses a polymer/metal insert molded hybrid frame for lighter weight (14% of steel) and better recoil absorption. Others now on the polymer bandwagon are HK (which used such first in their VP70), Walther, S&W, Colt, Kimber, CZ, Taurus, Ruger, SIG, EAA, Grendel, Kahr, Kel-Tec, and Patriot.

The slide is CNC-milled, so it's most efficient to produce. The Tenifer finish is 99% saltwater corrosion-resistant and 69 RC hard (a metal file is 62-65; an industrial diamond is 70), and just about rustproof. It field strips easier than any other handgun. It feels good and points well.

Yes, the Colt 1911 *was* a brilliant design (which is why it still shines 89+ years later), but, hey, progress *is* progress. In my handgun classes were students with Ø2,000 1911A1s constantly in the shop. (Too bad there's no Hi-Power in .45ACP or 10mm. The .40S&W model, however, is great.) A Ø450 Glock works out of the box, *period*, and I've owned or shot about *everything*. Only the SIGs and tuned Colts are slightly more accurate (though generally not quite as reliable).

Get a Glock, and be *done* with your semi-auto handgun needs so that you can move on to other matters deserving more time and money (like battle rifles). In summary, the Glock is accurate, insensitive to dirt, field-strips easily, and is as reliable as handguns get. There may be a better handgun for *you*, but there's none better than a Glock, and there won't be for a *very* long time. (Probably not until Gaston designs it.)

Shooting the Glock

This handgun is the easiest for novices to train with, as it has none of the difficulties of the SAs and DAs. There are now drop-free mags, so empty reloads are just as fast as with a 1911.

The students who've had problems with the Glock are usually ones who didn't use a *firm* grip. Since the Glock is so lightweight, it has less mass of its own to recoil against and needs your firm grip as a backstop. With proper training and practice, most small-framed shooters can master it.

If you absolutely *cannot* "resonate" with the grip size, then try the grip reduction process from Robar (602-581-2648/2962) which makes the G20/21/29/30s feel like a Hi-Power. Go to another handgun if you must, but *do* give the Glock a fair try. (I'd nonetheless train with SAs and DAs for familiarity's sake.)

Which Glock for *you*?

The Glock numerology is purely sequential in order of design. (The handgun was Gaston Glock's 17th patent, hence the beginning number.) Models in bold are the best choices.

G17	9mm full size (17+1)
G17L	9mm full size (17+1) long slide
G18	9mm full size select-fire for cops
G19	9mm compact (15+1); 9x21 in Europe
G20	10mm full size (15+1)
G21	.45ACP full size (13+1)
G22	.40S&W full size (15+1)—size of the 17
G23	.40S&W compact (13+1)—size of the 19
G24	.40S&W target long slide (15+1)—*very accurate*
G25	.380ACP compact (not available here), 19/23 size
G26	9mm subcompact (10+1)
G27	.40S&W subcompact (9+1)—size of the 26
G28	.380 on 26/27 frame sold in Central/S. America
G29	10mm compact (10+1)—size of the 19 and 23
G30	.45ACP compact (10+1)—size of the 29
G31	.357 SIG full size ("15"+1)—22 size and mags
G32	.357 SIG compact ("13"+1)—23 size and mags
G33	.357 SIG subcompact (9+1)—27 size and mags
G34	9mm IPSC-class gun with 5.32" barrel
G35	as the G34, but in .40S&W
G36	.45ACP compact, but with single-column 6rd mag

So, we've decided on .40S&W, 10mm, or .45ACP. This gives us *seven* choices (not counting the G24, or G29).

Why not the Glock 29?

In 10mm we have the compact G29, which holds 10+1. It's the same size as the G23, but with a bit fatter grip and slide. This is an awesome conceal piece, though it has one big problem: the shorter barrel (3.78" vs. 4.60") reduces velocities by 100fps to nearly .40S&W levels—so what's the *point* of it being in 10mm? None, really. Carry a G27 or G23 in .40S&W, or a G30 in .45ACP. Sorry, Gaston. (One *could* install a G20 barrel in a G29, and the protruding .82" wouldn't much hamper concealability, though it'd look funny.)

Why not the Glock 31/32/33s in .357 SIG?

While I've every confidence in the .357 SIG's effectiveness, let's wait for more street data, just to be sure. Ammo is still uncommon, although that will change. Finally, these are too new to find on the used market.

Just get a G23 or G27 and install a .357 SIG barrel (Ø75 from CTD). The .357 SIG uses .40S&W mags. The .357 SIG loses 70fps from the G33's 3½" barrel vs. the G32's 4" barrel, so just install a G32 barrel in a G27. (The G31's 4½" barrel only gains 40fps at best and isn't worth the length.) This is a fine plan for those with both a G27 and a G23. Every .40 Glock owner should have a .357 SIG drop-in barrel.

compact (.40: G27 or G23), (.45: G30 or G36)

Concealability is the goal here. (If you can *reliably* conceal a *full*-size handgun, then by all means carry that, as they hold more rounds, are easier to control and more accurate.)

.40S&W

The .40S&W subcompact G27 is tiny yet holds 9-10+1—a superb *deep* cover handgun which can use the 13-15rd mags of the G23 and G22. I highly recommend the Ø9 Pearce grip extension (from CTD) which improves feel. (Don't use a +2 floorplate in the G27 because the mag spring is too short.) For the novice, the G27's heavier recoil is more challenging to master than the G23, though it's no problem for any dedicated student.

If you can conceal a mid-size gun, the G23 is hard to beat. It holds at least 13+1, and can use the 15rd mag of the G22. Though not tiny, it conceals very well.

.45ACP

The .45ACP G30, which is similar in size to the G23, is a real winner. It conceals well enough, yet holds 9-10+1 (depending on the mag, or 13+1 if using the G21 mag). You won't likely find any used ones for sale for a long time, so that means a papered sale. If adding the .40 is out of the question and you're sticking with the .45, then the G30 is your compact handgun. They work *perfectly* right out of the box, whereas the 1911s are much more finicky. The G30 is also the most controllable compact .45, given its superb telescoping recoil spring. (It's actually *more* gentle to shoot than its G21 big brother!)

If you have deeper concealment needs, then consider the G36. While it's more uncommon and expensive, it wears and shoots very nicely. (I was a little too harsh on it in 2000. Sorry.)

"So, which is it?"

For *deep* concealment, the G27 is just unbeatable.

For larger conceal guns it's a choice between the G23 or the G30. The G23 holds 3 more rounds, is a bit thinner and has a little narrower grip which feels better to me. Therefore, between a G30 and G23, I'd choose a G23.

More on the G36

The single-column 6rd mag sacrifices 3-4rds from the G30 to reduce grip girth. (Add a Pearce or Scherer +1 floorplate.) However, it's the *slide* that's wide and difficult to conceal on the G30, not so much the grip. Contrasted to the G30, the G36's slide is 0.14" thinner and nearly 4oz lighter. The G30, however, holds 3-4rds more, and can use G21 mags (the G36 cannot).

The G36 conceals better and is noticeably more comfortable than even the G27 micro. After wearing mine for a while, I can state that the 0.14" slide width reduction truly makes a difference. In contrast, the G27 is a block, and the G30 is a *brick*.

Also, the G36 is surprisingly pleasant to shoot given its small size. (The telescoping recoil spring really does its job.) One thing to mention, however, is that your gun pinky gets pinched between the mag well and floorplate, which is easily fixed by building up the mag well with some neoprene, etc. (Or, when you send yours to Robar for a grip reduction—which I highly recommend—ask them to address this issue.)

I'm starting to see more G36s in the private-sale market, and you'll find one for Ø500-600 if you're diligent. Mags, however, remain pretty scarce, so pounce on any you find.

full size duty   (G23/.40S&W)
(G20/10mm)   (G21 or G30/.45)

A "duty" handgun is one worn daily in a belt holster, therefore, the smaller size of the concealables isn't needed. The G23 and G30 are more concealable duty sized handguns, and they do hold 10-13+1, which is probably sufficient. Any of them would be a fine choice if you could afford only *one* defensive handgun for alternative belt and concealed carry.

The G20 and G21

The G20 and G21 are great, though grip fat (send to Robar for grip reduction, which transforms the gun into the feel of Browning Hi-Power—you'll love it!). They carry 13-15+1 (or 15-17+1 with the +2 floorplate) without being much larger than a 1911. Sixteen rounds of .45 or eighteen rounds of 10mm should please *any* hostile crowd. If you *never* envision having to conceal your belt handgun, then a G20 or G21 is for you.

The G23 and G30

For *me*, however, I'd probably prefer a more compact G23 or G30 since mag capacity is sufficient (you can use the longer mags, anyway), and they're more concealable. You never know when you'll have to hide your handgun in a hurry. (Why have a G22 when a G23 is just as accurate and conceals better?)

So, what's *my* choice of Glocks?

If I could afford only one, *and* I were conceal carrying most of the time, it would be the G27. (If deep concealment were not paramount, then the G23.) Two, I'd add the G23 (for cartridge and mag commonality with the G27). Three, the G30. Four, the G20. Five, a G19 (or G26), just to have a 9mm. Six, the G21. Seven, the G24. Eight, the G36.

The bedroom Glock

New Glocks have a built-in frame rail mount for flashlights, so I might consider a making a dedicated housegun from a G22 (or G24L for less muzzle flash) holding a Sure-Fire light (with pop-off IR filter), 15+2rd mag, and tritium sights (which can be used very effectively with a pair of night vision goggles). Such a rig with NVDs would be an excellent weapon to hunt down intruders, using your IR light without them knowing it.

Don't shoot lead bullets in a Glock!

Unless you have a spare aftermarket barrel, don't shoot lead bullets in a Glock, as the factory's hexagonal rifling leads badly, which produces unwanted higher pressures.

Customizing your Glock

Glock Works (800-710-5202; www.glockworks.com) has all the custom gear you could want, and then some. Glocks don't need much, so don't go crazy. Here are my thoughts:

ported or compensated barrels
They ruin your night vision, and are unnecessary with good training, a strong shooting grip, and sufficient practice.

extended mag (if you must) and slide releases (No!)
Generally unadvised—stock controls usually work fine.

3½lb triggers
I like these *very* much. Why keep the stock 5lb trigger bar? Ø25 from Scherer (POB 250, Ewing, VA, 24248).

recoil buffer   www.buffertech.com
Reduces felt recoil and stops frame battering. Only Ø10.

lasers
Don't you *dare*. Forget about the Buck Rogers junk. Lasers don't stay aligned, are hard to see in daylight, and the battery will crap out in the cold or when you need it the most.

sights
Adjustable rear sights are neither required nor suitable for combat handguns. Instead, I recommend a tritium Ashley Express available from Brownells. (I have recently come to prefer the small dot over the big dot, which is fast, though less precise at distance.)

A ghost-ring rear (Tactical 2; 818-962-8712) is also good.

Even if you don't go for tritium sights, at least replace the OEM plastic sights with steel ones (which are much more durable, especially in one hand malfunction and reloading drills where the rear sight is used as a belt catch to rack the slide).

Whatever you choose, make it universal for *all* your handguns and practice extensively.

grips
The rubber sleeve from Hogue is a must. Also, the grip plug (from CTD) seals up that needless space.

magazines
The newer factory Glock mags (with the squared "U" at the rear of the lips) will drop free when empty (compared to the rounded "U" mags). The steel body U.S.A. mags will also drop free, but are hard on the plastic mag catch. The aftermarket polymer normal-capacity mags are somewhat junky.

The post-ban factory 10rd mags (9rds in the G27 and G30) are very reasonable (Ø21 from CTD) and excellent for practice.

Save your Ø75 normal-capacity mags for actual duty carry. If you've got a G27 or a G23, you might as well get the *15*rd G22 mags for spares. (If you *have* to reload, then by definition you're in quite a firefight, so wouldn't you rather that second mag have *15*rds instead of a mere 9 or 13? Logical, eh?)

The +2 floorplates are clever, but sometimes come off the mag body when firing, so experiment thoroughly *before* relying on them for duty. Glue them in place with Loctite Surface Insensitive Formula. (Remember, +2 floorplates are not suitable for the subcompact G26/27/33 as their mag spring is too short.)

Scherer makes (order through Brownells) replacement full-cap mag bodies for Glock.

> *...If the original body has been damaged beyond repair, a replacement magazine body manufactured at any time, may be used to replace the body of a large capacity magazine that was manufactured before the effective date of the act.*
> — Edward Owen, Jr., BATF

MISCELLANEOUS SEMI-AUTOS

Bargain autos

If reliable, any gun is better than *no* gun at all. Remember the first rule of gun fights: Have A Gun.

.25ACP

The CZ45 is a lovely little DAO for only Ø250. While the sights are very poor, this is no target gun.

.30 Tokarev (7.62x25)

From J&G, the CZ52 is a very strong handgun for Ø125, and its 7.62x25 is a real zinger. (They're also in 9mm for Ø150, but I'd stick with the more powerful 7.62x25.) It's a large and rather clunky gun, but a rugged beast. Think of it as the "SKS of handguns." (Get a spare *forged* firing pin, as the OEM cast steel pin will break.)

.32ACP

The Ø100 CZ70 is a steal. In fact, *any* CZ handgun will be a well-made bargain.

9x18 (skip the .380 for this)

If you're on a *real* budget, then the Ø165 Makarov 9x18 pocket handgun (derived from the Walther PP) is a great bargain. The 9x18 is 100fpe more powerful than the .380, though not quite up to the 9x19 Luger. The quality is very good, with the best being East German, then Russian. MagSafe makes hot defensive ammo for the 9x18, and a 1,000rd case of training ammo goes for about Ø150 from J&G.

9x19
The Tokarev 9mm (or 7.62x25) is only Ø130, but is a fairly clumsy handgun which will not conceal like the Makarov.

There are a lot of surplus 9mm Browning Hi-Powers coming in for about Ø350. Fine guns, and mags/parts abound.

The Egyptian Helwan Brigadier is a clone of the Beretta M51 (sort of an SA M92), and a whopping bargain at Ø115. The latest ones imported are pretty rough, so shop for an earlier one.

The Hungarian KBI P35 clones are well made and very good values, although few P35 parts will interchange.

.45ACP
The Argentine *Modelo 1927* .45 1911A1 for Ø375 is a *very* solid auto, with full parts interchangeability. (Recognize them by the D.G.F.M. — (F.M.A.P.) on the left side.) The first 20K were made by Colt, and the remaining 80K in Argentina at Rosaria. These are *the* bargain gun in .45. Great quality! (Serial numbers under 24,501 are classified *"curio or relic."*)

The Ø275 Ballester-Molina is a hybrid of the 1911A1 and the Star Military Model C. It produced between 1937-53 and is very well made, although only the barrel, bushing, link, pin, recoil spring and guide, and mag will interchange with the American Colt. I'd save up the extra Ø100 and get a *Modelo 1927*.

The DA GKK45 from Birmingham Pistol (800-951-4867) is a red-hot bargain at under Ø250. Unfortunately, it is impossible to get spare parts, mags, and accessories for them.

Semi-autos to *avoid*
The **Ruger P series** run poorly, feel just *awful*, and have stupid controls. Can't stand 'em. Besides, Bill Ruger was making them with 10rd mags *before Congress even required it.*

S&W autos are generally poor. I like their *revolvers*, however. (The opposite is true for Colts—except for the Python and Diamondback, Colt are not known for their revolvers.) Notice how I didn't even mention the recent Ruger and S&W sellouts to Government demands?

Do *not* buy handguns by Davis, Lorcin, Jennings, Kahr, High Point, or Bersa. The *gangsta* TEC-9s are worthless crap.

Quality is almost always *discernible*. If you've never heard of a "Yugo Arms" and it looks crappy and feels crappy— then it probably *is* crappy. A decent quality auto will generally cost at least Ø150. Handguns less than Ø150 are usually priced that way for a reason. (Exceptions would be the Makarovs, CZs, and Hungarian PP-clones.) Autos demanding and getting over Ø300 are usually pretty good.

Collectible pistols (*circa* WWI, 1920-30s, WWII)

I have a fondness for these. If you're going to collect something, these handguns are at least serviceable as well as nice to look at. I recommend only matching numbered guns in 90+% condition without an import stamp. Such will go for Ø300-900+. (Get *Gun List* for current prices.) Find an original holster (while they're still affordable), mags, etc. for each to build a fun collection of historical shooting irons. Prices quoted reflect 95% condition from *Blue Book of Gun Values* (22nd Edition).

Most of the below qualify as a BATF *"curio or relic"* and can be bought interstate at wholesale if you're a licensed collector. (Visit www.auctionarms.com, the eBay of guns.)

The Broomhandles, Lugers, 1911s, and P38s are collector worlds in themselves, and you'll need several guide books.

C.96 Mauser Broomhandle

A wonderfully funky late-19th Century gun. Winston Churchill carried one in the 1899 Boer War. The Russian Communists favored them, hence the gun's nickname "Bolo" (from "Bolshevik"). Mauser delivered 130,000 in 9mm (the "Red Nines" from the grip) between 1916 and 1918. There are dozens of models, including Spanish Astra 900. (Given its superior ballistics from a 5" barrel, I prefer the .30 Mauser over the 9mm.)

A Chinese Shansei .45 (only 8,000 made in the 1930s) for Ø900 (plus Ø300 for the original wooden buttstock/holster) has been tempting me for years, but when I think of the M1A or FAL I can buy for the same money, I suddenly get realistic. I.A.R. (949-443-3642; www.iar-arms.com) has a few of them left. I can't think of a more cool and quaint handgun for the dough.

P08 Luger

While the Luger is too ammo temperamental for combat use, every collection should have one. If you merely want a non-collectible shooter, then there is a newly imported batch (most from the former East Germany) of import stamped/arsenal refinished guns for Ø350.

However, I'd recommend spending the coin for a truly nice P08 with matching numbers, a good bore, and no import stamp. Affordable collectible Lugers are the mid-late 1930s up to 1943 (the last year of production). You can find one in 90+% condition with holster for Ø500-800 if you beat the bushes. WWI-era DWMs are also lovely old Lugers for about the same price.

Savage 1907, 1915, 1917

These are elegant and unusual pocket pistols. They have a double column 10rd mag and a rotating-lock barrel. Very affordable at only Ø250 for even a nice one. Add 30% for a .380.

Model 1907	exposed cocking piece	
	209,201 made in **.32**	10,046 made in **.380**
	SNs 1-229,800	SNs 2001B-15,748B
	Ø175	Ø350
Model 1915	grip safey, internal hammer (rarest of the three)	
	6,520 made in **.32**	3,902 made in **.380**
	SNs 130,000-136,520	SNs 10,000B-13,902B
	Ø375	Ø500
Model 1917	trapezoidal grip, exposed hammer	
	89,671 made in **.32**	15,157 made in **.380**
	SNs 229,801-259,472	SNs 15,749B-29,862B
	Ø175	Ø350

By far the most common models are the 1907 and 1917, both in .32. Any of the Model 1915s are pretty scarce (I've seen only two for sale, and one seller had his priced at Ø175, which is what a plain-Jane Model 1907 fetches). All of the .380s are comparatively rare, although I personally wouldn't spend the extra money for one unless you're a Savage collector.

The Army tested a Savage in .45 for the pistol trials (which finished 2nd), but chose the Colt 1911. About 300 were made, and they command Ø3,000+ today. (I've only seen two, both in museums—the Davis Museum in Claremont, Oklahoma and the Buffalo Bill Museum in Cody, Wyoming.)

Colt 1903 (.32) and 1908 (.380)

Over 500,000 of these were made until 1946, so finding one is assured. If you're collecting pocket pistols, then this classic is a must. Prices will be Ø350+. The .380s are four times as rare as the .32s. There were four types:

Type 1   4" barrel, made from 1903-1908
71,999 made in **.32**   Ø425
SNs 1-71,999

Type 2   3¾" barrel with shorter frame, rarest of .32 Colts
33,050 made in **.32**   6,251 made in **.380**
SNs 72,000-105,050   SNs 1-6,251 (rare!)
Ø350   Ø550

Type 3   no barrel bushing, made from 1910-1926
363,045 made in **.32**   86,641 made in **.380**
SNs 105,051-468,096   SNs 6,252-92,893
Ø350   Ø450

Type 4   magazine safety, made from 1926-1946
104,117 made in **.32**   45,106 made in **.380**
SNs 468,097-572,214   SNs 92,894-138,000
Ø350   Ø450

Colt 1911 and 1911A1

These have not been cheap for 10 years, even though millions were made. Expect to pay at least Ø600 for a decent one. They are rugged combat pistols, with ample parts availability.

I have a crush on the M1914 Norwegian 1911A1-clones. Only 33,000 were made, and prices begin at Ø700.

Walther Model 8

This a jewel of a pocket .25—a sort of pre-PP. These were favored by *Luftwaffe* pilots for their small size. Since M8s were often carried inside the waistband, many of them have mild sweat pitting. Nonpitted models are hard to find, and will go for Ø400-450. Also, make sure that it has an *original* mag, and that the grip retaining clips are not broken.

Astra 400 (9mm Largo)

Made between 1921-45, the Astra 400 (also called the *Modelo 1921*) is a very interesting pistol. Not only is it a blowback (like the pocket pistols), it can fire nearly *any* .355 (*i.e.,*

9mm) cartridge. That includes the .380, 9mm Browning Long, 9mm Steyr, 9x18 Makarov, 9x19, 9x21, .38 Super, and 9mm Largo, and Winchester 9x23 (reduced load). It will reliably feed all but the .380 (which is must be singly chambered). Now *this* is a gun for a Road Warrior society wherein ammo is scarce.

Astras have an unfair and false reputation for being junky, when they're actually fine pistols made with Old World quality. They are very accurate when used with .38 Super and 9x23, and are certainly a better combat gun than the Luger. Although the 400 is not terribly common (only 106,175 were made), you'll find a nice one for under Ø250 if you're diligent.

The Astra 600 is a shorter/lighter 400 chambered in 9x19. Visit www.n-link.com/~largo/400_seri.htm for Astra info.

Remington Model 51
Only 65K were made from 1918-1927, this was a very slim .380 and superior to the Colt 1908. Gen. George S. Patton carried one in his waistband from 1944 on. I've seen only a few for sale (for Ø300+) over the years, and the .32ACP guns are *very* rare (add 30%). Three types of Model 51 were made:

Type 1	no patent date rollmark; ".32 CAL" on chamber	
	1,198 made in **.32**	37,925 made in **.380**
	SNs 60,801-61,999	SNs 25-38,000
Type 2	1921-1926; patent date; ".32 CAL" over "7.65mm"	
	8,281 made in **.32**	22,800 made in **.380**
	SNs 62,000-70,280	SNs 38,001-60,800
Type 3	1926-1934; serial numbers 90,501-92,626	
	2,126 made in **.32**	

Walther PP and PPK
Copied by many, the Walther pocket pistol design is a classic. Many PPs and PPKs exist, both pre-war and WWII. The most common caliber is .32, with .380 (9mm *Kurz*) being a distant second. It has a small beavertail, so the slide is known to bite larger hands.

A 95% gun with original flap holster begins at about Ø500. I prefer a pre-war model for its superior finish. Walther also made these in .22LR (most are PPs), which are highly sought after today (Ø700-1,100). I'd still hold out for a Sauer M38H.

Mauser HSc

Another well-made pocket pistol, usually in .32 or .380. They are not very comfortable to shoot, and have never been very popular with collectors, so nice ones can be found for under Ø400. I like them for their beautiful quality, nonetheless. The wooden grip models command a Ø50 premium.

Still, the Sauer M38H is superior in every way.

Browning P35 "Hi-Power" 9mm

A superior design to the 1911, and with a 13rd mag. Many affordable models exist, especially the Canadian models made for the Chinese with tangent sight (these are now widely available). Parts/mags abound. A very rugged combat handgun.

CZ38

This is a marvelous DAO .380 designed for the pre-WWII Czech Air Force. Made only from 1938-1939, it is very slim, and has snag-free lines. A thoroughly fine design (though large, ugle, and funky) made with great 1930s quality. They are fairly rare (I've seen only five). You'll be lucky to find one, and very glad, too! (The Bulgarian version, the VZ38, is *very* rare.)

Polish Radom

A fine combat handgun in 9mm made from 1935-1945. Often called the VIS-35, it was strongly patterned from the Colt 1911A1, and retains Browning's original design of having no manipulative safety. It was to be carried in Condition Zero, with the grip safety needing only to be disengaged with a firm grip. As a cavalry gun, this made good sense, and such is really no more unsafe than any Glock. (What *looks* like the safety is the hammer decocker.)

These very rugged pistols come in four collector grades. The pre-WWII Polish Eagle Radoms (dated 1936-1939; 1937 being the most scarce) are quite rare, and fetch Ø1,000+ in 95% condition. Nazi Type I Radoms (Ø450) are of very rare commercial quality, and some have shoulder-stock backstrap slots. Nazi Type II Radoms (Ø300) were of wartime finish and quality (these are the most common guns). Nazi Type III Radoms (Ø300-500) without takedown lever were made towards the end of the war and have wooden grips, abysmal phosphate finishes, and sheet roll pins (although they shoot fine).

All Type I, II, and III Radoms will have Nazi proofs, except for a few Type II guns which were apparently "lunch box guns" smuggled out by factory workers to the resistance movement (these fetch quite a premium).

Radoms used to be quite rare over here, but now can be found for Ø300-500. Most Radoms have atrocious bores so inspect carefully. Holsters are still rare, so snag one if you can.

In 1997 a limited run of the "VIS P-35" was made with a large Polish eagle on the left side of the slide. Ø850/95%.

Walther P38

This is a well-designed and rugged handgun, quite suitable for combat. Parts and mags abound, and original WWII holsters are still affordable (though increasing in price). You'll find non-stamped G.I. bringbacks at gun shows.

Three firms made the P38 in WWII, though I prefer Walthers (ac code) and Mausers (byf code) made between 1942-44 (these are going for about Ø400 today). The 1940 P38s are very expensive, the 1941 guns are moderately expensive, and the 1945 guns—especially cyq from Spreewerke in Berlin—are usually pretty crude.

If you're a P38 nut, then save up about Ø1,100+/95% for a lovely HP with high-gloss finish (SN <13,000). I saw an HP at a gun show, but it had been buffed and reblued. (It made me cry.)

The post-WWII svw-46 guns (made by the French on captured Mauser equipment) seem an interesting bargain to me.

Sauer M38H

The best pocket pistol of the 1930s, hands down. Made from 1938-1945, it has a loaded chamber indicator, mag release button, enclosed hammer, combination cocker/decocker, and can be carried in SA Condition 1, or DA Condition 2. Very slender, *very* accurate, and very reliable. The only fragile part is the extractor, so get a spare or two from Gun Parts Corp.

Nearly all were in .32. (The .22LR and .380 models fetch Ø2,000+, and are museum pieces. The Davis Museum in Claremont, Oklahoma has a .22LR model with *Duraliminum* frame, which is basically a Ø4,500 gun! Wow.) WWII issues are usually crudely finished (but can be had for as little as Ø225). Hold out for a nice pre-war model for Ø350-425. Forrest (888-372-5968) has Ø20 aftermarket mags.

The antecedent Model 1930, the *Behörden* ("Authority"), is also a very nice (and fairly uncommon) pocket .32 for Ø250. This was derived from the Model 1913 (175,000 made from 1913-1930), a real Junes Vearne-looking piece. (All pre-WWII Sauers exhibit fine engineering.)

Swedish Lahti Model 40

The Lahti was designed for sub-zero temperatures, and it *works*. Just 83,950 were made between 1940-1946. It's a big, blocky, rugged beast of a 9mm, which strongly resembles a Luger (even down to the same shoulder stock lug). When imported back in 1996, Lahtis could be had for just Ø350, but are now at least Ø425 these days. Original holsters and mags are still a bargain, however. Don't shoot +P loads, as many Lahtis suffered cracked frames from years of hot SMG ammo.

The *Finnish* L-35 Lahti (only 9,100 made from 1938-1954) is a *true* collector's piece, going for at least Ø1,000. (SNs under 4,701 get Ø1,800+ in 95% condition.)

REVOLVERS

While I enjoy revolvers, I'm really not crazy about them. To me, they have only two general purposes: a decent defensive handgun for those who cannot (or will not) spend the time needed to master an auto; and trail weapons against big cats, bears, etc. Certainly, in the wild an S&W 629 Mountain Gun in .44 Mag has little peer (but for something in .454 Casull).

Cartridges

In my opinion there are only several to consider. Underlined cartridges are my favorites.

.38 Special   (115/1200 for 368fpe)

Introduced in 1902, it's sort of the .30-30 of revolver rounds. While not a great stopper, the P+ load approaches a hot 9mm. A good cartridge for ladies and backup guns. Derringers in .38 Special are great hideout guns.

CorBon's 115gr does 1200fps from a 2" barrel for 368fpe.

.357 Magnum   (125/1450+ for 584+fpe)

Its case is 0.125" longer than a .38 Special, giving twice the energy. Its 125gr/1600fps load for 711fpe (from a 6" barrel) is historically *the best* one-shot stopper, at 98%. A 4" barrel will give "only" 1450fps, which is still 584fpe (96% one-shot stops). The 4" ballistics are approached (or matched) by the semi-auto .357 SIG, 9x21, and 9x23.

A fine round, but a bit light for a trail gun (*i.e.,* big cats, bears, etc.). A friend of mine out on a hiking trip once had to shoot a charging mountain lion with his Python, and it took all 6 shots to stop him. Carry a .44 instead.

.41 Magnum   (210/1400 for 914fpe)

Between the .357 and .44 Magnums in energy, it's powerful, accurate, tolerable and *uncommon.* While a fine round with great ballistics, it's sort of a *"neither-fish-nor-fowl"* 16 gauge. I'd carry the .44 instead, just like the 12ga over the 16ga. The .41 Mag does have a dedicated "cult" following, but I just can't see the point—not when the more common .44 Mag is *25%* more powerful.

.44 Special   (200/900 for 360fpe)

The .44 Special approaches the .45ACP in stopping power, and *far* outshines the .38 Special. A very good cartridge in a snub-nose, as a long barrel isn't needed for velocity. Also, it can be fired from .44 Magnums.

It can be easily handloaded to 200/1000 for 444fpe.

.44-40 (.44 W.C.F.)   (200/1150 for 587fpe)

An Old West round from 1873 offering 10mm-class energy. Uncommon in modern revolvers, but fun cowboy stuff. Handloading it is a bitch, and factory ammo is pricey.

.44 Magnum   (240/1450 for 1121fpe)

A *fantastic* cartridge—powerful, versatile, and easy to load. The classic revolver load of 240/1450 (for 1121fpe) is pretty stompy. 265/1400 (1154fpe) or 300/1250 (1041fpe) will take black bear and elk within 75yds, and deer out to 100. It is very easy and economical to reload, either in light or heavy loads. The round does *very* well out of a lever-action rifle, too.

.45ACP   (230/820 for 343fpe)

Colt and S&W both made revolvers in this, using ½ and full moon clips. Fun and gentle shooters with decent power.

.45 Colt   (250/950 for 500fpe)

The ".45-70" of revolver cartridges. Between the .44 Special and .41 Magnum in energy (and equal to the .40S&W), this century-old cowboy round is fun for the hobbyist, but better and more common cartridges exist. Still, many pre-1899 guns (*i.e.,* unregulated by the BATF) exist in the cartridge, so...

.454 Casull   (250/1800 for 1800fpe)

It's over *half* again as powerful as the .44 Magnum, and makes it look positively anemic. Sort of a ".45-70 Lite." Gee. (This would make a fantastic carbine cartridge.) The .454 Casull revolvers can also fire .45 Colt ammo. Unless you're in grizzly country, this monster is really too *beaucoup* for most souls.

snub nose (.38Sp., .357, .44 Sp., .45ACP)

(S&W 60 and 640; Ruger SP101, Charter Arms, Taurus, Rossi)

This is a great gun for the nightstand, as it can be kept loaded forever without stressing any springs. They're sometimes only 5-shot instead of six, but that's the price of small size. Go stainless whenever possible. Use MagSafes or Glasers.

.38 Special

I'd go for a 5-shot S&W 60 or 640. I prefer the hammer to be shrouded, if not fully concealed. Or, choose a 6-shot, as in the Colt Cobra. Taurus has greatly improved their quality (and, to a lesser extent, so has Rossi). I'd avoid the cheaper revolvers. (Guns, tires, and tools are *not* the things to sacrifice quality to price.) As the standard .38 Special round is pretty anemic, load it with MagSafe, Glaser Silver, or CorBon. Practice your two-shots-to-the-body in DA, and empty loading with strips and HKS speedloaders.

.357 Magnum

For the stainless .357 Magnum, in order of preference are the Ruger SP101, the S&W 640-1, and the Taurus 605. The 2½" barrel Python 6-shot stainless is also a beauty, though big ØØØ.

Barrel length should be as long as you can conceal. Compact .357s are a real handful, so attach some good grips by Pachmayr or Hogue. Practice with full-house loads. Muzzle-blast from 2" snubbies is literally stupefying, therefore a poor choice for low light conditions.

.44 Special
Best choices here are the 3" S&W 29-3, S&W 696, Taurus M431 or M445CH, Rossi M720, or older Charter Arms Bulldog. (Forsake the newer Charco Bulldog Pug and its abysmal quality for an older Charter Arms Bulldog. Shoot it sparingly.)

Revolver — Magnum (.357 or .44 Magnums)
(Colt Python; S&W 19, 27, 66, 29, 629; Ruger Redhawk)

Those in bear or big cat country should carry at least a .44 Magnum (or even a .454 Casull), as the .357 is *not* a reliable stopper for the big and mean stuff. In fact, the .44 is preferable to the .357 in about every situation, though I included the .357 for those who can't handle the .44. You won't need such a revolver unless you're often in the field. Load your first chamber with snake shot and the other 5 with game loads.

The best as are the S&W 29/629 and Ruger Redhawk. (Though the S&W is no weakling, the Ruger is stronger.) Ruger also makes great SAs, the Blackhawk and Super Blackhawk. I've got a 629 and Super Blackhawk, and love 'em both. I do not recommend the Colt Anaconda .44 Magnum.

Hunting with a good .44 Magnum is extremely gratifying. I'd choose a 629 or Redhawk with 6-7½" bbl. and a trigger job. Some swear by scoped models, but get proficient with iron sights, first. Use Hornady XTP 240gr bullets.

Bargain revolvers
There's an import glut of very decent WWII S&W Model 10 .38 Specials for Ø100 (two for Ø90) from SOG. These are nice collectible pieces and excellent values. For future *wampum* when private sales have been outlawed, a Model 10 and box of ammo will be *very* desirable. You might consider picking up a dozen or two, individually shrink wrapping them with 50rds, and burying them for that upcoming Rainy Decade.

The police trade-in .357 Magnum S&W 65s and 66s are very nice for Ø180-250. The 66 is more solid than the 65.

Revolvers to *avoid*

Same rules for autos apply to revolvers: If it feels like junk, then it probably *is*. All of the Spanish cheapies are abysmal. You can rarely go wrong with a Ø100-250 S&W which appears to be in decent condition.

The only Colt revolvers I like are the Pythons (.357 Mag) and the Diamondbacks (in .22LR and .38 Special). The modern King Cobra and Anaconda guns are pretty sloppy.

.22LR PISTOLS

While these aren't what you'd choose for defense (as it only *barely* meets the military's lethality minimum of 58fpe), .22LR pistols are good for initial training, plinking, and pest control.   At least one .22LR pistol is a necessary gun in most batteries. Also, they're just plain *fun*. I can train a novice for a .40 or .45 *much* more quickly by starting with a .22LR for an hour to shed fear and gain confidence.

.22LR ammo

Use any copper-coated ammo and avoid the leadfingers. The last time I checked, WalMart was selling a 550rd box of Federal for just Ø7.86, which is only 1½¢/rd (less than what I paid in high school!). Thus, you should always have onhand at least 10,000rds of .22LR (for use and for possible barter). Federal seems more reliable than Remington (though not quite as accurate), so check out what feeds and prints best in your guns.

Stingers, Yellowjackets, and Vipers are the hot loads for pests. *Avoid* the Mexican and Russian stuff—it's *bad*.

Auto — full size .22LR
Ruger Mk.II stainless

This is the way to go. Extremely accurate (particularly with a 5½" bull barrel) and good pointers. You'll pay Ø175+ for a used one. The Mk.II has a slide stop and can also use Mk.I mags, whereas the Mk.I can use only its own 9rd mags. The older Mk.I is fine, though I prefer the Mk.II.

holsters for the Ruger Mk.I and II

Get a Ø25 surplus Swedish Lahti leather holster from Sarco or Gun Parts Corp. The Ruger and mags fit perfectly.

Colt Woodsman 1st Series (including pre-Woodsman)

These are lovely old guns, made from 1915-1947. (All variants included, Colt made the gun for 62 years from 1915-1977.) A Targetsman was my first handgun. I was in 7th grade, and think that I paid Ø107 for it brand new. Although I invariably traded it off (stupid boy!), I now have a lovely old pre-Woodsman (1915-1927) made in *1923*. It's a jewel! An incredibly foolish college student sold it to me for only Ø295. Not only is it worth about Ø650, it was his *grandfather's*. (This "Generation X" just doesn't get it.) I will *never* sell it!

1915	1-	pre-Woodsman with lightweight pencil-thin barrel
1922	27,500-	pre-Woodsman with medium barrel
1927	54,000-	"The Woodsman" stamped on the frame left side
1932	83,790-	new mainspring housing for high velocity ammo
1934	90,000-	tapered barrel
1938	MT1-MT16,611	1st Series Match Target (1938-1944)
1944	158,000-	production ceased on 24 January due to WWII
1947	187,423	end of 1st Series, assembled from 1944 parts (sniff!)

A real honey is the 1st Series Match Target Woodsman which had a 6½" flat-side heavy barrel, target rear sight, and one-piece "elephant ear" walnut grips (which cracked easily). The action parts were expertly hand-fit, and the gun was highly polished and deeply blued (but the for the matte top and rear). Only 16,611 were made from 1938-1944, and the retail price was just Ø41.75. Today, 95% guns begin at Ø950, and I've seen a 99% gun in original box fetch Ø2,300. I found an 85% finish gun without original grips for Ø425, and it's a great shooter.

Other decent choices

Other good .22 autos are the High-Standard models, of which there were many. Some are collectors' guns, while some are affordable at Ø275-400.

I also like Erma's scaled-down Luger and P38 copies, although the quality is only good (*i.e.,* not excellent).

Auto — compact .22LR

Once you've got your Ruger, then you might like a compact .22LR. They're not vital, but they do have their place. They are good for snakes/pests, or for *deep* conceal backups. (Still, if you can afford a Ø275 KelTec .32, I'd recommend that.)

Beretta 21A (stainless if possible) or Taurus PT-22

One of these in blued finish will set you back Ø160, but they're worth it. The junky Ø60 Jennings (which costs only Ø3 to manufacture) are a false savings (they misfeed often). I've tried two of the Iver Johnson Walther PP clones, but both were malfers, to my sad surprise.

Walther TPH stainless

It's Ø350, but a real Mercedes. The American version malfunctions often, so stick with the *German* model.

Shot placement is *everything* with these gats!

Practice making *headshots*—forget the body, as the .22LR will *not* stop your bad guy there. If you can *reliably* place with eye-socket accuracy, then this handgun might someday save your life. The original sights will be tiny and dark, but Ashley Outdoors might be able to dovetail in one of their Express sights. A small dot tritium on a Beretta 21A would be just terribly cute, and I'd be real envious.

Maintenance is crucial!

Keep it spotlessly clean and only *very* lightly oiled—all .22s are sensitive to powder buildup. A thin film of NECO Moly Grease might be the best lubrication for it.

Use the hottest .22LR ammo

Something like the CCI Stinger or Remington Viper is what these little guys need. Muzzle blast is incredibly loud, so don't say I didn't warn you.

What about the .25ACP? *Nah!*

Ammo is 20¢/rd compared to 2¢/rd for .22LR, with no appreciably greater stopping power from its whopping 62fpe. Stick with a reliable .22LR.

HOLSTERS & CARRY GEAR

Here's a very important, though ignored, fact: Your gun gear is not separate from your gun, but *part* of it. It makes no sense to own a Ø550 Glock 30 with tritium sights and then stuff it into a Ø10 black nylon holster. Pay for the best carry gear possible, which will pay in superior comfort (which will invite you to wear your gun).

have a sturdy belt!

In my gun classes, you wouldn't believe the menagerie of silly belts the students show up with. Skinny 1" dress belts, 2" wide fabric fashion belts, gold lamé belts, all kinds of belts! Needless to say, those fashion plates had a very difficult time wearing their handguns. I say this, not to embarrass anyone, but to save *you* the later embarrassment (or injury/death from not being able to fight well).

A proper gun belt should be *thick,* 1½"–1¾" wide (a 1¼" belt is really too thin), and made of either leather or nylon (ballistic or Cordura). This will not only best support your rig, but will allow one-hand slide manipulation using the rear sight. Regarding width, the best compromise between function and fashion is a 1½" simple cowhide belt (Galco, Coronado, etc.). The "Instructor" belt from Wilderness (602-242-4945) is the best nylon belt going, available in both 1½" and 1¾", in tan or black.

pants

Only jeans usually have loops for 1¾" belts, so if you plan on wearing a belt gun with other pants you'll have to get 1½" gear. Since you should wear the gun just behind your hipbone, a belt loop precisely inline with your outer seam is what you need. (Wrangler jeans are one example, and the company does *not* support anti-gun causes as does Levi Strauss.)

belt holsters and mag pouches

Pay for top quality so you never have to blame your gear.

Kydex gear by Mad Dog Knives

With Glocks, Kydex-T® gear is the way to go, *period*. It's a tough thermo-molded polymer which is impervious to salt, sweat, water, oil, gun cleaners and most chemicals and solvents. Leather and Cordura just can't compare.

The indisputable progenitor of Kydex-T® gun/knife gear is SEAL A.T.A.K. knifemaker Kevin McClung of Mad Dog Knives (www.mdenterprise.com). Made in America by Americans with American materials, all Mad Dog products come with a no-sniveling Lifetime Guarantee. (Tell 'em Boston sent you!)

I like the Taylor ThunderBolt™ and the Tactical Low Ride™. Also get mag pouches, a Sure-Fire Flashlight holder, and a multi-tool pouch (Leatherman, Gerber, or Swiss Tool).

leather gear

Rosen or Milt Sparks is the main choice of professionals. Hoffners (281-353-6484) makes very affordable quality holsters. The only leather holster I'd want is an IWB model.

concealment gear

Two good books on concealed carry are *Hidden In Plain Sight* by Bloodworth and Raley (Paladin Press) and *CCW: Carrying Concealed Weapons* (ISBN 0-941540-24-3) by Ahern. Both discuss all the concealment options, and have many photos. I also like the annual magazine *Conceal Carry Handguns*.

inside-the-pants strong-side holster

Likely the best conceal carry method, and it has no drawbacks. Worn just behind the strong-side hip bone, it is comfortable, very concealable (when under a vest or jacket), very accessible, and very secure. On the other side of your body will be your mag pouch(es), flashlight, knife, and ASP.

A nice selection of vests: www.concealedcarry.com.

fanny gun packs

Fanny packs worn in front work well, but are by now very well known. So, if you're illegally concealing without a permit, understand in advance that the cops might spot the pack and ask to see your CCW permit. Nevertheless, these packs *do* have their place. I like the Bagmaster products (800-950-8181).

Insist on heavy YKK zippers; they're the best.

shoulder and ankle holsters

I *don't* care for shoulder holsters. They're off-balanced and print through your jacket too obviously.

Ankle holsters work only for small handguns and create a slight limp, but are fine for a backup micro .32ACP.

miscellaneous concealed carry options

For *best* deep concealment, Thunderwear (Ø54.45ppd.; 800-375-4433) has no equal. You'll need loose fitting slacks. I also like the Pager Pal (from CTD, 817-625-7557) and the faux cell-phone case (Phone-E-Pak; 800-209-7904).

For jogging, etc. the ActionPac™ for Ø54ppd is the ticket (800-472-2388; www.action-direct.com).

With an untucked shirt, vest, or jacket, a behind-the-back Inside Pants Mad Dog holster works very well. It's nearest your center of gravity, easy to hide, yet quick to draw.

CARRY MULTIPLE HANDGUNS!

Carrying *two* handguns

Two is one, and one is none.
— classic SEAL answer to *"How many ____ should I pack?"*

Anytime you are carrying one weapon, you should always carry two... Your primary weapon may become disabled, lost, or be incapable of being reached. You may run out of ammunition or may have an ally with you who needs an arm to defend himself... A healthy person has two arms, two legs, two eyes, two ears, etc. A similarly well-prepared individual should have two handguns also.
— Timothy Mullin, *Round Guns—Square Guns* (2000)

This makes a lot of sense, and is very common throughout global hotspots (such as Israel). Ideally, both guns should be not only cartridge common, but *mag* common. Mag commonality will limit your choices to certain systems, such as SIG, Colt, HK, and Glock. For example, some fine Glock pairs would be:

	Primary	Secondary
.45	Glock 21	Glock 30 (can use G21 mags)
.45	Glock 30	Glock 30
.40	Glock 23	Glock 23
.40	Glock 23	Glock 27 (can use G23 mags)
9mm	Glock 19	Glock 19
9mm	Glock 19	Glock 26 (can use G19 mags)

Both guns should be belt worn, with the second gun in a weak-hand draw position (*i.e.,* on weak side, or behind the back). A brace (*i.e.,* pair) of handguns is a very comforting thing.

Carrying a *third* handgun

Cartridge/mag commonality with the first two is not likely very feasible. This gun should be either a *very* small 9mm or .40 (*e.g.,* Kahr), or a snubnose .38 Special, carried in a pocket or ankle holster. (Any fourth handgun would be a .32 hideout.)

Carrying a *fourth* handgun (*i.e.,* the hideout)

These are smaller than even the Glock 27 subcompact. We're talking a *last-ditch* handgun, carried in the bra, groin, etc. This is what you'd use to fight your way back to a "real" handgun! *Extensively* practice your discreet, flawless drawing and shooting, as this is your *last* "last chance" firearm. You simply *cannot* fail with it.

The following .32ACP semi-autos serve well: Seecamp (Ø600+!), NAA .32 Guardian (a Ø350 Seecamp clone; www.naaminis.com), or the new Ø250 Kel-Tec (which is *very* reliable little gun!). I've heard conflicting reports on the Beretta Tomcat. The Autauga is highly malf-prone, so avoid it.

The Derringer (www.amderringer.com) is worth a look, slow as it is. I'd choose the stainless M-1 in .40, a common cartridge that doesn't need a lot of barrel to perform well.

One of those micro .22LRs, such as the Beretta 21A, could work as a hideout pistol, though the round *must* be well placed. I'd probably have an Ashley Express small dot tritium installed.

SIGHTS

As you learned from Chapter 4 *Tactics & Training*, your front sight is your entire world in Condition Black. How quickly it is acquired can really make the difference between life or death in a gunfight. I have come to prefer the Ashley Outdoors (now called AO) Standard (*i.e.,* "Small") Dot Tritium (without a tritium rear sight). I tried the Big Dot for a year, but found it too imprecise for headshots and distant bodyshots. Brownells has any AO sight you need, and most drop right in your gun.

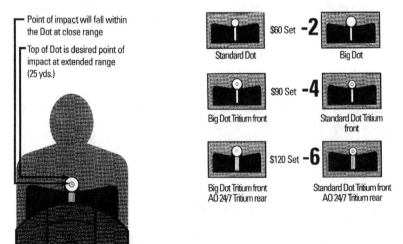

Point of impact will fall within the Dot at close range

Top of Dot is desired point of impact at extended range (25 yds.)

| Standard Dot | $60 Set -2 | Big Dot |

| Big Dot Tritium front | $90 Set -4 | Standard Dot Tritium front |

| Big Dot Tritium front AO 24/7 Tritium rear | $120 Set -6 | Standard Dot Tritium front AO 24/7 Tritium rear |

MY SHOPPING LIST

Every person of gunbearing ability needs, *at bare-bones minimum*, a handgun and a rifle. I'd get your necessary guns *today*. I'm looking at a July *1988* copy of the *Shotgun News*. All semi-autos were "pre-ban"; there was no import ban; mags were cheap and plentiful. The prices will make you weep:

Swedish M38 carbines in exc. condition	Ø 90
8mm Hakims	Ø100
FR-8 .308 carbines	Ø115
Remington .30/06 U.S. M1917s	Ø140
FN-49s	Ø126
Chinese AK47s	Ø275
M1 Garands	Ø299
M1As (w/Ø4 mags!)	Ø325
AR15s (w/Ø2 mags!)	Ø395
Belgian FALs	**Ø595!**
M1D Garands	Ø800
AUGs (w/Ø25 mags!)	**Ø870!**
Belgian paratrooper FALs	Ø875

Fourteen years later in 2002, pre-ban ARs fetch Ø1,300+; Belgian FALs are Ø2,500+; and AUGs *begin* at Ø3,700. Even SKSs are now getting Ø175+. *Do I have your attention?* Good.

Now listen to me *very carefully*:   The queasy wistfulness you feel *right now* over the 1988 prices is *exactly* how you'll feel in a few years over *2002's* prices. You may even feel *worse*.

At some point, *forget* about acquiring a private-sale M1A or FAL. What you have by 2003 is what you may be stuck with for many years, or even rest of your life. (At least *plan* on that.)

You can never have your guns *too* early. If you are unarmed, then guns are a bargain at *any* price because defending your family's lives is (or *should* be) worth *all* of your assets. I'd go into *debt* if necessary to arm my family and best friends.

SO, *WHAT* GUNS SHOULD I HAVE?

Everybody's needs and tastes differ. Here's a guide based on income and urban vs. rural:

Urbanites

Your weapon needs will be much different from those of us in the country. Your primary need is to repel boarders from very close ranges.

Dirt poor (only Ø80-165)

At the *very* least get an Ø80 Marlin Model 60 .22LR rifle. Better yet is a Ø110 S&W Model 10 .38 Special, or a more concealable Ø165 Russian Makarov 9x18 pistol.

Rather poor (above, plus Ø200)

Get a Winchester Defender 12ga or Rem 870.

Lower middle-class (above, plus Ø80-275)

The above pistol and shotgun, plus a rifle. Find an Ø80 Lee-Enfield No.4 Mk.I, a Ø175 SKS, a Ø275 SKS/AK mag, or a Ø175 Marlin .30-30. Also, get the Ø80 Marlin .22LR, if you can.

Middle-class (above, plus Ø1,500 on)

A Glock (21, 23, 27, or 30). An AMT 10/22. An M1A or FAL. Perhaps a backup handgun. Training and ammo.

Upper middle-class (above, plus Ø1,500 on)

The immediate above, plus two more rifles: an AR15 and a Level 1 scoped .308 bolt-action. Perhaps a second battle rifle.

Filthy rich

Buy a ranch and leave the city. The metros don't deserve you. At least have a helicopter on the roof to fly you out when the cities implode.

Rural folks

More emphasis on working and long-range weapons.

Dirt poor (only Ø160)

A Lee-Enfield No.4 Mk.I for Ø80. With this you can hunt and/or defend yourself. Cut it down to carbine length. Also get a Marlin 60 .22LR rifle for Ø80.

Rather poor (above, plus Ø110-200)

An inexpensive handgun (Makarov, S&W 10, CZ).

Lower middle-class (above, plus Ø365)

A Marlin .30-30 or SKS, and Ruger .22LR pistol.

Middle-class (above, plus Ø2,000 on)

A Level 1 scoped, bolt-action .308. A Glock (23, 27, 21, 30). An M1A or FAL. An AMT 10/22. Training and *lots* of ammo.

Upper middle-class (above, plus Ø2,000 on)

A Remington 870. An AR15. A Level 3 sniper rifle. Some backup handguns. More training.

If you can afford it, then also get a .44 Mag revolver, a Level 4 sniper rifle, and a duplicate battery for offsite storage.

Filthy rich

Have fun. Build a shooting range. Get a Level 5 .338L and a .50BMG. Night vision goggles and scopes. Radios. Ghillie suits. Get *all* the training. Invite me over for a visit.

Your handguns

Q: *"What if I could have only one handgun?"*
A: Get a Glock, in .40S&W or .45ACP (*e.g.*, G23 or G30).

Glocks work flawlessly right out of the box and rarely break. Having only 35 parts (versus 57 to nearly 80 for a Colt 1911A1), there are fewer *to* break, anyway. They are indifferent to poor and abusive conditions. In a word, you can't go wrong with a Glock.

Which cartridge?

It's between the 9mm, .40S&W, and .45ACP. (Although the .357SIG is an excellent caliber, it's too new for affordable training ammo. The 10mm, though also excellent, has yet to really catch on and isn't common at all.)

While **9mm** *might* have edge in ammo availability, the .40S&W and .45ACP are *significantly* better fight stoppers.

The **.45** Glock comes in the full-size G21, the compact G30, and the slimline G36 (which is still too new to appear on the used market in any numbers, but if you see one, snap it up).

The **.40S&W** is really the best of both 9mm and .45ACP worlds. It's got 87% the mag capacity of the 9mm and 95% the stopping power of the .45. It's also the cops' caliber of choice so ammo is/will remain common.

While most cops have gone to the G22, I prefer the compact G23. The G23 can use the 15rd mags of the G22, and is more easily concealable. The subcompact G27 is smaller still, but recoils more than the G23 and is more difficult to train with.

All things considered, I'd choose the G23 for my only handgun. Used, the G23 goes for Ø450-500. If *very* deep concealment is required, then get a subcompact G27.

Regarding .45 Glocks, if a private sale G30 were available, then such would be tied for first with the G23. G21s are superb pistols, though quite large and hard to conceal, and concealability will be *quite* important in the near future. Although I wouldn't choose the G36 as my *only* Glock, your concealment needs may differ. (Being the "Glockaholic" that I am, I own all the .45s, anyway. G21 in a tactical low-ride holster for field, G30 for house, and G36 for dress.)

Simply because of the vast ammo stocks, I'd also own Glocks in 9mm and .45ACP.

Attend Thunder Ranch for Defensive Handgun 1, *ASAP*.

Glock magazines

Although pre-ban full capacity mags are Ø50-85, post-ban 10rd mags are only Ø21 from CTD. Use full-cap mags for duty, and 10rd mags for training. While I'd love full-cap mags all around, I don't feel significantly underarmed with 10rd mags.

Q: *"What should be my 2nd handgun?"*
A: **A second model of your *first* handgun.**

This is your spare for caching or for a friend, or in case your first handgun is lost or stolen. Remember in the movie *Aliens* when Bishop had a second shuttle brought down from the mother ship to replace the one that had crashed? Inside was an identical full complement of weapons to replace the ones lost. Only then could Ripley lock-and-load. Have a spare handgun.

Q: *"What should be my 3rd handgun?"*
A: **A *quality* backup in at least 9mm/.38 Special.**

Sometimes, a backup handgun is the quickest way to "reload." Such has saved the lives of countless cops. Ideally, for inventory's sake, it should be in the same cartridge as your primary handgun (if not use the primary's mag), though this is not absolutely necessary.

Autos: The Glock G27 backs up the G23 nicely, as well as the G30 for the G21. (The G36 cannot use G30 or G21 mags.)

The East German or Russian (not Bulgarian, which malf) Makarov 9x18 is a reliable bargain at Ø175-225.

Revolvers: A *quality* snub-nose .38 Special or .44 Special. (The .357 Mag has too much muzzle flash—stupefying, actually—which will temporarily blind you at 2:00AM.)

Q: *"What should be my 4th handgun?"*
A: Probably a .22LR, such as the Ruger MarkII.

These are excellent for training, plinking, and pest control. Younger children can shoot it.

For a full size pistol, get a Ruger MarkII for Ø175-200. For a tiny back up, get a Beretta 21A or Taurus PT-22 for Ø165.

Ammo for your handguns

Have several thousand rounds of quality FMJ (full metal jacket) ball. While the specialty defensive ammo (MagSafe, CorBon, etc.) are better stoppers than FMJ, FMJ is the most *reliable* ammo and it's also the least expensive.

Why several *thousand* rounds? Because there's no such thing as "too much" ammo—ever. One can easily go through 200rds in an afternoon of practice. You'll shoot 1,000-1,500rds during 5 days of Thunder Ranch. Have oodles of ammo. What you don't need, somebody else *will*. Count on it.

For your .22LR, get 10,000rds (relax, this will cost only Ø200) of copper-plated (to avoid lead on your fingers) ammo. Each brick of 550rds will run you only Ø8 at any WalMart. If there's no such thing as "too much" ammo, then there's *really* no such thing as "too much" *.22LR* ammo because nearly *every* gunowner has a .22LR of some kind. We may be using .22LR shells like nickels during some future depression.

Gear and spare parts for your handgun

Kydex® belt holsters and mag pouches from Mad Dog Tactical (520-772-3021/3022fax). They're simply the best.

Have a Model 6Z Sure-Fire flashlight and pouch (from CTD), several spare bulbs, and *dozens* of Duracell 123A 3V lithium batteries (they store for years).

Advisable spare parts are mag springs, mainsprings, firing pins, and extractors. (Glocks rarely break at all. The only part I've ever broken was an old G23's extractor.) Have an extra set of sights since they can break (and always at the worst moments). An extra barrel also couldn't hurt in case yours is damaged from an overpressure load.

Your shotgun

Skeet and dove hunting shotguns have long, unwieldy barrels, 5 shell capacity, and poor sights. Trying to fight with one of these is like taking a 4x4 trail in a Porsche 911. Why own incapable equipment that works *against* you?

If you live in the city, get one of these "riot" 12 gauge pumps with an extended mag tube: a Remington 870 or a Winchester 1300 Defender. It must have a full-length pistol-grip rear stock (Choate), Ashley Outdoors sights, SideSaddle, forestock Sure-Fire flashlight, and sling. CTD has most of this.

Your rifles

If I could have only *one* firearm, it would be a *rifle*. A rifle is what you *go* to a fight with; a handgun is what you get *caught* in a fight with. Your rifle must be able to quickly and reliably deliver an incapacitating blow to distant lethal threats. It must be rugged, reliable, accurate, and sufficiently ergonomic.

Q: *"What if I could have only one rifle?"*
A: Make it a *very* accurate .308 semi-auto battle rifle.

With such a rifle, I could hunt or defend myself. Mounted with a quality scope (*e.g.,* I.O.R. M2 4x24mm, or Shepherd P2), I could be quite formidable out to at least 600yds. This is an incredible amount of capability for one gun.

My first choice would be the M14/M1A. It is accurate, reliable, and easy to service. Smith Enterprise scope mount.

I also like the FAL because of its excellent ergonomics, reliability, accuracy, <Ø10 mags, and vast parts availability.

An original HK91 would be my third MBR choice.

A 1950's Springfield Armory or H&R M1 Garand would also make a very fine choice. I'd rebarrel it in .308.

Q: *"What should be my 2nd rifle?"*
A: An AR15A2 (or A3), preferably pre-ban.

This is a good CQB carbine for the ladies or teenagers.

Q: *"What should be my 3rd rifle?"*
A: An *extremely* accurate scoped bolt-action .308.
Any accurate Winchester M70, Savage M110, Ruger M77II, or Remington M700BDL will serve well. These are the most common bolt-actions with the best selection of stocks, triggers, scope mounts, etc. My preference is a stainless steel rifle in a synthetic stock, camo painted with Bow-Flage paint.
Don't skimp on **barrel** length. Length means velocity (and the .308 isn't a Magnum caliber). 19" is the *minimum*, and 22" is much better. Have a Douglas, Shilen, etc. barrel cryo-treated and professionally installed.
The ideal **scope** is a Leupold Mark4 M1-10X with Mil-Dot reticle and BDC. U.S. Optics also make very fine scopes, as does I.O.R. and Shepherd. Dope it, dial it, dump it. If you can't spend the Ø1,000, then any 3-9x Leupold scope will do fine (send it to Premier Reticle, 540-722-0601, for Mil-Dots). Even the Ø100 Tasco World Class 3-9x-40mm scope is pretty decent. Buy the best scope you can *painfully* afford.
For Ø450 you can have a good quality 400yd rifle out of the box (with Tasco scope). For Ø800 you can have a very nice 600yd rifle (I.O.R. scope, synthetic stock, Timney trigger). For Ø1,200 you can have a truly fine 800yd rifle. For Ø3,000+ you can have a *really* trick custom rifle. **How much accuracy can you afford *not* to have?**
In truth, you could do fine with a scoped bolt-action .308 *instead* of the .308 battle rifle. While I certainly wouldn't feel uncomfortably *underarmed* with "only" an AR15 and M70 Winchester in .308, I'd sure miss my M1A or FAL. This affordable combination is more sensible for families who just cannot spend Ø1,100+ for a quality .308 MBR.
A .30/06 would also be fine. Though it's another cartridge to stock, it's always been *slightly* more common than the .308, gives another 150fps, and can throw the heavier 180-220gr bullets (for elk or black bear). With a Ø15 chamber adapter, a .30/06 can fairly accurately (2½MOA) fire the shorter case .308. If I could have only *one* bolt-action rifle for uncertain times and remote places, the .30/06 really is more common and versatile than the .308. (I'd stock the odd camper or cabin with .30/06s.)
The 140gr .270 would be a close second choice.
Stick with the .308 for your boltgun if you *also* get an M1A, FAL, or HK91. If you *can't* do it with a .308, then a .30/06's extra 150fps *won't* make the difference.

Q: *"What should be my 4th rifle?"*
A: **Probably a semi-auto .22LR.**

These are necessary for training, plinking, and pest control. If you camp or hike often, choose the take-down Marlin M70 Papoose (preferably in stainless). Otherwise the Ø85 tube-fed Marlin M60 or Ø150 mag-fed Ruger 10/22 are the way to go.

Q: *"What should be my 5th rifle?"*
A: **Something exclusively for routine travel.**

A dedicated car or airplane rifle may just one day save your life in some distant big city. An inexpensive M1 is a great car rifle (and legal in more states due to its lack of QD mag). A cut-down Lee-Enfield carbine would also serve well.

Q: *"What should be my 6th rifle?"*
A: **A spare battle rifle (*e.g.*, M1A) for yourself or friend.**

Battle rifles will be worth their weight in gold in 10 years. They may be worth a cabin and several acres of property. No other hand-held weapon can effectively neutralize multiple aggressors out to 600yds. Such rifles are the queen of battle. Have at least one spare salted away in a safe place with its own ammo, mags, cleaning kit, and spare parts.

Q: *"What should be my 7th rifle?"*
A: **If in the city, a third AR15, M1A, or FAL.**

Being able to arm another friend could prove invaluable

If in the country, probably a bolt-action .50BMG.

To bust up vehicles and equipment at distances up to *1½* miles you just *gotta* have a .50BMG. It's the most powerful weapon you can own without a federal license. Unsurpassably serious weapons for unsurpassably serious folks.

"Gee, Boston, that's a lot of rifles!"

Yeah, it *is*. Rifles are merely tools, and no *one* tool can do it *all* (although a scoped M1A or FAL comes close...). Think of rifles like shoes: how many pairs of *shoes* do you have? You've got tennis shoes, running shoes, dress shoes, beach sandals, hiking boots, work boots, and house slippers. That's seven pairs of footwear, and you're not even Imelda Marcos! Now, does seven *rifles* sound so extreme?

At least three of them could be in .308 (the M1A, the bolt-action, and the Lee-Enfield travel rifle), four if you get a second M1A. The only other cartridges are .22LR, .223, and .50BMG.

I *could* have urged you to get two other bolt-actions (in .300Win Mag and .338 Lapua Mag), an AK47-clone (for training), and a Scout Rifle. That would have been *eleven* rifles in three additional cartridges. A scoped .223 bolt-action would also be nice for the ladies and children.

Even though an AR15, a scoped .308 bolt-action, and a .22LR rifle can handle 95% of all rifle needs, only your family's *lives* depend on your weaponry. Will three rifles giving 95% be enough? Is that a gamble you can make in good conscience? If those three rifles are all that you can truly afford, then they'll have to suffice, but know in advance that 95% is all they'll give.

Ammo for your rifles

For .223, choose the newer 62gr SS109 ball *if* your AR15 has a barrel twist rate of 1:7" or 1:9". (1:12" is too slow and good only for 55gr bullets.) Your 1:9" barrel will also shoot the cheaper 55gr rounds (for training) well enough.

For your .308 MBR, any modern FMJ is fine. Good bargains are the Malaysian, British, and Portuguese ammo for Ø160ish per 1,000rds. U.S. Lake City is the best FMJ, but more expensive. Have some black tip AP, too.

For the .308 bolt-action, most BDC scopes are calibrated for the Federal Match load of a 168gr Sierra MatchKing. This is a fine round, very accurate, and easily duplicated in handloads. The 175gr bullets, however, buck the wind better over long distances. If I could have only *one* load for *everything* (deer, elk, and Dad Guys), I'd use the 165gr Sierra GameKing.

THINGS TO BUY *NOW!*

First of all, get your unpapered handguns and battle rifles. Then, buy plenty of ammo, spare parts, mags, etc. for each. Next, get trained at a quality shooting academy.

The following list is based on what will likely be outlawed *sooner* versus later. **Bold items you should get *first*.**

Rifles

Get a .50BMG while you *can*. With some diligence, you might actually find them for private sale in your local paper. I urged this of you in 1998, and time is running out! Two noisome Senators are now calling these target rifles *"terrorist weapons,"* even though there is no evidence of a .50BMG ever having been used in a crime. If you can't afford a rifle, go in on one with some buddies. At least buy some API and Raufoss rounds!

Mag-fed semi-autos (M1As, FALs, and AR15s). Stick with .223 and .308 rifles, as imported 7.62x39 and 5.45x39 ammo (steel-cased, and thus nonreloadable) will dry up quickly.

Handguns

Unpapered quality guns. Pick up every 9mm/.40/.45 Glock you can afford, as they work perfectly right out of the box, rarely break, and are easiest to train with. Unpapered 26s and 27s you should immediately snap up, as well as the 21s and 30s. (The 10mm 20/29s are too caliber uncommon, sadly.)

Stock up on bargain trading *wampum* guns (S&W 10, Makarov, FEG, CZ, etc.).

Finally, highly *concealable* pistols will be *very* desirable in the coming years as the open bearing of arms will become highly taboo, if not restricted. There are only 24 open-carry States, and even there the practice of such is usually uncommon.

Shotguns

Rifled slug barrels and mag tube extensions are eventually to be *cosas non grata*. Buy Brenneke slugs now.

Ammo

I forecast that **.50BMG ammo** will be outlawed soon. Have 200rds of *very* accurate handloads, and 1,000rds of API. Get a couple dozen rounds of Raufoss. Dial in and practice with this rifle while you can.

Stock up on defensive handgun bullets, match rifle bullets (Sierra HPBT MatchKing), primers, and the powder you need.

Parts and accessories

Full-capacity mags. Soon, you'll wish you bought even some of those cheesy 10rd mags.

Spare parts for all your guns. Scopes and rings.

Miscellaneous gear

Night vision devices and infrared lasers. Great high-tech stuff which offers a huge tactical edge to the user. We soon won't have access to this. Expensive, but worth it. Sell your jet ski if you have to.

Bulletproof vests are a must. One gun and one vest beats two guns and no vest. (Details later in this chapter.)

Reloading equipment. Dump your uncommon cartridges and concentrate on the common stuff.

GUN GEAR

Stuff you wear

BDUs (Battle Dress Utilities)
Military camo clothing. Nothing else works as well for patrolling and combat. Rugged and versatile.

Eagle chest pouch for battle rifle   (www.streetpro.com)
For training, around-the-yard use, perimeter patrol, brief errands, etc. It will hold eight 30rd AR15 mags or four 20rd FAL mags right next to your body's center of gravity. In time, you'll never know it's there. An absolutely *essential* piece of gear. Have an extra in every vehicle for every person.

I also like the *Bundeswehr* pouch (Tapco; #PCH301; Ø40).

SKS ammo chest pouch
These are only Ø2.75 from CTD. They have 10 pockets, each holding (in stripper clips) 20rds of 7.62x39 or 30rds of .223. All your rifle's unloaded ammo should be in stripper clips to quickly top off mags. With every chest pouch, paracord a mag loading tool. Have a *minimum* of 3 loaded pouches per rifle.

These chest pouches are also useful as tool/parts kits, first aid kits, etc. Rugged and inexpensive; have *dozens*.

Eagle tactical vest
For extended patrolling, light missions, etc. It has a CamelBak sleeve, mag pouches, and extra pockets. Comfy!

CamelBak
Indispensable for easy and continuous hydration. Get the 100oz. bladder, and have some extra valves.

2 quart bladder canteen
Use this to replenish your CamelBak. Squeeze out air to eliminate the sloshing sound (impossible with hard canteens).

Survival tabs
Contains 15 days of food energy and nutrition in a pleasant malt ball taste. Their plastic bottles fit in the 1qt. canteen pouches. Ø24 per bottle from Nitro-Pak. Buy a case.

Headgear
Boonie hat
Lightweight camo hat that bunches up for packing. Add a couple of feet of camo netting material to break up outline.

PASGAT Kevlar helmet
Although I probably wouldn't wear it every day (unless under mortar/artillery fire), it might be good to have one.

Kevlar flak vest (Army or Marine Corps issue)

While these are *not* bulletproof, they *do* offer some resistance to rounds, and will stop most shrapnel. Heavy and cumbersome, they are still a necessary bargain at Ø75.

Bulletproof vest

Pistol caliber vests are under Ø350, but Level IV rifle caliber vests are Ø1,275. What's your *life* worth? Vests are discussed in detail later in this chapter.

If you get head shot, *tough luck*. A PASGAT helmet might deflect a glancing round, but it'll still ring your bell.

Binoculars

A must. Don't skimp on quality—buy a pair of Steiners. (The Tasco copies are also quite good for the money.)

Don't skimp on size—get the 7x50s. A 50mm objective lens transmits much more light than do 20mm or 35mm lenses, which makes the difference in forests and other low-light environments. Combat vets have convinced me that the superior performance of armored 7x50s or 8x56s (both with exit pupils of 7mm) is well worth the extra weight.

If you see a pair of Steiners with *gold* mirror lenses, snap them up immediately! They are laserproof models (to eliminate laser blindness from the enemy) and *very* hard to find. The gold coating scratches at a harsh word, so don't touch it!

Life Pack

If you're on foot for days or weeks, the Life Pack 100 contains the necessary materials to sustain an individual for 30 days. It's got food, water tablets, cook stove, vitamins, first aid kit, and even a gas mask. A great pack to have in the car, cabin, etc. From Millennium (800-500-9893) for Ø477 + Ø25 S&H.

gun-shot wound (GSW) trama kit

The Blow-Out Kit contains sterile gauze pads, petrolatum gauze, conforming gauze, Betadine solution, antimicrobial wipes, bandage scissors, Bloodstopper trauma dressing, elastic-wrap dressing, nitrile gloves, triangular bandage, and instructional Fast-Action card. (Pro-Med Kits; 530-750-1158)

Stuff you carry

The list can be quite extensive:

Cleaning gear, cartridge converters (from MCA; 907-248-4913), radios, bandanas, sewing kit, foot powder, socks, sunglasses, camo facepaint, multitool, Sure-Fire flashlight, eye protection (shatterproof, 99% UV blockage—sunglasses, and yellow lens for night), ear protection (orange foam earplugs for rifle work, muffs for pistol; Walker's Tact'l-Ear for tactical work, 800-424-1069), etc.

Cache tubes

PVC sewer pipe works great. A tube 58"x8" holds four AR15s and 2000rds of ammo. A tube 40"x8" holds three .50 ammo cans. Sealing them with caps is the only critical task.

GUN SAFES

Anyone can slap together six pieces of steel and call it a safe. Innovative technology offers much more security than raw weight. Once you get above 10-gauge steel, a burglar needs a carbide cutting tool or torch to cut through the wall. If he has those kinds of tools, a safe's thickness or weight won't matter; he's getting in [if he has sufficient time]. We have to look for other ways besides thicker steel to keep him out, or at least slow him down so that the risk of detection is too great. Look for things like hidden hinges, drill deflectors, positive locking systems, hardplates over the locking mechanism, central placement of the door handle to disguise the direction of the door swing, or recessed ball bearings to deflect a drill attack.

— "Safe & Sound," *American Guardian,* January 2000

burglary certification

The Underwriters' Laboratory's 2/1992 "Residential Security Containers" certification is given to a safe only if the U.L.'s team cannot crack it with simple tools in a specific amount of time. Armed with the safe's blueprints, high-speed carbide drills, hammers, chisels, pry bars, punches, etc., the team defeats many safes. Make sure that yours is U.L. certified!

fire certification

Several reputable labs perform such by wiring the interiors with thermometers and then placing the safes into a furnace for a specific amount of time. If the safe's interior exceeds 350°, the safe fails.

the heat curve
Just because two safes are both rated at 1,550° for 30 minutes does not mean that they are equal. One safe probably withstood that max temperature longer than the other. Always ask the salesman to give you a particular safe's heat curve.

the interior temperatures
How many thermometers and their location within the safe (and how hot they each got) is more important to know instead of just the *average* interior safe temperature.

gun safe sources

A.G. English	918-251-3399	www.agenglish.com
AMSEC	800-423-1881	www.amsecusa.com
Browning	800-333-3288	www.browning.com
Cabela's	800-237-4444	www.cabelas.com
Cannon Safe	800-242-1055	www.cannonsafe.com
Fort Knox	800-821-5216	www.ftknox.com
Frontier Safe	800-461-6131	www.frontiersafe.com
Liberty	800-247-5625	www.libertysafe.com
Melink Safe	800-634-5465	www.melinksafe.com
Mossberg	800-795-7893	www.mossberg.com
Southern Security	800-251-9992	
Sportsman's Guide	800-888-3006	www.sportsmansguide.com

NIGHT VISION DEVICES

There are several pieces of equipment which will give you what I call an order of magnitude advantage over likely opponents. Encrypted radio communications are one. Bulletproof vests are another. Night vision devices are another.

Zero Generation
Non-U.S. spec stuff made in the U.S.S.R. Very low light gain, and fun-house lens optics. Inexpensive, and not worth it.

First Generation
Our first NVDs. Heavy and bulky, using vacuum tubes.

Second Generation

The minimum standard, in my opinion. Gen II devices use micro-channel plate (MCP) intensifiers, which are lighter, more sensitive, and longer lasting than Gen I tubes. U.S. Gen II NVDs will satisfy most applications. An affordable value. (Note: 2nd gen Russian is often equivalent only to our 1st Gen.)

Third Generation

Wow! State-of-the-art, amazing equipment. A gallium arsenide (GaAs) photocathode replaces the Gen II multialkai version, providing increased photosensitivity. An improved MCP greatly enhances resolution, and tube life is extended by an ion barrier. Very expensive and *very* worth it .

Uses of NVDs

Name it. Gunsights, hand scopes, goggles, and camera applications. Hunting, surveillance, and patrolling.

Shopping for NVDs

Even among identical makes and models, tube clarity varies. Some have more spots, chicken wire, or honeycomb (fixed-pattern noise) than others. Compare, *compare, compare.*

Unless they've got a great return policy, I don't buy from mail-order since I can't compare actual devices.

Turn on your NVD at least monthly!

Don't think you can buy an NVD and cache it. NVDs must be at least occasionally fired up (*i.e.,* 5-10 minutes/month), else their components will deteriorate. One wealthy fellow found this out when he left his Ø4,000 Aguila night vision scope in his gun safe for over a year and ruined the tube.

NVD hand scopes

Fine for surveillance, but requires a dedicated hand. Choose goggles instead, especially for tactical needs. If you want a hand scope, check out TNT's selection.

NVD goggles

This should be your *first* NVD, as it's the most versatile because of the hands-free headmount. Coupled with an IR laser gunsight, you won't need a night vision scope. You can go with either the PVS-7s, or the monocular PVS-14s.

3rd Gen goggles

ITT PVS-7B (ITT, 800-448-8678)

Absolutely *the* coolest thing you can buy for Ø2,500. You can drive, patrol, and shoot at night with these goggles in their headmount. (One guy used his to hot-wire his county's heavy grader at night and build himself a private road. He would top off the fuel tank after each use, and nobody was the wiser.)

The tubes last 10,000 hours (that's almost 3½ *years* of nightly 8hr use!). They are warranteed for two years. They have a small, built-in IR light for increased illumination up to 7yds. The 2 AA batteries will power for 20-40 hours, depending on much you use the IR light.

I'd get the Ø100 add-on compass, and some IR filters for your Sure-Fire flashlights and 12VDC spotlights. Having some extra sacrificial lenses isn't a bad idea.

Commercially, the military PVS-7Bs are called the 5001 series. The Ø2,500 5001Bs have a guaranteed *minimum* lp/mm (line pair per millimeter resolution) of 45 (the newer tubes are often closer to 50); the Ø3,500 5001Js are 58 lp/mm; the Ø4,500 5001Ps are 64+ lp/mm (wow!). **B, J, or P series?** While the 64+ lp/mm 5001P goggles are just fantastic, the 45-50 lp/mm 5001Bs are 90% as clear and sharp for Ø2,000 less money. Unless you're quite wealthy, stick with the 5001Bs.

A few suppliers are N.A.I.T. (800-432-6248), Morovision (800-424-8222), TNT (800-644-4867), The Camping Supply Store (800-998-7007; www.campingsupply.com), and Ready Made Resources (800-627-3809).

2nd Gen goggles

ITT 200

2nd Gen version of the ITT 210. From TNT.

Russian Night Owl goggles

By comparison, the Russian stuff is 2nd Gen 34 lp/mm at best. Still, if that's all you can afford, it's certainly better than being totally blind at night. CTD offers the Ø590 Night Owl (designed for helo pilots) with 35,000X amplification and 1X magnification for real-time use. They weigh 2lbs. with headmount, and use 2 AA batteries.

The Russian 2nd Gen stuff pales in comparison to the American 2nd Gen NVDs. While *any* NVD is better than *none* at all, I'd nevertheless save up for the ITT 3rd Gen PVS-7Bs. For night ops you need every edge possible.

NVD scopes

The advantage of an NVD scope is that no IR laser target designator is required, thus targeting is totally passive. (If your enemy has NVDs, then they can see your IR laser.) The disadvantage of NVD scopes is that you cannot look through the thing for very long (much less hold up your rifle for hours), so they are not very useful for patrolling.

Get a pair of PVS-7B goggles *first*. They're *much* more versatile than an NVD scope alone. If you've still got the money for a night fire team, *then* get an NVD scope. A 4x Aguila is probably the best choice.

In 1998 I handled a new state-of-the-art Aguila Ø8,000 6x scope, courtesy of a friend who was an expert in the industry. With this unit 200yd headshots and 400yd torsoshots are not a problem. The clarity was astounding. What a righteous piece of kit! He finally got it back, though not without my teethmarks on it. Since an Ø8,000 scope is financially out of the question for nearly all of us, what are the more affordable alternatives?

3rd Gen NVD scopes
Python (from TNT)

This 3X scope with 36-45 lp/mm sits atop a Hughes Elcan mount (which fits on any flattop base), uses a Duracell 123A battery, and weighs just 0.8lb. Very compact at 5½"x3"—like a fat can of beer. The best scope for the money (about Ø3,000).

Aries MK440

From CTD, it's a pretty good NVD scope for Ø1,100. It's got 34 lp/mm, 4.5X, 50,000X amplification. It's a *much* better device than the 1st Gen MK208 and provides viable tactical performance (50yd headshots; 100yd torsoshots). Has built-in illuminator. It's quite heavy, however.

Cheaper Than Dirt (888-625-3848), America's leading sports discounter, were the pioneer in bringing in Soviet NVDs after the Berlin Wall fell. They offer two scopes which have chevron reticles and internal windage/elevation adjustments, use common batteries, have a 2-year warranty, and mount on Weaver bases. There's an 800 number for service questions.

2nd Gen NVD scopes
DarkStar (from TNT)

Weighing 1¾lb, this Elcan-mount scope (with 4X and 28 lp/mm) is very capable for Ø1,200. Uses 2 AA batteries.

1st Gen scopes
AN/PVS-2 (from TNT)
Huge and heavy (2.7lbs.) but only Ø600, and it's Elcan mounted. Uses 4 AA batteries. A cool bit of early 1970s rebuilt surplus which would look great on a wall-hanging M1 Carbine.

Aries MK208
From CTD for Ø550, it's 40 lp/mm, 2.6X with 35,000X amplification. It's a pretty basic unit and only 50yd torsoshots are possible. Weighs 1¾lbs—half the weight/size of the PVS-2.

IR laser gunsights (target designators)
I covered these in Chapter 12, as they are most suitable for a flash-suppressed AR15.

KNIVES

A knife is the most basic and most important tool you can own. Besides a rock or club, it's also the most basic weapon. Having a top-quality knife can make the difference between living or dying. Have a knife on you *always*! Finally, *never* skimp on your knives!

Knives fall into two general classes: utility and fighting. No knife will excel at *both*, although some utility knives are fairly good fighters. Avoid bargain production knives as your *primary* knife, meaning no Buck, no Gerber, and no Cold Steel. Cheaper knives have their place, but don't bet the ranch. My primary fixed blade knife is always a Mad Dog SEAL A.T.A.K.

Swiss Army knives (Wenger or Victorinox)
A must. While the knife blades are rather brittle, the cornucopia of tools make these knives indispensable. Do *not* buy the cheap copies; insist on the original Swiss brand.

folders
I like the half serrated edge blades for heavier materials. A handle clip is quite useful for pockets and inside waistbands.

The Spidercos are good, but way overpriced, and Japanese. The Gerber folders are a good bargain.

Avoid the cheap copies of the Spiderco, *unless* they are relegated for mere letter opening/box cutting.

Mad Dog SEAL A.T.A.K. (928-772-3021/3022fax)

The best utility knife made, *period*. Chosen in the famous 1992 Navy SEAL knife trials. Materials, design, and workmanship are all unsurpassed. Until the U.S. Navy nearly bankrupted him by their slow payments, Mad Dog's A.T.A.K. was the SEAL's sole-source justification knife by grueling trials (in which it beat out 31 competitors, including Buck, SOG, Gerber, etc.). When McClung couldn't be the Navy's "banker" *and* keep up with demand, the Navy in a snit went to SOG. (Many SEALs still order A.T.A.K.s out of their own pocket.)

Any knife is only as good as its materials, design, and workmanship. Mad Dog knives are superior in all three. Kevin uses only Starrett 496-01 high carbon tool steel (hardened and selectively tempered, then industrial hard-chromed), G11 glass epoxy composite handles, and Kydex-T® for sheaths. Their design is no B.S., no buckskin fringe, real-world stuff. The workmanship is second to none. Kevin is a true materials scientist and knifemaker, not some ex real-estate hairball who sells mass-produced Japanese stuff through saturation marketing as the "Ronald McDonald" of knives.

All of his knives and Kydex-T® holsters are backed by a no-sniveling lifetime guarantee. You can will your knife to your great-grandchildren, and the 23rd century paleontologist who digs it up will have quite a usable treasure.

If you want a Mad Dog knife, *hurry*. His knives are sold only through authorized distributors, so call the shop for the nearest order point (or visit www.mdenterprise.com). Get your order in ASAP as the wait can be quite long given his small custom shop. And tell him Boston sent you.

MISCELLANEOUS WEAPONRY

Sometimes a gun will not be tactically or legally the best choice, so your defensive weaponry continuum must include some other weapons (and the training to use them). In this book, I can only touch on several. Paladin Press offers many books on edged and impact weapons.

Telescoping batons

A great deep cover concealed weapon. ASPs are the best. Coupled with a fighting knife in the other hand (and the training to use them), you'd be very formidable. An ASP is one of my favorite substitutes for a gun (such as in foreign countries). Choose the largest model you can conceal.

PR-24, or *tonfa* (hard wood, fiberglass, aluminum)
This is the side-handled baton used by police. A fantastic striking weapon. Buy a training video and practice with it.

Spears
Can be made 4-5' long from green wood, and the sharpened end heated over hot coals to harden it.

OC pepper spray
An excellent non-lethal weapon. Some very rare Bad Guys have built up somewhat of a tolerance to OC, so don't count on 100% street effectiveness.

Blowguns
While I haven't had much experience with them, some folks really like their blowguns. Good for *very* small pests and birds at *very* close range, but that's about it.

Slingshots
The "WristRocket" slingshots with surgical tubing power bands are quite powerful and accurate. A ⅜" steel ball at 500fps packs a real wallop (*i.e.,* a .38 caliber 125gr ball at 500fps gives 69fpe, nearly as much as a .22LR), and can be deadly if well-placed. Stock up on several feet of extra tubing, as there's really no substitute for it.

Bow and arrow
A fine weapon, assuming you've the training and practice. I personally prefer a crossbow over a longbow for its superior accuracy and better sighting options. Have *lots* of quarrels (*i.e.,* crossbow arrows) and tips, as homemade versions can't compare with commercial quality.

Body Armor
to Put the Odds in YOUR Favor
(by www.BulletProofME.com)

This Guide draws on our experience, and the excellent research from the National Law Enforcement and Corrections Technology Center to give you some real fact and insight into ballistic protection. The following also contains opinions on choices and tradeoffs in ballistic protection on which reasonable people can differ. There is always a trade-off to be made between protection and wearability (and NO armor is ever 100% bullet-PROOF). Thus, how you apply this Guide to your specific circumstances is solely your responsibility and legal liability.

Do YOU Need Body Armor?

Well, what is your life worth? (Or peace of mind?) What is it worth to know that you can survive even a SURPRISE criminal attack? Consider that criminals prefer to strike when circumstances put you in the most vulnerable position. You are at a twofold disadvantage:

❖ When you are the target of a criminal attack it may very well be at a time and place chosen by the criminal—to maximize their advantage.

❖ Even worse, law-abiding citizens and police operate under strict ethical and legal constraints to using deadly force. While *morally* correct, *tactically* this puts you at a huge disadvantage.

By criminal design and legal constraint, you are often forced to REACT in catch-up mode.

Body Armor puts the odds back in YOUR favor

An order of magnitude advantage
— Boston on Surviving Y2K

Even if you are "only" in a situation where you are threatened, the confidence that comes from knowing you are protected can be decisive. Tactically *and* psychologically, body armor gives you a huge advantage, because you know your armour can give you a second chance.

It's kind of like poker...
One vest and one gun, beats NO vest and two guns!

Think about the minutes that will elapse between the sound of glass breaking at 3 a.m., and the arrival of police (regardless of the speed of police response, there are unavoidable time lags). Would you rather enter that scenario with JUST a $600 gun—or a $300 gun, and a $300 vest?

Body Armor WORKS...

❖ *"...as of January 1, 2001, a total of 2,500 "saves" have been attributed to the use of body armor. 58% of these saves were connected with felonious assaults..."*

(Of the felonious assaults: 69% firearms, 21% cutting or slashing, and 10% other.)

❖ *"...42% with accidents, such as car crashes."*

v   *"...the risk of sustaining a fatal injury for officers who do not routinely wear body armor is 14 times greater than for officers who do"* (FBI study)

❖ *"No documented fatal injury has ever resulted from a round of ammunition penetrating body armor that NIJ had approved as protection against that level of threat."*

> — *Guide to Police Body Armor*, National Law Enforcement and Corrections Technology Center, www.nlectc.org

Vests protect against:

❖ **blunt trauma**, e.g., fists, clubs and car steering wheel columns!

❖ slashing **knife** / edged weapon attack (though NOT thrusting/stabbing unless special stab-resistant material)

❖ most **pistol** ammunition (and '00' Buckshot)—the regular 3 to 6 lb. soft body armor vest...

...and with Rifle Plates you can also stop:

❖ **FMJ Rifle rounds** - Threat Level III
❖ **Armor-Piercing Rifle**—Threat Level IV

...But NO Armor is 100% Bullet-PROOF

A "bulletproof" vest is technically only "bullet-resistant"—push the velocity high enough, and most projectiles will penetrate *any* armor. There is always a tradeoff between more protection and more wearability (and the constraint to stay within your budget). However, a bullet-resistant vest (Level II-A or higher) *will* protect you from the vast majority of pistol ballistic threats you are ever likely to face. Do know that:

❖ rifle rounds
❖ unusual high velocity pistol ammunition (*e.g.,* from a rifle barrel)
❖ armor piercing ammunition
❖ sharp-edged or pointed instruments (*e.g.,* knives, icepicks, etc.),
❖ and other unusual ammunition or situations...

CAN defeat body armor.

Also, at some angles, projectiles can slide, or deflect off the edges of Body Armor—or ricochet. Furthermore, projectiles that are successfully stopped by the vest will always produce some level of injury, resulting in severe bruising, broken bones, and possibly serious internal injury or even death. Soft body armor vests defeat *most* pistol and shotgun projectiles, but NO vest on earth makes you invulnerable. **To state the obvious, getting shot ALWAYS carries some risk!**

What Vests Are Tested to Do...

The National Institute of Justice (NIJ Standard 0101.03, and 0101.04) rates body armor on ballistic protection levels. As you add layers of a ballistic fiber, such as DuPont Kevlar®, you add protection.

Vests are tested not just for penetration, but also for blunt trauma protection—the sledgehammer-like blow suffered by the body from the bullet's impact on the vest. Blunt trauma is measured by the dent suffered by a soft clay backstop to the vest—a maximum of 1.7" (44 mm) is allowed.

NOTE: The standard NIJ test rounds are listed below—tested vests stop many other comparable rounds, and lesser threats, some listed separately below.

Level I
❖ .22 at 1,050fps
❖ .38 Special at 850fps

(For the latest NIJ Standard 0101.04, the .38 round is .380 ACP at 1,025fps.)

NOT RECOMMENDED: Early generation ballistic fibers, though bulkier, only stop fragmentation and low velocity pistol ammunition. Sometimes army surplus PASGT flak jackets are passed off as "about Level II-A", but in our tests 9mm penetrated easily. Excellent birdshot protection, riot gear, or paintball equipment, but NOT recommended for pistol ballistic protection.

Level IIA   ~16—18 layers of Kevlar 129®
❖ 9mm FMJ at 1,090fps
❖ .357 Magnum JSP at 1,250fps

(For 01.01.04, instead of a .357, a .40 S&W FMJ at 1,025fps.)

Adequate protection for the vast majority of pistol threats encountered on the street (plus 12 gauge 00 Buckshot), though you would sustain more blunt trauma injury than Level II or III-A. Perhaps the best choice if thinness, comfort and/or concealability are the most important factors.

Level II   ~22–24 layers
❖   9mm FMJ, at 1,175fps
❖   .357 JSP at ~1,395fps

(For 01.01.04, the .357 velocity is 5 fps higher.)

A great balance between blunt trauma protection, versus cost, and thickness/comfort/concealability. **What we most often recommend.**

Level III-A   ~28–32 layers
❖   9mm FMJ at 1,400fps
❖   .44 Magnum Lead Semi-Wadcutter at 1,400fps

(For 01.01.04, a .44 Magnum Semi-Jacketed Hollow Point bullet is used. 1,400 fps is to cover the velocity of 9 mm FMJ from a submachine gun.)

The highest blunt trauma protection rating in soft body armor. The best for very high-risk situations, or to cover more of the uncommon or unusual threats. Less blunt trauma injury to allow more effective return fire.

These ratings often have a large safety margin for penetration, because blunt trauma is usually the limiting factor in certification. For example, Level II body armor would likely stop the III-A test standard, (9mm submachine gun, at 1400 fps) from actually penetrating through the Level II vest. But, the Level II vest would definitely fail the test on blunt trauma impact (the NIJ deems any dent greater than ~1.7" (~44 mm.) on the soft clay test surface, a FAIL).

So, the advantage in increasing protection Levels from II-A, to II, to III-A, is NOT so much protection from penetration of pistol fire, but a significant reduction in the blunt trauma received.

Rifle Protection Levels — HARD Body Armor

Level III

Six spaced rounds of .308 Winchester FMJ (7.62 X 51 mm NATO / U.S. M80) at 2,750fps

- ❖ ~1/4" Ballistic Steel (~6 mm)
- ❖ ~1/2" Ballistic Ceramic (~13 mm)
- ❖ ~1" Ballistic Polyethelene (~27 mm)

Level IV

One round of .3006 Armor-Piercing(U.S. M2 AP)
One round at 2,850 fps (~868 mps)

- ❖ ~ 1/2" Ballistic Steel (~12 mm)
- ❖ ~ 3/4" Ballistic Ceramic (~18 mm)

The highest rating for Body Armor.

(For comparable threats also stopped, visit our website.)

Knife / Stab Protection

It's important to know that pointed or streamlined objects such as an ice picks, arrowheads, and knives can penetrate if THRUST with enough force. Because of the "pointedness" they can get in-between the Kevlar® weave to penetrate. Prison guards use special stab-resistant armour with a much tighter, stiffer fabric weave or actual metal mesh or plates.

Obviously having just a ballistic vest on is better than nothing—but the knife protection is not as "bullet-proof" as the pistol protection offered. Kevlar® does work well to protect against slashing knife attacks:

> ...ballistic-resistant body armor is potentially vulnerable to knife attack; hence, all officers should exercise due caution when confronted with these situations. However, numerous incidents have been documented in which body armor lessened injury.
> — *Guide to Police Body Armor*, www.nlectc.org

Generally we don't recommend the added cost of Stab-Resistance unless there is a serious knife threat. The tighter weave makes the vest much stiffer and therefore less comfortable and concealable. Secondarily a regular ballistic vest does offer some (some, not 100%) knife protection. Usually, it's more important to have some protection that's worn regularly, than more complete protection that isn't. Of course, YOU must evaluate the threats you are likely to face.

An IN-DEPTH Buyer's Guide
What Do You Need to Worry About?

Aramid fibers include the original Kevlar® from DuPont, and Twaron®, from Akzo, the European brand. Both have the advantage of excellent flexibility for greater comfort.

The Polyethelene fibers Spectra® by Allied Signal, or Dyneema® (by DSM in Europe) offer both advantages and disadvantages: ~25% lighter, better multiple hit and blunt trauma performance—but also more expensive, and stiffer with a corresponding reduction in comfort. Later generation ballistic panels (such as GoldFlex® by Honeywell) incorporate both Spectra® and Kevlar®. Zylon® from Toyobo is the latest high tech fiber entrant, the lightest, and also the most expensive.

(2004 BTP Alert! Avoid Zylon! We now know them to fail from heat/humidity/UV degradation! Avoid Spectra. Buy *only 100% aramid vests*, such as Kevlar and Twaron! I recommend only U.S. Armor vests—*not* Second Chance. Go to www.tacticalforums.com and explore the M.D. Labs page threads. Kevin McClung has, at no pay, spent the past several years warning the public about non-Kevlar materials, and now that police officers are dying from Zylon vest failures, many state AGs are suing. Dozens of PDs are dumping their Zylon vests for Kevlar replacements. *60 Minutes 2* is considering a segment, and has talked to Kevin. This issue will soon explode nationally. **Get your Kevlar vest *now*, before the rush!**)

What you SHOULD worry about is armor construction as it relates to the coverage of the armor on your body (see below) and the vest's softness and comfort / concealability. Vests can be made lighter and thinner—to look good on paper—with less Kevlar and more stitching (or more Spectra, or even a stiff laminated film construction). But when you wear the vest for a length of time the stiffness and comfort penalty becomes obvious (plus a possible concealability problem).

There is really no substitute for trying on your vest—and ensuring you have a money-back guarantee. (You should have a guarantee for fitting issues anyway.) Body armor is quite flexible to size, as front and back panels connect with elastic and adjustable Velcro straps. A size Large person could wear a Medium with a gap on the sides (for more ventilation, freedom of movement and concealability). A size Large could also wear an Extra-Large with overlapping sides (more coverage, but also more bulk, less ventilation and less concealability). But with life-saving equipment like Body Armor, you want an excellent fit, not just adequate.

What are the Threats YOU Face?

It is possible with current, off-the-shelf technology to be covered with pistol-level protection for helmet, faceshield, neck, torso, upper arms and groin, plus Rifle Plates on the chest and back—but this is not always practical for several reasons...

Practical Considerations

❖ HEAT BUILD-UP— is the number one problem for vest users. Putting on a vest is a welcome replacement for a jacket or sweater for much of the year, but during the summer, heat is the limiting factor in use.

No vest on earth can honestly claim to be comfortable when it is hot and/or you are exercising and sweating. The thickness of the ballistic panel insulates you, and the waterproofing of the ballistic panel simply prevents effective cooling through the vest.

❖ COMFORT / WEARABILITY— is a function of the vest's fit, coverage and softness. if you aren't wearing the vest, it isn't protecting you!

❖ FREEDOM of MOVEMENT— is a function of the vest's thickness or bulkiness, softness and design and fit. If you are hindered in the movement required, your vest can become a liability as well as an asset.

❖ WEIGHT— affects your fatigue level after prolonged wear, and your physical speed of movement. More of an issue with Rifle Plates than a pound or so difference in soft Body Armor protection Levels (or models).

❖ CONCEALABILITY— firstly, your situation may demand the discretion of a concealable vest. Secondly, if an armed criminal notices your body armor, they can threaten or aim at, unprotected areas. You have just wasted part of the advantage of wearing a vest (though you have reduced your target area by half!)

Vests are only ~0.25" thick (~6mm) so just a shirt can cover it up nicely if the shirt is loose, and not too thin. A thin dress shirt may need a T-shirt over the vest to conceal well. A sweater, or suit jacket makes it easy. Rifle Plates are an extra 0.25"' to 0.5" to 1" thick (6—25 mm) and thus require a jacket to conceal.

❖ COST— if you can't afford it, it isn't protecting you! As a consumer, you must realistically judge what threats you face, and make rational choices. 100% protection is not possible no matter how much you spend, but you can get ~80% of the max protection available, for half the cost.

The best vest for you is the one you're wearing when shot!

So, how do you make a rational tradeoff between all the choices, with all these constraints? By the percentages...

REAL PROTECTION =

1) % of Threats Stopped by Vest, and
2) % Coverage of Vest on YOUR Body, and
3) % of Time Exposed that Vest is Worn

Assuming the threat doesn't notice your armor, and target unprotected areas!

For example, if your vest...

1) stops 95% of the threats you face, and...
2) covers 70% of your upper body, and...
3) is worn 100% of the time in a potential threat environment...

You've achieved 67% coverage. (95% x 70% x 100% = 67%.)

67% is a superb score, but, if nothing else, this example should remind you of the importance of training, tactics and common sense. Body Armor will put the odds in your favor— very substantially— but (just as in life) there are no 100% guarantees.

1) % of Threats Stopped by the Vest

Even Level II-A vests are adequate for the vast majority of pistol ammunition usually seen on the street. Level II and III-A offer more blunt trauma protection, and stop more of the unusual threats. But really the decision here is not so much a percentage protection decision, as personal preference—pay a little more, for a slightly heavier and bulkier vest—and know that if you ever take a hit on the vest you might possibly get off with a 3" or 4" bruise (~8 or 10 cm.), versus a cracked or broken rib. We can't make that call for you, other than to say we feel well protected with a Level II vest— a nice balance between competing priorities.

If all you can afford is Level II-A, yes, you might be missing a few per cent of pistol threats (the more exotic ammunition threats)—but in the big picture wearing your vest 100% of the time is MUCH more important. If you simply feel better knowing you have a III-A (the maximum in soft body armor) we can't argue with peace of mind.

The one hard rule of thumb is— get a vest tested to stop the weapon you, or your partner, carries:

> *one in six officers killed with a handgun was killed with his or her own service weapon*
> — *Guide to Police Body Armor,* www.nlectc.org

Tactically, one factor does strongly recommend higher Protection Levels—being able to return fire more quickly and/or effectively. The extra thickness means more blunt trauma protection and less felt impact or injury from bullets striking you. Thus you may be able to react faster and more effectively after being hit— critical if you need to prevail in the confrontation, as well as just survive the hit.

Armor-Piercing Threats?

Some aficionados are fond of expounding on the fact that their special Armor-Piercing (AP) 9mm, or 7.62mm Tokarev pistol ammo, etc., etc., can "go through that vest like a hot knife through butter"! Indeed, you should be aware that some very rare and specialized pistol ammo CAN penetrate soft body armor. But what also needs to be said is that, in the US, AP pistol ammo is illegal and difficult or impossible to obtain (also all the calibers of rifle AP usable in pistol variants).

How often does the armed criminal take the time and trouble to find such rare ammo? Not very often, though obviously you must evaluate the threats YOU are likely to face. If you are a narcotics police officer after hard-core biker drug-gangs— AP is possibly a concern. (In 1999 one officer was just barely saved by his vest from a drug dealer with a 7.62x25 Tokarev.)

So, for example, SWAT teams, and police officers making high-risk traffic stops, may be well advised to get Level III-A armour, just to be on the saf-ER side. For the majority of law enforcement, security guards, and civilians, getting a Level III-A is money well spent for peace of mind and extra blunt trauma protection—but probably not required on a percentage analysis. You must evaluate the threats YOU are likely to face.

What About Blunt Trauma Pads?

Not to be confused with Rifle Plates, these 5" by 8" (~13 by 20 cm.) Steel, Kevlar®/Spectra® or even Titanium/ Kevlar® inserts are designed for extra protection of the vulnerable mid-chest/sternum area from blunt trauma. A great idea and highly recommended, but the icing on the cake— not the cake. Vests are NIJ-certified WITHOUT a Blunt Trauma Pad.

> *NIJ has not conducted research to determine the effectiveness of such inserts. In general, NIJ believes that agencies should select armor that provides the rated level of protection over the entire area of coverage, not just isolated areas.*
> — *Guide to Police Body Armor,* www.nlectc.org

Rifle Protection

The big question in Threat Levels is do you need Level III or IV rifle plate protection? Adding a PAIR of 10" by 12" Ceramic plates will add ~11 lbs. (5kg) to your 4 lb. vest (1.8kg)! (Plus it will add ~$500 to the cost!) You can cut the weight down to ~6.6 lbs. (3kg) for a PAIR of Ultra-light Polyethelene plates—but then the extra cost is ~$800.

Generally, in U.S. urban areas, short-barreled firearms are the main threat because they are the type of weapon most often used by criminals. Worse, they are concealable—you can't avoid something you can't see. You can more easily avoid the criminal with a rifle, seen from a distance.

Once again, you must evaluate the threats YOU are likely to face. If rifles are a possible or probable threat, get some Level III or IV protection, as this is often the only option short of your vehicle's engine block. (Or hoping that your car door will cut ~2,300–3,300 fps of muzzle velocity more than 50%—so that your soft body armor *might* handle it!)

A good compromise is a soft body armor vest for regular wear, with an optional carrier with built-in rifle plate pockets. Or, more convenient for quick throw-on use, Rifle Plates in a separate 'modular' Over-vest Carrier. This allows you to quickly add Rifle Plates when the tactical situation demands.

2) % Coverage of Vest

Rather than focusing on marginal differences of what the vest stops (outside of rifles), it is far more important is to focus on the percentage of your vital areas that are covered by the vest.

Many concealable vests skimp on the amount of coverage of your body. A lot of people are worried about whether their vest will stop the exotic, uncommon threats— but what's usually more important is to cover MORE of your body against the COMMON threats. By all means get a Level III-A for the uncommon threats, but the more important factor is how well the vest covers YOUR body (and that it is comfortable and concealable enough so that you actually wear it).

Side Coverage

If you hold your weapon in the side-angled "Weaver" stance, the target area exposed to the threat is your SIDE as much-or more-than your front. Full-wrap side protection is critical to achieve a good percentage coverage of the body.

Many vests are marketed that are just front and back coverage, or only have "extended", or partial, or "scalloped" side coverage. Look in the mirror when holding your weapon in a side-angled Weaver stance— the large percentage of your upper body that would NOT be covered makes the problem obvious.

However partial side vests do serve a purpose in high heat environments because they offer more ventilation and heat dissipation. If you can't, or won't, wear a full side protection vest in the summer—get a partial side coverage vest that will be worn (and train yourself to face the threat in a front-facing, isosceles stance—and then hope it's just a single threat!)

Width

Firstly, is the vest cut narrowly across the chest, to give maximum freedom of movement and comfort— or cut widely for maximum protection? The coverage across the chest can vary by up to an inch or two (3–5 cm.) between brands—for the same size.

What is best for you really depends on the softness of the vest, your body type, how long you wear the vest each time, the level of threats, and your personal preference for more comfort and arm freedom, vs. more protection. Have the vest you are going to buy measured across the chest between the armpits (the ballistic panel, NOT the cloth carrier).

Length

Most vests are designed short to ride comfortably above a patrol officer's duty belt. This is ideal for comfort for patrol officers on long shifts—but, if you don't wear a duty belt (or have a long torso), you are missing an extra 1 to 3 inches (~3 to 8 cm.)

of coverage on your abdomen. It is also critical to avoid a vest is too long, that will ride up when you sit or bend, and jab you in the throat.

Unless you see it in writing otherwise, you can safely assume that a vest is the standard, shorter, duty belt length. (And just to add confusion, one company's Regular can be another company's Short.) Generally, a standard, size Large vest is ~12.5" to 13" (~32—33 cm.) measuring the ballistic panel (NOT the cloth carrier) front *centerline,*— the SHORTEST distance from the bottom of the neck scoop to the bottom of the vest.

An extra one to three inches (~3 to 8 cm.) increases the coverage area of the vest by ~5% to ~15%. This is not an earth-shaking difference, but the feeling of coverage you get can be illustrated by holding 13" (~33 cm.) of a tape measure from the bottom of your throat down to the belly, versus 14" or 15" (~36 or 38 cm.) of coverage for an Extra-Long vest. This exercise usually convinces those who don't wear a duty belt to get Extra-Long coverage!

Tactical Vests

An exterior tactical vest with neck, shoulder and groin protection will weigh ~50% more than a concealable vest, and cost you ~ $700 or more. But you leave the criminal with little to aim at, other than your head, arms and legs. (And you can even cover the bicep, tricep, deltoid and armpit area with Upper Arm Protectors!)

The percentage coverage is superb—although heat build-up is more of a problem, and comfort and freedom of movement is slightly more restricted. But nothing beats that turtle-shell feeling, if you are investigating the sound of breaking glass at 3AM!

Will you have it on when the threat arrives? For SWAT teams who have transit time to gear up, the answer is obviously yes, but for others highly dependent on the particular situation. Thus for tactical vests, the ease and quickness of getting the vest on is critical. Front-opening vests are a very attractive (though more expensive) option here. If you are buying a tactical vest— find out EXACTLY how it is put on, to evaluate quickness.

The other argument against exterior tactical vests is that it is visually obvious to the criminal to aim at unprotected areas. However, it can also be argued that it is unlikely that this visual clue will be acted on effectively in an adrenaline-charged confrontation.

Regardless, our suggestion is that even tactical armor is best worn in the same color as the usual uniform or clothing to minimize the giveaway. Even better is to cover up with a loose jacket. Even if criminals know in the back of their mind that law enforcement almost always wear vests— why remind them in the middle of a gunfight!

3) % of Threat Time Vest is Worn

This is THE most important factor. Whether your vest covers 90% or 95% of pistol ballistic threats is marginal. And whether you are covering 50% or 70% of your vital areas is still less critical than going to ZERO protection with NO vest. Whatever vest you buy— make sure it is comfortable enough to wear for the duration required.

**The best vest for you
is the one you are actually wearing when shot!**

Also, it's often the practical considerations listed above that are the most important, and can really only be thoroughly checked out on your body, with the vest in hand. Thus you should only buy a vest with a clear return policy, in case the vest won't work on your body, or in your situation.

Heat Discomfort vs. Vest Use

If you don't wear your vest in the daytime, or during the summer heat, you have cut your average protection in half or less. A solution could be a partial side model for summer, daytime use, keeping a full side protection model for the winter, and at night when it's cooler.

Before sacrificing this much protection, it would be advisable to try adapting to a full side protection vest. Firstly, wearing the vest more loosely helps to allow a little more air to circulate under the vest, and helps keep it from getting so "sticky". Secondly a moisture-wicking CoolMax® undershirt, and/or a CoolMax® vest carrier will move and evaporate sweat three times faster than cotton, and can make a tough situation bearable. Finally, you can get a cooling system for your vest—one of the new devices that plug into your vehicle's AC vents to put cool, dry air BEHIND your vest, next to your body.

If Your Vest is NOT Worn Routinely...

...but kept at hand for emergencies, how fast you get it on is THE critical factor. While it would be nice to have a $1500 Tactical Ballistic Shield at hand, before house-clearing at 3AM, the moderately-priced quickest solution here is a front-opening jacket vest. Instead of slipping on over your head, you can throw it on like a jacket, and quickly close the overlapping Velcro front flaps. Just as importantly, the concealment is built-in with the jacket. It doesn't do quite as much good to get a vest on fast—visible overtop of your clothes—and then have the criminal take head and groin shots!

If you simply cannot wear a vest due to circumstances, an inexpensive back-up plan is a Briefcase (or Backpack) Ballistic Shield Insert to give at least some protection to get behind in an emergency. You can even get briefcases which serve triple duty—briefcase, ballistic shield, and discreet concealed carry holster!

A Final Word...

Remember that armor is insurance to "put the odds in your favor"—but it is NOT a guarantee of invulnerability. NO vest is ever 100% "bulletproof". ANY impact of a bullet on your vest causes blunt trauma injury, and requires a trip to the hospital. And, of course, your head, neck, hips, groin, arms and legs, etc., etc. are always vulnerable.

So, you can "put the odds in your favor" with Body Armor—but remember that your training, alertness and common sense is always your first—and BEST- defense. Make putting on your vest a mental reminder of the dangers you face—not a substitute for caution.

Be safe, and stay cautious.

For More Information see our website at:

www.bulletproofme.com

If you own a vest (or are getting one), email our auto-responder for more Body Armor Care, Tips, and Tricks. Just send a blank email to: subscribeb@bulletproofme.com

Our Privacy Commitment is posted online at:

http://bulletproofme.com/Privacy-Commitment.shtml

(BTP Note: The folks at BulletProofMe are like-minded souls, and American Patriots. Tell them Boston sent you!)

YOU & THE BATF

I have included the former chapters 12, 21, and 29 here.

DEALING WITH POST-BAN BLUES

In Chapter 30 I quote the various regulations affecting so-called *"assault weapons"* (*i.e.*, semi-auto/detachable mag). Here I will explain just what you can/cannot own or do. First, here's an exclusive *Boston's Gun Bible* guide through the rats' warren of *"assault rifle"* laws.

If the rifle (*i.e.*, receiver) was imported,

was it imported (not merely made) *by* 30 November 1990?
If Yes, then it is pre-import ban and can have *all* features.

If No, was it imported *by* 13 September 1994?
  If **Yes**, then it's pre-Crime Bill and *can* have all features *if* the 27 CFR §178.39(c) imported parts count is 10 or less.

  If No, then it *can have only one* 18 USC §921(30)(B) feature (*i.e.*, folding/telescoping/pistol grip stock, bayonet mount, flash suppressor or threaded barrel, or grenade launcher) *if* the 27 CFR §178.39(c) imported parts count is 10 or less.

If the rifle (*i.e.*, receiver) was made in U.S.A.,

was it assembled as a complete rifle *by* 13 September 1994?
If Yes, then it is pre-Crime Bill and can have *all* features.

If No, then it *can have only one* 18 USC §921(30)(B) feature (*i.e.*, folding/telescoping/pistol grip stock, bayonet mount, flash suppressor or threaded barrel, or grenade launcher).

The import ban found at 18 USC §922(r) applied the *"sporting purposes"* cosmetic crap to foreign semi-autos imported (not merely manufactured) after 30 November 1990. The *"Crime Bill"* (18 USC §922(v&w)) did the same to *domestic* semi-autos assembled after 13 September 1994. In some cases, post-ban rifles may legally have certain (but not all) pre-ban parts (and even imported ones, at that).

The above flowchart is quite accurate and thorough, but doesn't provide us with much practical detail. So, let's amplify. The military-style features affected by the Crime Bill are:

> folding or telescoping stock
> pistol grip
> bayonet mount
> flash suppressor, or threaded barrel designed for such
> grenade launcher

Regarding three out of five features, I sarcastically say *Boo, hoo!* Most of us will probably never miss a folding/telescoping stock, a bayonet mount, or a grenade launcher. *However,* a pistol grip and flash suppressor are *essential* to a combat rifle. Hereafter, I will speak only of these two necessary and affected features, and will ignore the other three largely irrelevant ones.

Foreign semi-auto/detachable mag rifles
imported (not just manufactured) *by* 30 November 1990
It is pre-import ban and can have all the "nasty" features. *"Can I trick out my AK with a folding stock and flash suppressor?"* Yes, *if* it was imported *by* 30 November 1990.

imported *between* 1 December 1990—13 September 1994
Because the 11/90 import ban and the 9/94 *"Crime Bill"* differently affect semi-autos, there exists a curious regulatory "loophole" for imports between 12/90 and 9/94 which can (under strict conditions) legally adopt *all* pre-import ban features.

The *"from imported parts"* of 18 USC §922 (r)is the key. An imported rifle assembled or configured from *10 or less* of the imported parts listed in 27 CFR §178.39(c) is not subject to 18 USC §922(r)—the import ban. **These imported parts are:** frames; receivers; receiver castings/forgings/stampings; barrels; barrel extensions; mounting blocks (trunnions); muzzle attachments; bolts; bolt carriers; operating rods; gas piston; trigger housings; triggers; hammers; sears; disconnectors;

buttstocks; pistol grips; forearms; handguards; magazine bodies/followers/floorplates.

What's the point? By substituting some of the original imported parts with *American-made* parts, the total imported parts count of §178.39(c) can be reduced to 10 or less, so you can legally revert the rifle to pre-import ban configuration. Here's the catch: the reversion had to have been done *by* 13 September 1994, as the *"Crime Bill"* prevents such after that.

after 13 September 1994

Reducing the import parts count to 10 or less *after* 9/94 lets you install *either* a pistol grip *or* a flash suppressor (but not both). Again, *as long as* the 27 CFR §178.39(c) imported parts count is 10 or less, it is exempt from the import ban—*however,* it remains subject to the *"Crime Bill"* ban on *"assault weapons"* and thus can have *only one* 18 USC §921(30)(B) feature. (Take your pick.) Is all this clear to everyone?

American parts kits for imported rifles

FAC (612-780-8780) sells a Ø100 American-made parts kit to allow a pistol-grip reversion of the imported Canadian/British FALs, and First Son Enterprises (770-497-0204) offers the same for Daewoos and AKs. Other firms selling such kits are RPB (404-297-0907) and TG (423-577-1939).

Be advised that the less expensive kits are usually so because they use mag followers and floorplates instead of more expensive *internal* gun parts (such as trigger groups). For optimum legal CYA protection, I'd choose the *internal* parts (which, by definition, would always be gun-present), versus, for example, an American *mag* which likely would get separated from your rifle. (Not to put too fine a point on all this, but that *is* what you pay me for.)

The FAL made in Brazil by Imbel (licensed by FN, so the quality is great) is a very fine rifle, and new versions have sufficient American parts to legally circumvent the import ban.

Beware: some gunphobic members of Congress are already whining about this *"loophole"* and want to close it. Further, the parts kit concept is perhaps ultimately futile as the feds will eventually restrict or ban *all* mag-fed semi-auto rifles, regardless of imported parts count. But, it allows you to get by without legal peril for just one more day. Consider using it.

Domestic semi-auto/detachable mag rifles

by **13 September 1994**

It's pre-*"Crime Bill"* enjoying all the features. Happiness.

after **13 September 1994**

On post-9/94 rifles, regulations allow you to have *either* a pistol grip *or* a flash suppressor, **but not *both.***

American ingenuity at work

As Tim Mullin is fond of saying, *"Any law that can't be circumvented should be complied with."* Meaning, there's usually a way to lessen any stupid law's effect: if not by circumventing it, then by *complying* with it to the letter.

Some American companies are making domestic H&K and FAL *receivers* to which they add a foreign parts kit, thus completing a *domestic* post-9/94 rifle which may legally have a pistol grip or flash suppressor. Dealer cost on these very serviceable rifles is only Ø600 (only a third or fourth the cost of a pre-import-ban gun), so the "adding American parts to foreign receivers" idea is getting some new competition. These new rifles are priced even lower than those Century Arms Model 58 "Frankenstein" FALs (now demanding Ø650-800, which originally sold for a mere Ø400 in 1996).

So, you have four ways to avoid 1990-98 imported rifles with their dumpy thumbhole stock: add an American parts kit to a foreign receiver, buy a foreign rifle with such parts already installed, buy an American rifle, or pay ØØØØ for a pre-ban.

Gun regulations are always changing, so research!

Gun regulations are tedious and subject to differing interpretations. Therefore, consult a lawyer and the BATF, do your *own* research, and arrive at your *own* conclusion. The below websites can update you on any new laws:

www.gunowners.org	(Gun Owners of America)
www.bloomfieldpress.com	(publishes *Gun Laws of America*)
www.findlaw.com/scripts	(to read any federal court case)
www.atf.treas.gov/core/firearms/information/	(BATF)

The 1994 *"Crime Bill"* and you

This hideous Act hampered properly equipped combat rifles, and requires some gymnastics to live with. Pistol grip or flash suppressor—*which* one to choose? If you choose the flash suppressor, then (to remain legal) you'll have to dump the pistol grip for a thumbhole "sporter" buttstock.

flash suppressors

Because 70% of defensive shooting is done in conditions of low/altered/failing light, and because muzzle flash temporarily blinds the shooter (try it if you don't believe me!), an effective flash suppressor is more important than a pistol grip. (I'm *assuming* that you can easily operate the safety from the post-ban thumbhole stock. If you cannot, then replacing the stock is paramount.)

Furthermore, an effective flash suppressor is *essential* for using NVDs. (Get a genuine Vortex or Phantom from QP. Accept no Ø25 Vortex copies, as they splay open from firing!)

Although the *"Crime Bill"* affects post-9/94 flash suppressor or barrels threaded for such, one could salt away for that Rainy Decade a set-screw attached flash suppressor and thus keep your post-ban barrel threadless.

If you don't want to bother flash-suppressing a post-ban AR15, then try Hornady's low-flash TAP Urban .223 ammo.

Post-ban FALs

As I mentioned earlier, there are today (6/2000) some very fine newly-made U.S. receivers with foreign parts kits (including pistol grip) which can be had at Ø600 dealer cost. Also, the Brazilian-made Imbel FAL with sufficient number of American parts is a very good gun. (Check out the *Shotgun News* for the latest offerings.) Although they cannot legally *also* have a flash suppressor, you could swap the pistol grip for such and still comply with the regs.

While thumbhole stocks generally feel pretty awful, they all can be tolerated, save one—the Century Arms FAL (which prevents the use of the rifle's safety). DSA makes a legal and tolerable replacement, the Dragunov stock (#090-DI for Ø75).

Choose either an Imbel or an American receiver FAL with the excellent Austrian StG58 kit, and replace its get-hot-quickly steel handguard with a synthetic version (DSA; Ø60).

Beware of retrofitted post-ban rifles posing as pre-bans!

This is especially true with those Century Arms imported Canadian uppers! No such pre-ban rifles exist; they were merely retrofitted with pre-ban flash suppressor, pistol grip, and buttstock (all for Ø15) and the price jacked up to Ø1,500. (The big giveaway is the word "Sporter" stamped on its upper. No pre-11/90 gun would have such a thing, as the word didn't then *exist* in connection with military rifles!)

If you ever run across one, politely inform the seller (as he may have cluelessly bought it from somebody else) of its *real* status, and ask that he *immediately* cease misrepresenting a felony pre/post hybrid as a true and legal pre-ban gun. Furthermore, ask him to take it off his table, as you don't want some poor *schmuck* to buy it and then get busted. The seller is likely to be a horse's ass about all this, so tell the show promoter, who has a vested interest in keeping his show clear of such stuff. (I wouldn't threaten going to the BATF, as not even a horse's ass deserves *that*.) If the show promoter does nothing (highly unlikely), then at least warn your friends not to even touch it.

Post-ban HKs

I know of no thumbhole sporter buttstocks for the HK91 clones, so there is no way to add a flash suppressor on a post-ban gun. The clones are generally problematic rifles, anyway, so you're not missing anything.

Post-ban AR15s

Since all ARs are American-made, post-9/94 rifles may have *either* a pistol grip *or* a flash suppressor, but not both. Manufacturers have mistakenly opted to give us the pistol grip. For you owners of post-9/94 ARs who want to *legally* enjoy a flash suppressor, simply replace the factory buttstock and grip with a post-ban thumbhole stock from DPMS (#BS-30 for about Ø100). Then, remove the upper, have its barrel threaded ½"x28 D.E.F. x 0.630 +/- 0.005", and install a Phantom flash suppressor from QP. (As not every gunsmith may understand the fine-toothed legality of this plan, you might simply tell him that it's for a pre-ban lower. Since he's only seeing the upper, how would he know any differently?)

If you have a 20" barrel but want a 16" CQB rifle, *do not* have the barrel cut down, as there *won't* be sufficient gas pressure to cycle the action. Get a true Bushmaster Dissipator 16" barrel (with proper gas block and gas tube).

If you don't have access to a quality gunsmith, then just install a pre-ban threaded barrel. For CQB I recommend the

16" Dissipator from QP. For field use, a 20" barrel. *Avoid* the short-stocked 16" Carbine barrel, which needlessly sacrifices handguard length and 5¼" of sight radius.

Now *this* may be going too far...
An option for those wanting *all* pre-ban features is the *pump*-operated AR15 from DPMS. Remember, the *"Crime Bill"* affected only *"assault weapons"* (*i.e.,* the semi-autos). *Manually*-operated (*i.e.,* bolt, pump, or lever) long guns may enjoy pistol grips, folding stocks, bayonet lugs, flash suppressors, and grenade launchers. While a pump AR15 is for me simply too expensive (dealer cost is Ø1,395, and you can find a true pre-ban AR for that!) and too wussy (there should be a limit to one's post-ban contortions), if *you* want to be the first (and *only*) one on your block, then...

muzzle brakes
Post-ban muzzle brakes are fine, *unless* such incorporate a flash suppressor into their design (*e.g.,* the MuzzleMiser). Fake flash suppressors (Ø20; RPB; 404-297-0907) conceivably may be added to threaded pre-ban barrels to allow their mating to a post-ban receiver, but the BATF probably won't go for it.

Know if the AR lower is pre- or post-ban!
You certainly don't want to unintentionally put a pre-ban upper on a post-ban lower, so being able to distinguish between lowers is very important. How to tell a pre-ban from a post-ban? At least one manufacturer (*i.e.,* Olympic) actually year-prefixes their serial numbers, but most do not, so you should know the serial number cut-offs for each factory. Even still, it's not that straightforward:

*Previously, a rifle was a serial numbered receiver. After the Crime Bill became law, [the BATF] defined a rifle as an assembled rifle, or a parts kit together as a package. That means, if you were making ARs and had 5,000 finished receivers in inventory, but had only enough parts to assemble 1,000 receivers into complete rifles, you now had 1,000 Pre-ban rifles and 4,000 Post-ban receivers in your shop, **even though the receivers were manufactured before the bill had been signed into law.** (Such bullsh*t is typical. BTP)*
— Vol.1, No. 1 of the Fall 1997 issue of Brownells *BenchTalk*

"But wait, there's <u>more!</u>"

*The requirement that semiautomatic assault weapons be marked "RESTRICTED LAW ENFORCEMENT/GOVERNMENT USE ONLY" **was not effective until July 5, 1995. Thus,** [these rifles]*

manufactured from September 13, 1994-July 4, 1995 may not
[always] *be marked with the restrictive markings.* ...*Licensees
obtaining semiautomatic assault weapons which do not have the
restrictive marking should obtain from the seller an invoice, bill of
sale, or other documentation indicating that the weapon in its
present configuration was lawfully possessed on or before
September 13, 1994.*
            — www.atf.treas.gov/core/firearms/information/faq/faqo.htm

Those *pre*-9/94 receivers deemed *post*-ban (because they
weren't *assembled* into complete rifles by 9/94) are called
"floaters" as they do not have a post-9/94 date on them. Such a
receiver built as a pre-ban gun would pass all but the most
careful of BATF scrutiny (*i.e.,* after some kind of confiscation
where they had lots of time). So, *beware.*

Regarding post-ban lowers and separate pre-ban parts,
you must take caution:

*Semiautomatic assault weapons in knockdown (disassembled)
condition consisting of a receiver and all parts needed to complete a
semiautomatic assault weapon are subject to regulation* (i.e.,
prohibition after 9/94) *if the parts are segregated or packaged
together and held by a person as the parts for the assembly of a
particular firearm.*
            — www.atf.treas.gov/core/firearms/information/faq/faqo.htm

If you have a post-ban AR15 receiver and pick up a pre-ban
upper, make sure they are packaged separately and held by two
different people. *Never* store them *together* under *one* roof!
(Later in this chapter I outline several possible defenses against
an arrest for possession of an illegal pre-/post-ban hybrid.)

The following are last pre-ban numbers, unless said
otherwise. (Note: This information was mostly excerpted from
BenchTalk and *The Small Arms Review* of 8/99.) As you can
see, except for Bushmaster, Colt, and PWA, cutoff numbers can
be elusive. While some risk is inherent, a pre/post hybrid rifle
will likely be discovered *only* under great scrutiny (*e.g.,* if the
rifle were ever seized for evidence from a shooting incident,
raid, traffic stop, vehicle impoundment, etc.).

American Spirit (888-GUN-KITS)	All are post-ban.
ArmaLite/Eagle (800-336-0184)	Just over 30,000 is the cut-off, but call to verify. (ArmaLite sells Eagle lowers.)
Bushmaster (207-892-2005)	Below L051000 are assembled pre-ban rifles. L051001—L063000 mixed pre-ban rifles. L063001—up definitely post-ban.

Colt
(203-236-6311)

BD000134	LH011326	SP360200
CC001616	MH086020	ST038100
CH019500	NL004800	TA10100
GC018500	SL027246	

All "Match Target" rifles are post-ban.
All MT, BK, CST, and CMH are post-ban.

DPMS (612-261-5600)	Most below 1030 are pre-ban, but call. (Beware, as date can be under pistol grip.)
E.A. Co.	All are pre-ban.
Eagle Arms (309-944-6939)	Call with specific serial # for them to check.
Hesse Arms	All are post-ban.
J.L.M. & Sons (603-425-1860)	SC001—250 are pre-ban.
KAC (561-562-5697)	All are post-ban.
Lone Star	All are post-ban.
Olympic Arms (206-459-7940)	4 #s only are all pre-ban. 1 letter + 4 #s are all pre-ban. 2 #s (the year) + 2 letters + 4 #s. 2 letters + 2 #s (the year) + 4 #s. 1-2 letters + 5 #s nearly all post-ban. BL serial #s are transitional, so call! (Visit www.olyarms.com/prepost/html.)
Pro-Ord	All are post-ban.
PWA	35,222 definitely last pre-ban lower, and some post-ban lowers are year-prefixed. Call.
Sendra	Most are pre-ban. Post-bans have circle milled on magwell.

Watch out for this possible scam!
The above knowledge is especially vital because of today's atmosphere of pre-ban pricing hysteria at gun shows. Here's what to beware of: Somebody buys a private sale post-ban AR lower (one with no date stamp) for Ø275-375 and then tosses on a *pre*-ban upper for Ø400-550. So, for only Ø675-925 he's made what *appears* to be a genuine *pre*-ban AR15—a rifle now fetching Ø1,000-1,400. Meaning, he stands to profit up to Ø725 by scamming *you*, the buyer. When the unscrupulous can potentially *double* their money with only a few minutes of work, they'll no doubt try.

Yes, the rifle will probably feed and function just fine, but *that's* not the issue. The problem is that you're unknowingly walking around a gun show (which is quietly swarming with BATF agents) with a 7½lb *felony* bust just waiting to happen. Such a theoretical risk is one of the many reasons why it is rarely sound policy to show your AR, FAL, or H&K to strangers. (I'd also put a sticker saying *"Not for Sale!"* right over the receiver's serial number—that way, no casual observer could glean any info about your gun's status. Address labels or name badge stickers work well for this sort of protection.)

Post-ban AR10s
The DPMS thumbhole stock (#BS-30) will also fit the AR10, which would then allow you to legally have the barrel threaded for a Vortex flash suppressor from QP (made for the FN-FALs; they offer four different thread specs, 14mm x 1.0 or 9/16" x 24, right or left hand threaded, so ask your gunsmith).

To protect yourself, never keep the old stock and pistol grip on your own premises (*i.e.,* home, office, cabin, storage unit, etc.), but at a friend's.

Special note on Kalifornia
After 1/1/2000, it is no longer legal to sell military-style rifles in People's Republic of Kalifornia. This now includes, *ex post facto*, the SKS (which they later deemed an *"assault rifle"*).

As they've already mandated registration, guess what'll follow? Yep, *confiscation*. Since, however, only about 3% of owners have registered these particular household firearms, this mass noncompliance bodes well. Stay tuned!

ILLEGAL POST/PRE-BAN HYBRIDS

I do not recommend illegal hybrids!

While one could *theoretically* buy a surplus FAL parts kit (which has everything but the upper receiver) such as the Ø200 Steyr StG58 (the best), and assemble it on a new metric upper (an FFL purchase)—don't do it. Assembling a pre-ban rifle from a post-ban receiver is a felony—and isn't worth it at this point.

All a BATF agent would have to do is spot multiple pre-ban features on a post-ban receiver, and you'd be in some (unnecessary) hot water. While this is *not* a common bust at gun shows (you'd have to wave it under a fed's nose), such is a risk if your home were raided and your guns confiscated (to be scrutinized, or even tampered with, at the BATF's leisure).

In short, given the current (though temporary, to be sure) choices in pistol-grip stocked FALs, ARs, H&Ks, and AKs (which feature can be legally exchanged for a thumbhole stock and flash suppressor), there is no compelling reason at this time to risk a felony by reverting a post-ban rifle to pre-ban status.

Final comments

When after having thus successively taken each member of the community in its powerful grasp, and fashioned him at will, the supreme power then extends its arm over the whole community. **It covers the surface of society with a network of small complicated rules,** *minute and uniform, through which the most original minds and the most energetic characters cannot penetrate to rise above the crowd.* **The will of man is not shattered but softened, bent and guided; men are seldom forced by it to act, but they are constantly retrained from acting.** *Such a power does not destroy, but it prevents existence; it does not tyrannize, but it compresses, enervates, extinguishes, and stupefies a people,* **till each nation is reduced to be nothing better that a flock of timid and industrial animals, of which government is the shepherd.** *I have always thought that servitude of the regular, quiet, and gentle kind which I have just described* **might be combined more easily than is commonly believed with some of the outward forms of freedom** *and that it might even establish itself under the wing of the sovereignty of the people.*

— Alexis de Tocqueville, *Democracy in America* (1835)

Just in case you're thinking that my will has been *"softened,"* let me finish my point here. There is a clear line crossed by the

Government when we should no longer be *"bent and guided"* by that *"network of small complicated* [post-ban] *rules"*:

The Day of Confiscation. When they come for your *"assault rifles"* you've got only one *last* chance to use them.

It seems very possible, if not likely, that military-style rifles will first be coercively registered, then banned, and then confiscated. At *that* **point,** it will make no difference whether your FAL *was* hitherto a *legal pre*-ban or a *post*-ban with *illegal pre*-ban parts. **It will be felonious *contraband*, either way.** (If this occurs, the pre-ban parts kits will price zoom overnight to eliminate any price disparity between pre- and post-ban parts.) At that point, what you'll *wish* you'd have done is stocked up on those excellent quality Ø175 bargain kits.

Does the date of 19 April 1775 mean anything to you? If so, then you probably will have no qualms with salting away a Ø15 pre-ban pistol grip, buttstock, and flash suppressor for your post-ban FAL (which you bought just in time). **Moral: Stock up on these bargain parts kits, *and bury them* until the Day comes.** Such are legal and inexpensive now, but will be priceless and unavailable later when sorely needed.

Now and later, I urge you to always keep things in proper perspective. Yes, *"Discretion is the better part of valor"*—**until there is no *choice* but to be brave.** If and when that time ever comes, we will surely know it.

May God grant us the wisdom to discover the right, the will to choose it, and the strength to make it endure.
— King Arthur, from the movie *First Knight*

PRE-1899 GUNS

(According to federal regulations, guns produced prior to 1899 are not *"firearms"* and thus have no interstate transfer restrictions. James Wesley, Rawles (author of *Patriots: Surviving the Coming Collapse*; ISBN 1-56384-155-X; Huntington House; 800-749-4009) has kindly allowed me to reprint his FAQ on the subject. The following text is his.)

I have put my mailorder business (Clearwater Trading Company) on hiatus. I am no longer producing a catalog. Because of my numerous writing commitments, I won't have the time to reanimate the mailorder biz until 2001 at the earliest.

Revised January 1, 1999

In response to numerous requests, here are the answers to the questions that I most commonly get on pre-1899 firearms. The second half of this FAQ posting lists serial number cut-offs for the 1899 threshold for many guns.

Q: What constitutes *"antique"* under U.S. law?

A: Although your State and local laws may vary, any firearm with a receiver actually made before Jan. 1, 1899 is legally "antique." and not considered a "firearm" under Federal law. This refers to the actual date of manufacture of the receiver/frame, not just model year or patent date marked. (For example, only low serial number Winchester Model 1894 lever actions are actually antique.) No FFL is required to buy or sell antiques across state lines—they are in the same legal category as a muzzle-loading replica. I regularly ship them right to people's doorstep via UPS, with no "paper trail." Think of it as the last bastion of gun ownership privacy.

Q: I saw a post that said that pre-1899s are considered modern *"firearms"* if they are chambered to fire ammo that is available off-the-shelf. Is this correct?

A: That is absolutely incorrect. ANY gun manufactured before Jan. 1, 1899 (other than a machinegun or other NFA category, such as a short-barreled gun) is NOT controlled in any way by Federal law. There is NO Federal requirement for sales of these guns to be handled by Federally licensed dealers. They may be freely bought and sold across State lines by private parties, regardless of what cartridge they are chambered in. (However, State or local laws vary.)

Q: Does sporterizing or re-chambering an antique end its exemption?

A: Sporterizing, re-barreling, or re-chambering an antique gun does not effect its legal status. Thus, I can sell folks Mauser sporters that have been converted to modern cartridges (like .308 Winchester!), without having to go through the "FFL to FFL" hassle. (I have a BATF letter confirming this, that I send on request. Just send me a SASE if you'd like a copy.)

Q: Would an antique...gun be worth more than an otherwise identical gun made just a few years later?

A: Pre-1899 production guns now bring a 20 to 60% premium over identical condition guns made AFTER 1898. Based on market trends, I expect that premium to increase considerably in the next few years. Many of my customers are commenting that they previously had no interest in *"antique"* guns, but now want one or more because they are paranoid about additional gun laws. For the time being at least, pre-1899 are completely EXEMPT from all federal laws. Presumably, this would also mean that they would be exempt from registration if they ever have nationwide gun registration. Think of the possibilities.

Q: But what if I find a pre-1899 gun at a gun shop that was mistakenly logged into the dealer's "bound book" of post-1899 firearms? Won't I have to fill out a Form 4473?

A: No. All the dealer has to do is log the gun out as: *"Inadvertent entry. Pre-1899 manufactured receiver. No FFL required."* (If the dealer gives you any grief and insists on the yellow form, a call to any ATF branch office will confirm this.)

Q: Will the prices of pre-1899s continue to go up?

A: Yes, and the rate of increase is likely to accelerate! On Nov. 30, 1998, a mere few months away, the permanent Brady rules come on line. On that date all post-1899 gun sales—long guns and handguns—will fall under the federal control of "national instant background checks." It is obvious that when that happens there will suddenly be a bigger interest in guns that are Federally exempt and that can be bought via relatively anonymous mail order!

Q: Are pre-1899s included in the Brady II background check law?

A: No. They are exempt.

Q: How does the law on pre-1899 antiques and replicas actually read?

A: From the *"Gun Control Act of 1968"* (which modified Title 18, U.S. Code):

18 USC 921 (a)(16)
(A) any firearm (including any firearm with a matchlock, flintlock, percussion cap, or similar type of ignition system) manufactured in or before 1898; and
(B) any replica of any firearm described in subparagraph (A) if such replica—
        (i) is not designed or redesigned for using rimfire or conventional centerfire fixed ammunition, or
        (ii) uses rimfire or conventional centerfire fixed ammunition which is no longer manufactured in the United States and which is not readily available in the ordinary channels of commercial trade.

Q: What are the primary advantages in investing in pre-1899 guns rather than modern (post-1898) guns, or replicas?

A: They are not considered *"firearms"* under Federal law. Thus they will most likely be exempt from any new Federal gun registration law. (Sadly, registration looks inevitable within a few years unless there is a massive swing of the pendulum back toward a constitutional republic.)

I can literally send you a pre-1899 handgun or rifle right to your doorstep without a lick of paperwork. (Unless your live in for example New York City or D.C.) It is a great loophole.

The Dec. 31, 1898 cut-off date has been in existence, unchanged, since 1968. Thus the pool of available pre-1899s continues to shrink with each passing year, and because of it they A) Look more and more antique/obsolete to lawmakers—*i.e.* not worth bothering about, and B) Grow more valuable with every passing year. Pre-1899 guns are already bring a considerable premium. People are willing to pay more for privacy.

Several States (including Texas and Florida) use the Federal definition of *"firearm"* as the basis for the CCW laws. Hence, pre-1899 guns can be legally carried concealed and loaded in your car or under your coat in those States WITHOUT A PERMIT.

So the bottom line is that with pre-1899s you are buying both privacy (the lack of a "paper trail" and probable exemption from future registration) plus a great investment. Why buy a replica (such as the Trapdoor Springfield, Winchester, and Schofield top break revolver replicas currently on the market —and requiring the Federal "Yellow" Form 4473), when you can buy the real thing (with far greater long term investment value, and NO paperwork) for just a little bit more money?

I hope that you find this information useful. Your comments, additions, and corrections are appreciated (send to rawles@usa.net). Thanks again to Jim Supica, proprietor of The Old Town Station (OldTownSta@aol.com) snail mail: c/o P.O. Box 15351, Lenexa, Kansas [66285], Dennis Kroh, and Ben Sansing swsansing@juno.com.

(BTP Note: For lack of space, I have not reprinted Rawles's extensive list of pre-1899 guns. See the 2000 edition of *Boston's Gun Bible*.)

"CURIOS OR RELICS"

My Foreword author Tim Mullin told me about these, and the federal license to collect such. While I am not the kind of guy who goes *looking* to get licensed for anything, a *"Collector's License"* confers two significant advantages:

❶ Licensed collectors may buy or sell firearms classified as *"curios or relics"* interstate. That means he/she can order such direct from any out-of-State seller (dealer, licensed collector, or not). No Form 4473 is required; no NICBC hassles! He has merely to keep a *"bound book."*
He can also sell such guns to in-State private parties.
He may *not* use this license to buy and sell as a business.
The license is just Ø10/year.

❷ Mullin (an attorney) claims that no State (or political subdivision thereof) can forbid a licensed collector to own such *"curios or relics"* even though such a gun may otherwise be illegal in that State (or city)! This means that a licensed collector living in Kalifornia or Neu Jersey may legally own, for example, a Russian SKS or FN-FAL—even though *"assault weapons"* are illegal there!
If he lived in—*horrors!*—Washington, D.C., Chicago, or New York City he may own, for example, a Luger, Walther P38, Argentine Colt .45, or a wartime Browning P35 Hi-Power—even though handguns are illegal there!
While the transportation and use of such *"curios or relics"* in prohibited States is probably dicey, you may be able to keep such at home or work without local interference.

(BTP Note: Any text in this font is verbatim from BATF website—typos, goofs, etc. Headings and bold emphasis are mine.)

FEDERALLY LICENSED FIREARMS COLLECTORS

A collector of curios or relics may obtain a Collector's License under the Gun Control Act of 1968, 18 U.S.C. Chapter 44 and the regulations issued thereunder in 27 CFR Part 178. The privileges conferred by this license extend only to curio or relic transactions. **The principal advantage of a Collector's License is that a collector can acquire curios or relics in interstate commerce.** A licensed collector may acquire and dispose of curios or relics at any location; however, dispositions to nonlicensees must be made to residents of the same State in which the collector is licensed. The licensed collector has the same status as a nonlicensee with respect to transactions involving firearms that are not classified as curios or relics. An individual must be licensed in order to lawfully receive curios or relics in interstate commerce, i.e., from outside his or her State of residence.

"Curios or relics" is defined in 27 CFR § 178.11, as follows:

Firearms which are of special interest to collectors by reason of some quality other than is associated with firearms intended for sporting use or as offensive or defensive weapons. **To be recognized as curios or relics, firearms must fall within one of the following categories:**

(a) Firearms which were manufactured at least 50 years prior to the current date, but not including replicas thereof;

(b) Firearms which are certified by the curator of a municipal, State, or Federal museum which exhibits firearms to be curios or relics of museum interest; and

(c) Any other firearms which derive a substantial part of their monetary value from the fact that they are novel, rare, bizarre, or because of their association with some historical figure, period, or event. Proof of qualification of a particular firearm under this category may be established by evidence of present value and evidence that like firearms are not available except as collector's items, or that the value of like firearms available in ordinary commercial channels is substantially less.

If a particular gun *should* be on the list, but isn't, ask the BATF to make a determination (their website has details).

The best *"curios and relics"*

Below are a few guns I culled from the *hundreds* on the list (which the BATF admits is not all-inclusive, as new entries are made continually). While you're welcome to scour the list yourself, rest assured that 99.9% of the good stuff is here. I have owned (or at least fired) all of the below.

Handguns

Colt 1911	C1-C130000 (commercial)
Colt 1911A1	WWII guns
Argentine D.G.F.M. (FMAP)	<24501 ("Ejercito Argentino")
Argentine D.G.F.M. (FMAP)	(all commercial)
German P-38	<1947 mfg.
Luger	<1946 mfg.
Swedish M40 Lahti	<1968 mfg.
Browning P35 Hi-Power	all military models
Makarov (East German, Russian)	all
CZ27, CZ38, CZ50, CZ52	all
Walther	all mfg. <1946
Sauer & Son	all mfg. <1946
Colt models 1903 and 1908	all
Savage models 1907, 1915, 1917	all
Colt Woodsman	1-157000 (*i.e.*, 1915-1943)

Shotguns

Winchester 12	mfg. 1-1962017
Winchester 37	mfg. 1936-1963
Remington 31	mfg. 1931-1950

Rifles

Mauser models 88-98	mfg. <1945
.308 Ishapore Lee-Enfield	mfg. <1965
.303 Lee-Enfield No.4	mfg. <1958
Egyptian Rasheed, Hakim	all
most Mosin-Nagants	
Russian SKS, Tokarev, Dragunov	all
Brazilian .30/06 copy of G43	G43-1 to G43-95
FN49	all
M1 Garand (USGI only)	mfg. <1956
Savage 99	1-450,000
Winchester 88	all rifles and carbines

HOW THE BATF OPERATES

Although I'm sure the feds have a "legal" way around this, I'm curious how a Title 26 USC (*NFA34*) *tax*-collecting bureau can legally enforce Title *18* USC criminal gun statutes (*e.g.,* the 1990 import ban and the 1994 *"Crime Bill"*). Just wondering...

Most BATF busts are based on stings and entrapments. BATmen won't scour the urban ghettos for *gangstas'* Uzis, but they *will* try to lure the uninformed and stupid into traps. It's not about fighting violent crime (which is dangerous work), but about hounding peaceable gunowners out of existence.

They can only bust three kinds of folks: the sellers, the buyers, and the owners. Regarding such busts, there's the to/from *whom*, the *what*, the *when*, the *where*, and the *how*.

spotting the BATF agent(s) at gun shows

These people have *no* love for guns or their history, and it shows. They handle guns like they were soiled diapers. Usually working in pairs, they are often abrupt, impatient, and arrogant. Preoccupation with unknown matters (*i.e.*, they're calculating how to best bust you) can be a clue to their identity. If he initiates a dialogue (with you, a *stranger*) about illegal items or activities, then it's 90% sure that he's a fed.

If you suspect a buyer or seller to be an agent, ask if he is a local. If answers affirmatively, then ask to see his driver's license (ostensibly to verify his State residency). He will be quite reluctant to do this, for several reasons. One, cops and feds often keep their DL inside their badge case to smoothly identify themselves during traffic stops as brother officers (thus avoiding the ticket). Two, his DL *might* show his home address (though their office address is more likely). Third, he's used to demanding *other* people's DLs, not vice versa. (It'll rankle him.)

If the guy (or woman) still seems hinky, politely decline to transact. Then, have a friend follow him around the show, or even to his car.

The agent's car

Because of their arrogance and low mental wattage, these people are tactically sloppy. Count on his many mistakes. Look for cop paraphernalia in the car interior. Some clues are: radio mikes, windshield/dashboard notepads, law enforcement paperwork or magazines, handcuffs, batons, Maglites, etc.

External clues are: blackwall tires, A-pillar spotlights, roof/trunk lid telltale round spots in the dust where the magnetic antenna mount was, and a general cop presence to the car.

Look at the rear license plate and its screw heads for evidence of frequent plate swapping (undercover feds have a trunkful of plates from many States). Get the dashboard VIN. If it's not a dedicated undercover vehicle with bogus registration, then running a "10-27" check might prove useful.

DO NOT BUY/SELL OUT-OF-STATE

Under federal law (based on interstate commerce clause regulations), you must be a resident of that State to directly transfer any firearm (even one bought or sold privately), else you'll fall within the *interstate* regulatory grasp of Title 18. From ATF Form 4473 (4-97) Definitions:

> 6. State of Residence - *The State in which an individual resides.* **An individual resides in a State if he or she is present in a State with the intention of making a home in that State.** *If an individual is on active duty as a member of the Armed Forces, the individual's State of residence is the State in which his or her permanent duty station is located. An alien who is legally in the United States shall be considered to be a resident in the State for a period of at least 90 days prior to the date of sale or delivery of a firearm. The following are examples that illustrate this definition:*
>
> > **Example 1.** *A maintains a home in State X. A travels to State Y on a hunting, fishing, business, or other type of trip. A does not become a resident of State Y by reason of such trip.*
> > **Example 2.** *A is a U.S. citizen and maintains a home in State X and a home in State Y. A resides in State X except for weekends or the summer months of the year and in State Y for weekends or the summer months of the year. During the time that A actually resides in State X, A is a resident of State X, and during the time that A actually resides in State Y, A is a resident of State Y.*
> >
> > **Example 3.** *A, an alien, travels on vacation or on a business trip to State X. Regardless of the length of the time A spends in State X, A does not have a State of residence in State X. This is because A does not have a home in State X at which he has resides for at least 90 days.*

While I have *never* advocated committing crimes which are *mala in se* (*i.e.*, evil in themselves), freedom-loving Americans should routinely challenge all *mala prohibita* (wrongs, though not evil, yet prohibited). I can think of no better example of such "victimless crime" legislation more deserving of our contempt than the interstate commerce gun control regulations. While it is never "evil in itself" (*malum in se*) for a peaceable American to buy a gun across State lines (just like a bottle of beer), Congress has deemed such a "wrong prohibited" (*malum prohibitum*) with prison and fines. As Emerson wrote:

> *Every actual State is corrupt. Good men must not obey the laws too well.*

If questioned for transacting out-of-State

First, *never* tell attendees that you're nonlocal. (At a Reno show, you're from Vegas.) If asked if you are a State resident, you might reply *"Of course!"* and say/offer/explain/amplify *nothing further.* If the agent already knows (or seems to know) who you are and in which State you reside, then you've probably been under investigation for some time and they feel confident of making stick an out-of-State transaction bust. (This is a rare thing. Usually, they merely spot one's out-of-State plates.)

What is a *"resident"*?

Remember, *"being present in a State* **with the intention** *of making a home in that State"* makes you a resident of that State under Title 18. Discussing with an out-of-State friend during a visit that you plan to relocate there and make a home should qualify as *"intention."* Moreover, there is *no* statutory requirement of having resided in a new State for any particular length of time before making legal firearm transactions.

Your response

To the agent, assert that you *are* a resident *and then clam up.* It's easy enough to later substantiate that you are a *"resident"* (*i.e.*, your friend could confirm that you just moved in with him, or were about to). Finally, it's *worth* doing so in order to avoid a *felony* conviction based on violating some cheesy interstate commerce regulation involving a *malum prohibitum*, or victimless/non-evil "crime."

Reducing your out-of-State exposure

Park any out-of-State car blocks away from the gun show (or go with a local friend). Remove all ID and papers from your person (which will deny the BATF agent any presumptive evidence). You do not have to carry ID with you in America (read my *You & The Police!* on this point). If you give the fed no instant way to dispute your claim of residency, then he cannot on the spot easily concoct probable cause for any arrest.

The out-of-State bust is *very* rare, and you'll have to draw inordinate attention to yourself to even become noticed at all, so don't get all paranoid at gun shows.

I wouldn't, however, make a habit of exhibiting at shows outside your home state(s). You certainly do not want to give the promoter any address or phone number in a State other than the one hosting the show. This is just common sense.

AVOID ENTRAPMENT!

If *anybody* tries to chat you up about illegal stuff, such as: machine gun parts and conversions, suppressors, sawed-off barrels or stocks, pre-/post-ban hybrids, explosives, stolen goods, "taking action" against the government or its officials, etc.—*firmly* announce your ignorance and disinterest.

If any of the above *persist*, threaten to immediately inform the police and/or a BATF agent. (Regardless of whether he is or isn't a plant or snitch, he will quickly scurry off.) If he persists after your warning, then follow through on your threat. If at a gun show, go to the promoter's desk and ask for a BATF agent. (John Ross's *Unintended Consequences* has a great scene about this sort of thing, on pages 451-53.)

As long as you're within your home State(s), *and* the guns are perfectly legal, *and* you use caution with whom you deal, and you don't say anything fatuous, then you should have little to be concerned about.

BUSTING THE SELLER

to *whom*

Enticing the ignorant, stupid, or greedy seller to break a federal firearms law is the most common of BATF stings.

Do not sell to *"straw man"* purchasers

If anybody asks if he can buy your gun *for* somebody *else*, refuse, even if such is not a *"prohibited possessor."*

Do not sell to *"prohibited possessors"*

"Even though" the party is from out-of-State, underage, a felon, etc.—absolutely refuse to transact! (See Chapter 30 for a list of *"prohibited possessors."*)

the *what*

The obvious are: unregistered full-auto stuff, illegal pre-/post-ban hybrids, short barreled/overall length long guns, or other miscellaneous *NFA34* stuff. First of all, you shouldn't be owning such, and secondly, you'd be a fool to try to sell it.

the *where*

If you reside in Kalifornia, then don't sell guns in Nevada. If your BATF agent customer has reason to believe that you're from out-of-State, then *"Lucy, ju gos som splaining to do!"*

the *how*

6. DO YOU NEED A FIREARMS LICENSE? - *Under 18 U.S.C. 922 and 923, it is unlawful for a person to engage in the business of dealing firearms without a license. A person is engaged in the business of dealing in firearms if he or she devotes time, attention, and labor to dealing in firearms* **as a regular course of trade or business with the principal objective of livelihood and profit through the repetitive purchase and resale of firearms.** *A license is not required of a person who only makes occasional sales, exchanges, or purchases of firearms for the enhancement of a personal collection or for a hobby, or who sells all or part of his or her personal collection of firearms.*
— ATF Form 4473 (5300.9) Part I (4-97)

Never admit to *any* profit on *any* transaction. *Never* claim that you are supporting yourself through private gun trading. (Even though an occasional transactional profit should not constitute a *"principal objective of livelihood and profit"* the BATF can possibly rule otherwise.) Be *very* wary of selling a gun at the same show where you bought it, especially if a profit from a *stranger* is involved (he could be a BATman). Don't *ever* divulge what you paid for a gun, or what you sold it for. Don't haunt the gun shows to the point that everybody thinks that you're a dealer. Don't buy and resell with great frequency.

A typical bust of illegal *"nonlicensed"* gun profits

To bust a seller would take two agents—one to sell an underpriced gun, and the other to buy it later at the market price (which means a profit for the victim, and thus an arrest). A possible way to avoid this is to share a table with a buddy. When one of you buys a gun, *trade* it to the other and let *him* sell it. Proving a monetary profit in that scenario would be difficult.

If you're from out-of-state, don't be stupid

As I earlier explained, the out-of-state bust is pretty rare, but showing up at the Nevada flea market with Oregon plates week after week will get somebody's attention. Registering for Georgia gun shows with a Florida address and phone is just begging for trouble.

Don't...be...*stupid*.

BUSTING THE BUYER

from *whom*

Do not buy from a *"prohibited possessor"*

Obviously, don't buy from somebody you know, or have reasonable cause to believe, is a *"prohibited possessor."*

the *what*

Don't buy illegal guns or full-auto parts, especially from strangers. The BATF has ruled that owning a semi-auto rifle (say, an AR15) with even *one* full-auto part (*e.g.,* a hammer, disconnector, etc.) constitutes an illegal full-auto gun—*even if the gun cannot fire full-auto!* Heck, they've ruled that *one* full-auto part in the home of a semi-auto owner is a felony!

Inspect military SLRs for full-auto parts *before* you buy!

The chances of this for AR15s are as high as 5%, given public ignorance and parts interchangeability. If you're shopping for a military-pattern SLR, inspect the trigger group and bolt carrier. If the selector moves to the "auto" position, avoid!

Reproduced below are drawings of the differences in AR15s. (I'd photocopy this to have it, and the pre-ban serial number cutoff list on page 27/9, with you at gun shows.)

Note the ★ differences in the full-auto M16 parts

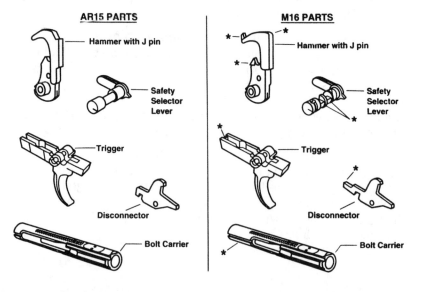

AR15 PARTS
- Hammer with J pin
- Safety Selector Lever
- Trigger
- Disconnector
- Bolt Carrier

M16 PARTS
- Hammer with J pin
- Safety Selector Lever
- Trigger
- Disconnector
- Bolt Carrier

the *where*
Don't buy outside your State(s), especially from strangers.

the *how*
Don't buy in such a way as to illegally evade the NICBC or Form 4473 requirements, or to evade them for somebody else.

Do not buy a gun *for* somebody else.
A nonlicensed person cannot buy a gun *for* anybody, except to *give* as a gift. So, if any stranger or "new" friend asks you to buy a gun *for* him (this is called a *"straw man sale"*), you should politely refuse, even if the end recipient is allegedly not a *"prohibited possessor."*

BUSTING THE OWNER
Since owning something bypasses any *transactional* risk, the BATmen will either have to spot you with something, or get a tip from a snitch. Don't let strangers handle or inspect your guns (especially semi-autos). Don't talk about sensitive items, not even to friends (as their phones may be tapped).

the *who*
"Prohibited possessors" may not own guns or ammo.

the *what*
Do not own illegal full-auto guns, or even full-auto parts!
This is a stupid and unnecessary risk. Avoid! And if you do, certainly do *not* tell your wife or girlfriend:

> *Of interest, is that most cases* [in which I testify as an expert witness] *have to do with the possession of an unregistered machine gun. In almost every instance a crime of violence was not committed but rather a wife, ex-girlfriend, etc., got angry and turned their husband or boyfriend in for possession.*
> — John Norrell, *The Small Arms Review*, 11/99, p. 39

Do not own illegal hybrid pre-/post-ban guns!
As I outlined earlier, only Bushmaster, Colt, and PWA lowers are easily distinguished, which makes it easy for a BATF sharpy (and they do exist, though not in any numbers) to spot their illegal hybrids. Know what your AR lower is.

the *where*
Do not take legal guns to restricted areas!
Such may include government buildings, school property, bars, polling places on election day, etc. Know before you go.

Do not take illegal guns to gun shows or ranges!
You shouldn't be owning them in first place, but taking them out in public is just begging for trouble.

IF EVER QUESTIONED

All this is fully covered in my *You & The Police!* (which I urge you to get), but I'll outline the basics here.

If you are ever questioned by a law enforcement official (or by anybody who merely *seems* to ask too many personal questions), *beware!* You may be moments away from a felony arrest based on some violation (mistakenly perceived, or even maliciously concocted) of the gun regulations found in Title 18.

Ascertain his identity. Don't cower!
Once he formally announces himself a BATF agent, politely yet firmly insist to inspect his credentials. (To "inspect" means exactly that—not letting him merely "flash" his "fold.") He will usually do this, albeit reluctantly. Since you've probably never seen a federal badge before, you might then (if you feel like pushing things a bit) firmly ask for corroborating ID such as his driver's license (which might have his home address on it). *This* he will rarely show you! How you play it from there is your choice; you could accept his badge, *or* you could maintain his badge to be phony and that he's *not* a federal agent (which will *really* piss him off). Either way, you've made your point.

What's the relationship? Arrest? Detention?
Immediately ascertain if it's an arrest, detention, or contact. Then you'll understand his powers are versus your rights.

First, ask if you are under arrest
He'll ask for your full name, ID, an address, how long you've lived there, etc. *Do **not** answer!* Instead, "answer" a question with a question. **Ask if you are under *arrest.*** (What

you are doing is acting like a Free American who demands to know why his Liberty is being interrupted.)

If not under arrest, then ask if you are being detained

If you are not under arrest, then ask if you are being *detained*. (He's more likely merely *"contact"* fishing, during which you may cheerfully bid him *"Good day!"* and walk away.) If he replies that you *are* being detained, ask him to articulate his reasonable suspicion. This will give him great pause, as most Americans, law-abiding or not, do not know to demand this. He might then ask if you are an attorney. Coolly reply, *"That is not relevant to the issue at hand. What is your reasonable suspicion?"* Only attorneys speak this way, and his confidence will *really* begin to ebb at this point, trust me!

Reasonable suspicion is the "little brother" of probable cause, and gives the officer the authority to detain you (20-30 minutes will be considered acceptable by any court). During this time you may not leave, and he is permitted to physically restrain you if necessary. He is trying to build reasonable suspicion into arrestable probable cause, and will bombard you with many questions in an intimidating manner. (During a detention, he is not required to "Mirandize" you; that's only *after* arrest.) **Know this: You cannot *ever* be forced to give testimony about *yourself!*** You do *not* have to answer questions during a contact, or during a detention, or during an arrest. Reply that *if* he has valid probable cause to arrest, then he's welcome to do so, but you've got *nothing* to say without your lawyer present. *Period. End of story.*

If detained, repeatedly ask if you're free to go

At first he will likely say *"No"* and follow with yet another question. (He might then pat you down for concealed weapons, but he cannot actually search your pockets, wallet, or sealed/locked containers.) You should reply, *"I have nothing to say without my lawyer present. Am I free to go?"* That's your mantra. Don't deviate from it. "Run out the clock" and he will eventually *have* to release you. He can't detain you forever.

Once free to go, don't hang around

As soon as he says that you're free to go, the relationship has changed from detention to mere contact (from which you may leave). First, call your lawyer and explain what happened.

Then, exit the premises immediately. If the scene was eerie enough (or if they're following you to the parking lot), then take a taxi and have a friend pick up your car later.

While all this may sound extreme, **nobody *else* can equally protect your own rights and liberty.** *Any* personal questioning by police is an adversarial relationship, and you must utterly be on guard. Please read my *You & The Police!* to fully understand your rights during any police confrontation. To quote myself, *"Cops work for the State, and the State is in search of bodies."* Don't be a "customer" of the State!

IF ARRESTED, EXPLAIN *NOTHING!*

You have only two duties during a search or arrest: to shut up and to stay alert. If ever arrested, *offer or explain nothing*! They went to a *lot* of trouble to get a signed warrant, and they're not going to be talked out of their hard work by even the most plausible of excuses. There is *nothing* you can say at the Scene to make them undo what they've just done. It's *their* party. You're already in a hole, and each word you say is shovelful of dirt to dig yourself even deeper. The only thing to say is *"I haven't done anything wrong. I do not consent to any search of my premises or property. I do not desire to answer any questions. I want to call my lawyer immediately."*

Don't give them *any* clues to your possible defense

If you do, they will undermine it (and they are very good at that). They surprised *you*, so your lawyer should surprise *them* later in court. *Nobody* can think of everything—not the criminals, and even not the *cops*. Believe me, they'll have goofed on *something*, and with diligence you'll discover it.

Do not be tempted by an urge to mentally spar with them

They do this for a living—you *don't*. The most brilliant display of intellectual swordsmanship I ever saw was in *The Man For All Seasons* (Sir Thomas More played by Paul Scofield). What succulent dueling with Master Secretary Cromwell and the court! Did he win? *No*. While he won all his battles, he lost the war by needlessly debating with a King's agent (who later perjured himself). Moral: If Sir Thomas More can be hung by his own tongue, then surely *you* can be, too!

"Never interrupt an enemy while he is making a mistake"

Wise advice from Napoleon. If they are breaking the law, or even proper procedure, allow them to continue. It'll somehow backfire on them later to either destroy their assertion of *"good faith"* or to weaken/negate material evidence.

Control your attitude! Stay calm and alert!

Be calm (keep the Scene to a minimum), polite (it can never hurt, and it often helps), and *alert*.

Observe and listen to *everything* going on. (Since you're not running your mouth, this ought to be easy.) They are as excited as you are (though obviously from a different perspective), and they too will make mistakes. (Trust me on this!) Demand to know who is in charge, and to see his badge. Demand to see the warrant. Listen for other names (they won't always be wearing name tags or badges). Try to glean a sense of what they *know* versus what they only *suspect*.

Beware of tricks!

If they ask you to handle an item, *refuse!* (Why put your prints on something that did not necessarily have them before?) Don't admit to any technical or legal expertise, which could be later used against you. If they claim that so-and-so has already implicated you in some alleged crime, shrug your shoulders and blandly reply, *"See you in court, then."* If they claim to *"know all about it,"* calmly reply, *"Good, then you can explain it all to me. I'm clueless here."* You get the idea.

Admittedly, these lines verge on the smartass, so if you don't feel comfortable with using them, fine. Just keep saying that you've *"done nothing wrong"* and refuse to answer any questions before speaking to your lawyer. (Truly, you need my *You & The Police!* for the fullest discussion of all this. Who knows how much trouble that 15 bucks might save you later!)

Ownership vs. *"possessory interest"*

If they ask if a particular thing belongs to you, *beware!* Refuse to answer, but if for some reason you felt *truly* compelled to claim it, admit to merely a *"possessory interest."* (This is, for example, what a coatcheck girl should say if drugs were found in a patron's garment.) *"Possessory interest"* means that you have temporary control or responsibility over something that isn't yours (or isn't yours yet). Point being, the phrase justifies an item being in your possession, but leaves an "out" regarding ownership and full knowledge of its nature or contents. (Or, as our Government loves to say, *"plausible deniability."*) It also allows you to exercise 4th Amendment rights on behalf another's property, as you have temporary custody for it, remember? Still, I wouldn't admit to even *"possessory interest"* of an item unless you *absolutely* knew what you're doing.

Legal defenses against a pre/post hybrid bust

Just as there are many ways to skin a cat, the cat has many ways to *avoid* being skinned. (This explains its 9 lives.)

"It had no post-9/94 date, so how could I have known?"

Title 18 USC § 923(i) requires gun makers and importers to date stamp all post-ban (*i.e.,* after 13 September 1994) full capacity mags and *"assault weapons."* Those *without* such a stamp may be presumed by the owner to be legal pre-ban items. This is your "ace in the hole" and few exist within the gun laws.

> **18 USC § 923(i)**
> *Licensed importers and licensed manufacturers shall identify, by means of a serial number engraved or cast on the receiver or frame of the weapon, in such a manner as the Secretary shall by regulations prescribe, each firearm imported or manufactured by such importer or manufacturer.* ***The serial number of any semiautomatic assault weapon manufactured after the date of the enactment of this sentence shall clearly show the date on which the weapon was manufactured.*** *A large capacity ammunition feeding device manufactured after the date of the enactment on this sentence shall* [also be so identified].

> **18 USC § 922(w)(4)**
> *If a person charged with violating paragraph (1)* ***asserts*** *that paragraph (1) does not apply to such person because of paragraph (2) or (3), the Government shall have the burden of proof to show that such paragraph (1) applies to such person.* ***The lack of a serial number as described in section 923(i) of Title 18, United States Code, shall be a presumption that the large capacity ammunition feeding device is not subject to the prohibition in paragraph (1).***

Notice that § 922(w)(4) specifies *"if"* one *"asserts."* This means that you must assert paragraph (2) or (3) to rebut the *prima facie* assumption of illegality. Without such assertion, such assumption is considered valid. (This is a perversion of that legal maxim *cui tacit consentire,* or he who is silent consents.)

The date stamp requirement expires on 13 September 2004, so expect its continuation or replacement before then.

"I understood it to have 10 or fewer affected import parts"

If such a bust ever *does* happen, a possible defense against prosecution or conviction would be that you understood the gun's 27 CFR § 178.39(c) imported parts count to be 10 or less. (This defense is feasible *if* the gun has *only one* "Crime Bill" feature.) Have your lawyer thoroughly research this argument, and make it *for* you, *after* the rifle has been photographed and can't be altered in order to preclude such a defense.

Protecting yourself in advance with photos/witnesses

Regarding any military-pattern SLR, it's a good idea to precisely document its legal status. Then, you can later allege any tampering of it by the authorities.

Make a detailed description of the gun. Have only one file per gun (and don't give the files obvious gun names!), encrypt it with PGP's biggest key, and store the file(s) only on a floppy diskette (never on the hard drive). Store the diskette offsite.

Next, take quality photos (make triple prints) of its semi-auto trigger group and receiver. If post-ban, get photos of its lack of multiple *"assault weapon"* features. Use *film*, not digital photos (which can be alleged to have been computer-altered).

Staple each photo set to a printed description of the gun, and have two or more witnesses date and sign the lot. Give one copy to your lawyer, and the others to your witnesses. *"Why not keep a copy for yourself?"* Because during a search or raid, it would likely be found and thus tip off the feds to your protection (which they might then illegally circumvent to keep their case).

Imagine the Government's surprise when their bogus case (based on an altered gun) falls apart in court with the testimony of two witnesses and photo evidence! (At the minimum, such evidence would clearly establish *"reasonable doubt."*) In any victory, preparation is everything.

Proving criminal intent (*mens rea*)

Actus non facit reum, nisi mens est rea.
The act does not make a man guilty, unless the mind be guilty.

Remember, the law usually requires you *"know or have reasonable cause to believe"* that your actions were illegal. This element (one of several) is under the *Government's* burden of proof. An otherwise viable prosecution can easily stumble and fail on the *mens rea* burden, even if the other elements are indisputable. Unless the defendant has admitted (in a diary, over the phone, to a witness, etc.) that he *knew* his actions were illegal, such is very difficult to prove. (All the more reason for watching your tongue!)

On this note, it's probably a good idea to purge your home of any evidence that you understood the regulations, such as law books, news articles, letters, and even this book.

Know a good gun-rights lawyer

The JPFO or GOA can help you find one. I'd look for one now, *before* you ever possibly need him. If you believe that you *are* under investigation or the potential victim of a sting, then get the relationship going immediately (while you store offsite any "extra" guns). Make sure that your family and friends know how to contact him, in case you can't.

(On the following pages are some related newsclippings which you may not have yet read.)

ASSAULT RIFLE CONFISCATION RESISTED BY ARMED EXTREMISTS

BOSTON (AP)—National guard units seeking to confiscate a cache of recently banned assault weapons were ambushed on April 19th by elements of a paramilitary extremist faction. Military and law enforcement officials estimate that 72 were killed and more than 200 injured before government forces were compelled to withdraw.

Speaking after the clash, Massachusetts Governor Thomas Gage declared that the extremist faction, which was made up of local citizens, has links to the radical right-wing tax protest movement.

Gage blamed the extremists for recent incidents of vandalism directed against internal revenue offices. The governor, who described the group's organizers as "criminals," issued an executive order authorizing the summary arrest of any individual who has interfered with the government's efforts to secure law and order.

The military raid on the extremist arsenal followed widespread refusal by the local citizenry to turn over recently outlawed assault weapons. Gage issued a ban on military-style assault weapons and ammunition earlier in the week. This decision followed a meeting earlier this month between government and military leaders at which the governor authorized the forcible confiscation of illegal arms.

One official, speaking on condition of anonymity, pointed out that *"none of these people would have been killed had the extremists obeyed the law and turned over their weapons voluntarily."*

Government troops initially succeeded in confiscating a large supply of outlawed weapons and ammunition. However, troops attempting to seize arms and ammunition in Lexington met with resistance from heavily-armed extremists who had been tipped-off regarding the government's plan.

During a tense standoff in Lexington's town park, National Guard Colonel Francis Smith, commander of the government operation, ordered the armed group to surrender and return to their homes. The impasse was broken by a single shot, which was reportedly fired by one of the extremists.

Eight civilians were killed in the ensuing exchange. Ironically, the local citizenry blamed government forces rather than the extremists for the civilian deaths. Before order could be restored, armed citizens from surrounding areas had descended upon the guard units. Colonel Smith, finding his forces overmatched by the armed mob, ordered a retreat.

Governor Gage has called upon citizens to support the state/national joint task force in its effort to restore law and order. The governor has also demanded the surrender of those responsible for planning and leading the attack against the government forces. Samuel Adams, Paul Revere, and John Hancock, who have been identified as "ringleaders" of the extremist faction, remain at large.

(The day and month you know, but the year was 1775.)

OMB NO. 1512-0129

DEPARTMENT OF THE TREASURY
BUREAU OF ALCOHOL, TOBACCO AND FIREARMS

TRANSFEROR'S TRANSACTION
SERIAL NUMBER

FIREARMS TRANSACTION RECORD PART I - OVER-THE-COUNTER

NOTE: Prepare in original only. All entries on this form must be in ink. **See Important Notices, Definitions and Instructions**

SECTION A - MUST BE COMPLETED PERSONALLY BY TRANSFEREE (BUYER)

1. TRANSFEREE'S *(Buyer's)* NAME *(Last, First, Middle)*	☐ MALE ☐ FEMALE	2. HEIGHT	3. WEIGHT	4. RACE

5. RESIDENCE ADDRESS *(No., Street, City, County, State, ZIP Code)*	6. BIRTH DATE	7. PLACE OF BIRTH *(City)*
	MONTH / DAY / YEAR	STATE OR FOREIGN COUNTRY

8. OPTIONAL INFORMATION - The information requested in this item (8) is strictly **optional** but will help to ensure the lawfulness of the sale and avoid the possibility of being misidentified as a felon or other prohibited person.

SOCIAL SECURITY NUMBER	ALIEN REGISTRATION NUMBER	MISCELLANEOUS NUMBER *(Military ID, etc.)*
	A __ __ __ __ __ __ __	

9. CERTIFICATION OF TRANSFEREE *(Buyer)* - Questions a. through l. must be answered with a "yes" or a "no" in the box at the right of the question.

a. Are you the actual buyer of the firearm indicated on this form? If you answer "no" to this question the dealer cannot transfer the firearm to you. *(See Important Notice 1.)*

g. Have you been discharged from the Armed Forces under **dishonorable** conditions?

b. Are you under indictment or information in any court for a crime for which the judge could imprison you for more than one year? An information is a formal accusation of a crime made by a prosecuting attorney.

h. Are you an alien **illegally** in the United States?

c. Have you been convicted in any court of a crime for which the judge could have imprisoned you for more than one year, even if the judge actually gave you a shorter sentence? *(See Important Notice 5 and EXCEPTION.)*

i. Have you ever renounced your United States citizenship?

d. Are you a **fugitive** from justice?

j. Are you subject to a court order restraining you from harassing, stalking, or threatening an intimate partner or child of such partner? *(See Important Notice 6 and Definition 4.)*

e. Are you an unlawful user of, or addicted to, marijuana, or any depressant, stimulant, or narcotic drug, or any other controlled substance?

k. Have you been convicted in any court of a misdemeanor crime of domestic violence? This includes any misdemeanor conviction involving the use or attempted use of physical force committed by a current or former spouse, parent, or guardian of the victim or by a person with a similar relationship with the victim. *(See Definition 5.)*

f. Have you ever been adjudicated mentally defective or have you been committed to a mental institution?

l. Are you a citizen of the United States?

m. What is your State of residence? _____
(State)

If you are not a citizen of the United States, you have a State of residence only if you have resided in the State for at least 90 days prior to the date of this sale. *(See Definition 6.)*

I CERTIFY THAT THE ABOVE ANSWERS ARE TRUE AND CORRECT. I UNDERSTAND THAT A PERSON WHO ANSWERS "YES" TO QUESTION 9b IS PROHIBITED FROM PURCHASING A FIREARM. I UNDERSTAND THAT A PERSON WHO ANSWERS "YES" TO ANY OF THE QUESTIONS 9c THROUGH 9k IS PROHIBITED FROM PURCHASING OR POSSESSING A FIREARM. I ALSO UNDERSTAND THAT THE MAKING OF A FALSE ORAL OR WRITTEN STATEMENT OR THE EXHIBITING OF ANY FALSE OR MISREPRESENTED IDENTIFICATION WITH RESPECT TO THIS TRANSACTION IS A CRIME PUNISHABLE AS A FELONY. I FURTHER UNDERSTAND THAT MY REPETITIVE PURCHASE OF FIREARMS FOR THE PURPOSE OF RESALE FOR LIVELIHOOD AND PROFIT WITHOUT A FEDERAL FIREARMS LICENSE IS A VIOLATION OF LAW. (SEE IMPORTANT NOTICE 7.)

TRANSFEREE'S *(Buyer's)* SIGNATURE	DATE

ATF F 4473 (5300.9) PART I (10-98) PREVIOUS EDITIONS ARE OBSOLETE

SECTION B - TO BE COMPLETED BY TRANSFEROR (SELLER)

10. TYPE OF FIREARM(S) TO BE TRANSFERRED:

☐ HANDGUN ☐ LONG GUN ☐ BOTH

11a. TYPE OF AND NUMBER ON IDENTIFICATION *(Driver's license or other valid government-issued photo identification. See Instruction to Transferor 1.)*	11b. TYPES AND DATES OF ADDITIONAL IDENTIFICATION REQUIRED FOR ALIENS *(e.g., utility bills or lease agreements. See Instruction to Transferor 2.)*

ITEM 12, 13, OR 14 MUST BE COMPLETED PRIOR TO TRANSFER OF FIREARM(S) *(See Instructions to Transferor 4-7.)*

12a. THE TRANSFEREE'S IDENTIFYING INFORMATION IN SECTION A OF THIS FORM WAS TRANSMITTED TO NICS OR THE APPROPRIATE STATE AGENCY ON _____ .
(Date)

12b. THE NICS OR STATE TRANSACTION NUMBER *(if provided)* WAS: _____ .

12c. THE RESPONSE INITIALLY PROVIDED BY NICS OR THE APPROPRIATE STATE AGENCY WAS AS FOLLOWS:

☐ PROCEED ☐ DENIED ☐ DELAYED

12d. IF INITIAL NICS OR STATE RESPONSE WAS "DELAYED," THE FOLLOWING RESPONSE WAS RECEIVED FROM NICS OR THE APPROPRIATE STATE AGENCY ON _____ .
(Date)

☐ PROCEED ☐ DENIED ☐ NO RESPONSE PROVIDED WITHIN 3 BUSINESS DAYS

13. STATE PERMIT TYPE *(no NICS check required because transferee has a valid permit which qualifies as an exemption to NICS)*	DATE OF ISSUANCE	EXPIRATION DATE *(if any)*	PERMIT NUMBER

14. ☐ NO NICS CHECK WAS REQUIRED BECAUSE THE TRANSFER INVOLVED ONLY NFA FIREARM(S)

SECTION C - IF THE TRANSFER OF THE FIREARM(S) TAKES PLACE ON A DIFFERENT DAY FROM THE DATE THAT THE TRANSFEREE SIGNED SECTION A, THEN THE TRANSFEREE MUST COMPLETE SECTION C IMMEDIATELY PRIOR TO THE TRANSFER OF THE FIREARM(S) *(SEE INSTRUCTION TO TRANSFEREE 3 AND INSTRUCTION TO TRANSFEROR 9)*

I CERTIFY THAT THE ANSWERS I PROVIDED TO THE QUESTIONS IN ITEM 9 OF SECTION A OF THIS FORM ARE STILL TRUE AND CORRECT.

TRANSFEREE'S *(BUYER'S)* SIGNATURE	DATE

SECTION D

On the basis of (1) the statements in Section A; (2) the verification of identity noted in item 11 and my verification again at the time of transfer *(if the transfer does not occur on the same day as the verification noted in item 11)*; and (3) the information in the current list of Published Ordinances, it is my belief that it is not unlawful for me to sell, deliver, transport, or otherwise dispose of the firearm(s) described below to the person identified in Section A.

15. MANUFACTURER AND/OR IMPORTER	16. MODEL	17. SERIAL NO.	18. TYPE *(Pistol, Revolver, Rifle, Shotgun, etc.)*	19. CALIBER OR GAUGE

COMPLETE ATF F 3310.4 FOR MULTIPLE PURCHASES OF HANDGUNS *(See Instruction to Transferor 11.)*

20. TRADE/CORPORATE NAME AND ADDRESS OF TRANSFEROR *(Seller) (Hand stamp may be used.)*	21. FEDERAL FIREARMS LICENSE NO. *(Hand stamp may be used.)*

THE PERSON ACTUALLY TRANSFERRING THE FIREARM(S) MUST COMPLETE ITEMS 22 THROUGH 24.

22. TRANSFEROR'S *(Seller's)* SIGNATURE	23. TRANSFEROR'S TITLE	24. TRANSACTION DATE

ATF F 4473 (5300.9) PART I 10-98

IMPORTANT NOTICES

1. **WARNING - The Federal firearms laws require that the individual filling out this form must be buying the firearm for himself or herself or as a gift.** Any individual who is not buying the firearm for himself or herself or as a gift, but who completes this form, violates the law. **Example: Mr. Smith asks Mr. Jones to purchase a firearm for Mr. Smith. Mr. Smith gives Mr. Jones the money for the firearm. If Mr. Jones fills out this form, he will violate the law. However, if Mr. Jones buys a firearm with his own money to give to Mr. Smith as a birthday present, Mr. Jones may lawfully complete this form.** A licensee who knowingly delivers a firearm to an individual who is not buying the firearm for himself or herself or as a gift violates the law by maintaining a false ATF F 4473.

   Question 9a is not applicable to returns of firearms, e.g., holders of pawn tickets or consignors of firearms. Accordingly, such transferees should answer Question 9a as "N/A."

2. Under 18 U.S.C. 922 firearms may not be sold to or received by certain persons. The information and certification on this form are designed so that a person licensed under 18 U.S.C. 923 may determine if he may lawfully sell or deliver a firearm to the person identified in Section A, and to alert the transferee *(buyer)* of certain restrictions on the receipt and possession of firearms. This form should not be used for sales or transfers where neither person is licensed under 18 U.S.C. 923.

3. The permanent provisions of the Brady law, 18 U.S.C. 922(t), became effective on November 30, 1998. The law requires that prior to transferring any firearm to an unlicensed person, a licensed importer, manufacturer or dealer must first contact the National Instant Criminal Background Check System (NICS). NICS will advise the licensee whether the system contains any information that the prospective purchaser is prohibited by law from possessing or receiving a firearm. For purposes of this form, contacts to NICS include contacts to State agencies that have been designated to do NICS checks for the Federal Government.

4. WARNING - Any seller who knowingly transfers a firearm(s) to any person prohibited from receiving or possessing any firearm violates the law even though the seller has complied with the background check requirements of the Brady law.

5. The transferee *(buyer)* of a firearm should be familiar with the provisions of law. Generally, 18 U.S.C. 922 prohibits the shipment, transportation, receipt, or possession in or affecting interstate commerce of a firearm by one who has been convicted of a crime punishable by imprisonment for a term exceeding one year; by one who is a fugitive from justice; by one who is an unlawful user of, or addicted to, marijuana, or any depressant, stimulant, or narcotic drug, or any other controlled substance; by one who has been adjudicated mentally defective or has been committed to a mental institution; by one who has been discharged from the Armed Forces under dishonorable conditions; by one who has renounced his or her U.S. citizenship; by one who is an alien illegally in the United States; by one who is subject to certain restraining orders; or by one who has been convicted of a misdemeanor crime of domestic violence. Furthermore, section 922 prohibits the shipment, transportation, or receipt in or affecting interstate commerce of a firearm by one who is under indictment for or information for a crime punishable by imprisonment for a term exceeding one year.

   EXCEPTION: For one who has been convicted of a crime for which the judge could have imprisoned the individual for more than one year, or has been convicted of a misdemeanor crime of domestic violence, the prohibition does not apply if, under the law where the conviction occurred, the individual has been pardoned for the crime, or the conviction has been expunged or set aside, or the person has had civil rights restored, AND the person is not prohibited by the law of the jurisdiction where the conviction occurred from receiving or possessing any firearms. Persons subject to one of these exceptions should answer "NO" to questions 9c or 9k, as applicable.

6. Under 18 U.S.C. 922, firearms may not be sold to or received by persons subject to a court order that: (A) was issued after a hearing of which the person received actual notice and had an opportunity to participate; (B) restrains such person from harassing, stalking or threatening an intimate partner or child of such intimate partner or person, or engaging in other conduct that would place an intimate partner in reasonable fear of bodily injury to the partner or child; and (C)(i) includes a finding that such person represents a credible threat to the physical safety of such intimate partner or child, or (ii) by its terms explicitly prohibits the use, attempted use, or threatened use of physical force against such intimate partner or child that would reasonably be expected to cause bodily injury.

7. DO YOU NEED A FIREARMS LICENSE? - Under 18 U.S.C. 922 and 923, it is unlawful for a person to engage in the business of dealing in firearms without a license. A person is engaged in the business of dealing in firearms if he or she devotes time, attention, and labor to dealing in firearms as a regular course of trade or business with the principal objective of livelihood and profit through the repetitive purchase and resale of firearms. A license is not required of a person who only makes occasional sales, exchanges, or purchases of firearms for the enhancement of a personal collection or for a hobby, or who sells all or part of his or her personal collection of firearms.

8. Persons acquiring firearms for the purpose of exportation should be aware that the State Department or Commerce Department may require a license to be obtained prior to exportation.

INSTRUCTIONS TO TRANSFEREE (BUYER)

1. The transferee *(buyer)* of a firearm must personally complete Section A of this form and certify *(sign)* that the answers are true and correct. However, if the buyer is unable to read and/or write, the answers may be written by other persons, excluding the dealer. Two persons *(other than the dealer)* must then sign as witnesses to the buyer's answers and signature.

2. When the transferee *(buyer)* of a firearm(s) is a corporation, company, association, partnership or other such business entity, an officer authorized to act on behalf of the business must complete and sign Section A of the form and attach a written statement, executed under penalties of perjury, stating (A) that the firearm(s) is being acquired for the use of and will be the property of that business entity, and (B) the name and address of that business entity.

3. If the transfer of the firearm(s) takes place on a different day from the date that the purchaser signed Section A, then the licensee must again check the photo identification of the purchaser prior to the transfer, and the purchaser must complete the certification in Section C at the time of transfer.

INSTRUCTIONS TO TRANSFEROR (SELLER)

1. KNOW YOUR CUSTOMER - Before a licensee may sell or deliver a firearm to a nonlicensee, the licensee must establish the identity, place of residence, and age of the buyer. The buyer must provide a valid government-issued photo identification to the seller that contains the buyer's name, date of birth, and residence address. A driver's license or identification card issued by a State in place of a license is particularly appropriate. Social security cards are not acceptable because no address, date of birth, or photograph is shown on the cards.

2. SALE OF FIREARMS TO ALIENS - A transferee *(buyer)* who is not a citizen of the United States must provide additional identification in order to establish that he or she is a resident of a State. *(See Definition 6.)* Such a transferee must provide a valid government-issued photo identification to the seller that contains the buyer's name, date of birth, and residence address. In addition, such a transferee must provide documentation such as utility bills or lease agreements that would establish that he or she has resided in a State for at least 90 days prior to the date of this sale.

3. If the buyer's name is illegible, the seller must print the buyer's name above the name printed by the buyer in Item 1.

4. NICS CHECK - Prior to transferring a firearm to a nonlicensee, the licensee must contact the National Instant Criminal Background Check System (NICS) for a criminal background check on the transferee (buyer). After the purchaser has completed Section A of the form, and the licensee has completed Items 10 and 11, the licensee should contact NICS in accordance with the instructions received from ATF. At the time that NICS is contacted, the licensee should record in Item 12 the date of contact, the NICS *(or State)* transaction number, and any response provided by NICS. If the licensee receives a "delayed" response, the licensee must also record any subsequent response provided by NICS. **NOTE:** In some instances, States acting as points of contact for NICS checks may use terms other than "proceed," "delayed," or "denied." For example, a State may provide an "approve" response that is equivalent to a "proceed" response; a "pended" response that is equivalent to a "delayed" response; or a "non-approval" response that is equivalent to a "denied" response. In such cases, the licensee should check the box on the form that corresponds to the State's response. Licensees should also note that some States may not provide a transaction number for denials. However, in any case where a firearm is transferred within the three business day period, a transaction number is required.

5. NICS RESPONSES - If NICS provides a "proceed" response, then the transaction may proceed. If the licensee receives a "denied" response, then the licensee is prohibited from transferring the firearm to the buyer. **If NICS provides a "delayed" response, the licensee must delay the transaction until he is contacted again by NICS or 3 business days have elapsed. See 27 CFR 178.102(a) for an example of how to calculate 3 business days.** If NICS does not provide a response after 3 business days have elapsed, the seller may transfer the firearm unless, prior to the transfer, NICS has advised the seller that the buyer's receipt or possession of the firearm would be in violation of law.

6. EXCEPTIONS TO NICS CHECK - A NICS check is not required if the transfer is subject to any of the alternatives in 27 CFR 178.102(d). Generally, these include transfers: (a) where the transferee has presented to the licensee a permit or license that allows the transferee to possess, acquire, or carry a firearm, and the permit has been recognized by ATF as a valid alternative to the NICS check requirement; (b) of National Firearms Act weapons approved by ATF; or (c) certified by ATF as exempt because compliance with the NICS check requirements is impracticable. See section 178.102(d) for a detailed explanation of these alternatives.

7. If the transfer is subject to one of the exceptions to the NICS check requirement outlined in paragraph 6 above, the transferor must obtain the supporting documentation required by 27 CFR 178.131. A firearm must not be transferred to any buyer who fails to provide such information.

8. If more than four firearms are involved, the identification required by Section D, items 15 through 19, must be provided for each firearm. The identification of the firearms transferred in a transaction which covers more than four weapons may be on a separate sheet of paper, which must be attached to the form covering the transaction.

9. Immediately prior to transferring the firearm, the transferor (seller) must complete and execute Section D of the form. If the transfer takes place on a different day from the date that the purchaser signed Section A, then the licensee must again check the photo identification of the purchaser prior to the transfer, and the purchaser must complete the certification in Section C at the time of transfer.

10. Additional firearms purchases made by the same buyer may not be added to this form after the seller has signed and dated it. A purchaser who wishes to buy additional firearms after the seller has signed and dated the ATF F 4473, must complete a new ATF F 4473, and a new NICS check must be conducted on this separate transaction.

11. In addition to completing this form, you must report any multiple sale or other disposition of pistols or revolvers on ATF F 3310.4 in accordance with 27 CFR 178.126a.

12. The transferor (seller) of a firearm is responsible for determining the lawfulness of the transaction and for keeping proper records of the transaction. Consequently, the transferor should be familiar with the provisions of 18 U.S.C. 921-929 and the regulations, 27 CFR Part 178. In determining the lawfulness of the sale or delivery of a rifle or shotgun to a nonresident, the transferor is presumed to know applicable State laws and published ordinances in both States.

13. After you have completed the firearm transaction, you must make the completed, original copy of the ATF F 4473, Part I, and any supporting documents part of your permanent firearms records. Forms 4473 must be retained for at least 20 years. Filing may be chronological (by date), alphabetical (by name), or numerical (by transaction serial number), so long as all of your completed Forms 4473, Part I, are filed in the same manner.

14. FORMS 4473 FOR DENIED TRANSFERS MUST BE RETAINED - If the transfer of a firearm is denied by NICS, or if for any other reason the transfer does not go through after a NICS check is conducted, the licensee must retain the ATF F 4473 in his or her records for at least 5 years. Forms 4473 with respect to which a sale, delivery or transfer did not take place shall be separately retained in alphabetical (by name of transferee) or chronological (by date of transferee's certification) order.

DEFINITIONS

1. Over-the-counter Transaction--The sale or other disposition of a firearm by the transferor (seller) to a transferee (buyer), occurring on the transferor's licensed premises. This includes the sale or other disposition of a rifle or a shotgun to a non-resident transferee (buyer) occurring on such premises.

2. Published Ordinances--The publication (ATF P 5300.5) containing State firearms laws and local ordinances which is annually distributed to Federal firearms licensees by the Bureau of Alcohol, Tobacco and Firearms.

3. Under indictment/information or convicted in any court -- An indictment/information or conviction in any Federal, State or foreign court.

4. Intimate Partner -- With respect to a person, the spouse of the person, a former spouse of the person, an individual who is a parent of a child of the person, and an individual who cohabits or has cohabited with the person.

5. Misdemeanor Crime of Domestic Violence -- A crime that is a misdemeanor under Federal or State law and has, as an element, the use or attempted use of physical force, or the threatened use of a deadly weapon, committed by a current or former spouse, parent, or guardian of the victim, by a person with whom the victim shares a child in common, by a person who is cohabiting with or has cohabited with the victim as a spouse, parent, or guardian, or by a person similarly situated to a spouse, parent, or guardian of the victim. The term includes all misdemeanors and lesser offenses that involve the use or attempted use of physical force (e.g., simple assault, assault and battery), if the offense is committed by one of the defined parties. The person is NOT considered to have been convicted of such crime unless the person was represented by a lawyer or gave up the right to a lawyer, and, if the person was entitled to a jury trial, was tried by a jury or gave up the right to a jury trial.

6. State of Residence - The State in which an individual resides. An individual resides in a State if he or she is present in a State with the intention of making a home in that State. If an individual is on active duty as a member of the Armed Forces, the individual's State of residence is the State in which his or her permanent duty station is located. An alien who is legally in the United States shall be considered to be a resident of a State only if the alien is residing in the State and has resided in the State for a period of at least 90 days prior to the date of sale or delivery of a firearm. See 27 CFR 178.11 for examples of this definition.

PRIVACY ACT INFORMATION

1. AUTHORITY. Solicitation of this information is authorized under 18 U.S.C. 923(g).

2. PURPOSE. To determine eligibility of the transferee (buyer) to receive firearms under Federal law.

3. DISCLOSURE OF SOCIAL SECURITY NUMBER. Disclosure of the individual's social security number is voluntary. The number may be used to verify the individual's identity.

PAPERWORK REDUCTION ACT NOTICE

The information required on this form is in accordance with the Paperwork Reduction Act of 1995. The purpose of the information is to determine the eligibility of the transferee (buyer) to receive firearms under Federal law. The information is subject to inspection by ATF officers. The information on this form is required by 18 U.S.C. 922.

The estimated average burden associated with this collection is 19 minutes per respondent or recordkeeper, depending on individual circumstances. Comments concerning the accuracy of this burden estimate and suggestions for reducing this burden should be directed to Reports Management Officer, Document Services Branch, Bureau of Alcohol, Tobacco and Firearms, Washington, DC 20226.

An agency may not conduct or sponsor, and a person is not required to respond to, a collection of information unless it displays a currently valid OMB control number.

HOW TO
BUY, SELL, & TRADE

THE PRIVATE SALE MARKET
IS QUICKLY DRYING UP!

23 States allow record-free private sales. Where else on the planet can you respond to a newspaper ad, drop by a flea market, or attend a gun show to buy a battle rifle from a total stranger with utterly *no* permission or record? This makes the Klintonistas incandescent with rage:

> *Some people who don't like guns can't stand the idea of so many gun owners in one place* (at gun shows), *buying and selling their wicked products.* **It's how some communists feel when they visit the New York Stock Exchange.**
>
> — David Kopel, *The American Guardian,* January 1999

Since 1998, private sale prices have been going up as people are catching on to the future *potential* cost (*i.e.,* registration and confiscation) of *papered* guns. The days of the Ø400 Glock are gone; today, you'll pay up to Ø475 for a plain old G17 and up to Ø550 for a G21—and you'll be giddy to have seen it first. (Some Good Advice: Snap up every private sale Glock you can. A Glock will work forever, and you'll never lose your investment.)

Battle rifles and carbines in particular have gone through the roof. No more Ø700 post-ban Bushmasters and Ø1,000 pre-ban Colt HBARs. (If you find even a *post*-ban AR15 these days for under Ø900, consider yourself very fortunate.) More disturbing still is that nobody is selling really *good* stuff these days. M1As, FALs, and H&Ks you almost never see any more. (An AR10? Dream on!) You *might* see an SKS (*"Only 250 bucks!"*), a Ø400 thumbhole stocked MAK90, or a Century Arms FAL for Ø850, but that's about it. (A couple of years from now, you'll probably wish you'd bought that FAL.)

RULES FOR BUYING

With today's (and tomorrow's) perilous and dynamic legal climate regarding gun transactions, I've laid out some helpful rules. Follow them, and you'll likely never have any trouble.

Be wary of the seller

Don't buy from obviously criminal types with jailhouse tatoos. Don't buy from anybody obviously underage, and if you've any doubt, then insist on ID. Don't buy from anybody who seems oddly nervous. Don't buy from anybody who seems to ask too many personal questions. Don't buy from an insistent buyer who is clearly disinterested in guns and is strangely pre-occupied (likely a BATF agent).

You're *not* there to chat or to make a new friend

Divulge little/no info to the buyer. Smoothly non-answer personal questions. Don't talk about the Government, politics, *"gun control,"* etc. You're buying it as a gift or for "protection."

Trust your instincts

If you get *any* kind of weird feeling about the deal, then *trust* it and politely decline to transact—no matter how badly you want the gun.

Carefully inspect the item

I'll go over this in great detail in just a few pages.

If you don't buy it, wipe off your prints

If you've handled the gun but passed on it, be sure to casu-ally wipe off your fingerprints (under the guise of politely re-moving rust-causing oils). If that gun were ever to be involved in a crime, you don't want to be linked to it by your fingerprints.

Pay cash, always

A check or M.O. creates a paper trail, and such could re-turn some day to haunt you if the seller ever commits a crime.

After you've bought the gun

Notate the make, model, serial #, caliber, date, and price

You need to have some sort of record of it in case it's ever lost, stolen, or unlawfully confiscated. I'd store this information in an encrypted file.

Secure it in a locked case while driving

Even if your State allows the open vehicular carry of firearms, why complicate any traffic stop?

Test immediately, and return or dump a lemon

If you've purchased a gun with chronic malfunctions, then high-tail it back to the seller and demand a refund (especially if he guaranteed its functionality).

If returning it is not possible, then promptly sell it.

If the gun is *not* part of the primary home battery, store it

As I've often said, the only guns which should remain at home are those needed for home defense (*i.e.,* 2-3 handguns and 1-2 long guns per family member). Everything else should be stored away from your home and office, for safety's sake.

RULES FOR SELLING

Deciding on whether to sell a favorite gun

You never regret the guns you keep, just the ones you sell. If you ever have qualms about selling a cherished gun, *don't.* Ask yourself:

"If I sell it, will I want to replace it later?"	(Certainly!)
"Is this the nicest one I'll likely find?"	(Probably.)
"Will it be more expensive and harder to find later?"	(No doubt!)

If you answer yes/probably to all three, then keep it! I, for example, can't look at a nice U.S. .30-06 M1917 (they're now over Ø400) without pangs of regret. Another choice piece I dumped (just because I then didn't want the extra caliber; what a whiner!) was a 98% Mauser HSc pistol with pre-WWII proofs that I'd bought for only Ø250. *Arrrggh!*

Transport it to the meet in a locked case

Even if your State allows the open vehicular carry of firearms, why complicate any traffic stop?

Be wary of your buyer

Don't sell to obviously criminal types with jailhouse tatoos. Don't sell to anybody obviously underage, and if you've any doubt, then insist on ID. Don't sell to anybody who seems oddly nervous. Don't sell to anybody who seems to ask too many personal questions. Don't sell to an insistent buyer who is clearly disinterested in guns and is strangely preoccupied (likely a BATF agent).

You're *not* there to chat or to make a new friend

Don't divulge much info to the buyer. Don't talk about the Government, the BATF, militias, etc. You're selling it because you need the money for bland, suburb an reasons.

If you get *any* kind of weird feeling about the deal, then *trust* it and politely decline to transact—no matter how badly you need the money.

Demand and accept only cash

Don't fall for stories like *"I didn't have time to get to the bank."* Motivated buyers bring cash. (A check is only a *claim* to money, and creates a link between buyer and seller.)

Wipe off your fingerprints

Just before relinquishing a gun for cash, be sure to casually wipe off your fingerprints (under the guise of politely removing rust-causing oils). If that gun were ever to be involved in a crime, you don't want to be linked to it by your fingerprints.

If he doesn't buy it, then wipe off his prints before packing.

When selling a papered/registered gun

You should always write out a receipt to protect yourself. With the gun's make, model, serial #, and caliber, you should also notate the buyer's name, address, DL#, and DOB.

If he balks at this, explain that the gun's last Form 4473 has your name on it, and that this receipt would never be given to the authorities unless the gun were sought after for its criminal use. If that doesn't satisfy him, then refuse to transact.

After you've sold the nonpapered gun

Delete its computer entry ASAP. Do not enter when, where, to whom, or for how much you sold it—this information is in no way helpful to keep (in fact, it could be incriminating if that gun is ever misused).

NEWSPAPER ADS

Buying

It pays to consistently check the "Guns" or "Sporting Goods" classified ad sections. I've seen some *amazing* items in local newspapers: Ø900 FALs, Ø600 ARs, Ø300 Glocks—even a .50BMG bolt gun (something you don't want any purchase transaction of). Be vigilant, have cash ready, and pounce on the great deals. Make your call to the seller from a payphone only, and never leave your home or office number.

Selling

Never, *never, never* list an ad with your home, office, or cell number! Ever! First of all, you could be targeted by thieves looking for the rest of your guns. Second, the BATF has been compiling a database of ad listings for The Day. (I know this for a fact from a law enforcement insider.) So, get a temporary voice mail under an alias and use that number. Tell the service that you're just in town briefly visiting friends and don't want to tie up their phone. Since you'll pay for that month's service in advance, no credit check (and thus no ID) is necessary. (Get my *Bulletproof Privacy* to learn more about tactical procedures.)

Pick up and return your messages from varied payphones, never from your home or office. Explain that you accept only cash. Never meet potential buyers at home or work. Instead, arrange to meet them in an outdoors public place (a discreet parking lot works well). If you can park elsewhere and walk over with your items in a case, then so much the better (as your car and plate aren't seen).

FLEA MARKETS

Gun show tactics generally apply, except that you must be more careful of avoiding a more common criminal element. Stolen weapons are more likely to be there (though they're not by any means prevalent), so beware.

Buying

Usually the seller has backed his car up to his spot. Look at his license plate. Is it from another State? If so, do *not* buy from him. He may claim to have just moved in town, or that he has a second home there. Such may indeed be the truth, but you probably shouldn't take the chance. Nonlicensed private citizens cannot buy from or sell to whom they *"should reasonably believe"* is an out-of-State person, and such a license plate would certainly qualify. Yes, you may have to forsake a nice deal, but a felony arrest just isn't worth it. (If, however, the seller showed you a local DL, then you're probably O.K.)

If you get *any* kind of weird feeling about the deal, then *trust* it and politely decline to transact.

Selling

Remove your front license plate, if any. Choose a perimeter spot (with no tables behind you), and nose in. Set up a chair, table, or blanket to cover your rear license plate. Over your dashboard VIN toss a paper napkin, map, etc.

Don't set up in out-of-State flea markets (especially if your car is registered as such). Don't sell a gun you just bought at the same market, else the profit involved may get you busted for operating a firearms business without an FFL (it's a stretch to convict, but it's happened). Accept only cash.

When packing up, wipe down all your guns for public prints (you don't know who's handled them).

If you get *any* kind of weird feeling about the deal, then *trust* it and politely decline to transact. (Yeah, I've said this several times already, but it's some of the best advice I have.)

Is all this "paranoid?"

No, but it *is* intense preparation to reduce the risk of a BATF sting. *Too* intense? Hey, that's up to you. What's your freedom worth? My job is to try to think of everything so that you don't have to. Therefore, my books are served "piping hot" from my mind's kitchen and it's your choice how much to let them "cool" before dining. (Conversely, a lukewarm dish cannot be heated up at the table.)

GUN SHOWS

Enjoy them, while they last. (This may be the final year.) In 1999 Congress very nearly eliminated gun show private sales by requiring NICBCs. (This is already the law in Kalifornia, which banned private transactions years ago.) Our illustrious President Klinton, that serial lecher, had this to say recently:

But at too many gun shows, a different, dangerous trend is emerging. Because the law (actually it's the Second Amendment) *permits some firearms to be sold without background checks, some of these gun shows have become **illegal arms bazaars for criminals** and gun traffickers looking to buy and sell guns on a cash-and-carry no-questions-asked basis.* (The National Institute of Justice's own 12/97 study found that only 2% of criminal guns came from gun shows. Hardly *"illegal arms bazaars for criminals."* BTP)
I believe this should be the law of the land: No background check, no gun, no exceptions. Therefore, I am directing Secretary Rubin and Attorney General Reno to report back to me in 60 days with a plan to close the loophole (sic) *in the law and prohibit any gun sale without a background check. We didn't fight as hard as we did to pass the Brady Law only to let a handful of unscrupulous gun dealers disrespect the law* (Oooh!), *undermine our progress* (No!), *put the safety of our families at risk.* (Puhleeze!) ***With this action, we are one step closer to shutting them down.***
— Bill Clinton, 7 November 1999 radio address

"Shutting them down" sounds like child pornography rings! They honestly believe that gun shows are *evil*. How did such philosophical weeds ever sprout and flourish in *American* soil?

To the un/underinformed, a "background check" sounds reasonable and responsible. What they don't understand is that the associated FBI recordkeeping is nothing but a national registration scheme. Before the Government can ever move to confiscate firearms, it must first know who has what. (*Heh!* Too late for that! Such won't stop them from trying, however.)

That's why we're now hearing the new misleading catch-phrase *"unlicensed dealer."* If you put an ad in the paper to sell your used car, would it be accurate to call you an *"unlicensed dealer?"* No, because you're not in the *business* of selling cars. It's the same with private folks buying and selling guns, as is their right. And all this crap about a *"loophole"* really cheeses me off. It's called the Second Amendment!

On a related note, Ruger just announced that their guns are not to be sold by FFLs at gun shows. We're all baffled at what that's supposed to accomplish since the NICBC procedure is the same for *all* FFL transactions—storefront or gun show! (Yet another reason not to buy a new Ruger.) If this isn't 2nd Amendment treason, then I don't know what is.

Folks, the handwriting is on the wall: First restrict imported guns, then choke off the domestic output. It's a diabolically clever plan, but it won't work. We're *already* armed.

Venting aside, my point is that the private sales at gun shows are under attack, and there's little joy in dealer-only gun shows. Only since the 1986 *Firearm Owners Protection Act* have FFLs been allowed to sell at gun shows (which were formerly *private* affairs with a much better selection), and it's my sneaking suspicion that many FFLs are licking their chops over the monopoly prospect. Go soon and go often, while you can.

Get there *early*

Gun shows are usually weekend events, which means that exhibitors set up on Friday afternoon (usually from 3-8PM). Lots of horse trading is done then, so why miss out? Either pay for your own table, or help out an exhibitor.

If you can't somehow swing a show badge, then you'll have to line up on Saturday morning with the rest of the public. I've found some great deals in line outside before the show even opened! Keep your eyes open and politely ask if things are for sale. *"If you don't ask, then the answer's always 'No'."*

Go *both* days

Most people attend only one day, which means that Sunday's crowd will be different from Saturday's. Why chance missing out on that *one* private sale pre-ban AR15 at the show? The fine deals don't last more than 30 minutes, and sometimes not even that. You've must be there all day, every day—which is why you should...

Get your own table

This has many, many advantages: you can be in the building on Friday afternoon during setup, you can arrive an hour earlier than the public on show days, you are treated better by other exhibitors, you get to see all the walk-by traffic and chat them up, you meet more people, and you have a base of operations. Finally, it's cost effective. Instead of you and several buddies paying Ø10 apiece to attend for the weekend, why not spend a mere Ø50 and get your own table?

The most compelling reason to have your own table is to more easily buy and sell. All the public comes to *you*—versus milling around the show on foot and missing out on 70% of the hand-carried goodies. Some examples: a Ø150 *mint* M1917, a

Ø90 Swedish M38, a Ø300 Glock 17, and a Ø625 AR—just to name a few I've seen.

Late Sunday often has the best deals

Many attendees pop in Sunday late afternoon, dump their guns, and leave. Most exhibitors are more interested in taking home additional money than guns and they'll often prefer to make a quick Ø25-50 on something they just bought 10 minutes prior. If the show was really slow, they might even sell an item to break even. Otherwise, they'll have to inventory it, pack it, cart it home, and then try to sell it at the next show.

How to scour a show

Gun shows are not carnivals to amble about; gun shows are *serious* business and a dwindling opportunity. Don't squander them!

Rule 1. Have lots of cash

Cash *works*. It's private, powerful, and has no substitute.

Rule 2. Be efficient and ruthless

Have a master shopping list that's prioritized by sublists of **A** (*e.g.,* private-sale Glocks, FALs, ARs, .50BMG rounds, etc.), **B** (*e.g.,* bargain mags, fast-selling ammo, collectibles, etc.), and **C** (*e.g.,* everything else). Conduct your A-sweep first, then B, and then C. Then, start again at A, as at least an hour will have passed and new stuff will have arrived in that time.

Instead of working the hall left to right or right to left (as do most of the public), work *back to front* and snap up those bargains before the public filters there. Get floor maps from the show promoter to ID a table location, or else you can easily forget where it was. Hit the private-sale table areas first!

Do not buy, or even examine, B and C items on an A sweep as you risk losing out on an A-item by mere seconds. (I once lost a Ø125 .308 Spanish FR8 that way. It would have been a perfect truck rifle.) Do not chat, do not sign petitions or fill out raffle cards. Do not dally. You're on a *mission*.

Scouring quickly (*i.e.,* at a fast walk), a person can learn to A-sweep 12 tables per minute. Five seconds per table is all an experienced eye needs for A-level items. The trick is to walk down aisles only once per trip, looking side to side at the tables. Keep your pace up, which helps to move through clogged traffic.

Some tables have only Cowboy stuff, or books, or parts, or jewelry and can be ignored on the A-sweep. Other tables are obviously FFL dealers, and you can ignore them, too. A-sweeps (the main reason for attending the show) are for private sale tables and individuals with goodies. I can, by myself, A-sweep a 200 table show in just 15 minutes. (One friend of mine described my relentless focus and pace as like a horse on its way to the water trough at day's end.)

By the time you've gone through your first A- and B-sweeps, you've probably spent most of your money, so the C-sweep can be a very leisurely stroll where you really take your time and examine every interesting table.

Rule 3. Have help

It's difficult, if not impossible, to single-handedly quickly and thoroughly scour any show of more than 200 tables. Take a buddy or two along, divide up the show into sections, and dive in. Three good people with radios can A-sweep a 1,000 table show in under a half hour.

Rule 4. Communicate by radio

Try it once and you'll be sold forever. (The Motorola Talk-Abouts are perfect for this.) If you're an exhibitor, then radios are absolutely vital so that your tablemates can stay in touch.

Rule 5. Advertise!

Trying to sell without advertising is like winking at a girl in the dark—*you* know what you're doing, but she *doesn't*. Make a placard with two headings, *Buying* and *Selling*, with a list under each. Wear this sign on your back. Visibly wear your handguns, and have *For Sale* flags in your rifle barrels.

Rule 6. Always take trading *wampum* with you

I once bought a mint, 4-digit (made in 1914) Winchester Model 11 shotgun (the Browning A5 design, but without bolt handle) for "only" Ø350, thinking I'd found a Ø500+ collectible. Turned out, I got skinned. *Nobody* wants those shotguns. Because it had no bolt handle and was designed to be cocked by pulling the barrel back (it's a recoil-operated gun), so many people negligently blew their fool heads off with it (by placing the buttpad on their shoe and then trying to barrel cock it) that Winchester frantically traded brand new Model 12 pumps for them, just to get the 11s off the streets. By the 1990s, it seemed that everybody had received a bulletin about this but me. The highest cash offer I ever got was only Ø225, and this gun was a beauty which functioned perfectly!

I began to gloomily conclude that I'd have to put the thing in my Last Will and Testament to ever be rid of it. So, I'm leaving this little gun show, having struck out on selling it, and just outside the door is a guy on a nicotine break holding a wooden pistol case. *"Say, what kind of shotgun is that?"*

Why, it's an antique Winchester, I replied. He asked to look at it, and immediately began heavily praise it, saying that he was looking for a nice shotgun for his dad so they could dove hunt together. Needless to say, I instantly warmed to his plan. It *was*, after all, a beautiful old gun and perfectly safe *if* (as with any gun) you kept your face out of its muzzle. I told him that it was one of John Moses Browning's first gun designs, which had also been made by Remington, Savage, and FN. I explained that the recoil operation was less fussy about ammo variances than modern gas-operated shotguns, such as the Rem 1100. I assured him that his father would treasure this lovely old gun which reeked of early 20th Century quality (and it sure *did*).

He began to look somewhat depressed, which I mistook for waning interest. Turns out I touted the gun so highly that he didn't think he could *afford* it! *"Would you be interested in trading for it?"* he asked, holding up his pistol case. *"Maybe, what's in the box?"* I languidly inquired. What he had was a new condition Dan Wesson .357 Magnum with five barrels, from 2" to 12"! I didn't know exactly what the package was worth, but knew that I didn't have the cash to make up the difference. I told him that he indeed had a very nice revolver, but that I probably couldn't trade. As the Winchester lingered in his hands, and dejection fell on his face, he said, *"This sure would be a nice shotgun for my dad. Are you sure you wouldn't trade for it?"* Only then did I finally understand that he meant trading *even*!

If you ever saw the movie *Trading Places* where Eddie Murphy is in the limousine with Randolph and Mortimer Duke saying, *"Uh, no, no...I think I can hang wit you fellas!"*—you know exactly what happened. My reflexes, honed by 25 years of flea markets and gun shows, kicked in immediately. In short, my worst gun show purchase turned into my best trade.

Did I skin the guy? Who can say, as nobody knows what he had in the Dan Wesson. A book value comparison indicated that I'd made a screaming deal, but book values are only transactional composites—averages which mean little in real-life. *"Beauty is in the eye of the beholder"* and what I *do* know is that he *really* wanted that old Model 11 and was absolutely *delighted* to get it. As long as he and his dad enjoy it, then everybody won. The moral of this long story is to *always* take gun show trading *wampum*, no matter how allegedly undesirable. You never know *what* will light up peoples' eyes.

Rule 7. Know the show
Shows are run by a particular promoter, and are filled by particular exhibitors (who usually reserve the same tables). Therefore, the private sale tables will usually be clumped in the same certain areas, so head for these archipelagoes first.

Rule 8. Be polite, nonantagonistic, and unremembered
Quietly work the show like a machine. Blend in and blend out. You don't want anybody later remarking about you.

Rule 9. Take somebody to their *first* gun show
These shows are an authentic, though probably doomed, bit of Americana. Introduce new shooters to the fun and living history of gun shows, while we can still enjoy them. I just took a friend to her first gun show (although she has her own guns), and we had a great time. She chatted with the Old Duffers, and especially liked the antique rifles (*"beautiful!"*—which they certainly were).

Gun show etiquette
Leave your "bad ass" attitude at home. Go to have a good time, to learn something, and to make new friends. If a seller is asking an exorbitant price, resist the urge to cut him down to size. Also, don't be overly critical of a seller's wares. If something isn't for you, then be polite, and move on. If another buyer is inspecting something you're interested in, it is impolite to try to buy it out of his hands. Wait until he's set it down to bid on it.

INSPECTING THE GOODS

Caveat emptor! Let the buyer beware!

Assume nothing!
Another time I jumped all over a WWI-era Walther .32 for Ø180, thinking it was the rare Ø400 Model 3. It was instead the *very* common Model 4. It took forever to get rid of that gun!

Inspect carefully!

Appearances are often deceiving. Half the effort in this world goes into making things seem what they are *not*. **While you can't *polish* a turd, you can surely *bronze* one.** I've caught cold blue touchups, grips glued on handgun frames (to hide their broken retaining ridges), actions cable-tied open to hide the fact that they wouldn't *close*, aftermarket parts on ostensibly 100%-original collector guns, and more.

Keep your focus

If you're not careful, you could buy a lemon or a felony. Take your time and don't let the seller distract or misdirect you with chatter.

Is it legal?

Before you even touch it, eye it carefully. Is it an illegal pre-/post-ban hybrid? Does the barrel or overall length seem too short? Only then do you pick it up. If a battle rifle or carbine, open the action to make sure that it has no full-auto parts. The selector should be blocked off from the "auto" position. (If there is any question about its status, wipe off your prints and politely put it back on the table.)

Is it in the caliber you want?

I once saw a guy walking around a gun show with a "For Sale" flag on his AR10. (Its green furniture was hard to miss.) A private sale AR10—*Gee, willikers!* It was in like-new condition, had three mags, and the price was a very reasonable Ø1,400. I very nearly ended up with it before I realized that it was in *.243* and not .308. (While the .243 is a fine round, it's not what I wanted, especially since it would have taken *months* to get a .308 barrel from ArmaLite.) Had the seller tried to deceive me? Nope. I saw an AR10 and *assumed* it was a .308, even though his sign and the rifle's own receiver clearly said .243. As Heinlein once wrote, *"Hear hoofbeats. Expect horses, not zebras."* The seller was a good chap and took it all very well—probably better than I would have!

Does it seem fully functional?

Work the action and *all* the controls (especially the safety and feeding device), and even strip it down. Insist on dry firing it at least once.

Carry extra cable ties with you to replace the one you cut off, that way the seller can't object to a full inspection by claiming that he has no more ties. I once nearly bought a Glock 30, but fortunately I insisted on removing the cable tie to work the action and discovered its faulty trigger mechanism. (The seller had tied the action shut to conceal this, and acted all surprised when I pointed out the problem.)

How is the bore?

Inspect the bore (have your own borelight with you). It takes some experience to discern between a bore that pitted, fouled, or dirty. Any conscientious seller will have scrubbed out the bore beforehand. Use an indeterminable bore as a bargaining chip.

Inspect for problems, hidden and not

Look for worn/gouged screwheads which evince much disassembly (and therefore likely problems).

Look for missing/incorrect screws and small parts, and don't believe that a missing slide stop is *"only Ø4 from Gun Parts Corp."* (Maybe it *is*, but that's not a risk *you* should be willing to take. Still, having a Gun Parts Corp. catalog back at your table can be an invaluable reference.)

Look at the sights carefully. Skewed sights mean a problem gun, and you should pass.

On scoped rifles, do a quick bore sight. If the reticle is off, then the seller merely threw on some scope to enhance the rifle and he has no way of knowing that *"it's a tackdriver"* (regardless of his claims).

Does the gun have matching numbers?

This is a *vital* consideration for collectibles. Check all the small parts, for even one mismatching number will reduce the gun's value considerably. (The numbers match, or they don't.)

Are all the parts original?

Very carefully inspect the grips (remove them to read any markings on the inside).

Inspect the mags for fit, function, and authenticity. (Beware the seller switching them at the last minute.)

Is the finish original?

This is also vital for collectibles, unless you merely want an affordable shooter. Look for evidence of buffing and rebluing (the rollmarks will be smooth and some pitting will have remained under the bluing). Always *smell* a gun for that telltale cold-blue odor (it's worth buying some just to know the odor).

If you catch a seller *lying* about *any* part of his story...

...you've uncovered merely the tip of the sh✳tberg. Consider yourself fortunate to have done so *before* you lost your money. Move on, and *never* buy *anything* from him. Tell others.

Have a current *Bluebook of Gun Values* and use it often

While the listed values are often 10-20% high, the figures will at least get you in the ballpark. My copy has saved me several times from buying an overpriced gun which I would have otherwise considered a bargain. (From CTD; #ZAA-391; Ø23)

Don't buy what you don't know about

There are thousands of different guns out there, many of which seemingly desirable. Know at least *something* about a gun before you buy it. For example, I once traded for a .22LR Remington Speedmaster rifle, only to discover that they malf frequently. It took months to finally dump it!

Ask questions!

What you ask, and in what order, is very important to helping you discern a problem gun:

> *"Have you fired it?"*
> *"How did it function?"*
> *"How many malfunctions did you have?"*
> *"What kind of groups did you shoot with it?"*
> *"Does point of aim equal point of impact?"*   (e.g., CETMEs)
> *"What did you notice that was wrong with it?"*

If you sense any lying or evasion, move on. (He'll understand.)

ON TRADING

Sometimes, you just can't sell a gun at *any* fair price. The gun show urge to come back with a new gun is admittedly a powerful one, and even I have succumbed to it more than once. The trouble is, this urge will often cloud your judgment, causing you to make a poor trade. (Trust me, I know.)

To minimize the risk of this, ask yourself the following test question: **If you actually had the *cash* for it, would you *buy* the tradeable item?** The answer will illuminate its true value to you. If you would *not* buy it outright at the trade value, then you're more likely just itching to trade for the trading's sake and thus risk swapping poorly.

If, however, you trade A for B in order to then trade B for C (knowing that you could *not* have *directly* traded A for C), then that's a different story. Such shrewdness takes much experience to develop, in conjunction with a regular thumb on the gun market pulse. Unless you have firsthand knowledge of reliable A→B and B→C opportunities, I'd be reluctant to take the chance on such a "Gin Rummy" game.

If you're stuck with something locally undesirable, then trading out from under it is often the only way to get into something else more easily saleable. That's happened to me over a dozen times, and usually (with patience and diligence) I've come out quite well. One particular trade was an A→B→C→D affair, with D being *much* more desirable than A.

HAGGLING

Bargaining (*i.e.,* negotiation) skills are *extremely* important in life, not just at gun shows.

As a cash buyer

Don't appear more prosperous than everybody else. Wear older clothing and no jewelry. Learn to haggle. Never pay the first, or even second, asking price—and often not even the third. Offer ⅔ and pay ¾. Remember, unless buyers are standing in line, there are *always* more sellers than buyers. You have the leverage, and never forget that. **If his stuff were so choice, then he'd *keep* it.** So, the most important question to ask is:

"Why are you selling it?"

If he hems and haws, or seems evasive, then *beware*. Remember, he likely knows *much* more about the item than you do.

Inspect the item very carefully. *Caveat emptor!* Once you've decided to bid on it, *put it back on the table.* This is very powerful psychologically—you haven't yet accepted the goods. Find a palpable defect and *harp* on it in disappointed tones.

Act more disinterested than not, and keep looking about as if searching for a friend. No seller can stand such "iffyness" and will work harder to reel you in. Before you make your first

offer, slowly count your money (inside the wallet) with a scowl,
pull out the offered amount and put it on the table. He's tempting you with his displayed goods, so you should tempt him with
your displayed money. **Always *show* him the money.** That
makes it easily *his* money with a simple *"Yeah, O.K."*

If he doesn't bite, then walk away. He'll often call you
back. Here are some of my best lines as a buyer:

"What repairs does it need now? What will it need later?"
You'll be amazed at what you can learn by asking these two.

"What's your best cash price, right now?"
Very powerful. It often forces the seller to his bottom dollar.

"Can you work with me on price?"
A very low-key line, as nobody wants to seem inflexible.

"It's something I kind of like, but don't really need."
A great way to explain your modest, yet remaining, interest.

"Is there anything you'd like on trade?"
Very interesting transactions can thus derive.

"I'm not sure I can swing it..."
This forces the seller to help solve your "dilemma."

"Can you sweeten the pot with something?"
A smooth way to get an extra mag or something thrown in.

Here's a technique against the *really* hard-core seller if
your bid is firm. Let's say he's asking Ø225 and the most you'll
pay is Ø150, and you're not in the mood to haggle. Tell him, *"I'll
give you Ø150 right now. That's what it's worth to me."* Plunk
down the Ø150. He'll no counter with Ø200, figuring you'll meet
at Ø170-185. You reply with, *"Was I not clear? I told you that it
was worth Ø150 to me. That's it. Now it's worth Ø145. My time
is not free."* Now remove Ø5. This will blow him away; no buyer
haggles *down*! This is a hard-core tactic, to be used sparingly.

Times may be tough and you must stretch your funds, but
do try to create only Win-Win deals. Don't haggle some old guy
down to his bones. Once you've reached a fair price you can
happily afford, *pay it.* It's cruel to demand everybody's bottom
dollar. Let him make a modest profit. **Be *fair* to sellers; you
never know when you might be one *yourself.***

Final bit of advice: *Never* divulge how much you paid for something, as doing so might kill the chance of a profit later, plus you risk being labeled an illegal *"unlicensed dealer."*

Ask to part out the item to break up "package" deals

Never forget that the seller's goal is to *sell*. Which will move more quickly: a Ø700 gun with Ø300 of accessories for Ø1,000, *or* the items offered separately? Usually, the second. I bought a Sure-Fire forestock flashlight this way for only Ø80 by persuading the seller to remove it from his shotgun.

As a seller

Same rules apply, but in reverse. Act fairly disinterested, but not overly so (that's rude). If an offer is not even close, don't mull it over or hesitate to reject it (although halfway politely). Only when an offer is "in the ballpark" do you begin to haggle. Never accept a first bid or the buyer will have immediate "cognitive dissonance" by imagining some hidden defect or cursing himself for not offering less. Make him haggle a bit and he'll be much happier with his purchase.

When he asks why you're *selling* such a treasure, reply that you need the money and *"can't keep everything."* Say or imply *nothing* to even indirectly disparage your goods, or to communicate that you desperately need the cash.

If he doesn't bite and walks off, don't follow him with your eyes or he may notice and correctly figure you to be a motivated seller. He's walked off and you've forgotten all about him—that's your attitude. When he returns acting all disinterested, you only barely remember him. My best lines for sellers:

"I'd be losing money at Ø100."
This politely informs the buyer of your (alleged) "bottom dollar."

"Don't you think Ø125 is fair?"
This politely encourages the buyer not to be such a tightwad.

"Hey, I'm not here for the fun of it!"
Reminds the buyer that you need to make a profit, too.

"I just got here. I think I'll hear some other offers, thanks."
A very smooth way to decline, yet not slam shut the door.

"Can you sweeten the pot with something?"
You never know what else he might toss on your table.

KEEP AND BEAR ARMS *PRIVATELY*

"Keep and bear" means to own and carry.

Gossips and snitches

Never underestimate the power of these worms. They are hard to squelch, as fear has a very short half life when you're not constantly around to reinforce it. The best tactic is to *never* let *anybody* know *anything* juicy or compromising about yourself. What they don't know, they can't *tell*. As I wrote in *Bulletproof Privacy*, *"Trust only when you can, and then only when you <u>have</u> to."*

Customer lists

One day, you may encounter a fairly enterprising "crat" or investigator who can actually conduct some decent field work. Therefore, organize your affairs so that records lead *nowhere*.

The neat thing about databases is that they only "know" what they've been *told*. If, for example, you ordered your AR parts under an assumed name, paid with a money order (bought with cash), had it shipped to Mail Boxes Etc. in another town where you're not personally known, and took delivery discreetly, then your supplier's records will offer nothing but *dead ends*. It will be as though the order disappeared into thin air.

Make a habit of quickly burning labels, receipts, M.O. stubs, and catalogs. Either flush the ashes, or soak them well. (Dry ash flakes are often amazingly readable.) Do this perfectly and consistently for many years, and no outside picture can possibly be assembled of your buying history. *Heh!*

Ammo

Until 1986, ammo sellers had to notate the buyer's name and DL number with every purchase. Today, you can order thousands of rounds of quality bargain ammo with no paper trail. While many mail-order suppliers insist on your faxing them a copy of your DL, a few do not. Besides, you can get almost the same deal at gun shows and pay cash for anonymity.

Guns & Gear

As listed in Chapter 34, some 23 states require no record kept of private sales (which are *intrastate* and thus properly unregulated by the feds). Gun shows, flea markets, and garage sales in those states are where you should buy your guns.

Your local gun club

Don't have your real name, phone, etc. on their list. Sign up under an alias, or go as a guest. Or, send the club their dues by anonymous M.O. and get the gate combo from a friend.

SALE OF FIREARMS

SELLER (Please Print)   Date_____
Name

_____
Address

_____
City and State   Zip

_____
Phone | Identification

PURCHASER (Please Print)
Name

_____
Address

_____
City and State   Zip

_____
Phone | Identification

ITEM PURCHASED:
Make | Model | Serial No.

_____

CAL _____ BARREL LENGTH_____

NOTICE TO THE BUYER:
Do not sign this agreement before you read it.

I certify that I am 21 years or more of age, that I have never been convicted of a crime punishable by imprisonment for a term exceeding one year — that I am not a fugitive from justice; that I am not a mental incompetent, a drug addict or an adjudged drunkard, or convicted of a felony, and that I am not prohibited from legally acquiring a firearm by state or local laws.

_____   _____
Signature of Seller   Signature of Purchaser

HANDLOADING, ZEROING, SHOOTING, CLEANING, & CACHING

If you think *Boston's Gun Bible* is an ambitious book, then this is likely one of its most ambitious chapters. There have been dozens of good books written on the above subjects. I will try to encapsulate what I've learned from my reading chair, as well as from my reloading bench, range, and field.

HANDLOADING

While I don't bother handloading my practice pistol and battle rifle FMJ (life is short; get it by the case), I do handload my bolt and lever action rifle ammo.

Handloading books

This is a subject in which you should invest *much* study *before* you handload your first round. Although handloading is not rocket science and the mechanics are fairly simple, it does require well thought-out and careful technique. Also, there are many excellent tips from books which will save you much time, expense, and aggravation.

Buy some good basic reloading manuals and apprentice under a buddy who has the experience. If you're handloading for only a few calibers, then the cartridge-specific manuals by Loadbooks USA (Ø8; 800-676-8920) are a bargain. You'll see them often at gun shows.

By *far* the best handloading guide I've found is:

Any Shot You Want: The A-Square Handloading and Rifle Manual
edited by Arthur B. Alphin

Written by five highly experienced hunters and riflemen: Finn Aagaard, Col. Arthur Alphin, Craig Boddington, Dr. Gary Minton, and Terry Wieland. Each of them have safaried in Africa more often than you or I have been to Canada or Mexico.

> *We saw this manual as an add-on to the other manuals. In order to get started in handloading from scratch, you will need other manuals (such as the Hornady, Nosler, or Sierra manuals), and/or* The ABC's of Reloading. *The A-Square manual has plenty of hints and nice-to-know things which are of great value to the beginning handloader. At the same time, we have developed other subjects much further than most manuals take them.*

Engagingly written, nicely compiled, and very well illustrated, this book is a treasure trove of information and experience not available elsewhere. It's not only got handloading data, but rifle and cartridge selection for target shooting and hunting everything from prairie dogs to cape buffalo. I learned things I never would have thought to contemplate.

There is even a distillation of the Four Rules of Safety:

> *The safety switch on your rifle is located between your ears. In the event of malfunction, the safety switch is adjusted through the use of sharp blows to the temple with a blunt object.*

Editor Alphin inscribed my copy *"Ama yena zingela uMagazini khulu!"* (Zulu for *"Shoot him with the big rifle!"*) I highly recommend this book! Available directly from:

A-Square Company   502-255-3021   www.a-sqarecompany.com

A-Square is primarily known for their "Triad" bullet concept. The "Lion Load" (highly frangible and very destructive), the "Dead Tough" (general purpose with great penetration and tightly controlled expansion), and the "Monolithic Solid" (an unbreakable bulldozer of a bullet for smashing bone of big game). If you hunt (especially medium and heavy game), give their superb bullets (or loaded ammo) a try.

They also offer custom rifles for any kind of hunting, and are experts on African safari needs.

Handloading safety rules
Be organized and self-disciplined

Not everyone is cut out for this. Some people just cannot remain in a conscious state for very long, and slip into daydreaming. Furthermore, some people are far too cluttered and messy. (If you ever see a chaotic handloading bench, *run!*)

Always use proper equipment

Handloading is not an area to skimp money on. Buy it right, buy it once, buy it safe.

Pay attention to detail

Pilots have printed checklists for takeoff and landing procedures. Even though a pilot with 10,000 hours in the same aircraft knows these procedures by heart, he will nevertheless read from the checklists just like a novice.

Do not smoke or eat during handloading

This would seem unnecessary to state, but many folks have ended up in the Darwin Awards by smoking around open tins of gunpowder.

Don't eat during a handloading session, as bullets are made of lead, which is not only toxic but has been proven to shave off IQ points over time. One former owner of a prestigious shooting academy (I can't divulge his name, but it rhymes with "pee") used to eat sandwiches while handloading, his fingers dark gray from the lead bullets! His behavior grew so odd, erratic, and counter-productive, that it became legendary in the gun world. One colleague of mine posited that it was from lead poisoning, and I think he may have been right.

Stay alert

The longer you've done something, the more it's imprinted in your subconscious. This is both a good and bad thing. Good, in that you "own" the knowledge. (As I explained in the *Training & Tactics* chapter, you learn in order to "forget.") Bad, in that your conscious will at some point begin to wander as it is not needed for the rote task at hand.

This is why motorcyclists typically have three accidents: the first at 6 months (when skills are still undeveloped), the second at 2 years (the mind wandered too far/long at the worst moment), and at 10 years (the mind wandered again, but the lesson from the 2nd accident lasted 8 years!).

As soon as you have handloaded enough that you can do it on "autopilot"—beware! The moment your mind begins to wander, immediately reinstate consciousness and focus.

Be patient

Don't wait until the last moment to handload. Have acres of time in front of you, with nothing pressing on your schedule.

Record *everything*

Though not to brag, I have an astounding memory for figures and names. I can recall phone numbers of childhood friends whom I haven't called in 25 years. I never have to look up 5-place values for pi or MOA or metric conversions. (My friends think it's rather eerie.)

However, do I trust this facility for my handloads? No way! If I mistake a powder weight by just 1gr (much less the powder type!), I could create some real trouble for myself. A student/friend recently emailed me for my pet .45-70 handload, and even though I was 99.9% certain of it from memory, I preferred to look it up just to make sure.

So, if *I* record all my handloading data, then *you* should.

Handloading supplies

Although not a handloading outfit, Brownells has a wide variety of miscellaneous tools and gear, plus their very useful and entertaining four volume *Gunsmithing Kinks*.

Press

For the beginner, a simple single-stage press is fine. (I actually got started with a Lee hand press.) With scale, Redding powder measure, case trimmers, priming tool, dies, tumbler, caliper, kinetic bullet puller, screwdrivers, punches, etc. you can get started for well under Ø300.

If you need a progressive reloader, then go Dillon Press (800-762-3845; www.dillonprecision.com). I like the RL650. Dillon has the best warranty service in the business, and is also a staunch RKBA supporter. Their monthly catalogs feature good shooting gear, accessories, books (perhaps even this one)—as well as pictures of beautiful women. What more could one ask?

Other quality handloading equipment suppliers are:

Hornady	www.hornady.com
Lee Precision	www.leeprecision.com
Lyman	www.lymanproducts.com
RCBS	www.rcbs.com
Redding	www.redding-reloading.com
Sinclair	www.sinclairintl.com

Dies

Get carbide dies (they last longer) for straight-walled cases, and a neck-sizer die for your bottleneck cases (for more consistent brass with less stretching).

Visit www.huntingtons.com. They have dies for *everything*.

Brass

Buy new brass and chamber fire-form for each rifle (don't mix them up). Count how many times each case has been reloaded. Brass varies significantly by manufacturer. Military brass is usually heavier (less case volume, thus more pressure) than civilian brass. Research and test thoroughly. For near-max loads, pay *strict* attention to the make of brass.

Powder

While powder drops are accurate, I prefer to *individually* weigh by digital scale all countersniper and near-max loads.

Lean towards the more versatile powders, such as 3031 and 4895, which can nicely load a variety of different rounds.

The Finnish VihtaVuouri powders are excellent, providing the highest velocities and best accuracy. VV gives a .308 an extra 100fps velocity to nearly match the .30-06. It's a dollar more per pound, but in .308 that works out to only ½¢/rd.

Primers

From a survivalist standpoint, I'd stock up on primers. It's the most difficult component to remanufacture. For example, our military has used lead styphnate primers since 1948:

Lead Styphnate, Normal	36.8%
Barium Nitrate	32.0%
Antimony Sulfide	15.0%
Aluminum Powder	7.0%
PETN	5.0%
Tetracene	4.0%
Gum Arabic	0.2%

Try to make these at home for 1.6¢ each! *"Honey, are we out of PETN?"* Buy them for Ø16/1000. 50K are only Ø800.

Brands are more critical than you might think. For best accuracy, Federal Bench Rest primers are king. For everything else, I like Winchester, but Remington is fine, too. CCI primers have a reputation for being rather soft.

Bullets

No gun, no particular shot, is better than the bullet it throws. What's the point of a great caliber, an accurate load, and a perfect shot if the bullet breaks up in your elk without damaging a vital organ? The inverse is also true: what's the point of a bullet which just zips right through your Bad Guy without him even noticing? (This was common in Somalia with the 62gr M855 .223 round. Some "skinnies" had to be shot several times before they dropped. Read *Blackhawk Down*.)

Expansion and penetration are two mutually exclusive properties, which must be kept in proper balance for different uses. Know *exactly* what is required of your bullet (especially in terminal ballistics), and pick the best one for the job.

If explosive frangibility is required (*i.e.*, for varmits or very light game), then you have many choices.

However, for hunting medium-heavy game, pick a bullet which will penetrate deeply without breaking up or expanding too much (which not only slows it down, but increases precession and veers the bullet path). The random bullet will likely be more frangible than tough, so if you're looking for tough choose the A-Square Dead Tough or Monolithic Solid. The Nosler Partition or Barnes X (if your rifle likes them) are also pretty good.

Reloading components vary between mfg. lots

You can load ammo with identical bullets, cases, powder, and primers and get 5-10% variations in chamber pressure and MV between different production lots from the *same* manufacturer. Primers seem especially known for this, and I've read of up to 12,800psi differences.

Moral: Reload in batches from the *same* production lot of components. **Make *very* detailed notes!** Just because you use up an old can of 4831 during a session, don't keep going with a newer-made can of 4831. This is most important for max loads.

If you have to incorporate a different lot of some component, back off 5% for case/primer/bullet, and 10% for powder. Chrono them and gradually work your way back up to desired MV. Does all this seem overly cautious? Well, what's a hand, or an eye, or a life worth to you?

Handloading for accuracy

In the September 2001 issue of *Guns & Ammo*, Wayne van Zwoll had a nice article called *6 Steps to Great Handloads*. I'll paraphrase it for you here.

Start with cases from the same maker/lot
Cull by weight to within 0.5gr.

Check flashhole diameter
Use #45 wire size drill bit as a gauge. Make primer pockets uniform with Sinclair tool.

Measure cases from base to mouth
Trim to equal length.

Deburr flashhole

Deburr case mouth, inside and out
Take is easy; a couple of twists with a tool is plenty.

Measure neckwall thickness and trim if necessary

If handloading for same rifle, neck size only
Since the case body will have been fired-formed to the gun's chamber, there is no need to resize the entire case. Just resize the neck. This will not only increase case life by not work-hardening the brass, but also improve accuracy.

Prime with hand-priming tool
Although not as fast as a progressive press, this tool gives you a precise feel. (I prime cases while watching videos.)

Weigh all powder charges
This is especially good advice with stick powders, and with all max or near-max loads. It's slow, but it's the only way to ensure consistent powder charges.

Ballistics software

Now you can have a ballistics lab in your own computer! Once you're an experienced handloader, this software is invaluable for playing "what-if" and working up new loads.

QuickLOAD   707-747-0897   www.neconos.com
This program installs through Windows, and is easy to use. The cartridge case selection includes 750 choices; the bullet selection 135 choices; the powder selection 80 choices.

Once you've chosen the combination of case, powder, bullet, and barrel length, QuickLOAD gives you muzzle velocity and chamber pressure, as well as a host of other ballistic data.

Also included is the external ballistics QuickTARGET, which gives all trajectory data in tabular and graphical formats.

AMMO

You *must* test your ammo in its gun. You must have reliable, *firsthand* knowledge that it fits in your mag, feeds perfectly, fires accurately to POA, extracts easily, and ejects cleanly. If using any defensive ammo other than FMJ, then spend the Ø on at least three test boxes. Don't trust your life to any assumptions!

In a pinch you should at least rack test several mags (with the safety on), but live fire is the only way to make *absolutely* sure. I learned this on an SKS which dry-racked perfectly but failed to feed at the range.

Buy only reputable ammo. Saving 2¢/round with Earl's Ammo is *not* the place to be economical. I once bought 100rds of generic 62gr .223 at a bargain price, only to learn that 3" groups at 50yds were the norm.

Save your brass. Even if you don't reload, somebody else does. One day, brass will be like gold. During non-dynamic shooting drills, you might attach a brasscatcher.

ZEROING

Your zeros will change with different bullet weights, powder loads, case brand, and even primers. Every rifle is an enigma regarding its optimal load. You'll have to experiment with handloads to find the tastiest combination. Start with the proven winners in the reloading guides, and work from there.

Battle rifles

For military-style rifles with adjustable rear sights, the front sight is usually adjustable for basic elevation. An AR15 is adjustable with a bullet tip, whereas the FAL, SKS and AK all need a front sight tool (Ø10-20). Using the most reliably feeding and consistently accurate ammo available for your rifle, set the rear sight at 100 and adjust the front sight if necessary.

Rule: Move the front sight *opposite* to how you want the bullet to move. (If impact is too high, then front sight is too low.) Move the rear sight in the *direction* of desired bullet impact.

Once zeroed at 100, test at all rear sight ranges to confirm that POA equals POI at distance. Only your life depends on it.

If you might use different ammo (e.g., 55 *and* 62gr .223), then test them against your primary ammo and make notes for field use. Tape a card to your rifle's buttstock.

How much to lower or raise your front sight

To determine how much change is needed, multiply (in inches) the amount of correction needed at the target by the sight radius (*i.e.,* the distance between the front and rear sight). Divide this by the inch distance to target (*i.e.,* 3,600" = 100yds).

$$\frac{(POI\ correction") \times (sight\ radius")}{(distance"\ to\ target)} = sight\ change"$$

For example, if your rifle has a sight radius of 20" and you're shooting 10" high at 100yds, the math would be:

$$\frac{10" \times 20"}{3600"} = 0.056"$$

Regardless of whether the front sight needs to raised or lowered, my first step would leave the sight about 0.010" higher than the strict math would dictate—which would cause you to shoot a bit lower (about 1.8" lower in the above example). You can always remove more of the front sight, but it's a real pain to add on metal. Low POI (versus high POI) is much more easily compensated for (*i.e.,* by raising the rear sight).

Focus on the *top edge* of the front sight

This will give you the most precise/consistent groups.

Scoped rifles

First, center the reticle

This is vital if you have purchased a used scope. Who knows *where* the reticle will be from the previous owner!

Start with windage. Click it all the way to the right, and stop. Now click it all the way to the left, *counting clicks as you do.* Once all the way left, go right half the number of clicks.

Now do the elevation. The reticle is now centered.

Boresighting

This is a technique to get you on 100yd paper with your first shot. Remove the bolt and the scope's turret caps. Rest the rifle on some sandbags as you sight on the target through the bore. (If the target is so small that you cannot easily center the image, simply use a decapped case in the chamber and peer through the flashhole.)

Now, *without disturbing the rifle*, look through the scope and move the reticle on target. Confirm that the bore remained sighted. Your first shot should be on paper. If it isn't, then fire a round at a 50yd target to show your POA/POI discrepancy.

Scopes with BDC cam or reticular holdover

Set at 100 and test with the necessary ammo. Once zeroed at 100, test at all other cam/holdover distances. Although the compensation is usually spot-on, you should have firsthand knowledge of this.

Most BDCs are graduated in only 100yd/100m increments, so you must be familiar with POIs between such even numbers. This become increasingly vital past 400yds as the trajectory drops at an increasing rate. Elevation clicks of ¼MOA are required for truly precise work past 800yds.

Scopes without BDC, zeroing for MPBR

Depending on barrel length, bullet, MV, and temperature, this is usually 225-300yds (check the reloading manuals). You must also know the maximum ordinate of the bullet (its highest point in flight):

> It is our belief that more game is missed because the hunter overestimated the distance, and shot the animal, than for any other single reason. A-Square's Art Alphin is most emphatic about this. He's trained hundreds of riflemen and tank gunners and he doesn't mince words.
>
> "The old saw about zeroing 3" high at 100 yards may have been great for iron sights and a 220 grain round nose at 2000fps. Today it's garbage. If used with a high velocity spitzer bullet fired from a rifle with a scope mounted 1.5" to 2.5" above the axis of the bore, you'll have a maximum ordinate anywhere from 6" to 14". This means you'll shoot over everything and an over is the absolute worst miss to make. With an over you normally do not see the strike of the bullet on the ground and you can't make any correction for the second shot since you have no idea where the first bullet went.
>
> When deciding on the distance to zero your rifle, the most important single factor to consider is the bullet's maximum ordinate—the highest point it will reach in its trajectory before

*beginning its descent back to the line of sight (zero point). If you
zero the rifle at too great a distance, the bullet will have to climb too
high to get there, and you run the risk of shooting over the animal at
intermediate distances.*
— *Any Shot You Want* (1996) p.109, A-Square Company

The kill zone of a deer is about 8" in diameter, of a Bad Guy
about 12", and of an elk about 20". Thus, max ordinates for each
would be zones' radii of 4", 6", and 10".

Let's say that your elk rifle is zeroed for a max ordinate of
10". That means that it's sighted in for some distance to which
the bullet never rises above or falls below 10", meaning that if
you hold dead center within that range your POI will be within
that 20" kill zone. That's fine...for *elk*. If, however, you
encounter a deer or Bad Guy with your elk rifle, you will have to
recalculate the trajectory and hold *under* (which is difficult).

The moore looping the trajectory of the bullet, the higher
the max ordinate for any given distance.

Let's use the .30-30 as an example. A 170gr/2200fps .30-
30 load zeroed for 200yds has a max ordinate of 4" at 112yds.
O.K., no problem—that's exactly what .30-30s are good for:
getting deer out to 200yds. Rezero for 250yds and the max
ordinate increases to 7.5" at 140yds. Rezero for 300yds, and the
max ordinate is now a whopping 12" at 165yds, which is plenty
high enough to shoot right over the back of a deer.

Any Shot You Want recommends zeroing your rifle so that
your max ordinate is never more than 3". This is a pretty good
rule of thumb for the flatter shooting loads, and will allow very
tight shots without need of compensation. If, however, your
rifle has a more looping trajectory (*e.g.,* a .45-70), then a max
ordinate of 4-5" may be more appropriate.

Basically, the max ordinate should not be greater than the
kill zone radius of the *smallest* thing you hunt.

Calculating scope/bore offset

Although most ballistic tables and programs assume 1.5"
above bore axis, your rifle may (and likely will) be different.
You must know for sure and plug in the correct offset, else your
downrange numbers will be quite off.

I learned the following method from *Any Shot You Want*
on page 110. You need to measure three things: the diameter of
the bolt body, the diameter of the scope tube (it's either 1", or
30mm/1.181"), and the distance between the top of the bolt body

to the bottom of the scope tube (not the objective lens). Once you have these three numbers, plug them into this formula:

(bolt body "/2) + bolt-scope" + (scope tube"/2) = scope offset"

Zeroing for 300yds, and using holdovers

If you envision shots past MPBR, then simply pick an even-number distance close to the round's maximum zero distance, and then rely on holdovers. Holdovers can be marked on a card, which is laminated and then taped to the buttstock.

This works fine out to 400yds or so, but then holdovers become too great to estimate. Holdovers more than 36" are very difficult to make. You'll need a Mil-Dot reticle past 400yds.

If your scope has Mil-Dots, then zero at 300yds and know your comeups. Mark them on a taped card. (Premier Reticle can add Mil-Dots to any quality scope for Ø100. A "must.")

A really neat item is the Mil-Dot Master, an analog slide-rule computer with a working range of 1-20mils (in 1/10th mil increments) for target measurement up to 2000yds. It's only Ø29.95ppd from Mildot Enterprises (505-565-0760; POB 1535, Los Lunas, N.M. 87031).

I also like the temperature-calculated Ballisticard Systems from Schwiebert Precision (805-461-3954) for only Ø15. They are designed for specific loads, such as the 168gr Sierra .308, etc.

SHOOTING

Eye protection

Buying discount eye protection is about as brilliant as buying a discount *parachute*. Don't let me catch you on my range with Ø5 gas station Chinese sunglasses! (Oh, and don't believe the little "100% UV" sticker found on cheap glasses. Some rice-paddy peasant is getting 35¢ a day to slap those on.)

You want a distortion-free, wraparound polycarbonate lens which has 99%+ UVA/UVB protection, and ANSI Z87.1 impact protection. *Period.* **Nothing less should *ever* be on your head.** If the frame is not stamped with "Z87.1", then move on. I got into the habit of wearing industrial-quality eye protection when I used to blow glass, and our team all wore UV/IR protection stuff. (IR protection was vital given the 2000°+ reheat oven.) Heck, they even *looked* stylish, too!

Crews   www.crewsinc.com

Crews is an industrial eye protection firm which has branched out into the shooting world. They now make glasses of all lens shades for Winchester. Their ratchet-action temple frames adjust for any head, and are very comfortable.

Radians   www.radians.com

Radians offers a full line of eye and ear protection. My favorite are the Sabre one-piece combination glasses/earplugs. Instead of frame legs which wrap over the ears like most glasses, they instead end in earplugs (NRR 26, and replaceable). A real *"Why didn't I think of that?"* kind of idea. These are great for shooting schools, machine shops, etc.

AOSafety   www.aosafety.com

I like their Lexa eyewear, which are industrial glasses with an optional PVC-foam Dust GoggleGear attachment. Great for dusty and desert conditions.

Ear protection

Ever been exposed to high-level noise to be rewarded with ringing, buzzing, or whistling in your ears? That's called tinnitus, and it's a symptom of hearing loss. Your inner ear contains millions of microscopic hairs called *cilia*. Sound (which is merely an expression of pressure) makes them wave like a wheatfield. Cilia of different lengths transmit to your brain different frequencies of sound. Overpressure blows cilia out of their "ground", and they don't grow back. (This is why people suffer hearing loss in only certain frequencies.) Tinnitus tells you that you just lost some cilia. Are you "hearing" me?

If you are subjected to a daily noise level greater than 85dB, you must protect your hearing. **Hearing loss is progressive and irreversible. Fortunately, it is largely *preventable*.** I've been wearing earplugs religiously in all high noise environments/activities since 1985. Flying, motorcycles, machine shops, long car trips, Nancy Sinatra concerts, etc. It's paid off. My hearing is much more acute than that of my peers.

A dozen foam earplugs from WalMart are only Ø1.50, and four pair fit nicely in a 35mm film cannister. I keep them in every bag, briefcase, fanny pack, jacket, and car I own. Most of my long guns have their own earplug container paracorded to the sling swivel. I am never without earplugs!

Noise Reduction Rating (NRR)

This is measured in an acoustical lab, and expressed in decibels (dB). Just like the Richter Scale, the dB scale is not linear, but logarithmic. Sound *doubles* in volume every 3dB. 83dB is *twice* as loud as 80dB.

For shooting, you need protection rated at least NRR25.

If shooting indoors, wear plugs *and* muffs

Earplugs protect only the ear canals, but sound is still transmitted to the inner ear through the mastoid bone. Wear earmuffs indoors to reduce this.

A warning about muzzle brakes

Recorded noise levels (on certified audiological instruments) at the muzzle of a magnum or high velocity rifle with a muzzle brake installed normally exceed 160 decibels. Permanent ear damage occurs at 120 decibels. If you read the fine print on the finest set of ear plugs and ear muffs available, you will find the total noise reduction only between 22 and 31 decibels. **This means that on a rifle with a muzzle brake, even if you are wearing hearing protection, you are suffering permanent ear damage.** (p.175)

— *Any Shot You Want* (1996)

Boston's target notation system

After shooting hundreds of targets, I devised a simple (though typically clever) way to quickly notate all pertinent variables in a logical order. These variables are:

Date	(if such cannot be likely used against you later)
Gun	(if such cannot be likely used against you later)
Ammo	(make, bullet type/weight, production lot#)
Target	(distance of target)
Sights	(*i.e.,* which setting? 200yd iron? 300yd scope?)
Position	(standing? squat? standing-to-squat?)
Hold	(6 o'clock? center? 12 o'clock? head? neck?)
Remarks	(*e.g.,* front sight needs adjustment, wind, temp, etc.)

I know that DGATSPHR might be difficult to remember, but it's easy for me as I went to high school with an exchange student from Bangladesh—Fred Dgatsphr (the "ph" is pronounced like an "f"). When people couldn't say his name, Fred would explain, *"It's like somebody from New Jersey talking about his kitty's coat—'Da gat's fur!'"* Anyway, however you remember it, simply draw the below on your target, and fill it in:

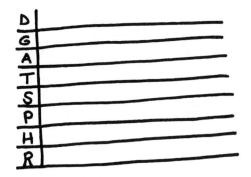

If you keep your targets, store them in a safe place. Somebody discovering a stack of them may get all weird about it. If under any kind of investigation, be prepared to burn your targets on short notice. I am loath to mention all this, but it's not 1952 anymore, and the gun culture has shrunk since then. Many Americans have never fired, or even held, a gun, and they just don't have any positive cultural frame of reference.

How to keep track of your shots on the same target

During the 200/300yd Speed Shoot, I needed a way to record my shots per silhouette. Each paper has 4 silhouettes, and I would shoot 2 papers (*i.e.*, 8 silhouettes) per drill. I'd shoot 4 drills per pair of targets, so each silhouette would have 4 holes. Since I would record elapsed time and number of hits, I had to keep track of which holes belonged to which drill.

On the holes from the 1st drill I would place a tick mark at the 12 o'clock position. The second drill, 3 o'clock ticks. Third, 6 o'clock. Fourth, 9 o'clock.

Use a Fisher Space Pen!   www.spacepen.com

For the range (and elsewhere), I use only Fisher Space Pens. They write at any angle (even upside down), at any temperature, on any paper, wet or dry. Paul Fisher (a true American who cares about the USA!) developed the pen for the space program (U.S. Patent #3,425,779), and since 1967 they've been used on *all* manned Space Flights (including Russian).

I don't understand why Fisher has only 2% of the ballpoint pen market, as why would anybody use anything *else*? You can get refills for your Mont Blanc, Cross, Parker, Paper Mate, etc. (By the way, I like pen #400BCL.)

Loaded chamber indicator   www.safrgun.com

Orange chamber indicator of unloaded status. Available in all common calibers. Great for shooting classes.

Mark A Shot™   800-235-8076

Colored ink daubers to mark your target holes. No more masking tape or stick-ons (which don't work in the cold or wet). Use orange, green, pink, and red to mark each group with a different color. Track groups by color for later analysis. Each tube will make 12,000 impressions. Great idea, and very affordable. *My* range box has them!

CLEANING

Since modern American primers have not been corrosive or rust-causing since 1948, immediate and thorough bore cleaning is not vital. (Bolt-actions I clean after every session.) My Glocks easily go past 500rds without needing attention, but I keep them spotless, nonetheless. I am not suggesting laziness, but you don't have to break open the bore cleaner within minutes of your last round.

Cleaning products

Bore cleaners

Use Dewey nylon-coated cleaning rods and guides. You'll need brass jags and brushes. (Dillon Press has it all if your local gunshop doesn't.)

The **Boresnake** ("World's Fastest Bore Cleaner") is a pull-through braided cord floss. With 160x the surface area of a cloth patch, 2-5 passes clean brilliantly. Then, simply wash the reusable cord. From CTD.

Bore solvents   www.shooters-choice.com

In my opinion, the best all-around bore solvent is **Shooter's Choice MC#7**. It is non-corrosive (no ammonia) and dissolves/removes powder, lead, copper fouling, carbon deposits and corrosion. Shooter's Choice also has specific solvents for copper or lead fouling.

Sweet's (for copper fouling) is good, but ammonia-based.

Bore cleaning technique

Rule: Clean from chamber towards muzzle (the direction of the bullet), even if you have to attach the jag at the chamber (as with an M1/M14).

Apply bore solvent onto your brass brush (do *not* dip the brush in the bottle, contaminating all), and one-way scrub the bore, detaching the brush at the muzzle. Spray off the brush. Next, attach the jag and alternate wet and dry patches through one pass each until *clean*. (This'll take 10-20 patches. Be patient.) When clean, send a wet brush through again, and repeat with wet and dry patches. Finally, *lightly* coat the bore with an oiled patch.

Or, you can "cheat" and use a BoreSnake, which I do (especially in the field). Two to five passes, and you're done.

Degreasing solvents

My favorite all-around gun cleaner is **Simple Green**. It is nontoxic, has no harmful fumes, and can be used without gloves. Spray on, or soak. It won't harm any finish or material.

Shooter's Choice Quick Scrub III is also very good. Fast drying, no redidue, non water based, and non-flammable.

In a pinch, use aerosol CRC brake cleaner (only Ø2/can). It'll really cut through caked powder residue (*e.g.,* AR15 or HK91). It also removes *all* old lubrication, so reapply diligently.

For greasy military stuff, use a disposable paint brush, plastic pan, and a gallon of low-odor mineral spirits (Ø2.50). In a well-ventilated area, soak the parts to cheaply and easily loosen and melt the gunk, then clean as usual and lubricate.

Lubrication: oil

For wet lubricant, BreakFree (you must shake *vigorously* to mix in the white Teflon beads!), Tetra, Prolix, or Shooter's Choice FP-10. Military LSA works fine, too.

Sentry Solutions (800-546-8049) makes superb *dry* lubricants using moly. Such work great on Glock feed ramps.

Lubrication: grease

Oil is fine for small working parts not under much pressure, but a high-temp grease is necessary (in my opinion) for the heavier moving parts (slide, bolt/carrier, locking lugs, etc.). Some guns (*e.g.,* M1/M14) truly *require* grease.

I use a CV joint grease from Valvoline called *DuraBlend*, which gives temperature protection from -54° to 400°F. A 1lb tub is only Ø3.50, which will last you years. A grease that will protect *CV joints* (with their incredible bearing surface pressures and temperatures) will protect *anything*.

I'm also trying this grease out on other guns (such as Glock, AK74, and even an AR15), and I am so far *very* pleased. The grease remains in place better than oil (which tries to migrate away), and the parts move like, well, greased lightning.

Derrick Martin of www.accuracyspeaks.com is an AR15 High Power shooter and gunsmith, and he greases up his AR upper, buffer tube, buffer, buffer spring, and drawbar. Eliminates the *Boing!* and scratchiness, although the gun gets filthier.

Lubrication techniques

Clean and lubricate your slide/bolt and its rails. Rack several times, and then remove any excess.

Most guns have a few unique spots which require lube or oil, and you must ask around or do some reading. On the AR15, for example, few shooters know to yearly oil the front sight threads, else they'll rust (and *then* try to adjust the sight!).

Misc. cleaning and storage

Any rust spots should *immediately* be removed with oil and 0000 steel wool. (Flitz metal polish also works well, and without wool. It's safe on all finishes.) Spray exposed surfaces with a *light* coat of Shooter's Choice Rust Prevent.

Occasionally, you should remove the stock and clean out all the accumulated gunk. If the gun is to be stored, cover the muzzle with a piece of tape or stick in a foam earplug. (You can safely shoot through such if you forget to remove it.)

Final word on cleaning

Yeah, all this is a pain, but reliability and accuracy aren't convenient. (Beats throwing rocks.) Spend the time and money your quality guns deserve, and they won't let you down.

MISCELLANEOUS

Spare parts

Gun parts *will* break and wear out. Expect it. Also, count on the availability of spare parts to evaporate because of the increasingly hostile regulatory environment. If the feds ever locked up the Gun Parts Corp., thousands of gunowners would have paperweights overnight. Get the parts you'll need, *now*.

Firing pins, extractors, and small internal springs are the most universally needed parts. A gun's mainspring is its "engine" so have spares (especially for the M1/M14). Full-capacity mag springs will weaken from lengthy loadings (Glocks in particular). Having a spare barrel or two is a great idea.

Finally, every gun has its "Achille's heel" or two, so find out now and stock up. CZ52s have cast firing pins, and they break often (replace with forged pins). ARs use up gas rings. You should also have exploded parts diagrams for each weapon.

Coating and finishes

OEM bluing or stainless steel is not satisfactory in the long run. Some guns have notoriously thin bluing (*e.g.*, Savage). Your gun's finish *must* be rustproof and nonreflective. (Only Glock's Tenifer finish meets the grade. Superb!)

Sending your gun to a smith is not legally a *"transfer,"* so no NICBC approval is required before you get it back.

Robar (602-581-2648)

Robar offers NP3 (a satin gray P.T.F.E./electroless nickel, suitable for all gun metals, and best for internal parts), and their excellent proprietary exterior finish, Roguard (available in most colors and camos). Robar also offers blueing, electroless nickel, stainless steel blackening, and parkerizing.

Teflon coating

Rocky Mountain Arms (800-375-0846) offers DuPont Teflon-S coating for all firearms in many colors.

Springfield Armory (309-944-5631) offers several colors.

Stainless steel bluing and oxidizing

Ed's Shooter's Supply (505-445-8404).

Parkerizing

An affordable and decent finish. Many firms can do this for under Ø100 (scour the *Shotgun News*). If you've got a favorite SKS (often weakly blued), this is the way to go.

CACHING

It's just plain foolish to keep *all* your guns in one place. At home, have only what is needed to defend yourself and, if necessary, fight your way out. Store the rest *elsewhere*.

Storing spare weapons

A secure storage unit, rented under an alias or by a friend, is a good option. Long-term food (if the unit stays cool enough), extra ammo, documents, etc. should also be stored there.

In my *Bulletproof Privacy* I discuss the RV-in-the-country idea, which is very practical. Buy a Ø3-8,000 RV and park it on some old rancher's property for Ø50/month. Keep your mouth shut about it! You'll have a cheap, self-sufficient retreat site.

Caching (burying) weapons

While I don't recommend that you own any illegal weapons (*e.g.,* unregistered Title II stuff, full-auto parts and plans, silencers, reverted post-ban guns, etc.), if you do then they should be *buried.* Don't store any such items at home.

What to cache

Include ammo, mags, mag pouches, spare parts, cleaning and loading supplies, tools, and latex gloves with each gun so that every cache is self-sufficient. Every rifle cache should also include a spare pistol, mags, ammo, and holster.

Try to imagine under what situations you'd have to retrieve your cache, and what your physical condition might be. Will you be tired, hungry, cold, or broke? Some cash, gold coins, food bars, Sure-Fire flashlight (with spare lithium batteries), Caluyme lightsticks, boots, socks, water, radios, first aid, etc. might be handy. Remember, retrieving a cache is a last-resort *Oh, sh✷t!* option, so think it through well.

Guns should be lightly coated with BreakFree and sealed in waterproof plastic gun bags with desiccant. (You could also coat with grease or Cosmoline for very long-term storage.) Ammo should be separately packed.

Use disposable latex gloves to leave no fingerprints on the contents or the pipe.

Caching materials

PVC 8-10" sewer pipe with silicone-sealed watertight caps and internal desiccant is the best thing for caching. Buy this pipe out of town with cash; multiple, traceable purchases are a red flag to caching activity. Burn the receipts.

For an inexpensive desiccant pouch, simply buy silica desiccant in bulk from your local hobby shop and duct-tape it inside coffee filters.

Where to cache

If cached stuff is found on private property, the land could be seized. Use National Forest or BLM land. Pick a spot *far* from any hiking trail or inviting campsite, where runoff is not a problem. Besides making a detailed map, I'd GPS notate the location and encrypt it. Trees and rocks are *not* utterly permanent landmarks, so don't rely too heavily on them. Use a posthole digger, and dig deeply enough to have at least 2' of earth on top of your container. A nylon rope or strap looped underneath with an extra 3' on top will assist in pulling out the pipe when you retrieve it (use a notched 2x4 to lever up the thing). Cover the container with a small tarp to deflect water.

Visually check every year that the site is undisturbed. Obviously, make certain that you're not followed.

❖ 30

FEDERAL
"GUN CONTROLS"

Lex Malum, Lex Nulla.   *"A bad law is no law."*

Don't look to the courts to strike down modern gun control legislation. They've had dozens of chances, but denied *certiorari* every time since 1939. This is no accident:

> *I cannot help but suspect that the best explanation for the absence of the Second Amendment from the legal consciousness of the elite bar, including that component found in the legal academy, is derived from a mixture of sheer opposition to the idea of private ownership of guns and the perhaps subconscious fear that altogether plausible, perhaps even "winning," interpretations of the Second Amendment would present real hurdles to those of us supporting prohibitory regulation.   ...[T]he Amendment may be profoundly embarrassing to many who both support such regulation and view themselves as committed to zealous adherence to the Bill of Rights (such as most members of the ACLU).*
>
> — Stanford Levinson, *The Embarrassing Second Amendment*,
>   sourced from *Safeguarding Liberty*

Meanwhile, become educated. Visit www.atf.treas.gov/core. The best digest is *Gun Laws of America* by Alan Korwin (www.bloomfieldpress.com). It covers *all* federal gun laws, and although I resent the fact that I must pay Ø20 for a book on federal gun laws (because there shouldn't *be* any), this book is a must. The summaries alone are invaluable. The novel *Unintended Consequences* by John Ross also contains excellent narratives on gun control laws. I'll cover the main laws which affect us generally. For wider or deeper detail, you'll have to dive in yourself.

NATIONAL FIREARMS ACT of 1934

Until 1933, you could order a new .45 Thompson submachinegun from the Sears catalog for Ø125, *with leather case.* You could own a BAR or an M1919A4. Silencers (or, more accurately, gun *mufflers*) were sold at the hardware store for under Ø10. You could even have $20 gold pieces in your pocket. What a great time to be a gunowner!

Since Prohibition had been repealed by the 22nd Amendment in 1933, thousands of Treasury agents were idle by 1934 and, golly, they needed *some* kind of work. So, create a new class of criminals. (What else is new?)

The *NFA34* was our first serious federal gun law. Unless you have paid a Ø200 Treasury tax stamp, you cannot legally own an automatic weapon, silencer, or any long gun less than 26" overall or with a barrel less than 18" (this was amended to 16" for rifles in 1958). Privately-owned gold had been generally restricted just one year earlier. (Good thing that alcohol had been decriminalized—*I'd* sure want a drink after Congress passed the *National Banking Act* and *National Firearms Act!*)

Not generally known is that the *original* language would have included *all handguns*, but women made such a proper and righteous stink that the handgun inclusion was stricken.

The phony rationale for *NFA34*

It was the Valentine's Day Massacre of 1929 and other similar gangster machinegunnings, but these infrequent incidents had all but ceased with Prohibition's end a year earlier. As Vin Suprynowicz rhetorically asked in his *Send In The Waco Killers*, why don't beer distributors today gun each other down?

So, what was the *real* reason?

The National Firearms Act fit in perfectly with the systematic creation of government programs and deficit spending that Franklin Roosevelt immediately began to institute the instant he took office. The NFA was a model vehicle for the continued expansion of government power: It was arbitrary (i.e., the 18-inch rule); it gave the government sweeping authority over something very common; it focused on inanimate objects rather than criminal behavior; it levied draconian taxes on these objects; and most certainly, it created millions of criminals with the stroke of a pen, just as Prohibition had.
— John Ross, *Unintended Consequences* (1996), p. 356

There are nearly 200,000 *NFA34* weapons on record. Only *one* has ever been used to commit a crime, according to the BATF. Nevertheless, the feds will eventually try to confiscate these weapons *without compensation* just as they did in 1994 with the Striker and Street Sweeper shotguns.

GUN CONTROL ACT of 1968

The Congress hereby declares that the purpose of this title is to provide support for Federal, State, and local law enforcement officials in their fight against crime and violence, and it is not the purpose of this title to place any undue or unnecessary Federal restrictions or burdens on law-abiding citizens with respect to the acquisition, possession, or use of firearms appropriate to the purpose of hunting, trapshooting, targetshooting, personal protection, or other lawful activity, and that this title is not intended to discourage or eliminate the private ownership or use of firearms by law-abiding citizens for lawful purposes, or provide for the imposition by Federal regulations of any procedures or requirements other than those reasonably necessary to implement and effectuate the provisions of this title.

— *Gun Control Act of 1968* preamble

Bullsh✷t. *Unbelievable* bullsh✷t. This preamble reminds me of the FBI at Waco on 19 April 1993 shouting through their tanks' bullhorns *"This is not an assault!"* (The Davidians should have fired back, shouting, *"These are not bullets!"*)

In 1968, Senator Dodd remembered Hitler's 1938 gun control legislation from the Nuremberg trials and requested its translation for his study. Just a few months later Congress passed a virtual clone of Hitler's gun registration scheme (designed to prohibit guns to Jews and other minorities). Chillingly, the Nazi *"sporting purpose"* rationale was used in *GCA68*. Aaron Zelman's "Jews For The Preservation of Firearm Ownership" (www.jpfo.org) proved this in their *Gateway To Tyranny* with its side-by-side comparison of both laws.

Zelman sent a copy of *Gateway* to every Congressman, Senator, and Supreme Court Justice, and to all the media. Silence. Not even the *conservative* and *libertarian* press dared to touch this bombshell. First, Nazi-style gun regulation. Then, the camps. In 1998 there were guys in Montana welding shackles to the insides of railroad boxcars. (I spoke to the brother of one the welders, so this isn't rumor.) Folks, do the math.

Using the *"interstate/foreign commerce"* clause for the second time in gun regulation, *GCA68* prohibited the mail-order receipt of firearms, the importation of foreign weapons *"unsuitable for sporting purposes,"* and the ownership of unregistered *"destructive devices"* (*e.g.*, mortars, bazookas, smokeless powder weapons with a bore in excess of ½").

It mandated the BATF Form 4473 and prohibited the sale of firearms and ammunition to certain *"prohibited persons."*

The phony rationale for *GCA68*

The murders of JFK, RFK, and MLK.

So, what was the *real* reason?

To create the beginnings of a national firearm registry, the means to a confiscation end.

18 USC §922(d) *"prohibited possessors"*

(d) it shall be unlawful for any person to sell or otherwise dispose of any firearm or ammunition to any person knowing or having reasonable cause to believe that such person—

(1) is under indictment for, or has been convicted in any court of, a crime punishable by imprisonment for a term exceeding one year;

(2) is a fugitive from justice (BTP note: This means, according to §921(15), having *"fled any State to avoid prosecution for a crime or to avoid giving testimony in any criminal proceeding."*—so remaining in hiding within your State is O.K.?);

(3) is an unlawful user of or addicted to any controlled substance (as defined in section 102 of the Controlled Substances Act (21 U.S.C. 802));

(4) has been adjudicated as a mental defective or has been committed to any mental institution (political dissidents beware of Soviet-style psychiatric sentences);

(5) who, being an alien, is illegally or unlawfully in the United States;

(6) who has been discharged from the Armed Forces under dishonorable conditions;

(7) who, having, been a citizen of the United States, has renounced his citizenship (word your untaxation and rescission affidavits very carefully), *or;*

(8) is subject to a court order that restrains such person from harassing, stalking, or threatening an intimate partner of such person or child of such intimate partner or person, or engaging in other conduct that would place an intimate partner in reasonable fear of bodily injury to the partner or child, except that this paragraph shall only apply to a court order that—

(A) was issued after a hearing of which such person received actual notice, and at which such person had the opportunity to participate; and
(B)(i) includes a finding that such person represents a credible threat to the physical safety of such intimate partner or child; or
(ii) by its terms explicitly prohibits the use, attempted use, or threatened use of physical force against such intimate partner or child that would reasonably be expected to cause bodily injury.

The "Lautenberg Amendment"

§658 was snuck in the 1997 *Department of Defense Appropriations Act.* This ugly bit added to the *"prohibited possessor"* list anybody convicted of a **misdemeanor** *"crime of domestic violence"* involving the use or attempted use of physical force, or the threatened use of a deadly weapon, among family members (spouse, parent, guardian, cohabitor, or similar). Spouses slapping each other, or spanking their child, can be such a *"crime."* I'm not making light of actual wife *battering*, but to ban somebody from owning guns because they threw a cereal bowl at their spouse is going to ridiculous extremes.

Never **before has a *misdemeanor* offense, and an *ex post facto* one at that, been grounds for denial of the constitutional right to own and carry guns.** According to Alan Korwin, *"It is as if a former speeding ticket were now grounds for felony arrest if you own a car or gasoline."* It denies *"due process"* (felony accountability without Grand Jury indictment; dispossession of lawful private property without *"just compensation"*; equal protection of the law, right to accusation, counsel, trial, and jury; among many others).

18 USC § 922(g)(8) struck down by a U.S. District judge

This subsection forbade those under domestic restraining orders from owning a gun, was struck down by a U.S. District judge on 2nd Amendment grounds:

> *It is absurd that a boilerplate state court divorce order can collaterally and automatically extinguish a law-abiding citizen's Second Amendment rights, particularly when neither the judge issuing the order, nor the parties nor their attorneys are aware of the federal criminal penalties arising from firearm possession after entry of the restraining order. That such a routine civil order has such extensive consequences totally attenuated from divorce proceedings makes the statute unconstitutional. There must be a limit to government regulation on lawful firearm possession. This statute exceeds that limit, and therefore is unconstitutional.*

and 5th Amendment grounds:

> [Since the statute is an] *obscure, highly technical statute with no mens rea requirement, it violates Emerson's Fifth Amendment due process rights subject to prosecution without proof of knowledge that he was violating the statute.*
> — *U.S. v. Emerson*, Northern District of Texas, San Angelo
>   7 April 1999

Judge Sam R. Cummings deserves our respect and praise for his fine ruling. The 5th Circuit held that the 2nd Amendment protects an *individual* right to keep and bear arms, although such could be regulated in certain cases. Look up the case on www.sas-aim.org or www.gunowners.org. Stay tuned...

THE "BRADY BILL"

Signed into law on 30 November 1993 and found at 18 USC §922(s&t), *The Brady Handgun Violence Prevention Act* mandated (for states without an instant-check system) waiting-period provisions for dealer handgun purchases after 28 February 1994. (These expired on 27 February 1999.) It contains extremely tortuous language. One sentence has *532* words.

Brady attempted to require the states to enforce Federal law at the states' expense, and the Supreme Court struck this portion of *Brady* down 5-4 on 27 June 1997 (***Printz v. U.S.***) as an improper use of the *"interstate commerce"* regulatory power. This is no real setback for the feds, as their *National Instant Criminal Background Check* (NICBC) system has been up since 30 November 1998. (This NICBC will predictably auger in a national ID with biometric numbering of your thumbprint.)

The phony rationale of "Brady"

The attempted assassination by John Hinckley, Jr. of President Reagan, and the wounding of James Brady.

So, what's the *real* reason?

To infringe more on your 2nd Amendment rights.

Changing from NICBC to NICS

The law named the check system the *"national instant criminal background check"* system (NICBC), but the feds are now calling it the National Instant Check System (NICS). Notice how they've eliminated *"criminal background"* from the name? They did this so that the system can be later *expanded* to a system of withholding *permission* for reasons *other* than an applicant's criminal background. Such could be suspected (not convicted) *"crimes"* of tax evasion, *"money laundering,"* or even political dissention. Just you wait, NICBC will prove to be the camel's nose under the tent.

LAWS ON *"ASSAULT WEAPONS"*

While this chapter will describe the various legal restrictions on so-called *"assault weapons,"* Chapter 27 explained exactly how law and metal meet in battle rifles. Learn how to deal with the "Post-ban Blues" by lawful conversion of your battle rifles. (Also explained is how to avoid illegal conversions.)

18 USC §922(r)

*It shall be unlawful for any person to assemble **from imported parts** any semiautomatic rifle or shotgun which is identical to any rifle or shotgun prohibited from importation under section 925(d)(3) of this chapter as **not being particularly suitable for or readily adaptable to sporting purposes**...*

It is because of this that post-11/90 mag-fed foreign semi-autos must have that "sporter" stock. §925(d)(3) long guns are 26 USC §5845(a) *1934 National Firearms Act* weapons (machineguns, <18"bbl shotguns, etc.) and surplus military firearms. Non-*NFA* and nonmilitary firearms which are *"particularly suitable for or readily adaptable to sporting purposes"* may be customized.

The so-called *"Crime Bill"*

The Orwellian title is *The 1994 Public Safety and Recreational Firearms Use Protection Act.* 18 USC §922(v&w) allows us to possess nasty looking "assault weapons" and their accessories only if they were completed *prior* to 13 September 1994. (In pages 27/1-12, I explain in full detail the tactical information you need.) The act expires on 13 September 2004, but it'll be renewed or replaced with something even *worse* (just after some glassly-eyed nut opens fire on a crowd with a Mini-14—*hmmm*).

Semiautomatic rifles (18 USC §921(30)(B))

Congress wet their panties over the military-style rifles. So, after 13 September 1994, the following rifles can no longer be imported, manufactured, or converted:

[A] **semiautomatic** *rifle that has an ability to accept a* **detachable magazine** *and has at least 2 (i.e., no more than* one*) of—*
(i) a folding or telescoping stock;
(ii) a pistol grip that protrudes conspicuously beneath the action of the weapon (oooh!—how scary!)*;*
(iii) a bayonet mount; (!!)
(iv) a flash suppressor or threaded barrel designed to accommodate a flash suppressor; and
(v) a grenade launcher; (!!!)

Reverting a post-ban gun to pre-ban status is a felony—conviction of which cancels your 2nd Amendment rights. *Cuidado.* A domestic semi-auto with a sporter stock *could* have *one* (but not two) of the above features, such as a flash suppressor.

Semi-auto rifles which *cannot* take a detachable mag of more than five rounds are excluded (*e.g.*, Remington 740, etc.).

Semiautomatic pistols (18 USC §921(30)(C))

Congress also wet their panties over the *gangsta* TEC-9 9mms, so, after 13 September 1994, the following pistols can no longer be imported, manufactured, or converted:

a semiautomatic pistol that has an ability to accept a detachable magazine **and** *has at least 2 (i.e., no more than* one*) of—*
(i) an ammunition magazine that attaches to the pistol outside of the pistol grip;
(ii) a threaded barrel capable of accepting a barrel extender, flash suppressor, forward handgrip, or silencer;
(iii) a shroud that is attached to, or partially or completely encircles, the barrel and that permits the shooter to hold the firearm with the nontrigger hand without being burned;
(iv) a manufactured weight of 50 ounces or more when the pistol is unloaded; and
(v) a semiautomatic version of an automatic firearm;

Semiautomatic shotguns (18 USC §921(30)(D))

Not only did the SecTreas *retroactively* outlaw the Street Sweeper and Striker 12 revolver shotguns, and the USAS-12 AR15-style shotgun, Congress outlawed these future shotguns:

a **semiautomatic** *shotgun that has* **at least 2 of**—
(i) a folding or telescoping stock;
(ii) a pistol grip that protrudes conspicuously beneath the action of the weapon;
(iii) a fixed magazine capacity in excess of 5 rounds; and
(iv) an ability to accept a detachable magazine.

Don't put a mag tube extension *and* folding stock on your post-9/94 Remington 1100. (Bayonets, apparently, are O.K. for now.) *Pump* shotguns can have extended mag tubes, folding stocks with pistol grip, etc., and I'd stock up on those parts *now*.

+10rd mags (18 USC §921(31)(A&B))

Now, *this* is irksome. While I had already purchased all the nasty *"assault weapons"* I needed (though not all I *wanted*), you can never have enough mags.

The term "large capacity ammunition feeding device"—
(A) means a magazine, belt, drum, feed strip, or similar device manufactured after [13 September 1994] *that has a capacity of, or that can be readily* (whatever that means) *restored or converted to accept, more than 10 rounds of ammunition; but*
(B) does not include an attached tubular device designed to accept, and capable of operating only with, .22 caliber rimfire...

(Note: It is *not* illegal to use a pre-9/94 +10rd mag in a post-9/94 weapon. I was wrong about this in the 1998 edition, sorry.)

If a +10rd mag does *not* have an 18 USC §923(i) post-ban serial number or date of manufacture, then the owner can assert under 18 USC §922(w)(4) that lack of such *"shall be a presumption that the large capacity ammunition feeding device is not subject to the prohibition of possession in paragraph (1)* [of 18 USC §922(w)]. *"* This is a handy bit of info to know.

"armor piercing ammunition" (18 USC §921(17)(B))

(B) The term "armor piercing ammunition" means—
(i) a projectile or projectile core which may be used in a handgun and which is constructed entirely (excluding the presence of traces of other substances) from one or a combination of tungsten alloys, steel, iron, brass, bronze, beryllium copper, or depleted uranium; or
(ii) a full jacketed projectile larger than .22 caliber designed and intended for use in a handgun and whose jacket has a weight of more than 25 percent of the total weight of the projectile.

Congress cannot document a *single* case of police homicide from these so-called *"cop killer bullets"*—but, *so what*?

The phony rationale of the *"Crime Bill"*

Taking *gansta* weapons off the streets, just like the *NFA34* supposedly did to the mob. L.A. and NYC are now safe.

So, what's the *real* reason?

Since AR15s are used in *3* murders a year, it wasn't crime. (Bowling balls kill more people than AR15s.) Rather, it was to relieve certain Congressmen from their bed-wetting nightmares in which they were attacked by irate Citizens with battle rifles. Such "legislative sedatives" are common for this ilk.

"GUN-FREE SCHOOL ZONES"

The Florida tourist-shooting epidemic is also relevant in another way. Once the airport rental lots started removing their big fluorescent rent-a-car stickers, Florida's "tourist-murder crime wave" disappeared virtually overnight. (Because criminals rightly figured that out-of-town tourists weren't armed like the Floridians were.) *Similarly, one of the last places a criminal knows he can find unarmed victims in an increasingly well-armed and peaceful America today...is in the "gun-free school zones" in which the snivelliberals have locked up our children.* (BTP Note: The correlation between school zone gun bans and school shootings is far too high to be ignored. Somebody should figure the "r" value on this.)
    — Vin Suprynowicz, *Send in the Waco Killers* (1999), p. 384

The *Gun-Free School Zones Act of 1991* (which was found at 18 USC §922(q)) prohibited the knowing possession of a firearm on or within 1,000 feet of a school. America had 121,855 schools as of 1994, and their 1,000' zones covered just about anywhere a gunowner would typically drive or travel. This was no accident. It's already illegal in every State to use a gun recklessly *on* school property, so Congress *didn't* have children's safety in mind. Since concealed-carry permit holders were exempted, it was an obvious ploy to herd all the other gunowners into the artificial CHL corral (eventually to be eliminated).

In *Hologram of Liberty* I thoroughly covered the Supreme Court's reversal (1995 *U.S. v. Lopez*) of this act. Undeterred, Congress simply repassed the struck down act in §657 of the 2,000 page DoD Appropriations Act of 1997. Congressmen voted for this Act without even having read the thing. Typical.

The only difference in this new version is that the phrase *"that has moved in or that otherwise affects interstate or foreign commerce"* was added in two places. Since this new language alone would not seem to affect the Supreme Court's *Lopez* 5-4 decision, I suspect that Rehnquist and/or O'Connor have been privately dealt with and that a 5-4 or 6-3 reversal of *Lopez* can be expected. Even if the 5 Justice *Lopez* majority holds fast, Congress will nevertheless enjoy 2-4 years of "free" enforcement and many innocent people will become convicted felons.

To avoid a needless felony arrest over this, you *must* get my book *You & The Police!* for its invaluable info and tips on car travel while armed.

The *"Self-defense Free Zones"*

The recent spate of school shootings has been, in a way, predictable. Peaceable folks are forbidden to be armed on school property, and the murderous maniacs have taken notice. (Israel used to suffer from terrorist attacks on her schools and airliners, until Israel got wise and began to arm teachers and pilots. The attacks quickly stopped.) In Texas, which passed its CHL in 1996, guns are banned from several types of establishments, including churches, sports arenas, government offices, courts, airports and restaurants serving alcohol.

I wanted to know why the state treats teachers like second-class citizens, when plumbers and doctors are allowed to protect themselves on the job. I would be happier sending my child to a school where a teacher whom I trust is armed and well prepared.

We have created a shopping list for madmen. *If guns are the problem, why don't we see things occurring at skeet and trap shoots, at gun shows, at NRA conventions?* ***We only see it where guns aren't allowed.*** *The sign of a gun with a slash through it is like a neon sign for gunmen—'We're unarmed. Come kill us.'*

— Texas Representative Suzanna Gratia Hupp

The fallacy of this was utterly proven on 9/11 when 19 terrorists armed with boxcutters took over and destroyed four airliners.

IS THE 2nd AMENDMENT AN INDIVIDUAL OR COLLECTIVE RIGHT?

A well-regulated militia, being necessary to the security of a free state, the right of the people to keep and bear arms shall not be infringed.

— Second Amendment to the Constitution

[Textual exegesis] *suggests that "the people" protected by the Fourth Amendment, and by the First **and Second** Amendments, and to whom rights and powers are reserved under the Ninth and Tenth Amendments, refers to a class of persons who are part of a national community or who have developed sufficient connection with this country to be considered part of that community.*

— *U.S. v. Verdugo-Urquidez,* 494 US 259,265 (1990)

*It would...be strange to find in the midst of a catalog of the rights of individuals a provision securing to the states the right to maintain a designated "Militia." **Dispassionate scholarship suggests quite strongly that the right of the people to keep and bear arms***

> **meant just that.** *There is no need to deceive ourselves as to what the Second Amendment said and meant.*
>   — Justice Antonin Scalia, *A Matter of Interpretation: Federal Courts and the Law* (Princeton University Press)

> *This Court has not had* (i.e., more like "chosen") *recent occasion to consider the nature of the substantive right safeguarded by the Second Amendment. If, however, the Second Amendment is read to confer a* <u>personal</u> *right to "keep and bear arms," a colorable argument exists that the Federal Government's regulatory scheme, at least as it pertains to the purely intrastate sale or possession of firearms, runs afoul of that Amendment's protections.*
>   — *Printz v. U.S.*, 521 US 898, 937-38 & n.1,2 (1997)
>   (Thomas, J., concurring)

As languidly as the 2nd Amendment was written, the *"People"* of the 2nd are the same *"People"* as in the 1st, 4th, 9th, and 10th. Any intellectually honest scholar must agree.

Was the 2nd Amendment deliberately sabotaged with imprecise language?

I touched on this in *Hologram of Liberty*. While the thought is unpleasant, please at least hear me out.

Save for a few, the 55 Philadelphia delegates did not *want* a Bill of Rights in the Constitution. Not only did they exclude such from the document, they fought against adding one before the Constitution was ratified by the States. Hamilton in *Federalist* #84 insisted that *"bills of rights,...are not only unnecessary in the proposed Constitution but would even be dangerous."*

Only when five of the 13 States made ratification contingent (though unenforceably so) upon a Bill of Rights did Representative Madison convince Congress of the matter's political necessity. Grudgingly, and with much more haste than concern for our rights, did Congress finally pass 12 *very* scrappy proposals to the states. (Read pages 4/1-5 of *Hologram of Liberty*.)

When five of the ratifying states urged amendments of rights to the Constitution, *all* of them included the right to bear arms, whereas only *three* mentioned freedom of speech—which would suggest that private armament was constitutionally more important than even free speech. Pennsylvania, for example, was quite explicit:

> *That the people have a right to bear arms for the defense of themselves and their own State, or of the United States, or for the purpose of killing game; and no law shall be passed for disarming the people or any of them, unless for crimes committed, or real danger of public injury from individuals; and as standing armies in time of peace are dangerous to liberty, they ought not to be kept up; and that the military shall be under strict subordination to and be governed by the civil power.*

— Pennsylvania's 1788 proposed amendment

Largely copied by the other four states was New York's version:

> *That the people have a right to keep and bear arms; that a well-regulated militia, including the body of the people capable of bearing arms, is the proper, natural, and safe defense of a free state.*

Madison's original proposal to the House was:

> *The right of the people to keep and bear arms shall not be infringed; a well-armed and well-regulated* (i.e., well-trained, well-disciplined, effective) *militia being the best security of a free country; but no person religiously scrupulous of bearing arms shall be compelled to render military service in person.*

Because the semicolon after *"shall not be infringed"* is grammatically equal to a period, the individual right is not even *theoretically* conditional upon the rest of the sentence. The Congress later altered the syntax to:

> *A well-regulated militia, being necessary to the security of a free state, the right of the people to keep and bear arms shall not be infringed.*

Even though contemporaries of the First Congress (*e.g.*, St. George Tucker and William Rawle), along with the populace at large correctly viewed the 2nd Amendment as an *individual* right, the germ of ambiguous syntax was set for eternity.

That change of sentence structure was crucial. No longer was the right *"to keep and bear arms"* listed first and independent. By vaguely couching the right within the duty of a common militia, the 2nd Amendment can be theoretically read to mean that people may only keep and bear arms *for militia purposes only and no others.* The Congress of 1789 likely *knew* that the 2nd Amendment was slightly ambiguous, giving future courts an excuse to sanctify federal infringement of that right.

The courts have done precisely that. In the 1939 case of *U.S. v. **Miller,*** 307 US 174, the Supreme Court unanimously held (out of sheer ignorance) that a short-barreled shotgun (controlled by the *NFA34*) was *not* a weapon suitable for militia purposes (even though shotguns had been used in the Civil War and in WWI), and therefore *no* right to possess such a shotgun existed. Gun ownership was declared to be indirectly conditional on militia practices (although the feds are ignoring this).

> *It is difficult to interpret* Miller *as rendering the Second Amendment meaningless as a control on Congress. Ironically, one can read* Miller *as supporting some of the most extreme anti-gun control arguments; for example, that the individual citizen has a right to keep and bear bazookas, rocket launchers, and other armaments that are clearly used for modern warfare,* **including, of course, assault weapons.** *Under* Miller, *arguments about the constitutional legitimacy of a prohibition by Congress of private ownership of handguns or, what is much more likely, assault rifles, thus might turn on the usefulness of such guns in military settings.*
>
> — *U.S. v. Emerson,* Northern District of Texas, San Angelo
>   7 April 1999

The Congress of 1789 knew how to write the 2nd Amendment to set in stone our right to keep and bear arms, *period*—but they did not *choose* to write it that way.

> *Every man, woman, and responsible child has a natural, fundamental, and inalienable human, individual, civil, and Constitutional right to obtain, own, and carry, openly or concealed, any weapon—handgun, shotgun, rifle, machinegun, anything—anytime, anywhere, without asking anyone's permission.*
>
> — L. Neil Smith, 1995 Arizona Libertarian Convention

Heck, even *I* could have written a sabotage-proof Amendment:

> *Neither Congress, nor the President, nor any State shall deny, infringe, regulate, or tax the absolute right of the people, in either their individual or collective militia capacities, to own, convey, carry, and use weapons and their accoutrements. Any congressional act, executive order, or State legislative act which would, directly or indirectly, or under any guise or pretense, deny, infringe, regulate, or tax this cornerstone right is null and void at moment of passage, and may lawfully be, without pain of prosecution, ignored, or, if deemed necessary by the people or any of them, forcibly resisted.*

Now *that's* a *real* 2nd Amendment!

Given the Federalists' desire and plan for a supreme, unchallengeable central government—vs. an armed citizenry's opposition to such a future government—I believe that the 2nd Amendment was *intentionally* "watered down" to make possible the gradual judicial whittling away our right of private armament. **Has this not happened *exactly*?**

Now that the common militia has unlawfully been usurped by the *select* militia of the National Guard, militia-type weapons such as the full-auto M16A2 are no longer judicially warranted. And, since the 30rd *semi*-auto AR15 with flash suppressor is not *"suitable for sporting purposes"*—there's no longer any legal rationale for owning one of these, either. The next step will be to outlaw hunting, target-shooting, etc. to eliminate the *"sporting purpose"* application, and thus ban all remaining guns (bolt-action rifles, shotguns, pistols—*everything*).

How does a boa constrictor kill a pig? The snake doesn't really have the strength to crush the ribs of any good-sized prey. But it doesn't need to. Once it has its body coiled around the victim, it simply waits. As the victim struggles, the poor thing uses up oxygen, even as its bloodstream continually transports more carbon dioxide from the struggling muscles to the lungs. Eventually, the piglet must exhale that exhaust gas, partially collapsing its lungs. Then it quickly tries to inhale again, to replace the vented carbon dioxide with fresh life-giving oxygen.

But it's not fast enough. **As it exhales, the snake tightens its grip. The pig can't inhale.** *It struggles harder, which only forces it to try to breathe again, leading to a further tightening of the coils.*

In precisely the same manner does government—once it is allowed to escape from the cage of a written Constitution that once allowed it to fund and do only a specific limited *number of things —coil around us,...*

It may be patient, but it never backs off. Someday, it knows, it will have finally grown large enough for the big meal it has in mind.

— Vin Suprynowicz, *Send in the Waco Killers* (1999), p. 14-15

All this was made possible by the deliberate wimpy verbiage of the 2nd Amendment. It left an "out" for the feds, and possibly on purpose. Had it been as strongly written as the states' version or as Madison's version, I'd be shooting a Ø400 BAR right now at 5¢ a round. (No, I take that back. *I'd* actually be shooting a Ø3,000 Solothurn 20mm cannon at Ø5 a round...)

SO, WHAT RIGHTS ARE *LEFT?*

Not many, but it could be much, much worse.

You may ship a long gun *intrastate* through the mails

Send it by registered mail with no outside "gun" markings. Handguns cannot be mailed, but must be sent by common carrier such as FedEx, RPS, UPS, etc.

You may ship interstate to *yourself* in care of the recipient

If shipping to yourself out of state, address it to yourself c/o the recipient (who cannot open the box). This can be useful if you don't want to chance losing a gun in a checked airline bag.

Buying ammo privately (preferably at a gun show)

Until 1986, you had to fill out a form to buy ammo, but no longer. You can even order the stuff by the case from out of State and have it sent right to your door (although I'd order it under an alias and receive it at a Mail Boxes Etc. for Ø3). Stock up *now* on affordable, quality, anonymous ammo—while we can.

Transferring intrastate firearms privately, without an FFL

The feds do not yet regulate the private, *intra*state transfer between nonlicensed adults. As long as the buyer or recipient is not an 18 USC §922(d) *"prohibited possessor" and* the nonlicensed transfer is legal in your home state and city, you may privately buy/sell used firearms as you can used books or clothing. You may buy/sell from classified ads, garage sales, flea markets, gun shows, etc.

The other party must be from your home state, to avoid the applicability of *"interstate commerce"* federal gun laws.

Do not expect this right to last much longer. The gun haters are beside themselves that in 23 States no record of sale is required to be reported to the State or local government. (As of 10/99, these states were: Alaska, Arizona, Arkansas, Colorado, Delaware, Florida, Georgia, Idaho, Kansas, Kentucky, Louisiana, Maine, Mississippi, Montana, Nebraska, Nevada, New Mexico, Oklahoma, Texas, Utah, Vermont, West Virginia, and Wyoming.) Since most of these states will *never* ban record-free private sales, the feds will try to, some day.

Out-of-State transfer through a bequest

You'll need to go through a local FFL and fill out a BATF Form 4473 to legally send or receive (even as gifts) firearms from out-of-state. The only exception to this is a bequest.

A temporary loan or rental of a firearm for lawful sporting purposes can be made interstate.

Interstate shipment of firearms for repair, etc.

You may send *and receive* a firearm through a common carrier (*e.g.*, FedEx, RPS, UPS, etc.) to a repair facility directly from your home without an FFL intermediary. When sending to a non-FFL, you must declare in writing to the common carrier that you are sending a firearm.

Interstate transportation of firearms

The NRA has a good pamphlet on this. *Generally*, if your gun is legal at your destination, then you may carry it *unloaded, cased, and locked in the trunk* of your car.

Many states (MA, NY, NJ, CA, etc.) are quirky about this with handguns and semiautomatic rifles. *Beware.*

You may take an unloaded/cased/locked/declared gun in your checked-through airline baggage. The airline may *not* place on your bag any identifying "steal me!" gun tag, but they *will* code the tag, usually with an "FFFFFFFFFFF."

Open carry of firearms (as of 10/99)

Only 28 states allow this. States in **bold** also allow the unrecorded private transfers of firearms. States *italicized* have strong preemptions against local infringement of gun rights:

Alabama, **Alaska, Arizona, Colorado, Delaware,** *Idaho,* **Kansas,** *Kentucky, Louisiana,* **Maine, Mississippi,** Missouri, **Montana, Nebraska, Nevada,** New Hampshire, Ohio, **Oklahoma,** Oregon, Pennsylvania, *New Mexico, North Carolina, South Dakota, Vermont,* Virginia, **West Virginia,** Wisconsin, and *Wyoming.*

Obviously, the best States here are Idaho, Kentucky, Louisiana, New Mexico, Vermont, and Wyoming.

Concealed carry of firearms (as of 10/99)

Some 27 states have a *"shall issue"* concealed handgun license (CHL) system. (4 others have discretionary, though relaxed, systems which are considered *de facto "shall issue."*) Generally, as long as you're not a *"prohibited possessor"* and you take a safety training course, the State *must* approve your CHL permit application.

In a dozen or so states, the local police chief or sheriff has the arbitrary power of refusal (and they use it *frequently,* most infamously in Kalifornia).

In Illinois, Kansas, Missouri, Nebraska, Ohio, Wisconsin, and D.C. there is no provision for CHLs. *Zip. Nada. Keine.*

Only *Vermont* perfectly recognizes your right to be peaceably armed *without* permit—openly or concealed. So, Sarah Brady and Josh Sugarmann—why isn't *Vermont* a hotbed of gun violence when it *should* be by your arguments?

Conversely, why is Washington, D.C., where they've *banned* handgun ownership, our nation's *murder* capital? CHL states have lower crime rates. This is indisputable. Every Swiss male keeps at home his *fully-automatic,* militia-issued rifle (along with grenades, mortars, etc.), and Switzerland has the lowest crime rate of the West.

Look, Brady and Sugarmann, you clowns—opposing political views are one thing, but you don't have the *decency* to be intellectually *honest!* You are liars, creeps, and cowards. You pervert our language through your Orwellian, neurolinguistic programming in order to make us all defenseless against criminals and government thugs alike. *Jackals!*

NOW HERE'S A THOUGHT...

Never forget that "your" Congress and President *forbid* you to own the *best* tools for defending your family. Thanks to them, you'll likely never own an AUG, SIG550, G36, H&K91, Belgian FAL, or a milspec AR10.

A crappy Ruger Mini-14 is permissible because it's a domestic rifle without a scary pistol grip and folding stock. It's also manufactured by an historic traitor to your 2nd Amendment rights, Bill Ruger. *Hmmm, coincidence?*

It must be quite embarrassing for Ruger that his own guns are the common choice of mass murderers, such as:

Bad Guys	Location	Ruger used
Platt	Miami, Florida	Mini-14
Hennard	Killeen, Texas	P85
Ferguson	Long Island subway	P85
Johnson, Golden	Jonesboro, Arkansas	Ruger .44
Carneal	Paducah, Kentucky	Mk.I
Kinkel	Springfield, Oregon	10/22
Barbarin	Salt Lake City, Utah	Mk.II
Smith	Illinois and Indiana	Mk.II

His firearms engineering prowess notwithstanding, perhaps Congress should vote to ban Bill Ruger...

WHAT ABOUT OUR RECENT SUPREME COURT "VICTORIES?"

Technically, we're 4 for 4 since 1992:

Thompson Center in 1992 (BATF rules on short-barreled rifles)

Staples in 1994 (knowledge required to prove illegal possession of an automatic weapon)

Lopez in 1995 (overturning the *"Gun-Free School Zone Act of 1991"*)

Printz in 1997 (overturning the background checks by CLEOs)

Boston sez: Hold off on the party balloons

> *The federal judiciary these days is not a competing power, anxious to keep the executive and legislative branches hemmed inside Constitutional bounds. It is a co-conspirator, sternly holding the people down while allowing our voracious oppressors to commit unbridled mayhem any way they please.*
> — Vin Suprynowicz, *Send in the Waco Killers* (1999), p. 465

I had observed the same thing two years earlier in *Hologram of Liberty*, so I am heartened that others are also realizing it.

Point #1: A new broom sweeps clean. Four victories in several years does *not* constitute a solid, irreversible trend.

Point #2: They were all 5-4 decisions. Expect Rehnquist or O'Connor to flip soon. The Scalia/Thomas "glue" won't hold.

Point #3: Two of those cases involved *federalism* challenges, *not* 2nd Amendment challenges. The Court *could* have by now struck down *NFA34* and *GCA68*, but has so far denied *cert* to the potential landmark gun cases.

Point #4: The Court is unwilling to go "too far" in restoring our 2nd Amendment rights. For example, it *could* have killed Brady's 5-day waiting period by now, but has not. Nobody, not even Scalia, has ever joined Thomas's concurrences.

Point #5: Even if these victories *are* a trend, and even if the 5-4 majority *does* hold firm, and even if the Court *were* serious about upholding our rights, there's still the presidential power of executive order (based on some nebulous *"national emergency"*). Show me just *one* executive order overturned by the Supreme Court in the last 60 years!

I trust I make my melancholy case. Even if I'm wrong, it's still no huge problem for the more pesky Justices to drown in 2" of bathtub water, have a fatal one-car accident, or, best yet, shoot themselves in an unprecedented, baffling moment of suicidal despair. (Ask Vince Foster how this works.)

After 9/11, commercial pilots are pleading for their right to protect their planes and passengers, **but *evil* Congressmen are still trying to block a pilot's right to be armed.** Yes, I said *"evil"* because not even Congressmen can be so stupid. Look Charles Schumer, we tried your *"gun free zone"* and it got 5,000 people killed in 90 minutes! There is not *one* compelling reason for keeping our airline pilots disarmed (we trust them with our lives anyway!), and armed pilots would eliminate the silly and expensive plan for 20,000 new sky marshals.

Americans should be in an *uproar* that our pilots are forbidden to be armed. They're not. **The pilots' unions should be on strike over this.** They're not. The USA is full of cowards, and I am profoundly ashamed about this.

The victim disarmament clan have a timetable to keep, they're on a roll, and, most importantly, they're not afraid of us. With or without the Court's blessing, the feds are going to try to strip away more and more of our self-defense rights.

They won't stop until—*unless*—they become afraid of us. History has proven that in countless examples. In *The Gulag Archipelago*, Alexander Solzhenitsyn persuasively argued that had Stalin's goons been assaulted at least with wooden chairs and kitchen knives during the initial raids, the police state would have collapsed from a lack of thugs willing to volunteer for such hazardous duty. Thugs became thugs in the first place because they're *jackals* at heart. They shoot nursing mothers in the face from 200yds and pour helicopter machine gun fire on helpless families in homestead churches. *Cowards.*

We'll have *no excuse*. We have the best firearms in history, we are the most armed people on the planet, we have an ingrained tradition of Liberty, and we have the priceless benefit of historical hindsight to understand not just the *process* of gradual tyranny, but its ugly finale of demonization, ostracization, roundups, camps (ask the Japanese-Americans of WWII), "reeducation," confinement, torture, and executions.

We will have *no excuse* not to resist.

Politically Corrected Glossary

by Alan Korwin

Dear friends and fans,

We've all talked about how we're losing the war of words in the struggle for our liberties. Well here comes the cavalry.

I'll have the first part formatted as a two-column table you can download from my site, http://www.gunlaws.com, just as soon as I can get it posted (use the New Stuff button).

For Publication, 3,449 Words, 2/29/00
One-time North American Serial Rights
Copyright 2000 Alan Korwin
Not-for-profit circulation is approved.

POLITICALLY CORRECTED Glossary of Terms

by Alan Korwin, Author
Gun Laws of America

Part One—The Concept

Certain words hurt you when you're talking about your rights. People who would deny your rights have done a good job of manipulating the language so far. Without even realizing it, you're probably using terms that actually help the people who want to disarm you. To preserve, protect and defend your rights in this critical debate, you need effective word choices.

They *want* you to say (and you lose if you say):	**It's *better* to say (and they lose if you say):**
pro-gun	pro-rights
gun control	crime control
anti-gun movement	anti-self-defense movement
semiautomatic handgun	sidearm
concealed carry	carry, or right to carry
assault weapons	household firearms
Saturday Night Specials	racist gun laws
junk guns	the affordability issue
high capacity magazines	full capacity magazines
Second Amendment	Bill of Rights
anti-gun	anti-gun bigot, or anti-rights

When *they* say...	**You reply...**
"Guns kill."	*"Guns save lives."*
"Guns cause crime."	*"Guns stop crime."*
"Guns are too dangerous to own."	*"Then you should take a safety class."*
	"Then don't trust the boys and girls in the military and police with them."
"People shouldn't have guns."	*"Only the good people should have guns."*
"The only purpose of a gun is to kill."	*"The main purpose of a gun is to protect."*
"Guns should go away."	*"Then you should personally sign up to never have a gun in your life, under penalty of felony arrest, as you would ask of me."*
"They should take all the guns away."	*"Bad guys first."*
"We need more gun laws."	*"Everything criminal about guns is already illegal."*
"Why would anyone want to own a gun?"	*"You're kidding, right?"*
	"You mean you really don't know?"
	"Well, why do you police have guns?"
"Do you really have a gun?"	*"Of course, don't you?"*

Then just give it a rest and watch where it goes. You'll hear their litany, replete with flaws. Don't rebut, seize the moment, listen hard and learn—then just raise an eyebrow and think, *"How 'bout that. Feller doesn't even own a gun. It takes all kinds."* Then talk about something else. And boy, does the disjoint hang in their craw.

Part Two—The Glossary

PRO-RIGHTS

A more accurate, and far more compelling term than the common "pro-gun." The reverse term, which describes them, is "anti-rights." Misguided utopian disarmament advocates love the phrases "pro-gun" and "anti-gun", because they automatically win when they're used. They believe the righteous path is to be anti-gun, because only devils would be pro-gun. You flat lose if you allow a debate to be framed that way.

The debate is really between people who are "pro-rights" and "anti-rights" (and then you automatically win), because the righteous choice between pro-rights and anti-rights is obvious. You're pro-safety; pro-self-defense; pro-freedom; pro-liberty; pro-Bill of Rights (correctly casting them as anti-safety; anti-self-defense; anti-freedom; anti-liberty; anti-Bill of Rights). This is an accurate depiction of people who would restrict, repress and flat-out deny civil rights you and your ancestors have always had in America.

ANTI-RIGHTS

A more accurate, and far more compelling term than the common "anti-gun." The reverse term, which describes you, is "pro-rights." Fight the desire to cast repressionists as "anti-gun" (and by so doing casting yourself narrowly as "pro-gun"). Instead, always refer more broadly to the "anti-rights" posture they take. Make them argue rights, not guns.

CRIME CONTROL

What "gun control" used to mean, and a generally good idea (the phrase "gun control" has morphed to mean "disarm the public" and thus should be avoided, more on this later). Everyone basically agrees there should be crime control, so it is good grounds for détente. A common sense and reasonable proposal. Includes forcibly disarming criminals. Emphasizes the differences between criminals and an armed public.

GUN BIGOT

A person who hates guns. Typically has little or no personal knowledge of guns, may never have even fired one, certainly doesn't have any. Would subject innocent people to defenselessness without compunction. An elitist. One with an irrational and morbid fear of guns that is ignorant and immoral. Spews bile and venom at guns, gun owners, gun-rights advocates, gun-rights associations, pro-Bill of Rights legislators. Striking similarity and direct parallels with racial bigotry before (and even after) the civil rights efforts of the 1960s.

GUN BIGOTRY
The notion that you can only own a gun if it is expensive, or passes a drop test, a melting point test, a consumer products test, a government design test, a caliber size, an ammunition capacity, a lock test, etc. The notion that only idiots, miscreants, red necks, dim bulbs and other nasty-named people would own guns. The notion that you can only vote, oops, I mean have a firearm, if you pass a test run by your government, and pay the tax, often called a "fee." The notion that anyone who fails the tests—or any other qualifications—automatically forfeits their rights "for the common good." An inability to distinguish honest people from criminals.

GUN PREJUDICE
Discrimination against honest people merely for their legal ownership or possession of firearms. A common occurrence in society today. A violation of your constitutional and natural rights. Gun prejudice appears to be a federal civil-rights offense, punishable by prison and fine. Now there's a thought. Repressionists have attempted some very novel court challenges to laws that protect our liberties. Turnabout's fair play. If there were, say, a city bank somewhere that refused customers simply because they legally handled firearms...

AFFORDABLE FIREARMS
Anti-rights bigots curse these as "junk guns" and "Saturday night specials," racial epithets you should never use. The racist goal of outlawing guns unless they're expensive is self evident and reprehensible. A woman who eats inexpensive food and drives an inexpensive car doesn't lose her right to protect her family because she can only afford an inexpensive gun.

SIDEARM
Or would you rather use the complex and dangerous sounding (though accurate perhaps) "semiautomatic handgun,"

a term which many people think means machine gun, according to Handgun Control (who recommends use of the term "semiautomatic handgun"). Unfortunately, "handgun" has been vilified beyond usability, and needs to be retired or at least back-burnered for now. Remember, it was the so-called Brady "handgun" law that federalized all retail sales of rifles and shotguns.

PISTOL
Or would you rather use the complex and dangerous sounding (though accurate perhaps) "semiautomatic handgun." A basic, reliable, standard type of pistol, a regular pistol, an ordinary pistol, the same kind of pistol anyone would normally own. A basic, reliable, standard type of sidearm, a regular sidearm, an ordinary sidearm, the same kind of sidearm anyone would normally own.

HOUSEHOLD FIREARMS
The type any household is likely to have. All the firearms you own, despite constant name-calling from the media, are just household firearms.

GOVERNMENT GUN
The only kind you can now buy in America at retail.

BASIC SELF-DEFENSE GUN
Any type of firearm that could save your life in an emergency.

CARRY
Expunge the word "concealed" because so many people hear it and believe only a criminal would conceal something. It implies you have something to hide. Because being discreet is a common sense, reasonable measure, there's no need to demean it with an ugly adjective (in this use anyway) like "concealed." "Carry license," not "concealed-carry license."

LETHALITY
The quality of a gun that makes it useful as a crime-stopping, life-saving, defensive tool. A point that is attacked subtly in most anti-rights arguments. When met head on, the issue works against the anti-rights position. Caliber and capacity restrictions reduce lethality and your ability to save

yourself or the state. Reducing lethality costs lives. Why should police need more capacity than you, when you both face the same criminals? How few bullets may a person use against an attacker, and how small should they be?

Guns are dangerous. They're supposed to be dangerous. They wouldn't be any good if they weren't dangerous. Anything that makes them less dangerous by reducing lethality puts you (or police officers) at unacceptable risk.

ANTI-SELF-DEFENSE MOVEMENT

People who believe you have little or no right to defend yourself if attacked, because social order may only be imposed by an authority, and that such authority is superior to your right to exist (if push comes to shove). Also sometimes referred to as socialists. Sometimes expressed as your right to keep a cell phone handy to dial 911. The anti-self-defense movement is often deceptively portrayed as the "anti-gun movement." Never let them hide behind their comfortable disguise as anti-gun.

POLITICALLY CORRECTED

Language that does not automatically bias a debate about the Bill of Rights against individual liberty and freedom. Opposite of "politically correct" language, which is basically socialist in nature. We all recognize that "political correctness" is "incorrect," and then we sneer and dismiss it. We do this at great peril, however, for PC statements treated that way don't just go away, they fester and insidiously modify the paradigm, and bend our thinking into acceptance of that which we have verbalized as "correct."

You want a good example of neurolinguistic programming and transformational grammar on a national scale, there it is to a tee. It's how we get to the Orwellian point where war is peace, freedom is slavery, ignorance is strength.

BILL OF RIGHTS

More broadly appealing and less polarizing than "Second Amendment." Sure, I like the Second Amendment, and talk about it all the time. But saying "Bill of Rights" protects you from malicious stigma and stereotyping as a gun nut. Much more difficult to oppose, slows the bigots down. All the rights count, don't they, and they're all under attack. Bill of Rights Day. Pro-Bill of Rights. I support the Bill of Rights, don't you? Actually, even virulent gun haters and gun bigots champion the

First Amendment and other parts of the BOR, which, if you'll recall, was a single amendment (with separate articles) to the Constitution.

SUNSHINE GUN LAWS
Laws that encourage gun safety training and responsible firearms ownership, as opposed to repressive laws that criminalize honest gun ownership and infringe civil rights. Civil rights.

THE FIRST AMENDMENT
Stop saying Second Amendment so much, since the other side tunes this out immediately, and marginalizes you as a gun nut. Say "First Amendment" instead, and make your comparisons there—does the government jeopardize your First Amendment rights? You betcha! Should you be concerned? Of course! What would you think of Internet censorship, government approved religion, font size limits, restricted word choices, acceptable word counts, licensed writers, training and testing before publishing controversial editorials, and tests for accuracy—now there's a nice parallel.

People on all sides recognize there are threats to free speech, religion, privacy and more from our friends, the government. The same root problems affect the whole Bill of Rights, gun rights are no different than other rights under attack.

GUN-SAFETY CLASSES
Something that, with all the accidents reported in America, all Americans should be taking—from the tens of thousands of trainers out there. Always encourage people on both sides of a debate to take a real class. Why wouldn't an honest person take a gun-safety class? Going out for some wholesome and relaxing target practice, with friends. Getting good at marksmanship. Target practice. Marksmanship. These words have not been defiled and cast a good light; use them. Privately promoted gun-safety training days. Talk up the goal of "National Accident Reduction" through education and training. Private enterprise should vigorously swell to fill the gaping theater called, *"We need more safety."*

ROWANITES

Anti-rights bigots who secretly own guns themselves, rely upon armed guards for security, or live inside communities with private security forces, but decry your right to arms. Closet gun owners. Named in honor of Carl Rowan, a vicious anti-gun bigot whose syndicated newspaper column vilified guns and gun owners for years, to a vast audience, until he one day fired at a trespasser near his home.

GUN BUY-UPS

Gun buy-back programs are misnamed. You cannot buy back something you didn't own in the first place. Since the Brady law prohibits dumping such guns into criminal lairs (gun buyers must be certified by the FBI these days), there is no longer justification for destroying firearms collected in buy-ups. That's right, there is no longer any justification at all for destroying firearms collected in buy-ups. When buy-ups are government funded, meltdowns are therefore wanton destruction of a public asset, and someone deserves to be held liable. Tax dollars are buying legal property simply to destroy it, when the only way to sell it is to certifiably law abiding individuals. What an outrage.

Where I live, savvy collectors have set up shop at widely publicized gun buy-ups to make competitive bids and cherry pick the merchandise, pre-smelter.

DEMOCIDE

Murder committed by government. The most prevalent form of murder, responsible this century alone for 170 million deaths. Regime-ocide.

GUN CONTROL

Now generally synonymous with "disarming the public." Using the phrase "gun control" in its currently twisted form distorts the debate and should be avoided; it is the other side's rallying flag, bolstered every time the words leave your lips; argue about *"gun control"* and you've already lost. Use "crime control," "accident reduction" and "disarming the public" to distinguish issues and preserve accuracy.

Listen hard when you hear the term *"gun control"* in the news. You'll notice they're basically not talking about controlling crime. They're talking about controlling you.

Always start by asking what a person means when they say this phrase, then shut up and see. Often, people who think of themselves as being anti-gun, unwittingly adopt the position that only the rulers should be armed (cop and army guns OK, but not you; such a person isn't anti-gun at all, they're simply anti-rights—your rights). When a "gun-control law" regulates or demeans honest people in the false name of controlling crime, that's actually tyranny. When "gun control" controls your right to have a gun, that is people control. The phrase "gun control" is a dangerous misnomer (some would say euphemism) for an agenda now actively pursued by a segment of society—that would consolidate power solely in "official" hands.

Help seize the metaphor back:

❶ Drop into conversation how your gun control at target practice recently was better than usual, or how you have pretty good gun control but you still need some lessons. Invite someone to your gun-control class at the range next Tuesday—free style target practice. A well advertised gun-control class might attract some pretty interesting neighbors. Jokes about gun control ("a steady hand") are neurolinguistically challenged and don't help. Say something else funny if you must be funny.

❷ When reporters and others inevitably ask, *"Are you in favor of gun control?"* they often don't realize their question is as biased as, *"Are you still beating your wife?"* So it's up to you to show them. They're looking for a pro-or con answer, and then a question of how much. Don't play into it. Instead, say, *"Well, I'm in favor of crime control. How about you?"*

❸ When you write about so-called *"gun control"* or so-called *"gun-control laws"* always put it in quotes, to disparage it.
        (BTP Note: West Germany did this to East Germany, the so-called *"German Democratic Republic."*)

THE HENIGAN/BOGUS THEORY
        Named by Dave Kopel in honor of its two leading proponents (Dennis Henigan and Carl Bogus). This is the notion, first arising a few decades ago, that the Second Amendment does not protect an individual right. It stands in opposition to the fact that *"the people"* means all of us, and is responsible for the widely armed population we observe today. Covered more thoroughly in an earlier article of mine, *The Big*

Lie (posted under Position Papers at http://www.gunlaws.com). Kopel's recent paper on this, for the St. Louis University Public Law Review, is nothing short of brilliant. David can be reached at http://www.independenceinstitute.net.

COGNITIVE DISSONANCE

A tool for reaching closed minds. The use of questions to point out fundamental illogic, which can then topple the notions a person builds on that flawed base. An application of the Socratic method. The mental awareness that forms when a simple question challenges fundamentally held beliefs. Here are many. One at a time is usually enough for most minds.

"If a registration list makes sense for the Second Amendment, would it make sense for the First Amendment?"

"Are criminals and an armed citizenry the same thing?"

"So why do people today carry guns anyway, and does it ever work?"

"Should it be against the law to defend yourself?"

"If a person can't have a gun, why should the police have them?"

"So if you're allowed to defend yourself, how many bullets can you use?"

"Shouldn't we disarm the criminals first?"

"Why haven't we disarmed the criminals?"

"Why don't they arrest all the Brady criminals they find?"

"Are you against an armed citizenry?"

"Do you believe that only the rulers should have guns?"

"Now let me see if I understand this; when you say "gun control," do you mean "stop crime" or "disarm the public?"

"Now let me see if I understand this; when you say you're anti-gun, do you mean you want to disarm the police and the armed forces?"

"If you don't want to disarm the police and military, you're not really anti-gun at all. You're anti-private gun. Why is that?"

"You know, after listening to you for a while, you've convinced me that you should never own a gun."

"I'm against the idea that you should be forced to own a gun, and I would stand up for your right to not be armed."

"Maybe you could sign up to be permanently disbarred from ever owning a gun. Would you do that (as you would ask me to do)?"

Closing Note:
This article doesn't end here. In attempting a document like this, I know I can never reach its ending. It defines a path which simply stretches forward.

If I wait until I have this evolved to my satisfaction it will never wrap. These ideas are too important to let wait that long. Consider it an early peek at a work in progress.

Alan.

Social balance has evolved into a war of the metaphor—neurolinguistic programming meets George Orwell.

— Alan Korwin

Alan Korwin is the author of seven best-selling books on gun law, including *Gun Laws of America—Every Federal Gun Law on the Books, with Plain English Summaries,* and gun owner guides for AZ, CA, FL, NY, TX, UT, VA. This paper is part of an ongoing series, click Position Papers on the home page, or write or call for copies.

BRAND NEW
Licensed to Carry, by Greg Jeffery
Check out this 30-State Shall-Issue License Guide, find out what it takes to get a carry license in each state.

LOOK AT "GUN LAWS OF AMERICA" YOURSELF:
If you knew all your rights you might demand them.

Alan Korwin
BLOOMFIELD PRESS   http://www.gunlaws.com
"We publish the gun laws"
12629 N. Tatum #440
Phoenix, AZ 85032
602-996-4020 Phone
602-494-0679 FAX
800-707-4020 Book orders

Sign up for future updates on our home page.

LETTER TO A COLUMBINE STUDENT

Dear Devon,

I read your well-written essay printed on page 41 of the 23 August 1999 issue of *Newsweek*, and felt led to write you. I was sickened by the murderous rampage suffered by students and faculty of the Columbine High School.

As a gunowner, gun books author, and defensive shooting instructor, there are some thoughts I'd like to share with you about Columbine and your essay. This letter is much longer than I had expected it to be, but my readers tell me that my style is very easy to read, so I hope that you'll give it a chance.

Emotionalist arguments have been effective...on *you*

Although you are obviously a sincere and articulate young lady traumatized by a terrible event, much of your essay regarding suggested new *"gun controls"* was misguided, ill-reasoned, or based on emotionalism. (Are you brave enough to read on and give me the chance to prove it?)

This may sound like stern talk. It is. But since you have joined a political lobbying group and have had a full page essay printed in a national magazine, you're now in (at least for awhile) the "big leagues." Hearing criticism is part of that new arena. If you're mature enough to purport to speak to America and influence national legislation directly affecting nearly *half* of her households, then you're mature enough to hear me out. (And I promise not to be mean or ugly, O.K.?)

Another thing that I promise is that I'll be *honest* with you. I won't lie; I won't exaggerate. The 2nd Amendment issue has truth on its side, and I won't jeopardize a perfectly defensible position by using specious reasoning or half-truths.

The real meaning of *"gun control"*

Probably without realizing it, you use the catchphrases of others. As I'll explain later, catchphrases are designed with political agendas in mind. If *"gun control"* meant only keeping guns out violent hands, I'd not only use the phrase, I'd support it. But *"gun control"* means much *more* than that. It *has* to, **because every criminal use of guns is *already* against the law!** It is *already* unlawful to use a gun to: rob, intimidate, rape, assault, kidnap, hijack, murder, etc. Think about that.

So, there is more to that seemingly innocent catchphrase. Its purpose is *not* to control guns, or even criminals. It's purpose is to control *people* by making them helpless, and thus requiring police (*i.e.,* government) protection. It is statistically irrefutable that those American cities with stringent *"gun control"* (*e.g.,* N.Y.C., D.C., Chicago, L.A.) have higher crime rates. It is also irrefutable that those 31 states which have made concealed carry of handguns easy for law-abiding citizens have correspondingly enjoyed significant drops in their crime rates. Finally, if you look at the British and Australian recent experiments with gun confiscation (not just *"control"*), those two countries are suffering from a new crime *wave.* The evidence is clear and unanimous:

"gun control" is actually "victim disarmament"

It is government's *nature* to want to control its citizens beyond any level proper for fighting crime. Government wants to be like a bossy mother who can't see "her" kids as grown adults:

> *Parents keep poison, knives, and matches out of the reach of two-year olds because of the high probability of injury or death.*
> — Pete Shields; *Guns Don't Die—People Do*

(...and therefore the government should keep guns out of the "childlike" hands of private citizens.)

Politicians and the media

I also believe that victim disarmament politicians and "advocacy journalism" media are shamelessly using you and the Columbine tragedy to further their own goals—goals which *many* people see as wholly unconstitutional. Had Columbine not occurred, do you honestly think that you would have been invited to the White House or published in *Newsweek*? The moral high ground of a victim is a powerful and heady thing, but it has a *very* short half-life. To them, your grief was useful *then*. For example, Pete Shields of Handgun Control, Inc. brazenly uses emotionalism to further HCI's agenda. He called it their "Victims Strategy":

> *It is the emotional appeal of the victim's story which assures communication, attention, and an emotional involvement on the part of those who are already known to be sympathetic on an intellectual level.* **Using victims is the most effective way,** *I believe, to conduct an educational campaign that will result in a constituency willing to vote on the basis of this issue.* (p.57)
> — Pete Shields; *Guns Don't Die—People Do*

Since facts and common sense are enemies of "victim disarmament," its proponents cannot make any sustainable *intellectual* argument. That's why they must resort to the shameful use of victims, exploiting their gore and grief in order to "educate" through emotions (which is an oxymoron).

Another professional victim disarmament lobbyist argued for applying the same emotionalist tactic to semi-auto military-pattern firearms:

> *The* [assault] *weapon's menacing looks, coupled with the confusion over fully automatic machine guns versus* [semi-automatic] *assault weapons—anything that looks like a machine gun is assumed to be a machine gun—can only increase the chance of* [ignorant] *public support for restrictions on these weapons.*
> — Josh Sugarmann, Violence Policy Center

Christians, self-defense, and guns

In your magazine picture you are wearing a cross on your necklace. On the assumption that you are a Christian (as am I), I will begin there.

In the Garden of Gethsemane, when Jesus knew that He would shortly be arrested, He gave His disciples what He knew would be some last minute instructions. In Luke 22:36, He admonished them to buy a sword, even if they had to sell their *coat* to afford it. (The disciples said that they had two swords among them, and Jesus replied, *"It is enough."*) This was an amazing command, for two reasons.

The coat

First, back then a coat also served as one's groundcloth and sleeping blanket for the freezing desert nights. It was no trivial matter to go without one—one could die from exposure.

The sword

Second, that Jesus specified a *sword* over other weapons is particularly significant. Jesus could have urged the carrying of a pocketknife, dagger, or axe—but He didn't. He said *sword.* A sword's only real purpose is for combat; for killing people in self-defense. Before the invention of the longbow, the sword was *the* most capable weapon an individual could carry and wield. Few people could afford one, as they cost many months of wages. I do not exaggerate in the slightest when I equate the 1st Century sword to the 20th Century military-style full-auto rifle. The sword of Judea was the fully-automatic M16 of today.

When the use of weapons is *inappropriate*

Once the mob came to arrest Jesus, Peter sliced off the high priest's servant's ear with his sword, a personal weapon *already* on Peter's person. Jesus's rebuke in Mark 26:52 of *"Those who take the sword shall perish with the sword"* had to do with Peter's *substitution* of a weapon for his lack of faith, and his lack of understanding of God's sacrificial plan for Jesus. (Note that Peter did not attack a *soldier*, or even the high priest. He attacked a defenseless servant, in an empty gesture of rage. No doubt because of this, Jesus also disapproved.)

If Jesus had objected to general sword *carrying* by His disciples, He wouldn't have commanded them to buy swords, and Peter would *not* have been allowed to be armed in the Garden.

The difference between "kill" and "murder"

Finally, the correct Hebrew translation of *Thou shalt not kill* (Exodus 20:13) is *Thou shalt not murder*—a different matter entirely than justifiable homicide during self-defense. Numbers 35:16-29 explains the difference between killing and murder. Christians are not to permit their own murders.

Even the Talmud and the Koran plainly state that it's no sin to kill a killer, so I really can't see how anybody can have, after much study and thought, a problem with self-defense. Since you *"can even see someone having a handgun in the home for protection,"* we probably somewhat agree on this issue.

Good Guys and Bad Guys

Devon, there are people in the world who delight in doing evil and harming others. There always have been, and there always will be. Only half of them are in prison at any given time.

Fortunately, these evil people are outnumbered *400* to 1 by ordinary folks like you and me who don't want to hurt anybody. You might not know that peaceable, law-abiding Americans use their personal firearms about 5,500 times a *day* for self-defense. (This was discovered in the now-famous Kleck study, which won a prestigious award for its research quality.) Not that there are 5,500 defensive *shootings* a day, as the mere display of a gun and verbal warning to an attacker usually resolves the situation without any shots fired. In fact, private citizens justifiably shoot nearly *three times* more violent criminals than do the police, while wounding far fewer bystanders than do the police. (The media doesn't admit this, but the NRA compiles news clippings of such incidents in *The Armed Citizen.*)

If only *1%* of decent folks will bother to learn how to safely use a pistol and carry it daily, they will *still* outnumber the Bad Guys 4 to 1. Carrying it in public is a must, as 87% of violent crime happens *outside* the home.

At Pearl High School in Mississippi on 1 October 1997, Assistant Principal Joel Myrick prevented, with his own handgun, further bloodshed by Luke Woodham. Mr. Myrick was a true hero, but that's very rarely admitted in the media. (It wasn't explained in that *Newsweek* article, which did mention Woodham but *not* his apprehension by a brave, armed citizen who had his gun in his car and had to run ¼ mile off school grounds to get it.)

If only *one* teacher that morning at Columbine was armed to have reduced (or prevented) all those deaths and injuries.

What's *really* the problem

Evil men can *always* get a weapon. They do so even in prisons (the most controlled environment possible), so how can any mere *law* (which criminals do not obey, because they're criminals) stop them?

But laws and regulations *do* hinder (if not prevent) many peaceful Americans from owning and carrying the most efficient tool for daily possible self-defense—a handgun.

So, if we really want to be honest, it's not so much that the *Bad* Guys are armed (because there's little to stop them), it's that the *Good* Guys are *not.*

"Leave the Bad Guys to the police. That's their job!"

Yes, it's their "job," but keeping the *peace* is the responsibility of all adults. The police force as we know it today is a *recent* institution (beginning in the early 1900s in the large cities). Back then, Americans understood their responsibility to apprehend criminals if the opportunity occurred. In a way, the whole country was like a Neighborhood Watch program.

95% of all 911 responses are too late to stop the crime!

So, the average 911 caller, terrified for his/her life, has only a 1-in-*20* chance of having the police arrive in time.

(But, why call the police in the first place? Because the police are *armed!* Well, why are so many people *unarmed?* Often, because the law required it! *Hmmm.*)

The police don't *have* to protect you!

Here's something else. During the research for my first book, I was shocked to learn that the police have *no legally enforceable duty* to protect any individual from criminals. If an attacker broke into your home and you frantically dialed 911, and the police were too late (or never showed up) to prevent a tragedy, you could not sue them and win.

This is because you had no *"specific relationship"* with them. You are merely part of society at large. I wish that this were just some weird exception, but this is how the courts have *always* ruled (*e.g., Hartzler v. San Jose, Warren v. D.C.,* and dozens of others).

It's up to *us* to defend *ourselves.* This has been true *before* police, and since. (A great book on this issue is called *Dial 911 and Die—The Shocking Truth about the Police Protection Myth* from the Jews for the Preservation of Firearms Ownership. www.jpfo.org)

> *Gun laws are an attempt to nationalize the right of self-defense. Politicians perennially react to the police's abject failure to prevent crime by trying to disarm law-abiding citizens. The worse government fails to control crime, the more politicians want to restrict individual's rights to defend themselves.*
>
> *But police protection in most places is typical government work —slow, inefficient, and unreliable. According to laws on the books in many states and cities, government has a specific, concrete obligation to disarm each citizen,* **but only an abstract obligation to defend each citizen.** *The government has stripped millions of people of their right to own weapons—yet generally left them free to be robbed, raped, and murdered. "Gun control" is one of the best examples of laws that corner private citizens—forcing them either to put themselves into danger or to be a lawbreaker.*
>
> *Even the most advanced cellular phone is no substitute for a good .38 Special.*
> —James Brovard, author of *Lost Rights*

One final question on police protection: Are the people of Littleton satisfied with the response of their local police and SWAT teams on 20 April 1999? (Not from what I've read.)

"Hear the other side."

In the 1960s, Jane Fonda admitted in a rare moment of candor that she made it a point to *not* read anything that opposed her views, because she feared that conflicting information might weaken her resolve. Today, this attitude is rampant. Does Columbine have a debate team? Probably not. These days, few high schools (or even colleges do). They weren't all that common when I was your age. But up until the 1960s, nearly *every* high school had a debate team. In fact, in debate tournaments only the subject was known in advance—*who* would argue Pro versus Con was chosen only just before the debate. You had to know *both* sides, each as well as the other!

Do you know why debate teams were so important? Because Americans contemplated important issues through a particular process. People did *not* take a position on an issue *until* they had studied *all* sides to it so well that they could, in a debate, argue any side with equal persuasiveness.

By *"well"* I don't mean merely parroting the general point. I mean a passionate, *thorough* argument, down to even quoting facts and statistics from memory. *Only* when they had educated themselves to *that* level of comprehensive knowledge would they *then* choose *their* side on the issue. Wow!

Have you ever heard of *anybody* doing that today? I rarely do. My first experience with it was in a college law class with this amazing professor. During case discussions he would elicit every possible view, and then have us defend *and* challenge them all! To this day, I have no idea where *he* stands on *any* issue. He was *that* neutral in class. *Every* side got fairly heard, because that's what court judges are supposed to do. More to his point, that's what *people* are supposed to do, as he knew that very few of his students would actually go on to a law career. His course was *so* refreshing that they jammed full every first day of registration from applicants of all majors. If you go to college, I hope you have at least *one* professor like him.

With TV and "news" magazines looking for the goriest photo and the juiciest soundbite, the truth usually gets lost in the stampede. (No doubt you saw a lot of that yourself.) **As a result, Americans have lost their ability to *think*.** Only the rare mind can put away its prejudice and emotions to *dispassionately* study a painful issue. But that's exactly what I'm asking *you* to do. I feel that it's my duty to ask this of you on many levels: from older generation to younger, from peaceable gunowner to one who has suffered from lawless gun users, and from one American to another.

Prejudice (Latin; *prae-* before + *judicium,* judgment)

We are told not to be prejudiced against black people because their skin color is different, but it's *O.K.* to be prejudiced against an *opinion* because *it* is different? Racial bigotry is evil, but *intellectual* bigotry is not only acceptable, but encouraged? Is the double standard here not obvious?

Pre-judgment (prejudice) is *not* the same as taking one position over another *after* researching *all* sides.

Did you research the pro-Bill of Rights side, or did you merely accept what Messrs. Head and Grossman told you?

Did you chat with lawful gunowners as much as you did with victim disarmament advocates?

Have you spoken with Hotchkiss high-schooler Desirae Davis? She, with over 100 other Colorado teenagers, signed a letter asking politicians *not* to pass further *"ill-conceived, feel-good"* victim-disarmament legislation.

Did you spend as much time at gun shows as you did at SAFE meetings? (Have you ever *been* to a gun show?)

Did you ever click on www.nra.org or www.gunowners.org or www.jpfo.org or www.wagc.com or www.sas-aim.org?

Have you ever spoken to Dr. Suzanna Gratia Hupp? She left her handgun in her car because of Texas restrictive gun laws, only to watch both of her parents murdered right before her eyes while at Luby's Cafeteria in Killeen. She is now a Texas congresswoman, and a highly vocal champion of gunowners' rights. Her email is suzanna.hupp@house.state.tx.us

If you answered "No" to any of these questions, then guess what: *you* are intellectually prejudiced. This is something that nobody can afford to be, especially a *young* person soon to embark on independent life. We have two eyes, two ears, and *one* mouth. The input/output ratio is 4:1 for a reason.

Your essay asks *us* not to see Eric and Dylan as monsters; not to be prejudiced. Well, I am asking *you* not to pre-judge guns and lawful gunowners as the root of Columbine, or of any other similar tragedy. This will be difficult, but please *try*.

Devon, I say all this *not* to condemn you, but to illuminate that other side which you have so far left in the dark. If, after reading this letter and doing some new research, you still feel that restrictive gun laws should be applied to law-abiding folks, that will be your opinion. **But, at least it will be *your* opinion,** and not one spoon-fed to you by professional politicians and lobbyists with their own, often hidden, agendas.

"reasonable gun legislation"

Your essay did pretty well in not being overly strident or preachy, which would have been the typical route of a victim. Instead, you asked that both sides *"compromise"* to achieve *"reasonable gun legislation."* Examples were mandatory waiting periods and licensing, and limits on magazine capacity.

Many people would probably agree that such seem reasonable. I don't, for one simple reason: Regarding the fundamental right of peaceable Americans to own and carry weapons, there is no such thing as *"reasonable gun legislation."* The vast majority (*i.e.,* 99.99999+%) of the 75,000,000 American gunowners are *law-abiding,* and thus no threat to you or me. Therefore, *any* gun legislation hindering *them* is **unreasonable**.

The term is an oxymoron (*i.e.,* something that internally contradicts itself). You've heard and laughed at other oxymorons: jumbo shrimp, freezer burn, athletic scholarship, etc.

But to me and millions of other lawful gunowners, the oxymoron of *"reasonable gun legislation"* is not at all laughable, as I'll later explain why. First, let's analyze the term.

Buzzwords and catchphrases

Before I do that, please know that I am *not* throwing your own words back in your face. First of all, I wouldn't be so rude to a young person, and second, they aren't *your* words. I've been reading that sly little phrase for years.

"Reasonable gun legislation," which you picked up and used twice, but did not invent, is a modern *catchphrase* made up of *buzzwords,* invented for a purpose. I am a professional book author and words are the tools of my trade, so I know.

Its purpose is this: If somebody is opposed to *"reasonable gun legislation"* then what does that make them? Why, *"unreasonable,"* of course! What right does anybody have to lump somebody else into the category of *"unreasonability"* just because they don't agree with *their* version of *"reasonability"*? The phrase also asserts that, regarding law-abiding folks, restrictive gun laws can be *"reasonable"*—when they cannot.

Other examples of buzzwords and catchphrases

Americans not pro-Clinton are *"right-wing radicals."*

Those who maintain a healthy patriotism and love for their country (though peaceful dissatisfaction with their government) are demonized as *"dangerous Patriots."*

A member of a group with unusual or unpopular beliefs (even if such are clearly nonviolent) belongs to a *"cult."*

When besieged by federal agents, that group's simple plywood home or church magically becomes a *"compound."*

Semi-auto military-style rifles (which are not machine guns or *"automatic"* rifles) are deemed evil *"assault weapons."*

Those with nonviolent moral or religious objections to homosexuality are somehow *"purveyors of hate and intolerance."*

Two very angry and disturbed young boys who murdered a dozen fellow students and a teacher are called *"monsters."*

Remember what I said earlier about learning *all* sides of an issue *first,* and *then* deciding on it? Regarding guns, you have not done this. But this is understandable. You are a young person traumatized by a terrible experience, and you never want it happen again. (If I had suffered this at 17, I, too, might have joined SAFE and flown to D.C. to meet with congressmen.) You didn't know any better then, which is why I'm writing you.

Analyzing *"Sane Alternatives to the Firearms Epidemic"*

Take your own organization, SAFE, for example. That particular acronym was chosen for a *reason*; to create in the reader a certain emotion. (The founders *could* have chosen "gun" instead of "firearms," but *SAGE* just doesn't really have the same *effect,* eh?) Now let's analyze its composition:

"Sane" connotes possible *in*sanity of SAFE *opponents.*

"Alternative" implies that *"shall not be infringed"* in the 2nd Amendment doesn't really mean *"shall not be infringed."*

"Epidemic" equates inanimate physical objects (incapable of autonomous harm) with a deadly virus. This is not only specious, it is rank neurolinguistic programming.

The power of *words* and *images*

We are being trained to act on *emotions,* without all the facts, and that is very, very dangerous in a democratic society. For a democracy to stand requires the *finest* thinking from its members. It requires that we vote from our *minds*—not from our visceral reactions.

If you learn anything from my letter to you, I hope it is this: Guard your mind very jealously, as *words and images* are used to color perceptions, and thus emotions, and thus actions. Learn to filter the spin from what you read and hear. Begin to discern and decipher *what actually happened (i.e.,* the facts) versus swallowing whole the *story* of what allegedly happened.

If you take my challenge seriously, even for just one week, you will be amazed how seldom the full truth about *anything* gets heard. I'll leave you with two quotes on this subject:

> *Everything you read in the newspapers* (or see on TV) *is absolutely true except for that rare story of which you happen to have firsthand knowledge.*
> — Erwin Kroll

To somebody watching the TV coverage of Columbine, for example, the news reporters *seemed* very upset and concerned. However, those actually at the scene (such as yourself) heard with their own ears, *"Do I look devastated enough?"* The *story* was broadcast over TV; the *truth* was evident only if you were *there.* (How does every EyeWitness TV News lead in? *"Our top story tonight..."*) On this very point, didn't you *"happen to have firsthand knowledge"* as the Kroll's quote described?

Here's the second quote:

> *Life is an entanglement of lies to hide its basic mechanisms.*
> — William S. Burroughs

This may strike you as highly cynical, but the older you get you'll find it to be more true than not. *"Things are not always what they seem; skim milk often masquerades as cream."*

My whole point, Devon, is: **Learn to think for *yourself.*** Don't believe me; don't believe your SAFE colleagues. Believe only your *own* well-researched conclusions, and even *then,* keep your mind open for new information in the future. (Think before you speak, and think before you think.)

Professional victim disarmament advocates

As a member of SAFE, no doubt that you have spoken with various colleagues. They have claimed for years that all they want is *"reasonable gun legislation."* Ha!

Every new act of victim disarmament is but a stepping-stone to their *real* goal of the total elimination of guns in law-abiding private hands. And they sometimes *admit* it:

> *We're going to have to take one step at a time, and the first step is necessarily—given the political realities—going to be very modest. Of course, it's true that politicians will then go home and say, "This is a great law. The problem is solved." And it's also true that such statements will tend to defuse the gun-control issue for a time. So then we'll have to start working again to strengthen that law, and then again to strengthen the next law, and maybe again and again. Right now, though, we'd be satisfied not with half a loaf but with a slice. **Our ultimate goal—total control of handguns in the United States—is going to take time.** My estimate is from 7-10 years.*
>
> **The first problem is to slow down the number of handguns produced and sold in this country. The second problem is to get handguns registered.** *The final problem is to make possession of all handguns and all handgun ammunition—except for the military, police, licensed security guards, licensed sporting clubs, and licensed gun collectors— totally illegal.*

— Nelson "Pete" Shields,
Handgun Control Inc. Founder and President
New Yorker, 26 July 1976, p. 58

Point #1: They're often hypocrites

A hypocrite says one thing but *does* another. For example:

Senator Edward Kennedy (D-MA), one of the biggest champions of victim disarmament, was outraged when his personal bodyguard, Charles Stein, was arrested at the Capitol for having an illegal handgun and a fully-automatic submachine gun. Bob Mann, the senator's spokesman, said that Stein was arrested because of a *"technical glitch"* in the law. Stein's six felony counts were reduced to one misdemeanor.

(Kennedy doesn't mind guns...when *his* bodyguard carries them. If an *average citizen* had been caught at the Capitol like Charles Stein, do you think his *6 felony counts* would have dumped for a $1,000 misdemeanor? Could he have successfully whined about a *"technical glitch"* in the law?)

Senator Jay D. Rockefeller IV (D-WV) signed the 1994 *"assault weapons"* ban. Later, it came out that he illegally kept one (an AR15) at his D.C. home. The *Washington Times* wrote:

> *If the senator appears to be in an awkward position here, it's because he is. It's bad enough to sign off on legislation banning law-abiding citizens access to weapons they may want... Even more difficult is trying to explain why the senator's constituents should not be allowed to obtain a weapon that he himself enjoys.* **Why is he to be trusted with one any more than they are?**

Anti-self-defense actress **Jennifer O'Neill** negligently discharged her revolver into her own stomach, claiming that it *"went off."* New York requires handguns to be registered. Hers was not. Her lawyer argued that famous actresses have a right to own a gun for protection.

(So, what was to prevent her from registering her gun and applying for a license—which she and her victim disarmament colleagues worked so hard to require for everybody *else*?)

On 14 June 1988 *Washington Post* anti-Bill of Rights columnist **Carl Rowan** used his illegal gun to shoot an 18 year old kid he caught in his pool. He got off, and defiantly asserted that he'd always have a gun—illegal or not. Seven years earlier, however, when the anti-gunners gave First Lady Nancy Reagan hell for having a pistol on her nightstand, Rowan wrote:

> *We must reverse this psychology. We can do it by passing a law that says anyone found in possession of a handgun except a legitimate officer of the law goes to jail—period!*

(Rowan got off with no punishment. Handgun prohibitions don't seem to apply to Rowan. Rowan's *own* assertive opinion's don't seem to apply to Rowan! This is typical...)

San Francisco mayor and noted victim disarmament advocate **Diane Feinstein** got the city's only gun permit issued in 1980 for her own .38 Special. Still, she saw no paradox two years later in banning handguns for everybody else in San Francisco.

Other notable victim disarmament figures who hypocritically own firearms include: Sidney Baumgarten (NYC politician), *New York Times* publisher Arthur Ochs "Punch" Sulzberger, actor Bill Cosby, Jane Fonda and husband Ted Turner, Fernando Mateo (NYC "Toys for Guns Bonus Amnesty"), 1993 Illinois Attorney General Roland Burris, and former Chief Justice Warren Burger. You see, Very Important People can own guns (even when they claim guns are bad), but us Little People must not. What they mean is:

> Do as I *say*; not as I do! Guns are for *me*, but not for thee!

One author has an plan for dealing with such hypocrites:

> I suspect that even most Gun Controllers recognize the efficacy of possessing the means of self-defense. I think that while they enjoy the positive social benefits of an armed populace (less crime and freedom), they also want to believe themselves moral beings. And since they have adopted an altruist morality (through the coercive sacrifice of others), *they feel pious when they believe themselves above guns and self-defense.*
>
> Imagine that instead of voting for blanket gun control, that the government, instead, published a directory that listed each individual as either armed or a Gun Control pacifist who refuses to be armed. This Directory of Gun-Free Individuals (the application of the Nuclear-Free Zone concept applied to the smallest minority) is made readily available throughout the U.S. and in libraries. What then happens to those remaining Gun Control advocates who stick by their ethics? Whose homes are burglarized? Who is most likely to be raped? Who will suffer the most murders? More importantly, who surrendered their pious anti-gun stand in the interest of protecting their lives? **Such a proposal would show that Gun Controllers want to enjoy the protective umbrella afforded by firearms, while at the same time denying firearms so that they can, by their ethics, maintain a feeling of moral superiority.**

— Mark A. Laughlin; www.ebarricades.com

Point #2: They're lazy and biased researchers

Their "scholarship" and "research" are too abysmal for words. For example, in your *Newsweek* issue, my pen nearly ran dry from marking up the numerous inaccuracies, stolen concepts, half-truths, *ad hominems*, *non sequiturs*, false alternatives, insinuations, emotionalisms, and evasions. (If you don't know what some of the terms mean, get David Kelley's *The Art of Reasoning*. If your local bookstore doesn't have it, call Laissez-Faire Books at 800-326-0996.)

Point #3: They are usually *untruthful*

They mouth support for lawful self-defense and promise that they would *never* confiscate the guns of ordinary Americans. I'll level with you, Devon—generally, they are *lying*. While I believe that *you* and many others are sincere in your feelings, those who are *professional* victim disarmament lobbyists, authors, and speakers are *lying.* (No, it's not a very nice word, but it's not a very nice *thing.*)

> *Ultimately, a civilized society must disarm its citizenry if it is to have a modicum of domestic tranquility of the kind enjoyed by sister democracies such as Canada and Britain. Given the frontier history and individualist ideology of the United States, however, this will not come easily. It certainly cannot be done radically. **It will probably take one, maybe two generations. It might be 50 years before the United States gets to where Britain is today.** Passing a law like the assault weapons ban (the "Crime Bill") is a symbolic—purely symbolic—move in that direction. **Its only real justification is not to reduce crime but to desensitize the public to the regulation of weapons in preparation for their ultimate confiscation.***
>
> — Charles Krauthammer, "Disarm the Citizenry,"
> *The Washington Post,* 5 April 1996

Please read that last sentence again, *very* carefully. The *"assault weapons"* ban was *"not to reduce crime"* but to condition us that *"reasonable"* gun controls are effective (when they're really just stepping stones to *"ultimate confiscation."*)

Here's an example of blatant statistical fraud:

> *2) Contrary to popular perception, most homicides do not occur as the result of an attack by a stranger but stem from an argument between people who know each other and are often related. For murders in 1995, almost half of the victims were either related to (11 percent) or acquainted with (34 percent) their killers. **Only 15 percent were killed by strangers.***
>
> — www.vpc.org/fact_sht/firearm.htm

Do the simple math here: relatives (11%) + acquaintances (34%) = 45%. That means the remaining killers (*i.e.,* strangers) constitute *55%* of women's killers—*not 15%!* (I doubt that this is was a mere typo. Further, women have a right to defend themselves against *any* potential assailant, stranger or not.)

Here's an experiment for you. Pick a colleague who has claimed that they do *not* support confiscation of guns from *law-abiding* Americans. Then, go to that person in private conversation and eventually ask them *"Don't you believe that total elimination of guns is the only way to <u>really</u> keep them out of criminal hands?"* Privately, they'll likely concur with you. *Publicly,* they don't *dare* say it because Americans wouldn't agree.

So, what would *you* call somebody who believes one thing but *advocates* another? *Hmmm?* A...liar?

Australia's victim disarmament

As a result of one mass murderer, the Australian government coercively bought up 640,381 personal firearms at a cost of more than $500 million dollars. This was supposed to have reduced crime. Did it?

Australia-wide, homicides are up 3.2%, assaults up 8.6%, and armed robberies are up 44%! In the state of Victoria, homicides with firearms are up 300%!

Australian politicians are at a loss to explain this rise in violent crime after such monumental effort and expense was successfully spent in *"ridding society of guns."* (It's real simple: The unarmed are defenseless. If you look like food, you'll be eaten. Nothing personal—it's a food-chain thing.)

England's victim disarmament

While the number of legal firearms owners in Britain has been declining due to a hostile gun control bureaucracy, crimes involving firearms increased 196% between 1981-1992.
— "Criminal Statistics England and Wales" 1992, p.34,65

Recently disarmed British are now suffering a dramatic rise in violent crimes, especially "hot" robberies of homes known to be *occupied.* Today, the only thing a British victim can do to their assailant is yell, *"Stop! Or, I'll yell 'Stop' again!"*

Chief Inspector Colin Greenwood of the West Yorkshire Constabulary spent six months at Oxford, studying restrictive gun laws in many countries. He concluded:

At first glance, it may seem odd or even perverse to suggest that statutory controls on the private ownership of firearms are irrelevant to the problem of armed crime; yet that is precisely what the evidence shows.

Armed crime and violent crime generally are products of ethnic and social factors unrelated to the availability of a particular type of weapon.

The number of firearms required to satisfy the crime market is small, and these are supplied no matter what controls are instituted. (Note: Please reread this sentence many times!)

*Controls have had serious effects on legitimate users of firearms, **but there is no case,** either in the history of this country or in the experience of other countries **in which controls can be shown to have restricted the flow of weapons to criminals, or in any way reduced crime.***

Other researchers agree:

Many advocates of gun control point to Great Britain as an example of a gun free paradise where violence and crime are rare. Well, there may be trouble in paradise. Our friends across the Atlantic did tighten their already strict gun laws, with the Firearms Act of 1997, making self defense with a firearm completely impossible for ordinary people. Obedient British subjects generally maintained a stiff upper lip as they surrendered their guns and their rights. **How much did crime drop as a result of this sacrifice? It did not drop at all.** *In fact, according to the local newspapers, England is being swept by a wave of crime,* **including plenty of gun crimes.**

This recent rise in crime is part of an upward trend that correlates well with the gradual tightening of gun control over the last several decades. The relationship between increasing gun control and rising crime is well documented in a scholarly 1999 report by Olsen and Kopel, "All the Way Down the Slippery Slope— Gun Prohibition in England". [http://www.goa-texas.org/kopel-2.htm] The traditional view of England as a low crime society has also been seriously damaged by the 1998 study titled, "Crime and Justice in the United States and in England and Wales", which is available from the U.S. Bureau of Justice Statistics. This report concludes that English crime rates in the period from 1981 to 1996 were actually higher than in the United States due to differences in the way crimes are reported.

The negative result from gun control laws should not surprise us. American cities have had similar counterproductive results whenever gun control has been implemented locally. Reports from Australia are similar. **It is no coincidence that crime typically goes up after a government enacts new gun restrictions.** *Several American researchers and criminologists have explored this effect. Whenever people give up their right to self defense in return for a promise of government protection, the results have been negative. No amount of social engineering will change this basic consequence of human nature.*

Unfortunately, the downward progression of gun control goes only one way. British subjects will never regain the basic human right to armed self defense.

Proponents of gun control in America have a lot of explaining to do. *Unfortunately, with the aid of their media allies, this new information will probably be ignored completely or brushed off with a few carefully chosen sound bites.* (mb@e-z.net)

— Dr. Michael Brown, "Results are in on British Gun Laws"

In recent months there have been a frightening number of shootings in Britain's major cities, despite new laws banning gun ownership after the Dunblane tragedy. Our investigation established that guns

are [still] *available through means open to any criminally minded individual.*
— *The Sunday Express,* 20 June 1999

Crime in America, however, has been *falling* for years, mostly thanks to an increasingly armed citizenry. Anti-self-defense groups such as HCI and VPC put themselves through incredible contortions of fact and statistics to deny this truth.

Think of it this way: Why don't the police get mugged? Is it perhaps because they are armed?

Britain's campaign against self-defense

Today, you can't even carry a *pocketknife* on your person in Britain. Dean Payne was arrested and jailed for two weeks. His crime? His job at a newspaper distributing plant necessitated a small pocketknife to cut bundling straps, and this "dangerous weapon" was found in his car during a "routine search." Though Payne was clearly nonviolent, the magistrate declared:

I have to view your conduct in light of the great public fear of people going around with knives...I consider the only proper punishment is one depriving you of your liberty.

In another case, an American woman tourist was convicted for carrying an "offensive" weapon after she defended herself against several attackers with a pen knife.

With gun ownership for self-protection now completely illegal (unless one works for the government), Britons have begun switching to other forms of protection. **The government considers this an intolerable affront.** *Having, through administrative interpretation, delegitimized gun ownership for self-defense, the British government has been able to outlaw a variety of defensive items. For example, non-lethal chemical defense sprays, such as Mace, are now illegal in Britain, as are electric stun devices.*

At the dawn of the twentieth century, Great Britain was the great exemplar of liberty to continental Europe, but the sun has set on Britain's tradition of civil liberty. The police search people's cars routinely. **Public hysteria against weapons is so extreme that working men are sentenced to jail for possessing the simple tools of their trade.** *The prosecutions of a newspaper delivery men who carries some knives, or a business executive who saved his own life, would likely have horrified the British gun control advocates of the early twentieth century. There is no evidence that most of these gun control advocates, who only wanted to keep firearms out of the hands of anti-government revolutionaries, ever wanted to make it illegal for tradesmen to carry tools,* **or for women to stab violent predators.** *The gun control advocates of 1905-1920 could distinguish a Communist with a rifle from a tourist with a pen-knife.*

But while the early weapons control advocates made such a distinction, they could not bind their successors to do so as well. Nor could the early weapons controllers understand the social changes that they would unleash when they gave the right to arms the first push down the slippery slope.

— *All The Way Down The Slippery Slope: Gun Prohibition in England and Some Lessons for Civil Liberties in America;* www.2ndlawlib.org/journals/okslip.html

The slippery slope of regulations and controls

Similarly, in the United States, few Congressmen who voted for the first federal controls on how Americans could consume medicine could have foreseen the "War on Drugs" that they were unleashing. Who could have predicted that a law requiring a prescription for morphine would pave the way for masked soldiers to break into a person's home because an anonymous tipster claimed that there were hemp plants, which were entirely legal in 1914, in the home? Who could have predicted that the Harrison Narcotics Act would pave the way for a Food and Drug Administration that would deny terminally-ill patients the medicine of their choice because the FDA had not satisfied itself that the medicine, available throughout Western Europe, was "safe and effective?" Who could have predicted that doctors would not be able to prescribe the most effective pain-killers, opiates, to the terminally ill who were suffering extreme pain? Who could have predicted that legislative action on opiate prescriptions would pave the way for a federal administrative agency to claim the right to outlaw speech about tobacco? Predictions of such events, had they been raised in 1914 on the floor of Congress, would have seemed absurd.

However, as too many Britons and citizens of the United States have learned the hard way in this century, **extreme consequences may flow from apparently small steps.** The [British] Firearms Act of 1920 was just a licensing law; the [U.S.] Harrison Narcotics Act was just a prescription system; **and the serpent only asked Eve to eat an apple.**

— *ibid*

Devon, will your proposed *"reasonable gun legislation"* be the end of it? No, it won't be—it never *is*. That's because victim disarmament doesn't reduce crime, it increases victims. American Liberty now sags under the weight of over 20,000 gun laws which have utterly failed to make a safer society. *"Gun control"* doesn't work, so its proponents always have to demand more.

Any structure is built one story at a time. Metaphorically, each *"We just need one more gun law and that will be it"* is never a ceiling. It is always the next "floor" for the next "story" in our prison—the prison *you* unwittingly help to build for us all. (Just so you know, *Americans* will not surrender their firearms to a Police State as did the craven British and Australians. We're on to your game, and we won't play along.)

The unreasonableness of waiting periods

It was clearly unreasonable to Bonnie Elmasri of Wisconsin. Her husband repeatedly threatened to kill her, so she got a restraining order. She tried to buy a gun for protection, but there was a 2-day waiting period. **The *next* day**, Bonnie and her two sons, aged 7 and 13, were murdered by her husband.

Waiting periods have cost other innocent lives, such as Deborah Randall of Virginia, and Igor Hutorsky of New York. (Would a gun have *definitely* saved all of their lives? Maybe not, but they certainly would have had an excellent *chance!*)

Devon, these innocent people had the right to *instantly* take possession of a gun if they felt threatened. We don't require waiting periods for fire extinguishers, do we? (Both *save* lives, and privately-owned guns save more lives than fire extinguishers.) Besides, nobody can document even *one* case of a waiting period saving a life.

"Since the Brady Bill, background checks have prevented hundreds of thousands of felons from getting guns!"

No, they *haven't*. If so, then why aren't those *"hundreds of thousands of felons"* in prison for having committed the felony of trying to buy a gun and getting caught by the NICBC system? (I mean, come on—can anybody *really* believe that so many felons are *so* stupid as to go through a *background* check?)

President Clinton claimed *"hundreds of thousands"* in a recent speech, only for his own Government Accounting Office to refute it the very next day. An initial NICBC denial *rarely* means that a *"prohibited possessor"* was caught trying to buy a gun. Such denials are mostly from faulty paperwork or computer data. 93% of them get sorted out and those sales are then approved. This comes from a recently released FBI report:

> *The FBI reports that while 27% of applications were delayed under NICS, 93% of the delays were eventually cleared. (This means a* **98.1% clearance rate**, *not counting successfully appealed denials.) Additionally, 26% of appealed denials were reversed. Clearly, only a small percentage (i.e., only 1.3%) of those who attempt to purchase firearms under the NICS system are prohibited possessors. There is nothing to prevent those persons from being tracked down,*

arrested and prosecuted for committing the multiple federal felonies that are inherent in their attempts to buy firearms from dealers.
— *American Guardian,* January 2000, p.22

The unreasonableness of mag restrictions

Again, let's be precise. *"Bullets"* do not go in *"clips."* A bullet is *part* of a "cartridge" or "round," which is held in a "magazine." Mags are usually detachable, but not always.

Since 13 September 1994 (the *"Crime Bill"* which Krauthammer admitted was never supposed to reduce crime), private citizens cannot purchase *new* mags holding more than 10 rounds. (+10 round mags existing before then were allowed to remain, but they have naturally risen in price to become unaffordable. The law transformed a $20 item into a $70-100 one.)

First of all, a maniac can kill with a single-shot gun. Magazine capacity, whether 6 or 10 or 17, has nothing to do with it. Further, it is no real hinderance for him to quickly change mags. So, mag capacity restrictions do not restrict the criminal. (And I'm not even addressing the point that many *other* types of weapons, *i.e.,* impact and edged, are available to criminals.)

Magazine capacity restrictions *do,* however, restrict a gunowner acting in self-defense. A sidearm is tool carried for defensive use in a lethal emergency. It must be handy, and it must be effective. By effective, I mean that it must fire a round sufficiently powerful to incapacitate an aggressor.

The magazine must have as *high* a capacity as possible, because nobody can forecast how many rounds it will take to stop one's Bad Guy. For these very reasons, the police now generally use pistols chambered for the .40S&W cartridge, held in 15 round mags. Street experience has shown that such is a good blend of cartridge power and mag capacity.

However, since 9/94 lawful private citizens have been *denied* their right to load their guns to full capacity. This reduces the time they to have defend themselves (the number of rounds equals time in the fight), thus jeopardizing their lives.

How would you like your mom's car gas tank unfairly restricted to just *59%* capacity, even though she had to drive through dangerous areas? Well, that's how *I* feel about *my* mom's 9mm Glock mags being restricted from 17 to 10 rounds.

"The only purpose...is to kill lots of people quickly."

Here's where you *really* didn't know your subject matter. First of all *"automatic guns"* (as you put it) have been highly regulated since 1934. There are about 190,000 privately-owned full-auto guns in the National Registry. (Only *one* has ever been used in a crime, in 66 years!) What you meant to say is *"semi-autos,"* which are not machine guns, but self-loading guns that fire one shot per trigger pull. Please get this straight.

Anyway, the argument against normal (*i.e.,* *"high"* to the gun-phobes) capacity magazines goes like this: In most defensive incidents, only a few rounds are fired, versus up to *dozens* by killers on a shooting spree. Therefore, the Good Guys don't really *need* *"high-capacity"* mags, which are something only mass murderers use. This is a specious argument which needs to be firmly refuted before it festers into "fact."

Statistically, there is some truth to such numbers, but we don't live in the *statistical* world. (Do you have 1.2 siblings?) Just because *"most"* defensive gunfights are won with only 2-4 rounds doesn't mean that *mine* will be, or that my *mom's* will be. Only 2-4 rounds will *not* prevail against: poor shot placement; multiple attackers; their use of bulletproof vests; or their strength, stamina, resolve, and damage resistance being heightened by drugs. Also, having only 2-4 rounds allows *no* margin for possible *misses*. Ask any cop or soldier who's been in a gunfight if knowing that they were down to just a few rounds wasn't a truly terrifying feeling.

A handgun round actually isn't all *that* powerful, which is why 80% of those shot by them survive. That's why it often takes *several* rounds to incapacitate an energized and dedicated assailant (regardless of what the movies portray).

"Oh, but you just said that a maniac can reload quickly and not be slowed down. Why can't she?"

A nut on a shooting spree is typically the *only* one armed, thus *he* is in control. *He* is not receiving fire; *he* is not in danger.

However, a woman being attacked is suffering very *different* dynamics. *She* is facing an attacker who is more physically powerful (so she can't risk getting near him). She is *reacting*, and thus behind the "power curve." And, she needs as many rounds as her sidearm can hold, *because reloading costs time* —and time is the one thing that she doesn't *have*.

That 10rd mag which Congress has forced on her since 1994 may be just *one* round short of what she needs to survive. If her gun runs dry *before* she has stopped the aggression, then she's in very *serious* trouble. Any cop will confirm that:

Gunfights are usually won by the *last* shot fired.

I'd rather *she*, versus her attacker, were able to fire that last shot because *her* gun had plenty of ammo. A 10 round mag may *not* be enough. **Why should *she* be *forced* to take *any* such chance when policemen and soldiers are *not*?**

Look, in any fight you are delivering kinetic energy to your attacker. The *delivery* vehicle of that energy is *irrelevant*, whether punches, a swung stick, thrown rocks, or fired bullets. (A gun is just a modern way of throwing a rock.) Do you want Congress mandating that you could swing only 2 punches or throw only 4 rocks at a rapist? Then *how* is it moral to discuss 10 versus 13 or 15 or 17 rounds in an innocent victim's gun?

Restricted-capacity mags jeopardize people's safety. That's why the police and military *don't* use them. By prohibiting the full mag capacity that is my mom's *right,* Congress has decreed that the lives of government employees are more valuable than hers, and that's just plain wicked.

Am I being melodramatic to keep using my mom as the example? No, because she has been assaulted and now carries a 9mm Glock with her, every day. If she ever comes up against a dirtbag who somehow thinks that her purse is worth more than her life, I want her to have what it takes to stay alive. (What assailant would let her dial 911 on her cell phone?)

Without an *instantly* accessible handgun and *sufficient* ammo capacity, my mom could get killed if she's ever in the wrong convenience store or gas station at the wrong time.

Licensing & registration are unreasonable

This is a complex issue made of up several sub-issues, so please bear with me.

What the Second Amendment protects

A well-regulated militia, being necessary to the security of a free state, the right of the people to keep and bear arms shall not be infringed.

The Second Amendment confirms and protects two things: ❶ The existence of an *individual* right, which ❷ can be exercised in a *collective* manner (to form militias, which are also protected elsewhere). The militia is made up of all able-bodied men 18-45 capable of bearing *personally owned* arms for national defense.

*...civilians primarily, soldiers on occasion...**bearing arms supplied by themselves** and of the kind in common use at the time...*
— *U.S. v. Miller,* 307 US 178-9 (1939)

Because the 2nd Amendment speaks of *two* things, victim disarmament advocates have chosen to give it solely the *collective* interpretation and ignore the individual right, which is incorrect. Court decisions such as 1990 *U.S. v. Verdugo-Urquidez* (110 S.Ct. 1056,1060) have confirmed that *"the People"* of the 2nd Amendment are the same *"the People"* of the 1st, 4th, 9th, and 10th Amendments. In a recent San Angelo, Texas case (*Emerson v. U.S.*), Federal District Court Judge Sam R. Cummings struck down a federal disarmament law because it violated the 2nd and 5th Amendments. (I *strongly* urge that you read this case. Go to www.gunowners.org/legal.htm and down to below the "Educational Links.")

If anybody persists claiming that the 2nd Amendment protects only the National Guard (which didn't even exist until before WWI), then know that they are grossly in error. Even *liberals* are now admitting that it protects individual rights:

> *The truth about the Second Amendment is something that liberals cannot bear to admit:* **The right wing is right.** *The amendment* **does** *confer an* **individual right to bear arms, and its very presence makes effective gun control in this country all but impossible.** *The individualist interpretation, the one that holds that Americans have a right to bear arms whether they're serving in an official state militia or not, has been more or less vindicated.*
> — Daniel Lazare, "Your Constitution is Killing You"
> *Harper's Magazine,* October 1999

"Rights are not absolute.
You can't yell 'Fire!' in a crowded theater."
Of course you can yell *"Fire!"* in a crowded theater—when there *is* a fire! Remember, don't take slogans at face value. They are too often merely *half-truths* at best.

Just because certain rights have been restricted, such as freedom of religion (*e.g.,* Mormon husbands may not have more than one wife), doesn't necessarily mean that such restrictions are morally right. If two adult women decide that they wish to be married to the same man, what *right* does anybody else have to prohibit them? Is polygamy unusual, or even distasteful, to many Americans? Certainly, but that's not the point. The law is supposed to forbid only theft, fraud, and the use of initiatory force—it is *not* to be a moral busybody in peoples' harmless lives.

Aside from that, the Founders considered our 2nd Amendment rights to be "more special" than our other rights:

Second Amendment rights may NOT be *"infringed"*

The right of the *people* to *"keep"* (own) and *"bear"* (carry) arms *"shall not be infringed."* To *"infringe"* means to encroach, trespass, or intrude *to any degree.* **There is no such thing as a *"reasonable"* 2nd Amendment infringement.** If there were, then the Founders would have written *"shall not be unreasonably infringed."* The Founders knew when and how to allow necessary reasonable intrusions on personal liberties (*e.g.,* the 4th Amendment forbidding *"unreasonable"* searches and seizures). **They pointedly refused to qualify the 2nd Amendment with *"unreasonable"* and that's *very* significant.**

The reason why our Founders used the unequivocable and absolute language of *"shall not be infringed"* is because they always wanted the citizens to be able to outgun the government in case in case it ever grew tyrannical (as governments always have throughout history). Government was always to remain our *servant.* What servant can be allowed to overpower its employer? While this notion may sound radical today, it remains highly relevant. They understand this in *Switzerland.*

The armed and nonviolent Swiss

Every Swiss man from 18 to 50 has a *fully* automatic *"assault rifle"* with 25-round mags, and ammo. His rifle is not stored at the army base (as here)—he gets to keep it *at home!* (And this is no cheapy rifle. The SIG550 would cost us over $8,000. *We* can't afford them because of federal anti-gun laws.) Some militiamen have even mortars, grenades, and bazookas. Yet, criminal use of these powerful weapons is almost unheard of. Also, the Swiss have no gun restrictions for sane non-felon adults. Buy what you want, and carry it where you want to.

You see, the Swiss government and the Swiss citizens *trust* each other, because they're are the *same people.* In fact, the Swiss often carry their rifles with them *to the polls on election day* to remind politicians of their God-given right to be armed. (In America, it is *illegal* to be armed at polling places!)

The president of Switzerland, for example, merely presides over an executive council, and goes to work on the public tram (with no bodyguard). In Switzerland, the people *are* the government, versus here where we suffer a professional political class ruling from on high what they see to be their "subjects."

When only the police have guns, it is a *Police State*
I've travelled to a few, and they're hellish. In the former East Germany, for example, the government was *so* suspicious of its own people that film developing (black and white only) could be sent to only *one* lab (a government lab, of course) in the entire country, and it took 6 weeks to get the pictures! Why so long? Because the government lab made *copies* of them all for their files! (How's *that* for scary?) When I told my East German friends about our 1-hour color labs all over town, they nearly fell out of their chairs in shock.

Government officials, even American ones, cannot be totally trusted with a *monopoly* of force. They cannot be trusted to possess *all*, or even most, of the guns. (An example of this was post-WWII Athens, Tennessee, when veterans returning home found Athens taken over by the local police. After many abuses, the vets had to run them out of town at gunpoint.)

One nation that recently *did* have all the guns was Nazi Germany. They used them to round up nearly every minority possible and slaughter them in camps. (I've twice been to the Auschwitz extermination camp in Poland, and the spirit of death still permeates that cursed ground over 50 years later.)

Conversely, the Nazis did not invade Switzerland because the whole country was (and is) a nation of militia riflemen. **Swiss Jews did *not* go to Auschwitz.** And that's the point: armed free people tend to *stay* free.

"*regulated*" does not mean "to be regulated by Congress"
The Bill of Rights was passed by Congress in 1789 and ratified by the States in 1791, so the Second Amendment is over 200 years old. When reading law (which includes the Constitution), one must employ the word meanings operating during the *authors'* day, not years or generations later during the *readers'*. This is why lawyers and judges own reprinted copies of *Webster's 1828 Dictionary,* for example. They must understand a law as the *creators* intended when it was written.

Many word meanings have changed in 211 years, and in even *less* time. (When I was a boy watching the *Flintstones* on black and white TV, the last line in the song was *"We'll have a gay old time!"* "Gay" used to mean lighthearted and carefree.)

Back in the 1790s, the word *"regulated"* meant "well-trained" or "well-disciplined." Until recently, when somebody *"kept their affairs regular"* it meant that they were organized and efficient. To use even a more modern example, anti-diarrhea product commercials market to those who aren't feeling "regular" (which is a polite way to put it).

By using the word *"regulated"* the Framers encouraged the many militia companies across the land to meet often, train effectively, use common caliber lead ball, etc. (They often trained once or twice a month on Sundays after church. The whole town would turn out to watch their militia drill.)

Only out of sheer scholastic laziness or political duplicity have certain modern legal pundits (including some judges, unfortunately) incorrectly interpreted *"regulated"* to justify the 1934 oppressive taxation of military-pattern full-auto firearms for civilian ownership. (Further manufacture/importation was banned in 1986.) It is the full-auto M16 that private citizens should constitutionally be training with as an effective militia force for the potential defense of the nation. What's worse, since 1994 no new *semi-auto* version of military-pattern rifles may be sold to the public.

It comes down to a matter of *trust*

By prohibiting such rifles to the average citizen (who composes the militia), the Government is not only violating the Constitution, but is admitting that it doesn't *trust* the People. (Historically, such has *always* been followed by that government swelling up to an utter tyranny.)

Britain is a good example of a country that doesn't trust its people. The Brits were mostly disarmed after WWI. Just a few years later, Nazi Germany had occupied all of Western Europe and was poised to invade England. In retreating from Dunkirk, the British soldiers had left most of their rifles behind. The British people could not contribute any, because they had no rifles either! They had no armed militia. So, in a panic, Prime Minister Churchill begged us to sell them 1,000,000 of our WWI surplus Enfield P17 rifles, which we did. We could do so because many (if not most) American men had their *own* rifles and shotguns. *We* had an armed militia, and we still do.

But today, Congress (with presidential support) is working to disarm the American people, thus disarming the constitutional militia. They are doing this for the *sole* reason that they are afraid of future Americans having no choice but to remove them from power just like we did to the 1770's British.

What's in it for *government* if crime is eradicated?

I'm going to tell you something that will probably shock you: Most governments don't *care* all that much about *really* reducing crime. If the crime rates *really* dropped, then *tens of thousands* of policemen, prosecutors, judges, and prison guards would have to look for other work, wouldn't they? Taxes would have to be *reduced*. **What government in history *ever* voluntarily downsized?** None. They *can't*. It goes against government's very *nature*, which is to *grow*.

Government *could* eliminate probably 70+% of violent crime in just 5 years by promoting an armed citizenry and by giving *real* prison terms for violent offenders. They won't do this, because it would *work*. I'm not saying that politicians actually *desire* people to suffer from rape, robbery, and murder. (They could never internalize such a possible truth.) But, despite all the evidence to the contrary, they have *convinced* themselves that only the *police* should have guns.

By "evidence" I offer Kennesaw, Georgia, which in 1989 passed a law that mandated all homeowners to have a gun in their house. Burglaries dropped by *89%*. (Conversely, Morton Grove, Illinois *banned* handguns and crimes of all sort went *up!*) Your victim disarmament colleagues won't tell you about that.

They also won't tell that in Florida, when 2,500 women were instructed in the defensive use of handguns in a highly publicized program by the Orlando Police Department, rapes decreased the following year by *88%!*

They won't tell you that recently disarmed Australia and Britain now have higher rates of burglary than we do, and people were home nearly half the time when those burglaries were committed! In America, it is less than 13%, because of the burglars' fear of homeowners' firearms.

Finally, your victim disarmament colleagues won't admit to you that in *every* state that has passed *"shall issue"* concealed carry permit bills, violent crimes have dropped by about a *third* (which is much more than the other states).

The Government *knows* all this, but would rather *deny* you the right to privately and discreetly arm yourself. Instead, all sorts of "feel good" victim disarmament measures are trotted out to be embraced by sincere, but uncomprehending, voters.

> *For every thousand hacking at the branches of evil, only one is hacking at the roots.*
> — Emerson

> *The greatest dangers to liberty lurk in the insidious encroachment by men of zeal, **well-meaning but without understanding**.*
> — Supreme Court Justice Louis Brandeis

The Wild West

You wrote that Littleton was not the Wild West. You're right. The Wild West was *safer.* 1880 Western U.S.A. had an average per capita murder rate of under 2 per 100,000. Even *before* Columbine, Littleton's was higher than that. As the late science-fiction author Robert A. Heinlein once wrote:

An armed society is a polite society.

The "Wild West" certainly had its wild *moments,* but it was as civilized as rural America is today. The "Wild" image is false.

The *real* "Wild West" is...Washington, D.C.!

When you visited Washington, D.C., did you know that you were in our nation's *Murder* Capital? Instead of a Wild West murder rate of only 2 per 100,000 people, D.C.'s is *78* per 100,000! But how can that *be* when Washington, D.C. has a total ban on privately-owned handguns?

"Because criminals get them from neighboring Virginia!"

Virginians *can* own handguns, that's right. And, yes, criminals often *do* get their illegal guns from Virginia and other neighboring or nearby states.

But here's what I can't figure out: If guns cause crime, or if easy criminal access to guns causes crime, **then why doesn't *Virginia* suffer a murder rate like Washington, D.C.'s? Why is Virginia's murder rate only *20%* of D.C.'s?**

Criminals in both places can get guns. In Washington, D.C., however, law-abiding citizens *cannot* get guns. Thus, they can't protect themselves, so they *much* more often get murdered. Simple, isn't it?

Guns don't cause crime; criminals do. And, as opportunists, criminals flourish where people are typically *unarmed.*

The futility of gun registration for reducing crime

As far as I've heard, the people who sold Eric and Dylan those guns bought them legally. Where they *broke* the law was by selling them to minors. They broke a federal law which *already* existed! What's to stop people from breaking laws—making such *illegal?* I'm being facetious to make a point: Gun laws did not stop the illegal transfer to Eric and Dylan. More gun laws would not have, either. Eric's and Dylan's gun suppliers had originally bought those guns from *licensed* dealers in *regulated* transactions. Outlawing unregulated *private* sales would not have prevented Eric's and Dylan's actions.

Private sales at gun shows are *not* the problem!

Here's something *else* your victim disarmament colleagues won't tell you: according Clinton's own 12/97 National Institute of Justice study, *only 2%* of criminally-used guns came from gun shows, yet he falsely accused the shows as being *"illegal arms bazaars for criminals."* (Nice catchphrase.)

Devon, I've been to literally *dozens* of gun shows throughout my life. Never *once* have I ever observed (or even heard about) an illegal transaction. In fact, quite the contrary.

One time, I saw three obvious gang members going to all the private-sale tables (they usually make up only 10-20% of any show), trying to buy a gun (which was their right, unless they were one of the *"prohibited possessors"* such as felon, fugitive, etc.) **Nobody would sell them anything!** Not a gun, not a holster—*nothing!* They left in frustration, cursing. This sort of thing was not the exception, it is the rule. Gun show patrons, buyers and sellers, are overwhelmingly honest folks. I've never met *anybody* who would sell to a criminal.

Felons are not required to register their guns!

Since felons are prohibited from owning guns, to force their registration would be compelled self-testimony, which is an unconstitutional violation of the 5th Amendment. The Supreme Court ruled so in *Haynes v. U.S.* The same holds true for licensing; felons can't be forced to apply for one, and they can't be prosecuted for not having one.

There you have it, gun registration and licensing apply only to the *law-abiding*. But, if they're law-abiding, what's the *point* of forcing *them* to register their guns or suffer licensing? I'll explain that mystery in just a second.

Laws do not prevent *any* serious crimes, because...

...serious criminals do not obey laws in the first place! Every nasty criminal activity possible is *already* prohibited by law, so there's really no further way to legislatively affect the criminal. (Some psychiatrists explain insanity this way: *repeating* an action over and over again with the expectation of *different* results. Restrictive laws relating to peaceful American gunowners have *never* reduced crime, yet with each new law a *"different result"* of crime reduction is anticipated! Sounds crazy to me!)

Besides, it is criminals' *nature* **to** *be* **lawless.** No legislation can suspend or eradicate something's very *nature*.

Could a law successfully make water dry, or suspend gravity? Then why do legislators continually pass laws and expect criminals to *obey* them? They *don't* expect obedience from the criminals. The only people who would possibly abide by new gun laws are...*law-abiding* people. But why regulate *them* further when they were never a criminal problem to begin with? So, *why* do legislators still do it?

Because after some point, laws are not written to catch *existing* criminals, but to manufacture *new* ones. Novelist Ayn Rand presciently observed this 43 years ago in *Atlas Shrugged*. Here's a quote from a government official speaking to a businessman:

> *Did you really think that we want those laws to be observed? ...There's no way to rule innocent men. The only power any government has is in the power to crack down on criminals. **Well, when there aren't enough criminals, one makes them.** One declares so many things to be a crime that it becomes impossible for men to live without breaking laws. **Who wants a nation of law-abiding citizens? What's there in that for anyone?***

Making *new* "criminals" out of innocent, honest people—*that's* the goal of gun control legislation. The Government knows that most gunowners will *not* register their guns (because they'll simply be confiscated later, once the lists have been compiled), so that will justify Government's future "War On Guns."

Regulating private sales is a hidden form of registration

The gun control politicians want to unconstitutionally regulate private sales for the *registration* value. There are over 240,000,000 guns in the hands of 75,000,000 Americans, and the Government has no idea who or where more than about 40% of them are. This is very unsettling to those in Washington. All that hysteria about *"unregulated sales at gun shows"* stems from Government's vested interest in registering *all* guns, so that citizens may eventually be disarmed.

Registration today *always* leads to confiscation later

"We're only asking for registration because we want to be able to trace a stolen gun back to its rightful owner," they claim. That's what the City of New York told *its* residents years ago. That's what Great Britain and Australia told *their* citizens years ago. And in all those places, the government went back on its word and banned guns. Sometimes they (partially) reimbursed the owners, sometimes not. Naturally, compliance has not been 100%, so the government threatens the holdouts with

4 years in prison and $100,000 fines. It then uses the registration lists to go house-to-house and forcibly steal private property. The guns then went to the smelters, leaving the people defenseless against the new violent crimes that predictably followed. (I have friends there, so I get firsthand reports.)

Historically, governments are the worst murderers

Honest, peaceable folks don't want to register their guns, because they properly do not trust "their" government. And generally, they shouldn't. Not counting wars, in the 20th Century alone, governments have murdered 56 *million* people. (Including wars, the total is *170* million.) A list of only the major actions (*e.g.,* Stalin's starvation of Ukrainian farmers, the Communist Chinese massacres and genocides) would literally fill an entire page! Governments have killed *far* more people than criminals ever have.

Government is the most dangerous threat to human life

If you study the many genocides of the 20th Century, *every one of them* was preceded by gun registration and confiscation. (Visit www.jpfo.org for the full story on this.) Think of it this way: What do governments all over the world apparently have *planned* for people that first requires them to be disarmed? The prospect is very frightening to many of us.

Armed citizens do not allow themselves to thrown out of their homes because they're black or Jewish. *Armed* citizens do not allowed their children to be dragged away for political *"reeducation."* *Armed* citizens do not allow themselves to be herded into cattle cars for the death camps.

"This is America! That can't happen here!"

Because enough Americans believe that is precisely *why* it *can* happen here.

It's *already* happening here. Devon, when you were 10 years old, *your* federal government gassed, burned, bombed, and machine-gunned to death *dozens* of helpless men, women, children, and *babies* huddling together terrified in their own homestead church. This was recently proven using the Government's *own* videotapes and by its *own* agents and employees (who came forward to tell what happened). It took years to prove this because the FBI concealed and destroyed crucial evidence, and only a recent court order has forced them to release some of it.

A documentary film of the massacre was made in 1997. *Waco: The Rules of Engagement* was nominated for an Academy Award. (To order call 800-466-6868.)

A newer and even more compelling documentary is called *Waco: A New Revelation*. (National media people got to see it in Washington, D.C. at a special screening. After watching it, many of them left in tears. These hardened reporters didn't have to *"look devasted"*—they were! *That's* how powerful this film is!) Your parents can order this from MGA Films in Ft. Collins at 877-511-4848 (www.waco-anewrevelation.com).

The murders at Waco do not excuse the Oklahoma City bombing, but they *do* shed light on the outrage felt by McVeigh and Nichols. If only for that reason alone, the *Waco* tapes are required viewing for every American, especially the youth.

Raising the age from 18 to 21 is unreasonable

You asserted, *"If you're not responsible enough to drink alcohol, you're not responsible enough to buy a gun."*

The reason why adults under the age of 21 cannot buy alcohol in Colorado is *not* because they're *"not responsible enough"*—it's because a sufficient number of legislators in Denver *voted* it so. And there's a difference! (Politicians have decreed all *sorts* of nonsense: that the world was flat, and that black people could be enslaved. What makes you think their opinion on a proper *drinking age* has automatic validity?) The day any upcoming generation takes the actions of *politicians* as credible evidence of truth or reality is a day of mourning. Perhaps it has been an impressive experience for you to have met national politicians (including the president), but hang around with them long enough and the awe will wear off, believe me.

Personally, I favor *lowering* the drinking age to 18. If 18 year olds are old enough to enter into binding contracts, vote, and die for their country, then denying them the right to drink seems hypocritical, at best. (If, however, an *individual* proves to be irresponsible with alcohol and causes damage or injury, then obviously there should be proper consequences.)

Any year of demarcation seems arbitrary to me. I know of "children" who are in their *30*s, and "adults" (*i.e.*, fully self-sustaining) who are only 17. Probably the fairest *conceptual* thing is to treat individuals as adults when they *behave* as adults in all respects (*e.g.*, independence, abiding by contracts, etc.).

Forbidding private gun sales is unreasonable

*The whole aim of practical politics is to keep the populace alarmed (and hence clamorous to be led to safety) by menacing it with an endless series of hobgoblins, **all of them imaginary.***
— H.L. Mencken

First of all, please understand that the governments (State and federal) have elbowed their regulatory way into an individual *right* protected under the Constitution. They have also convinced some of the population that such is not only constitutionally permissible, but socially necessary (even though less than 2% of criminals' guns come from gun shows).

As I explained earlier, it is the constitutional *right* of any sane, nonfelon adult to buy, sell, or trade firearms *without* government permission or delay. When a free people allow the licensing of their rights, their Liberty is in trouble. How would *you* have felt if you had been required to submit your *Newsweek* essay to a federal agency for approval before it could be published? (In many countries, such would have been mandatory.)

"70 to 80% of Americans support reasonable gun legislation"

No, they don't. There are about 170 million American adults and they haven't all been asked. A *sample* of them were polled, and there's a *huge* difference. A sample of the population is not the same as the population itself.

Your *own* figures are indistinct

Which is it, Devon, 70% or 80%? Is it 75%? 74.8% SAFE founder John Head claims that it's *90%*! (Both of you wrong.)

Polls are nearly *always* inaccurate and misleading

Poll results are purposely skewed dozens of ways (*e.g.,* picking a particular ZIP code, or city, or State). For example, those living in the upper East side of NYC feel differently about guns than those living in the Wyoming countryside.

How questions are *worded* can shift up to 40 percentage points from one side of an issue to another. For example, here are just five different ways to poll on new gun laws:

Would you support more victim disarmament, even though many policemen have found the existing ones ineffective in reducing crime?

Would you support more victim disarmament, even though many policemen have found the existing ones not only ineffective in reducing crime, but endangering innocent people by unconstitutionally infringing on their right to defend themselves against assailants?

Would you support more gun controls?

Would you support reasonable gun controls for safer schools?

Would you support reasonable gun controls for safer schools, happy kids, a strong economy, and sunny weather?

I trust I make my point. The last questions don't ask if you support the alleged *means* to the goal; what they *really* do is ask if you support the *goal* (who wouldn't want safer schools?) and *then* link the "means" *to* the goal.

Moral: Polls are a seriously tricky business. I would not recommend using them to try to prove your point. (*I* haven't.)

Even still, just because 70-80% of people favor something doesn't make it *right,* or even lawful

Democracy is *not* supposed to be about two wolves and a sheep deciding on what's for dinner. But that's what tends to happen over time. The majority devours the minority. That's why the Founding Fathers avoided creating a democracy, and chose instead a representative republic.

Not all laws are equal

There are two kinds of crimes:

mala in se	wrongs evil in themselves (*e.g.,* murder, rape)
mala prohibita	wrongs prohibited (*e.g.,* speeding on the highway)

The Ten Commandments prohibit mostly *mala in se* crimes. **All *mala in se* crimes have *long* since been outlawed.** What has been keeping lawmakers busy for generations is creating *mala prohibita.* Gun laws merely *decree* things and activities (which are *not* evil in themselves) to be "crimes." See the difference? Owning a post-1994 *"assault weapon"* or an unregistered machine gun are clearly *mala prohibita.*

People don't obey *mala prohibita* (such as speeding on the highway) out of guilt; they obey out of *fear.* So, instead of laws dealing only with *mala in se* and thus enjoying the moral high ground, modern regulations (especially the gun regs) are evil interferences of harmless activities, enforced by thugs. A very wise Roman (Tacitus) once wrote:

The more numerous the laws, the more corrupt the State.

I'd rather *respect* my Government than fear it. How about you?

What's "legal" is not necessarily *right*
What's right is very often "illegal"

Adolf Hitler gained office in 1933 through an honestly won election. He legally used his emergency powers to constitutionally dispense with the legislature. Then he set up a police state. The Nazi's quickly enacted restrictive gun registration:

This year will go down in history. **For the first time, a civilized nation has full gun registration.** *Our streets will be safer, our police more efficient, and the world will follow our lead in the future.*

— attributed to Adolf Hitler, 1935

As "good, law-abiding Germans," they complied. And, as we all know, Nazi police *did* become *"more efficient."* They became highly *"efficient"* in separating Jews and many other minorities from society, and packing them into ghettos. These people were then rounded up at gunpoint, stuffed into cattle cars for distant death camps in Poland, and systematically murdered.

This was all done *according to German law and the popular support of at least 70% of the people.* **But was it *right*?**

Just a few generations ago, over 50% of Americans sincerely believed that Africans were subhumans fit for slavery. The Congress, the President, and the Supreme Court agreed. **But was it *right*?**

No, *none* of it was right. And neither is *"reasonable gun legislation."* Here's why:

Individual rights are *not* subject to *collective* permission.

When they become so, that society exchanges a rule of *law* for a rule of *men,* and then it's *finished.* While we have rejected the folly of one man (a king) ruling many, we have forgotten ancient Greece's folly of many (a democratic majority) ruling the few, or the one. Evil is evil, whether enforced by one despot (monarchy) or by a *multitude* of despots (democracy).

Political fairness is not achieved by 51% outvoting the other 49%. It is achieved by keeping law at the State and county levels, thus allowing differing philosophies to *each* have their *own* haven. I don't want to rule *other* folks, and I don't want them to rule *me. That* used to be America.

Nazi victim disarmament laws were copied *here* in 1968!

If what I'm about to share with you doesn't totally shock you, then you might have to check your pulse.

Holocaust survivor Jay Simkin got a copy of the entire text of the Nazi gun laws of 1938, translated it, and reprinted it side by side with our *"Gun Control Act"* of 1968. **Its organization and phraseology were nearly *identical!*** "Thanks" to Senator Dodd, our Congress in 1968 used Nazi laws, even down to that insidious (and constitutionally irrelevant) concept of requiring guns to have a *"legitimate sporting purpose."*

For example, the Nazi Weapons Law (18 March 1938; § 25(1)) forbade the manufacture and importation of firearms which: *"fold-down, break-down, are collapsible, or are dismantled—beyond the common limits of hunting activities..."*

Similarly, our *"Gun Control Act"* of 1968 (at 18 USC § 925(d)(3)) permits the importation of firearms only if they are *"of a type...generally recognized particularly suitable for or readily adaptable to sporting purposes."* Further, our *"Crime Bill"* of 1994 forbids the manufacture and importation of semiauto rifles and shotguns with a *"folding or telescoping stock."*

Sound familiar?

The Nazi Weapons Law (§§ 15, 25, 26) vested the power to decide the fitness of weapons (and their owners) in the unelected bureaucracy and the Nazi courts.

The *"Gun Control Act"* of 1968 (at 18 USC § 925(d)) also purports to vest the power to determine whether a firearm has a *"sporting purpose"* in the Secretary of Treasury, in the unelected BATF bureaucracy, and in the federal courts.

Sound familiar?

Don't believe *me* on this. Get Simkin's book *Gateway to Tyranny* from the Jews for the Preservation of Firearms Ownership (www.jpfo.org; 800-869-1884). If you tell them that you're a Columbine student and *"gun control"* activist, they'll probably even *donate* one to you for your research. Show it to SAFE founder John Head. He's an attorney; I'd like to see him try to explain away all this as a "coincidence."

The *National Instant Criminal Background Check System*

In a 15 May 1998 letter to the BATF regarding the proposed NICBC system, Aaron Zelman of the Jews for the Preservation of Firearms Ownership (www.jpfo.org) wrote:

> *It is an undisputed fact that the overwhelming majority of firearms owners are not violent criminals or firearms abusers. The proposed de facto national registration plan therefore is largely irrelevant to crime detection or prevention. **The plan must have some other purpose.** The effects of the national "instant check" system are:*

❶ *to register nationally as many firearms owners as possible without their knowing assent,*

❷ *to accustom Americans to federal government intrusion into their minute daily affairs,*

❸ *to stigmatize firearms as dangers to society requiring federal control,*

❹ *to stigmatize firearms owners as criminal suspects needing federal monitoring and control,*

❺ *to serve as an intermediate step toward total federal control of firearms ownership, and*

❻ *to pave the way for future firearms confiscation and/or future persecution of firearms owners.*

The national "instant check" regulations proposed by the BATF eerily follow the path of Nazi Germany. In his scholarly account of how the Nazi German government accomplished the Holocaust, Richard Lawrence Miller identified the five step process of genocide:

The 5-step process of genocide
From *Nazi Justiz: Law of the Holocaust,* p.3:

❶   Identification/registration of targeted group as public menace.
❷   Ostracism of the targeted persons.
❸   Confiscation of property of the targeted persons.
❹   Geographical concentration of the targeted persons.
❺   Annihilation of the targeted persons.

"Gun control" historically leads to genocide
Simkin also wrote a second book called *Lethal Laws* which shows that all modern genocides were preceded by gun bans. As he once said, *"How is it physically possible that so many people could be murdered in a so short a time by a mere handful of oppressors?* ***The answer is gun control. You cannot have a genocide without having gun control.***"

Simkin sent copies to the President and *every* Congressmen, Senator, and Supreme Court Justice. Silence from all but a few of those 545 government "leaders." Simkin also sent the evidence to the major media. (They ignored it. They *had* to.)

Now do you understand why gunowners get pretty upset when talk of more *"reasonable gun legislation"* is casually mentioned? *They* know the historical end result of such is *death.*

Schindler armed his Jews after Germany's surrender
The movie *Schindler's List* left out a crucial part of the true story: After his factory floor speech upon Germany's sur-

render, Oskar Schindler distributed firearms to his former workers! Director Steven Spielberg, no friend of our right to self-defense, pointedly chose *not* to dramatize this! (When asked why he supported *"gun control"* even though he owns many machine guns, Spielberg replied, *"That's for them!"*)

The Constitution

Because of Article V, the Constitution is *very* difficult to change, for a good reason. Since just 13 States (regardless of size) can prevent the adoption of *any* amendment, it is expressly *un*democratic. This was so designed on *purpose*. We were to have the benefit of honest and moral law for the *ages,* which *transcended* changing popular opinion and the mood of the day. Only when 38 of the 50 States feel strongly enough on an issue, is the Constitution (including the 2nd Amendment) allowed to be amended.

Congress and the President are illegally trying to amend, if not abolish, part of the Constitution through legislation.

Gun violence and children

Yes, I've also read that 13 young people die every day in this country from gun violence. But *why*? *Who* are they? First of all, that statistic has been enlarged by including young *adults* up to *19* years of age. When the Jews for the Preservation for Firearms Ownership challenged the figure, Sarah Brady of HCI lowered it to 11.56. (Visit www.jpfo.org/alert, 6 March 2000, for the full story.)

Second, most of the deaths are from suicides and gang-related murders. The *manner* of death (from a gun) is incidental to the *real* issues of suicides and gang violence.

Tragedies such as Columbine are the ultra-rare exception, but even still, the guns involved are *incidental.* If they are not, then why is nobody demanding that propane bottles like the ones which Eric and Dylan used be banned for everyone?

Kids-with-guns are *not* the problem. There have *always* been guns in schools, such as rifle teams, hunting safety classes, ROTC, and .30-30 Winchesters in high-schoolers' pickups.

Guns are not at fault; guns are simply being misused. **The problem is *bad* kids with guns.** We're seeing a dramatic increase in the number and viciousness of troubled kids. What's *creating* all these highly disturbed youths who are dousing sleeping parents with gasoline, shoving elderly people down stairs, and shooting up their high schools in a blaze of suicide?

Columbine does not justify further gun restrictions

If I or any other gunowner had been in a position to stop Eric and Dylan, we would have tried, just like Assistant Principal Joel Myrick did in Pearl, Mississippi. But the fact that too *few* honest folks are daily armed does not justify insisting on their *further* disarmament. Because Eric and Dylan chose to criminally use firearms, why are America's 75,000,000 *lawful* gunowners being unfairly linked to this tragedy?

The warning signals were there...

Why did two obviously disturbed and seethingly angry boys get no help in time? Dylan was your *friend.* Didn't you at least *sense* that he was so troubled? Did you think that Eric was a healthy friend for Dylan? If not, did you ever *tell* him?

As you wrote, *"But someone had to make monsters out of them."* Well, just who *did*, and how can we prevent them from making more? Parents are (or at least *should* be) responsible for the diets (body, mind, and spirit) of their kids. On this point, I'm *very* curious why nobody is asking:

Why *didn't* the Harris and Klebold families *vigorously* prevent their own son's *poisonous* interests, such as extremely violent video games and websites?

Why is nearly every commentator on Columbine *"hacking at the branches of evil"* and leaving the roots untouched?

"Gun control" helps massacres to succeed

Analyzing history's mass murders for common criteria has proven very illuminating. There is a formula, and it is nearly 100% accurate. It is this:

> Person with evil intent to kill many people
> + Any deadly weapon
> + Guarantee that the intended victims can't fight back
> + Expectation that the police won't prevent the killing
> = **Mass murder**

The formula "worked" in Littleton, it worked on 2 November 1999 in Hawaii at the Xerox building—it has worked nearly every time it has been tried. The *"gun free school zones"* are places where mass murderers *know* they won't be resisted. (Conversely, they *don't* go to gun shows, police stations, or military bases—*do* they?) Disarming ordinary Americans isn't the answer—it is the *problem!* (Declaw your housecat and see how long she lasts in the wild.)

THE RISK OF MORE GUN CONTROL

That the United States was born out of an armed rebellion fueled, in large part, by resentment over excessive taxation is a bit of history that ***makes statists extremely uncomfortable.*** *It should, therefore, come as no surprise that congressmen and senators who dream of an ever-expanding welfare state consistently vote to restrict individual gun ownership or even ban the production of certain classes of firearms.*

As we enter the 21st Century, rates of taxation have reached oppressive levels. To statists (who seek only to expand government power), growing resentment on the part of people who work, produce wealth, and pay oppressive taxes presents a serious threat. Disarming ordinary Americans who will be called upon to pay ever higher taxes is seen by them as necessary to minimize that threat.

— Howard J. Fezell, Esq., "Early American 'Gun Control'"
www.2ndamendment.net/2amd8.html

Have you or anybody else at SAFE *really* analyzed what the end results of your *"reasonable gun legislation"* might be? Has anybody actually done the "math" on all this?

As I said, there are about 240,000,000 guns in the hands of 75,000,000 Americans (nearly 1 in 2 adults, and more than the populations of Britain or France). If the Second Amendment ever *were* somehow repealed through Article V (or explicitly ignored by Congress and the President), it would cause Civil War 2, with many States seceding—I kid you not.

Further, even if it *were* somehow possible (which it's not) to eliminate *99%* of all lawfully-owned guns (and neutralize 99% of the gunowners), that would still leave *2,400,000* guns in the hands of 750,000 *very* upset citizens.

Do you for one moment believe that those 750,000 armed people would simply *lay down*? No, they would proceed to fight and win a *Second* American Revolution. (Sure, the Government has tanks and jet aircraft. So did the Soviet Union when it invaded Afghanistan, and look what happened to them. They got waxed by untrained peasants with bolt-action rifles.)

Armed Americans will *stay* armed—*period.* The gun haters are banking on the *docile cooperation* of gunowners, and they're dreaming. It *won't* happen. **What they don't appreciate is that gunowners enjoy an actual *culture*.** The Government *could* successfully outlaw, for example, the wearing of orange shirts, because there's no culture involved (much less a deeply entrenched one). *Cultures,* however, do *not* die easily— especially when they can and will defend themselves.

Devon, you must understand how very seriously *tens of millions* of Americans view their God-given right to self-protection from criminals and tyrannical government. They have been putting up with your so-called *"reasonable gun legislation"* for as long as your grandparents have been alive, and they are *not* going along with any *more* of it.

They are tired of hearing from professional media liars (*e.g.,* Dan Rather, 2 August 1999 *CBS Evening News*) that the Second Amendment does not protect an *individual* right, when these same hypocrites have no problem owning and using guns *themselves* (*e.g.,* with his semi-auto Browning shotgun, Dan Rather scared away burglars from his home on 8 April 1972).

American gunowners have been squeezed for two generations, and we've arrived at the irreducible core. There will be no more *"compromises."* They've been doing that since *1934.*

They are sick and tired of excessive taxes, crushing and contradictory regulations, and a haughty, unaccountable Government which scoffs at both the Constitution and its *own* laws. Trying to take away their guns *will* be the last straw. My advice is to leave the 75,000,000 law-abiding American gunowners *alone.* They are a sleeping giant that you don't want to awaken.

They will *never* meekly disarm as the Brits and Australians have, and as the Canadians are about to. Never. (Oh, *some* might disarm, but not enough. Not 99%—not even 50%.)

It's *your* choice

He who will not reason is a bigot; he who cannot is fool; and he who dares not is a slave.
 — William Drummond

So, Devon, how *far* do you want to push for more victim disarmament which does *not* affect criminals, costs *innocent* people their lives, is *unconstitutional*, and increasingly *alienates* 75,000,000 peaceable but armed citizens from the Government?

Further 2nd Amendment violations are a *big* mistake. They may be the biggest mistake a foolish America ever commits. Do you *really* want that on your conscience?

There's a book I highly recommend (but not to young people because it's R-rated) called *Unintended Consequences* by John Ross. I can summarize its 861 pages for you: Quit squeezing something that's not even a pimple (though you *think* it is), or else it will soon turn into a very messy *boil.*

One book I *can* recommend to you is *The Mitzvah.* It's a tiny paperback and easy to read. Get it from www.jpfo.org.

Think this through some more—a *lot* more

Although 17 years of age is *young* enough to "know every-thing," it is not *old* enough to know everything. There's a very fine saying, *"A little knowledge is a dangerous thing."* People with *no* knowledge don't act or express opinions because they can't. People with a *little* knowledge are suddenly imbued with huge moral convictions, usually ill-founded.

Devon, please consider *all* sides to the gun issue before you commit yourself to any train of thought (much less, a course of action). I ask this of you, not only in *my* interests, but in yours. Life is too short to be led through the nose by catch-phrases and false alternative arguments, and you're barely old enough to know that it's happening to you. But it is.

Finally, please keep this in mind...

I can't begin to explain to any high-schooler how much they will change over their next 10 years. (I'm sure that any parent would agree with me!) The younger one is, the more one should keep complex issues "on a shelf" for lots of pondering.

Don't be insulted by this. I mean no insult, as this letter was written with respect and courtesy. I know that you take your feelings on guns very seriously, but given that you are but 6 years out of the 6th grade and still supported by your parents, I (who have been an adult longer than you have been alive) nec-essarily have a different perspective.

O.K., I'm done writing

Thank you for reading my letter. I didn't plan on it being so long, but I wanted to clearly and thoroughly make my points. I spent quite literally an entire day (and a beautiful sunny one, at that!) writing to you, and that's a lot of valuable time for a professional author. I mention this not to impress you with how important I think I am, but how important I think *you* are.

If you and your family have never attended a gun show to see what all the (needless) fuss is about, I will be happy to be your guide. (Denver has a show nearly every month.) You all would meet some really nice people, and they would no doubt like to personally express their sadness at Littleton's tragedy, and reassure you of the fact that they do everything they can to prevent criminals from getting guns.

Further, if you and your family have never shot a gun be-fore, I offer to take you all to the range for an afternoon to show you the basics of safety and handling. (There's a good chance that you'd even find it fun!) I've taught dozens of people over the years, and am regarded as a very good instructor. (Even if one chooses not to own a gun, one should still know how to safely handle and unload them.)

Was my letter at least more interesting than your homework? (If so, then I accomplished *something*!)

I hope that you will give me the courtesy of a full reply.

Very truly yours,

Kenneth W. Royce

P.S. I've always liked this quote:

> *The mind will be governed. If it finds no government within it will embrace whatever government offers itself from without* (by others).
> — R. Mitchell, *The Underground Grammarian*

I wish you a long and happy life of good *self*-government.

THE *REAL* GOAL
OF *"GUN CONTROL"*

The evils of tyranny are rarely seen but by him who resists it.
— John Hay, *Castilian Days II* (1872)

In case you've fallen for the lie that *"just one more law is needed, and then everything will be fine,"* here are a few quotes of theirs to set you straight:

> We're going to have to take one step at a time, and the first step is necessarily—given the political realities—going to be very modest. Of course, it's true that politicians will then go home and say, "This is a great law. The problem is solved." And it's also true that such statements will tend to defuse the gun-control issue for a time. So then we'll have to start working again to strengthen that law, and then again to strengthen the next law, and maybe again and again. Right now, though, we'd be satisfied not with half a loaf but with a slice. **Our ultimate goal—total control of handguns in the United States—is going to take time.** My estimate is from seven to ten years. (BTP Note: They're a little behind schedule!)
> **The first problem is to slow down the number of handguns produced and sold in this country.** (BTP Note: This is happening now, with city lawsuits against the domestic gun manufacturers.) **The second problem is to get handguns registered.** (BTP Note: The first phase of this is the NICBC system which is quietly, though illegally, registering all new owners of any firearm.) The final problem is to make possession of all handguns and all handgun ammunition—except for the military, police, licensed security guards, licensed sporting clubs, and licensed gun collectors— totally illegal.
> — Nelson "Pete" Shields,
> Handgun Control Inc. Founder and President
> *New Yorker*, 26 July 1976, p. 58

The prohibitionists actually *believe* that in order for our society to become "civilized" (*i.e.,* like Britain and Canada), peaceable citizens must first be disarmed. But what about the 2nd Amendment? Doesn't it explicitly protect the individual's right to keep (*i.e.,* own) and bear (*i.e.,* carry) arms. Yes, it *does* and the liberals now *know* it:

> *The truth about the Second Amendment is something that liberals cannot bear to admit:* **The right wing is right. The amendment does confer an individual right to bear arms, and its very presence makes effective gun control in this country all but impossible.** *The individualist interpretation, the one that holds that Americans have a right to bear arms whether they're serving in an official state militia or not,* **has been more or less vindicated.**
>
> *So why must we subordinate ourselves to a 208-year old law that, if the latest scholarship is correct, is contrary to what the democratic majority believes is in its best interest? They (the Founding Fathers) are dead and buried and will not be around to suffer the consequences. We the living will.*
>
> — Daniel Lazare, "Your Constitution Is Killing You,"
> *Harper's Magazine*, October 1999

Daniel Lazare? Now I remember that name! He is the author of *The Frozen Republic* whom I quoted on page 10/6 of my *Hologram of Liberty*. (Danny proposed that a future House of Representatives just ignore whatever parts of the Constitution it found archaic or inconvenient, the Supreme Court be damned. This tiresome worm is getting *far* too much ink.)

O.K., time for an "expert opinion." A psychiatrist speaks:

On page 49 of the 23 August 1999 issue of *Newsweek* is found an essay "The Psyche of a 'Gunocracy'" by Robert Jay Lifton, M.D. of John Jay University in NYC. It is a particularly sly essay, full of stolen concepts, revisionist history, and false premises. I hope you're sitting down for this:

> *Indeed, the gun has become close to a sacred object, revered by many as the essence of American life. The sources of our "gunocracy" date back at least to the Revolutionary War* **and our romanticized visions of citizen militias,** *which place the gun at the center of our national creation myth.*

"Romanticized visions of citizen militias"? Throughout the day of 19 April 1775, militiamen by the *thousands* swarmed like bees around the retreating Redcoats and fought them over 20 miles back to their boats. This was no *"vision"* (much less a self-serving *"romanticized"* one)—this is historical fact! However,

Lifton (yet another pansy NYC liberal we see so often in the media) maintains that such a display of desperation and courage didn't really happen, and that we made it all up in order to create a _"mythology"_ on private ownership of firearms.

Killers like Furrow and McVeigh have long since upgraded their arsenals from flintlock rifles and Colt pistols to assault weapons and fertilizer bombs.

Follow the "reasoning" here: As marijuana is allegedly the "gateway drug" to cocaine and heroin, handheld firearms are "gateway weapons" for weapons of mass destruction.

*The latter are lethal enough, but we should not delude ourselves into believing that weapons worship stops there. Aum Shinrikyo, the fanatical Japanese cult that released sarin gas in the Tokyo subways in March 1995, killing 12 and injuring 5,000, has another lesson to teach us. **Its gurus and his disciples had no equivalent tradition of gunocracy to draw upon.***

Well, if the Japanese have no firearm "gateway weapons" for weapons of mass destruction, then how did a cult magically springboard into using sarin gas? Lifton, apparently without realizing it, destroys his own silly argument of _"the worship of the gun can be extended to weaponry of any kind, including that which may destroy everything."_

Still, even Lifton had to admit that not every American gunowner is fanatical or mentally disturbed:

...many ordinary Americans have also become caught up in the cult of the gun. For them, it is not a jarring source of violence but as much an accepted part of the landscape as forests and rivers. Such people often resist controls over the objects they revere. But human beings are capable of modifying their own mythologies.

Gee, Lifton is so sharp! He's figured out why Americans are so upset with proposed gun registrations and gun bans—we just don't like having our _"mythologies"_ tampered with. (Naturally, it has nothing to do with freedom or self-defense from both criminals and government...) _"Gosh, leave our 'accepted part of the landscape' alone!"_ (Only in NYC can somebody so craven and clueless actually retain air in his fatuous pair of lungs.)

Americans (i.e., the gunphobic ones) have shown signs of a change in their feelings about guns, seeing them increasingly more dangerous than sacred. That kind of collective psychological shift is necessary is we are ever to transcend the crippling fraternity of the gun.

Since we live in a "democratic" society where government tyranny is deemed conceptually impossible (*"Why, the voters would never allow it!"*), since everybody can now carry a cell phone to dial 911 (*"Why do you 'need' a gun when the police will protect you?"*), guns are allegedly no longer necessary. Those who loath the Bill of Rights actually expect gunowning Americans to give up the *"myth"* of their *"gunocracy,"* to cease this senseless *"weapons worship,"* and to relinquish their *"icons of freedom and power."* (Give me a minute here to stop this convulsive laughter. O.K., I'm back.)

Well, Bobby, you can whine about the *"crippling fraternity of the gun"* in *Newsweek* all you want—it will take an impossible level of force to disarm 75,000,000 gunowners, no matter *how* many Ø27,000/year SWAT thugs you send. Further, we're not going to disarm *voluntarily*. We're staying armed; get used to it.

Cloister your little self in NYC teaching psychiatry, feeling all warm and safe and fuzzy. Oh, and by the way,

A fear of weapons is a sign of retarded sexual and emotional maturity.
— Dr. Sigmund Freud, *Introductory Lectures on Psychoanalysis*

So, Robert Jay Lifton, psychiatrist—heal *thyself.*

Wussies of a feather, flock together

Have you noticed that nearly all those paranoid about guns live in big cities, and usually eastern ones, at that? To live in Rural America requires toughness and responsibility, which these petunias don't have. Lazare and Lifton couldn't *hack* it in Billings, Montana or Moab, Utah—or anywhere in between. It takes an *adult* to live in the country. As unformed larva, these Alan Aldas must stay in their familiar metropolitan cocoon, where reality is desperately suspended. Only from there can they safely typewriter snipe at us butt-crack country folk. These guys aren't men; they're women with erroneous plumbing. During a lethal emergency, you and I don't squeal for a cop or dial 911. They *have* to. Sick.

Honestly, these people cannot do *anything* for themselves. They are adolescents inhabiting adult bodies, still living in their crib. I was once at a Manhattan party when the stereo went out. While they were milling about or busy thumbing through the Yellow Pages for a repairman, I merely plugged back in the speaker wires that somebody had tripped over. The other guests had never seen such an unexpected display of random competence, and I was thereafter treated as a *god.* *"Hey, meet Ken Royce—he fixed the stereo!"* It was both heady and revolting. A similar thing happened again years later when on a movie set I fixed the grip truck's frozen starter solenoid by pounding on it. By their awe, you'd have thought I built space shuttles out of beer cans.

Not only is metro life a virtual reality, it's a form of insanity *("a sustained disassociation with reality").* Life in NYC or LA is not real, but do they ever *think* it is! And they want us to be just like them. As I once quipped:

> *The mole hates not only mountains, but* mountaineering.

Lazare and Lifton cannot bear to know that rugged and independent people not only persist in being born, but still enjoy huge geographical areas in which to generally thrive:

> *Gun Control advocates are first cousins to those people who "cannot stand to know that someone, somewhere is happy."* *...***Gun controllers "cannot stand to know that someone, somewhere is capable of defending themselves."***
>
> **Gun Control advocates envy those who are happy and willing to defend their lives for they recognize that these are people able to deal with the world.** *In other words, that which they view as evil they believe to be efficacious.*
>
> *The envy they feel leads them not to seek similar abilities for themselves, but to bring the target of their envy down to their level.* **They don't want to be as able at self-defense as you, they want you to be rendered as defenseless as they.** *Basically they harbor a fundamental hatred of life* (and of those who would dare to live one), *which translates into an unwillingness to permit others the right to self-defense. They recognize protection as a value for human life, but they are the ones who do not value human life as such; therefore their hostility to handguns, for protecting human life; and industry, for supporting human life.*
>
> **Gun Controllers fear guns for two basic reasons.** *By their ethical standard (altruism) guns are evil because they are meant for preventing the sacrifice of the individual....*
>
> **Others fear guns because the presence of a gun brings them to face the means of forcing their whims on others.** *These are the modern day Hitlers that haven't the courage to identify the means of their goals.* **They want to keep the means, guns as weapons of initiatory violence, discreetly hidden from sight.** *These are the smiling bureaucrats, the ones flanked by armed thugs; who, when physically confronted with firearms as one of the tools of subjugation,* **are forced to see and recognize their own adopted but hidden means.** *They are unable to maintain the illusion within their own mind, they can no longer evade the fact that*

*firearms represent to them not a means of defending man's rights
but of violating them. They fear the firearm because it forces them
to acknowledge their evasions.*
— Mark A. Laughlin
www.ebarricades.com/root/POF7.html

My *"best interest"* is to be armed and remain armed

I don't care if 99% of the electorate demand that I dump
my guns into the ocean, or turn them in for Ø5,000 each—*I will
remain armed.* The purpose of our Constitution is to ensure
sufficient political *ballast* to weather the constantly shifting
winds of democratic opinion. If the free speech right of the
KKK, for example, were left to Lazare's *"what the democratic
majority believes is in its best interest"* then the KKK could
never publish anything, much less stage their silly little
marches. That accomplished, the piously empowered majority
would then continue to nibble at the fringe, until they began to
consume themselves. The truth of the matter is this:

Individual rights are *not* subject to collective permission. *Period.*

O.K., gunowners one day get outvoted; so what? I mean,
really—what can an *unarmed* majority do to an *armed* minority? Not much. And *that* is what liberals are really fuming over.

Gradual *"gun control"*

*The time to guard against corruption and tyranny is before they shall
have gotten hold of us. It is better to keep the wolf out of the fold
than to trust him not to draw his teeth and talons after he shall have
entered.*
— Thomas Jefferson

In response to this harsh reality, liberals have had to convince
themselves that citizen disarmament can be accomplished with
no backlash through "gradualism" (*i.e.,* one slice at a time).
(The *last* time a central government tried to forcibly round up
firearms on *these* shores was an early morning on 19 April 1775,
and we all know just how well *that* turned out.) Here's a quote
from another mouthy gunphobe:

*Ultimately, a civilized society must disarm its citizenry if it is to have
a modicum of domestic tranquility of the kind enjoyed by sister
democracies such as Canada and Britain.*

(BTP Note: The recently disarmed British are now suffering a
dramatic rise in armed crimes, especially "hot" robberies of
homes known to be occupied. If you look like food, you'll be

eaten. Crime in America, however, has been *falling* for years, thanks to an increasingly armed citizenry.)

*Given the frontier history and individualist ideology of the United States, however, this will not come easily. It certainly cannot be done radically. **It will probably take one, maybe two generations. It might be 50 years before the United States gets to where Britain is today.*** (BTP: Not if I can help it!) *Passing a law like the assault weapons ban is a symbolic—purely symbolic—move in that direction. **Its only real justification is not to reduce crime but to desensitize the public to the regulation of weapons in preparation for their ultimate confiscation.***

— Charles Krauthammer, "Disarm the Citizenry," *The Washington Post,* 5 April 1996

Hear that? The *"Crime Bill"* was just a *"symbolic"* gesture which had nothing to do with crime, but was just part of the de-sensitizing continuum. As Nazi Propaganda Minister Josef Goebbels was fond of saying, lie to the people often enough and boldly enough and they will eventually believe.

"Civil society" means sheep ruled by wolves

The falcon cannot hear the falconer;
Things fall apart; the centre cannot hold;
Mere anarchy is loosed upon the world,
The blood-dimmed tide is loosed, and everywhere
The ceremony of innocence is drowned;
The best lack all conviction, while the worst
Are full of passionate intensity.
And what rough beast, its hour come round at last,
Slouches towards Bethlehem to be born?

— William Butler Yeats, "The Second Coming" (1921)

[N]o reform can be meaningful without a tough program for disman-tling existing arsenals (sic), applying not just to handguns but to all assault weapons (and ammunition). After a brief amnesty, the dis-mantling of all unregistered and unregulated weapons must be swift and thorough. (Heh! Good luck!)

— Attorney Ronald Goldfarb, "Domestic Disarmament," *The Washington Post,* 21 November 1993, page C3

*In the short term, of course, the police must be given the firepower that's required to combat the firepower they now face. In the long run, however, we need fewer guns. **Semiautomatic weapons and other weapons of war have no legitimate place in civil society and ought to be banned outright, right now...***

— Hubert Williams, "End the Domestic Arms Race," *The Washington Post,* 26 March 1997, page A19

If being *"civilized"* means being at the defenseless mercy of criminals and government, I'll stay a "savage," thank you.

> ...when the struggle seems to be drifting definitely towards a world social (i.e., socialist) democracy, there may still be very great delays and disappointments before it becomes an efficient and beneficent world system. **Countless people—will hate the new world order —and will die protesting it.** When we attempt to evaluate its promise, we have to bear in mind the distress of a generation or so of malcontents, many of them quite gallant and graceful-looking people.
>
> — H.G. Wells, *The New World Order* (1939)

> The totalitarians have followed this rule [of isolation to induce a conditioned reflex] and know that they can condition their political victims most quickly if they are kept in isolation. In the totalitarian technique of thought control, the same isolation applied to the individual is applied also to groups of people. This is the reason the civilian populations of totalitarian countries are not permitted to travel freely and are kept away from mental and political contamination.
>
> That is the reason, too, for the solitary confinement cell and prison camp; and what of the neighborhoods were people are afraid of each other, where every one is a stool pigeon? Do you really think that the 800 telephone numbers about child abuse, elderly abuse, environmental abuse, are to protect the public? **I propose to you that they are designed to create a state of isolation where no one trusts anyone else.** The bounty given to the stool pigeon in all of these schemes makes us all afraid, keeps us isolated and,...better subjects for menticide (i.e., to murder the mind).
>
> — Thomas Dorman, M.D.
> www.zolatimes.com/V4.13/dignity2.html

They are now turning in *pocketknives* in Britain. Is there a knife ban? **No, it's *voluntary*, as *preemptive* compliance.** The correct visual metaphor is a dog, lying on its back, wagging its tail, exposing its urine-soaked pink belly. When those cowards go the camps, they'll no doubt motor there in their own cars. And they'll thoughtfully leave the keys in the ignition, I'll bet. (*"Do take care, Officer—the tyres are a bit thin! Oh, and she's low on petrol. Here's a tenner to see you home. Cheerio!"*)

"Civil society" indeed.

Folks, don't be fooled. It all boils down to the same thing: a *gun ban*. Yesterday, the full-auto M16. Today, the semi-auto AR15. Tomorrow, the scoped *"sniper"* rifle. Next week, the skeet shotgun. Next month, the fixed-blade knife. This is nothing new; history is merely repeating itself:

The people of the various provinces are strictly forbidden to have in their possession any swords, short swords ("sawed off" swords?), bows, spears, firearms, or other types of arms. **The possession of unnecessary implements** (without legitimate *"sporting purpose"* ?) **makes difficult the collection of taxes and dues, and tends to foment uprisings.**

   — shogun Hideyoshi Toyotomi (1536-1598)
     8th day of the 7th month, Tensho 16

Oh, 16th Century feudal Japan is not an appropriate example? Well, victim disarmament has a long history in America:

That no negro or other slave within this province shall be per-mitted to carry any gun, or any other offensive weapon, *from off their master's land,* **without license from their said master;** *and if any negro or other slave shall presume to do so, he shall be liable to be carried before a justice of the peace, and be whipped,* **and his gun or other offensive weapon shall be forfeited to him that shall seize the same and carry such negro so offending before a justice of the peace.**

   — Chapter XLIV, Section XXXII, Maryland Acts of 1715

Nice incentive program for police; the arresting officer got to keep the slave's confiscated weapon. (*Hmmm*, sounds similar to civil forfeitures under our so-called "War On Drugs.")

One hundred and fifty years later, black Civil War veter-ans (two-thirds of whom were freed slaves) were *"full of the im-pudent notions of a freeman,"* thus forbidden to own weapons. Today, we're *all* slaves—regardless of skin color. Government is our *"said master,"* trying to require a *"license."*

"Gee, Boston, 'slaves' is a extreme. How can Americans, living in the freest country in the world, be 'slaves'?" We don't even enjoy the liberty of *serfs.* (A serf paid "only" 25% of his earnings to his feudal lord. How much income tax do *you* pay?) Don't kid yourselves, we're slaves. Slaves with weekends off.

But we're *armed* slaves. *"Master"* forgot to disarm us. Oh, the *NFA34* and the *GCA68* and the *"Crime Bill"* have been a pain, but they haven't really disarmed us. I can't easily (*i.e.*, legally) own an M2 .50BMG or an M16. *Boo, hoo.* Between my FAL, AR15, Glock, and scoped bolt-action .308, I'll do just fine.

In response to the recent rash of police shootings of un-armed people (holding a wallet, fork, cell phone, etc.), here's a new insight from a professionally cretinous gunphobe:

The problem—or a large part of it—is precisely that there are guns out there, by the thousands and the millions. **Police in other countries do not have to assume that anyone they question is likely to have a gun and likely to use it.** *That is one of the many effects of our gun culture—that the guns are so plentiful they first terrorize the police, and then the police terrorize the citizenry. It is a vicious circle, of accelerating viciousness.*

...[G]uns, by their very number and omnipresence, make people fearful, and fearful people act in dangerous ways.

The guns that gun cultists treat as sacred are the cause of a national sickness, one manifested in many ways, beginning with the vile rhetoric of the NRA.

— Gary Wills, "Police Brutality or Gun Brutality?"
31 March 2000, Univeral Press Syndicate

The statists haven't been able to disarm us because gun ownership is part of this nation's "DNA." Not only that, this right was *explicitly* protected in the Bill of Rights. Finally, more and more American gunowners are waking up to the gunhaters' end goal. They're seeing firsthand that registration is merely a cheap ploy for the hidden purpose of future confiscation (*e.g.,* New York City), and they are now properly refusing to register their guns. (Registering guns is like sending a list of your household valuables to a burglars' guild. Why invite—*guarantee*—a visit?) So, the gunowners are becoming more resolute, and the gunhaters are growing more desperate. Schumer and all his little cockroach friends (my apologies to cockroaches) *know* what they've got planned for their unarmed America, but they're *way* behind in implementing it:

That the United States was born out of an armed rebellion fueled, in large part, by resentment over excessive taxation is a bit of history that makes statists extremely uncomfortable. It should, therefore, come as no surprise that congressmen and senators who dream of an ever-expanding welfare state consistently vote to restrict individual gun ownership or even ban the production of certain classes of firearms.

Claims by extremist groups such as Handgun Control, Inc. (HCI) that "just one more" gun law is necessary to "fight crime" or "reduce the level of violence" are simply a smoke screen. HCI is run by statists whose objective is the total disarmament of ordinary people. They are savvy political professionals with enormous patience who are willing to disarm you in increments, if need be. However long it takes, to HCI the best "gun control" is gun prohibition.

In the minds of people who promote the expansion of government power at the expense of individual liberty, gun prohibition makes perfect sense. **In fact, it is essential.** *Middle class welfare programs (e.g., Medicare and Social Security) along with interest payments on the national debt currently consume more than half of all federal expenditures. It is only a matter of time, perhaps less than a decade, until "discretionary" spending on defense, law enforcement, parks, roads, etc. is relegated to less than one-third of the total.* **Sooner or later something has got to give.** *Either the federal welfare apparatus will have to shrink dramatically or taxes will have to go up. But what would happen if 50,000,000 Americans "just say no" to forking over more of their hard-earned money?* **Massive civil disobedience by ordinary people who, if necessary, could defend themselves is a statist's worst nightmare. On the other hand, the populace will be much easier to intimidate if it has already been disarmed.**

Disarmament of people kept (or to be kept) in servitude has historical precedent dating back to ancient times. *The history of "gun control" in America shows that is has been used repeatedly as an authoritarian and elitist device to favor the powerful and politically well-connected and keep supposedly less worthy people "in their place."*

"Gun control" in America has often meant gun prohibition for people who, because of their race, religion, ethnic origin, or condition of servitude, were considered a threat to those in power. As we enter the 21st Century, rates of taxation have reached oppressive levels. To statists (who seek only to expand government power), growing resentment on the part of people who work, produce wealth, and pay oppressive taxes presents a serious threat. **Disarming ordinary Americans who will be called upon to pay ever higher taxes is seen by them as necessary to minimize that threat.**

— Howard J. Fezell, Esq., "Early American 'Gun Control'"
www.2ndamendment.net/2amd8.html

Of course, our masters claim that victim disarmament is *"necessary"* to bring out a *"safe"* society (for them). Well, William Pitt and Thomas Jefferson disagree with the statists:

Necessity is the plea for every infringement of human freedom. It is the argument of tyrants; it is the creed of slaves.

— William Pitt, House of Commons, 18 November 1783

No free man shall ever be debarred the use of arms.

— Thomas Jefferson, Proposal for Virginia Constitution

I am a political dissident. (Given the atrocities of our times, every thinking American should be, too.) And I know what happens—what *always* has happened—to *unarmed* political dissidents. I will not stand in line for a cattle car aimed at some extermination camp. I will not be led blindfolded to a bullet-pocked brick wall.

"We have met the enemy, and the enemy is us." There are no liberating forces on the horizon. We're on our own.

❖ 34

GUN LAWS IN THE 50 STATES & D.C.

While most Bill of Rights issues have been ironed out at the national level by the Supreme Court and applied to the 50 States (*e.g.*, search and seizure, due process, etc.), the Court has studiously *avoided* so applying the *2nd* Amendment. Therefore, gunowners have no local 2nd Amendment protection and are at the legislative mercy of their State, if not their county or city. This foments random peril for any traveling gunowner:

> *A businessman from North Carolina was traveling to Maine via New Jersey when he was stopped by a New Jersey state trooper for a speeding violation. During the routine questioning, the trooper asked the North Carolina man if he had any firearms in the vehicle.*

(The correct answer is *always* "No." I cannot conceive of a single instance when admitting to a cased, locked weapon would be to the gunowner's advantage. Properly secured, a cop would need *"probable cause"* (PC) to search the container. With or without righteous PC, any such search (which would be rare) could be later challenged by your lawyer.)

> *Having a concealed carry permit from North Carolina, the traveler assumed he was operating well within the law. He told the trooper that he had a Glock 19...in his briefcase which he was licensed to carry and would...allow the trooper to inspect it.*

(Not only did he *"assume"* that he was within the law, he assumed that the trooper was reasonable. Few cops are these days, especially state troopers in the East. The traveler from North Carolina is about to have a Reality Check.)

> *Before the traveler could utter another word, the trooper had drawn his sidearm, pointed it at the traveler and begun shouting at the man to exit the vehicle at once with his hands in the air. The stunned businessman, who had never had so much as a parking ticket, did as the officer demanded. He soon found himself spread eagle on the ground while the agitated trooper called for assistance. ...[T]he traveler was charged with a felony and spent three days in a Newark jail. ...[T]he felony charge was pled down to a misdemeanor. However, if the traveler had not possessed such an exemplary prior record, he may have faced the original felony and prison time.* (at 1)
>
> — J. Scott Kappas, Esq.
>
> *Traveler's Guide to the Firearm Laws of the Fifty States*

Attorney Kappas has provided us with a unique and fairly comprehensive manual for understanding the myriad gun laws. Call 606-647-5100 to order it, or get it from a gun store for Ø13. The *Guide* is, however, unevenly written, weakly organized, and poorly typeset. No table matrix is given. Its 0-100% ranking system is unexplained in its subjectivity. In short, it is not very user friendly. This chapter supplements the *Guide*.

While I gleaned heavily from the *Guide* and table summarized its info (which is likely sufficient for most readers), consult the *Guide* and/or your lawyer and/or the State AG if you've any questions beyond my summary.

The *McClure-Volkmer Act of 1986*

> *This bill will remove bad laws that were passed during a period of hysteria.*
>
> — President Ronald Reagan, 19 May 1986

The so-called *Firearms Owner's Protection Act* amended the *GCA68*. It did two good things: It eliminated the interstate commerce restrictions on ammo sales. (No more ridiculous retail recordkeeping!) It also created a federal "umbrella" for interstate gunowners in transit. If you are legal where you live and where you are going, States in between (such as Neu Jersey) can't arrest you if your guns are unloaded and cased.

It did, *however*, do one very bad thing. Snuck in during the last seconds of debate by a career gun bigot from NJ was an amendment to prohibit after 19 May 1986 further manufacture or conversion of full-auto weapons. (Within a month, *NFA* manufacturers, working frantically, increased the National Registry numbers from 90,000 to 190,000.)

No firearms rights in State Constitution
CA IA MD MN NJ NY WI

Transfer record?
no record for guns	AK AZ AR CO DE FL GA ID KS KY LA ME MS MT NE NV NM OK TX UT VT WV WY
record required in cities	OH VA
required record for guns	AL CA CT DC HI IL IN IA MD MA MI MN MO NH NJ NY NC ND OR PA RI SC SD TN WA WI

Purchase, importation, or ownership
Handguns
unrestricted	AL AK AZ CA CO CT DE FL GA ID IN KS KY LA ME MD MS MT NE NV NH NM ND OH OK OR PA RI SC SD TN TX UT VT WA WV WI WY
permit required	HI IA IL MA MI MN MO NJ NY NC VA
banned after-_____	DC-1975

Long guns
unrestricted	AL AK AZ CA CO CT DE FL GA ID IN IA KS KY LA ME MD MI MN MS MO MT NE NV NH NM NY NC ND OH OK OR PA RI SC SD TN TX UT VT VA WA WV WI WY
permit required	DC HI IL MA NJ

"assault weapons"
unrestricted	AL AK AZ CO DE FL GA ID IN IA KS KY LA ME MD MI MS MO MT NE NV NH NM NY NC ND OK OR PA RI SC SD TN TX UT VT VA WA WV WI WY
permit required	HI IL MA MN
city permit required	OH
banned after-_____	CT-1997?
totally forbidden	CA DC NJ

NFA34 weapons
unrestricted	AL AK AZ CO FL GA ID IN KY ME MD MS MT NE NV NH NM ND OH OK OR PA SD TN TX UT VT VA WV WI WY
"curios or relics" only	MN MO
restricted to *"war relics"*	LA
C&R and *Class III* licensees	MI
permit required	AR CT MA
with local sheriff's permission	NC
banned after-_____	CT-?
totally forbidden	CA DE DC HI IL IA KS NJ NY RI SC WA

On foot carry
Handguns
open, loaded, anywhere*	ID KY LA NM NC SD VT WY
open, loaded, unless locally prohibited	AL AK AZ CO DE KS ME MI MS MO MT NE NV NH OH OK OR PA VA WI

open, loaded in rural areas only	CA WA WV
open, loaded for licensed hunting/fishing	AR GA MN UT
open, unloaded	ND
open forbidden	CT FL HI IL IN IA MD MA NJ NY RI SC TN TX
concealed, no license required	VT
concealed, no license in rural areas	ID MT
concealed, license required	AL AK AZ CA CO CT DE FL GA ID IN IA KY LA ME MD MA MI MN MS MT NH NJ NY NC OK OR RI SD TN VA WA WV WY
concealed, with affirmative defense	MS MO NE OH
concealed, unloaded	NM
concealed not at all possible	DC HI IL KS WI

Long guns

open, loaded anywhere*	GA ID IN KY LA NV NM NC TX VT WI WY
open, loaded, unless locally prohibited	AL AK AZ CO DE KS ME MI MS MO MT NE OH OK OR PA SD VA
open, loaded in rural areas only	CA IA WA
open, loaded, for hunting, etc., only	MN UT WV
open, unloaded	ND
open forbidden	CT DC FL HI IL MD MA NJ NY RI SC TN UT

Vehicle carry
Handguns

open, loaded	AK AZ DE FL GA ID KS KY LA MS MT NV NM NC VT WY
open, loaded, unless locally prohibited	CO MO NE OR
open, chamber and mag empty	ME NH OK UT VA
open forbidden	AL AR CA CT DC HI IL IN IA MD MA MI MN NJ NY ND OH PA RI SC SD TN TX WA WV WI
concealed, no license required	VT MS NM
loaded in glove box O.K. w/o license	AK AZ FL GA KS KY LA NV SC
concealed, loaded, license required	AL AK AZ AR CA CO CT DE FL MN ID IN IA KY LA ME MD MA MI MT NV NH NJ NY NC ND OK OR PA RI SC SD TN TX UT VA WA WV WY
concealed, with affirmative defense	AR CO MO NE OH TX
concealed, unloaded in locked trunk/case	HI IL KS NE OH WI
locked in trunk only for passing through	NJ
concealed not at all possible	DC

Long guns

open, loaded	AZ FL ID KS KY LA MS MT NM NC SD TX WY
open, loaded, unless locally prohibited	MO OR
open, loaded (except during hunting season)	AR
open, chamber empty	CO NV ND
open, chamber and mag empty	AL AK DE ME MD NE NH OK VT VA

open forbidden	AL CA DC HI MN NY OH PA RI TN WV WI
concealed, loaded, no license required	MS NM SD
concealed, loaded, in rural areas only	MT
concealed, unloaded	VT
concealed if unloaded in locked case/trunk	AL CA CO DE FL HI IL IN IA ME MD MA MI MN MT NV NH NY NC ND OH OK OR PA RI SC TN TX UT VA WA WV WI WY
locked in trunk only for passing through	CT NJ
concealed impossible	DC

Uniformity

Preemption of local laws by State

preemption strict—all local laws preempted by State	FL GA IA ID KY LA ME MI MN NM NC ND OK SC SD TN TX UT WA WY
preemption by judicial ruling	CT NJ NY
preemption general, but for local discharge ordinances	MD VT
preemption since-____;previous laws "grandfathered"	DE-1985 IN-1995 NV-1989 VA-1987 WV-1999
preemption softened by court	AZ
preemption, except for handguns or certain places/events	AL MS MO MT OR
preemption, except for large cities	PA
preemption only with State legislature concurrence	MA
preemption general, but for certain areas (call AG)	AR
preemption, but State laws are draconian anyway	CA RI WI

No preemption of local laws

no preemption; local legislation possible, but infrequent	AK NH
no preemption; local legislation possible and common	CO HI IL KS NE NY OH VA
a moot point, since anything that shoots is restricted	DC MA NJ

Concealed handgun license

Issuance

none required; concealed carry without permit	VT AK
"shall issue"	AZ CO CT FL ID IN KY LA ME MN MS MT NV NH NC ND NM OK OR PA SC SD TN TX UT VA WA WV WY
discretionary and common issued (States in bold are nearly *"shall issue"*)	**AL AR** DE **GA** MI
discretionary and rarely issued	CA HI IA MD MA NJ NY RI
often issued to nonresident Americans	AZ FL ME NH PA UT WA
rarely issued to nonresident Americans	IA NJ OR
none offered	DC IL KS MO NE OH WI

CHL reciprocity

automatic for all State permits	ID IN KY MI VT WY
for States with like standards (call AG)	AK AZ LA MT OK PA SC TN TX UT
for mutually recognized States (call AG)	AR FL GA NH ND WV
for identical standards *and* mutuality	MS VA
automatic, for vehicle carry only	PA RI
ad hoc for recognized firearms competitions	CT
highly discretionary (call AG)	MA
none	AL CA CO DE DC HI IL IA KS ME MD MN MO NE NV NJ NM NY NC OH OR SD WA WI

RANKING THE STATES & D.C.

I scored them on 10 criteria, rated 0-10 (worst to best):

❶ Private sale record required?
Purchase of: ❷ handguns ❸ long guns ❹ *"assault weapons"*
❺ On foot open carry
❻ Car open carry
❼ Uniformity
❽ Concealed carry
❾ CHL issuance
❿ CHL reciprocity

How my scoring differed from Kappas *Guide*

First of all, he did not take into account what I consider a crucial concern—recordfree private sales. No government should know which citizens are buying which guns, as no government can be *trusted* with such information.

Secondly, I consider respecting the right to open carry not only important, but highly indicative of a State's overall attitude towards gun ownership.

Lastly, I did not take into account one of his variables: the unrestricted ownership of full-auto weapons. Since it goes against my grain to get licensed for *anything*, Class 3 firearms are not my bag. I also believe that such privileged ownership is soon to be revoked, possibly within 10 years.

So, my State scoring was stricter than that of Mr. Kappas, usually by 10-15 points and often 22-27 points. Still, there is a very strong correlation between our scores.

BOSTON T. PARTY'S RANKINGS

❶ Private sale record? (Purchase of: ❷ handguns ❸ long guns ❹ *"assault weapons"*)   ❺ On foot open carry ❻ Car open carry ❼ Uniformity ❽ Concealed carry ❾ CHL issuance ❿ CHL reciprocity

	❶	❷	❸	❹	❺	❻	❼	❽	❾	❿	100%
AL	0	10	10	10	8	0	8	3	5	0	54
AK	10	10	10	10	9	10	5	10	10	10	*94*
AZ	10	10	10	10	9	10	8	6	10	8	*91*
AR	10	10	10	10	5	0	7	3	5	6	66
CA	0	10	10	0	5	0	2	1	2	0	30
CO	10	10	10	10	8	9	5	7	10	6	**85**
CT	0	10	10	2	0	0	2	3	9	1	37
DE	10	10	10	10	8	10	5	1	5	0	69
DC	0	0	2	0	0	0	0	0	0	0	2
FL	10	10	10	10	0	10	10	7	10	6	**83**
GA	10	10	10	10	5	10	10	6	7	6	**84**
HI	0	5	5	5	0	0	0	0	1	0	16
ID	10	10	10	10	10	10	10	7	10	10	*97*
IL	0	5	5	5	0	0	0	0	0	0	15
IN	0	10	10	10	0	0	5	5	10	10	60
IA	10	5	10	10	0	0	10	2	6	0	53
KS	10	10	10	10	8	10	8	4	0	0	68
KY	10	10	10	10	10	10	10	7	10	10	*97*
LA	10	10	10	10	10	10	10	7	9	8	*94*
ME	10	10	10	10	8	2	10	3	10	0	*73*
MD	0	10	10	10	0	0	9	0	2	0	41
MA	0	5	5	5	0	0	0	0	1	1	17
MI	0	5	10	10	8	0	10	2	5	10	60
MN	0	5	10	5	5	0	10	7	10	6	58
MS	10	10	10	10	8	10	8	8	9	4	**85**
MO	0	5	10	10	8	8	8	2	0	0	51
MT	10	10	10	10	9	10	8	7	9	8	*92*
NE	10	10	10	10	8	8	5	3	0	0	64
NV	10	10	10	10	8	10	5	4	9	0	*76*
NH	0	10	10	10	8	2	7	5	10	6	68
NJ	0	5	5	0	0	0	0	0	1	0	11
NM	10	10	10	10	10	10	10	7	10	0	**87**
NY	0	5	10	10	0	0	0	0	1	0	26
NC	0	5	10	10	10	10	10	2	9	0	66
ND	0	10	10	10	3	0	10	3	9	6	61
OH	5	10	10	7	8	0	5	2	0	0	47
OK	10	10	10	10	8	2	10	3	9	8	**80**
OR	0	10	10	10	8	8	8	2	9	0	65
PA	0	10	10	10	8	0	6	3	10	4	61
RI	0	10	10	10	0	0	10	0	1	4	45
SC	0	10	10	10	0	0	10	7	9	8	64
SD	0	10	10	10	10	5	10	5	9	0	69
TN	0	10	10	10	0	0	10	3	9	8	60
TX	10	10	10	10	5	5	10	6	9	7	**82**
UT	10	10	10	10	5	0	10	3	10	8	*76*
VT	10	10	10	10	10	10	9	10	10	10	*99*
VA	5	5	10	10	8	2	5	3	9	4	61
WA	0	10	10	10	5	0	10	2	10	0	57
WV	10	10	10	10	5	0	5	2	9	0	61
WI	0	10	10	10	8	0	10	0	0	0	48
WY	10	10	10	10	10	10	10	4	9	10	*93*

What a range, from 2% (D.C.) to 99% (Vermont)! Half the States are at least "tolerable." Two-thirds are in the South and West. Three are each in the Midwest and East.

95+	Slices of Heaven		VT ID KY
85-94	Havens		LA AK WY MT AZ AK MS CO
75-84	Quite Comfortable		GA TX FL OK NM NV UT
65-74	Tolerable		ME DE SD KS NH AR NC OR

BTP #		BTP %	pop./ mile²	What's still needed there
1	**Vermont**	99	61	loaded car long guns
2	Idaho	97	12	Vermont conceal carry
3	Kentucky	97	93	Vermont conceal carry
4	Louisiana	94	97	Vermont conceal carry
5	Alaska	94	1	preemption
6	Wyoming	93	5	Vermont conceal carry
7	Montana	92	6	Vermont conceal carry
8	Arizona	91	32	preemption; Vermont conceal carry
9	New Mexico	87	12	preemption; Vermont conceal carry
10	Mississippi	85	55	preemption; Vermont conceal carry
11	Colorado	85	32	preemption; Vermont conceal carry
12	Georgia	84	112	preemption; Vermont conceal carry
13	Florida	83	240	open carry; Vermont conceal carry
14	Texas	82	65	open carry; Vermont conceal carry
15	Oklahoma	80	46	car open carry; Vermont carry
16	Nevada	76	11	preemption; reciprocity
17	Utah	76	21	on foot and car open carry;
18	Maine	73	40	car open carry; reciprocity
19	Delaware	69	341	preemption; *"shall issue"*; reciprocity
20	S. Dakota	69	9	record-free transfers; car open carry
21	Kansas	68	30	*"shall issue"*; reciprocity
22	N. Hampshire	68	124	no records; car carry; *"shall issue"*
23	Arkansas	66	45	car open carry; *"shall issue"*
24	N. Carolina	66	136	no records or handgun permit; reciprocity
25	Oregon	65	30	no records or handgun permit; reciprocity
	pop./mile² average		**47**	(*i.e.*, fewer people equals more freedom)

The "Top 10" Losers

Six are in the Northeast, two are in the Midwest, and two are out West. If you cherish freedom, these areas are not fit for habitation. Any professed gunlover should pack up and leave.

42	Ohio	47	265	
43	Maryland	41	489	*"Where no one can hear you scream."*
44	Connecticut	37	678	Constitution State?
45	California	30	191	Settled by freedom-seeking pioneers?
46	New York	26	381	Fought for by Minutemen?
47	Mass.	17	768	Birthplace of the American Revolution?
48	Hawaii	16	173	Now owned by the anti-gun Japanese
49	Illinois	15	206	Land of Lincoln?
50	New Jersey	11	1,042	Consecrated by blood of 1770s Patriots?
51	**D.C.**	2	9,949	One can own (disassembled) long guns
	pop./mile² average		**466**	(not including D.C.)
	pop./mile² average		**1,414**	(including D.C.)

State		Attorney General
Alabama	AL	334-242-7300
Alaska	AK	907-465-3600
Arizona	AZ	602-542-4266
Arkansas	AR	501-682-2007
California	CA	916-324-5437
Colorado	CO	303-866-3052
Connecticut	CT	860-808-5318
Delaware	DE	302-577-8400
D. of C.	DC	202-727-6284
Florida	FL	850-488-5381
Georgia	GA	404-656-4585
Hawaii	HI	808-586-1282
Idaho	ID	208-334-2400
Illinois	IL	312-814-2503
Indiana	IN	317-232-6201
Iowa	IA	515-281-3053
Kansas	KS	785-296-2215
Kentucky	KY	502-696-5300
Louisiana	LA	225-342-7013
Maine	ME	207-626-8800
Maryland	MD	410-576-6300
Massachusetts	MA	617-727-2200
Michigan	MI	517-373-1110
Minnesota	MN	651-296-6196
Mississippi	MS	601-359-3692
Missouri	MO	573-751-3321
Montana	MT	406-444-2026
Nebraska	NE	402-471-2682
Nevada	NV	775-684-1100
N. Hampshire	NH	603-271-3658
N. Jersey	NJ	609-984-9579
N. Mexico	NM	505-827-6000
N. York	NY	212-416-8519
N. Carolina	NC	919-716-6400
N. Dakota	ND	701-328-2210
Ohio	OH	614-466-3376
Oklahoma	OK	405-521-3921
Oregon	OR	503-378-6002
Pennsylvania	PA	717-783-9995
Rhode Island	RI	401-274-4400
S. Carolina	SC	803-734-3970
S. Dakota	SD	605-773-3215
Tennessee	TN	615-741-3491
Texas	TX	512-463-2191
Utah	UT	801-538-1326
Vermont	VT	802-828-3171
Virginia	VA	804-786-2071
Washington	WA	360-753-6200
W. Virginia	WV	304-558-2021
Wisconsin	WI	608-266-1221
Wyoming	WY	307-777-7841

CANADA

All handguns and semi-auto military-pattern long guns are prohibited. If you get caught, your weapons will be confiscated, your vehicle may be impounded, and you could face prosecution under Canadian law. Have a nice day, *eh*?

There is no legal concealed carry. Disgusting.

The only firearms allowed entry are *"regular sporting rifles or shotguns with barrels over 18.5 inches and longer than 26 inches in overall length."* As self-defense is *not* considered a legitimate reason for gun importation, the only "correct" reasons are hunting or officially-sanctioned target shoots. Putrescent.

Until 31 December 2000 no permit was required, but now you have to cough up Ø50 for a declaration permit. (Call 800-731-4000 for more information.)

MEXICO

While special permits may be wrangled for hunting rifles (call the consulate at 202-736-1000 for more info), anything else is *prohibita*. Unless you're willing and able to shoot your way out of any potential arrest, don't take in firearms or ammo.

WHAT ABOUT OTHER COUNTRIES?

From what I've heard and read, there are only a few foreign countries which even somewhat recognize one's right to keep and bear arms: Bolivia (no laws!), Crete (*de facto* free), Czech Republic, Finland (5m people; 4m guns), Israel, Norway, Poland, and Switzerland.

Ragnar Benson is researching a book on this very subject, so keep your eye out for it.

CONCLUSION

As restricted as firearms are in much of the USA, this is still the best country in the world for gunowners. *So far...*

CREEPING CITIZEN DISARMAMENT

For several reasons, the freedom-hating gunphobes cannot pass (much less enforce) an outright national ban and confiscation program for all firearms.

Gun ownership is supported by about two-thirds of Americans. About 1 out of 2 households own a gun. 27 States now enjoy *"shall issue"* concealed carry permits, 4 States still use discretionary (though fairly reasonable) systems, and Vermont has never required a permit. Meaning, in 32 States (64%) is it not only possible for sane, non-felon adults to legally carry for protection, it's socially *acceptable.* Handgun ownership is growing (especially amongst women).

Translation: **We are *winning* the conceptual battle for practical self-defense.** The next phases should be automatic CHL reciprocity, and then national Vermont-style carry. Then, we can seek the repeal of the *"Crime Bill"* and the 1990 import ban and the *GCA68.* With the right Supreme Court victory, perhaps even the *NFA34* will be struck down.

Military-style rifles, however, seem to be slowly losing mass acceptance. While most Americans can understand the need for a handgun to protect against criminals, they have yet to realize the need for an FAL or H&K91 or M1A to protect against *government.* And they won't likely make that leap unless government oppression becomes (or at least seems) *personal,* just like street crime did. Except for a few major gaffes like Ruby Ridge and Waco, the USG has generally kept its systemic oppression to somewhat muted levels and thus has not terribly alarmed the general public. While the feds have inexorably been erasing bits of liberty, they are far too impatient to remove the entire edifice brick by brick. At some point, they will have to employ the wrecking ball, if not dynamite.

This is particularly true in the matter of eliminating residual *de facto* 2nd Amendment enjoyment. As you'll see from the table on page 7, they have few remaining "easy squares" to fill in relating to equipment not widely enjoyed by gunowners. Examples of these are .50BMG rifles, NVDs, laser sights, bulletproof vests, and possibly even semi-auto battle rifles. Banning the importation and domestic manufacture of such would likely be their last bloodless victory.

Eventually, they'll have to bring out the wrecking ball of mandatory registration. Registration is a prerequisite to their *real* goals. Without full registration, they cannot fully enforce a ban on private transfers in those 23 States which require no records. Without registration, no coercive buy-up scheme (like Britain's) would have any leverage. Without registration, they cannot bring off a national confiscation.

If we successfully thwart registration, then they will have only two alternatives: **Give up, or *up* the ante.** By "up the ante" I mean proceed directly to a ban and confiscation (which will undoubtedly be a monumental catalyst for citizen reaction).

The reason why gun bans in their areas have *not* caused mass uprisings is that affected gunowners can simply *move* to another State. As Chapter 34 showed, gunowners have 25 States which range from Tolerable to Slices of Heaven. The gunowning *diaspora* can choose from Alaska, 9 Western States, 3 in the Midwest, 8 Southern ones, and even 3 in the East. Most are within a day's move from any gun-hating State. (Kalifornia, for example, has lost many thousands of productive gunowners to Oregon, Nevada, and Arizona.) Accomplishing a national citizeny disarmament through the States has achieved only a 50% moderate success and such clearly cannot be counted on for more than 65-70%. (At least 15 States will *really* dig in on the 2nd Amendment issue from here on out.)

Anti-gun bigots will thus have to attack the very foundation of it all: the 2nd Amendment itself.

Repealing the 2nd Amendment

Since State-level gun restrictions can only go so far, the freedom-haters are now talking about legislative amputation:

*Gun control advocates...should squarely face the need to deconstitutionalize the subject **by repealing the embarrassing Second Amendment**.*

— George F. Will, 21 March 1991

*There is no reason for anyone in this country, anyone except a police officer or a military person, to buy, to own, to have, to use, a handgun...The only way to control handgun use in this country is to prohibit the guns. **And the only way to do that is to change the Constitution.*** (From the guy who faked those pick-up explosions.)

— *NBC News* President Michael Gartner
USA Today, 16 January 1992

*The truth about the Second Amendment is something that liberals cannot bear to admit: The right wing is right. The amendment does confer an individual right to bear arms, **and its very presence makes effective gun control in this country all but impossible.***

So why must we subordinate ourselves to a 208-year old law that, if the latest scholarship is correct, is contrary to what the democratic majority believes is in its best interest?... They (the Founding Fathers) *are dead and buried and will not be around to suffer the consequences. We the living will.*

— Daniel Lazare, "Your Constitution Is Killing You"
Harper's Magazine, October 1999

Going through the State legislatures

Technically, Congress must successfully propose such a constitutional amendment and the President must sign it. Then it is sent out to the 50 States where at least three-fourths of their legislatures must ratify it. Meaning, as few as 13 States (with as little as 4.5% of the population) can prevent its ratification. We certainly have those numbers (and more), and will continue to have them for at least another generation.

Thus, I do not see a proposed repeal likely to succeed, though they may indeed try. Such a naked attempt would likely galvanize into action many of the fence-sitting gunowners.

Calling for a Con-Con

When two-thirds (34) of the States call for a constitutional convention, the entire Constitution is up for grabs. Two sly attempts were made since the mid-1980s. The first was a wholly needless Con-Con to pass a Balanced Budget Amendment.

The second was the trick of Utah Governor Leavitt calling for a "town meeting" of the States to discuss issues of federalism. Thanks to quick action by Patriots and Conservatives through the Net, faxes, and newsletters, the public quickly got wind of this scheme in time to voice sufficient outrage. Leavitt was quite floored with the negative reaction and weakly countered that—*My goodness!*—they weren't trying for a Con-Con, and even if they were they would *never* tamper with the Bill of Rights, and even if they *did* such had to be ratified by at least three fourths of the States.

The People, however, understood that it's far better to keep the wolf *outside*, rather than to let him in (trusting him to never get hungry, or if he did, to never eat *you*).

While I don't discount future attempts at a Con-Con, it's a "hair-trigger" issue for too many Americans to easily succeed.

The gunphobes' best chance to get the 2nd Amendment actually repealed through constitutional procedure lies in the use of State conventions.

Going through *ad hoc* State conventions

*..., or by conventions in three fourths thereof, **as the one or the other mode of ratification may be proposed by the Congress;...***
— Article V; *The Constitution for the United States of America*

This succeeded in 1787-88 when the proposed Constitution sent itself (through Article VII) to State *conventions* and not to the legislatures (which were understandably hostile to relinquishing their State's autonomy). The Federalists skillfully packed enough of these conventions with enough of their people for the Constitution to squeak by.

In my studied opinion, a repeat of this offers the most hope to the gunphobes, and thus we should anticipate it.

In *Hologram of Liberty* I postulated that Con-Con conventioneers, mindful of their treason, would "meet" in cyberspace to avoid receiving rifle fire had they met at a hall. The State conventioneers might also resort to such a security measure.

I certainly am *not* advocating the Federal crime of terrorism, which is (according to Public Law 104-132, Title VII, Section 702(g)(5)(A)) an offense that *"is calculated to influence or affect the conduct of government by intimidation or coercion, or to retaliate against government conduct."* I am merely discussing possible actions/reactions within theoretical scenarios.

Repeal of the 2nd Amendment or not, the gun-haters have no conceptual choice but a *national* ban and confiscation.

A national ban and confiscation

The illegal we can do immediately; the unconstitutional takes a little longer.
— Henry Kissinger (He would know...)

A *national* ban does not leave us with the viable response of moving. There are very few other countries which would welcome American gunowners and their hardware, and even if there were, the only practical way to relocate would be to *sail* there (as we would not be permitted to fly out with our FALs). How many of you own or have access to ocean-going craft?

Translation: It would be far "easier" to simply remain in the USA and finally fight for our liberty.

Any national ban would result in massive noncompliance

If historical noncompliance examples of the *NFA34* and the *"assault weapons"* bans of NYC and Neu Jersey and Kalifornia hold true, under 5% would voluntarily register their guns.

Going house-to-house would be a meat-grinder

Without a registration data list, limited enforcement police would not have the numbers to go house-to-house. Only an *army* conceivably has those numbers, and such has only succeeded when the population were only *very* lightly armed (*e.g.,* Haiti and Panama). When even mildly armed (*e.g.,* Somalia), gun stealing troops got waxed and quickly left.

The rifle "cat" is out of the victim disarmament "bag"!

As Afghanistan proved, the *real* danger to any oppressive government is the widespread citizen ownership of centerfire rifles. As I earlier wrote, while a handgun can protect your life, only a powerful *rifle* (*i.e.,* an MBR) can defend your *Liberty*. No wars, not even guerrilla wars, have ever been won with pistols. If you're serious about staying free, then get an MBR and become "one" with it—*quickly*.

It doesn't even have to be a .308 battle rifle, although such is certainly the tool of choice. A bunch of hicks with mere lever-action .30-30s could probably prevail against a modern army using .223s. As long as the rifle is in a common cartridge with muzzle energy of at least 1700fpe and is accurate to at least 3MOA, then it's probably capable enough.

Still, if you can at all afford a .308 MBR, do so. Hurry.

One possible disarmament timetable

6/34	*NFA34*	*National Firearms Act of 1934*	(mid-term Roosevelt)
6/68	*GCA68*	*Gun Control Act of 1968*	(lame duck Johnson)
5/86	*MV86*	*McClure-Volkmer Act of 1986*	(lame duck Reagan)
11/90	*IB90*	Import Ban of 1990	(mid-term Bush)
11/93	*BB93*	Brady Bill of 1993	(congressional mid-term)
9/94	*CB94*	*"Crime Bill"* of 1994	(mid-term Clinton)

presidential lame-duck (2004-05, 2008-09)

New executive orders or bill signings would be quite possible (*e.g.,* sweeping import bans of mag-fed SLRs and AP ammo). Also, a President's *second* (*i.e.,* final) term is a lame-duck 4 years, in which he has no political accountability.

congressional lame-duck (2002-03, 2004-05)

If a large number of liberal congressmen were voted out of office, they could pass draconian gun laws before January.

just after congressional elections (2002, 04, 06, 08, 10)

A new (or reelected) Congress could flex its muscles with sweeping anti-gun legislation. The 11/90 import ban of military SLRs was the prime example (and during Bush's mid-term).

just after presidential elections (2005, 09)

While this has not been used before, if a Democratic President were elected in 2004 to take office with a liberal Congress, then early 2005 could see disastrous new controls.

presidential mid-term (2006-07, 2010-11)

An arrogant Congress and Clinton tried this with their 9/94 *"Crime Bill"* only to result in the "Republican Revolution" just months later in November. Presidential mid-term years can be *election* years for Congress, thus it's best to wait until *after* the congressional elections (*e.g.,* the 11/90 import ban).

possible future anti-gun legislation of the near future

Here is my read on their goals, and the likely sequence of how they'll try to pass them. A-C are easiest. D-J are difficult.

A	late 2002 (presidential mid-term, just after congressional elections)
B	late 2004/early 2005 (after elections; lame duck President Bush?)
C	mid 2005 (after presidential inauguration)
D	late 2005
E	late 2006 (presidential mid-term, just after congressional elections)
F	???
G	???
HIJ	???

	ban imports	ban U.S. manu.	ex post facto NFA34	mandatory registration	ban future transfer	ban current possession
full-autos	GCA68	1986	NFA34	NFA34	C	E
short barreled rifles/shotguns	GCA68	B	NFA34	NFA34	C	E
"destructive devices"	GCA68	B	NFA34	NFA34	C	E
silencers	GCA68	B	NFA34	NFA34	C	E
DEWATs	GCA68	N/A	GCA68	GCA68	C	E
>.50 caliber guns	GCA68	GCA68	GCA68	GCA68	C	E
USAS-12, Striker, etc.	1990	1994	1994	1994	C	E
"cop killer ammo"	1994	1994	N/A	N/A	N/A	1994
semi-auto "assault weapons"	1990	1994	D	D	D	E
"high-capacity" mags	A	1994	N/A	N/A	C	E
.50BMG ammo	A	B	B	N/A	C	E
.50BMG rifles	A	B	B	B	D	E
"armor piercing" ammo	A	B	B	N/A	C	E
military rifle ammo	B	C	N/A	N/A	D	E
detachable mag semi-auto rifles	A	C	unlikely	unlikely	D	E
shotgun slugs & slug barrels	C	D	E		E	F
"sniper ammo"	C	D	N/A		E	F
"sniper rifles"	C	D	E		E	F
semi-auto handguns	B	E	N/A		E	F
semi-auto centerfire long guns	B	E	N/A		E	F
bulletproof vests	C	D	E		E	F
night vision devices	C	D	E		E	F
laser sights	C	D	E		E	F
pre-1899 guns	D	N/A	N/A	F	G	H
reloading components	C	E	N/A	F	G	H
centerfire handguns	C	F	N/A	F	G	H
centerfire rifles	D	F	N/A	F	G	H
.22LR handguns	C	G	N/A	G	H	I
shotguns	D	G	N/A	G	H	I
blackpowder guns	D	H	N/A	H	I	J
.22LR rifles	D	H	N/A	H	I	J
BB and pellet guns	E	I	N/A	H	I	J
"assault slingshots"	E	I	N/A	H	I	J
"assault blowguns"	E	I	N/A	H	I	J
"assault knives"	E	J	N/A	H	I	J

The above is merely *one* scenario

While I wouldn't be surprised if the successive waves of anti-Bill of Rights legislation didn't follow a similar flow, my crystal ball is just as murky as the next. Things could sour even more quickly than that, or they could (with a Supreme Court case victory) level out (or even *improve*).

Any one of a dozen scenarios could unfold. The one I just outlined seems the most plausible to *me* at *this* time.

MANDATORY REGISTRATION

While the feds can probably get away with import and domestic manufacture bans of mag-fed SLRs, and even *NFA34* classification of .50BMG rifles—mandatory registration of household firearms is the brick wall that will prove unclimbable and unbreakable. Not even the NRA will likely budge on registration. Registration has indisputably been proven to be a mere stepping stone to the *real* goal of confiscation, and the public is quickly realizing this. So, I think the gunhaters will try to *avoid* the "Maginot Line" of gun registration in one of two ways.

a national firearms owner's card

Instead of registering guns, register their owners. After a national gun ban, "visit" everybody on the list to make sure that they've turned in all their guns.

The NICBC system is the first step in this goal. Even though approved records are required by law to be destroyed and not compiled, the FBI is ignoring this.

State CHLs are another form of gunowner registration, providing a list of high-level owners (*i.e.,* those who have the temerity to actually *carry* a handgun).

banning private gun sales

23 States do not require permits or records of private gun transfers. Few of those States will ever do so in the future, so a national ban is required to close that *"loophole."*

Given that all gun control laws since *GCA68* have been (erroneously) based on the foreign/interstate commerce regulatory powers, it will prove difficult, if not impossible, to apply such to private gun sales (especially after ***Lopez***). Banning private sales will probably only succeed if done by executive order.

However accomplished, a transfer ban would eliminate 85% of private sales (*e.g.*, gun shows, flea markets, classified ads, etc.). The 15% of residual, and suddenly illegal, private gun transfers would be "committed" by both the true criminal class and the newly artificial *mala prohibita* "criminal" class (peaceably folks who sell amongst their trusted selves).

More importantly, a national ban on private sales would neatly bypass the brick wall of registration. Whether or not they would have the confidence to actually pass and enforce a ban is another matter. (I suspect not.)

WATCH YOUR TONGUE!

As more and more anti-freedom laws are passed, gunowners will understandably and rightfully grow angrier. You may feel led to write your newspaper or even give a press interview. Fine, but do *not* admit to committing any crimes, don't promise to disobey any future gun laws, and don't bluster or threaten.

Remarks like *"Assault rifles are made to shoot gun-grabbing thugs, and I can't wait for the day when they try to take mine!"* are heartfelt, but stupid. At the least, the media gets its juicy soundbite; at the worst, you become a target for investigation (and possibly a raid). Instead, use counter-questions like:

"Everything criminal about guns and their use is already illegal."

"What does the government have planned for us that we must first be disarmed?"

"If the government's goals are harmless and will have the support of the people, then what's the problem with us remaining armed?"

"If so-called 'assault rifles' cause crime, then why does Switzerland not only allow, but require, all adult males to keep one at home?"

"Did Swiss Jews go to Hitler's death camps? No? Why not?"

"If Germany's Jews had owned guns to defend themselves, would there have been a holocaust?"

"Did you know the world's first gun registration was in the 1930s? In Nazi Germany?"

"Did you know that our federal Gun Control Act of 1968 *came from the Nazis' gun control laws designed to disarm the Jews?"*

"So, the central government wants to ban and confiscate guns from law-abiding Americans? Didn't they try that back in April of 1775?"

"So you're saying that the Minutemen of Lexington and Concord were wrong *to resist their own disarmament by the British? So, you support the colonization of people against their will?"*

"Don't you believe that good people have the right *to protect themselves from the Bad Guys?"*

"Isn't government *sometimes the Bad Guys? How about* often*?"*

"Tell me again why the Swiss *Jews didn't die in the holocaust?"*

How to deal with baited questions

If you're asked if you *personally* would ever use your guns to fight government confiscation, reply that it is your personal policy *not* to answer *hypothetical* questions, and leave it at that. If asked whether you own any *"assault weapons,"* reply that all of your "household firearms" are perfectly lawful, and leave it that. If asked if you *daily* carry a gun with you, reply that such you couldn't say because no day is the same. You get the idea.

BANNING GUNS, AMMO, & GEAR

We've got a tidal wave of more *"gun control"* on the way, with the sequential goals of:

banning imports	(stop the flooding from outside)
banning domestic production	(stop the flooding from inside)
national registration	(identify the soaked areas)
banning private transfers	(prohibit water movement)
national confiscation	(mop up & blot with paper towels)

This has *already* happened in NYC and Neu Jersey. Visit www.gunowners.org and www.jpfo.org for the latest on the national level. (I *highly* recommend joining Gun Owners of America and the Jews for the Preservation of Firearms Ownership, the most effective gun rights lobby groups.)

Here's my forecast of what to expect, and in a logical sequence. (Remember, the enemy has to have a plan, and much of it can be inferred. Certain things are prerequisites for others, and some guns are more of a priority.) I think we have about 1-3 years before any registration attempts, and 2-4 years after that before they try confiscation. Post-2006 should be "fun."

semi-auto *"assault weapons"*

Instead of trying to close the "cosmetic loophole" (through which we can still buy new quasi-MBRs, American-made or not), all detachable mag semi-autos will eventually be banned from further importation and manufacture.

banning importation

Amazingly enough, it is 2000 and we can still buy FALs, H&K91s, AK47s, AK74s, and other foreign rifles (if the foreign parts count is 10 or less). Don't expect this fluke to last. All the President has to do is sign an executive order (to fight terrorism, you see). If you haven't yet bought a parts kit, do so at once!

banning domestic manufacture

If not a total ban, than at least a ban of certain receivers, such as the AR15, M96, FAL, H&K91, SKS, and AK. Yes, folks will howl, but that's about it.

mandatory registration of *"assault weapons"*

Next will have to be some sort of registration (in order to provide for future transfer ban and then confiscation). Semi-auto mag-fed rifles will be transformed into quasi-Title II weapons. Kalifornia, Connecticut, Neu Jersey, and NYC have already done this. You'll have 30-90 days to register yours, or they're contraband. (In those Hitlerian states of Kalifornia and Neu Jersey, less than 3% have so far complied, so the "ball" is in the state governments' court. They'll need federal help.)

ban future transfers

Banning private sales might be achieved easily. Banning dealer transfers would be much more difficult, legally.

ownership ban and confiscation

Since probably less than 5% of the owners will have registered their rifles, a ban won't have much enforcement leverage. The raids are coming. It'll be interesting. I suspect that some (maybe many, but not most) people will resist and the state governors will declare martial law and cry to the feds.

"high-capacity" (*i.e.,* normal capacity) mags

First, they've banned further imports. That, coupled with the production ban of 9/1994, has frozen the civilian supply.

Then, they'll ban *transfers* of pre-1994 full capacity mags. (If you think that prices are steep *now...*) This will also increase the price of 10rd mags (stock up now while they're still Ø20 and under). Since registration of mags is infeasible, a transfer ban will have to suffice until possession is finally banned (probably along with their respective guns). In the meantime, they might also require that new handguns be incompatible with pre-9/94 full capacity mags. (S&W agreed to such in I:2:e.)

They'll likely get away with these two restrictions with little risk. However, going to the *next* step and declaring them contraband will *really* cross the line for many gunowners.

.50BMG rifles and ammo

These rifles are currently making the gun haters froth at their lying mouths. .50BMG target rifles have come under the recent attention of *CNN, The Wall Street Journal*, and other anti-self-defense megaphones. Since few of the public (gunowning or not) own or have even shot such a *"military heavy sniper rifle"* they are a potentially "easy" gun to attack. Fortunately, an intelligent and tight-knit .50BMG target shooting community (the Fifty Caliber Shooting Association, or FCSA) has firmly justified these rifles' *"sporting purpose"* and is poised to defend the tools of their sport.

It seems nearly inevitable, however, that these rifles will be soon restricted. (The precedent was established in 1994 by artificially declaring—without warning—USAS-12, Striker, and Street Sweeper shotguns to be *"destructive devices."*) Such is already a goal of the so-called "Violence Policy Center":

> *Bring heavy and intermediate sniper rifles under the control of the National Firearms Act.*

— www.vpc.org / studies / sniper.htm

Notice that they also mentioned *"intermediate"*? Such would likely mean any caliber between .308 and .50. The VPC also implied that the Branch Davidians used .50BMG rifles on the BATF, which is simply *untrue*. They also claim that there is enough sniper instructional material *"to roil troubled minds and teach home-grown terrorists or impressionable juveniles."* Further, the sniper subculture *"has a mordant appeal for unstable personalities."* Just so you know.

On 10 June 1999 Representatives Blagojevich, Waxman, and Norton introduced HR2127, the so-called *"Military Sniper Weapon Regulation Act of 1999"* which proposes to *"amend the*

Internal Revenue Code of 1986 to regulate certain 50 caliber sniper weapons in the same manner as machine guns and other firearms." Meaning, they'd become *NFA34 "firearms."*

> The Congress finds that—
> *(1) certain firearms originally designed and built for use as long-range 50 caliber military sniper weapons are increasingly sold in the domestic civilian market;*
> *(2) the intended use of these long-range firearms, and an increasing number of models derived directly from them, is the taking of human life and the destruction of materiel, including armored vehicles and such components of the national critical infrastructure as radars and microwave transmission devices;* (Funny, I didn't see that in the brochures. BTP)
> *(3) these firearms are neither designed nor used* **in any significant number** (here is the new standard, apparently) *for legitimate sporting or hunting purposes and are clearly distinguishable from rilfes intended for sporting and hunting use;* (This is horsesh✳t. They are <u>only</u> used for target sports and hunting! BTP)
> *(4) extraordinarily destructive ammunition for these weapons, including armor-piercing and armor-piercing incendiary ammunition, is freely sold in interstate commerce; and*
> *(5) the virtually unrestricted availability of these firearms and ammunition, given the uses intended in their design and manufacture,* **present a serious and substantial threat to the national security.**

They just had to throw in *"national security"* to get everyone all jittery. Now, after 9/11, they're claiming terrorists have them.

"armor piercing" ammo

The black-tipped AP .308, .30-06, etc. is destined to be banned, just like the so-called *"cop killer bullets."* Stock up.

most centerfire rifle ammo can perforate steel

Velocity is the key to penetration (ask any laser), and therefore *all* rifle ammo is somewhat "armor piercing" in a technical sense (though it's not designed to be). Pistol calibers pale in power and range compared to any centerfire rifle caliber. Expect Congress to realize this in a couple of years.

military rifle ammo

Meaning, 5.45x39, 5.56x45, 7.62x39, 7.62x51, 7.62x54R, .30-06, .303 British, etc. First, the import ban (which will be relatively easy to achieve). Chinese ammo has already been banned from further importation, so what's to stop Congress from cutting off the Russian, Czech, and South African stuff?

A ban on *domestic* production, however, will be *much* more difficult, so what they'll probably end up doing instead is banning sales to civilians and private transfers (figuring that we'll eventually exhaust our own supplies). They might later ban having more than, say, 1,000rds (to gauge public reaction).

detachable mag semi-auto rifles

These are *non grata* to the freedom haters. Since the post-1994 quasi-*"assault rifles"* (lacking only a flash suppressor or pistol grip) legally circumvent the ban, the gunhaters will have to restrict *all* mag-fed SLRs. Besides, the *"assault rifle"* cosmetic hysteria of 1994 was just a stepping stone, anyway.

Concentrate on owning *rifles*. Like the Afghans, if we're going to fight this thing, we'll win through the competent use of *rifles*. (60,000 dead Soviets can't be wrong.) Handguns are what you use to gain time and distance from your assailants to grab your rifle. You shouldn't be so close as handgun range to the enemy, anyway. Get a good .308 or .30-06 scoped bolt-action, a good .308 battle rifle, and *lots* of training ammo.

import ban

Easy to do and with little likely outrage (as few guns will be affected, such as the AK Hunter, etc.). In 1998 Klinton signed an executive order 120-day ban.

catching hunting semi-autos in the *"assault rifle"* net

Two major California gun stores (Turner's Outdoorsman and Trader Sports, Inc.) announced that they have indefinitely suspended the sale of semi-auto sporting rifles, such as the Remington 7400 and the Ruger Mini-14. The Kalifornia *"assault weapons"* ban is so vague that gun stores are not taking any chances with an overzealous interpretation regarding wholly cosmetic features.

"As California goes, so goes the nation." Given that Kalifornia is the mortally wounded canary in the coal mine, anticipate more State-level bans on military-pattern SLRs, which will eventually affect hunting and target rifles.

domestic production ban

Once foreign guns can no longer get in, they'll deal with domestic guns. This will be justified by their bleating *"Nobody needs a semi-auto rifle to hunt deer."* Technically, that may be true, but the greater issue of gun rights will be lost in the noise.

Now it begins to get *difficult* for Congress, as they're messing with *American* jobs and companies. Congress nearly banned new domestic *"assault rifles"* in 1991 (including the Colt AR15), but didn't quite have the nerve.

Look, the congressional graffiti is on the wall already. You're supposed to shut up and pay up. Why's a good little slave like you wanting a nasty *"assault rifle"* anyway?

registration

Oh, how the fascists are licking their chops over this! Millions of military-pattern SLRs are out there in unknown hands, and it just drives them nuts. Still, registration will be very tough to pass, even for these guns.

banning transfers

As with *"high-capacity"* mags, they'll likely bypass registration and simply ban transfers until a possession ban.

possession ban

The gunhaters will have a conceptual snag on banning these: if such rifles are deemed "bad" later, sharp folks will ask why they weren't "bad" back in 1994 and banned along with their military *"assault rifle"* brethren.

shotgun slugs & slug barrels

Even though a 12 gauge 1oz slug at 1400fps gives only 3047fpe (equal to a .30-06), it is .729 and will likely come under scrutiny and get on the fast track for *"destructive device"* classification. Even a 20 gauge is .615 caliber. Stay tuned...

"sniper ammo"

This could come to mean anything Sarah Brady says it means. Basically, any centerfire hunting cartridge will qualify. Naturally, this will really anger the hunters.

"sniper rifles"

Trying to distinguish between hunting rifles and *"sniper rifles"* for regulation's sake is impossible, but that won't likely stop the gunphobes. Given how entrenched hunting is in America, they probably won't be able to pull it off. They'll start with the .50BMG rifles (*"military heavy sniper rifles"*). Then, they'll work down to the *"intermediate sniper rifles"* of .309-.499 calibers, and *that* will wake up America's riflemen!   Few gunowners have a .50BMG, but *many* of them have an 8x57, .338WM, .35 Whelen, .45-70, etc.

mandatory registration

This will mean any centerfire rifle readily capable of accepting a telescopic sight—which means *all* of them.

The day some "Manchurian Candidate" (going through *Prozac®* withdrawal) snipes somebody, rush out and stock up on scopes, mounts and rings for Rugers, Winchesters, Remingtons, AKs, SKSs, Mini-14s, AR15s, etc.   You'll eventually be able to sell them for 2-3X times what you paid for them.

semi-auto handguns

Given the millions of recent CHL holders, an outright ban will be difficult, if not impossible. However, since these people are *already licensed*, registration (gun and/or owner) is a small and relatively painless conceptual step.

semi-auto centerfire long guns

For symmetry's sake, these will have to go, too. A .30-06 Browning BAR or Remington 7400 (or M1 Garand!) are powerful and accurate rifles with semi-auto firepower. While bans on importation and domestic manufacture for civilians might go through, registration and possession ban won't. (Bummer for the gunhaters; most of the easily restricted guns have already been affected. Now, their road quickly grows steeply uphill!)

bulletproof vests

"Only criminals are afraid of getting shot!" will be the way the gun bigots try to demonize the civilian ownership of vests. We're already seeing an early wind of this with Stupak's HR1423, the *"Body Armor Restriction Act of 1999,"* which would prohibit mail order sales to civilians.

Visit www.bulletproofme.com for updates on body armor.

night vision devices

They'll eventually have to get around to these. NVDs are one of the pieces of equipment which give the owner an order of magnitude increase in advantage. If you don't have a 3rd Gen American NVD, then get moving. Yeah, a pair of PVS-7Bs are Ø2,300+, but what *cooler* thing could you buy for that money? It's dark 40% of the time, and without an NVD you're blind 40% of the time.

laser sights

Tactically, I won't really miss these (except for IR laser target designators), but a ban will make Congress feel good (and that's what is important).

pre-1899 guns

Guns made before 1899 are not federal *"firearms"* and thus transfer unregulated. As I earlier explained, some of these are perfectly viable weapons, such as the Turkish M93. All can be mail ordered without paperwork or license and delivered right to your door! Take advantage of this opportunity quickly.

reloading components

While guns can last for generations, ammo is used up quickly. Although 1,000rds sounds like a lot, a week of intensive shooting can easily go through that. Before ammo is taxed out of existence, or banned, you should have a lifetime's supply (at least for your most important guns). I'd rather be ammo-heavy than gun-heavy.

tagging gunpowder for detection and ID

A report was due on 30 September 1997 from a special panel which investigated whether tracers in gunpowder will:

❶ pose a risk to human life or safety;
❷ help law enforcement;
❸ harm the quality and performance of gunpowders;
❹ harm the environment;
❺ cost more than its worth.

In addition, the panel must have projected:

❶ the cost to make tagged powders;
❷ the cost to regulate the system;
❸ the costs and effects on the consumers;
❹ the effect on consumer demand for ammunition;
❺ how hard it'll be for "terrorists" to evade taggants;
❻ if taggants could be evaded by homemade powders.

> *It would be an easy step to make taggants unavailable to anyone other than those four main manufacturers. Then, **perhaps as a condition for selling to government agencies,** [the federals could] require those manufacturers to stop selling to gun shops and the public, thus making ammunition unavailable to anyone outside of law enforcement.*
> — from *Send in the Waco Killers* (1999), p.435

The moral is: Stock up on ammo and gunpowder *today*. You can't lose with highly versatile powders such as Unique, H335, IMR4320, and IMR4895. (If you have a pet load with VihtaVuori or something else a bit exotic, be sure to get plenty of that, too.) Get a lifetime supply for you, your family, your friends, and any future family and friends. **There's no such thing as *too* much ammo.** Remember, guns can last forever, but ammo is *quickly* used up. Have at least 5,000rds per handgun, 1,000rds per scoped rifle, and 10,000rds per battle rifle.

What you don't use, others will eagerly buy or trade from you, as most people will *not* have stocked enough. *Count* on it.

U.S. military wants tungsten-core ammo

Due to ostensible environmental concerns, the DoD is replacing lead core ammo with tungsten. Tungsten is much more expensive than lead, and its melting point is 10 times higher (so much more energy will be required for production).

Why not use *steel*? Because we *have* steel; we don't have tungsten. Well, who has the worlds' reserves of tungsten? China. Which nation poses the greatest strategic threat to America over the next generation? China. Incredible, isn't it?

If this switch happens, then our ammo will be next as the ecofascists take up a new banner for victim disarmament.

centerfire handguns
mandatory registration

After the 30-90 day window, they're contraband. All CHL holders will have their handgun tied to their Card. Can't buy ammo or parts for handguns without a Firearm Ownership Card. Ask any Massachusetts slave how this works.

centerfire rifles

Even bolt-action rifles somehow escaping the *"sniper rifle"* classification will be targeted. A .308 round delivers 2700fpe, regardless what kind of rifle fires it, SLR or not.

.22LR handguns

Handguns are concealable, and any handgun can take out an occupying soldier. .22LRs will at last be restricted.

shotguns

Yeah, sure, the trapshooters will complain, but so *what?* They kept quiet all this time because their Ø6,000 Perazzis weren't affected, and now it's too late.

blackpowder guns
.22LR rifles
BB and pellet guns
"assault slingshots"
"assault blowguns"
"assault knives"

For the moment, this is all that the British can own. It's difficult to defend your right to keep and bear kitchen knives.

REGULATING ACTIVITIES

Many men are capable of dying on the barricades for a big issue, but few—very few—are able to resist the gray suction of small, unheralded, day-by-day surrenders.
— Ayn Rand, *The Ayn Rand Letter,* 22 May 1972

Eliminate gun show private sales

This could happen anytime (*e.g.,* S.890 from Lieberman and McCain). *Lots* of pressure and hysteria over 9/11 will be brought to bear on this very issue. Of course they're not calling it a "ban," but closing the *"loophole"* by requiring NICBCs. If this is achieved it naturally won't stop a single crime, so next will be flea markets, then newspaper ads, etc. Buy now!

Quantity limitation on dealer purchases

Currently there is a *"Twelve Is Enough"* H.R.12 bill introduced by Charles Schumer (who else?) which would limit buyers to no more than one handgun per month. Since most of the public doesn't relate to a need (or simple desire) to own multiple handguns, this bill might go through. *"Why, anybody buying more than twelve pistols in a year <u>must</u> have criminal purposes!"* (That's like saying anybody who buys more than 12 gallons of gas per week must be an interstate drug smuggler.)

Outlawing privately-sold handguns
This will probably be the first private sale ban, followed by semi-auto rifles. (This nearly happened in 1999.)

Outlawing private sales of *all* guns
Gun shows are almost totally free of state and federal regulation despite a 1993 federal investigation that found stolen military weapons being routinely sold at them. (Yeah, <u>suuuure</u>! BTP)
— 28 December 1997, *The Chicago Tribune*

In *Brady* Ø200,000,000 was allocated annually to the Attorney General for a NICBC system online by 30 November 1998. This affects *all* dealer firearm transfers, not just handguns. (If you're ever questioned after a possession ban regarding the whereabouts of your papered gun, you can say that you needed the money and sold everything at a gun show to private buyers.)

In the 1998 edition of this book, I forecasted that once the NICBC system is in place that private (*i.e.,* non-dealer) gun sales and transfers will at last be prohibited. In the 23 states (mostly in the South and the West) which do *not* restrict private transfers, this will kill the gun show and classified ad sales. It's no accident; it was *meant* to do so.

After that, how can *strangers* network? How will you *trust* one another during a forbidden private sale? You *won't*, so the only people you'll be able to buy from or sell to without federal paperwork will be *reliable* friends, neighbors and relatives. Will they have *exactly* what you need in the future? *Doubtful.* **The odds are against an excess supply amongst your trusted people.** Can pressure be exerted on them to give up your name and inventory? *Absolutely.* Buy now, *privately and without paperwork*, while you still *can*.

Further reduce the number of FFLs
[A] purposeful campaign was launched to jack up the annual FFL fee and to require FFL holders to prove they had a permanent place of business, a fixed address, at which the main activity was a "commercial gun store." By the end of 1997, the federals had

quickly succeeded in trimming the number of American FFL holders by two-thirds.

When was the last time you heard of a revenue agency complaining that too many people were paying their fees? *Also, now that the ATF's "regulatory burden" has been reduced by two-thirds (soon to become 95 percent), has their budget been trimmed by two-thirds? Ha!*
— Vin Suprynowicz, *Send in the Waco Killers* (1999), p. 364

Hound domestic gun makers out of business

Nuisance lawsuits have already affected Colt, Ruger, and Jennings. Force them out of business, or into being only government contractors (read the S&W agreement). (Colt seems halfway there. Bill Ruger would love to be a government contractor, but the feds don't want his crappy guns.)

Gun-Free School Zone enforcement

Even though **Lopez** struck down the 1991 Act, it was brazenly repassed in 1997, and is just waiting for illegal enforcement. (Who are you going to complain *to*? The Supreme Court already ruled in your favor, but is being ignored!)

Credit goes to GOA for killing HB163 which would have given BATF agents power to stop vehicles and seize otherwise legally owned firearms that were in violation of the school zone ban. I expect that a near-future Supreme Court will expand the *Terry* doctrine to allow the full search of autos (including the trunk and locked containers) *without* probable cause. This is *de facto* practice in Neu Jersey. Done nationally by the BATF, this may indeed prove to be the spark of insurrection.

When the BATF and your local police set up checkpoints within 1,000' of schools to search for weapons, I expect some shooting incidents. **Folks, if we allow gun-search checkpoints, then we've *lost*.** Cordoned-off blocks and house-to-house searches will be next.

Restrict or abolish the *"licensed collectors"*

For just Ø10/year you can become a *"licensed collector"* of *"curios and relics"* and legally avoid NICBCs and 4473s. As I covered in Chapter 29, many of these guns are very capable for self-defense (*e.g.*, P35, P38, 1911, Win. pre-64 M70, .308 Indian Lee-Enfield, Russian SKS, M1 Garand, and FN49).

No purchase of gun stuff without Card

No more filling up a basket at WalMart and paying with cash. Your Firearm Ownership ID Card will have its bar code scanned and the Federal computers will instantly upgrade your known inventory. Purchase permission can be denied onsite if the transaction is deemed *"suspicious or excessive."* *"Gun-related items"* will include books, paramilitary gear, reloading equipment, holsters, mags, firing pins, etc.

Mandatory *"arsenal"* license and inspection

The BATF already requires an additional form for 2 or more handgun purchases within 5 days from the same FFL. Someday, anybody with more than 2 guns or 1,000rds of ammo has an *"arsenal"* and must be visited by BATF prior to getting a Ø200 *"arsenal"* permit. Undeclared stuff will get you 10 years.

Severe regulation/closure of gun ranges

The EPA has already begun this tactic. Outdoor ranges are hassled over noise regulations, and indoor ranges are closed because of alleged lead pollution. If there's no public place to shoot, then we won't be able to sight-in and practice as easily. Shooting skills, like any other skills, erode from disuse.

Federal law banning the carrying of firearms

Senator Frank Lautenberg (D-NJ) proposed this in S.707, which would override state concealed-carry and open-carry laws. I warned you about precisely this in 1997 (*Bulletproof Privacy*; 14/2-3). It *will* happen someday, probably by UN resolution to give Congress its *"our hands are tied"* excuse. If you have a CCW permit your name will be on a handy list. Read my *Bulletproof Privacy* and disappear. Lock and load.

...but the federal judges should be able to conceal carry...

On 11 May 1999, HR1752, *"The Federal Courts Improvement Act of 1999,"* was introduced by Berman (D-CA) and Coble (R-NC). Buried in this seemingly innocuous bill is language allowing federal judges, both current and retired, to conceal carry firearms, regardless of any state or local laws or regulations. The temerity is breathtaking.

You see, the federal judges want to be able to protect themselves from the very irate citizens they helped to disarm.

THE MANIA FOR *"SMART GUNS"*

"Smart guns" which can only be fired by their *"authorized user"* will allegedly reduce or eliminate the possibility of a child or a burglar using somebody else's gun. This idea is being championed by that ignorant class of pseudo-intellectuals with no concomitant Real World experience. They habitually gravitate to *prima facie* elegant technological "answers" to questions and issues too silly to deserve being taken seriously. (On this point, it's bitterly ironic that the same pansy liberals who so strongly objected to SDI—Reagan's "Star Wars" anti-ICBM system—as being a technological pipe dream, are the same ones so revoltingly *gaah-gaah* over *"smart guns."* Hypocrites!)

There are only three forms of ID:

Something you *know*   (*e.g.,* a password or combination)
Something you *have*   (*e.g.,* a key or mag-strip ID card)
Something you *are*   (*e.g.,* biometric print of finger, voice, etc.)

"Authorized user" gunlocks can employ each of the above.

Something you *know*

This would be a combination lock. Trigger locks and lockboxes already exist and are inexpensive, and SIG plans to debut this year a 4-digit keypad pistol. Still, these do not meet Government's ulterior goals, as I'll soon explain.

Something you *have*

This would be a coded-transmitter wristband or magnetic ring. While such would theoretically significantly curtail the misuse of stolen guns, it does not satisfy ulterior goals.

The something you *are*

This form of ID is the most insidious, and the most effective in what Government is *really* after.

S&W's fingerprint scanner gunlock

S&W has spent Ø5 million since 1996 on *"smart gun"* technology, placing its silly hopes on a biometric ID system. Your fingerprint would be scanned, and a digital representation would then be downloaded into the gun's on-board computer. To unlock your gun, place your finger on the gun's scanner. (No, I'm not kidding—they're quite serious about all this!)

I think that part of the reason why this particular idea is being pursued is to perfect such for law enforcement.

Individual cops would love to carry a portable fingerprint scanner which is radio-linked with a national databank! (This technology would be the death knell of false ID and aliases, which circumvent controls of any tyrannical state.)

Another related goal of this technology is to condition all of us to be regularly fingerprinted. The banks are already doing a fine job of this for check-cashing requirements.

My philosophical objections

It's the *"authorized user"* language that gives me the chills. *"Authorized"* by *whom*? Gunowner or Government? To avoid public rejection of the scheme, authorization will first be voluntarily performed by the gunowner in some kind of in-house "self-registration." You'll scan your own fingerprint, or don your own wristband or ring transmitter.

Next, it will then be a simple regulatory matter to make mandatory what was previously voluntary. Finally, change the authorizing party from owner to Government, thus indirectly creating a databank of such gunowners (while simultaneously denying that such a databank in itself was ever a goal).

The whole scheme is a trap, and a clever one. Beware.

A small tactical concern

Through training we should gunproof our children, and not trying to "childproof" our guns. But, since Government is making it very difficult (if not illegal) to give children heirloom guns (as we received) or to take them shooting, modern youth are having less and less exposure to guns. This is unhealthy, not just from a civic standpoint (*e.g.,* for defense of self and nation), but in a *literal* sense by indirectly creating legislated gun ignorance which will increase negligent gun casualties.

My technological objections

No defensive firearm should ever rely upon any technology more advanced than Newtonian physics. That especially includes batteries, radiolinks, encryption, scanning devices, and microcomputers. Even if a particular system *could* be 99.9% reliable, that means it can be *expected to fail* once every 1,000 operations. That's not reliable enough—my life deserves more certainty.

DOWN THE SLIPPERY U.K. SLOPE

This section was lifted from an excellent essay by Joseph E. Olson and David B. Kopel called *All The Way Down The Slippery Slope: Gun Prohibition in England and Some Lessons for Civil Liberties in America.* You can download it from www.2ndlawlib.org/journals/okslip.html. I've spliced together some of the most concise sections, as the essay is 56 pages long.

Separating future generations from guns

The British government in the 1950s left the subject of gun control alone. Crime was still quite low, and issues such as national health care and the Cold War dominated the political dialogue. Even so, the maintenance of the existing, relatively mild, structure of rifle and pistol licensing would have important consequences. As the Firearms Act remained in force year after year, a smaller and smaller percentage of the population could remember a time in their own lives when a Briton could buy a rifle or pistol because he had a right to do so rather than because he had convinced a police administrator that there was a "good reason" for him to purchase the gun. As the post-1920 generation grew up, the licensing provisions of the Firearms Act began to seem less like a change from previous conditions and more like part of ordinary social circumstances. A similar process is at work in the United States, where only part of the population remembers the days before 1968 when federal registration was not required for people to purchase firearms.

The 1968 law contained one other provision that illustrated a key strategy of how to push something down a slippery slope: it is easier to legislate against people who cannot vote, or who are not yet born, than against adults who want to retain their rights. Reducing the number people who will, one day in the future, care about exercising a particular right is a good way to ensure that, on that future day, new restrictions on the right will be politically easier to enact. Thus, the 1967 law did nothing to take away guns from law-abiding adults, but the Act did severely restrict gun transfers to minors. It became illegal for a father to give even an airgun as a gift to his thirteen-year-old son. The fewer young people who enjoy the exercise of a civil liberty such as the shooting sports, the fewer adults there will eventually be to defend that civil liberty.

This conditioning young people not to believe they have rights can exist in other contexts, of course. For example, the current American practice of denying American schoolchildren constitutional protection from locker searches, dog sniffs, metal detectors, and random drug testing is a good way to raise a generation with little appreciation for the Fourth Amendment.

If, over the course of generations, the percentage of a population that is interested in a right can be gradually reduced, stricter controls become more politically feasible, and the stricter controls can further reduce the long-term number of people who exercise their rights. This suggests the long-term importance of young people exercising their rights. If high school newspapers have large staffs that fearlessly report the truth, the future of the First Amendment is better protected. If, conversely, laws prevent teenagers from target shooting or hunting, the future of the Second Amendment is endangered.

Britain becomes totalitarian

National security concerns do more than keep British citizens from learning about their government. The *Security Service Act of 1989* provides: *"No entry on or interference with property shall be unlawful if it is authorized by a warrant issued by the secretary of state."* If committed pursuant to an order from the secretary of state, acts such as theft, damage to property, arson, procuring information for blackmail, and leaving planted evidence are not crimes. In the United States, no official of the Executive Branch can authorize such actions. Only a court can authorize a government breaking and entering, and only if the government presents particular proof of necessity.

Security continues to eat away at other traditional rights of British subjects. In Northern Ireland the jury has been "suspended" for political violence cases. Confessions are admitted without corroboration. **Confessions are extracted through** *"the five techniques:"* wall-standing, hooding, continuous noise, deprivation of food, and deprivation of sleep. Convictions may be based solely on the testimony of "supergrasses" (police informers).

The Birmingham bombings that led to the *Prevention of Terrorism Act* resulted in the conviction of a group of defendants called the "Birmingham Six." The defendants confessed while being held incommunicado by the police. The various confessions were so factually inconsistent that they could not have been true. The forensic scientist whose testimony convicted the Birmingham Six later admitted that he lied in court. Amnesty International charged that the defendants' confessions were extracted under torture. Civil libertarians fear that the Birmingham case is only one of many instances of police obtaining coerced confessions.

Of course United States police have sometimes framed people and manufactured evidence. What is stunning about the Birmingham Six case is the rationale used by Britain's highest judicial body to deny the appeal:

> *If the six men win, it will mean that the police were guilty of perjury ...violence and threats, and the confessions were involuntary and improperly admitted and that the convictions were erroneous. The Home Secretary would have to recommend that they be pardoned or remit the case to the Court of Appeal.* **This is such an appalling vista that any sensible person in the land would say: It cannot be right that these actions should go any further. They should be struck out.**
> — *McIlkenney v. Chief Constable of West Midlands Police Force,* 2 W.L.R. 872 (C.A. 1980), at p.444

Failure of British gun control & prohibition

Have all these controls and abusive enforcement of controls actually made Britain safer? Armed crime in Britain is higher than it has been in at least two centuries. Armed crime is literally one hundred times more common than at the turn of the century when Britain had no weapons controls. Crime victimization surveys show that, per capita, assault in England and Wales occurs between two and three times more often than in the United States. These same surveys demonstrate that robbery occurs 1.4 times more, and burglary occurs 1.7 times more. In contrast to criminologists in the United States, British criminologists have displayed little interest in studying whether their nation's gun laws do any good. Accordingly, definitive statements about cause and effect should be avoided. One can, however, say that as British gun laws have grown more severe, the country has grown more dangerous.

The raw statistics do make some facts clear: when Britain had no gun control (early in the twentieth century) or moderately-administered gun control (in the middle of the century), Britain had virtually no gun crime. Today, Britain literally has substantially more gun crime, as well as more violent crime in general. From 1776 until very recently, the United States has suffered a much higher violent crime rate than Britain, regardless of whether British gun laws were liberal or strict. In recent years, however, the once-wide gap in violent crime has disappeared. **This gap was closed by a moderate drop in American crime rates, coupled with a sharp rise in the British rates.** One does not hear British gun control advocates touting statistics about how crime rates fell after previous gun laws were enacted. Rather, the advocacy is based on the "inherent danger of guns," and on the "horror" of Dunblane and Hungerford.

The *"sporting purpose"* trap

The British gun-owners must accept much of the blame for their current predicament because of their concession that guns were only appropriate for sports. When the Home Office in the 1980s began complaining that some people were obtaining guns for protection, British Shooting Sports Council joined the complaint: *"This, if it is a fact, is an alarming trend and reflects sadly on our society."* One hunting lobby official condemned *"the growing number of weapons being held in urban areas"* for reasons having nothing to do with sport. The major hunting lobby, the British Association for Shooting and Conservation, defended the right to arms, but only, in its words, *"the freedom to possess and use sporting arms."*

The BASC's stance may appear to be a "reasonable" position, which demonstrates that gun-owners are not bloodthirsty nuts wanting to shoot people. Rather, shooters are harmless sportsmen, and licensed guns belong in the same category as cricket bats or golf clubs. In practice, however, the concession that guns are only for sports undermines defense of the right to bear arms. If guns are not to be owned for defense, then guns make no positive contribution to public safety. If the sovereignty of the central government is absolute, then the people's ownership of arms makes no positive contribution to a sound body politic.

British libertarian Sean Gabb points out that the British gun lobbies' support of gun licensing undermines the lobbies' arguments that licensed gun owners are not part of the gun crime problem. As Gabb writes: "[b]*ut if control is needed, and if it can be made to work, the fact that it did not prevent Thomas Hamilton from shooting those poor children is surely an argument at least for tightening it in future.*" Gabb further argues that British gun owners have been losing battle after battle and have therefore shriveled in numbers because *"you all failed to put the real case for guns—that their possession for defence is a moral right and duty, as well as a positive social good."* Instead, the many eloquent MPs who spoke against handgun confiscation pointed to all the admirable sporting uses of sporting guns: by handicapped people in the paralympics; by British athletes in the Olympics and in the Commonwealth Games; and by ordinary Britons on a Saturday afternoon of innocent sport.

The anti-ban MPs spoke well, but the prohibitionists' argument, while simple, was intellectually stronger. There are substitutes for sports; displaced handgun shooters can still use rifles or shotguns or airguns. But there is no substitute for a child's life. Even if virtually all handguns are never misused, at the very least, once in a while a handgun will be. If complete prohibition saves one life, it's worth it. The score in this debate, for potential lives saved was Gun Ownership: zero; Gun Prohibition: perhaps one or more. If this is the only calculus, then prohibition is a clear winner.

The only practical way that British gun owners could have avoided abuse of the licensing laws would have been to resist the first proposed laws that allowed the police to determine who could get a gun license. However the gun owners never would have dreamed of resisting, because such a law seemed so "reasonable." Having meekly accepted the wishes of the police and the ruling party for "reasonable" controls, by the early 1970's British rifle and handgun owners found themselves in a boiling pot of severe controls from which escape was no longer possible. British shotgun owners, ignoring the fate of their rifle and handgun-owning brethren, jumped into their own pot of then-lukewarm water when they accepted the 1966 shotgun licensing proposals.

British gun prohibition in 2000 and beyond

Gun control in Great Britain now proceeds on two fronts. When a sensational crime takes place, proposals for gun confiscations and for major new restrictions on the licensing system are introduced.   During more tranquil times, fees are raised and increased controls are applied to relatively smaller issues.

The frog-cooking principle helps explain why America's Handgun Control, Inc. (HCI), and the other anti-gun lobbies are so desperate to pass any kind of gun control, even controls that most observers agree will accomplish very little.   By lobbying for the enactment of, for example, the Brady Bill, HCI established the principle of a national gun licensing system. Once a lenient national handgun licensing system was established in 1993, the foundation was laid so that the licensing system can gradually be tightened.   The push has already begun, as President Clinton echoes HCI's demand that Congress close the "loophole" in the Brady Act that allows private individuals, those persons not in the gun business, to sell firearms to each other without going through the federal Brady background check.

Legal British gun owners now constitute only four percent of total households, with perhaps another small percentage of the population possessing illegal, unregistered guns.   Given that many Britons have no personal acquaintance with anyone who they know to be a sporting shooter, it is not surprising that seventy-six percent of the population supports banning all guns.   Thus, the people who used long guns in the field sports—who confidently expected that whatever controls government imposed on the rabble in the cities who wanted handguns, genteel deer rifles and hand-made shotguns would be left alone—have been proven disastrously wrong.

Strong rights usually need a strong sociological foundation.   Approximately half of American homes contain a gun, and a quarter contain a handgun.   Thus, except in a few cities like New York where gun ownership is rare, gun bans in the United States are nearly impossible to enact; too many voters would be unhappy.   Consequently gun prohibition in the United States must focus on very small segments of the gun-owning population.   That is why "assault weapon" bans, which cover only about one or two percent of the total firearms stock, are so much easier to enact than handgun bans.   Even with "assault weapons," it is usually necessary to exempt the Ruger

Mini-14 and Mini-30 rifles since these rifles, while functionally identical to banned guns, have too large an ownership base.

Continued appeasement?

Almost every time the British government has demanded more power, the great mass of British gun owners have placidly accepted the government's action without protest. The 1996-97 push for handgun confiscation saw the first significant display of mass gun-owner activism in many years, with tens of thousands of law-abiding gun owners and supporters rallying at demonstrations, and letter after letter to M.P.s. It was the biggest and most powerful display of political activism by British gun rights advocates in the twentieth century. If the gun owners had rallied so effectively in 1967, or in 1920, they would not be on the verge of extinction today. If they can sustain the present level of political activism into the next century, they will at least have a chance of survival.

But the politics of British gun owners in most of the twentieth century are a failure. The consequence of the "reasonable" approach of the gun owners has not been a reasonable treatment by the British government. Instead, the government has pressed down restriction after restriction upon the British people, and as every restriction fails to halt the rising tide of crime, the British government invents still more "reasonable" gun controls to distract the public from the government's inept efforts at crime control.

As armed crime grows worse and worse, despite nearly a century of severe firearms controls, the British government expends more and more energy "cracking down" on the rights of the law-abiding British people. The undermining of the right to arms has paralleled the destruction of many other common law rights, including the grand jury right, freedom of the press from prior restraints, the civil jury, freedom from warrantless searches, the right to confront one's accusers, and the right against self-incrimination. People who want to argue that gun rights can be destroyed while other rights prosper must find some other country to use as an example.

The United States' gun control lobbies and their intellectual supporters brim with praise for Britain's "sensible" gun laws. In response, are citizens of the United States who cherish Second Amendment rights necessarily wrong for being reluctant to take any more steps down the slippery slope? Should those United States citizens who cherish other parts of the Bill of Rights look forward to their civil liberty standards becoming more like Britain's?

Towards Closer Analysis of Slippery Slopes

While slippery slopes are frequently invoked in political and legal debate, little attention has been paid to factors that contribute to the real, as opposed to the merely theoretical, danger that a first step down a slippery slope may lead to severe damage or even elimination of a civil liberty. This Essay has identified the following factors that helped lead to the destruction of the right to arms in Great Britain:

media sensationalism about abuses of the right and media hostility toward the exercise of the right;

technological changes that introduce new and socially controversial ways of exercising the right;

the hesitation of extending civil liberties principles developed under old technologies to new technologies;

the creation of government jurisdiction, in the form of a licensing system, that created a platform for administrative constriction of the right;

political leaders gaining political benefits (such as diverting the public from the death penalty, or demonstrating the leader's compassion) from attacks on the right;

restrictions aimed at teenagers, which over the long term reduced the number of adults interested in the exercising of the right, and, consequently reduced the number of adults interested in defending the right politically;

shifting the burden of proof away from the government, which no longer had to prove the need for new restrictions or for the denial of a permit to exercise the right, and placing the burden on the individual, who had to prove his or her need to own a particular item;

restrictions created by administrative fiat that further reduced adult entry into or continuance in the activity, thus driving the exercise of the right to levels so low that rights advocates became an insignificant political group;

the production of deliberately misleading data by the government in support of restrictive legislation;

registration of the property of persons who exercised the right, which was later used to facilitate confiscation of property;

the government's loss of trust in ordinary citizens.

In addition, we identified one other potential factor that might encourage movement down a slippery slope, that being the prominent success of an earlier step down the slope; this factor did not appear to be present in England. None of the British gun controls resulted in any statistically noticeable reduction in crime in the years after their enactment.

These factors are not the only factors that could make a slippery slope situation dangerous; but when slippery slope arguments are raised, the presence (or absence) of these factors may indicate how real the slippery slope danger is. The more factors that are present, the greater the potential slippery slope risk.

This Essay has also identified several structural elements in the British system of government that contributed to the gradual elimination of the right to arms in Great Britain:

rights are subject to balancing against perceived government or social needs;

the government is not constrained by internal checks and balances;

there is a consensus that Parliament, which is, in practice, a few leaders of the majority party, rather than the people or the law, is sovereign;

there is no written constitution;

the absence of a right in a written constitution impedes the growth of rights consciousness among the people.

Regarding most of these elements, the United States is radically different from Great Britain. Consequently, civil liberties of all types are stronger in the United States than in Great Britain. However, the erosion of federalism and of the separation of powers over the last half century in the United States should caution Americans against complacency regarding the security of their constitutional structure.

We also identified several factors about the political defense of gun rights in Great Britain that made the arms right vulnerable to the slippery slope. Most of these factors have parallels regarding the defense of other civil liberties in Britain:

the right was defended only on sporting grounds, and not on the basis that it protects people from dangerous criminals or from dangerously criminal governments;

the right's defenders accepted and even applauded a great deal of regulation of the right;

the right's defenders accepted the principle that the right could be further regulated whenever the government saw a need, rather than only when there was a genuine necessity for more regulation;

the right's defenders usually appeased the government, rather than resisting unjustifiable government demands for more controls;

people who exercised the right in one way were often unwilling to defend people who exercised the right in a different way.

As with constitutional structure, the American system is considerably more sound than the British one. Civil liberties organizations such as the National Rifle Association and the American Civil Liberties Union are bolder than their British counterparts, and better able to articulate strong theories of right that can withstand heavy political assault and pressure to balance the right against other interests.

In the United States' political and legal debate, arguments for or against slippery slopes have heretofore often been made in a simplistic manner, with little more than assertions that slippery slope dangers do or do not exist. We hope that this Essay can provide a step toward a more complex analysis of slippery slopes by highlighting some of the elements that can increase or decrease slippery slope risks.

Slippery slopes are not inevitable, but neither are they imaginary. The British experience demonstrates that many civil liberties, including the right to arms, really can slowly slide all the way to the bottom of the slippery slope. While we have not aimed to convince readers to value any particular civil liberty, such as arms, speech, or protection from warrantless searches, we have attempted to show that it is reasonable for groups that do honor such rights, like the NRA, ACLU, or NACDL, to refuse to acquiesce in "reasonable" infringements of those rights. Even though, as John Maynard Keynes observed, we are all dead in the long run, persons who cherish a particular civil liberty want that liberty to endure not just in their own lifetimes, but in the lives of subsequent generations. **In the** long run, the best way to protect a given civil liberty from destruction may be to resist even the smallest infringements in the short run.

BTP Note: Amen to that! Madison remarked on this very concept when explaining the reasons for our Revolution:

> *It is proper to take alarm at the first experiment of our liberties. We hold this prudent jealousy to be the first duty of citizens, and one of the noblest characteristics of the late Revolution. The freemen...did not wait til usurped power had strengthened itself by exercise, and entangled the question in* [legalistic] *precedents. They saw the consequences in the principle, and avoided the consequences by denying the principle.*

BATF-INDUCED NATIONAL I.D. CARD

The Government is using the BATF Form 4473 to cunningly implement a *de facto* national I.D. card (*i.e.,* the driver's license) and condition us all to its artificial importance. The 4/97 Form did not require gun buyers to have a State-issued I.D. card (which was merely *"particularly appropriate"*):

> *However, although a particular document may not be sufficient by itself to meet the statutory requirement for identifying the buyer* [as a resident of his State], *any combination of documents* [such as rental contracts and utility bills] *which together disclose the required information is acceptable.*

All that reasonableness was lifted out of the 10/98 Form 4473:

> *The buyer must provide a valid government-issued photo identification to the seller that contains the buyer's name, date of birth, and residence address.*

The 1981 version of Form 4473 even allowed the seller to dispense with seeing any I.D. if the buyer was *"known to me."* Creeping tyranny indeed! Although the SSN is not (yet) required on the current Form 4473, they strongly encourage it:

> [The SSN requested] *is strictly optional but will help to ensure the lawfulness of the sale and avoid the possibility of being misidentified as a felon or other prohibited person.*

Furthermore, the Forms' length of time to complete has increased from 6 minutes (4/97) to 19 minutes (10/98). This is not only an *"infringement"* counter to the 2nd Amendment, but an increasing one! It shouldn't take even 6 or 19 seconds.

FINE SUPREME COURT RULINGS

The below are all exemplary rulings. They are all ignored.

No State shall convert a liberty into a privilege, license it, and charge a fee therefor.
— *Murdock v. Pennsylvania,* 319 US 105

If the State converts a right (liberty) into a privilege, the citizen can ignore the license and fee and engage in the right (liberty) with impunity.
— *Shuttleworth v. City of Birmingham Alabama,*
    373 US 262

The Court is to protect against any encroachment of constitutionally secured rights.
— *Boyd v. U.S.,* 116 US 616

Where rights (liberty) *secured by the Constitution are involved, there can be no legislation which would abrogate* (abolish) *them.*
— *Miranda v. Arizona,* 384 US 436 (1966)

An unconstitutional act is not law; it confers no rights; it imposes no duties; affords no protection; it creates no office; it is in legal contemplation as though it had never been passed.
— *Norton v. Shelby County,* 118 US 425

Once, however, the 2nd Amendment is recognized by the Supreme Court to protect an *individual* right to own and carry guns, then all the above cases must then also apply. This explains why the Court has adopted its "hear no 2nd Amendment" stance (similar to why hotels have no 13th floor). To recognize the 2nd would undo the entire *"gun control"* apparatus, a main pillar of tyranny's New World Order.

COERCIVE BUY-UP PROGRAMS

First of all, we should *never* stoop to the gunphobe language of *"buy-back."* As Alan Korwin explained in Chapter 31, they can't buy "back" something that was never *theirs* in the first place! Call it a "coercive buy-up" or "disarmament by government check." Never surrender the battle for the metaphor.

Second Amendment challenge

The fight against a coercive buy-up should start here. We are not often enough first relying upon the Bill of Rights in gun cases, though that's changing (*e.g.*, the 1999 victory of *Emerson v. U.S.* in San Angelo, Texas).

The Supreme Court would *have* to hear such a case!

I don't think the Supreme Court could successfully duck this one by denying *certiorari*—the hue and cry would be deafening. Such a case would be one of the most important cases in our Republic's history, the feds know it. Therefore, given the present Court's recent decisions of *Thompson Center, Staples, Lopez,* and *Printz* (all of which were USG losses), a buy-up scheme is probably still years away (when the character of the Court has sufficiently altered).

Tampering with the Supreme Court

Or, has sufficiently *been* altered. I imagine that there's been a *lot* of vicious White House talk against Justices Scalia and Thomas in particular. Their premature deaths (along the lines of Vince Foster's) would be *highly* convenient for many members of the Federal Government and their fascist agenda. If any Supreme Court Justice dies soon (especially Scalia or Thomas), there should be much national suspicion and a demand for the *fullest* investigation with *lots* of independent oversight. I am not being melodramatic. Conceivably, only a couple of lives stand in the way a Supreme Court rubber stamp approval on a federal gun ban, and the professional gunphob⌐s *have* to know it. I do not at all put "executive action" past them.

A less-sure, though probably effective, way for rogue government agents to affect the Court is through extortion or the kidnapping of a Justice's family member. This has happened to State judges in organized crime cases.

Yes, all this is very ugly business, but it has never been beneath the scruples of tyrants. Hitler's minions set fire to the Reichstag and blamed it on the Communists to activate the emergency powers of the Chancellor and sweep away all civil rights. It worked, and that's the only thing that matters to the political pragmatists.

Fifth Amendment challenge

Given that the Constitution demands at least a *modicum* of fairness in the *"just compensation"* clause of the Fifth Amendment, the USG will very likely have to buy up banned firearms in private hands. (A coercive buy-up should be constitutionally challenged as these private guns would be headed for destruction, and not *"for public use"* as the 5th Amendment specifies.)

"We can't afford it!"
There's a hidden principle involved

This should be our *last* line of dialogue defense, because to embrace it *first* waives all defense under the Bill of Rights. I trust I make myself obscure. Here's a joke to illustrate my point: A man and woman meet at a party and converse. After a bit of mutual flirting the man asks her *"Assuming a serious offer, would you sleep with me for a million dollars in cash?"* Although taken back, she muses for a moment and then replies that she would. *"Well, how about for ten bucks?"* Predictably, she's outraged, *"What do you take me for?!"* He calmly replies, *"We've already established that. Now, we're haggling on price!"*

If we *begin* howling about the low dollar figure proposed for our guns, it's *"established"* that we'll whore away our 2nd Amendment rights and are thus only *"haggling on price."*

If we're left with *"haggling on price"*

Let's say that the Government stipulates only Ø100 per gun. *Not counting administrative costs*, that means *Ø24 billion* for the estimated 240 million guns. A more accurate average of Ø500+ would mean *Ø120+* billion—in one year! These are huge amounts of money, regardless, so a buy-up might also be challenged on fiscal grounds. While such a challenge might not actually prevail, it could prove to be an excellent delaying tactic (especially if the courts got involved).

If a coercive buy-up goes through

Once our guns are gone, they can never be replaced. Think of them like the Jews enroute to the death camps. (As history has always shown, when they start burning books or guns, they'll soon be burning people.)

Saving the guns

Every opportunity must be explored to save as many guns from the smelters as is possible. They should aggressively be bought from those owners who are giving them up. If you can get away with advertising or setting up near the collection stations, do so. Tactically, this will likely be difficult. It may even be illegal, so be smart. (If that putrid day ever arrives, there will be plenty of chatter on how to go about all this. Meanwhile, network with other gunowners in CA, NJ, UK, etc. who have gone through it.)

If a coercive buy-up ever happens, there will have been much public discussion about it beforehand. Meaning, we'll have lots of warning. At the first significant whiff, start buying up guns. Stick with reliable, rugged guns in common cartridges. I'd begin with .308 battle rifles, then .223 battle carbines, then Glock pistols (which virtually never break or malfunction). Be sure to also clean the seller out of all ammo, parts, gear, etc.

Saving parts and gear

Guns which are inevitably enroute for destruction should be stripped bare of sights, mags, slings, flash suppressors, muzzle brakes, stocks, etc. *No* **gear whatever should be turned in!** (Since gear is not regulated, the Government cannot know *what* holsters, extra mags, mag pouches, slings, spare parts, tools, cleaning equipment, etc. one ever had, if any.)

If the law's wording does not specify the whole firearm, then a *totally stripped receiver* is all that the gun grabbers should expect. Remove the barrel, the stocks, the trigger group, the internal parts, *everything*. (If they ask, reply that you parted out the gun years ago because you were going to upgrade it, but just never got around to it. Or, you could reply that you had bought only the stripped receiver and was planning to assemble it when you could afford it. You get the idea.)

Who would give up their guns?

There are two types of gunowners would sell their gun to be destroyed. One acts out of fear, the other disinterest.

"Upset, but more afraid than upset"

Those who enjoy their guns and disagree with the buy-up, but are afraid to be caught with "contraband." These are good folks, but are not very long on courage. They could not be expected to fight like the Minutemen did on 19 April 1775. They *might*, however, provide mild support and aid to future freedom fighters as long as the risk wasn't too great.

This group would very often sell (or give) their unrecorded guns to future freedom fighters. At the very minimum, they would allow cherry-picking trades (*e.g.*, your post-ban Olympic AR15 for their pre-ban Bushmaster or Colt) and they would strip their to-be-sold guns of all useful parts and accessories.

Estimated percentage of gunowners: 10-30%

"Incidental gunowners"

Those who inherited their guns, or bought one out of fear of increasing crime. They generally have little interest in their guns, rarely shoot them, and thus no strong emotional or philosophical ties to gun owning or the Second Amendment. The imminent "contraband" aspect will be all that's needed to make them give up their guns. They generally can't be counted on to help freedom fighters or sell us their guns.

Estimated percentage of gunowners: 20-45%

For tyranny's purposes, 30-75% still won't be enough...

So, in my totally subjective opinion, probably at least 30% and perhaps as much as 75% of American gunowners could voluntarily sell out their right to remain armed. That means at *least* 25% of gunowners would at least bury their guns (which is 50 million of them—many times over the numbers needed to successfully fight American Revolution 2).

The wildcards
The concealed carry permit holders
There are millions since the mid-1990s. They are a mix of the above types of gunowners. While many of them bought their handgun incidentally (as first time gunowners), having carried it daily has understandably created a bond, and thus they have *much* more emotional/philosophical equity in remaining armed.

While the State certainly knows that they are armed, it usually doesn't know precisely with *what* or with how many. Many permit holders might give up a cheapy handgun (a good reason for owning *one*) just to get their name crossed off the list, while retaining their Colt, Glock, SIG, etc.

The full-auto owners
Unless they are willing to literally run off to the mountains with their Steyr AUG or M1919A4, I don't see how these gunowners will escape incredible scrutiny and hassle.

It's probable that many Class 3 folks have salted away many unregistered goodies. In fact, when the *GCA68*'s amnesty for undeclared *NFA34* stuff was in effect, most owners did not know if it was merely a ruse to flush out weapons, so many of them "hedged" on both sides and registered only a few items. Thousands of DEWATs, cannons, and mortars went underground. These owners could give up the registered stuff yet still have serious weaponry which the Government does not know about (until it's too late).

The BATF's National Registry contains only 190,000 *NFA34* weapons. That's probably less than 20% of what's actually out there, and maybe not even 5%! Boo, hoo.

"But the government already knows that I have guns!"
If you live in one of the States which prohibits recordfree private transfers, and you are concerned that your resolve might be weakened since the State knows about all your guns, my strong advice to you is to *relocate* to one of the 23 recordfree States. This will give you "breathing room" to galvanize your courage.

I understand that having to potentially fight for your Liberty is a frightening prospect. Why stay in Massachusetts only to have your guns cleaned out by a raid team? Why not move to Vermont? Why stay in Kalifornia with your pre-ban Belgian FAL when you could—*should*—be in neighboring Arizona?

Are you a man or a mouse?

Do the math *right now* and figure out what your freedom is worth, and how much (or how little) you'll fight for it. (Be honest, as you won't be able to fool a harsh reality later.)

mouse

If you think that you'll likely give up your guns when things get hairy, then sell them to a more resolute fellow now.

man

Dedicated mariners don't live in Kansas. Gunlovers shouldn't live in those 10 (if not 25) States which don't support your right to self-defense. If, however, you *don't* yet own a battle rifle (but *would* use one if needed) and live in Connecticut, etc.—*move!* Yes, you'll have to quit your job and sell your house and move, but what's *that* compared to living as a *slave* later? If Liberty truly burns hot in your heart, then get to "high ground" no matter the cost.

Australia still has some men

After learning of some interesting statistics, there might be a bit of hope for Australia.

Out of an estimated 7,000,000 guns, 40% (2.8M) fell under the coercive buy-up. Of those 2,800,000, only 640,000 (25%) were turned in for a government check. The other 2,160,000 (many of which are on the registration lists) have apparently been salted away for their Rainy Decade. Good show!

❖ 37

Why I Will Not Obey California's Gun Registration Edict

by Brian Puckett

Date: Friday, November 12, 1999 5:51
(Sent directly to the California Governor)

A BRIEF SUMMARY OF THE SITUATION

The Democrat-controlled government of California has recently issued two edicts, one that bans ownership of SKS rifles with detachable magazines and requires their surrender to the state, and one that bans buying, selling, or lending of so-called "assault weapons" and that requires present owners of such arms to register them. The edicts take effect January 1, 2000. For all those who have in the past stated that, *"When the state starts confiscating guns, then I'll know it's time to fight back,"* that time in California will be January 1, 2000.

Many people oppose registration because it precedes confiscation. Indeed it does, as those who were foolish enough to register their SKS's are now discovering. However, that is a practical reason to oppose registration, not a legal reason. And while avoiding confiscation is tangentially a moral reason to oppose registration, neither is it a legal reason. Refusing to obey a law because of what might happen or what has happened in other cases will not stand up in court. But there is a reason not to register or turn in any firearm that is practical, moral, and legal.

TWO QUESTIONS TO ANSWER

As regards the Second Amendment, determining the constitutionality of the California edicts mentioned above forces the examination of two basic questions. One, which arms are protected by the Second Amendment? And two, is registration an "infringement" of the Second Amendment's right to keep and bear arms? Fortunately, answering these questions is not a difficult or mysterious task. But they should be answered thoroughly.

WHAT IS THE BILL OF RIGHTS?

The Bill of Rights is not separate from the Constitution but is an integral part of it, as are all the other amendments. However, the Bill of Rights is special in that—like sections of the Declaration of Independence—it contains many of the core philosophical underpinnings of our government (especially Amendments 1, 2, 9, and 10). Therefore, it is easily the most important part of the U.S. Constitution. The rest of the Constitution, along with most of the remaining Amendments, deals primarily with the mechanics of putting this philosophy into effect in the form of a republic.

In the original document that we call the Bill of Rights, the Bill's ten enumerated items are listed as "articles". Those familiar with the history of the Constitution are aware that these articles were not afterthoughts, but were crucial elements whose written inclusion in the Constitution was insisted upon before certain states would agree to ratification of the preceding text. Because of this, a powerful case can be made that none of these first ten articles may be modified or revoked, because that would alter the fundamental philosophy underlying the Constitution and would violate the original agreement among the states.

THE PURPOSE AND MEANING OF THE SECOND AMENDMENT

The laws of the pre-U.S. colonies and the writings of the Founders clearly reveal that they, like all civilized humans, embraced the personal, common-law right of self-defense and property defense. The Founders' writings, such as the Federalist Papers, also clearly reveal their belief that self- defense includes defending oneself against a government gone bad. In fact the evidence shows that this latter item is a primary reason they included the Second Amendment in the Bill of Rights, and the reason for the Second Amendment's reference to the militia—the "army of citizens" (as opposed to the regular army).

The Second Amendment specifies the right of the people to keep and bear arms. If the people are to keep and bear them this must include, at the very minimum, personal arms—that is, arms that a single individual may carry and employ. For hundreds of years prior to the writing of the Constitution, the Western world's most advanced and cherished personal arm had been the firearm. Furthermore, the firearm is the sole arm continually singled out in the Founders' writings. Owning firearms was a right exercised in North America long before the existence of the United States.

TO MEAN ANYTHING, RIGHTS MUST INCLUDE ASSOCIATED NECESSITIES

For any given right, it is meaningless to affirm that right if the tools or necessities of effecting that right are prohibited. Consider our Bill of Rights:

It is meaningless to affirm the First Amendment's right to free exercise of religion if people are prohibited to own Bibles, Korans, or Torahs.

It is meaningless to affirm the First Amendment's "freedom of the press" if people are prohibited to own printing presses (or today's electronic methods of mass communication).

It is meaningless to affirm the Third Amendment's right to refuse to lodge a soldier in one's home, or the Fourth Amendment's right to be secure in one's home, if people are prohibited from owning their own home.

It is meaningless to affirm the Sixth Amendment's right to defense counsel if people are prohibited to use their own or public money to pay for an attorney's services.

And it is beyond meaningless—it is absolutely absurd—to affirm the Second Amendment's right to keep and bear arms if people are prohibited from owning arms. Applying the above-mentioned general principle of rights to the Second Amendment, it would be correct to state that it is meaningless to affirm the right to self-defense if people are prohibited from owning the tools or necessities of self-defense.

For example, consider elderly people, women, the physically handicapped, small-statured men, or anyone who is not a master of unarmed combat being faced with a large, or muscular, or armed assailant, or multiple assailants. It happens every day in this country. It is absurd, illogical, illegal, and inhumane to uphold their right to self-defense while prohibiting them from owning the most portable, easy to use, proven, and inexpensive of instantly effective self-defense tools—guns.

WHICH ARMS ARE PROTECTED BY THE SECOND AMENDMENT?

Along with "the people", the Second Amendment specifically mentions the militia, consisting of armed citizens not enlisted in any regular military corps—the "citizen army". The militia's purpose is, as its name implies, a military one. The militia was—and still may be—pitted against other military forces. That was true in pre-U.S. North America, it was true during the Revolutionary War, and it is true today.

If the militia may be pitted against regular soldiers, whether of a foreign invader or of a tyrannical domestic government, then it follows automatically that at a minimum the citizens comprising the militia must possess personal arms (as opposed to large or crew-served arms like cannon) equal to those of the opposing soldiers. Equal personal arms means, of course, those that include all design features, capabilities, and ergonomics that make a military firearm suitable for modern battle. If this is not the case then there is no point in having a militia, as it will not pose an effective fighting force. For example, the extreme inadequacy of bolt action rifles in combat against semiautomatic arms is well known. But the Founders' firm insistence upon having an effective militia is absolutely clear from their numerous writings on the subject and from the existence of the Second Amendment itself.

That being so, military-pattern firearms are obviously protected by the Second Amendment. Therefore any restrictive legislation on military-pattern firearms, or on military design elements of other firearms, is completely contrary to the word and spirit of the Second Amendment and is therefore flatly unconstitutional. [*U.S. v. Miller*, 307 U.S. 174 (1939) completely supports this.]

REGISTRATION IS INCOMPATIBLE WITH RIGHTS

Consider the situation if a state declared that it was perfectly legal to own a Bible—or a copy of the Koran or the Talmud—but that you had to register it in order to keep and use it. Now, what if you did not register it—would you lose the right to own and read it? Of course not. The very idea is absurd. Under the laws of this nation you have the right to worship as you please. As we have seen, that right automatically includes articles necessary or associated with the right, such as books, crucifixes, stars of David, yarmulkes, and so forth.

In exactly the same way, if the state suddenly required registration of printing presses, would the owner of a press lose his right to own or use it by not filling out a registration form? Of course not. The right would still exist. No piece of paper affects it.

In exactly the same way, one does not have to register one's vocal cords, bullhorn, typewriter, pens, pencils, computers, movie cameras, etc, to exercise the right of free speech (or stated in modern terms, the right of uncensored communication).   Under the Constitution, if a state issued an edict demanding registration of such things that rule would be invalid as law. Your right to use them would still exist, completely unaffected.

In exactly the same way, prior registration of one's body, home, address, papers, possessions, etc, is not necessary in order to enjoy the Constitutional right to protection from unreasonable searches and seizures of one's person, house, papers, and effects. These various physical things are automatically included, automatically protected by the right.

In exactly the same way, one does not have to register anything or fill out any forms in order to have the Constitutional right to a speedy public trial. It is automatic.

Now consider the situation if you do not register a gun. Is the Second Amendment somehow instantly suspended? Did it vanish? Do you somehow lose the right to keep and bear arms? Certainly not.

If you can lose a "right" by not filling out a piece of paper, then it is not a right. It is a privilege granted by the government, which is a different thing altogether. In the area of government, a privilege is a special permission or immunity granted by a government, it is generally related to the use of some public facility (such as driving on the streets, or using the public library) and it may be suspended or revoked even for minor infractions or misdemeanors.

In sum: Rights do not require government registration, certification, or approval, and are not subject to any form of taxation—otherwise they are not rights, they are privileges granted at the discretion of the government, controlled by the government, and revocable by the government.

REGISTRATION IS MORE THAN AN INFRINGEMENT

The Second Amendment reads,

A well-regulated militia, being necessary to the security of a free state, the right of the people to keep and bear arms, shall not be infringed.

The question may be asked, *"Is registration of a particular gun truly such a burden that it can be called an infringement of the right to keep and bear arms?"*

To begin with, if we were speaking of registering religious items or communications devices, none but socialists would dare ask such a question. Yet the Second Amendment directly follows the amendment concerned with the free exercise of religion and freedom of the press. The Second Amendment holds a place of priority in the Bill of Rights, which is primarily a list of inalienable personal rights.

But to answer the above question—Yes. Registration is absolutely an infringement, on at least three grounds. In fact, we will see that the rights versus privileges issue makes registration far more than a mere infringement.

Information.
Registration of a firearm gives the government information that can be used (and has been used, and is being used right now) to confiscate that firearm or to pinpoint its owner for weapon seizure, fining, incarceration, or execution. Having the government in possession of this information is directly contrary to the Second Amendment's intent to ensure that citizens always possess the means to overthrow the government should it become corrupt or tyrannical.

Government control.
Allowing the government to seize a citizen's firearm, or to suspend, revoke, or diminish a citizen's ability to defend life, family, property, and country for paperwork omissions or errors, for regulatory violations, for minor infractions of the law, for misdemeanors, or arguably for anything less than conviction for a major crime of violence is also directly contrary to the intent of the Second Amendment. This is because virtually all citizens have committed, or will commit, one or more of the listed non-violent errors listed above, whereas the entire point of the Second Amendment is to place this same citizenry's right to keep and bear arms (and therefore the right of self-defense) out of the government's grasp.

RIGHT VERSUS PRIVILEGE

Critically relevant to all our rights, is that any edict that attempts to convert a right into a state-granted privilege by imposing prior requirements—such as registration—before it may be exercised goes far beyond mere "infringement" of that right; it becomes an attempt at outright abrogation of the right.

Therefore the state's demand to comply with the requirements of such an edict—no matter how physically easy compliance is—imposes not some mere inconvenience on the individual. It imposes the enormous moral, ethical, intellectual, and spiritual burden of denying the existence of the right.

It does not matter if the state demands that one simply tap one's nose five times in succession in order to be able to keep and bear a particular gun. This would still be a state-mandated prior requirement. Compliance would indicate tacit denial of the validity of the Second Amendment, and denial of the right it protects. Compliance would encompass an implicit acceptance of the right as a mere privilege, which is directly contrary to both the letter and spirit of the Second Amendment.

APPLYING THESE CONCEPTS TO CALIFORNIA'S EDICT

The argument against registration of, and restrictions on, military-style firearms may be approached by two logical paths that reach the same conclusions:

❶　If the supreme law of the nation protects a personal right to keep and bear arms (which it does), then the failure to comply with a state mandate to fill out some registration form cannot revoke this, or any other, right. If the right to keep and bear arms cannot be revoked (and it can not be), then the right to keep and bear militia arms, which are the very arms implicitly referred to in the Founders' writings and in the Second Amendment itself, cannot be revoked. If the right to keep and bear militia arms cannot be revoked (and it can not be), then we may own and use any military-pattern individually portable firearm, all of which are practical militia arms. If that is the case (and it is), then any restrictive legislation based on militarily useful design elements of such firearms is flatly unconstitutional.

❷　If the supreme law of the nation protects the personal right to keep and bear arms (which it does), then the right to keep and bear militia arms, which are the very arms implicitly referred to in the Founders' writings and in the Second Amendment itself, certainly exists. If that is the case (and it is), then we may own and use any military-pattern individually portable firearm, because all are practical militia arms. If that is the case (and it is), any restrictive legislation based on the militarily useful design elements of such firearms is flatly unconstitutional. If that is the case (and it is), then the failure to comply with a state mandate to fill out some registration form cannot revoke this right.

Again, the same situation prevails with all the personal rights. That is, no state mandate requiring registration—either of oneself or of things directly associated with a right—can be a prerequisite or condition of exercising a right, nor can it affect that right in any way. If it does, then the right has been unconstitutionally declared a state-controlled privilege.

SUMMARY

As we see from the above, no American can be legally compelled to register any militarily useful individual arm. That includes pistols, revolvers, carbines, semi-autos, military-style guns, hunting guns, self-defense guns, pump guns, lever guns, bolt guns, black powder guns, scoped guns, .50 caliber guns, .338 caliber guns, .30 caliber guns, .223 caliber guns, etc. All have been used, or are being used, as individual military arms, and therefore are implicitly referred to by the Second Amendment's militia clause.

Moreover, no American can be legally compelled to register any firearm of common design or function because the Second Amendment does not protect only guns that are useful in military affairs; it protects all guns. The militia reference is clearly meant as one important reason for protecting the right which follows: the right of the people to keep and bear arms.

The Second Amendment says simply "arms", which imposes no quantity or design limits. It says "bear", which in its narrowest sense would still include all firearms capable of being carried and used by one person. Therefore, under the supreme law of the land, the right to own one or several of any type of individually portable firearm exists permanently, inherently, automatically, without prior approval or conditions.

RELATED ISSUES

❶   Indiscriminate weapons—those whose effects are difficult to direct upon, or confine to, a discrete target (such as flamethrowers, fragmentation bombs, chemical and biological weapons, mortars) etc.—are arguably excludable from the full protection of the Second Amendment as posing an unreasonable danger to friend and foe alike.

❷   Individually portable machine guns are clearly allowed under the wording of the Second Amendment. However, under certain specific circumstances their employment might arguably be said to encroach into the area of indiscriminate weapons. Therefore, it is arguable that some extra care might be taken in the use of these firearms, but that any restrictions imposing an effective ban on their general ownership or general use would be unconstitutional. As this is a highly specific, highly debatable subject, it will not be, and need not be, delved into here.

Aside from the debatable exceptions of ❶ and ❷ above, absolutely no individually portable firearm of common design or function may be determined to be an indiscriminate weapon under any circumstances, nor to pose an unreasonable danger. This is because a ban on such a firearm could "logically" be extended to all other firearms of similar design and function (exactly what is occurring with California's edicts now), which would completely vitiate the Second Amendment. Thus, the 1994 Federal "assault weapon" ban and magazine capacity limit are both completely unconstitutional.

REGISTRATION—YOUR DECISION AFFECTS ALL RIGHTS

If a military pattern firearm, the firearm most suited to the militia mentioned in the Second Amendment, is not protected by the clear wording of the Second Amendment, then there is no meaning to the Second Amendment.

If there is no meaning to the Second Amendment, there is no reason to infer meaning in the rest of the Bill of Rights.

If converting the Second Amendment into a privilege by means of a registration edict is not the maximum "infringement" of that right, then nothing is.

If converting the Second Amendment into a privilege by means of an edict is possible, then it is possible to do so for any other right.

Therefore, regarding the Second Amendment, refusing registration affirms the right to own a militia firearm. It affirms the right to keep and bear all personal arms. It affirms the validity of the rest of the Bill of Rights. It affirms that attempting to convert the Second Amendment into a privilege is the maximum infringement of that right. It rejects a state's power to convert any right into a privilege. And lastly it affirms the validity of the Constitution, and the rule of law, not men.

DEMANDING OR COMPLYING WITH REGISTRATION IS BETRAYAL

Article VI of the Constitution designates the Constitution as the supreme law of the United States, and specifically states that it prevails over all state constitutions and statutes. Further, Article VI requires all legislative, executive, and judicial officers of the U.S. government and of the state governments to take an oath to obey the Constitution. Some of these officials may hate firearms and the power they give to the citizenry, but that is irrelevant—they must treat the Second Amendment as they would the rest of our Bill of Rights.

All state officials—judges, representatives, law enforcement officials—know these facts, but many are corrupt and ignore them. Their sworn word means nothing to them, nor does the Constitution, nor do the rights of the constituents for whom they work unless it suits their own political agenda. It is against this conscienceless species of human that decent Americans must continually fight, in California and in the rest of the United States.

If you believe you have the right to keep and bear proper militia arms in order to defend yourself, your family, your home, and your country, and if you believe this right is recognized in the Bill of Rights, then you cannot register or turn in any firearm whatsoever. You may rationalize it any way you wish, but if you register a firearm you are implicitly agreeing with the proposition that your right to own that firearm is nonexistent, and that such ownership is dependent upon permission from the government. Registration equals betrayal of yourself, your family, your ancestors, your birthright, your country, and your Constitution. Period.

A PERSONAL POSITION

Every new illegal gun control edict issued, and every day that existing illegal gun control edicts continue to be enforced, brings inexorable closer the time when firearms owners will train their guns on the politicians, judges, and other officials who have misled the rest of the public into giving up their sacred and ancient rights. A desire to avoid this terrible tragedy motivates my own actions regarding the Second Amendment and the rights it protects.

For nearly twenty years I have legally owned a militia rifle possessing the characteristics of the socialists' so-called *"assault weapon"*. Now my right to own this arm, a right that has existed far longer than the two centuries—plus that this nation has existed, is suddenly being challenged by corrupt politicians. But I vehemently reject any infringement of my rights. I will never register this or any other firearm. Nor will I ever turn it in, nor will I ever alter any characteristic or attachment to it.

I will never again concern myself with legislation about pistol grips, bayonet lugs, high-capacity magazines, flash suppressors, threaded barrels, folding stocks, pre-or post-ban manufacture, or any other irrelevant detail of my firearms.

I will certainly not do as the NRA Members Councils suggest on their internet site, which is to saw off the pistol grip of one's AR-style rifle to make it "legal". Understand this: in America it is already legal. I sometimes wonder whether the socialists will issue an edict requiring all firearms to have a pink ribbon tied to the barrel, just to get a belly laugh as the panicked descendants of once-proud American patriots scurry to comply.

California's current governor, attorney general, and legislators who voted for these edicts can undoubtedly find thugs as corrupt and anti-American as themselves to send to my home. I vow not to physically interfere with their illegal activities, because I wish to see this matter in court. I hope that other men and women will join me in this public declaration of civil disobedience, because it would be best to have ten thousand civil disobedience cases in court, not just mine. But I understand why, in this day and age of brutal, ethics-free "public servants"; citizens are reluctant to make themselves a target of the state. Fortunately, the citizens of California and other states demanding registration can strike a powerful blow for humanity simply by refusing to comply.

SEIZE THIS OPPORTUNITY

To those of you who whine, complain, and talk, talk, talk about your loss of freedom—I say now is the time to do something. There are few times in an average man's life when the occasion presents itself to take part in history. Here and now is such a time. This refusal to submit to tyranny is not simply about firearms. It is about human rights, it is about the rule of law, and it is about the continuance of this great nation. To what better use will you ever put you life than to stand up for these things? Will you look back on this moment and say, *"I wish I had done something,"* or will you step forward and seize this chance?

With the government having grown so powerful and corrupt, defying it is frightening. It is especially frightening because many Americans seem fairly content right now. But the feelings of the apathetic mass are irrelevant. They have never figured in history, and never will. The apathetic mass will go along with whatever system exists. It is the freedom-loving individual who, although part of a much smaller group, has guided every free nation toward the light.

Freedom is not maintained without taking risks and making sacrifices, without fighting for it. This has always been true, throughout history. If you are afraid to take a stand against this tyrannical government, if you excuse yourself by saying you must "take care of my family first", I say thank God there were men in the past who understood the priority of freedom.

Look at your children. Is it more important that they have an uninterrupted flow of plastic toys and the soft luxuries of modern American life, or that they grow up as free men and women, with all inherent rights and responsibilities? I say any man who does nothing while even a single basic freedom he has enjoyed is stripped from his offspring—a freedom secured by the blood of others—deserves no offspring.

As I said, I will turn in no firearms, ever. I will register no firearms, ever. My right to own and use firearms predates the Constitution. It existed before the corrupt socialists in Washington and Sacramento came to office, and it will exist forever afterward. The Second Amendment simply recognizes this right. I do not know where my civil disobedience will lead, but I am certain where the slavishness and cowardice of compliance will lead. I refuse to take part in this foul business of registration. I hope that you refuse also. If we stand together we will set fires of freedom burning across America.

Mr. Puckett is a free-lance writer whose past work includes articles on U.S. foreign, domestic, and military policy for the *Houston Post*. His firearms and Second Amendment articles have appeared in the magazines *Handguns, Combat Handguns, Guns & Ammo, SWAT, Police*, and numerous other publications. He is the author of the essay *"A Plan to Restore the Second Amendment,"* appearing in an upcoming issue of Handguns Magazine.

He is a co-founder of the gun rights resource organization GunTruths (*http://www.guntruths.com*) and the gun rights media action organization Citizens Of America (*http://www.citizensofamerica.org*). Mr. Puckett believes that much of the annual slaughter of Americans by criminals can be blamed directly on those who advocate gun control, and that any politician who advocates gun control neither trusts his constituents nor cares about their lives or property. The above statement/essay is an expression of his opinions alone. He may be contacted regarding this article at *guns1776@earthlink.net*   Put the word RESISTER in the subject line. You can read more of Mr. Puckett's work at *http://www.guntruths.com/Puckett/brian_puckett.htm*

The above essay, which includes the biographical note, may be reproduced in any medium provided it is reproduced in full. A copy has been sent via email and regular mail to the governor of California. Feel free to forward it to all gun rights activists and lists.

CONFISCATION

Good day to you. ...I am in Australia and the [gun] *amnesty is finished. Stick up for your rights now! Speaking out is easier than what we face here.*

Gun owners who did not comply with new regulations in Australia are now faced with the fact that their name is flagged on government computers (they <u>registered</u> their guns, remember?), [and] *they are liable to four years imprisonment and a fine that is about the cost of an average house.*

Those with firearms licenses and those who did not hand in their weapons are liable to search of person or premises without warrant.

People cannot organize because what the government has done is now legislated, enacted law. Therefore any attempt to communicate or organise is liable to the charge of subversion. (Lesson to Americans: Start organizing <u>now</u>, while you can.) *If an individual says to another, "I would suggest that you do not hand in your firearm," the speaker may be charged with subverting another to commit a criminal act.*

They have started mounting raids to retrieve firearms and that is likely to intensify. (BTP Note: The proper word would be "steal." One can "retrieve" only what originally <u>belonged</u> to oneself.)

WHATEVER YOU GUYS DO, FOR GOD'S SAKE DON'T REGISTER YOUR WEAPONS. *It* (confiscation) *really is happening and it seems to be global.*

U.S. brothers, watch your six. If you don't with your politicians, then you will have to watch it for real against your own troopers.

Australia to America: God bless you and pray for us poor bastards down under.

— Carolyn Dillon, posted on 9 May 1998

The slow torture and murder of the Branch Davidians in that town in Texas in April 1993 was, I propose to you, equivalent to the public burning of witches—everyone's eyes were glued to the image of the fire on their televisions. *It does not matter whether you applauded the government for burning "kooks" or whether you were horrified that people were sacrificed for their belief in Christ and, in their minds, his representative David Koresh.* **The purpose of the exercise was to** horrify **us.**

Now, let me ask you, why is Waco coming back to our television screens, this time with a wainscoting of courtrooms in the background? *The message of the horror was that those in power will do as they will, laws not withstanding. We need also to ask ourselves, if the purpose was simply to murder those people, could they not have dropped a bomb on the building? Of course they could have. Their use of the Delta Force, in breach of the Posse Comitatus Law, would be no different than using the Air Force. Why was it prolonged? Well, the answer is already in—In order to torture your mind; you, the observer. And why is it coming back? For the same purpose; to rub in to your subconscious that—nay, I should phrase it differently—***to brainwash us with the recognition that laws and rules are immaterial; it is power that governs in America these days.*** *The second message is that you had better be politically correct and that some forms of Christianity are now politically* incorrect. *What's wrong with Christianity* [from the Government's standpoint] *you might ask? Many Christians believe that they were given* inalienable rights *by their God.* This is the belief that needs to be destroyed; *this belief that is the core of* dignitas *and which makes up the citizens of each state. If you have stayed with me so far, I think you are coming to recognize the wondrous benefit of a concept* dignitas *and why it is under threat and by whom. Here is* [a commentary by Dr. Joost A.M. Meerloo, author of *The Rape of the Mind*]:

There is in existence the totalitarian "Document of Terror" which discusses in detail the use of well-planned, repeated success of waves of terror *to bring the people into submission. Each wave of terrorizing cold war creates its effect more easily—after a breathing spell—than the one that preceded it. Because people are still disturbed by their previous experience, morale becomes lower and lower, and the [conformity] becomes stronger; it reaches a public already softened up.* ***Every dissenter becomes more and more frightened that he may be found out.*** *Gradually, people are no longer willing to participate in any sort of political discussion or to express their opinions. Inwardly they have already surrendered to the terrorizing dictatorial forces.*

— Thomas Dorman, M.D.
www.zolatimes.com/V4.13/dignity2.html

Back in May 1995, President Clinton responded to the growing dissatisfaction of conservative Americans and their militias:

I say this to the militias and all others who believe that the greatest threat to freedom comes from the government.

(Well, where *else* has it historically always come from?)

If you say violence is an acceptable way to make change, you are wrong.

(Defensive violence is certainly an acceptable way to *prevent* change, *i.e.,* slavery.)

If you appropriate our sacred symbols

(No, we're *reclaiming* them; it was politicians like *you* who first stole them from the people.)

for paranoid purposes and compare yourselves to colonial militias who fought for the democracy you rail against, you are wrong.

(They would profoundly disagree; read their writings and speeches. And, they fought for a *republic,* not a democracy.)

How dare you suggest that we in the freest nation on earth live in tyranny?

(Bill, America is merely the healthiest patient in the cancer ward, that's all. That *"freest nation on earth"* stuff is just an echo of when we didn't suffer professional politicians like you.)

...There is no right to kill people who are doing their duty.
— Bill Clinton, 5 May 1995, East Lansing, Michigan

On page 416 of his fine book, *Send in the Waco Killers,* Vin Suprynowicz replies to Clinton's assertion:

Sure there is.
General Washington killed plenty of Redcoats and Hessians who were doing their duty—and in defense of the duly constituted government, at that.
The Jews in the Warsaw ghetto had every right to kill Nazis who were only doing their duty, enforcing duly enacted laws against Jews bearing arms. Our own prosecutions of the Nazis at Nuremberg in 1946 established a lasting precedent that men can and will be legally executed for "just following orders."

On page 368, Vin continues:

Yes, guns kill people. Sometimes, to preserve our freedom, some people need to be killed. *Occasionally, these are freelance bandits. But most often, down through the corridors of history, they have turned out to be uniformed agents of a tyrannical central government. That is precisely why the Second Amendment guarantees us that, in America, the government and its agents must never be al-*

lowed to outgun the common people...while it says not a word about "legitimate sporting use."

The Founders could not predict precisely when such a time would come again. But they knew for sure it <u>would</u> come again. Thus they guaranteed in the strongest terms each citizen his private arms, so that—whenever their treason against our God-given rights leaves us no other choice—we, or our children, or our grandchildren shall retain the ability to shoot government agents through the head, and kill them.

That is what firearms are for. And that is why no people can be without them, and long remain free.

According to James Madison in the *Federalist* #46, encroachments on our liberties should *"provoke plans of resistance"* and should be *"opposed [by] a militia amounting to near half a million citizens with arms in their hands."*

Asking soldiers if they'll fire on gunowners

Question #46 of the 1994 *Combat Arms Survey* given to U.S. Navy personnel said:

The U.S. Government declares a ban on the possession, sale, transportation, and transfer of all non-sporting firearms. A thirty (30) day amnesty period is permitted for these firearms to be turned over to the local authorities. At the end of this period, a number of citizen groups refuse to turn over their firearms. Consider the following statement:

I would fire upon U.S. citizens who refuse or resist confiscation of firearms banned by the U.S. Government.

The permitted answers were Strongly Disagree, Disagree, Agree, Strongly Agree, and No Opinion.

Notice that it said *"citizen groups"* and not simply *"citizens."* Apparently individual gunowners are expected to generally obey, but not *groups* of them? (By *"groups,"* obviously the militias are meant.)

The likely reason why *Navy* personnel were asked this alarming question is because the Posse Comitatus Act of 1878 (amended in 1956 at 18 USC § 1385) forbids only *Army* and *Air Force* troops from domestic law enforcement. Navy, Marines, and Coast Guard personnel are exempt.

THE STATES' RESOLVE GROWS

Although 9/11 has proven the deadly futility of gun-free zones and victim disarmament, the pols are again calling for Bill of Rights restrictions. (Apparently, they cannot help it.)

However, at least in Vermont and Arizona, legislators working to strengthen their citizens' right to keep and bear arms. Their efforts are indeed stirring:

Vermont

*From the state of Vermont comes the following reaction to the ongoing national assault on Second Amendment rights. In what can only be described as a 180-degree about-face reaction to the contemporary assault on the right to bear arms, a Vermont legislator introduced two bills in late January **that would make gun ownership mandatory and create a mandatory citizens' militia.** House Bill 760 would require state residents over 18 who do not own guns to register with the secretary of state's office and pay a $500 fine and House Bill 763 would make military training a prerequisite for a high school diploma in the state. State Representative Fred Maslack is the moving force behind both of these bills and has been characterized as a strong supporter of gun rights. Representative Maslack believes that the right to bear arms implies an obligation to serve in a militia and gave his opinion that neither of these bills will become state law. Currently, the state of Vermont has some of the least restrictive gun laws in the nation and permits all adults to carry a concealed gun without a permit.*

No state in the history of the USA has ever passed a law that makes possession of arms obligatory. Rights by their very nature must never be confused with obligations. Making gun ownership mandatory would remove citizens' discretion on the issue and would have the same moral result as banning gun ownership totally. Both positions are equally authoritarian and the very antithesis of the basic concept behind any right: freedom.

— from the internet, 2 / 2000

Regarding the second paragraph, I have mixed feelings. Inherent to any right is some reciprocal of *responsibility* (and thus *"obligations"* as the author put it). The right to be armed also includes the situational responsibility to use one's arms to prevent crime and arrest criminals.

Instead of making it illegal to *not* own a gun, which I cannot fully accept, I would prefer that objectors to gun owning be required to fund the police forces. After all, being unarmed it is *they* who will more likely be attacked by opportunistic criminals and thus need police protection. Further, to prevent an implicit umbrella of protection by those armed, their gun aversion would be public knowledge through signs posted on their stores, homes, and cars. (Perhaps they should have to also wear pink beanies!) Those who will not defend their *own* lives will not defend *yours*, and they should be instantly recognizable to all.

"*But they would be discriminated against!*" Yes, they would. That is rather the point. While government cannot discriminate, private citizens and companies have the *right* of association and *dis*association with whomever they please. Only the government cannot be a bigot. I would not buy from or sell to a pink beanie-wearing coward, and I have the right not to support my philosophical enemies. If the gunphobes didn't like it, they'd have two options: buy a gun, or move to Neu Jersey.

Arizona

Article V of the Constitution gives Congress the outrageous authority to prevent corrective constitutional amendments (by not passing them and sending them to the States). This is a blatant conflict-of-interest issue, like giving arrested criminals the power to decide whether their own case gets prosecuted. Almost three years ago, I proposed a way out of Article V's ratification straightjacket:

> *Rather, our "end run" would be that the states may themselves float their own proposed constitutional amendments, bypassing Congress. The Nevada legislature could, for example, pass a proposed amendment and offer it to the other 49 states. If 37 more states signed on, the proposal would be considered ratified by the requisite 3/4ths of the states. Borrowing from Madison's The Federalist #40, it's an "absurdity" that the popular mandate is subjected to the "perverseness and corruption" of two-thirds of Congress by virtue of Article V. Because 357 members of Congress don't utter a "Simon says" we're going to allow this nation to take a dirt nap? Therefore, I shall "dismiss it without further observation." Moral: two-edged swords are a bitch.*
> — Kenneth W. Royce, *Hologram of Liberty* (1997), page 10/8

This would allow the States to exercise their rightful prerogative of self-rule in a historically valid precedent, without initiating direct physical confrontation with the Federal Government. (Whether or not the USG would go *quietly* is another matter.)

Apparently, somebody in the Arizona legislature read *Hologram of Liberty*. When the following came across my desk, I nearly fell out of my chair:

State of Arizona
House of Representatives
Forty-fourth Legislature
Second Regular Session
2000
HCR 2034
Introduced by
Representatives Johnson, Cooley

A CONCURRENT RESOLUTION

PROPOSING THE DISSOLUTION OF THE FEDERAL GOVERN-MENT OF THE UNITED STATES OF AMERICA IF CERTAIN CONDI-TIONS OCCUR.

Whereas, on July 4, 1776, our founding fathers proclaimed that the people had the right to alter or abolish their government and declared thirteen British colonies to be free and independent, or sovereign, states; and

Whereas, on March 1, 1781, the thirteen states formed a central government they called the United States of America under a charter known as the Articles of Confederation and Perpetual Union, which stated that "each state retains its sovereignty, freedom and independence"; and

Whereas, on September 17, 1787, the leaders of the Continental Congress signed the present Constitution of the United States, which was then transmitted to the thirteen states for ratification and the formation of a new central government; and

Whereas, several of the states delayed ratification of the Constitution and three states made clear their position regarding sovereignty by stating that "the powers of government may be resumed by the people whensoever it shall become necessary to their happiness"; and

Whereas, eventually all thirteen of the independent states ratified the Constitution of the United States and joined the new Union, while retaining their sovereignty as states. The states made the new central government sovereign only to the extent that the states delegated to it limited and specific powers; and

Whereas, the Constitution of the United States is merely a treaty among sovereigns, **and under treaty law when one party violates the treaty the other parties are automatically released from further adherence to it unless they wish to continue**; and

Whereas, the fifty current principals, or signatories, to the treaty have done well in honoring and obeying it, yet the federal agent has, for decades, violated it in both word and spirit. The many violations of the Constitution of the United States by the federal government include disposing of federal property without the approval of Congress, usurping jurisdiction from the states in such matters as abortion and firearms rights and seeking control of public lands within state borders; and

Whereas, under Article V, Constitution of the United States, three-fourths of the states may abolish the federal government. In the alternative, if the states choose to exercise their inherent right as sovereigns, **fewer than thirty-eight states may lawfully choose to ignore Article V**, Constitution of the United States, **and establish a new federal government for themselves by following the precedent established by Article VII**, Constitution of the United States, in which nine of the existing thirteen states dissolved the existing Union under the Articles of Confederation and automatically superceded the Articles.

Therefore

Be it resolved by the House of Representatives of the State of Arizona, the Senate concurring:

1. That when or if the President of the United States, the Congress of the United States or any other federal agent or agency **declares the Constitution of the United States to be suspended or abolished,** if the President or any other federal entity attempts to institute martial law or its equivalent without an official declaration in one or more of the states without the consent of that state **or if any federal order attempts to make it unlawful for individual Americans to own firearms or to confiscate firearms,** the State of Arizona, when joined by thirty-four of the other fifty states, declares as follows: that the states resume all state powers delegated by the Constitution of the United States and assume total sovereignty; that the states re-ratify and re-establish the present Constitution of the United States as the charter for the formation of a new federal government, **to be followed by the election of a new Congress and President and the reorganization of a new judiciary,** similarly following the precedent and procedures of the founding fathers; that individual members of the military return to their respective states and report to the Governor until a new President is elected; that each

state assume a negotiated, prorated share of the national debt; that all land within the borders of a state belongs to the state until sold or ceded to the central government by the state's Legislature and Governor; and that once thirty-five states have agreed to form a new government, each of the remaining fifteen be permitted to join the new confederation on application.

2. That the Secretary of State of the State of Arizona transmit copies of this Resolution to the President of the United States, the President of the United States Senate, the Speaker of the United States House of Representatives and each Member of Congress from the State of Arizona.

I have just one word to say about all that: *Wow*.

They've even improved on my idea by requiring only 9/13's of the States (from Article VII) instead of the ¾'s stipulated in Article V. So, instead of 75% (38) of the States, only 69.23% (35) are required to dissolve the current compact and form another. Alexander Hamilton must be spinning in his Wall Street tomb.

If enough of the States begin to really feel encroached upon by the USG, this resolution could actually go somewhere. The fact that it was passed as a *joint* resolution is nothing short of astounding. Even if you don't live in Arizona, you should write Representatives Johnson and Cooley and praise them for such integrity and courage. They are truly American *statesmen* in the tradition of Thomas Jefferson.

GUN CONFISCATION ABROAD

Several countries are following the NYC model: registration, then confiscation. This works with the wimps.

England

Following the mass murder of 16 Scottish school children and their teacher by the homosexual child molester Thomas Hamilton, Britain rode the wave of media hysteria and collected over 100,000 handguns larger than .22 caliber.

Knives, pepper spray, etc. are also strongly discouraged. Unarmed victims *can* say, "*Stop! Or, I'll say 'stop!' again.*" In a

15 September 1997 *The London Telegraph* article *TEARS AS SPORTSMEN LAY DOWN THEIR ARMS* by Boris Johnson:

"They aren't too chuffed (pleased)," says Insp. Paul Brightwell. "I've seen grown men close to tears handing over a gun they've had a long time, saying 'this is the pistol my father had in the Second World War,' or 'my wife gave me this for our 25th wedding anniversary.'"...

Nanny is confiscating their toys. It is like one of those Indian programmes of compulsory vasectomy....

Law-abiding gun-owners are now handing over their weapons here at rate of 50 to 60 a day.

Of the 6,000 fullbore and smallbore handguns in the Thames Valley area, about 3,000 have already been surrendered. That includes about 550 examples of .22 pistols.

***"They're not banned yet, but some people are seeing the writing on the wall,"** says Insp. Brightwell. In two weeks the three-month surrender period will be up. The legal will have become illegal. An entire pastime will have been exterminated. Britain will be the only country in the world where it is forbidden to practise for an Olympic sport....(Not to worry, chaps. Australia joined you in 1998.)*

We, the taxpayers will have to cough up about £1 billion in compensation; and still the shooters will receive 25 per cent less than the full value of any improvements to their weapons.

"These people are being legislated against because of the insane actions of one or two people. There are ordinary people. Dunblane (the "Littleton" of Britain) affected them in the same way that it affected you and me."...

(Since British cops get to keep *their* guns, how were *they* "affected" by the ban?)

A man wearing cowboy boots, moustache and denims is walking denuded to the door. His eyes are moist as he proclaims that he is "absolutely fed up with the situation and the way everyone's been treated."

(No, he's not *"fed up."* If he *were*, then he wouldn't have surrendered his guns, or let them be taken.)

*He continues, " I've been shooting for 30 years. My eldest daughter shoots. I've never been in any type of trouble with the police. I've served two terms with the Army in Northern Ireland," he says, adding that he is about to resign from the Territorials. **"If I can't be trusted to put a few holes in a bit of paper, why should I be trusted to defend my country?"** (That's something his government should have more carefully considered.)*

Now his expensive leather holsters, bandoleers and belts are to be burned, even though they are "uncontrolled items."

(See, *this* is what I'm talking about: the *feistiest* citizen of the story *voluntarily* also brings in his *gear?* Those people are truly hopeless.)

His 9mm Lugers and bullet making equipment will either go to a foundry in South Wales or a crusher in the Midlands.

(Not unless one of the cops nabs them for his own, which I'll wager happens to much of the good stuff.)

Nothing will be excepted from destruction apart from Glock 17s, which the police use themselves, and any items of historic interest. (All guns are of historic interest!) But it is the melting pot for...this huge Smith and Wesson .45 with an eight inch barrel. "Feel the weight of that." says Insp. Brightwell, handing me a shiny two-tone slug. "You'd know if that hit you. **Why would you want something that massive to shoot at targets?"**

(Groan. You wouldn't. It was to shoot Bad Guys with, you dolt!)

Insp. Brightwell may feel sorry for the shooters; and yet at heart he is a policeman.... (Who's just following orders...) **"We support the** [confiscation] **measures in the greater interests of public safety."**

"In the greater interests of public safety" was first used by the Nazis to round up guns. You'll be hearing it over here soon.)

All the legislation means is no more mayhem by owners of legal handguns, since legal handguns will no longer exist. It is no use the shooters protesting that this will do nothing about the myriad of illegal weapons, or [temporarily] legal shotguns; or that the existing law should have ensured that Thomas Hamilton's guns were taken away.

The owners of all the 160,000 handguns are penalised for the dementia of a couple of their number, **and because no one, in the current climate, dare speak for them.**

(It was the handgun owners who didn't speak for *themselves!* Honest citizens with handguns should never need anybody *else* to speak on their behalf.)

Australia (www.ssaa.org.au/)

By September 1997, over 600,000 firearms were coercively purchased by the government following Australia's worst mass killing of 35 people in Tasmania by Martin Bryant.

On a humorous note, 40,000 Aussies used their government check to purchase another firearm. The buy-up merely assisted the "exchange" of one gun for a better one.

New Zealand (www.ssanz.org.nz/)

No confiscation yet, but their government is pushing for mandatory registration of all firearms. A mass murderer is obviously the next prerequisite... Stay tuned.

Canada (www.nfa.ca/)

After Marc Lepine slaughtered a number of college women with a Mini-14, the Canadian parliament passed Bill C-68 requiring the registration of all firearms by 1 January 2003. Warrantless home searches are now authorized. Half of all handguns are outlawed, and the other half cannot be sold but must be destroyed upon the owner's death. The province of Alberta (the "Montana" of Canada) has sued to block the plan.

Notice any *pattern* here? Armed madman with criminal record kills many people, creating outrage over gun ownership which results in new gun control laws. This formula was invented here in America. (One wonders if some of these murderers were not intentionally destabilized through *Prozac*® withdrawal, etc. Rent the movie *The Parallax View* sometime for a similar dramatic plot.)

UN GUN-CONTROL

...arms...discourage and keep the invader and plunderer in awe, and preserve order in the world as well as property. ...Horrid mischief would ensue were [the law-abiding] *deprived the use of them.*
— Thomas Paine

If the Japs should ever try to raid our Pacific coast they would find the west just as wild as it used to be.

Cow punchers, hard rock miners, farmers, even business men and factory workers, have oiled their rifles and are keeping them handy. Good hunters make good snipers and crack shooting is a tradition in the west. Right after America entered the war a spontaneous movement to put their rifles in good shape swept the western population. Armed men began to band together in many communities. (Note: This is a militia group.) *Now, efforts are being made to organize the groups into official home guard units.*

...Armed men in many Oregon communities have held organization meetings, 1,000 armed civilians having been rallied at the small town of Tillamook alone.

...It's hard to find a revolver or rifle for sale in the west today. Practically everything available has been bought up.   Standard calibers of ammunition are just as scarce.

— "Minute Men of 1942," *Popular Mechanics,* October 1942

What Congress doesn't have the nerve to ban, the UN will:

...there are wide differences among States (nations) *as regards which types of arms are permitted for civilian possession, and as regards the circumstances under which they can legitimately be owned, carried and used. Such wide variation in national laws raise difficulties for effective regional or international cooridination.*

States (nations) ***should work toward the prohibition of unrestricted trade and private ownership of small arms*** (defined as "...revolvers and self-loading pistols, rifles and carbines") *and light weapons.*

— "Report of the Group of Governmental Experts on Small Arms," issued by the United Nations

"Disarmament" doesn't mean just nuclear weapons—it also means your own firearms. On 22 December 1995, the UN announced a study of individually held small arms which:

are increasingly associated with crime, accidents and suicides, and form a major source of illicit profits for transnational criminal networks...

— www.un.org

I expect an international "War On Guns" soon. The only well-armed citizenries left are those of Switzerland and America (and to a lesser extent, Bolivia, the Czech Republic, Israel, and Norway). Wherever the UN moves in (*e.g.,* Somalia, Rwanda, Haiti, Bosnia) it forcibly disarms the populace. Independently armed citizens cannot be allowed, for the UN god must reign supreme.

We're eventually due for an international enforcement of a domestic gun ban. *Good.* It'll wake up millions of fence-sitters, and our vigilant Citizens won't mind defending their rights against baby-blue helmeted foreign troops from Bulgaria. (If we're lucky, the UN might even send the French, *oui?*) The Smurfs will have *big* problems.

WHEN THEY COME FOR YOUR GUN

That government, being instituted for the common benefit, the doctrine of nonresistance against arbitrary power and oppression is

absurd, slavish and destructive of the good and happiness of mankind.
— Tennessee Constitution, Declaration of Rights

Now that they know *who* you are, *what* you have and *where* you store it, the confiscation raids can begin. Will you "Pass" or will you "Play"? The English and the Australians went through this and they chose *"mouse"* without a squeak. Fine, those whimpering souls don't deserve their guns.

So, this could be *your* story—*our* story—if we don't wake up and grow some gonads, *quickly.* Or, be defanged and get sent to the camps. Your manacles are waiting. *"Hey, this is America! This can't happen here!"* That's exactly why it *can* happen here; because it's too incredible for most people to even contemplate.

*Don't ever think it can't happen here. It has happened here. **We have a shameful history—don't ever forget it.** In 1932, twenty thousand World War One veterans peacefully assembled...in Washington [D.C.] to urge Congress to give them their war bonus early. The military drove them out at gunpoint. General Douglas MacArthur had full armament, including foot soldiers with rifles and bayonets, cavalry with pistols and sabers, and tanks. MacArthur led his troops into a place where twenty thousand unarmed American war veterans were camped, and he burned them out. The soldiers shot and bayonetted some of the veterans, their wives, and children. Babies died from tear gas inhalation. The result of this horror is that Hoover was defeated and Franklin Roosevelt was able to seize power and drastically expand the government's reach into your lives. Part of that meant passing the unconstitutional National Firearms Act of 1934, which was the beginning of the terrible situation we now face. What happened at Waco and the disaster we face now is nothing new. It started sixty years ago with Franklin Roosevelt, it's gotten worse ever since, and we let it happen!*
— John Ross, *Unintended Consequences* (1996), p. 566

Gun registration and confiscation have preceded *every* modern genocide in history. Ask the murdered Sioux Indians of the 1870s. Ask the dead Moroccan Jews of 1912. Ask the starved Ukrainians of the 1930s. Ask the dead Jews of Nazi Europe. Ask the gulaged Soviet dissidents. Ask the 65,000,000 dead post-1948 Chinese anti-Communists, and the 2,000 massacred students of 1989 Tiananmen Square. If these groups had been *armed*, would they likely have been shot, flattened by tanks, or herded into gas chambers?

Prompt defensive measures (this means shooting back, folks) *are the most effective means for the prevention of genocide.*
— V.V. Stanciu, Secretary of the International Society for the Prevention of Genocide (Paris, France)

A society of sheep must in time beget a government of wolves.
— Betrand de Juvenal

Wisdom is knowing what to do next. Virtue is doing it.
— David Starr Jordan

Cowardice...in an individual, is the unpardonable sin.
— Theodore Roosevelt

The price of freedom is the willingness to do sudden battle, anywhere, anytime, and with utter recklessness.
— Robert A. Heinlein

If the representatives of the people betray their constituents, then there is no resource left but in the exertion of that original right of self-defense which is paramount to all positive forms of government, and which against the usurpations of the natural rulers may be exerted with infinitely better prospect of success than against those of the rulers of an individual State. In a single State, if the persons entrusted with supreme power become usurpers, the different parcels, subdivisions, or districts of which it consists, having no distinct governments in each, can take no regular measures for defense. The **[State]** *citizens must rush tumultuously to arms, without concert, without system, without resource; except in their courage and despair.*
— Alexander Hamilton; *Federalist Paper #28*

Stay armed and stay *free*. England was expelled from America in 1781, from Ireland in 1920, and from Palestine in 1948; France and the U.S. from Vietnam; Portugal from Angola; the U.S.S.R. from Afghanistan—all because the counter insurgents had both the will *and* the *means* to resist insurgent troops.

Within the society that still maintains a rational legal system, civil disobedience is justified to bring a bad law to court for a review. Civil disobedience is to force a review of bad legislation. This is an opportunity for the defenders of freedom and reason to prove their case and, thereby, repeal or nullify bad laws.

Civil disobedience in an irrational legal system serves an altogether different purpose. This is the simple rejection of the usurpations of an oppressive government. Disobeying this government is an act of self-preservation—for if the government is acting contrary to reality and reason, then its edicts, regulations, and commandments are dangerous and opposed to human life. Civil disobedience in this context is the psychological and physical preparation for civil war.

A policeman coming to take you to Auschwitz deserves to be shot. A policeman coming to steal your property deserves to be shot. A policeman coming to kidnap your children to haul them off to a government accredited indoctrination center deserves to be shot. A policeman coming to confiscate your means of self-defense, your guns, deserves to be shot.

As a government moves more and more toward the totalitarian state, it is increasingly inclined to intimidate the citizens by threatening resistance to the police with mandatory death. This is less than the Geneva Conventions guarantee to captured soldiers. So if you are going to resist, renounce your citizenship, start your own country, sign the Geneva Conventions and then declare war on the tyrannical government.

> — Mark Laughlin
> www.ebarricades.com/root/POF5.html

And here's the moral:

When they come for your guns, *give 'em the ammo first*.

If you haven't seen the film *The White Rose*, go find a copy. It's about the student anti-Nazi resistance movement of 1943, which was finally crushed by the guillotine. The White Rose's second flyer included the below text, which struck me as amazingly poignant for us today:

Wenn so eine Welle des Aufuhrs durch das Land geht,
wenn es in der Luft liegt,
wenn viele mitmachen,
dann kann in einer letzten, gewältigen Anstrengung
dieses System abgeschütelt werden.

If a wave of revolt rolls across the country,
if it is carried by the air,
if many people join us,
then in one last, powerful effort,
this system can be shaken off.

❖ 39

WHEN THE
RAIDS COME

A prudent man forseeth the evil and hideth himself; but the simple pass on, and are punished.
  — Proverbs 27:12 (KJV)

Pressure makes diamonds.
  — Gen. George S. Patton

First, they'll visit the homes on their gun registration lists. If you're on the list, prepare yourself for a knock at the door. **Do not let them in under any circumstance!** Speak to them through a closed door, and reply, *"If I were a gunowner, you can be sure that I would comply with all applicable laws. Beyond that, I've got nothing else to say. Good day, officers."*

Later, they'll get around to List #2—the problem children. By then, you should have *moved*, or at least hidden your prohibited guns out of town/state. If you haven't, then the choice of "Pass or Play" will be forced upon you. Know in advance what you'll do, and make necessary preparations.

The raids will come. The freedom-haters are far too committed to back down on the gun issue. If only to save face, the raids will be ordered. When that happens, the gloves are off, folks. Give up your guns and expect the camps a few years later. Do not be "declawed"! Get tough *now*, because you'll need to be tough later—and toughness (like a callus) is built up over years, not created in the moment. Steel yourself for all this now, as it'll be too late to get courageous later.

Yes, guns kill people. Sometimes, in order to preserve our free-dom, some people need to be killed. Occasionally, these are freelance bandits. But most often, down through the corridors of history, they have turned out to be uniformed agents of a tyrannical central government. That is precisely why the Second Amendment guarantees that, in America, the government and its agents must <u>never</u> be allowed to outgun the common people...while it says not a word about "legitimate sporting use."

The Founders could not predict precisely when such a time would come again. But they knew for sure it <u>would</u> come again. Thus they guaranteed in the strongest terms each citizen his private arms, so that—whenever their treason against our God-given rights leaves us no other choice—we, or our children, or our grandchildren shall retain the ability to shoot government agents through the head, and kill them.

That is what firearms are for. And that is why no people can be without them, and long remain free.

— Vin Suprynowicz; *Send in the Waco Killers* (1999), p.368

The below essay contains much good advice, which supplements my book *You & The Police!*

What To Do If The Police Come To Confiscate Your Militia Weapons

by Howard J. Fezell, Esq.

This essay originally appeared in the June, 1990 issue of DOWN-RANGE, the official publication of the Maryland State Rifle & Pistol Association. (Also check out a file put on the Net by the ACLU entitled *Your Rights in an Encounter with the Police* and download their pocket-sized Bustcard.) Go to www.2ndAmendment.net for other essays on your right to keep bear arms.

As California and New Jersey have enacted bans on the sale and unlicensed possession of militia-style semi-automatic rifles, every Marylander who professes loyalty to the Constitution should consider what action he or she will take in the event that Congress, or our own General Assembly were to follow suit. The points addressed in this article are premised on three assumptions.

❶ Either Congress, or our General Assembly has enacted legislation prohibiting or severely restricting the possession of weapons protected by the Second Amendment (*e.g.*, military pattern semi-automatic rifles).

❷ The reader has already decided to uphold the Constitution and not turn over his or her *"prohibited"* firearms under any circumstances, nor to register such weapons in order to facilitate their future confiscation. The reader has also failed to respond to government directives to dispose of or surrender such firearms.

❸ The reader has secured all *"prohibited"* firearms away from his or her principal residence so as to prevent their unconstitutional seizure by the authorities.

What do you do when the police show up on your doorstep demanding the surrender of your militia weapons? In responding, bear in mind that you have two important rights guaranteed by the Fourth and Fifth Amendments to the United States Constitution.

The Fourth Amendment protects you against unreasonable searches and seizures. If the police want to search your house without your consent, they need a warrant. Warrants may only be issued upon a showing of probable cause, supported by an affidavit. The facts contained in the affidavit must do more than support a mere suspicion. The test is whether the information in the affidavit would justify a person of prudence and caution in believing that an offense is being committed, *e.g.*, that *"prohibited"* weapons can be found on your premises. The requirement of probable cause for the issuance of warrants is one of your most precious constitutional protections.

NEVER GIVE THE AUTHORITIES YOUR CONSENT TO SEARCH YOUR HOUSE, YOUR CAR, YOUR PLACE OF BUSINESS, OR ANY OTHER PREMISES UNDER YOUR CONTROL.

Consent dispenses with the necessity of probable cause. While lacking probable cause, if the police conduct a search with your consent and seize evidence for use against you in court, your lawyer will not be able to suppress it on the basis that the search was warrantless.

The Fifth Amendment protects you against giving evidence against yourself, *i.e.*, your right to remain silent. Just as you cannot be compelled to testify against yourself in a criminal trial, neither can you be compelled to answer a policeman's questions about that AR-15 you bought a couple of years ago and never surrendered. Don't be bashful about invoking this right. **It's always better to remain silent and appear guilty than to open your mouth and prove it.**

At the outset of any contact with the police, ask them if they have a warrant to search your premises, or a warrant for your arrest. Without one or the other, don't let them inside your front door. If they have neither, politely request that they leave and gently close the door. If you have an attorney, keep one of his cards in your wallet. Give it to the officer in charge and request that all inquiries be made through your counsel. Remember, the police wouldn't be at your doorstep if you were not the target of a criminal investigation. You have no obligation whatsoever to cooperate with people who intend to unlawfully confiscate your property and put you in jail. They can't arrest you for keeping your mouth shut and going about your business.

The police may still persist in trying to question you, or ask your consent to *"take a look around."* Again, if you have an attorney, give the officer in charge one of his or her cards and request that all inquiries be made through your counsel. Above all, remember that you have the right to break off this conversation. Do so immediately.

In some instances where the police lack a search warrant, they will tell you that it's a simple matter for them to obtain one and they *"just want to save everybody a lot of time."* This is hogwash. Politely tell them to go get one, and close the door. If they suggest that it will *"go a lot easier on you"* should you give them your consent to search, tell them to call your lawyer, and close the door.

In the event the police do in fact have a warrant either to arrest you or to search your premises, do not offer any resistance. You will have other battles to fight (presumably with the weapons you have hidden) and you want to be alive and kicking when the time comes. You are a member of the militia and we don't want to lose you or your weapon. You also don't want to do anything to endanger your family or deprive them of a home. Don't be foolish and engage the authorities in a firefight that you have no chance of winning.

On the other hand, you are not obliged to do anything to make the officers' job easier, such as giving them the combination to your gun safe. You have the right to remain silent and should take advantage of it. That may cause the authorities to forcibly open your safe, with resultant damage. But let them work at their task. After all, it's their search warrant.

Politely request to see a copy of any warrants, and above all, remain silent. Anything you say can be used against you in court. Tell the officers that you do not want to say anything or answer any questions—and that you want to talk to an attorney immediately. If you already have a lawyer, request permission to telephone him or her. If you have been taken into custody, the police are obliged to cease and desist from interrogation once you have asserted your right to remain silent and requested the assistance of legal counsel.

Your spouse and children will be natural targets of interrogation for the authorities. Do they know where your firearms are hidden? Although Maryland law generally prohibits your spouse from testifying against you in a criminal trial, that will be of no help of he or she breaks down under questioning and the authorities know where to retrieve your guns. Never forget that your objective is to safeguard your weapons and ammunition for the defense of the Constitution against all enemies, foreign and domestic.

If you or a family members are subpoenaed to testify before a grand jury or other judicial or governmental body, get an attorney immediately. Legal counsel can be very helpful, either in trying to quash the subpoena or helping to invoke one's rights against self-incrimination. (BTP Note: The 5th protects against *all compelled self-testimony*—incriminating or not!)

Never, under any circumstances, should you lie to the authorities. Simply exercise your right to remain silent. Don't try to snow them with phony bills of sale that can easily be checked out and used to impeach your credibility in court should you decide to testify. Above all, don't file a false police report that your guns were lost or stolen. Making a false report to a police officer that results in an investigation being undertaken is a criminal offense in Maryland. Remember, you are not a criminal. Your ultimate goal is to defend the Constitution.

Likewise, don't fall for any of the authorities' lies. Police love to play "Mutt & Jeff" (also known as "Good Cop—Bad Cop").

One officer comes across as a real hardcase, telling you about all the jail time you're looking at. After a few minutes of this, his partner takes you aside, offers you a cigarette, and in a friendly tone tells you that he *"only wants to help you."* He only wants to help you confess. Tell Mr. Nice Guy you want to talk with a lawyer. Another police tactic is to tell you that a friend of yours has confessed and given them a statement implicating you for all kinds of things. They're just trying to rattle your cage and make you blurt something out. Keep your mouth shut and let your attorney handle the police. If they really have such a statement, your counsel will be able to discover it.

If the authorities have a warrant to search your home, they might imply (sometimes none too subtly) that if you do not come across with that they're looking for they will tear the place apart. Don't give in. Just keep your mouth shut. If you hand over your *"prohibited"* weapons, you've just given them all the evidence they need to put you in prison. Even if you fall for this scare tactic, the police may still trash your house. Although this is the rare exception, not the rule, such conduct is not unheard of.

In the event you are on the receiving end of a search warrant, do not be pressured into signing any inventories of property seized without first consulting with an attorney. There might be something on that list that is prohibited according to some obscure regulation that you've never heard of. Also be sure that you or some family member receive an itemized list of any property seized. Under Maryland law the police are obliged to sign one and leave it at the premises from which the property is taken. If it is subsequently determined that the authorities took anything that was not within the scope of their warrant, your attorney should motion the court for its prompt return.

Hopefully, you will never have to avail yourself of the advice set forth above. The best thing you can do to keep the Free State really free is to make a healthy contribution to the cause,...and keep up the pressure on your Delegate and Senator.

Remember, the battle to defend our liberties has already begun—and you are one of the Constitution's foot soldiers.

Dear Peace Officer:

(Note: This was sent to me, and I thought it fitting for this chapter. BTP)

I don't want to kill you. I don't even want to wound you. I admire your courage and the commitment you've made to help others, often at risk of own your life. I hope you won't come for me, because if you do, one of us will die. It may be you. I've done nothing wrong. I don't intend to. But the government that you serve has passed too many laws. I am sure to accidentally break one, some day. And that same government is systematically destroying the unalienable rights which our Constitution says may not be infringed—very specifically, my right to keep and bear arms.

I am not some wacko lunatic, but I can no longer stand idly by, while decent people are systematically enslaved by an out-of-control government. I cannot allow a corrupt judiciary to use its power to destroy my rights and my country. That government and that judiciary has begun to use you to arrest and kill people just like me—people who believe that the Declaration of Independence, the Constitution and the Bill of Rights mean what they say.

You don't know me, but you see me every day. I may be a businessman, a truck driver, an executive. I could be a housewife or a salesman. But I am armed, as Americans have been for over 250 years, and I am determined to keep the freedoms that only an armed people may retain. With a rifle, I can hit a man-sized target at 800 yards. At shorter distances, in the blink of an eye, I can hit a head-size target with a handgun. I don't wear a uniform. I don't drive a marked car. I don't wear camouflage. I could be your own secretary, or your barber. I might be the guy who delivers your bottled water, or the parcel delivery lady. You don't know who I am, or what arms I have, and you never will. I am millions. I am America.

But I know you. I know your uniform, your car, and your work schedule. I know where you work, and where you live. And that is good for you, because not only am I no threat to you, so long as you do the job for which you are hired, I am also prepared to assist you when you are threatened. There aren't many of me left, you may think, but believe me, there are many, many more than you can imagine. When the chips are down, we are the ones who are truly on your side. On your side, that is, so long as you honor your Oath.

We are on your side if you are one of the majority of peace officers who are not corrupt and who have not sold out to the socialists and communists who will do anything, say anything to destroy the America our fathers and grandfathers bequeathed us. No, I am no threat to you, but your bosses in government don't see it that way. They think that I, and my arms, are a threat to them, and they are planning to send you for me, just as they've sent armed, dangerous officers on select little missions for years, taking out targeted individuals. On their orders, you may succeed in murdering me for my beliefs. Or you may not.

Whether or not you succeed in murdering me, as federal agents murdered Vicki Weaver in Idaho; or as those same federal agents murdered 81 men, women and children at Waco, Texas; there will be others who will rise up in my memory, as I now rise up in honor of the innocent lives taken by the jack-booted thugs and black-clad imitation ninjas who think it is fun to murder Americans—who have somehow become convinced that it is their job to murder Americans.

I am prepared to die, honoring my sacred Oath as an American, to defend and protect the Constitution of the united States of America. Are you prepared to die to violate the Oath you took? You see, our government is out of control. You know it. You've seen it. But you, like many others, have been too concerned with your job, your family, and your pension, to say or do anything about it. Deep down, you know I am right. But you think you must follow orders.

Or must you? Are you going to murder me for having the courage to stand up for the country and the principles in which you believe? Are you going to go along with unconscionably illegal, unconstitutional orders, just as the "good" German soldiers followed their orders? Are you going to be a peace officer or a jack-booted thug? There is little difference between a street outlaw who murders and robs; and a uniformed thug who murders and robs under color of law. The result is the same. Property confiscated, lives ruined, families ripped apart, murder committed, and a free nation destroyed.

Look at history. Look around the world. As we move toward a lawless society, our country moves closer and closer to anarchy and then some form of fascism. Are you going to enforce unconstitutional laws? Are you going to be the private army of fascist dictators masquerading as democratic representatives? Or are you going to do your part to recapture America? Are you going to keep your eyes and ears open? Will you let me know when the jack-booted thugs in the SWAT teams have targeted me? Will you let your fellow officers know that they are being sold down the river by their corrupt masters? Don't come to kill me. Because I don't want to kill you. If you do come, you may succeed—if you get lucky. But don't count on luck, because it will probably be hard—damned hard. Like millions of other Americans, I am the son or daughter of a nation of riflemen—citizen-soldiers who have a rich heritage of beating the best the enemy can send against us. We are resourceful. We understand weapons and tactics. You are foolish if you intend to be our enemy. If you don't succeed in the long run, and you won't, here's what you can expect:

Ambushes of SWAT teams; the wholesale slaughter of all the jack-booted thugs who have murdered innocent Americans on the orders of their socialist masters; targeted assassinations and kidnappings of anti-Constitution judges; assassinations of anti-American, anti-gun politicians.

By your willingness to be a good little Nazi, you will have unleashed a civil war. It doesn't have to be that way. You can do something about it. It's easy. Read the Declaration of Independence, the Constitution and the Bill of Rights. Although you took an Oath to defend them, you don't see much of them in your training, do you? Today, these documents are considered dangerous by the government, just as King George found them dangerous over 200 years ago. Why do you suppose your leaders lead you to oppose the very rights you swore to protect? Why do they want a disarmed public? You know the reason. It has nothing to do with controlling crime. It has everything to do with using you to disarm and control your fellow American Citizens.

Don't fall for it. Don't force me to kill you.

(Signed, 100 Million+ American Patriots)

CCW Coalition: Citizens For A Constitutional Washington
John R. Prukop, Executive Director
11910-C Meridian Ave. E., #142
Puyallup, Washington 98373
(253) 840-8071/8074 fax   e-mail: ccw@wolfenet.com

STAY COOL, FOLKS!

We are still trying to educate our "representatives" not only in the *error* of their ways, not merely in the *folly* of their ways, but in the *danger* of their ways. Their self-serving and evil path of citizen disarmament can only lead to one disastrous end—a second civil war which they are destined to lose.

They are destined to lose for one unalterable reason: *We* have the numbers, and they *don't*. If only *1%* of American gunowners are left to fight for Liberty, that would mean *2,400,000* guns in the hands of *750,000* Patriots fighting a guerrilla war on their own territory. Think of it this way: even if the USG were ever *99%* successful, it still leaves nearly *21 times* the IRA's per capita numbers that has fought the British empire to a standstill for generations. (I am not championing the IRA or its terrorism. I'm only noting the historical fact that a handful of riflemen can mire whole armies.) So, please, *enough* whining about future gun confiscation efforts—*they cannot succeed!*

❖ 40

WEALTH
vs. LIBERTY

Here's how the 2nd Amendment was *supposed* to work:

> *The Second Amendment is a recognition of the danger of standing armies. Its purpose is to recognize that every citizen has the right to keep and bear the same type of basic arms as a soldier in the modern military. A militia embodies all able-bodied men over the age of sixteen.* **Therefore, a militia will always outnumber a standing army by at least twenty to one.** *If this militia is armed with weapons similar to those used by the individuals comprising the standing army,* **it will be impossible for that standing army to inflict the will of a tyrannical government upon the people.** *The Second Amendment is the guarantee behind all the other articles in the Bill of Rights. It is the ultimate guarantee that citizens in the United States [of America] will remain free.*
>
> — John Ross; *Unintended Consequences* (1996), p. 47

Well, what *happened*? **If we're so armed, then why aren't we *free*?** Because too many Americans are *wimps*. Arms are one thing; the *will* to use them is another. The 2nd Amendment doesn't actually assure freedom for it can guarantee neither the citizens' *dedication* to freedom nor their *courage* to maintain it at all costs. No constitutional amendment can do that. As Judge Learned Hand so eloquently explained it for the ages:

> *I often wonder whether we do not rest our hopes too much upon constitutions, upon laws and upon courts. These are false hopes, believe me, these are false hopes.* **Liberty lies in the hearts of men and women;** *when it dies there, no constitution, no law, no court can even do much to help it.* **While it lies there it needs no constitution, no law, no court to save it.**

We have grown to love ease and convenience more than liberty. Today, we can hardly be roused over *anything.*

*Yes, we did produce a near perfect Republic. But will they keep it, or will they, in the enjoyment of plenty, lose the memory of freedom? **Material abundance without character is the surest way to destruction.***
— Thomas Jefferson

*__What is lacking in this country is a climate of unrest.__ A certain air of mewling discontent does exist, but it is too similar to the affectionate bickering young lovers indulge in as they jockey for the role identities that will endure between them for the rest of their married lives. Except for your criminal elements, who through circumstances or choice are the pariahs of any society, **I defy you to find nowadays any of the implacable ferocity** that must have been extant in the Jacobin, Cromwellian, pre-Revolutionary American, and Czarist-ruled societies.*
— Oliver Lange, *Defiance* (1971), p. 417

Based on many years of having attended Patriot meetings, I can say with sad certainty that we will not be roused until we suffer a few more atrocities. We will have to reach some point of desperation to wake us. The next Waco-type massacre might do it.

We scaled the mountain but have grown fat, dumb, and lazy on the peak. Now, we're sliding back down. It's a human cycle, and we simply went through it faster than any other civilization, that's all. We're not *quite* through, but getting close.

*Part of any serious program of economic and political survival is that of mental and psychological conditioning. It is not sufficient to stock up on your supplies of dehydrated fruits and gold coins. **The rifle you bought is no better than your determination to use it and your ability to use it.** This means that you have to have some sort of guideline when and under what circumstances to use it. In a time of true terror, which I hope never comes, but which cannot be dismissed lightly, each man must have a mental line drawn, over which his opponent cannot step at zero risk. **The drawing of that line is probably more important than other physical preparations. Where a man's treasure is, there is his heart.** What am I getting at? Simple: all of your preparations should be aimed at preserving your freedom first, and only secondarily aimed at protecting your wealth. Your wealth is simply a tool for expanding your productivity under freedom. **Your wealth must not be allowed to capture you, to chain you to the ground while the wolves plan your demise.** Get this into your mind early: your wealth is your tool to utilize freedom, not your enemy's tool of dominion over you. **The soft underbelly of America is here: our***

inability to understand the proper use of wealth. *We cling to our wealth as if it could save us in a major crisis.*
We have confused means with ends, and we have worshipped means.
— Dr. Gary North; *The Pirate Economy,* pp. 180-1

Alexander Solzhenitsyn in his profound *The Gulag Archipelago* discussed the necessity of an *early* resistance to tyranny:

...At what exact point, then, should one resist...? *...How we burned in the prison camps later thinking:* *what would have things been like if every security operative, when he went out at night to make an arrest, had been uncertain whether he would return alive and had to say good-bye to his family?*

Or if during periods of mass arrests people had not simply sat there in their lairs, paling with terror at every step on the staircase, but had understood they had nothing to lose and had boldly set up in the downstairs hall an ambush of half a dozen people with axes, hammers, pokers, or whatever else was at hand... **The [police] would have quickly suffered a shortage of officers...and notwithstanding all of Stalin's thirst, the cursed machine would have ground to a halt.**

If...If... **We didn't love freedom enough.** *...We purely and simply deserved everything that happened afterward.*

Fellow Americans, we ultimately have *nothing* **to** *lose.* Quit worrying about your precious stuff—they don't put luggage racks on hearses. Our vast material wealth is Delilah's shears to our strength.

Better a sovereign in squalor than a slave in splendor.
— Dresden James

A slave with weekends off is not 2/7ths free.
— Boston T. Party

I've given a lot of thought to exactly *how* our wealth buys off our independent spirit, and I've come up with a few ideas on resetting our priorities. (And, no, we don't have to live in a cave with one set of homespun clothing.)

HAVING WEALTH *AND* FREEDOM

Long-term *liberty*, not comfort, is the goal

Modern slaves are comfortable. They don't even have to think for themselves; they only have to do as they're told. If, however, *you* want to deliberately live an "examined life" of your own, then freedom-of-action will supercede comfort. (For now, at least.) Liberty and comfort are *somewhat* mutually exclusive, so choose *now* and quit bitching. Besides, there's a peculiar comfort to liberty, so if you focus on liberty, comfort will follow.

Wealth is *expendable*
Wealth is not an end, but a *means* for Liberty

Get this through your head *now* if you've chosen Liberty. Regardless of what happens to us after we're dead, it seems fairly well settled that we *don't* get to use our earthly stuff. Our wealth is here while *we're* here, and moot when we're gone.

We don't actually get to own *anything* down here. We just get to *use* it for a few years. Everything is "rented" including our bodies, so treat "your" stuff like that rental car—pedal to the floor. If the tires aren't smoking when you turn it in, then you didn't get your daily Ø39.95's worth. Use wealth to maximize liberty for yourself and for your children. Wealth is *expendable*.

Maintain income. Lower your living standard.

My income could drop by half and I wouldn't know the difference. Why not? Because I live *beneath* my means. I do not "live for today." I forsake much of the comfort I *could* enjoy today for future value.

Don't waste your disposable income on transitory entertainment and luxuries. Don't put your investment capital in stocks, bonds, or mutuals. Invest in *yourself*—knowledge, training, and tools—things which will increase your chances of future survival and prosperity.

Your biggest expense is probably shelter. Living beneath your means requires shelter less than you "deserve." Trade down your 5/4 mansion for a 3/2 house, or your 3/2 house for a 3/2 mobile. After a bit of adjustment, you won't miss your fancy digs. As long as your home is sufficiently spacious, warm, and cheery—what else *really* matters? It's all *attitude*, folks.

For example, if you save Ø300 per month in rent or mortgage for just one year, then you can buy a .308 FAL battle rifle *and* send yourself to Thunder Ranch. In only one year, you will have acquired something priceless—especially since you will not be *allowed* to buy such a tool or its training for too much longer.

Do this for *two* years and you can include 12 months of excellent food storage, a good handgun, and some gold coins. Do this for *three* years, and you can go back to Thunder for Handun 1 and Urban Rifle 2. Do this for *four* years, and buy a small used RV and store it on somebody's country property. Do this for *five* years, and you can buy a few acres yourself to build on.

Actually, this could be done in just *two* years with deeper cutbacks and harder work. *Backwood Homes* had a story of an Oregon *waitress* who bought some country acreage and built her own log home in just a few years from tips and salary. If you want it badly enough, *anything* can be accomplished. What's *your* excuse—you're not some single waitress in rural Oregon?

You all would be surprised if you knew how modestly I live. This is not to brag, but to reassure you that Boston T. Party "walks the walk." Most Patriot authors *don't*. I know of one who can't find his Mini-14 right now. (Hint: It's either under the entertainment center or behind the waterbed.)

Fractionalize your assets
Have 2x50%, or 3x33%—not 1x100%

Remember our goal: Liberty, not comfort. Americans don't rock the boat because they don't want to lose their precious stuff. Their precious stuff is all in one big basket—and this is tactical leverage against the owner. One simple raid can clean out the unprepared dissident. He can go from fat and comfy to hungry and cold in an afternoon. The IRS has done this to *thousands* of Americans already.

The solution? Have smaller eggs in several baskets. I recommend living on 50% and having 2 other 25% places. Having ½ your assets elsewhere does two vital things for you:

❶   You won't likely make some tactically futile stand for 50% as you might for the whole 100%.

❷   It gives you someplace else of your own to go to if your public/primary domicile gets raided or seized.

What goes in your private hideouts

Most of your guns, food storage, how-to books, "subversive" materials, tools, cash, and gold. These are your "Mr. Hyde" places. Keep your "Dr. Jekyll" home squeaky clean.

What remains in your public/primary home

Guns: only enough to fight your way *out*. This means at most per person: two handguns and one long gun. Long guns for a family of four (assuming the children are of rifle-bearing age) might be a scoped boltgun, two battle rifles and a shotgun. You won't be able to lug anything more than that with you, much less wield it in your two busy hands. Extra guns should be stored at locations 2 and 3. If battle rifles are forbidden in your city/state and you don't want to be at risk, then have instead bolt-action Lee-Enfields or Mausers, or lever-action .30-30s. *Any* decent .30 caliber rifle will do if *you* will do.

Food storage for a month. If a crisis lasts longer than *that*, then you don't want to remain in the city, anyway. Don't prepare to outlast some siege. Get out when (preferably *before*) it looks ugly—you can always go back home later.

Bugout packs for every member. One should already be in every car (including rifle, though maybe not semi-auto). Notarized copies of all important documents. Passports. Spare eyeglasses. Medicines. Ø1,000+/person. Small gold bullion coins.

Vehicles: A 4x4 with trailer (already packed with "camping" gear, etc.). Gasoline for at least 600 miles per vehicle (1,000 is much better). Radios. Spare parts. Tools. Tires. Enough gear to get you out, but not so much to bog you down.

Now, get *rugged*

You've removed most of the negative tactical leverage of wealth and assets. You are the master of your stuff, not vice-versa. Now, you need to toughen up yourself.

I know many great Patriots and Libertarians who have all the right gear, but no calluses. Gear alone won't do it. **It's the *man*, not the gun. The *man* is the weapon system—the gun is just a tool.** Get to every shooting school you can afford. Take up martial arts, preferably at a *dojo* where there's *lots* of sparring. Shun modern comfort and camp out for a week or two at a time. Go the gym regularly, lose that gut and *get in shape*. Backpack with your rifle—become "as one" with it. Get *rugged*!

41

PREPARING FOR THE WORST

The strongest reason for the people to retain the right to keep (own)
and bear (carry) *arms is, as a last resort,* **to protect themselves**
against tyranny in government.
— Thomas Jefferson

We are fast arriving at our point of no return—if we're not there
already. I see little chance of successful reforms. The Freedom
Movement began too late, and we probably *won't* acquire the
necessary mass influence for national political change. We're
almost assuredly past political solutions, anyway, so let's now
focus on what we've probably been forced to resolve ourselves
to—a resistance movement.

    I estimate that there are about 500,000 hard-core,
"damn-the-torpedoes," liberty-loving Americans who will *never*
give in to tyranny. Maybe it's just 100,000. Well, then, what are
our chances? What odds do only 100,000 recalcitrant gun
owners have? An historical example offers a clue:

"Let me summarize: Ireland is an island [about the size of
Arkansas]. *Residents there have to store their weapons at
government-sanctioned gun clubs. Anyone with a relative even
suspected of belonging to the IRA cannot own a gun, cannot belong
to such a club, and must go outside the country if he wants to shoot
at paper targets. The Special Air Service has quite a bit
more...latitude in dealing with terrorists than we have here, and the
SAS is one of the finest fighting units in the world. It is fully the
equal of our own Special Forces.* **And for decades, the SAS has
been held at bay by a group...similar in number to the**

*spectators at an average American Little League baseball
game. Is that about right?" "Spot on," the SAS Major said...*
— John Ross; *Unintended Consequences* (1996), p. 730

Assuming only the IRA's *per capita* numbers extrapolated here,
that still means 36,000 guerrilla fighters (about a third of the
100,000+ I'm certain that actually exist). Although 36,000 is
only one in every 2,083 gunowners, it's still a lot of people,
numerically. Percentage wise, we're negligible, but that's really
only a *political* disadvantage.

There are 240 million guns in 75 million private American
hands. **Even if 99% of the guns could be collected, *there
would still be 2.4 million left* in the hands of 750,000 very
upset Patriots.** Even at a *99.9%* confiscation rate, that still
would leave 75,000 Patriots (over twice the IRA's *per capita*
numbers) with 240,000 guns. Nothing close to 99% will ever be
achieved, so what is everybody so jittery about? The simple
math of it all means that citizen disarmament cannot happen!

The only guns *successfully* confiscated will be from those
owners *who know in advance* that they will never resist—those
who value sandwiches over freedom, temporary comfort over
indelible honor. The rest of us (and I devoutly hope this
includes *you*) will not—will *never*—give up our arms. If liberty-
loving Americans are treated so shabbily *when we have guns*,
then how much *more* brutal will the treatment be if we are
disarmed? If the fedgoons are *this* bold, when they can be easily
shot at, imagine their savagery if we give up our guns.

*...Guard with jealous attention the public liberty. Suspect every one
who approaches that jewel.* **Unfortunately, nothing will preserve
it but downright force. Whenever you give up that force, you
are inevitably ruined.**

— Patrick Henry, 5 June 1788

No slave shall keep any arms whatever,...

— A Bill Concerning Slaves, Virginia Assembly (1779)

Some thoughts on the bureaucrats

*The bureaucrats and politicians do not fear armed criminals or
armed political zealots as much as they fear peaceful Americans
who will probably never use their* [so-called] *assault rifles, but whose
mental toughness may be enhanced by possession of military
weapons.*

*The gun controllers are not deterred by the facts about guns
and crime, **because their primary fear is not of criminals. They***

*fear ordinary Americans whose lives and freedom their policies
are destroying. In this fear and in their world, they are on target.*
— Arthur B. Robinson, Ph.D.; *Access to Energy*, Vol. 21, #11

The front cover of Dr. Gary North's excellent book *Government
By Emergency* beautifully illustrates this point: a bald, wimpy
bureaucrat with a clipboard flanked by two thug cops
brandishing shotguns to enforce his edicts.

Bureaucrats are *weenies*. I learned this firsthand in
1991 when I was writing *Good-Bye April 15th!* and had to get
some sample IRS forms at their district HQ. Having picked up
forms months earlier, I knew in which building they were kept,
but what I *didn't* know was that "customer service" had been
moved into *another building* entirely. I was at the wrong place.
I casually walked past the newly placed security guard and
entered. Although no forms were displayed as before and the
office had been rearranged, I nonetheless pleasantly and
confidently requested to be supplied with the forms on my list.
The drones seemed quite confused and asked if I was with the
EEOC ("Equal Employment Opportunity Commission"), which
confused *me*. When they finally realized that I was a mere
member of the *public*, they all but panicked and called for
security. I was escorted outside by the same guy who had let me
walk right in. You see, they felt all warm and safe and fuzzy
because of their "security"—until my visit. I have often savored
the memory of their faces flooding with terror, *over nothing*.

Congressmen, judges, bureaucrats—they're all *weenies*.
Without their black-suited ninja thugs, they're nothing. If the
government pushes things much further, these thugs will have
their hands full. **Even if American revolutionaries
number to only the IRA's per capita, it still equates to
36,000.** The feds simply don't have enough trained people to
handle 36,000 righteously pissed-off Americans. That averages
to 720 revolutionaries per state. So relax, but stay alert.

The federal ninja are preparing...
Honed. Honed to a fine edge. Honed to kill!
— a Kansas City FBI agent at Waco, waiting for action

The fedgoons take all this seriously. Long before the
OKBombings the *Waffen* FBI ordered almost 2,000 suppressed
.308 sniper rifles with night vision scopes. These rifles were
made by Brown Precision with AWC suppressors and STANO
image tubes. (The feds hope to "decapitate" the Freedom Move-

ment and gun culture by simultaneously arresting and/or eliminating and several hundred key people.)

This purchase order was placed at the same time the FBI was saying their sniper Lon Horiuchi maybe *shouldn't* have murdered Vicki Weaver, and they would keep tighter control on their "Rules of Engagement." *Wink, wink.* The BATF now has Bradleys. (They *almost* got OV-10D gunships, but *tooo bad!*)

> *It is my belief that we now have reached the point of diminishing returns in our battle to restore the Constitution.* **We would serve each other better to spend our time and energy learning how to survive in a country devoid of freedom,** *which is, I believe, the unstated goal of powerful interests who are now running our nation.*
>
> — Colorado state senator Charles Duke

In 1994 the Pentagon's deputy chief of staff for intelligence, a Major Ralph Peters, wrote a position paper *Warrior Class*:

> **The desire for patriotism is considered an enemy doctrine. The U.S. armed forces must be prepared to fight against all those who oppose the New World Order and who are holding out for nationalism...** *This new warrior class is most dangerous because they consist of those who fight out of strong religious beliefs... There is a worldwide class of patriots* (i.e., "terrorists") *who number in the millions, and if the current trend continues, there may be more of these who...love freedom and are now the target of the New World Order... You cannot bargain and compromise with these warriors... We, as the military, need to commit more training to counter these warrior threats. We must have an active campaign to win over the populace.* **This must be coupled with irresistible violence.**
>
> — from the *McAlvany Intelligence Advisor,* May/June 1994

There you have it. Patriotic American gunowners are the #1 Enemy of the New World Order. Since we can't be bargained or compromised with, prepare for *"irresistible violence."*

DON'T GET SKITTISH!

> *You will never know how much it cost...[us] to preserve your freedom.* **I hope you will make good use of it.**
>
> — John Quincy Adams

If we are left alone, either by truce or by inefficiency, so be it. However, *if,* despite our best efforts for peaceful privacy and gun ownership, we be hounded unmercifully, if we be raided for our guns—**then give 'em tooth and claw.**

I will not compromise, I will not grovel, I will not toady at the feet of mammon. I will give every man his due. I will honor my word even to my own hurt, and if these be insufficient grounds to be left alone, then somebody will have a seething problem on their hands. I *will* be left alone to cause no harm. I hereby pledge to you my life, my fortune, and my sacred honor that I will die on my feet before I ever cower on my knees. What about *you*?

The final, simple human truth

Today, we need a nation of Minute Men, citizens who are not only prepared to take up arms, but citizens who regard the preservation of freedom to be the basic purpose of their daily life and who are willing to consciously work and sacrifice for that freedom.
— John F. Kennedy, in defense of citizen militias (1961)

As the total subjection of a people arises generally from gradual encroachments, it will be our indispensable duty manfully to oppose every invasion of our rights in the beginning.
— Silks Downer; from *American Political Writing during the Founding Era, 1760-1805*, p. 1071

You *have* no rights unless you are willing to *fight* for them:

The price of freedom is the **willingness** *to do sudden battle, anywhere, anytime, and with utter recklessness.*
— Robert A. Heinlein

I *don't* mean to say that you have no rights *unless* you fight—I mean you must only be *willing* to fight, if necessary. The mere *will* to fight often avoids the fight itself. (Observe your neighborhood dogs on this point.) Obviously, the feds scoff at our will. Guns without the resolve to use them is perhaps worse than resolve without guns, for it creates a false confidence.

And yet no weapons, no matter how powerful, can help the West **until it overcomes its loss of will power.** *In a state of psychological weakness weapons become a burden for the capitulating side.* **To defend oneself one must be ready to die, and there is little such readiness in a society raised in the cult of material well-being.**
— Solzhenitsyn; *Warning To The West*

Never was anything great achieved without danger.
— Niccolò Machiavelli

Most gunowners will wet their pants when the raids come, and the feds *know* it. Many, however, will not.

I don't *want* to shoot *anybody*—not even fedgoons.
All I'm saying is that it's a real possibility that peaceable folks will be backed into an ugly corner by government—and we should mentally and physically prepare ourselves for this. I'd much rather that awful day never came, but *if* it comes, *fire*.

> *Fight, and you may die. Run...and you'll live. At least a while. Many years from now, would you be willing to trade all the days, from this day 'till that, for one chance—just one chance to come back here and tell our enemies that they may take our lives, but that they'll never take...our freedom!*
> — William Wallace before the battle at Stirling, *Braveheart*

I pray for the Lord's wisdom and courage. **We need *heroism* above all else.** Freedom cannot survive without it, no matter how brilliant a nation's constitution. (Freedom *clearly* cannot survive under *our* Constitution. It wasn't written tightly enough, as I proved in *Hologram of Liberty*. The feds always have a way out of their constitutional "straightjacket.")

> *Keep your overall goal in mind above all. Those who swerve to avoid a few cuts and bruises defeat themselves. Understand from the very minute the fight begins that you're going to take damage.* ***Accept it.*** *You'll suffer far worse from the idiots and cowards on your own side.*
> — L. Neil Smith; *Pallas*

> *I do believe that where there is a choice only between cowardice and* [defensive] *violence,* ***I would advise violence.***
> — Gandhi

> *Strike back when you're strong, and still have your wits about you, and the enemy isn't expecting it.* ***Give them your teeth, not your belly.***
> — John Ross; *Unintended Consequences* (1996), p. 618

> *The history of liberty is a history of resistance.*
> — Woodrow Wilson

> *When the tyrant comes for your guns, after all, you have only one more chance to use them.*
> — Vin Suprynowicz; *Send in the Waco Killers* (1999), p.308

> ***Live Free or Die.***
> — New Hampshire state motto

Hey, there's no immunity from historical constants just because we're *Americans*.

❖ 42

PATRIOT *LIGHT!*

That, too, was another self-deception,...on the part of those who thought they could get by without toeing the line. I mean the idiocy of the guerrilla business. **That's all it turned out to be: business** *—big business American-style, with endless promotion on all the junk, ranging from Geiger counters and do-it-yourself fallout shelters with revolving periscopes to James Bond folding rifles. Distilled water, fancy food concentrates, snakebite kits, vitamins, machetes, sunglasses. Goosedown sleeping bags, alpine rucksacks, Anzac campaign hats, with accompanying literature on how to assemble your own neighborhood* Maquis. *Batman in the Boondocks. To listen to some, if the day ever came, five hundred thousand citizens, all appropriately* Rogue Male *types, would melt into the hills, and when they weren't creating havoc among the brutal Occupation forces, they would be practicing the fine art of survival.*

Why, if a survival-and-guerrilla nut brought all the stuff the sporting-goods stores and catalogs said he needed, it would have taken a twenty-five-foot long U-Haul trailer and two weeks of packing to get him out of his damned carport....

There were gadgets...to keep...many men alive and operational, but there was one thing nobody considered—or maybe it was too grim to contemplate and so we conveniently wiped it out of our minds—one thing that had simply gone away from us.

What I'm referring to was the actual collective climate of temperament that existed at any given moment in this country: the real, as opposed to the fancied, state of mind.

Barring a few million in the armed forces who were coerced into at least perfunctorily practicing bravery in order to gain peergroup approval, **Americans, as it turned out were not tough.** *For us to leave comfortable homes and camp outdoors for longer than a week was a major adventure planned far in advance, and then the idea was to make wilderness camp as much like home as possible —tents, portable generators, folding chairs, tables, collapsible crappers, radio, television, the works.* **Ché would have flipped.**

— Oliver Lange, *Defiance,* p.83

A third less courage than the regular Patriot!
The spineless sellout "conservatives"

[The Nazis]...*came for the Jews, but I wasn't a Jew, so I didn't speak out. They came for the trade unionists, but I wasn't a trade unionist, so I didn't speak out. They came for the Catholics, but I wasn't a Catholic, so I didn't speak out.* **Then they came for me, and there was no one left to speak out!**
— Reverend Niemuller

...*between freedom and sandwiches, they will choose sandwiches.*
— Lord Boyd-Orr

When men reduce their virtues to the approximate, then evil acquires the force of an absolute; *when loyalty to an unyielding purpose is dropped by the virtuous, it's picked up by scoundrels— and you get the indecent spectacle of a cringing, bargaining traitorous good and a self-righteously uncompromising evil.*
— Ayn Rand; *Atlas Shrugged*

A society of sheep must in time beget a government of wolves.
— Betrand de Juvenal

Do you know *why* conservatives and Patriots get *so* upset at the passage of each new oppressive measure? Why do they become so utterly livid at the *"assault-weapons"* ban, at the *Exclusionary Rule Reform Act of 1995* (H.R. 666), at the *"Crime"* and the *"Anti-Terrorism"* bills? Granted, these acts *are* outrageous on their very face, but there's another reason. **They already know that they will likely *comply*.** Present outrage stems from the imagined pain of their future obedience. They already *know* that they'll redraw their line in the sand.

Folks, draw the line *somewhere* and keep things in perspective. If Congress passed a bill demanding that you throw your children off a cliff, would you comply—even if the fedgoons tried to enforce it? Of course not! So why is everybody so unhinged about some future gun ban? **Why should we even *care*, much less get our blood pressure up?** Draw your line in advance, firmly commit to your principles, make plans, and quit howling about what Congress does!

Quit playing Patriot or Libertarian or Republican or free-market advocate. Quit the NRA and sell your guns, assuming you had the nerve to ever own any. **Quit fooling your-self—*wimp*.** Tear up your von Mises Fan Club Card. Cancel your subscription to the *National Review*.

The country that draws a broad line between its fighting men and its thinking men **will find its fighting done by fools and its thinking done by cowards.**
— Sir William F. Butler

This is the Conservative Movement today—cuddled up in the American flag. All most folks have ever done is pay smarmy lip service to liberty and play "American" if it's not risky. Example: A man selling a mint pre-ban Colt AR15 at a 1998 gun show for just Ø600 was asked *why*. He replied, *"My son wants a jet-ski."* (Gosh, at least it wasn't for something *frivolous*...)

If ye love wealth greater than liberty,
the tranquility of servitude greater
than the animating contest for freedom,
go home from us in peace.

We seek not your counsel, nor your arms,
Crouch down and lick the hand that feeds you;
and may posterity forget that ye were our countrymen.
— Samuel Adams

If you penny-loafer conservatives—you slaves in splendor—ever had the courage of a housecat, we'd have a free America today. But, no, you chirped for the gilded cage. And you got it—*for all of us*. Our vile "leaders" are not the *real* enemy. *You* are.

The only man who makes slavery possible is the slave.
— John W. Campbell, Jr.

I will not, under the guise of politics, initiate force or steal, and I will resist those who do. I utterly despise thieves, liars, and bullies—*especially* when they sanctimoniously couch their immoral actions under "legal" government authority.

There are whole *families* out there—right now—striving for honest government and responsible leadership while you prance around in your Stars and Stripes costume. Quit playing "American" and step into the ring!

To rebel in season (i.e., when victory is sure) **is not to rebel.**
— Greek proverb

The Eastern Bloc "demonstrations" of 1989 were totally *"in season"* because the Communist regimes *allowed* the people to "rebel" in preparation for the politically-timed demise of the Soviet satellite governments. I know—I was *there*. They rebelled without risk. It wasn't like the *real* uprisings of 1953 East Berlin or 1989 Tiananmen Square where people were shot and killed for throwing rocks at tanks. Remember the photo of that lone courageous soul who stopped a column of Chinese tanks? Now *that's* desperation. That's *courage!* (The tanks didn't stop for long. They ran him down—made hamburger of him—because he stood his ground. We're not "there" yet.)

> [T]*he Socialists already have such complete control over the American news media and political processes that it is impossible to change our own government's policies by the customary means of politics and public opinion.* (at 151)
> *We're not advocating revolution—we're advocating counter-revolution! A socialist, one world revolution has evolved over the past few decades to within a few years of total success.* (at 224)
> — Nolan Wilson, *The Minuteman Handbook* (1999)

There were no "Patriot *Lights*" on 4 July 1776

The price paid by many signers of the Declaration of Independence was truly staggering:

Francis Lewis had his home burned and his wife tortured by the British for two years. She died shortly after her release.

John Hart's home was looted and burned, his ailing wife died and his 13 children were scattered. He eluded capture by sleeping in caves.

The 1,000 acre estate of **Lewis Morris** was ransacked and burned. His home was destroyed, his cattle butchered, and his family driven off.

Richard Stockton was imprisoned and repeatedly beaten at the brink of starvation. His home was destroyed, his papers burned.

Carter Braxton saw virtually every merchant ship he owned sunk or captured. He was forced to sell off his land.

Thomas McKean *"was hunted like a fox"* and once *"compelled to move my family five times in a few months."*

Thomas Nelson, Jr. led 3,000 Virginia militia against the British. Redcoats took refuge in his own home, so he turned a cannon on it.

Your assets have already been conscripted by the State. The UN bureaucrats are drooling over your children. **It's 2002 and we're in the calm before the stormtroopers.** Liberty has no friend but the simple, brave American. Rebel with me, with *us*, because it's *not* fashionable. Rebel *"out of season"* when it's truly necessary and truly risky. Get involved *now* so that we perhaps don't *have* to give 'em our teeth later.

> *On too many occasions in the history of civilization, people have accepted authority without subjecting that authority to rational*

examination. A complacent population leaves itself wide open to control. Eventually the abusive bureaucracy demands too much. The end is either revolt or subjugation. Perhaps the problem is not with the power of the abuser; perhaps the problem is with the individual who is willing to submit. Free men and women need not apologize for being enraged by arrogance in government.
   Look into your soul. Corner apathy. Root it out. The darkest hours of human history are marked by muted minutes of indifference. *(p. 108)*
   *I think I know what real courage is. **Real courage is to leave that nice chair and walk into the flame of history.** Real courage is to fight when there are so many places to hide, so many excuses. The halls of forever are long. Somewhere, far from this time, you may have to look into the eyes of your children once again. Somewhere, far from this time, you may have to look into the eyes of patriots. Somewhere, far from this time, you may have to look into the eyes of the young soldier who never got to hold the tiny hand of his firstborn; **who took the hit for you because he knew that somewhere, somehow, in all the confusion of his youth, freedom mattered.** (p. 207)*
   — Bill Branon; *Let Us Prey* (1994)

Get involved *now* so that *you* won't crumple and give 'em your *belly* later. We're all going to die some day. What counts, and what will count, is how you lived your life. How are *you* living *your* life right now? For honor and decency, courageously? Or for comfort, cowardly and shamefully?

*These are the times that try men's souls. The summer soldier and sunshine patriot will, in this crisis, shrink from the service of his country; but he that stands now deserves the love and thanks of man and woman. Heaven knows how to put a proper price upon its goods; **and it would be strange indeed if so celestial an article as Freedom should not be highly rated.***
   —Thomas Paine, *The Crisis*, 23 December 1776

How are *you* living *your* life right now? As Jefferson said:

What country can preserve its liberties if their rulers are not warned from time to time that their people preserve the spirit of resistance?

In the dark days of 1941, Winston Churchill admonished:

...this is the lesson: never give in, never give in, never, never, never, never—in nothing, great or small, large or petty—never give in except to convictions of honour and good sense.

If my talk of armed resistance is getting you squeamish—*good*. **It's better to discover your lack of mettle *now* than later.** Example: A Patriot Light was shopping for a lever-action .30-30 so he'll still have *some* kind of Politically Correct, unbanned rifle after they take away his H&K93. I told him to also shop for a BB gun so he'll have something after they confiscate his .30-30. (Skewered, he saw my point, though I felt like open-handing him across the face just to make it stick.)

Folks, when they come for your *"assault rifles"* either give them up and admit that you were just a wimpy hobbyist—or use them for their true purpose.

Oh, and by the way, decide *now*, please.

Every oppressed people in history was, at some point, forced to resort to arms. *We* were forced to 225 years ago, and it's almost certain to be our "turn" again very soon. Big deal. That's life. And death is part of life. It goes something like this:

> We weren't here.
>
> > We were here.
>
> > > We left.

You and I get 76 trips around the sun and then we check out. The world spun before our arrival, and it will spin after our exit.

What will *you* have accomplished during the interval? Don't let this scenario be your own:

> *The feds came for the White Separatists, but I wasn't a White Separatist, so I didn't speak out. They came for the Branch Davidians, but I wasn't a Branch Davidian, so I didn't speak out. They came for the militias, but I wasn't a militia member, so I didn't speak out. They came for the "assault weapons" owners, but I didn't own any "assault weapons," so I didn't speak out. They came for the rest of the gunowners, but I wasn't a gunowner, so I didn't speak out. They came for the holistic health practitioners, the home-schoolers, the ranchers, the Libertarians, the Buchanan Republicans, the Christians, but I wasn't one of them, so I didn't speak out. **Then they came for me, and there was no one left to speak out!**
>
> — any non-Socialist American, a few years from now...*

It's *not* how comfortable did you make yourself, or how much money did you earn, but *what* did *you* do to stand against evil?

> *Courage is the first of human qualities because it is the quality which guarantees the others.*
> — Aristotle

OUTRAGE,
THEN COURAGE

If you want a picture of the future, imagine a boot stamping on a human face—forever.
— George Orwell; *1984*

*We are trying to reinforce to them (the Branch Davidians) that we (the FBI) are in charge of the situation, that the compound (sic) is under the complete control of the Government. It is in fact no longer their compound (sic); that we have the ability to exercise whatever control we want over that compound (sic), and we will do that at various times to demonstrate to them the fact **they are impotent in their ability to control their everyday lives.***
— Bob Ricks, FBI spokesman at Waco, April 1993

*These, muh (BTP Note: She nearly said "military"), uh, pieces of equipment (the CS-injecting tanks from Ft. Hood, Texas) were unarmed, as I understand it, and were contracted...**I mean, it was like a good rental car.** Uh, they were...*
(Attorney General Janet "For The Kids" Reno)
Ah, a good...a good rental car? A tank going into a building?
(Congressman Bill Zeliff; R-NH)
Uh, ah, ah... (Attorney General Janet "For The Kids" Reno)
— from the House hearings on Waco

Men that are above all fear, soon grow above all shame.
— Trenchard and Gordon, *Cato's Letters* (1755), vol. I, p. 255

A *2nd* AMERICAN REVOLUTION?

*The Clinton era has spawned an armed militia movement involving tens of thousands of people. The last time anything like this occurred was in the 1850's with the emergence of the southern gun clubs. It is easy to dismiss the militia as right-wing nuts: it is much harder to read the complex sociology of civic revolt. **At the very least, the militias reveal the hatred building up against the irksome yuppies who run the country.***

It is under this president that domestic terrorism has become a feature of life in America, culminated with the destruction of the Oklahoma Federal Building on April 19, 1995. What set the deadly spiral in motion was the Waco assault two years before, and the cover-up that followed.

— Ambrose Evans-Pritchard, 1997 letter to America

Look, I am *not* advocating an armed rebellion or the lynching of officials. What I *am* saying is *this:* Do not cherish your own life or property *so much* as to be bought at the price of *slavery.* Quit worrying about your precious skin! As William Wallace said in *Braveheart, "Every man dies. Not every man really lives."*

*What country can preserve its liberties if their rulers are not warned from time to time that their people preserve the spirit of resistance? **Let them take arms...** What signify a few lives lost in a century or two? The tree of liberty must be refreshed from time to time with the blood of patriots and tyrants. It is its natural manure.*

— Thomas Jefferson; 13 November 1787, *Papers* (12:356)

You are a sovereign human being, created by God with unalienable rights as much a part of you as your lungs. **It is *not* wrong to *defend* these rights, force against force.**

*A strict observance of the laws is doubtless one of the highest duties of a good citizen, **but it is not the highest.** The laws of necessity, of self-preservation, of saving our country when in danger, are of higher obligation. To lose our country by a scrupulous adherence of written law, **would be to lose the law itself,** with life, liberty, property and all those who are enjoying them with us...*

— Thomas Jefferson; 20 September 1810, *Human Events*

Our lives are not blank checks for government. Our backs were not made to be saddled nor our mouths to be bridled! *We* are the sovereigns—*they* are the *servants.* When government is afraid of the people, it's Liberty. When people are afraid of the government, it's *Tyranny.* What our "last straw" will be, I do not know. Perhaps some new *"Anti-Terrorism"* Act with its suspension of *habeas corpus* and its new death penalties will snap the camel's back.

> *Those who profess to favor freedom, and yet depreciate agitation, are men who want crops without plowing up the ground. They want rain without thunder or lightning. They want the ocean without the awful roar of its waters. This struggle may be a moral one; or it may be a physical one; or it may be both moral and physical; **but it must be a struggle. Power concedes nothing without demand.***
>
> ***Find out just what people will submit to, and you have found out the exact amount of injustice and wrong which will be imposed upon them;*** *and these will continue until they are resisted with either words or blows, or with both.*
>
> ***The limits of tyrants are prescribed by the endurance of those whom they oppress.***
>
> — Frederick Douglass, a self-freed black slave, in 1857

I do not *seek* an armed rebellion, but I will *not* live as a *slave.* Not in *America.* Nor will I run off to Costa Rica in silly hopes of freedom, as if tyranny won't try to become global. (Besides, they wouldn't let me in with my guns...)

> *Individuals obtained recognition of their freedom by fighting and bargaining, or—failing in this—they could run away. This running was possible **because they had somewhere to go.***
>
> — L. Neil Smith; *Pallas*

Folks, America is truly the last stand. There is nowhere else *to* go. I will stay here and *work* for freedom.

> *If a nation values anything more than freedom, it will lose that freedom; and the irony of it is that if it is comfort that it values more, **it will lose that too.***
>
> — W. Somerset Maugham

> **Liberty is always unfinished business.**
>
> — anonymous

> *If you will not fight for right when you can easily win without bloodshed; if you will not fight when your victory will be sure and not too costly; you may come to the moment when you will have to fight with all the odds against you and only a precarious chance of survival. There may be even a worse case. You may have to fight when there is no hope of victory, **because it is better to perish** [free] **than to live as slaves.*** (As did Jews on 19 April 1943 in the Warsaw Ghetto uprising. They killed 80 Nazi troops! BTP)
>
> — Winston Churchill

We're probably already at that *"worse case."* In *Hologram of Liberty* I described how our constitutional system has allowed a federal stranglehold on America. But the *real* culprit *hasn't* been the Constitution. **We've only *ourselves* to blame.**

We *should* have strung up Congress for handing monetary control to a private consortium of bankers and then dragging us into WWI in 1917. We *should* have resisted in the 1930s during FDR's atrocious "social" programs and the confiscation of our gold. We *should* have shouted down the 1945 U.N. We *should* have pushed through the righteous tax revolt of the late 1970s instead of accepting the sop presidency of Ronald Reagan. We *should* have hounded out the Clintonistas after their murder of the Branch Davidians. Etc. Etc. *Etc.*

The only times when we stood up to the Government were in 1794 (Whiskey Rebellion) and 1860 (the secession of the South over economic autonomy—not slavery). Other than that, we have *chickened out* on a dozen crucial opportunities to rein in Washington. **Evil has triumphed because good men have done *nothing.*** We've become a paper tiger and Congress is no longer afraid of us. The servant now scoffs at his master, and the servant's bulldog routinely sinks its teeth in our legs.

If there's one constant to bullies it's that they're *bluff*. Knock their teeth in suddenly and they crumple every time. It's only difficult and scary the *first* time. All they need is some long-overdue fear and they'll run.

For example, the French could have nipped WWII in the bud by calling Hitler's 1936 Rhineland bluff. We could have easily pushed the Soviets out of Germany, Poland, Austria, etc. in 1945, kept our military strong, and avoided the Cold War. We certainly could have rolled into East Berlin in 1961 and smashed the barbed-wire wall with righteous impunity. (What starts out as mere barbed-wire is soon replaced with *concrete.*)

Jefferson spoke of occasional mild rebellions for a America's health. Rebellions are sort of like vomiting. The *prospect* is very unpleasant, but you feel so much better *afterwards*. We've been so queasy with political poisoning for so long, but we won't hug the toilet and stick a finger down our national throat. **We're *so* afraid of vomiting that we'd rather stay queasy.** Well, if we wait to vomit on the *poison's* timetable, we will be too weak and ill to recover by then.

We must heal ourselves—while we are *able*—or expire.

BOSTON IS *NUTS!*

I want to give you Liberals, Social Democrats, and other coercive collectivists a final chance to understand the Freedom Movement's mindset. Your political agenda, enforced by government thugs, *created* the Freedom Movement in the mid-1970s. We did not create you—you created *us*.

Had you modern Tories been content to let peaceable folks alone to raise their own children, control their own schools, attend church unmolested, use their own property, shoot their own guns, pay *reasonable* taxes and keep their own wages, and generally live their own lives—there wouldn't *be* a Freedom Movement. Such is superfluous in free countries. Thanks to you, America is now Land of the Fee, Home of the Slave.

As *kulaks* (Russian peasants who owned land and businesses, liquidated by Stalin in 1929) we have never injured you, but our independent spirit irritates your controlling nature. Since you Know Best, since it horrifies you that Americans actually have the *nerve* to live without your license, you have nearly bridled this glorious mustang of a people. We will never, however, take your saddle. You will never be our jockey. *Never.*

You're probably too committed to hear reason. You're probably too confident to believe the tremors. Nonetheless, for the sake of fairness and conscience, I offer you this warning:

> [Liberty minded people are] *all the same. And the kicker is, every single one of us believes that as honest adult citizens, we have the absolute right to own any and all small arms and shoot them just as often as we want.* **We have a specific culture.** *Guns and shooting are very important to us, just like...hunting buffalo was important to the Indians....*
> *Our culture is important, and we're willing to pay for it. We have above-average educations, above-average incomes, and almost*

*nonexistent criminal involvement. We pay far more taxes and re-
ceive virtually no subsidy payments. You'd think Washington would
be happy, but instead they are doing everything they can to destroy
our culture.*

*In the '20s, soldiers sat on their bunks in the cold at Camp
Perry, cleaning the handmade .22 target rifles they would compete
with the next day. When the President proudly announces that
today, seventy years later, he is ordering these same guns thrown
into a blast furnace, we in the gun culture feel powerful emotions.*
***They are the same emotions a Native American would feel if the
President proudly ordered the destruction of war clubs and
other sacred tribal artifacts. They are the same emotions that
the Jews felt watching...Nazi** Sturmtroopen **gleefully burning intricate copies of the Torah.***

*We offer to buy the government's surplus guns, and instead
they pay to have them cut up. We offer to buy their surplus military
ammo, shoot it, sell the brass to a smelter, and give the government
the proceeds, and instead they pay to have it burned.*

*These government slugs ban our guns and they ban our maga-
zines and they ban our ammo. They ban suppressors that make our
guns quieter and then they ban our outdoor shooting ranges because our guns are too loud. They ban steel-core ammunition because it's "armor piercing", then they close down our indoor ranges
where people shoot lead-core bullets because they say we might
get lead poisoning.*

*The people in the gun culture have a better safety record than
any police department in the nation, but several states actually prohibit us from using guns for self-protection, and in all the other states
except [Vermont] they make us buy a license. They tax us so we
can have more cops, and when crime still goes up, they tax us more
and ban more...guns.*

*[We] endure waiting periods that no other group would stand
for. We undergo background checks that no legislator, judge, doctor, or police officer has to tolerate, and we submit to it not once, or
once a year, but over and over again. Then, after we yield to this
outrage, they smile and forbid us from buying more than one gun in
a 30-day period.*

*If we sell one gun we own that's gone up in value, they can
charge us with dealing in firearms without a federal dealer's license,
which is a felony. If we get a dealer's license, they say we are not
really in business, and report us to our local authorities for violating
zoning ordinances by running a commercial venture out of a residence.*

*If the steel or the wood on our guns is too long or too short, they
make us pay $200 taxes and get fingerprinted and photographed.
They make us get a law enforcement certification from the local police chief. If he refuses to sign we have no recourse. If he takes the
forms in the next room and brings them back out, signed, he can*

later claim the signature is not his, and the feds will charge us with a felony.

We in the gun culture have played all their stupid games on [National Firearms Act of 1934 licensed fully-automatic] weapons for over half a century, without a single violent crime being committed by any person in the system. So when a bill comes up to keep travelers with guns locked in the trunk of their cars out of jail, what happens? A scumbucket from New Jersey,...puts an amendment on it that closes down the whole NFA process.

Then, if they even suspect we've ignored the $200 tax process altogether, on the guns where the wood and steel is too long or too short, they'll spend over a million dollars watching us for months, then they'll shoot our wives and children (i.e., Ruby Ridge) or burn us all alive (i.e., Waco). When the public gets outraged by these actions, the government issues letters of reprimand and sends the guys who did the killing on paid leave. In the decades that the feds have been raiding and killing people in the gun culture over suspected non-payment of $200 taxes, not one federal agent has been fined a single dollar or spent even one night in jail.

And you know something else that's never happened? To this day, not a single person in the gun culture has ever dropped the hammer on one of these feds. Not once.

Then, after these statist bastards have done all these things, they grin and tell us how they like to hunt ducks, and how the only laws they want to pass are "reasonable ones."

***One of two things** [is going to happen]. One of the political parties is going to have to wake up, smell the coffee, and start restoring all the articles in the Bill of Rights—the Second, Fourth, Fifth, and Tenth Amendments.*

***[And if that doesn't happen], then we're going to have a civil war.** (at pp. 555-6)*

***Stripping a motivated people of their dignity and rubbing their noses in it is a very bad idea.** (at p. 9)*

— John Ross; *Unintended Consequences* (1996)

In no time in history has an oppressive government been *so* thoroughly and fairly warned *to back off*. Not even the 1770s English were. When you weren't playing deaf to our pleas, you scoffed at them. We have not resorted to violence. We have only *rarely* resorted to righteous *self-defense*. No oppressed people, with the arms to resist, have ever been more patient. Your greed for Power and Control has nearly dried up our tolerance.

Americans will *not* take much more. Don't expect us to merely whine about the tune you fiddle while Rome burns. We won't let you strike the match. Your goons fight only for their next paycheck. *We* will be fighting for our culture, our rights, and our lives. Many in your military will defect.

You will *lose*. America is the greatest potential guerrilla base in history. You have transformed thousands of normal Americans into Patriots who spend every waking hour planning for your rout. One is Elmer Wade, a 61 year old farmer in North Carolina, whose farm you stole because of your conflicting regulations between the EPA and the Soil Conservation Service:

> *I am writing this letter so you won't have any surprises. Through no fault of my own I am being put upon.* ***I've had all I can stand from you in the front, and I do not plan to roll over.*** *So when you send your collector, have That Woman send your WACO KILLERS with them. They will need them.* ***Living is not very much fun with you standing on my neck.***

> — quoted from *Send in the Waco Killers* (1999), 237

You are making guerrillas out of whole families, counties, and states—*that's* how serious Civil War 2 will be, if you continue your oppression. ***"Stripping a motivated people of their dignity and rubbing their noses in it is a very bad idea."*** Keep squeezing us—keep fueling our desperation—and we'll make Afghanistan look like a spitwad fight. We have been preparing for your Soviet Amerika since the 1970s. Many of us are combat veterans, or have military experience. We have land, food, tools, guns, friends, and an unquenchable fire for Liberty.

You don't believe this, of course, and that's good. Because of our patience and long suffering, you continue to underestimate your opponents. You're in for a rude shock.

> *Again, it is under Clinton that an armed militia movement involving tens of thousands of people has mushroomed out of the plain, an expression of dissent that is unparalleled since the southern gun clubs before the Civil War. People do not spend their weekends with an SKS rifle, drilling for guerilla warfare against federal forces, in a country that is at ease with itself.* ***It takes very bad behavior to provoke the first simmerings or armed insurgency, and the militias are unmistakably Clinton's offspring.*** *Would they have happened if America were governed by a President Tsongas or a President Bush? Of course not.*

> *What is it about the combustible chemistry of Bill Clinton that causes such a reaction? What has he been doing to America?*

> *The original sin, I believe, was the FBI assault on the Branch Davidian community in Waco, Texas, on April 19, 1993. At least 76 people were incinerated, most of them women and children, after FBI tanks went smashing through the walls of Mount Carmel. The death toll adds up to the worst tragedy precipitated by government on American soil in this century. You have to go back to the slaughter of 200 Sioux Indians at Wounded Knee in 1890 to find an abuse*

of power on this scale. Just like Waco, Wounded Knee was desig-
nated a "battle" by officials; and just like Waco, the victims were de-
monized as sexual deviants. Some methods never change.
— Ambrose Evans-Pritchard, *The Secret Life of Bill Clinton —*
The Unreported Stories, p.xiv (1997)

You politicians have broken your American pact with us. Government was to be a means to an end, *not an end in itself.* We merely *delegated* our sovereignty to federal officials for courts, Congress, and national defense—*not* to be viciously ruled within our own homes, schools, businesses, and churches.

The United States owes its existence to the Bill of Rights. Were it
not for the Bill of Rights' explicit promise to limit government power
over the citizenry, the U.S. Constitution would never have been rati-
fied. Americans in the Revolutionary Era would only permit a na-
tional government to come into existence if...that government would
solemnly pledge to limit their power in perpetuity. But this sacred
compact is now violated by thousands of officials at all levels of gov-
ernment. **If the government will not keep its pact with the peo-**
ple, what do the people owe the government?
— James Bovard; *Lost Rights*, p. 333

You have broken your sacred trust, and you will pay a price far higher than that of tyrants. You will pay the *traitor's* price.

Even if you *do* successfully disarm the people, materially and spiritually, you will still lose. The more responsibility you take away from them, the more irresponsible they will become. At some point, you will reap the inverse of *"People have the government they deserve"*—you governors will have the *people* you deserve (and I suspect this has *already* begun to occur). In *On Liberty*, John Stuart Mill put it well:

A State which dwarfs its men, in order that they may be more docile
instruments in its hands even for beneficial purposes will find that
with small men no great things can really be accomplished; *and*
that the perfection of machinery to which it has sacrificed everything
will avail nothing.

Either way, you *will* lose, and that's the lovely irony of it all. Whether you geld or tolerate this independent mustang of the American people, you will lose. Either way, our presence *or* our absence will destroy you. (Irony's a bitch, ain't it?)

Back off.

Back off, *now*, before you step into the abyss.

Back off, *now,* while you are *allowed* to.

This is a
GUN FREE
Home

An invitation to assault, rape, rob and murder.

If you support Gun Control, put this yard sign in front of your home. If not, join us in our fight to preserve your right to keep and bear arms.

Citizens Committee for the Right to Keep and Bear Arms
Annual Membership $15 / 12500 N.E. 10th Pl., Bellevue, WA 98005 / (206) 454-4911

❖ 45

RESOURCES

Note: The listing of the following resources does *not* imply full and unqualified endorsement of the same. *Caveat Emptor!* People are verbs, and even good companies can sour, so keep visiting www.javelinpress.com for pertinent updates.

BOOKS

Molôn Labé!, **Boston T. Party**
Finally published in January 2004. See you in Wyoming!

Unintended Consequences, **John Ross**
A fantastic novel about American gunowners pushed too far by the feds. Unnecessarily risqué in parts and totally dismissive of any possible conspiracies, it's still "must" reading.

Civil War 2, **Thomas Chittum**
A Vietnam vet and professional mercenary makes a compelling case for America cracking at her ethnic seams in about 20 years. Not at all a racist book, but wholly logical. A very timely and unique title. From Loompanics.

101 Things To Do 'Til The Revolution, **Claire Wolfe**
Don't Shoot the Bastards (Yet)—101 More Things To Do 'Til The Revolution, **Claire Wolfe**
Fun and zippy stuff full of practical ideas and morsels of hilarious wisdom. For *Don't Shoot*'s Introduction, I contributed a rather piercing essay on the difference between Action Libertarians and Egghead Libertarians.

The State vs. The People: The Rise of the American Police State, Claire Wolfe and Aaron Zelman

Published by www.jpfo.org in 2002, this is Claire's newest (and best) book. An incredibly sweeping, detailed, and infuriating analysis of our emerging totalitarianism. I had a difficult time finishing the book simply because of the outrages so richly described. Things are worse than even *I* had thought. Ø19.95ppd.

Lost Rights, James Bovard

An excellent, sweeping overview of mindless federal tyranny. Not a Patriot work, but it might as well have been. Infuriating reading. At any bookstore.

His sequel, *Freedom in Chains*, is also excellent.

Defiance, Oliver Lange

Originally titled *Vandenberg*, this utterly absorbing novel describes Amerikan life in the U.S.S.A. and what a handful of average folks do about it. A must. At any used bookstore.

One curious thing: In the movie *Arlington Road*, the bomber's name was Oliver Lang. An intention slap in the face?

The Moon Is A Harsh Mistress, Robert A. Heinlein

The best novel I've ever read about a successful rebellion. A lunar penal colony in 2075 revolts from is Earthly masters. A marvelous story deserving to be a movie! At used bookstores.

The Probability Broach, L. Neil Smith

A real romp of a novel in which tandem-dimensional Americas exist—one Jeffersonian, one Hamiltonian—and battle each other. Great fun! From Laissez-Faire Books.

Followed by *The Gallatin Divergence*.

Snowcrash, Neal Stephenson

It's about 2050 in L.A., and the country has splintered into city states, fiefdoms, and enclaves. Virtual reality is *the* reality, which makes for a very odd society. The subplot of a *coup* via a neurolinguistic virus is fascinating.

The Diamond Age, Neal Stephenson

It's about 2150 in Shanghai, and nanotechnology is the primary force of existence. Governments have all collapsed, only to be replaced by sophisticated and elaborate tribes. The Central Economic Protocol (a libertarian commercial and criminal code) is the glue between them all.

Cryptonomicon, Neal Stephenson
His best work to date, and likely unsurpassable. A sweeping and totally engaging story of WWII encryption, hidden Japanese war gold, and an emerging data haven offering digital currency. One of the five best novels I've ever read.

Kill Zone, Craig Roberts
A Vietnam vet and police sniper looks at the JFK assassination at Dealey Plaza in Dallas. Highly recommended.

The Medusa Files, Craig Roberts
Roberts examines the PanAm bombing, Oklahoma City, the Amtrak derailing, Waco, and many other suspicious events which the feds have used to justify further controls. A sweeping and fascinating catalog of likely government complicity.

Patriots, Rawles
An informative and tidy tale of survival against tyranny.

Send In the Waco Killers, Vin Suprynowicz
Ballad of Carl Drega, Vin Suprynowicz
A superb essay collection of Nevada's leading libertarian columnist. I mined many excellent nuggets from this fine book. Uncompromising, sweeping, and witty stuff! From Mountain Media (POB 4422, Las Vegas, NV 89127-4422).

Safeguarding Liberty—The Constitution & Citizen Militias, edited by Larry Pratt of Gun Owners of America
A superb collection of essays on the 2nd Amendment. Visit GOA's Web Site at www. gunowners.org.

Target Switzerland: Swiss Armed Neutrality in World War II, Stephen P. Halbrook (Sarpedon Press)
A fascinating study of how well a citizen militia works.

The Samurai, The Mountie, and the Cowboy: Should America Adopt the Gun Controls of Other Democracies?, by David B. Kopel (1992)
This was named Book of The Year by the American Society of Criminology. A ground-breaking work.

Dial 911 and Die, Richard Stevens
The police are not required to protect any individual! A unique and cogent work on how governments avoid legal responsibility for their poor police forces. Its State-by-State analysis of court rulings is devastating. From JPFO.

Death by "Gun Control": The Human Cost of Victim Disarmament, **Aaron Zelman & Richard W. Stevens**
Devastating nation-by-nation proof that disarming a people is historically a prelude to their genocide. An utterly unanswerable treatise. Ø16.95ppd. from JPFO.

The Mitzvah, **L. Neil Smith and Aaron Zelman (JPFO)**
A Catholic priest discovers that he is Jewish, and thus rethinks his feelings on guns and pacifism. A fine and tidy little novel which should be given to any 2nd Amendment agnostic.

Invisible Resistance to Tyranny, **Jefferson Mack**
How to fight tyranny yet still appear to the State like a good, little citizen. Thought-provoking stuff. Paladin Press.

To Ride, Shoot Straight, and Speak the Truth, **Jeff Cooper**
A collection of fascinating essays on guns, travel, hunting, and philosophy from the Professor of the Modern Shooting Technique. I recommend all of Jeff's books. Paladin Press.

Art of the Rifle, **Jeff Cooper**
An excellent book on a long-overlooked subject, the Queen of weapons, by one of the Masters. From Paladin Press.

Life Without Fear, **Mike Dalton and Mickey Fowler**
An excellent beginner's book on the use of defensive handguns. Written by staff of the International Shootist Institute, it has dozens of superb pictures to complement its thorough coverage of lethal confrontations. Ø14.95 ppd. Call 818-891-1723.

Street Stoppers, **Marshall and Sanow**
A sequel to their *Handgun Stopping Power*, it gives the latest results of hundreds of shootings in every major caliber. Includes the seminal Strasbourg Goat Tests and a chapter on MagSafe Ammo. From Paladin Press.

The Ayoob Files: The Book, **Massad Ayoob**
Good cross-section of 30 shooting incidents.

Novels
Since America is unraveling at her seams, I've included many novels which dramatize political upheavels. Books in bold are my favorites.

Disaster preparation
Lucifer's Hammer, Niven and Pournelle
Farnham's Freehold, Robert Heinlein
Pulling Through, Dean Ing

Resistance movements with at least a somewhat happy ending
Atlas Shrugged, Ayn Rand
The Moon Is A Harsh Mistress, Robert A. Heinlein
Weapons Shops of Isher, A.E. vanVogt
Unintended Consequences, John Ross
Mirror Maze, James P. Hogan
The Gallatin Divergence, L. Neil Smith
Pallas, L. Neil Smith
When The Almond Tree Blossoms, David Aikman
Patriots, Rawles
The Postman, David Brin
The *Ashes* novels by William W. Johnstone
The Survival of Freedom, Jerry Pournelle
Kings Of The High Frontier, V. Koman (www.pulpless.com)
Paul Revere's Ride, D.H. Fischer
The Battle of Athens, Tennessee, Byrum

Libertarian utopias
Alongside Night, Schulman
The Probability Broach, L. Neil Smith
Voyage of Yesteryear, James P. Hogan
Hope, L. Neil Smith and Aaron Zelman
Molôn Labé!, Boston T. Party (published January 2004!)

Resistance movements with a less-than-happy ending
Defiance (also titled *Vandenberg*), Oliver Lange
Animal Farm, George Orwell
Amerika, Pouns
Let Us Prey, Bill Branon
Resistance, Israel Gutman
The Whiskey Rebellion, Thomas Slaughter

Dystopias
This Perfect Day, Ira Levin
1984, George Orwell
Brave New World, Aldous Huxley
Anthem, Ayn Rand
Man In A High Castle, Philip K. Dick
Oath of Fealty, Niven and Pournelle
The Trial, Franz Kafka

MOVIES AND VIDEOS

Red Dawn
A modern classic. Alpine high-schoolers fight the Communist invasion of America. An utterly unique film.

Amerika
Powerful mini-series on the Soviet takeover of the U.S.A.

Heat
Robert de Niro heads a team of bank robbers using battle rifles. The rifle fight in downtown L.A. is particularly well done. Director (and Gunsite graduate) Michael Mann's films are known for their realism, attention to detail, and intensity.

misc. videos
Militia of Montana (406-847-2735)
Ask for the video with official footage of *Operation Cooperative Nugget* at Ft. Polk, Louisiana where 4,000 soldiers of 14 Eastern European countries learned how to shoot American flag T-shirted *civilians*, many of whom are women and children. Also shows footage of the "nonexistent" American detention camps for us dissidents. M.O.M. also carries my books. Great folks.

Waco—The Rules of Engagement
This is the new documentary film, 136 minutes long, which has been sweeping the country at film festivals. It is *so* good, *so* convincing, that even California liberals are upset at the feds. It's now out on video. Get a copy and invite a crowd over to see it. Infrared footage of machine-gun firing executioners of trapped Davidians, feds caught lying through their teeth, a charred child bowed backwards from the hydrogen cyanide gas poisoning, *60 Minutes* refusing to touch the issue—*wow!* If this is ever aired on national TV, there will be a revolution the next morning. From Laissez-Faire Books.

Waco—A New Revelation   877-511-4848
A superb new documentary that picks up the story with information uncovered in 1999: that pyrotechnic devices *were* used at Waco, and that Delta Force soldiers were there pulling triggers. The FLIR evidence is much bolstered, too. If the tape is ever shown on national TV, it would mean the end of the regime. This video is a must in every American home!

FLIR Project

A Mike McNulty sequel to *Waco—A New Revelation*, which trashes the Government's staged reinactment of Waco. Using the FBI's own FLIR imagery, McNultry proves that the Branch Davidians were machine-gunned by ground and air personnel on 19 April 1993 during the fire.

The veracity of this was confirmed personally to me by an active-duty special forces operator who watched *Waco—A New Revelation*. During the viewing he remarked, *"See how the helo pitched up just before the muzzle flashes? We tell the pilots to do that to stabilize the helo as a shooting platform. That was definitely full-auto fire—they (i.e., the video's producers) are right on the money."* He also personally identified many of the Delta operators filmed at Waco—*"D-boys"* as he called them.

Available from Paladin Press.

Braveheart

Mel Gibson portrays William Wallace, the George Washington of 14th century Scotland. Outstanding!

The Patriot

Mel Gibson does it again! The *Braveheart* of the American Revolution. A beautiful and savage story of what it took to win our freedom. The movie has a perfect pace, drama, and deft realism. Take your family and friends to see this astonishing film!

Michael Collins

Liam Neeson portrays the 1920s founder of the IRA and its guerrilla resistance to the British occupation.

The Parallax View

A 1976 film with Warren Beatty. A corporation seeks out unstable sociopaths to be groomed for assassination duty. An eerie, disturbing film. (You'll have to special order it, as it suspiciously does not show up in most movie catalogs.)

A similar scenario is probably used today to create these mass murdering gunmen (many of whom, it's rumored, were on *Prozac*—"delayed violence") and killer schoolchildren (nearly 100% of whom, such as Kip Kinkel, were on *Ritalin* and/or *Prozac*). *Prozac*'s side effects can include: apathy, hallucinations, hostility, irrational ideas, paranoid reactions, antisocial behavior, hysteria, and suicidal thoughts.

A fine book on the subject is *Talking Back to Prozac* by Peter R. Breggin, M.D. whose organization *Children First!* fights against biopsychiatric intrusions into our children.

The Manchurian Candidate

A 1963 feature film starring Frank Sinatra. An American soldier from the Korean War is brainwashed and molded into a sleeper assassin of a presidential nominee. *Way* beyond its time. Frank personally had it suppressed for years, claiming that showing the film after JFK's assassination was distasteful. (Yeah, *right*. Whaddaya bet Frank got a little visit?)

Executive Action

A 1973 feature film on how JFK was likely assassinated. As a rifleman and mystery buff, I've been to Dealey Plaza and read many books. This film dramatizes a highly credible theory. If the Insiders succeeded in *1963*, just imagine how much better they are at it *today*. (They're still pretty sloppy—Ruby Ridge, Waco, Vince Foster, Oklahoma City, etc.)

Conspiracy Theory

A backhanded spoof on us nutty folks, yet with enough plausibility to remain interesting and thought-provoking. There *are* scheming Bad Guys, after all. *Gee, who'da thunk it?*

Dial 911 and Die

A 29 minute video interview of author Richard Stevens, who explains your responsibility for self-protection. Available from www.jpfo.org (800-869-1884).

MAIL ORDER BOOKS

Underlined companies carry my books.

Bloomfield Press 800-707-4020 www.bloomfieldpress.com

Great books explaining state and federal gun laws.

Laissez-Faire Books   800-326-0996   www.laissezfaire.org

A Libertarian/Objectivist oriented, highly intellectual catalog company. Top quality "food for thought."

Liberty Tree   800-927-8733   www.independent.org

The book catalog by the Libertarian think-tank *The Independent Institute*. A good selection of erudite material.

Loompanics   **800-380-2230**   **www.loompanics.com**
With over 700 titles carried in their 190+ page catalog, if it's unusual, they'll have it. *Really* eccentric stuff. Not only do they have books you didn't know existed, they've got books on *subjects* you didn't know existed.

Eden Press   **800-338-8484**   **www.edenpress.com**
A smaller, but more personal, alternative book catalog company. A good source for privacy and ID material.

Delta Press   **800-852-4445**   **www.deltapress.com**
New distributors of my all books, including *Good-Bye April 15th!* and *Hologram of Liberty*. Many fascinating titles.

Lancer Militaria   **870-867-2232**
Owner Jack McPherson is a true military history buff who scours the globe for unique titles. Great catalog.

Paladin Press   **800-392-2400**   **www.paladin-press.com**
Titles on weapons and tactics. They also carry all of my books but for *Good-Bye April 15th!* and *Hologram of Liberty*.

Fred's   **800-979-2144**   **www.fredsm14stocks.com**
He carries about a dozen of Freedom's best books, often at the best price. A Rifleman and Patriot. Check here first.

Knowledge = Freedom   **702-329-5968**
This is the Freedom Movement's "Yellow Pages." With over 2,000 listings (alphabetized and cross-referenced by subject matter and state/city), this continually updated compendium is a labor of love by Dennis Grover. A must.

CPA Book Publishers   **503-668-4941**
They carry nearly *every* Patriot/Freedom book.

Information Exchange   **800-346-6205**
Good selection on a variety of topics.

Freedom Bound   **888-385-FREE**
Your "untax" connection. Solid, hard-working folks.

The Free American   **505-423-3250**
Great national news magazine from New Mexico.

The Resource Center   **800-922-1771**
Mostly books on financial privacy, trusts, foreign banking, passports, etc.

Bohica Concepts   360-497-7075
Good selection on freedom-oriented subjects.

Militia of Montana   406-847-2735
Good selection of anti-NWO and survival books, gear, etc.

Gunowners of America 701-321-8585 www.gunowners.org
Great folks who carry *Boston's Gun Bible*.

JPFO   800-869-1884   www.jpfo.org
Headed by Aaron Zelman, a hard-working Patriot. They have been publishing some marvelous books lately, and their *Gran'pa Jack* comic series is brilliant.

NEWSLETTERS & MAGAZINES

Shotgun News
Published thrice monthly, the FFLs' source list. A "must."

Gun List
National classified ad gun paper. Excellent resource. *GL* and *SGN* are found at gun shops, gun shows, and newsstands.

The Anti-Shyster   214-418-8993
Highly original legal contrarian magazine.

Aid & Abet   602-237-2533
Put out by *Police Against the New World Order* ministry.

Media Bypass Magazine
Highly informative.

S.W.A.T.
Keep abreast on what the turbo-cops are up to. Good coverage of new gear and tactics.

SHOOTING GEAR

BlackHawk   800-694-5263   www.mdenterprise.com
Tactical Nylon gear of all description.

BlackStar Barrel Accurizing   218-721-6040
Electro-polishing of rifle bores to increase accuracy.

Brownells   515-623-5401
Fantastic catalog of parts and accessories. Best service in the business. Get your Ashley Outdoors sights and scope mounts here. Look for *Boston's Gun Bible* there soon.

CFI   817-595-2485   www.cfiarms.com
A great "one-stop" mail-order firm which handles most of the quality gun firms: Scattergun, Knights, ARMS, Choate, Sure-Fire flashlights, ArmaLite, Bushmaster, etc.

Cheaper Than Dirt   888-625-3848 (mention the GOA)
America's leading sports discounter, which donates a percentage of your total order to the Gunowners of America if mention the GOA during a phone order, or when you enter their online store at: www.cheaperthandirt.com/goa.htm

300 Below, Inc.   800-550-CRYO
Cryogenic treatment of rifle barrels to relieve stress.

D&L Sports   POB 651   Gillette, WY 82717-0651
Dave Lauck builds very fine custom 1911s and rifles.

Dillon Press 800-223-4570   www.dillonprecision.com
The best progressive reloading presses. Top quality with the best return/service reputation in the business.

Firing Pin Enterprises   602-275-1623 (Tu, Wed, Th)
Sells many books, parts, and gun show items.

Life Line (long-distance service)   800-311-2811
Why support anti-gun phone companies like AT&T and Sprint when there's a pro-2nd Amendment alternative? Life Line gives 10% of every call to Gun Owners of America. Call today and switch your long distance service!

Mad Dog Tactical, Inc.   520-772-3021/3022fax
Best knives and Kydex gun gear, hands down. Two good distributors: www.mdenterprise.com and www.streetpro.com

Major Surplus & Survival   800-441-8855
Good selection of outdoor survival gear.

Midway   800-243-3220
Reloading equipment and shooting accessories.

Premier Reticles   540-722-0601
They install the Mil-Dot reticle on scopes.

Robar, Inc.   602-581-2648/582-0059fax
Corrosion-resistant finishes. Grip reduction for Glocks.
M1A mags in bolt guns. "Snout" (scout/sniper) .308 rifles.

Shomer-Tec   360-733-6214
Fascinating selection of police and spy stuff.

Tapco   800-554-1445   www.tapco.com
Lots of gun parts and accessories.

The Survival Center   800-321-2900
Interesting survival gear.

U.S. Cavalry   800-777-7732
Great color catalog. Tactical Heaven.

GUN AND PARTS DISTRIBUTORS

They run ads in *Shotgun News* and *Gun List*. While you
must order their guns and receivers through your local FFL,
sometimes it's the only way to acquire something too new or uncommon to be found in the unpapered used market.

A.R.M.S.   508-584-7816   www.armsmounts.com
Burns Bros.   516-234-7676
Bushmaster   800-998-7928   www.bushmaster.com
CDNN   800-588-9500
Century Arms Intl.   800-527-1252   www.CenturyArms.com
CFI   817-595-2485   www.cfiarms.com
Cheaper Than Dirt   888-625-3848 www.cheaperthandirt.com
Classic Arms   800-383-8011
DPMS   800-578-3767
DSA Inc.   847-223-4770   www.dsarms.com
Fred's M14 Stocks 800-979-2144 www.fredsm14stocks.com
Fulton Armory   www.fulton-armory.com
Gun Parts Corp.   914-679-2417   www.gunpartscorp.com
J&G   520-445-9650   www.jgsales.com
Northridge   800-678-3931   www.northridge.com
Samco   800-554-1618
Sarco   908-647-3800   www.sarcoinc.com
SOG   800-944-GUNS

Springfield Armory   www.springfield-armory.com
Tapco   800-554-1445   www.tapco.com
World Wide Gun Parts   www.gun-parts.com

WEB SITES

www.i2i.org
   The Independence Institute. Great stuff, with great links.

www.laissezfaire.org
   Great links.

www.oughtsix.com
   Look for their fabulous jpg (picoweek6) of "Troops obeying
Orders. Citizens obeying gun laws."

www.shooters.com
   The most complete source of shooting info on the Net.

www.law.cornell.edu/uscode
   Search within the entire U.S. Code

www.findlaw.com/scripts
   Search for any legal case.

GROUPS & ORGANIZATIONS

Victim Disarmament Groups
   It is recommended that you visit their websites regularly,
to keep up with our enemies.

Coalition to Stop Gun Violence (CSGV)
Educational Fund to End Handgun Violence (Ed Fund)
1000 16th Street, NW
Suite 603
Washington, DC 20036
(202) 530-0340   http://www.gunfree.org

CSGV is a 501(c)(4) lobbying organization founded in 1974 as
the National Coalition to Ban Handguns. Endorses banning
the sale and private possession of handguns in America.
Founded in 1979, the Educational Fund to End Handgun

Violence is the 501(c)(3) educational arm of the Coalition. The Ed Fund operates the Firearms Litigation Clearinghouse, which maintains a database of depositions and court documents of firearm-related cases.

Handgun Control, Inc. (HCI)
Center to Prevent Handgun Violence (CPHV)
1225 Eye Street, NW
Suite 1100
Washington, DC 20005
(202) 898-0792   http://www.handguncontrol.org

Handgun Control, Inc. (HCI) was founded in 1974 by Mark Borinsky, who was later joined by Nelson T. "Pete" Shields. Shields founded the Center to Prevent Handgun Violence (CPHV) in 1983, which is the education, legal advocacy, and research affiliate of HCI. In 1985 Sarah Brady became its primary spokesperson and in 1989 succeeded Shields.

Violence Policy Center (VPC)
1350 Connecticut Avenue, NW, Suite 825
Washington, DC 20036
(202) 822-8200   http://www.vpc.org

A really noisome group headed by Josh Sugarmann.

Government Agencies
Bureau of Alcohol, Tobacco and Firearms (BATF)
650 Massachusetts Avenue, NW
Washington, DC 20226
(202) 927-7777
postmaster@atfhq.atf.treas.gov   http://www.atf.treas.gov

The Bureau of Alcohol, Tobacco and Firearms (ATF) is a law enforcement organization within the United States Department of Treasury. ATF enforces the federal regulations relating to alcohol, tobacco, firearms, explosives, and arson.

Bureau of Justice Statistics (BJS)
National Center for Justice Research Statistics (NCJRS)
810 7th Street, NW
Washington, DC 20531
800-732-3277
askbjs@ojp.usdoj.gov   http://www.ojp.usdoj.gov/bjs/

The Bureau of Justice Statistics (BJS), a component of the Office of Justice Programs in the U.S. Department of Justice, is the United States' primary source for criminal justice statistics. BJS collects, analyzes, publishes, and disseminates information on crime, criminal offenders, victims of crime, and the operation of justice systems at all levels of government.

National Centers for Disease Control and Prevention (CDC)
1600 Clifton Road, NE
Atlanta, GA 30333
(404) 639-3311   http://www.cdc.gov

The National Centers for Disease Control and Prevention (CDC) is located in Atlanta, Georgia, and is an agency of the Department of Health and Human Services.

Federal Bureau of Investigation (FBI)
935 Pennsylvania Avenue, NW
Washington, DC 20535-0001
(202) 324-3000   http://www.fbi.gov

The FBI is the principal investigative arm of the Department of Justice. At present, the FBI has investigative jurisdiction over violations of more than 200 categories of federal crimes. The FBI is also authorized to provide other law enforcement agencies with cooperative services, such as Uniform Crime Reports and the National Crime Information Center.

National Center for Health Statistics (NCHS)
6525 Belcrest Road
Hyattsville, MD 20782
Telephone: (301) 436-8500
Email: nchsquery@nch10a.em.cdc.gov
Website: http://www.cdc.gov/nchswww/nchshome.htm

The NCHS is a part of the Centers for Disease Control and Prevention, U.S. Department of Health and Human Services. NCHS is the federal government's principal vital and health statistics agency.

Pro-Bill of Rights Groups

American Shooting Sports Council (ASSC)
9 Perimeter Way, Suite C-950
Atlanta, GA 30339
(404) 933-0200   www.assc.org

The ASSC is the *"organized voice of the firearms industry"* and was established in 1989 to *"take pro-active steps to enhance the industry's ability to do business..., improve the public perception of the industry as a whole, and...provide a viable voice in the hearings preceding debate of statutes affecting the industry."* Its slogan is *"As Pro-Gun as Our Customers."*

The statute affecting the industry that resulted in ASSC's formation was a partial federal *"assault weapons"* ban sponsored by former Senator Dennis DeConcini (D-AZ) in 1989. Believing that none of the traditional pro-gun organizations were effectively defending the manufacturers of such weapons, the ASSC was formed as *"the only voice in the Capital that lobbies specifically for our industry."* Its promotional material promises that *"as a sophisticated registered lobby organization, ASSC monitors legislative trends and proposals at every level of government. We ACT BEFORE legislation is passed or opinions are formed. We are Pro-active not Re-active!"*

Citizens Committee for the Right to Keep and Bear Arms (CCRKBA) and the Second Amendment Foundation (SAF)
James Madison Building
12500 NE Tenth Place
Bellevue, WA 98005
(206) 454-4911 (CCRKBA)
(206) 454-7012 (SAF)   http://www.ccrkba.org

The CCRKBA is a 501(c)(4) lobbying organization founded in 1974 by activist Alan Gottlieb *"to defend the Second Amendment of the United States Constitution and to provide aid and information to individuals throughout the Nation seeking to maintain the right to keep and bear arms."* The Second Amendment Foundation (SAF) is the 501(c)(3) educational arm of CCRKBA and was founded by Gottlieb in 1974. Periodicals owned by SAF include *Gun Week* and *Women & Guns.*

Gun Owners of America (GOA)
8001 Forbes Place, Suite 102
Springfield, VA 22151
(703) 321-8585   http://www.gunowners.org/

Gun Owners of America (GOA) is a 501(c)(4) lobbying organization formed in 1975 to *"preserve and defend the Second Amendment rights"* of gun owners. Associated with GOA are: Gun Owners of America Political Victory Fund, Gun Owners of California, and The Gun Owners Foundation.

Jews for the Preservation of Firearms Ownership (JPFO)
2872 S. Wentworth Avenue
Milwaukee, WI 53207
(414) 769-0760   http://www.jpfo.org

JPFO was founded in 1989 by Aaron Zelman. The organization works to *"expose the propaganda and myths used by all anti-gunners, but particularly by some Jewish anti-gunners."* JPFO's key argument is that the *Gun Control Act of 1968* was taken literally from the gun control laws of Nazi Germany and that gun control is a prerequisite to genocide.

National Rifle Association (NRA)
11250 Waples Mill Road
Fairfax, VA 22030-7400
(800) 672-3888   http://www.nra.org

The NRA is the best known and most powerful organization working against firearm restrictions in America. The NRA is a 501(c)(4) lobbying organization with an estimated 2.8 million members that describes itself as *"the foremost guardian of the traditional American right to keep and bear arms."* The NRA's Institute for Legislation Action (ILA) advocates *"against federal and state gun legislation to protect and defend the Constitution of the United States, especially with reference to the rights of the individual American citizen to acquire, possess, transport, carry and enjoy the right to use arms."* Other related NRA organizations include the NRA Special Contribution Fund, International Shooter Development Fund, American Firearms & Shooting Foundation, Firearms Civil Rights Legal Defense Fund, National Firearms Museum Fund and The NRA Foundation.

National Shooting Sports Foundation (NSSF)
Sporting Arms and Ammunition Manufacturers Institute (SAAMI)
11 Mile Hill Road
Newtown, CT 06470-2359
Telephone: (203) 426-1320 (NSSF)
Telephone: (203) 426-4358 (SAAMI)   www.nssf.org

NSSF is the leading trade association of the firearms industry. The NSSF was formed in 1961 as a non-profit communications and marketing organization that manages a variety of programs designed to promote a better understanding of the shooting sports, as well as encourage participation in the shooting sports. In 1983, the NSSF created the Women's Shooting Sports Foundation (WSSF).

❖ 46

Molôn Labé! excerpt

Logan, Utah   **January 2010**

Frank Edwin Swan is a gun owner. Federal NICS records (that is, the ones which by law are to be destroyed after the purchaser's background check has been approved) show that Swan had purchased a Bushmaster AR15 and Beretta 92 in 1999. Thus, the FBI are expecting .223 and 9mm firepower. They do not know that in 2003 Swan bought a thick green paperback book which changed his life. He sold his AR and Beretta at a large Salt Lake City gunshow and traded up to a Springfield Armory® Squad Scout M1A™ .308 battle rifle and a .45 Glock 21. These guns he legally bought from private sellers with cash, thus creating no NICS records at all.

The .308 is over twice as powerful as the .223, and can perforate much more cover. One round from a .308 will drop a man for good, whereas a .223 needs two to five rounds. Similarly, the .45ACP is a significantly better stopper than the 9mm, especially when using FMJ.

Swan's Glock 21 needed nothing but tritium night sights. Before retiring for the night, he always attached to the frame rail a powerful tactical white light. Over 70% of defensive gunfire happens at night, so being able to illuminate your threat was paramount. Legally, morally, and tactically you cannot shoot at anything not positively identified as a legitimate threat.

Because it was an American-made rifle with no pistol grip, a post-ban M1A could (under the 1994/2004 *"Crime Bill"*) have a flash suppressor. Swan replaced the stock part for a Smith Enterprise Vortex. Made of forged 8620 hardened steel (just like the M1 and M14), the Vortex was brutally strong and totally eliminated muzzle flash from the 18" barrel. Thus, Swan would not blind himself during a nighttime gunfight.

With a hunting 5 round magazine, his defensive M1A even doubled as a deer rifle if necessary. Finally, he mounted the XS Sights 24/7 tritium stripe set, an Aimpoint CompM2 red-dot sight, and a SureFire tactical light.

Next, Swan experimented with different surplus ammo until he found that Portuguese FMJ was the most accurate in his rifle. Sold by mail order in

1,000 round lots for only 15¢/round delivered, Swan bought several thousand rounds. He could not even begin to reload his own ammo for 15¢/round, especially for what his time was worth. His friends kidded him for buying so much, but Swan had learned from that big green book that *"ammo turns money into skill"* and that it was preferable to have 900 rounds of skill and 100rds of ammo, versus 1,000 rounds of ammo and no skill.

Possibly being in a gunfight means risking incoming fire, so Swan thought it prudent to buy a bulletproof vest. He learned to avoid any vest made of Zylon or Goldflex (which permanently degrade from humidity and light over time, and got several cops killed or injured before being recalled). Kevlar aramid was the only way to go. Level IIIA protection (which will stop nearly all handgun rounds) was the best balance between cost, protection, and wearability. He picked a US Armor IIIA with a Level IV (rifle protection) titanium shock plate.

The vest carrier was also important. For home defense, he chose a police tactical model which had a built-in holster and several utility pouches. The garment hung on his bedpost by his nightstand. Also on the bedpost were a pair of Peltor electronic shooting muffs which amplified inaudible sounds but blocked out gunfire. Wearing his Peltors, Swan could clearly hear a whispered conversation in another part of the house. (He proved this with friends one evening, to their stunned amazement. They all bought their own.)

His final item of apparel was a bedside pair of slip-on boots.

If ever woken up in the middle of the night by something suspicious, Swan would need less than fifteen seconds to put on his boots, vest, and ears, to investigate matters. His M1A was under the bed if he needed it quickly.

Although his child support and alimony payments took much of Swan's income, he worked overtime for many months in order to afford training back in 2004 at the world-renowned defensive shooting academies of Gunsite in Arizona and Thunder Ranch of Texas. The handgun and rifle courses cost nearly $1,000 each in tuition, not including travel, ammo, lodging, etc. Swan considered the money well spent—the training invaluable. He felt confident that he could defend himself during a lethal emergency.

Unbeknownst to him, he would soon have his chance to find out.

Washington, D.C.
J. Edgar Hoover FBI Building   January 2010

The Assistant Director of the Criminal Investigation Division grimaces at the mountain of folders on his walnut desk. Violent Census 2010 protests, attacks on Federal Reserve officials and buildings, and civil unrest. *It never ends!* Jerome Devereaux oversees all intrusive techniques, such as wiretaps, Magic Lantern insertions, "sneak and peek" warrants, long-term undercover ops, stings, etc. He picks up two folders from the top of the stack.

The proposed joint raids in Utah and Wyoming. He's been under tremendous pressure for over a year to produce an arrest in the Krassnyite phenomenon. Finally, western agents are ready to search and question two suspects. They are both gun owners and members of 2nd Amendment groups. Both harbor anti-government views.

Both had been to Denver near the time of the three abductions.

Devereaux knows that the probable cause is based only on weak circumstantial evidence, but the Bureau cannot continue to be accused of "doing nothing." Not when judges, congressmen, and VIPs are being kidnapped and murdered at the rate of two a month.

The AD signs off on the two raids as Active SCI (Sensitive Compartmented Information). US Attorneys in Casper and Salt Lake City would strictly curtail dissemination of the case details.

Maybe we'll get a break.

Then the American people will see the Bureau taking action.

Positive public perception is the FBI's greatest asset. The Bureau learned this most poignantly as it had been gradually lost during years of scandals of Ruby Ridge, Waco, Whitewater-gate, Jewell-gate, Foster-gate, Laptop-gate, Missing MP5s-gate, 9/11-gate, Crime Lab-gate, etc.

It all began with Ruby Ridge. Back in the mid-1990s, Director Louis Freeh personally deemed HRT SWAT sniper Lon Horiuchi's second shot (which struck Vicki Weaver in the face and killed her) as *"unconstitutional"* but did not censure him.

It would have greatly dampened HRT morale.

No, the FBI must stand by its own. If it didn't, who would?

Freeh put great pressure on the Justice Department to kill the manslaughter charge filed by the state of Idaho. It worked. The matter was moved to federal court against Idaho's wishes, where it died by judicial decree. Federal agents have *"sovereign immunity"* while enforcing federal law and cannot be held responsible by the states or the people.

All who were paying attention got the message.

The Republic is dead. The gloves are off.

Logan, Utah   February 2010   4:28AM

FBI agents from Salt Lake City, Boise, and Pocatello have descended upon the sleepy neighborhood of Frank Edwin Swan. The FBI for weeks had surveilled the diesel mechanic, who lived alone since his divorce eight years ago. Intelligence showed that he awoke regularly at 0530 on weekdays. Accordingly, the FBI chose to execute the raid when he was most likely at the bottom of his longest and deepest REM cycle of delta sleep. Swan would be groggiest then. That meant 0430.

Salt Lake FBI SWAT "got the ticket" for the dynamic entry. They are "jocked out" and "on line" at Phase Line Yellow, the forward rallying point. They will not bother to knock.

"No knock" warrants were originally authorized by the Supreme Court only to: prevent the easy destruction of evidence, protect lives (*e.g.,* hostages), or prevent the escape of a dangerous suspect. Additionally, police are not required to knock/announce if the suspect already knows that the police are present.

None of these factors apply to Swan, but federal judges generally give the FBI whatever they request. Utah authorities were especially cooperative with the Government since the 2002 Winter Olympics. When the Salt Lake FBI SAC made the point that Swan was wanted for questioning in the abduction of three Denver men (one of them a sitting judge), the Federal District Court judge immediately approved a no-knock search warrant.

The softly snoring Frank Swan is aware of none of this.

Eighty-six yards away FBI SWAT commander Raymond Wilcox switches his encrypted Motorola headset radio to the channel used by the entry teams. "TOC to all units. You have compromise authority and permission to move to Green."

The SWAT operators begin to surround Swan's small home. Phase Line Green is their final position before dynamic entry. Team White will enter the front and Team Black the back. Simultaneously. (They don't call it "dynamic entry" for nothing.) Team Green will cover the left side and Team Red the right. These color codes for target buildings are standard SWAT jargon. The area is cordoned off for two blocks by over twenty FBI agents, sheriff's deputies, and police. Two ambulances are standing by. So many men and vehicles are bound to rile up the neighborhood dogs.

near Lander, Wyoming   4:29AM

FBI agents from Casper, Rock Springs, Laramie, Cheyenne, and Lander have converged on the small farm of Kyle and Susan Bradford. They timed the raid with Swan's so that the subjects could not warn each other. The Bradfords live at the end of a remote county road, and their nearest neighbor is several hundred yards away behind a small knoll.

For the FBI, it was ideal. Seclusion was preferred for such raids. It not only limited risk of collateral damage, but the subjects could be isolated from interfering third parties such as friends, media, etc. As the Weaver family learned at Ruby Ridge, a remote homestead is a mixed blessing.

Logan, Utah   4:30AM

Several dogs up and down the street begin to bark from all the activity, waking a blue heeler at the foot of Swan's bed. His intelligent brown eyes are alert, his ears radar dishes swiveling about. The dog jumps to the floor and runs to the bedroom window. He sees several dark shadows moving stealthily by his master's house. His low, soft growl snaps Swan instantly awake from a very deep sleep. After seven years he knew every nuance of every bark and growl. This growl meant *Danger!*

"What is it, Otto?" Swan whispers hoarsely. Otto is still on point, softly growling at the window. Still in sweatpants, Swan gets up and peeks slightly through the top of the drapes. *Shit! Burglars!* He forces himself to take deep breaths as he dons his emergency gear. He is dressed in seconds.

He unholsters his Glock and does a blind system check of mag and chamber. Holding the .45 in his right hand, he removes the magazine with his left and touches the top round with his index finger. Loaded. The ISMI chrome-silicon mag spring would last years fully depressed. He reinserts the magazine with a *Tap-Tug.* Fully seated. Then he grabs the middle of the slide with his left hand and pulls it back about a half inch. With his middle finger he feels the partially chambered round. He pushes the slide forward, feeling the flush barrel lockup to ensure that it's in battery. A man should be able to load, unload, check, and clear his weapons by tactile feel only. During a gunfight you cannot risk taking your eyes off your threats.

Swan sees his tritium night sights as the decaying hydrogen isotope of H^3 glows reassuringly inside its hardened sapphire vials. Swan reholsters the Glock. Fourteen rounds of Triton 200 grain hollowpoints. Night sights. Tactical light. Bulletproof vest. Peltors. Boots.

All Swan needs now is the proper *mindset*—the most important ingredient for victory. Without a fighting spirit the best gear is irrelevant. *With* a fighting spirit you can defend yourself with a rolled-up newspaper.

Always Cheat. Always Win. The only unfair fight is the one you lose.

He is halfway down the hall before he recalls something his Thunder Ranch instructor Clint Smith once said. From Swan's memory a small piece calves off: *There is a big difference in being in a fight and going to a fight. You get caught in a fight with a handgun. You go to a fight with a rifle.*

Why fight with 14 rounds of .45 when you can fight with 20 rounds of .308? Besides, rifles are much easier to hit with during great stress.

Swan stops in mid-stride, returns to his bed, holsters his Glock, and grabs his M1A. Again, he does a blind system check of mag and chamber. He keeps the rifle in Condition One, meaning cocked and locked. His instructors taught him that he may not have the luxury of time or silence to chamber a first round. Thus, a home defensive rifle should be kept in Condition One. Very few gunowners know to do this and the ones who do are often uncomfortable—feeling it's "dangerous" to keep a cocked and locked rifle in the house. Swan knows better because he has been trained better.

With the 11½ pounds of stock and steel in his hands he feels immensely more prepared. What a difference a *rifle* makes. He walks down the hall with his M1A shouldered in the High Ready position, safety off, trigger finger straight. His left hand is underneath the forestock—thumb on the flashlight's momentary ON/OFF rubber button.

near Lander, Wyoming   4:30AM
Raid leader Scott Malone checks his watch and nods to his men. An entry man with a battering ram steps forward on the front porch. There will be no knocking at the Bradford farm, either.

Logan, Utah
Commander Wilcox makes a radio call to his men. All silently click in to communicate that they are standing by at Green.

The White Team leader hand signals "breacher up!" and an operator moves forward with a sawed-off 12 gauge Remington 870 pump shotgun loaded with Hatton rounds. The powdered lead shells were specifically designed for safely blowing apart door hinges.

Wilcox checks his watch. It is precisely 0430. He looks at his Special Agent in Charge, who nods. Wilcox presses the transmit button and speaks.

TOC to all units. I have control. Stand by. Five. Four. Three.

near Lander, Wyoming
Five agents are "stacked" just beside the door's left jamb. Malone holds up his non-gun hand and counts down from five to one. Their tension doubles as they anticipate being released in seconds, like a coiled spring.

Logan, Utah
Two. One. Execute. Execute. Execute.

Swan is twenty feet from the kitchen back door when his home explodes from both ends with a stereophonic crash. His Peltors blank out from nearly a second of sonic overpressure. Both front and rear doors blow off the jambs and fly inside in a shower of splinters.

Home invasion!

Gruff voices are screaming but Swan cannot make out the words amidst the smoke and confusion. The front doorway is blocked by the heavy sofa which Swan had pushed aside earlier that evening for vacuuming. It is his great fortune that he'd been too tired to move it back. Because of the sofa, the armed men in front are delayed entry.

Cover! Swan ducks in a left-side bathroom doorway, keeping his rifle pointed down the hall towards the kitchen. He has an overwhelming urge to begin shooting at the burglars he knows are just a split-second away, but forces himself to wait for visibly armed and hostile threats.

Through the kitchen door several dark gun-carrying forms in black ski masks pour inside. Swan lights up the one in front, quickly takes up the first stage of the M1A trigger, focuses on his front sight, and squeezes out the rest of the trigger pull. *Front sight! Press! Front sight!* What happens in an eyeblink seems to take hours, but time distortions usually occur when you are fighting for your life. After a mini-eternity his rifle finally *Booms!* Swan sees and hears his assailant hit in the lower chest with the 2,500 foot pound impact of a rifle bullet at nearly point-blank range. As he falls, Swan visually picks up the front post through the Aimpoint, which he has not yet turned on. *Front sight! Press! Front sight!*

near Lander, Wyoming

The Bradfords' front door is bashed in and federal agents immediately pour through the house. *FBI! FBI!* They approach the master bedroom in an urgent tangle of flashlight beams as Kyle Bradford groggily reaches for his Ed Brown Kobra .45 on the nightstand.

Logan, Utah

Two other intruders become instantly visible and Swan shoots them both in the head within .52 seconds of each other. He notes that he saw his front sight before and after each shot, just like he was trained. The terminal ballistics of a .308 round to the human cranial cavity are stupefying. Their heads literally burst with loud *Thwhops!* and the men collapse like string-cut puppets. The kitchen walls are instantly painted in gore.

Swan hears much barking, pistol fire, and shouting from the front of his home and is suddenly aware of his dog attacking intruders in the living room. *Otto is buying me time!* He swats down the impulse to save his dog and instead rushes down the hall towards the kitchen, muzzle leading the way.

He remembers to switch on the Aimpoint, and its small orange-red dot comes immediately to life. Battery life of the CompM2 is literally thousands of hours, and the unit is quite rugged. Even if the device failed he could still use his iron sights. For the first three intruders he *had*, having forgotten all about the Aimpoint.

A fourth invader suddenly appears through the kitchen doorway, his Oakley goggles covered with the blood and brain matter of his colleagues. Screaming something unintelligible at the top of his lungs, he muzzles a black subgun at the homeowner. The FBI are not accustomed to being shot at during raids, and this agent, shocked at the deaths of his comrades, has forgotten to identify himself.

Swan marvels at burglars who can afford Heckler & Koch MP5s while centering the red dot on the invader's chest as he presses out the trigger. The impact makes an dull clanging sound, but the man drops instantly. Swan steps over the four bodies and stops next to the doorway. He has a difficult time not slipping on the tile. The kitchen floor is slick with blood, its copper stench heavy in the air with the smell of burnt gunpowder and hot brass.

The magnitude of events presses upon Swan's consciousness but he is too busy. *The answer to fear is preoccupation. Solve your problem!* He is more than preoccupied, he is furious. *They started this party, but I am going to finish it for them!*

He flips a wall switch, and a porchlight illuminates two other men partially concealed behind small trees. They immediately pour bursts of 9mm subgun fire at the rear of the house, shooting out the light. Through his Peltors Swan hears raspy chirps of the suppressed MP5s, their winking muzzles strangely captivating. 147 grain slugs shatter the kitchen window, raining glass on the besieged homeowner. *May your enemies be on full-auto!* as Jeff Cooper said. Single well-placed shots are what win battles.

Swan crouches, pies out slightly past the right door jamb, quickly lights up the kneeling man on the left and fires three aimed rounds through the tree. FMJ zip through the small tree as if it were balsa wood, striking the man behind and causing him to expose more of himself. *Shoot what is available, while it is available, until something else becomes available.* Swan fires twice more, knocking the man over in a lifeless sprawl.

Five down, one to go.

near Lander, Wyoming

FBI! Hands up, now! scream three agents more or less in unison. As the Bradfords are blinded by the powerful tac lights, Kyle slowly withdraws his hand from the .45 and pulls Susan to him. Agents yank away the down comforter and plaid flannel sheets to expose the terrified, naked couple, and roughly drag them from their warm bed. They are handcuffed and herded to separate areas of the house.

"Susan, say nothing to them!" Kyle yells from the hallway.

"Shut the fuck up, you!" snarls an agent as he shoves Kyle along.

In the background, Bondo the parrot is squawking at full volume.

Logan, Utah

From behind Swan a raking burst just over his head showers him with shards of dishes. *They're making their way from the front!* Swan understands at once that he will be overcome by the men coming down the hall. His world is violent chaos and it's getting worse by the second. He must flee and find cover *now*. He can take the remaining guy in the yard, but not the several in the house. There is Danger in front, but Death is clearly behind him. No choice but to charge the Danger. This clarity is oddly comforting...